VITAMIN C+

VITAMIN C+

Phaidon Press Limited
2 Cooperage Yard
London E15 2QR

Phaidon Press Inc.
111 Broadway,
New York, NY 10006

Phaidon SARL
55, rue Traversière,
75012 Paris

phaidon.com

First published 2023
Reprinted in paperback 2026
© 2023 Phaidon Press Limited

ISBN 978 1 83729 222 6

A CIP catalogue record for this book is available from the British Library
and the Library of Congress.

COMMISSIONING EDITOR: REBECCA MORRILL
ASSISTANT EDITOR: FRANKIE MOUTAFIS
EDITORIAL ASSISTANT: CAITLIN ARNELL ARGLES
PRODUCTION CONTROLLER: LILY RODGERS
DESIGN AND COVER ILLUSTRATION: JULIA HASTING
TYPESETTING: CANTINA

Printed in China

All measurements are given height × width × depth unless otherwise specified.

Current place names are used throughout unless otherwise specified.

If this book contains inaccurate information or language that you feel we should
improve or change, we would like to hear from you. Please email texts@phaidon.com

The publishers are indebted to the following contributors for their expertise
and collaboration, and for their texts.

GIOVANNI ALOI: 086, 192, 204, 210
SKYE ARUNDHATI THOMAS: 098, 142, 170, 258, 284
LUCIENNE BESTALL: 050, 140, 236
PAUL CAREY-KENT: 126, 194, 200
JANINE GAELLE DIEUDJI: 176
LOUISA ELDERTON: 122, 178
YUVAL ETGAR: 058, 076, 150, 158, 160, 174, 260, 290
FERREN GIPSON: 036, 112, 268
AJ GIRARD: 094, 226
KEREN GOLDBERG: 032, 138, 166
PIA GOTTSCHALLER: 082, 104, 250
ZOË GRAY: 030
CHARLOTTE JANSEN: 018, 128, 168, 206, 222, 230, 254
MARITZA LACAYO: 024, 196, 238
EDMÉE LEPERCQ: 028, 090, 272
GRACE LINDEN: 062, 134, 224, 274
CAOIMHÍN MAC GIOLLA LÉITH: 084
KATHLEEN MADDEN: 066, 148, 246
REBECCA MORRILL: 198, 244
FRANKIE MOUTAFIS: 046
TAUSIF NOOR: 052, 064, 270
HANA NOORALI AND LYNTON TALBOT: 078, 118, 154, 216, 240, 242
SEAN O'TOOLE: 144, 186, 264
JOHN OWOO: 182, 294
ALONA PARDO: 022, 146, 188
HABDA RASHID: 072, 212, 218
MICHELE ROBECCHI: 054
BARRY SCHWABSKY: 102, 286
GABRIELLE SCHWARZ: 068, 070, 180, 248, 278
SHAMITA SHARMACHARJA: 026
DAVID TRIGG: 042, 116, 124, 136, 276, 296
MARGRETHE TROENSEGAARD: 108, 280
GEORGE VASEY: 056, 096, 132
MADELINE WEISBURG: 020, 040, 232
POPPY DONGXUE WU: 114, 162, 292

We are most grateful to MICHELA PARKIN, JOANNE MURRAY
and VANESSA BIRD for editorial services.

And finally, we extend our thanks to all the nominators, the artists and their galleries,
for their participation and support.

VITAMIN C+

COLLAGE IN CONTEMPORARY ART

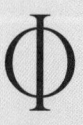

CONTENTS

NOMINATORS

CECILIA ALEMANI
Donald R. Mullen, Jr. Director & Chief Curator of High Line Art, New York, USA, and Artistic Director of the 59th Venice Biennale, 2022.

VINCE ALETTI
Photography critic, curator and writer, New York, USA.

GIOVANNI ALOI
Associate Professor, School of the Art Institute of Chicago, USA.

SKYE ARUNDHATI THOMAS
Writer and editor of *The White Review*, Goa, India.

ÇELENK BAFRA
Curator and director of SAHA, Istanbul, Turkey.

LARS BANG LARSEN
Director of artistic research, Art Hub Copenhagen, Denmark.

MARCELLA BECCARIA
Chief Curator and Curator of Collections at Castello di Rivoli Museo d'Arte Contemporanea, Turin, Italy.

NATASHA BECKER
Curator of African Art, De Young Museum, San Francisco, USA.

IWONA BLAZWICK
Curator, critic and lecturer, London, UK.

KATE BRYAN
Global Director of Art at Soho House, TV presenter, writer and curator, London, UK.

ZOE BUTT
Artistic Director, The Factory Contemporary Arts Centre, Ho Chi Minh City, Vietnam.

DAVID CAMPANY
Curator and writer, New York, USA and London, UK.

DIANA CAMPBELL
Artistic Director, Samdani Art Foundation, Dhaka and Chief Curator, Dhaka Art Summit, Dhaka, Bangladesh.

ANDRIANNA T. CAMPBELL-LAFLEUR
Scholar, curator, and critic, New Haven, Connecticut, USA.

JUDITH CARLTON
Director, Southwark Park Galleries, London, UK.

CLARE CAROLIN
Senior Lecturer in Art and Public Engagement, Department of Culture, Media and Creative Industries, King's College London, UK.

ANTONIA CARVER
Director, Art Jameel, Dubai, UAE.

DURGA CHEW-BOSE
Writer, Montreal, Canada.

RAPHAEL CHIKUKWA
Executive Director, National Gallery of Zimbabwe, Harare.

JULIE CROOKS
Curator, Arts of Global Africa and the Diaspora, Art Gallery of Ontario, Canada.

EOIN DARA
Head of Exhibitions, Dundee Contemporary Arts, Scotland, UK.

TANDAZANI DHLAKAMA
Assistant Curator, Zeitz Museum of Contemporary Art Africa, Cape Town, South Africa.

JANINE GAËLLE DIEUDJI
Independent curator and Co-founder, The Recovery Plan, Florence, Italy.

PATRICK ELLIOTT
Chief Curator of Modern and Contemporary Art, National Galleries of Scotland, Edinburgh, UK.

YUVAL ETGAR
Curator and art historian, London, UK.

REEMA FADDA
Curator and Director of Abu Dhabi Cultural Foundation, UAE.

FLAVIA FRIGERI
Curator, art historian and lecturer, London, UK.

AJ GIRARD
Curator, art historian and lecturer, Los Angeles, USA.

PIA GOTTSCHALLER
Technical art historian, London, UK.

CLARE GRAFIK
Head of Exhibitions, The Photographers' Gallery, London, UK.

ZOË GRAY
Senior curator, WIELS, Brussels, Belgium.

GARETH HARRIS
Chief Contributing Editor, *The Art Newspaper*, London, UK.

MAX HOLLEIN
Director, Metropolitan Museum of Art, New York, USA.

SARAH HUMPHREVILLE
Lunder Curator of American Art, Colby College Museum of Art, Waterville, Maine, USA.

DAKIS JOANNOU
Founder, DESTE Foundation for Contemporary Art, Athens, Greece.

JUSTE JONUTYTE
Curator and art historian, Vilnius, Lithuania.

HETTIE JUDAH
Author, and senior art critic, *The i*, London, UK.

GEETA KAPUR
Art critic and curator, New Delhi, India.

ANNA KŁOS
Founder, Retroavangarda Gallery, Warsaw, Poland.

MARITZA LACAYO
Curator, Pérez Art Museum Miami (PAMM), Florida, USA.

CLIFF LAUSON
Director of Exhibitions, Somerset House, London, UK.

CHRISTINE MACEL
Chief Curator, Centre Pompidou, Paris, France and Artistic Director, 57th Venice Biennale, 2017.

KATHLEEN MADDEN
Writer, lecturer, curator and editor, New York, USA.

ROXANA MARCOCI
The David Dechman Senior Curator of Photography, The Museum of Modern Art, New York, USA.

SARAH MCCRORY
Director, Goldsmiths Centre for Contemporary Art, London, UK.

BERNARDO MOSQUEIRA
Curator and writer, New York, USA and Rio de Janeiro, Brazil.

MARGOT NORTON
Allen and Lola Goldring Senior Curator, New Museum, New York, USA.

DURO OLOWU
Fashion designer and curator, London, UK and New York, USA.

SEAN O'TOOLE
Writer, editor and curator, Cape Town, South Africa.

JOHN OWOO
Writer and critic, Accra, Ghana.

ALONA PARDO
Curator, Barbican Art Gallery, London, UK.

IBERIA PÉREZ GONZÁLEZ
Andrew W. Mellon Caribbean Cultural Institute Coordinator, Pérez Art Museum Miami (PAMM), Florida, USA.

ROSIE RAM
Associate Lecturer in MA Curating Contemporary Art at the Royal College of Art, London, UK.

HABDA RASHID
Senior Curator, Modern & Contemporary Art, The Fitzwilliam Museum and Kettle's Yard, University of Cambridge, UK.

EMMA RIDGWAY
Chief curator, Modern Art Oxford, UK, and curator, British Pavilion, 59th Venice Biennale, 2022.

SCOTT ROTHKOPF
Senior Deputy Director and Chief Curator, Whitney Museum of American Art, New York, USA.

DREW SAWYER
Art historian and curator, Brooklyn Museum, New York, USA.

BARRY SCHWABSKY
Art critic, *The Nation*, New York, USA.

SHAMITA SHARMACHARJA
Curator, Wellcome Collection, London, UK.

JONATHAN SHAUGHNESSY
Director, Curatorial Initiatives, National Gallery of Canada, Ottawa.

BRIAN SHOLIS
Writer and editor, Toronto, Canada.

FRANCESCO STOCCHI
Curator, Museum Boijmans Van Beuningen, Rotterdam, The Netherlands.

RUSSELL TOVEY
Collector, actor and founder and co-host, TalkArt, London, UK.

NICOLA TREZZI
Director and curator, CCA Tel Aviv-Yafo and lecturer, BFA, Bezalel Academy of Arts and Design, Jerusalem, Israel.

NIKO VARTIAINEN
Editor-in-Chief, *Toombes* magazine, Turku, Finland.

CLARRIE WALLIS
Director, Turner Contemporary, Margate, UK.

ZOÉ WHITLEY
Director, Chisenhale Gallery, London, UK.

POPPY DONGXUE WU
Chief Curator, X Museum, Beijing, China.

HEIDI ZUCKERMAN
CEO and Director, Orange County Museum of Art, Los Angeles, USA.

WRITERS

GIOVANNI ALOI
Associate Professor, School of the Art Institute of Chicago, USA.

SKYE ARUNDHATI THOMAS
Writer and editor of *The White Review*, Goa, India.

LUCIENNE BESTALL
Writer, Cape Town, South Africa.

PAUL CAREY-KENT
Writer and curator, New Forest, UK.

JANINE GAËLLE DIEUDJI
Independent curator and Co-founder, The Recovery Plan, Florence, Italy.

LOUISA ELDERTON
Independent writer and art critic, and Managing Editor, Institute for Cultural Inquiry Berlin Press, Germany.

YUVAL ETGAR
Curator and art historian, London, UK.

FERREN GIPSON
Art historian, writer and presenter, London, UK.

AJ GIRARD
Curator, art historian and lecturer, Los Angeles, USA.

KEREN GOLDBERG
Art critic and PhD student, the Hebrew University, Jerusalem, Israel.

PIA GOTTSCHALLER
Technical art historian, London, UK.

ZOË GRAY
Senior curator, WIELS, Brussels, Belgium.

CHARLOTTE JANSEN
Arts writer and author, London, UK.

MARITZA LACAYO
Curator, Pérez Art Museum Miami (PAMM), Florida, USA.

EDMÉE LEPERCQ
Writer, London, UK.

GRACE LINDEN
Writer and art historian, London, UK.

CAOIMHÍN MAC GIOLLA LÉITH
Associate Professor of the School of Irish, Celtic Studies and Folklore at University College Dublin, Ireland.

REBECCA MORRILL
Writer and editor, Gateshead and London, UK.

FRANKIE MOUTAFIS
Writer and editor, London, UK.

TAUSIF NOOR
Critic, curator and doctoral student at the University of California, Berkeley, USA.

HANA NOORALI AND LYNTON TALBOT
Writers and curators, London, UK.

SEAN O'TOOLE
Writer, editor and curator, Cape Town, South Africa.

JOHN OWOO
Writer and critic, Accra, Ghana.

ALONA PARDO
Curator, Barbican Art Gallery, London, UK.

HABDA RASHID
Senior Curator, Modern & Contemporary Art, The Fitzwilliam Museum and Kettle's Yard, University of Cambridge, UK.

MICHELE ROBECCHI
Curator, writer and editor, London, UK.

BARRY SCHWABSKY
Art critic, *The Nation*, New York, USA.

GABRIELLE SCHWARZ
Writer and Deputy Editor of Outland, London, UK.

SHAMITA SHARMACHARJA
Curator, Wellcome Collection, London, UK.

DAVID TRIGG
Writer, critic and art historian, Bristol, UK.

MARGRETHE TROENSEGAARD
Curator and art historian, London, UK.

GEORGE VASEY
Curator and writer, Saltburn-by-the-Sea, UK.

MADELINE WEISBURG
Curatorial Assistant, New Museum, New York, USA.

POPPY DONGXUE WU
Chief Curator, X Museum, Beijing, China.

NOMINATORS AND WRITERS

008.009

This is the latest in the series of acclaimed 'Vitamin' art surveys that explore trends in contemporary art through the lens of a particular medium. Since the first edition was published in 2002, these books have focused on the categories of painting, drawing, photography and '3D' (sculpture and installation). More recently, the series expanded to encompass materials and processes that might once have been classified as 'craft' rather than 'fine art' – textiles and ceramics – but are now also central in contemporary art practice. ▬▬ *Vitamin C+ Collage in Contemporary Art* introduces another new subject to the series. Collage first gained 'fine art' status in early-twentieth-century Europe when artists in modernist movements such as Cubism, Dada and Surrealism saw its potential as a means of challenging traditional image-making techniques and created dynamic experimental visual forms that captured the spirit of modern life by literally incorporating elements of the real world within them. ◣ Collage, of course, existed long before then in many cultures worldwide, with a history stretching as far back as that of its basic components: paper and glue. In his introductory essay, collage expert Yuval Etgar describes its 'long history of illicit acts: cutting, tearing, stealing, covering up, pretending, and above all disrupting expectations that things can be whole, and perfect, in one piece.' ◣ Many twenty-first-century collage artists work with the same fundamental tools and methods as their predecessors: gathering printed imagery, photographs and other ephemera that is then physically cut-and-pasted together to create something new. However, artists today might equally be working digitally, making still or moving-image artworks that are composed from fragmentary elements arranged on screen and output as a print, video, animation or online project. ▬▬► This volume showcases over one hundred living artists from across the globe, who were nominated for inclusion by an esteemed panel of museum directors, curators, critics and collectors. The artist names were put forward because of the central role that collage plays in their recent visual art practice and the end result features both analogue and digital approaches, overturning any narrow definitions and revealing collage as one of the most exciting and varied art creative processes used by artists today. ▬▬◣

REBECCA MORRILL, EDITOR

BORDER CONTROL:
TESTING THE LIMITS OF COLLAGE
BY YUVAL ETGAR

Collage, as it turns out, is a synonym for trouble. It is a term tainted by a long history of illicit acts: cutting, tearing, stealing, covering up, pretending and, above all, disrupting all expectations that things can be whole, and perfect, in one piece. Over the years, critics have offered various definitions for this term, hoping to discipline the word at least, if not the object itself. But still today consensus seems far from reach. Is collage a technical term to be recognized according to a set of materials or tools? Is it a strategy that can be applied based on conceptual principles? And should it be regarded as an historical object that belongs to a specific material and technological era?

AN EXPANDED FIELD

In 1975 the Canadian-born, American artist Jack Goldstein (1945–2003) produced a short video titled *The Chair* (fig.1). In it, multi-coloured feathers slowly descend from an unspecified source above the frame onto a freshly painted black chair placed in a dark room. One by one, the feathers stick to the paint in various places or drop to the floor around it, gradually decorating the dark setting with blue, red, green and yellow patches of colour. *The Chair* is an enigmatic work, difficult to contextualize or narrate, but its historical roots are clearly exposed. They lead directly back to the series of collages by Jean Arp (1886–1966), famously 'arranged according to the laws of chance', executed more than half a century earlier by dropping pieces of cut or torn paper onto a surface and fixing them wherever they landed (fig.2). Like Arp's pioneering work in collage from the first decades of the twentieth century, Goldstein's chance experiment reflects on notions of displacement and the artist's ability to relinquish control over the outcome of their actions. *The Chair*, however, is fundamentally different in terms of medium from its historical precedent executed with paper and glue. It is at once a sculpture, a performative action and a film depicting the process of making a collage under challenging material and technical conditions. ▌Goldstein's work sets the tone for this survey of living artists using collage in contemporary art. Aptly located on the historical seam between the analogue and the digital eras, *The Chair* offers one possible interpretation of what collage might be able to offer this practice as part of an expanded field (to borrow the terminology of theorist Rosalind Krauss, originally used in 1979 to describe medium-breaking tendencies in sculpture) in the aftermath of the postmodern moment, the advent of digital media and the radical structural changes in the economy of art production and its display from the 1970s onwards. *The Chair* also encourages one to abandon what now seems like an outdated ambition to define collage in strict material or technical terms, and to try and imagine instead what it might mean to inhabit the process of making one. The following is an examination of selected case studies from the history of collage in modern and contemporary art gathered with the aim to expose the delicate balance between the potential and limitations implied by this term. These extend to and overlap with the mediums of moving image, photography, sculpture, writing, sound production and live performance, as well as social and environmental projects. But, as such, they also provide a frame of reference to some of the tendencies manifested in this book.

THE NEW SCULPTURE

The first question to address when trying to imagine what scope of practices might be included in a survey of collage in contemporary art is a spatial one. At what point does a construction of pasted papers, pieces of wood, cloth or fragments of other found objects and materials cease to be a collage and become an assemblage, a *bas-relief*, a sculpture or full-blown architecture? Examples of borderline cases are widespread today as this survey confirms. Consider, for example, Anita Witek's (pp.290–1) sprawling architectural collage-installations in which photographs of built spaces are spliced and reconfigured to undermine differences between bodily and visual experience. Other examples include

fig.1

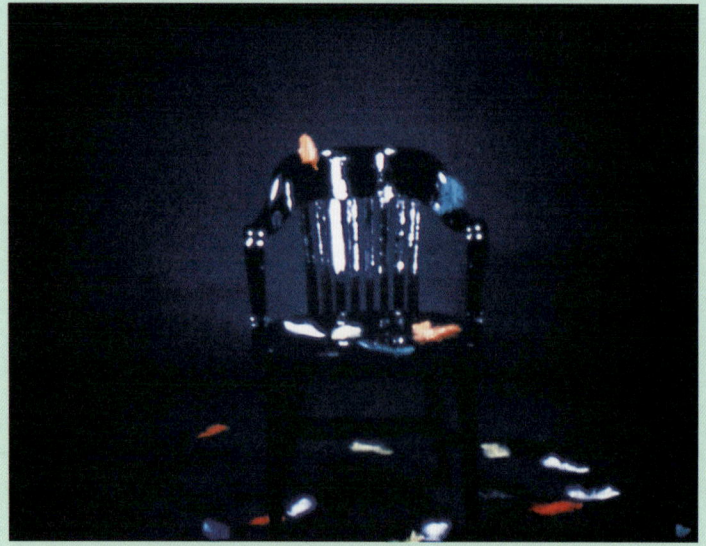

fig.2

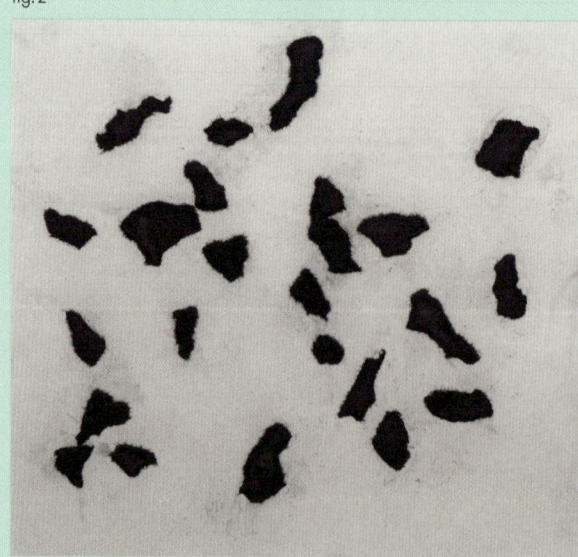

    Jack Goldstein, *The Chair*, 1975, 16mm film, colour, silent, 5 minutes

↑   **Jean Arp**, *Selon les lois du hasard (According to the Laws of Chance)*, 1933, sugar paper on plyboard, 15.9 × 17.3 cm (6¼ × 6¾ in), Tate, London, UK

→   **Georges Braque**, photograph of a 'painted paper' construction in Braque's studio (now destroyed), 1914

→→   **Kurt Schwitters**, *The Hanover Merzbau*, 1933 (destroyed in 1943), installation made with paper, cardboard, plaster, glass, mirror, metal, wood, stone, painted materials and electric lighting, 393 × 580 × 460 cm (153½ × 228⅜ × 181⅛ in)

Kahlil Robert Irving's (pp.116–7) sculptural conglomerations made of crafted and found ceramics with food and other product wrappings pasted across their surface, and Guanyu Xu's (pp.292–3) series of photographs capturing his clandestine installations of images and documents associated with his sexual identity, which he is forced to conceal in the domestic environment of his parents' home in a Beijing military base. These examples of three-dimensional collages, however, draw on the legacy of a significant branch in the history of this practice that is worth revisiting. The art critic Clement Greenberg touched on this subject already more than half a century ago in an essay titled 'The New Sculpture', where he argued that it was the adoption of collage by members of the European and Russian avant-garde in the 1910s that enabled sculpture to escape its monolithic origins (as chiselled stone, carved wood or cast bronze) and assume a constructed and materially diverse form.[1] Unfolding the historical process of this transition, Greenberg suggested that it was Pablo Picasso (1881–1973) who pioneered the experiment by 'raising collage's affixed material above the picture surface, thus going over into *bas-relief*. And soon after that he subtracted the picture surface entirely, to let what had originally been affixed stand free as a "construction".[2] The example Greenberg was alluding to is a suite of guitar-shaped constructions developed by Picasso between 1912 and 1914. In these works, the artist gradually transitioned from drawing, through collage, to sculpture-making. He began by adding pieces of newspaper clippings to charcoal drawings of guitars in order to emphasize certain parts of the instrument. Soon, more and more materials were added to works in order to create volume and texture, including paper, cardboard, glue, tape, painted wire, pins, twine and string, and in one final version from 1914. the construction was entirely transformed into a sculpture made of sheet metal and wire.[3] But Picasso's guitars were not, as Greenberg suggested, an entirely original invention or an isolated case. As the artist's letters confirm, the idea of making a three-dimensional collage was something he borrowed from his closest colleague, friend and competitor, Georges Braque

(1882–1963), who had already constructed several objects of a similar nature the year before in his studio at Sorgues, France, and continued developing these until sometime in 1914. But Braque's sculptural collage experiments were all destroyed shortly thereafter, and it appears that he attached little importance to them as they had 'merely helped him to solve pictorial problems'.[4] Today, only a single photograph (fig. 3) survives as proof of the experiment dated around 1914. It depicts a corner still life sculpture of a newspaper, bottle and glass on a table installed in a corner of the artist's studio. Other attempts at making three-dimensional collages during the early 1910s were undertaken by artists who sought to expand the spatial inclination of the new practice and to integrate 'real space' into their pictures in different ways. One particularly interesting example can be found in the work of Juan Gris (1887–1927), who incorporated a piece of mirror into one of his paintings, titled *Le Lavabo* (*The Washbasin*) of 1912. Gris's addition not only transformed an oil painting on canvas into a collage, but also created a spatial intervention that implicated the work in the context of its display and the presence of the viewer.[5] ◢ The most radical step from collage into three-dimensional construction in this definitive period, however, did not take place until a few years later in 1923, when the German artist Kurt Schwitters (1887–1948) started building the first of four immersive architectural environments executed over the next twenty-five years in a collage-like manner. The *Merzbau*,[6] as Schwitters named the first fabricated interior, was conceived as an ongoing project, in which fragments of leftover materials such as boxes, cardboard, paper, and the debris of furniture and panels gradually covered every part of the artist's studio in Hanover (fig. 4). For fourteen years Schwitters worked on the piece before it was tragically destroyed during a bombing of the city in 1943 by Allied forces, an event that took place shortly after he had fled Germany. By then, however, the idea of collage as a lived environment had already become part of Schwitters's way of life, and three further attempts to build similar structures followed during the artist's years in exile between Norway and

fig. 3

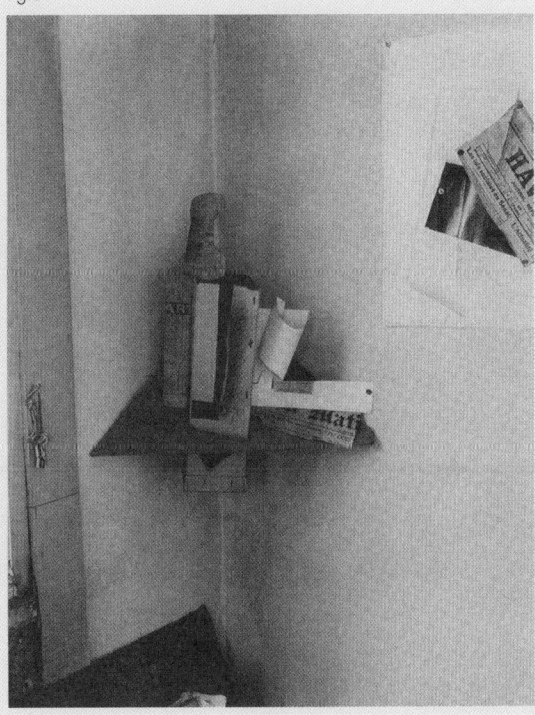

fig. 4

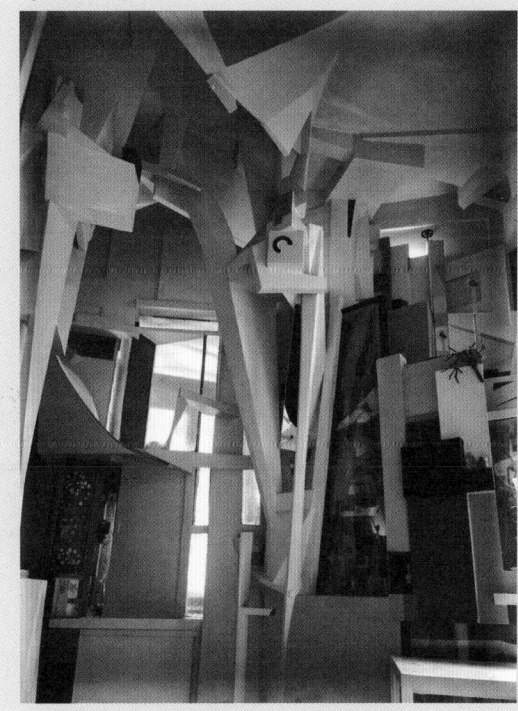

England. The obsession with collage that led Schwitters to expand his practice to such a scale, it is said, was at least in part a reaction to the destruction he witnessed during the First World War and the need he felt to transform detritus into positive creation wherever he went. Only a few projects can be compared with Schwitters's *Merzbau* in the years leading up to the Second World War, none of which is so clearly invested in its reinterpretation of the spatial boundaries of collage. By the 1950s, however, a greater tendency to engage with this practice on a large scale and in almost architectural terms was gaining momentum, and the implications of this expansion continue to manifest today.

▰ Despite these examples, the prevailing tendency within collage's history is to be suspicious of three-dimensional space. The appeal of collage to artists and architects alike more often lies in its ability to offer alternatives that overcome the impossibility of physically creating or inhabiting architectural environments by methods of image manipulation and construction. This survey is full of such examples, many of which draw on the lessons of Surrealist collage with its fantastic sensibilities, its legacy and derivatives – artists such as Max Ernst (1891–1976), Nusch Eluard (1906–46), Joseph Cornell (1903–72), Toshiko Okanoue (b.1928) and others thus inform the work of Noémie Goudal (pp.90–3), David Maljkovic (pp.158–9), Yamini Nayar (pp.178–9), Ventura Profana (pp.206–9), Anastasia Samoylova (pp.224–5) and John Stezaker (pp.260–3) among others. Other notable examples that fall outside of the scope of this book in terms of their creation dates, include C.K. Rajan's (b.1960) series of 'Mild Terrors II' collages from 1991–6 (fig.5.) and Ellsworth Kelly's (1923–2015) series of postcard collages from the 1960s through to the 1980s, both of which depict hypothetical and paradoxical inversions of scale between body parts, public sculpture and urban landscape. ▰ The tensions between simulated and real space as well as material are central to the history of collage. Indeed, one of collage's greatest contributions to modern art is the ability to establish a genuine connection between artworks and the material reality they address but without losing their

critical distance from the appropriated materials and objects altogether. Commonly cited in this respect are the works of the décollagists (better known for their affiliations with Fluxus and Nouveau Réalisme) who set out to tear the layered surfaces of advertising billboards in major cities across Europe in the post-war decades of the 1950s and 1960s before bringing the lacerated results into the gallery space for display.[7] But while a great deal of scholarship has been dedicated to the nature of the materials documented and unveiled by these artists, and the way they reflected the wounded cities of Europe in the aftermath of the war, I would like to suggest that such materialistic analysis largely overlooks the performative value of collage, and certainly décollage, as a political and artistic action in its own right. The violent and illicit destruction of public advertising panels in cities such as Rome, Paris, Berlin and Cologne during the 1950s and 1960s by the likes of Jacques Villeglé (1926–2022), Raymond Hains (1926–2005), Mimmo Rotella (1918–2006) and Wolf Vostell (1932–98) was undoubtedly a performative and indeed also ritualistic act for which real-time experience and public attendance was given primary importance (fig.6).[8]

▰ Another artist to which this argument should be extended is Niki de Saint Phalle (1930–2002), who operated in tangent to the abovementioned groups of Nouveau Réalistes and Fluxus artists. Among her composite creations, de Saint Phalle created a series of large-scale assemblages in the early 1960s known as '*Tirs*' (French for 'Shootings'). In these works, she attached small bags of fresh paint along with various found objects (from pieces of furniture through to raw materials and even food) onto large wooden surfaces that she then covered with layers of white plaster before making these the targets of a shooting exercise. Using her rifle, de Saint Phalle thus transformed her unusual white reliefs into wounded objects, marked by their perforated, paint-dripping surfaces (fig.7). When asked about her motivation to use destruction as a method in her work, the artist spoke of a triumph of the female sex over its male counterpart, and emphasized the importance of violent action to this process: 'It was a moment

fig.5

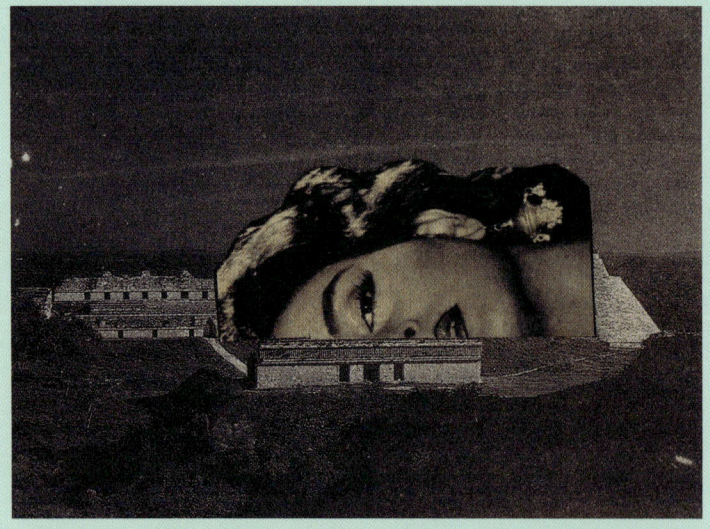

fig.6

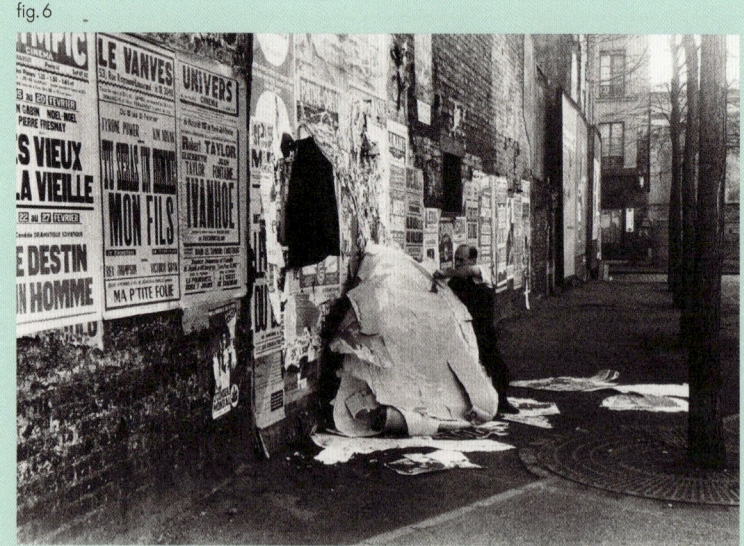

↖ **C.K. Rajan**, *Untitled*, from the series 'Mild Terrors II', 1991–6, collage from print media on A4 sheet, 21 × 29.7 cm (8¼ × 11¾ in)

↑ **Jacques Villeglé** working, Montparnasse, Paris, France, 1961. Photograph by Harry Shunk and Janos Kender, Centre Pompidou, Paris.

→ **Niki de Saint Phalle** shooting session, Impasse Ronsin, Paris, France, 1961. Photograph by Harry Shunk and Janos Kender, Centre Pompidou, Paris.

→→ **Louise Nevelson**, *Untitled*, 1956, cardboard, metal, paper, plastic and wood collage on board, 91.5 × 61 cm (36 × 24 in) of fantastic exaltation to see these works become something real before my eyes, my sentiments of aggression finally found a form of sublimation.'[9] ◆ Destruction, however, can also manifest itself in positive terms. In fact, when addressing the relationship between collage and leftover materials, detritus and, indeed, even ordinary domestic trash, the inevitable link to recycling and ecological thinking is a point that deserves serious consideration. In this respect, one of the most consistent and dedicated practitioners to engage with recycling in her practice and to also attribute an environmental vocabulary to her work was the American (Ukrainian-born) artist Louise Nevelson (1899–1988).[10] As Pia Gottschaller points out in an essay on the artist's unusual material sensibility, Nevelson's 'collages consist of what many people would call trash or detritus from the street', but 'What is interesting to note… is that Nevelson herself rarely referred to her materials as "junk", "trash" or "urban waste" – critics did. The closest she came to using a pejorative term was when she stated in 1977 that she was less inspired by "period pieces"… and "more inspired by the crap I see out of my window, so help me God".'[11] Nevelson's collages, assemblages and free-standing constructed sculptures were the outcome of a methodical process of sourcing and ordering items of varying quality, kind and condition – from old furniture to torn pieces of plywood panels, carpenters' rejects, paper wrappings, posters and newspaper pages (fig. 8). The abstract nature of the compositions she then created with these materials came to emphasize, rather than conceal, their functional origins. The shape of her sculptures, in turn, soon also began to imitate that of walls, extending from floor to ceiling and along the periphery of entire rooms. Nevelson's sculptures ended up replacing the contours of her home as well as those of the gallery, and she came to declare that 'when I clean house… I am not really cleaning house. I am building architecture.'[12] ▬ Today, a much broader range of 'found' materials whose symbolic value is indicative of environmental, social and geopolitical issues can be found in galleries and museums across the world, exposing the injustice and travesty

implicated in an accelerated global economy in which the packaging industry is bigger than most of those it sets out to serve. Under such conditions, subjective memory and identity are at risk of becoming invisible. In response, the Algerian-French artist Mohamed Bourouissa (pp. 46–9) imbeds his photographic documentation of marginalized communities onto the surface of large-scale collage-like constructions made of steel and aluminium plates, various car body parts and other unusual supports. Corresponding with the legacy of John Chamberlain (1927–2011), César (1921–98), Andy Warhol (1928–87), Robert Rauschenberg (1925–2008), Hisachika Takahashi (b. 1940, fig. 9) and indeed also Louise Nevelson, Bourouissa's practice is nevertheless profoundly different from that of his predecessors because his relationship with material is so deeply connected to the social circumstances of his subjects and the reality he seeks to document.

▬◆ EDGES ARE BORDERS ▬◆

Spatial or material concerns are key to understanding how collage extends beyond its conventional scope. But what might the minimal conditions be for a work to qualify as a collage? Albeit this is dangerous terrain on which to tread, one thing is certain: collage must have more than one element in order to be regarded as such, even if one of these elements is nothing more than a background or a neutral support, or if the elements have been processed to form a seamless composition by way of printing or digital retouching. This inevitable reliance on conjunction of distinct parts easily lends itself to political interpretation as a method that expresses difference, friction or kinship between foreign bodies. But while collage history is full of stories about displacement, migration or dissidence as a result of this characteristic, some others. This maintains a sense of prejudice and hierarchical imbalance that still taints the discipline of art history and is contrary to the spirit of collage as an artistic practice. In reaction, however, different artists throughout the history of collage have found ways to employ the attributes of this practice in order to make their arguments heard. This is true for Lyle Ashton Harris (pp. 98–101), for example, whose work explores representations

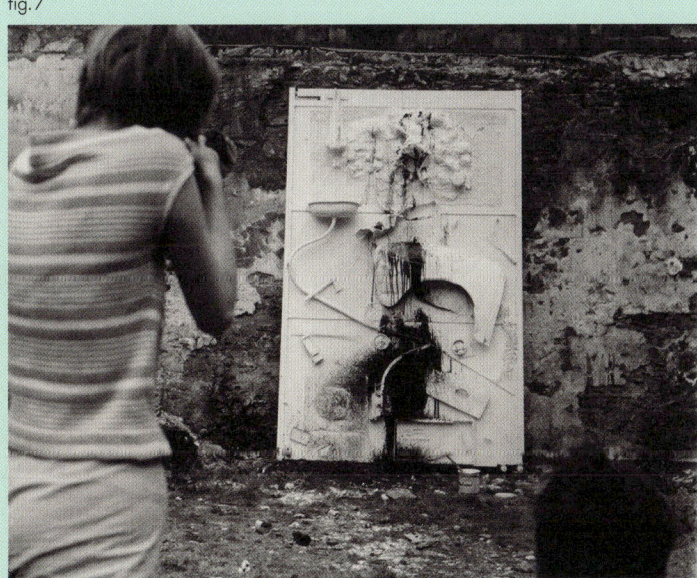
fig. 7

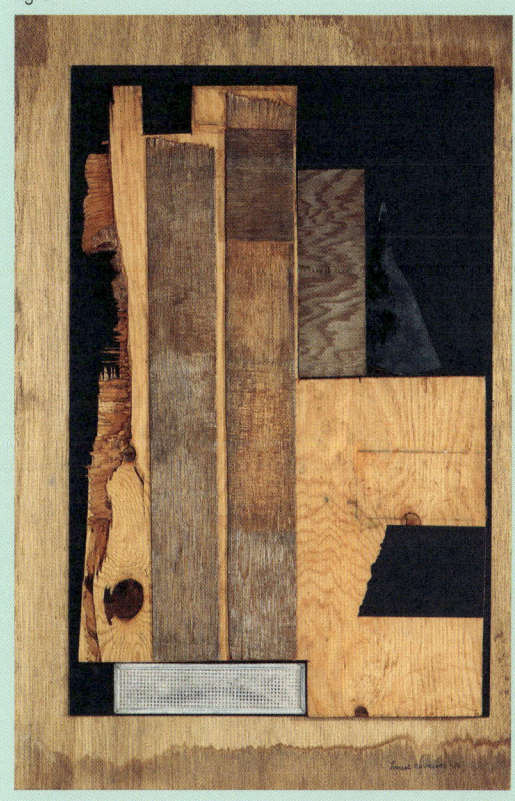
fig. 8

of queer sexuality visible outside the constraints of the art object since the 1990s, by pasting images, documents, fabrics and pamphlets directly onto the supporting walls of homes and galleries. In this way, Harris makes the site of display part of his work and unpacks the multifaceted constructions of his personal, ethnic, sexual and national identity as something that has to become part of the physical environment in which the work is presented. ▬ Harris's approach to collage as a sprawling entity that spreads across entire walls raises another important and distinctly political aspect inherent to the qualifying conditions of collage as the meeting point between at least two foreign pieces of material. Normally associated with margins, or periphery (whether in a picture, text, document or even our field of vision), edges in collage are easily transformed into the main event, the place of meeting or breaking apart of different elements and realities. The Scottish author Ali Smith, whose writings have long been invested in the relationship between edges and geopolitics by way of textual collage, had previously accounted for this attribute in one of her essays, declaring that 'edges are borders. Edges are very much about identity, about who you are. Crossing a border is not a simple thing. Geopolitically, getting anywhere round the world in which we live now requires a constant producing of proof of identity. Who are you? You can't cross till we're sure. When we know, then we'll decide whether you can or not.' [13] Smith's interpretation of edges as thresholds is particularly interesting as it raises questions about the identity of the authorities that determine whose narrative can be admitted into the canon and whose is not, and whether one can cross a border without permission. ▟ A particularly telling example of such an attempt to redefine the politics of centre and margins can be traced back to Noah Purifoy (1917–2004) and Judson Powell's (1933–2021) project *66 Signs of Neon* (1966). This series of assemblages, collages and found objects was executed in the aftermath of the Los Angeles 'Watts riots' (also known as the 'Watts Rebellion') of 1965. Artists and educational activists in the predominantly African American Watts neighbourhood

in LA, Purifoy and Powell witnessed the civil uprising caused by the violent arrest of local resident Marquette Frye. The confrontations between local members of the community and police as well as military forces that took place on 11 August 1965 escalated in a matter of hours to colossal dimensions and continued for five consecutive days without stop, causing the death of thirty-four individuals, with more than a thousand injured, and unprecedented damage to public and private property. In the months that followed these catastrophic events Purifoy and Powell created art from the lead drippings of melted neon signs that were burnt during the riots and other found debris that was left on the streets (fig. 10). These were then presented in an exhibition *Junk Art: 66 Signs of Neon* in summer 1966 ,which went on to tour widely until 1972. The artists' aim was to express 'the imposition of order on disorder' and 'the creation of beauty from ugliness', as Purifoy explained in an official statement.[14] For the sake of their project, the two artists recruited six other skilled workers to help them sculpt and write slogans in preparation for an exhibition that they insisted on realizing within thirty days, employing burnt pieces of wood, melted neon signs, contorted steel, cutlery, graffiti, tyres, steel frames and many other found objects more or less recognizable for what they originally were. ▬ *66 Signs of Neon* was an attempt to oppose the discrimination and marginalization of African American communities in the United States by bringing the physical remnants of the riots into the centre of an exhibition to provoke debate about oppression. Much of the time, however, oppression and marginalization of minority communities occurs implicitly in everyday life, and is therefore invisible to large parts of society. Romare Bearden (1911–88), another artist who used collage, was addressing precisely this issue in his work: the persisting side-lining of African Americans from the national narrative during the 1960s. Bearden was born in North Carolina, grew up in Pittsburgh and eventually settled in New York, becoming an important figure in the Harlem Renaissance of the 1920s and 1930s. He adopted collage as a practice that enabled him to sample patterns and photographs to reflect his personal

fig. 9

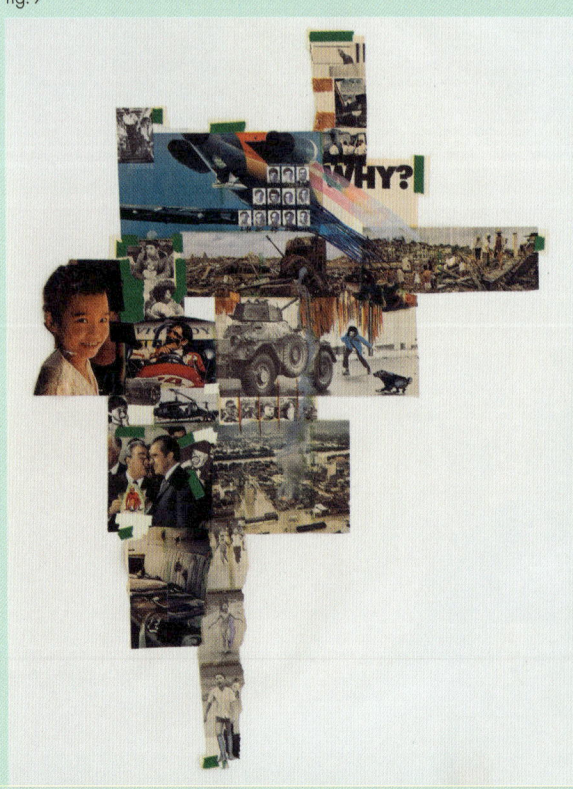

fig. 10

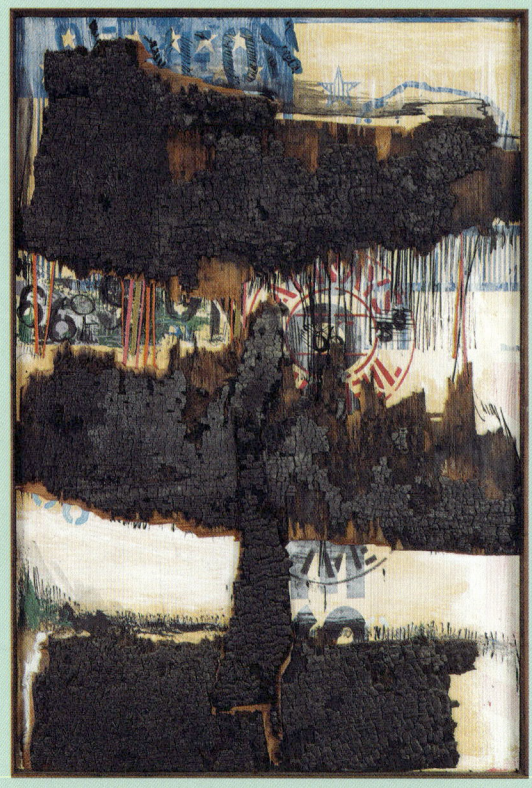

experience of community life at this time. Bearden's collages are depictions of culture, ritual and leisure – seemingly apolitical themes. However, images of African American lives were absent from the walls of public museums, the pages of textbooks or the teachings Bearden had been exposed to at school and university. Finding a strategy to address these concerns, however, proved more complicated than it might seem in hindsight. The process began to take shape in 1936, when Bearden enrolled at the Artists Students League. There he met the German Dada and New Objectivity artist George Grosz (1893–1959), whose teachings helped him define his stylistic vocabulary – to embrace collage as a method, and to use his art as a magnifying glass for society's virtues and misgivings. After some years of experimentation, Bearden began to compose depictions of *Young Students* (1964), *The Street* (1964) or a local congregation on *Sunday After Sermon* (1969), arguing that for him 'an artist is an art lover who finds that in *all* the art that he sees, he sees something is missing. And to touch at the core of what he feels is missing, what needs to be there, becomes the centre of his life's work.' [15] A particularly potent example of Bearden's poignant critique can be found in the collage *Evening 9:10, 461 Lenox Avenue* of 1964 (fig. 11), in which three figures are playing cards around a table surrounded by ordinary domestic objects and furniture. The simple setting, however, manages to hold high tension in its merger of African American connotations and Eurocentric modernist traditions, most notably the mirroring of Paul Cézanne's famous *Card Players* paintings of 1892–4. The iconic image of typical French farmers sitting around the table and playing cards is replaced in Bearden's composition by three Black figures and a traditional banjo resting on one of the chairs as if in a nod to Picasso's most famous collage compositions of his beloved Spanish guitars.

FROM PAPER TO PIXEL

Questions of a political nature are always also questions of media. Namely, what are the vehicles available for the delivery of information, protest, inquiry and creativity. Some of the examples explored in the opening of this introduction touch briefly on the relationship between collage, moving image and the screen, but the subject merits further elaboration. Historically speaking, the terms 'montage' and 'photomontage' indicate a crossover between several different practices whose results are manifested on and off the screen. The first use of the term 'photomontage' is attributed to a series of experiments in photography from the mid-nineteenth century, by the likes of Henry Peach Robinson (1830–1901) and Oscar Gustave Rejlander (1813–75), artists and innovators who attempted to overlay photographs one on top of the other to create fantastic compositions that outwit the eye. The term 'montage' was then adopted in the first decades of the twentieth century by Soviet filmmakers and theorists, most notably Sergei Eisenstein (1898–1948), who spoke about montage in film as 'the collision of independent shots' wherein 'each sequential element is perceived not next to the other, but on top of the other'. [16] While similar in principle to its historical precedent, Eisenstein's notion of 'collision' – a surprising and often conflicting union of images – gave his work a completely different tone. Montage was a method of contrasting images rather than one of merger. Eisenstein's film theory was far more in tune with the worldview of the Russian and European avant-garde, and it seems to echo similar developments in photographic collage of the 1920s among artists associated with Dada, such as Hannah Höch (1889–1978, fig. 12), Raoul Hausmann (1886–1971), John Heartfield (1891–1968) and the abovementioned George Grosz, among others. These artists adopted the term 'photomontage' for its connection with 'assembly lines' (*monter* is French for 'to assemble'), promoting a new perspective on the role of artists as mechanics or engineers of the image rather than as craftspeople. [17] The overlap between film, collage and photomontage, and the respective industries that employ these techniques, unfolds a fascinating history of cross-pollination. [18] But this crossover has been complicated in manifold ways since the introduction of several technological developments from the late 1970s onwards, including hardware (the VCR (video cassette recorder) and domestic personal computers)

fig. 11

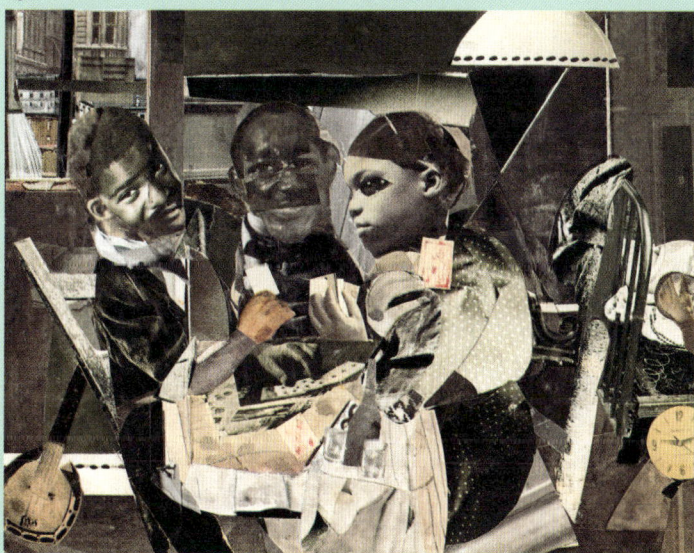

fig. 12

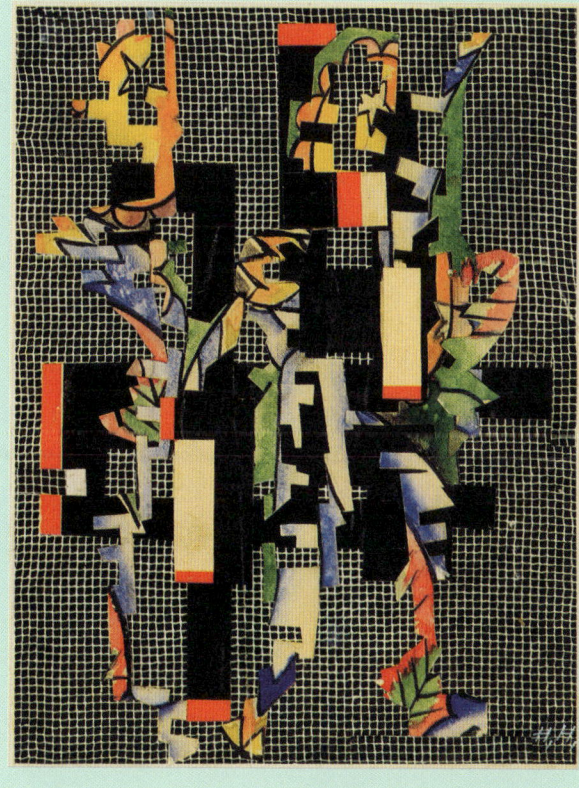

←← **Hisachika Takahashi**, *Untitled*, 1973, crayon, pastel, Scotch and masking tape on magazine cutouts (taken from *Life*, *Esquire*, *Playboy* and *Scientific American*), 152.4 × 127 cm (60 × 50 in)

← **Noah Purifoy**, *Untitled (66 Signs of Neon)*, c.1966, mixed-media assemblage, including burnt wood, acrylic, stencil and coloured felt on plywood board, 142.2 × 91.4 cm (56 × 36 in)

↑ **Romare Bearden**, *Evening 9:10, 461 Lenox Avenue*, 1964, collage of various papers with paint, ink and graphite on cardboard, 21.6 × 27.9 cm (8½ × 11 in), Van Every/Smith Galleries at Davidson College, North Carolina, USA

↗ **Hannah Höch**, *Collage II (On Filet Ground)*, c.1925, cut-and-pasted printed and painted paper on printed paper, 24.5 × 19.2 cm (9¾ × 7⅝ in), Museum of Modern Art, New York

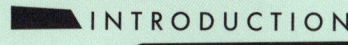 INTRODUCTION

and software – the 'windows' format of the operating systems of Apple and Microsoft, and, of course, the World Wide Web and its multiplicity of browser interfaces. These platforms, facilitating combination, juxtaposition and exchange of visual or auditory communication, also changed the material composition of images and the ability to compare, juxtapose or merge pictorial and textual content from various sources. The French artist Camille Henrot (b. 1978) addressed the implications of this transition in her work *Grosse Fatigue* (French for 'exhaustion') of 2013, which was developed during a residency at the Smithsonian Institution in Washington DC, the world's largest museum and research complex. Henrot pulled together a wealth of images and video excerpts depicting objects and specimens, rituals and cultural traditions, ranging from the fields of anthropology, natural sciences, astrology and history, adding to these video excerpts and images she both made and found online (fig. 13). The result is a thirteen-minute-long video that follows the process of browsing and scrolling through available content on a computer desktop whose background is a picture of the Milky Way galaxy. Images are then overlayed, replaced or juxtaposed with one another in a manner that is now considered natural to how information is consumed. Divided into three parts: Emptiness, God and Exhaustion, these stages are expressed not only through the choice of imagery but also with the help of a multi-layered soundtrack – a spoken-word poem written in collaboration with poet Jacob Bromberg and performed in a slam rhythm by artist Akwetey Orraca-Tetteh, to a throbbing musical beat composed by Joakim. To Henrot, *Grosse Fatigue* is 'an experience of density itself' more than any specific commentary about the content displayed throughout the film. It is a mirroring of a navigation system created in order to map the world and manage an overwhelming exposure to content. If *Grosse Fatigue* is in any way a collage, however, its edges, borders or margins are in constant flux as they dissolve into the pixelized matter of the screen, opening and closing from and to their desktop icons. ▬ One of the most notable things in Henrot's film, however, is her constant depiction of hands

(presumably her own) that are holding, peeling, touching, handling objects or browsing through books and documents. The physical presence of manual activity, literally speaking, can be interpreted as a trace of resistance to the digital takeover, but also a sign of complacency. In *Gross Fatigue* the hands, the body's most tactile part, are embedded into the molecular surface of the image, they form part of it, obey its conditions, become a strategy of its display mechanisms, a trope. Henrot's meditation on the loss of manual creative tools in the process of art-making as well as research is symptomatic to a whole group of artists operating since the 2000s with the aim to negotiate the conditions of physical and tactile sensibility in art and visual culture at large. This tendency is evident in Thomas Hirschhorn's (pp.108–1 reflections on censorship, social media and the aesthetics of politics, or Sara Cwynar's (pp.58–61) filmic and photographic work, which infiltrates the smooth and seductive appearance of online communication in which advertisement, learning, sense of personal worth and the potential to make meaningful connections are all enmeshed into polished constructions of brands and individuals. ▬ A similar trajectory, it should be noted, can be identified in the field of sound and audiovisual collage, where the processes of sampling, mixing and appropriating auditory content have undergone a transition from manual through analogue and eventually to digital methods of sound production and editing over the last century: from the first experiments in deconstructing the iterations of language by Dada artists and performers such as Hugo Ball (1886–1927) and Kurt Schwitters, through the development of Concrete music by the likes of Pierre Schaeffer (1910–95) and later also Henri Chopin (1922–2008) who spliced bits of recorded material and joined these together using analogue technologies, all the way to contemporary artists who, once again, like Henrot, Hirschhorn and Cwynar, operate on the seam between live disc-jockeying and digital processing, as well as appropriation of found imagery and footage associated with sound. Notable examples of this tendency include the work of Christian Marclay (pp.160–1), who has consistently occupied

fig. 13

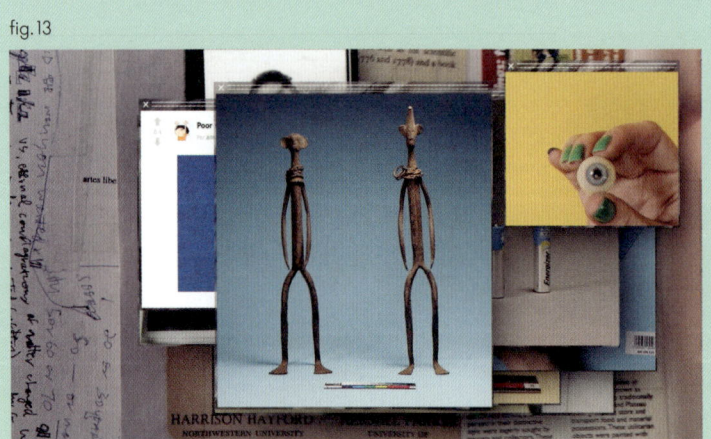

fig. 14

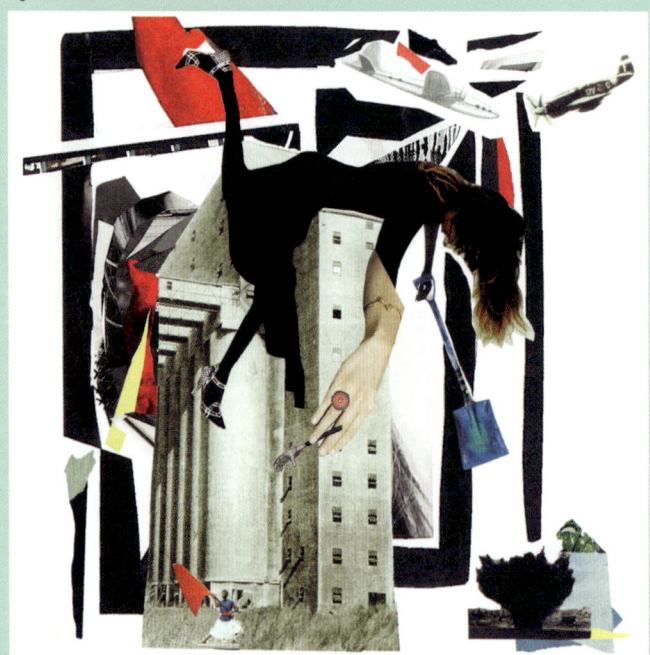

↖ **Camille Henrot**, *Grosse Fatigue*, 2013, still from video, 13 min, original music by Joakim. Voice by Akwetey Orraca-Tetteh. Text written in collaboration with Jacob Bromberg

↑ **mira calix**, ~~absent~~ origin, 2021, collage for inner sleeve of album released by Warp Records the liminal space between outmoded and innovative sound technologies since the late 1970s, and mira calix (1969–2022) whose musical practice came to rely on the adaptation of strategies from the visual field of collage into the auditory one.[19] (fig.14) ◣ Indeed, questions concerning the paradoxical relationship of collage to medium specificity are central to this book. As such, its survey format is compatible with the subject, offering a wide range of interpretations to the term 'collage', but also constituting a reminder of what is most at stake in contemporary collage – namely, the marking of edges and periphery in a field of creativity whose territorial outlines are almost impossible to identify and in constant change. As the following pages confirm, the question that artists continue to pose still today, and despite the notion of post-medium art, relies to a great deal on how the juxtaposition of seemingly unrelated materials can enable original connections and resist dilution, or mere sleight of hand. Collage, as the range of examples outlined here suggests, is a practice defined by a continuous process of challenging the borders of the artistic spectrum and the visual field. This comes into play in formal terms relating to scale, spatial orientation and material composition, but also in ideological terms where hierarchies – social or other – can be undermined or inverted, and margins are constantly pulled into the centre. After all, and despite constant reminders that we live in the age of globalization, 'crossing a border is not a simple thing'.[20]

YUVAL ETGAR is a curator and art historian who specializes in the history and theory of collage and image appropriation. His curated and published work includes *The Ends of Collage*, an anthology of writings on the history and theory of this practice, as well as monographic projects dedicated to the work of Louise Nevelson, Jake Chapman, John Stezaker, Fischli & Weiss and René Magritte, among others.

1 Clement Greenberg, 'The New Sculpture', 1948/1959, in Clement Greenberg, *Art and Culture: Critical Essays* (Beacon Press, Boston, 1961), pp.139–45.
2 ibid., pp.141–2.
3 Pablo Picasso, *Guitar* of 1914, executed sometime around January–February 1914 using ferrous sheet metal and wire. It was later gifted by the artist to the Museum of Modern Art, New York, www.moma.org/collection/works/80934.
4 John Richardson, *A Life of Picasso, Volume II: 1907–1917, The Painter of Modern Life* (Jonathan Cape, London, 1996), pp.252 5.
5 There is an elaborate history of artists using mirrors in collage, including Max Ernst, Enrico Baj, Louise Nevelson and Robert Rauschenberg, among others. Within the context of this book, the work of Sammy Baloji (pp.30–1) stands out, where historical photographs depicting the lives of Congolese miners from the 1930s as well as scans of minerals and other natural resources are printed atop mirrors that implicate the viewer as an active participant in the legacy of colonialism.

6 The word *merzbau* is composed of two utterances. The first, *merz*, was invented by the artist in order to describe his approach to art-making as one that employs a broad range of materials and methods of construction. As such, it forms part of Schwitters's interest in nonsensical language and its potential role for poetry and art. The term *bau* however, simply means 'build' in German.
7 For more on this subject, see Benjamin H. D. Buchloh, 'From Detail to Fragment: Décollage Affichiste', *October*, vol.56, 1991, pp.99–110, and Brandon Taylor, 'The Critique of Cities', in *Collage: The Making of Modern Art* (Thames & Hudson, London, 2004), pp.145–64.
8 Vostell's documentation of his décollage happenings in a series of publications from the first half of the 1960s provides a good indication as to the importance of audience participation in this history.
9 Interview between Niki de Saint Phalle and Maurice Rheims, 'Niki de Saint Phalle l'Art et les Mecs', *Vogue* (Paris, 1965), pp.92–4.
10 An elaborate account of Nevelson's engagement in collage can be found in

Out of Order: The Collages of Louise Nevelson, ed. by Yuval Etgar (Fondazione Marconi and Mousse Publishing, Milan, 2022).
11 Pia Gottschaller, 'Your Trash is My Treasure', in ibid., p.45.
12 Louise Nevelson, *Dawns and Dusks: Taped Conversations with Diana MacKown* (Charles Scribner's Sons, New York, 1976), p.184.
13 Ali Smith, 'On Edge', in *Artful* (Hamish Hamilton, London, 2012), p.125.
14 Noah Purifoy and Judson Powell, *Junk Art, 66 Signs of Neon*, 1966 (66 Signs of Neon, Los Angeles), n.p.
15 Romare Bearden, *The Romare Bearden Reader*, ed. by Robert G. O'Meally (Duke University Press, Durham, NC, 2019), p.20.
16 Sergei Eisenstein, 'A Dialectic Approach to Film Form', in *Film Form: Essays in Film Theory*, ed. and trans. by Jan Leyda (Harcourt, Brace, Janovitch, New York and London, 1977), p.49.
17 For a more elaborated discussion on terminology associated with collage and photomontage, see the author's essay 'On Edge: Collage Tactics and Terminology', in *Cut and Paste: 400 Years of Collage*,

ed. by Patrick Elliott (National Galleries of Scotland, Edinburgh, 2019), pp.35–50.
18 Filmmakers and artists who occupy this intermediate position include Luis Buñuel (*Un Chien Andalou*, 1929), Hans Richter (*Ghosts Before Breakfast*, 1927), Maya Deren (*Meshes of the Afternoon*, 1943), Arthur Lipsett (*21-87*, 1964), Stan VanDerBeek (*Movie-Drome*, 1965), Bruce Conner (*A Movie*, 1969), Frank Mouris (*Frank Film*, 1973) and more recently also Christian Marclay (*The Clock*, 2010), John Stezaker (*Blind*, 2012) and Arthur Jafa (*Love is the Message, The Message is Death*, 2016).
19 Mira Calix and Yuval Etgar, 'Running with Scissors', warp.net/editorial/running-with-scissors, 2021.
20 Ali Smith, 'On Edge', in *Artful* (Hamish Hamilton, London, 2012), p.125.

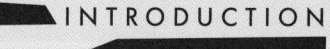

SARAH
ABU ABDALLAH

In Sarah Abu Abdallah's multimedia works – ranging from intimate to massive in scale – collage is a way to forge connections that are impossible in the real world. Her early performance-based video works tackled her position as a woman in Saudi society with direct gestures and actions: for *Saudi Automobile* (2011), presented at Sharjah Biennial 11 (2013), Abu Abdallah painted a crumpled and incomplete shell of a car in light pink paint – a way of taking ownership of a vehicle she, as a woman, would not be allowed to drive. In an equally defiant gesture in the 2013 video work *Salad Zone*, which was shown in the group exhibition 'RHIZOMA (generation in waiting)', a collateral event of the 55th Venice Biennale, two women smash a TV with sticks. Inspired by an argument recounted to her by a friend, Abu Abdallah transformed the domestic, communal space of the living room into a highly charged site of social exchange where female rebellion is possible. Abu Abdallah's more recent collage works are subtler reflections on the artist's position in the world, evolving a complex and often highly personal language. Returning to her initial training as a painter, Abu Abdallah incorporates traditional techniques in the collaborative work *Horizontal Dimensions* (2021), made with her mother, the artist Ghada Al Hassan. The viewer travels along a curving installation that unfurls like a scroll, finding acrylic and ink paintings and pencil drawings as well as cut photographs embedded in the papier-mâché surface. The physical space the work inhabits stands in contrast to the private, codified meanings the work holds, serving as 'sort of a dialogue between us, like a manuscript, a documentation or a map of our conversations', as Abu Abdallah described it in a 2022 video interview for the Diriyah Biennale Foundation. This tension between form and meaning, between privacy and the public space, and between comprehension and the indecipherable, plays out constantly in Abu Abdallah's collages. The cartographic, mixed-media paintings *Karam* and *Capacity* (both 2019) are in fact visual journals inspired by the artist's own everyday experiences, webs of dreamlike abstract and figurative images connected by a signature line or thread that draws free associations between them. There is often a meandering, experiential quality to Abu Abdallah's works, each one a complex mesh of figments and fragments that reflects a networked yet disconnected digital world. Her references draw on personal encounters and memories, as well as family photographs from before she was born – such as the pictures of her father as a young man that appear in the 'q-VR' series of 2015. Elsewhere, the regional pop culture of the Gulf (where Abu Abdallah lives) meets the infinite, globalized matrix of virtual reality. By taking control of these disparate parts, Abu Abdallah re-establishes the connection between herself and the world. But crucially, in her works, the image is never complete, multiple narratives coexist – a visual puzzle in which the viewer must find their own coordinates too.

CHARLOTTE JANSEN

Born 1990, Qatif, Saudi Arabia. Lives in Riydah, Saudi Arabia.

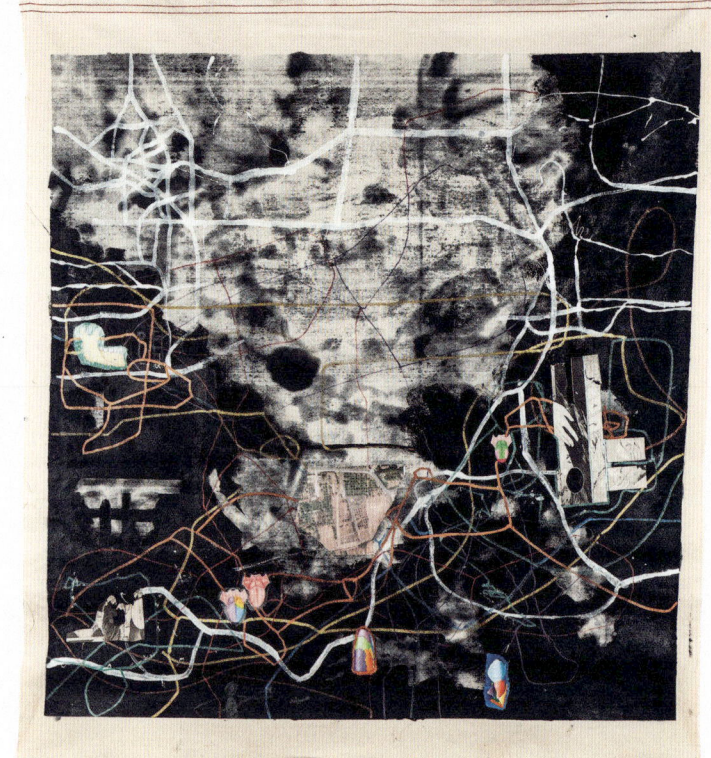

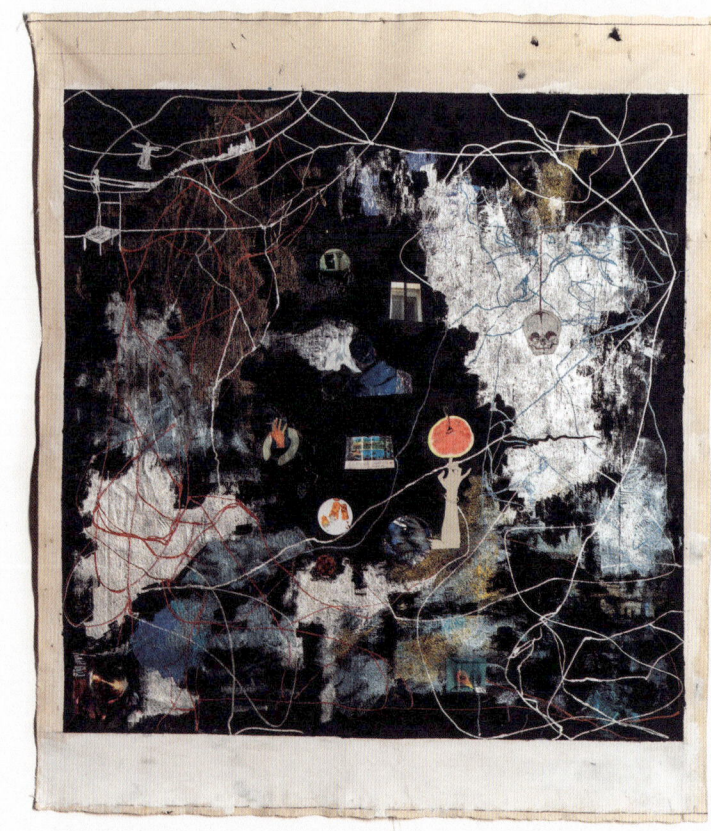

↑↑ **Capacity**, 2019, mixed media, 120 × 120 cm (47¼ × 47¼ in)

↑ **Karam**, 2019, mixed media, 120 × 120 cm (47¼ × 47¼ in)

↗ **q-VR 02**, **q-VR 03** and **q-VR 04**, 2015, digital prints, each 45 × 45 cm (17¾ × 17¾ in), editions of 4

→ **Horizontal Dimensions** (detail), made with **Ghada Al Hassan**. 2021, acrylic, ink, pencil and papier-mâché on canvas, 1.7 × 25 m (5¼ × 82 ft), installation view, 'Feeling the Stones', First Diriyah Biennale, Saudi Arabia, 2021

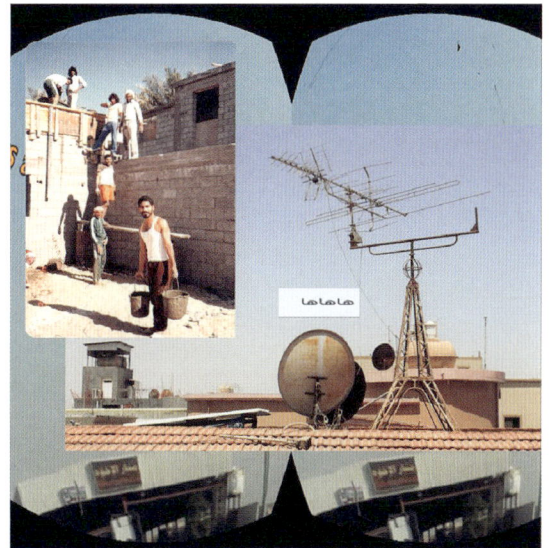
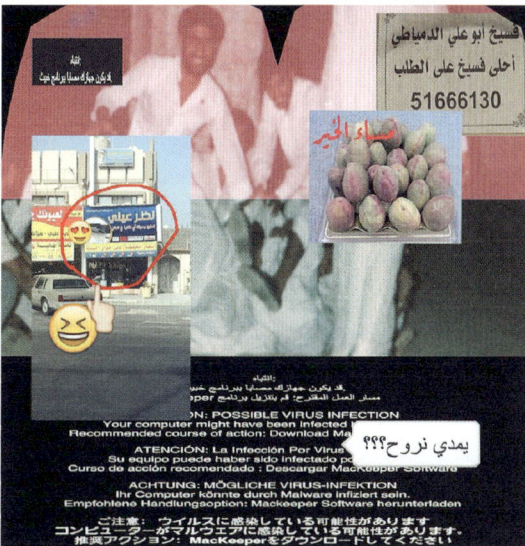
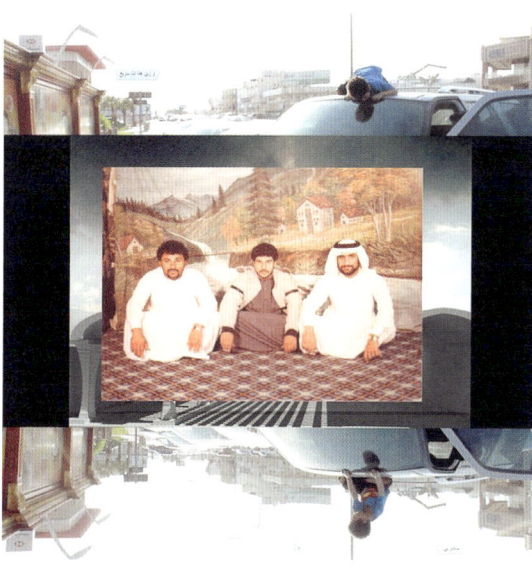

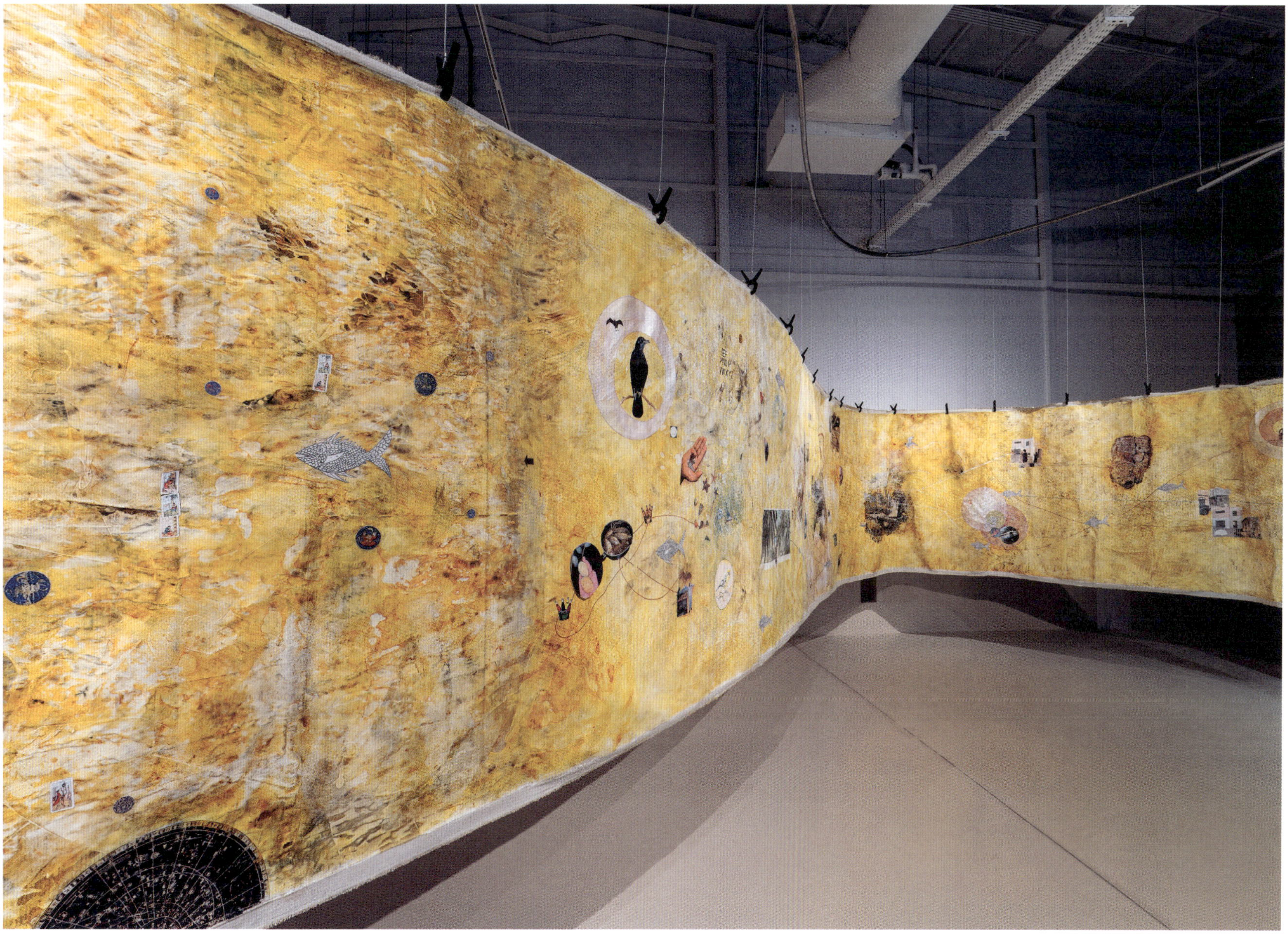

SARAH
ABU ABDALLAH

DERRICK ADAMS

Since the late 1990s Derrick Adams has created a vast oeuvre, characterized by strategies of fragmentation and recombination, that encompasses painting, textile- and paper-based collage, sculpture, sound, video and performance. Engaged in an ongoing dialogue with the changing modes of representation of the Black figure as reflected through popular culture, mass media and entertainment, Adams deftly reinterprets and updates common tropes, creating images of subjects engaged in everyday rituals or joyfully luxuriating during moments of leisure. Although his lively colour palette refracts the heightened chromatic world of television and media platforms – *Colorbar Constellation 6* (2016), for example, depicts the SMPTE colour bars of an analogue television set, juxtaposed with a *TV Guide* cover and strips of brightly coloured African dashiki cloth – his references look back much further: the simplified rhythms of Constructivism, the geometries of African masks, the documentary impulse of Dadaist photomontage and improvisational cut-paper collage work of American artist Romare Bearden (1911–88). As with Bearden, Adams's practice is entrenched in the philosophical ethos of fragmentation. For Bearden, collage offered a means to construct an image while destabilizing prevalent views relating to issues of race and identity through the recontextualization of images informed by his dynamic and layered style. For Adams, aesthetic discontinuity, and the collision of complex forms – typically exercised through shifts in colour, shape and pattern – beckon to the construction of the self, too. As seen in these examples from the series 'We Came to Party and Plan' (2019–20), these images frequently appear as colourful bust-length portraits, set against monochrome backgrounds, in which human faces read as geometric or architectural facets. Made from paint, cut paper and swatches of fabric, these portraits oscillate between pattern and a type of sculptural relief. Flatness and depth are expressed through architectonic shifts in swathes of colour, indicating light and shadow through shapes that form elements like a figure's shoulder pad or the flat of the forehead. While Adams utilizes the visual strategies of recombining images that have been used throughout twentieth-century art history as a critique of popular culture, his works also employ these strategies in the service of affirmation. His ongoing series 'Floaters', which he began in 2015, comprises a variety of playful collaged paintings that depict figures swimming and idling in calm waters. Although pointing to the insidious history of swimming pools in the United States as inaccessible sites for Black Americans, works such as *Floater 89* (2020), in which two figures lounge on a colour-blocked inflatable swan, express a quiet radicality in their refusal to depict instances of suffering or trauma. As Adams said in a 2021 *ARTnews* interview, 'That's the benefit of being an artist: you can actually create the environment you want to experience every day.'

MADELINE WEISBURG

Born 1970, Baltimore, Maryland, USA. Lives in Brooklyn, New York, USA.

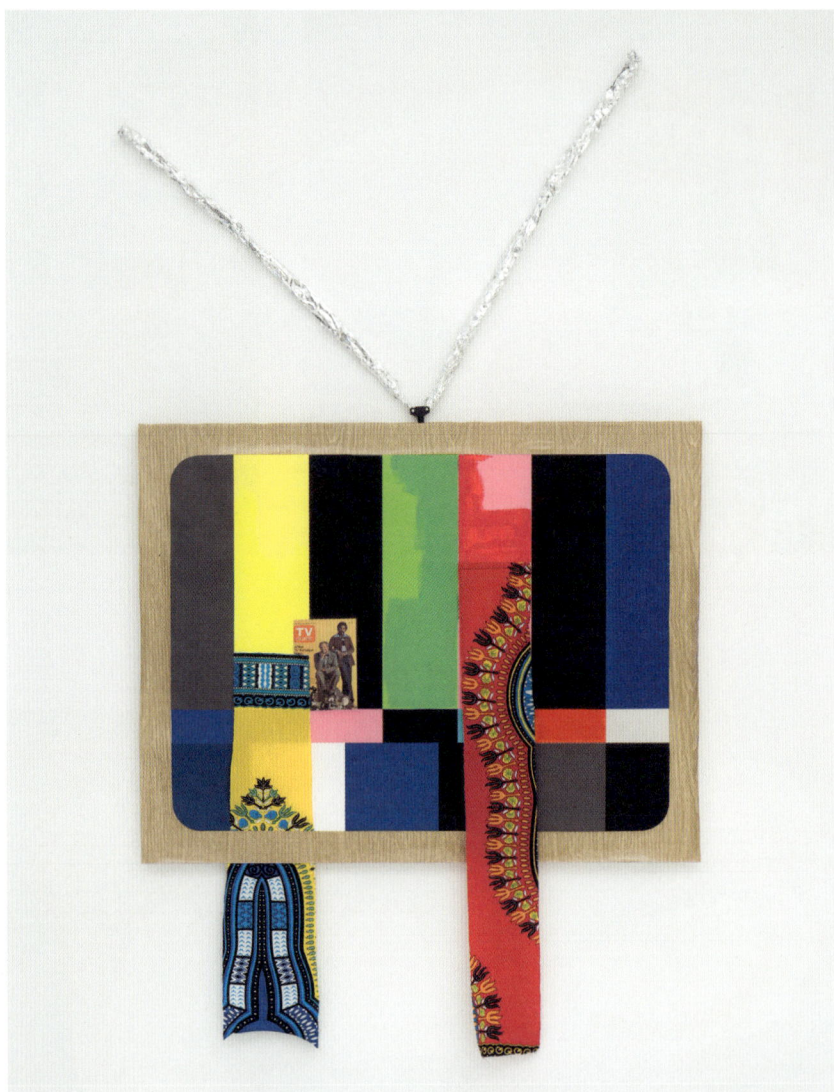

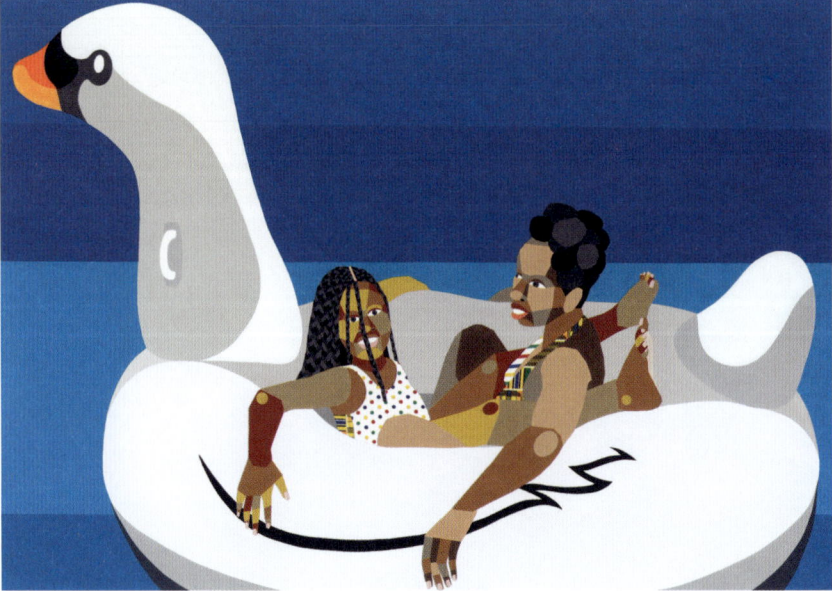

↑↑ **Colorbar Constellation 6**, 2016, acrylic paint, paper vintage *TV Guide* cover, fabric, on pigment printed canvas, with wood-grain-patterned fabric-backed vinyl, TV antenna, aluminium foil and wood cleat, 198.1 × 111.8 × 2.5 cm (78 × 44 × 1 in)

↑ **Floater 89**, 2020, acrylic paint, pencil, fabric and paper collage on paper, 132.1 × 188 × 2.5 cm (52 × 74 × 1 in)

↗ **We Came to Party and Plan 18**, 2020; **We Came to Party and Plan 32**, 2019; **We Came to Party and Plan 31**, 2019, acrylic paint, fabric and paper collage on paper, each 61 × 45.7 cm (24 × 18 in)

→ **Tables Turned 1**, 2016, mixed media and collage on hardboard panel, 91.4 × 182.9 cm (36 × 72 in)

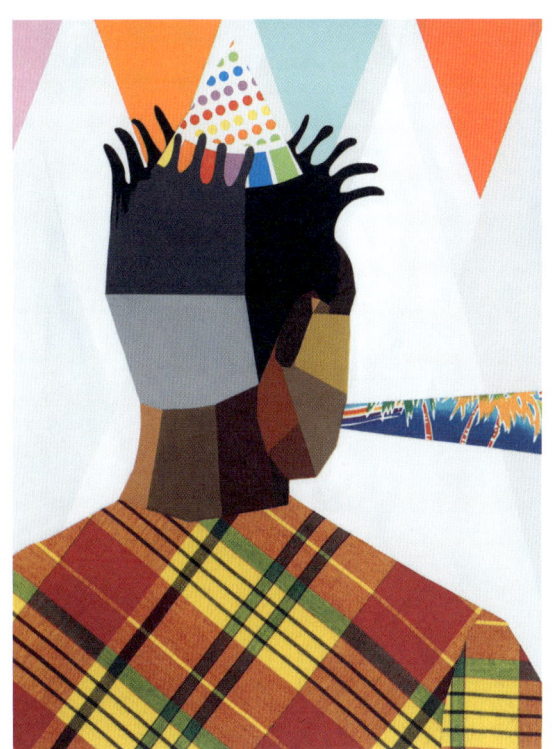
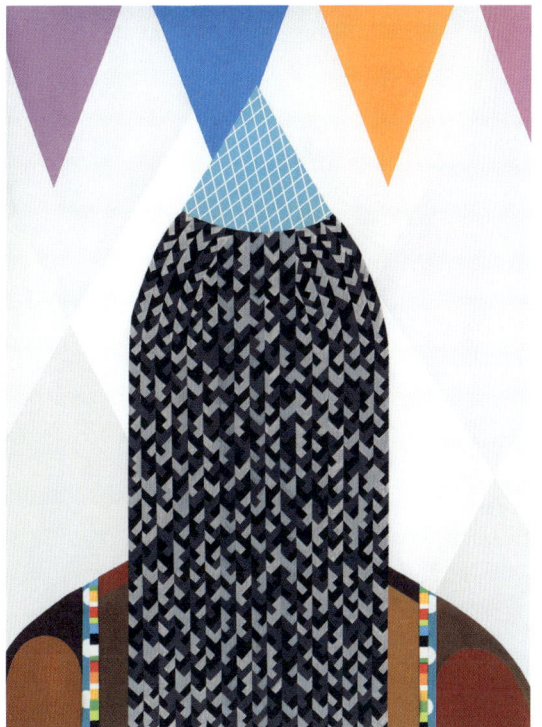
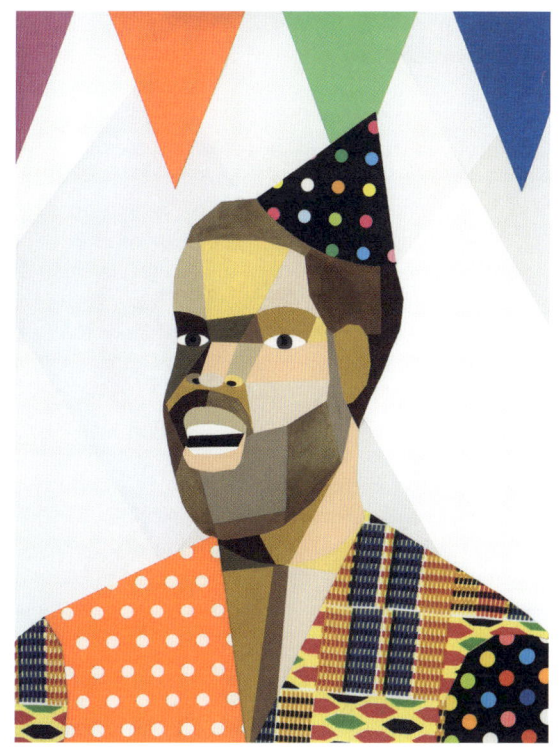

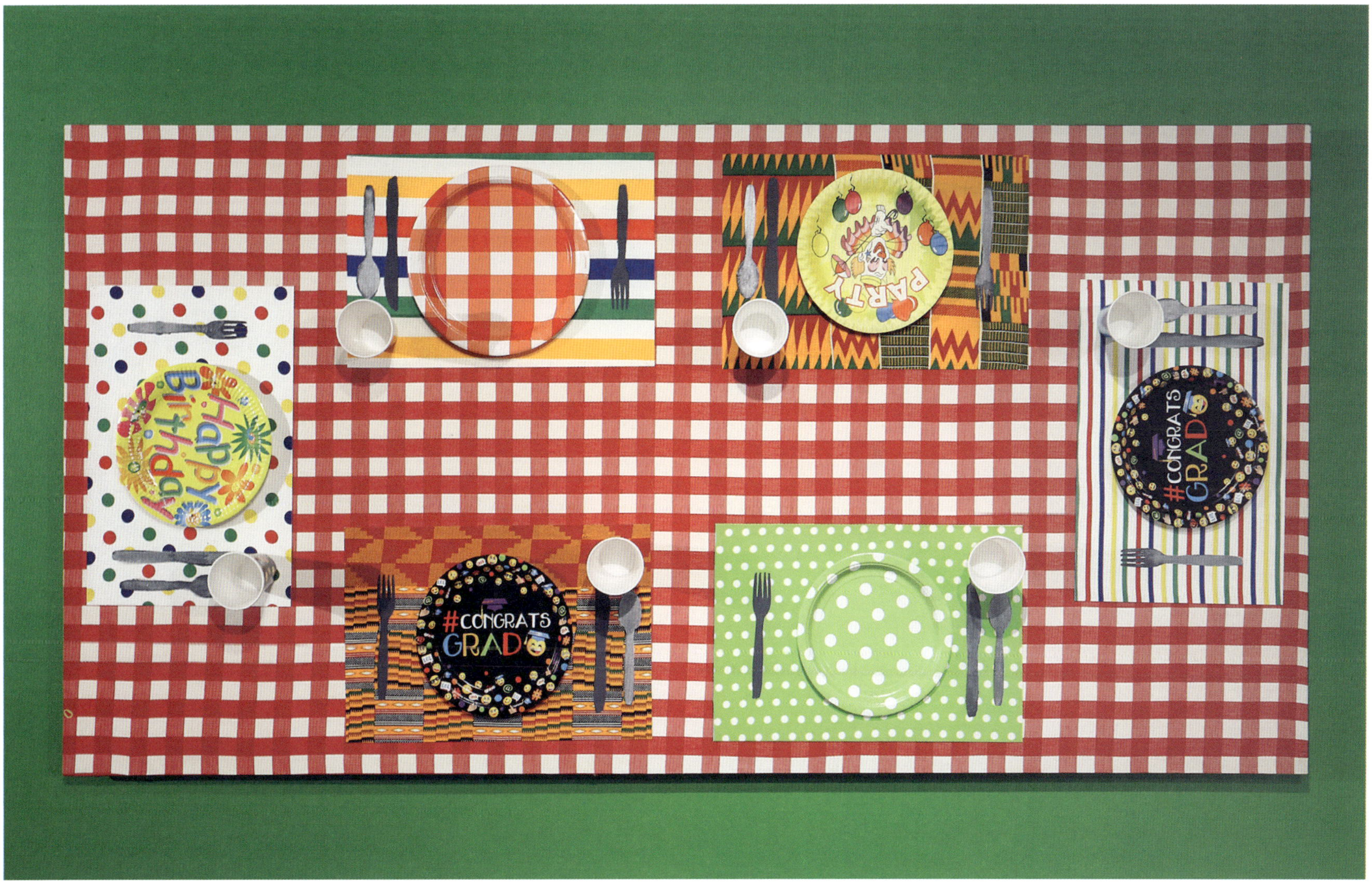

DERRICK ADAMS

IBRAHIM AHMED

Informed by forensic research into the histories of his family, the material reality of the Nile Delta region and the objects and monuments that populate his immediate urban environment, Ibrahim Ahmed's expansive collage practice wrestles with legacies of colonialism, structures of power, migration and masculinity, and how these ideas intersect with notions of self and nationhood. Using his father's extensive photographic archive as his source material, which includes thousands of photographs taken as the artist's family migrated freely between Kuwait, Bahrain and the United States, Ahmed sutures, splices and samples images to conjure up a new reality, full of generative possibilities that destabilize the Western-centric hegemonic gaze. Taken across different temporal and geographic zones, these images collapse the space-time continuum and offer up a hybrid space that rejects fabricated borders and singular identities. Across the series 'I never revealed myself to them' (2012–21), Ahmed analyzes the similarities and differences between Egyptian and American male bodies set against civic, military, religious or urban modernist architecture. Through a process of compare and contrast, he draws attention not only to their sartorial differences – men in military uniform, sporting suits or wearing djellaba – but more significantly directs the viewer to examine his subjects' physical patterns of behaviour to understand how men are socially conditioned to behave depending on their cultural norms. In *Figure #7* images of cars signifying the American Dream are juxtaposed against images of flags that reflect on imperial sovereignty, while headless men in military regalia gaze upon the surreal scene unfolding as children in silhouette share the frame with a faceless man holding a baby. Ahmed here is interested in the meaning of bodily gestures, in this case scrutinizing the supposed tenderness between father and child. Questions of visibility and invisibility are critical to Ahmed's way of presenting the world and he invariably conceals his figures' faces. This act of collaged masquerade speaks to ideas of being excluded from the regime of visibility while also being a mechanism of resistance against state-sanctioned nationalism and mythic fabulations of borders. Equally, by obliterating his subjects' identities, Ahmed denies the Orientalist gaze that consistently vilifies the North African male as a subject of sexual danger or political violence. The construction of gender is a recurring motif in Ahmed's practice and the 'assemblage' quality of collage operates as a mimetic trope, calling to mind the performative and unstable nature of both gender and photography. In *Figure #50, you can't recognize what you don't know* (2020–1), Ahmed edits, cuts, reassembles and layers a full-body, black-and-white self-portraits taken in the studio, set against a white curtain, to further reinforce the theatricality of gender. Distorted, fractured, multiplied or erased, the male form here becomes a fugitive entity, evading any fixed definition and therefore liberated from the straitjacketing of heteronormative masculinity.

ALONA PARDO

Born 1984, Kuwait City, Kuwait. Lives in Ard-el-Lewa, Giza, Egypt.

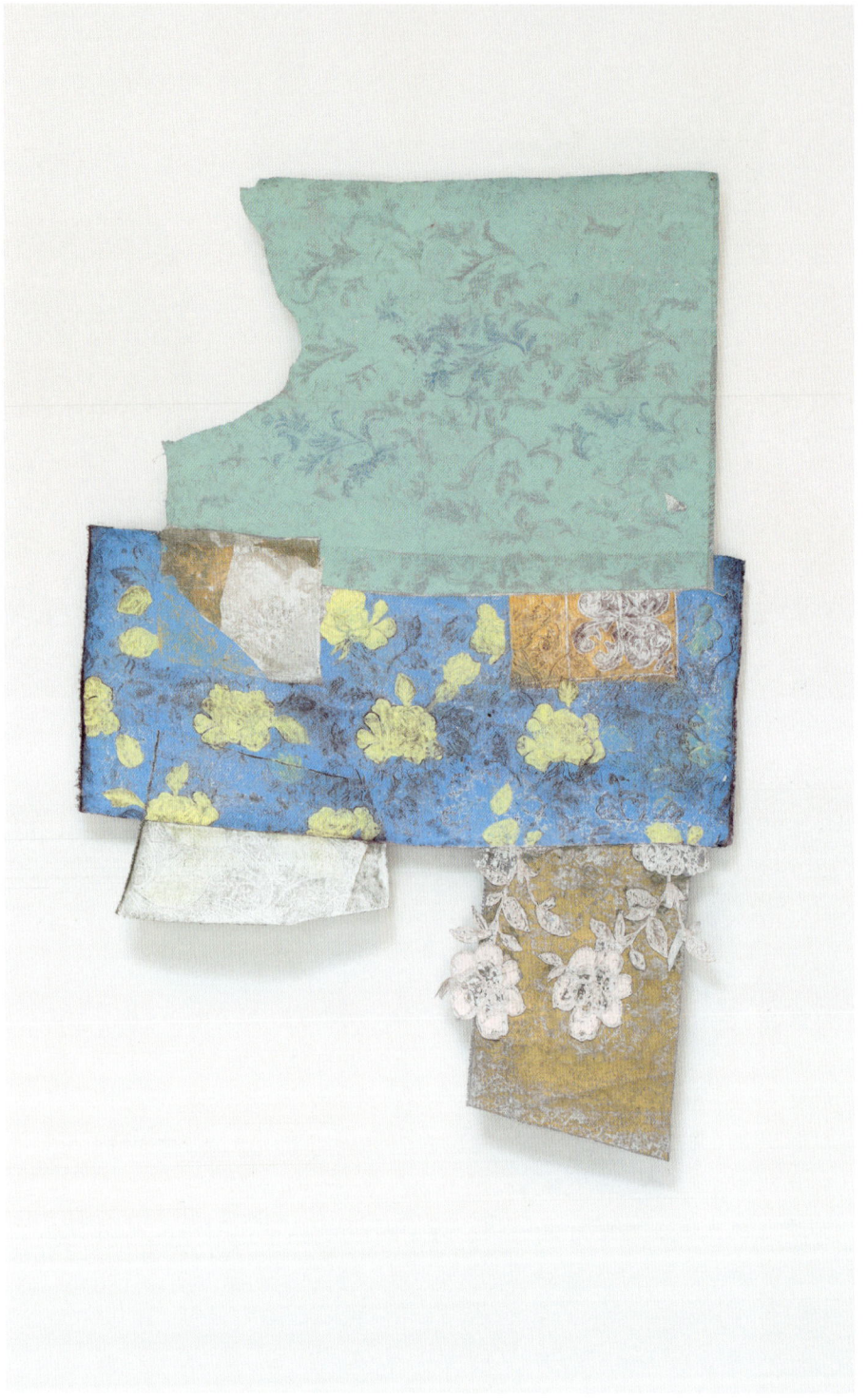

↑ **Ard el Lewa #2**, 2016, mixed media, 214 × 153 cm (84¼ × 60¼ in), installation view, 'Ibrahim Ahmed: It Will Always Come Back to You', Institute for Contemporary Art at VCU, Richmond, Virginia, USA, 2021

↗ **Figure #7, quickly but carefully cross to the other side**, from the series 'I never revealed myself to them', 2012–21, unique photo-collage, 54.4 × 50.3 cm (21⅜ × 19¾ in)

↗↗ **Figure #50, you can't recognize what you don't know**, from the series 'I never revealed myself to them', 2012–21, unique photo-collage, 49.4 × 29.8 cm (18¼ × 11¾ in)

→ **Figure #3, some things seem forgotten**, from the series 'I never revealed myself to them', 2012–21, unique photo-collage, 34.4 × 47 cm (13½ × 18½ in)

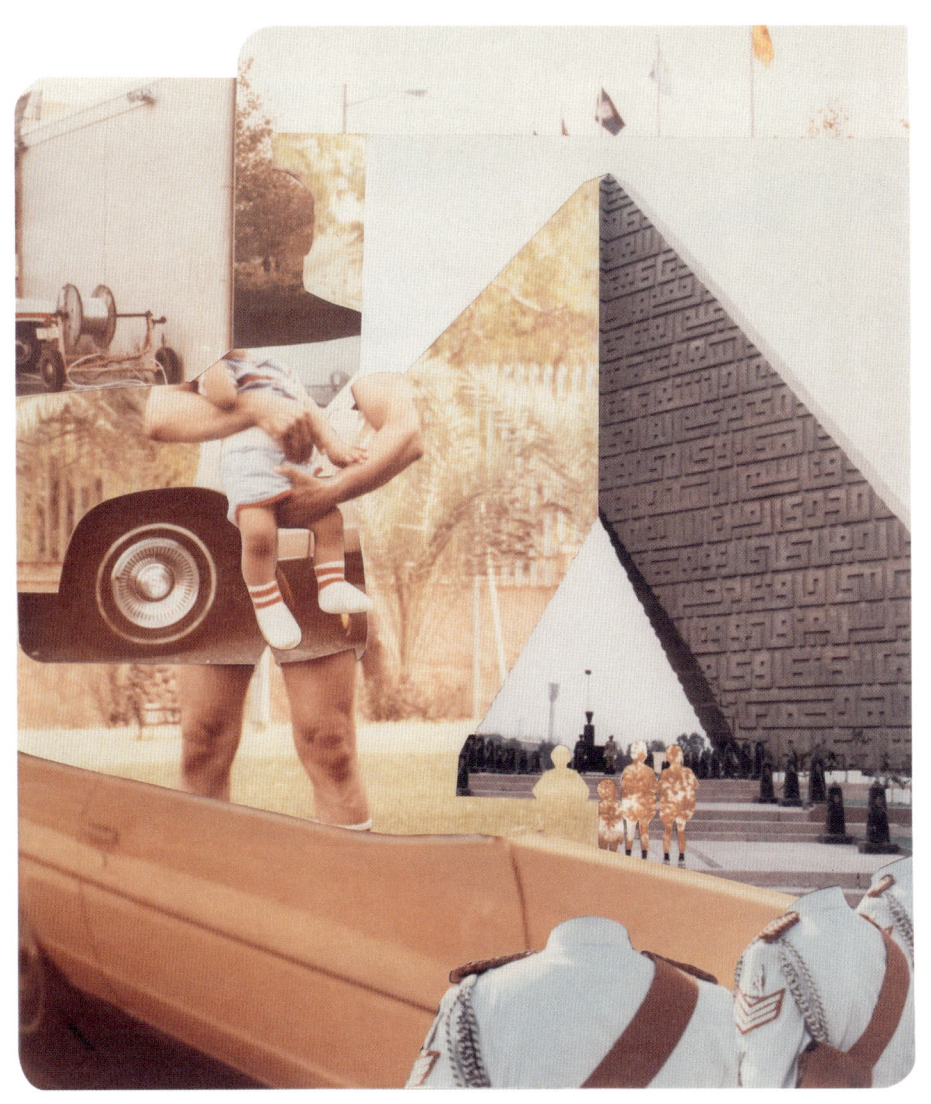

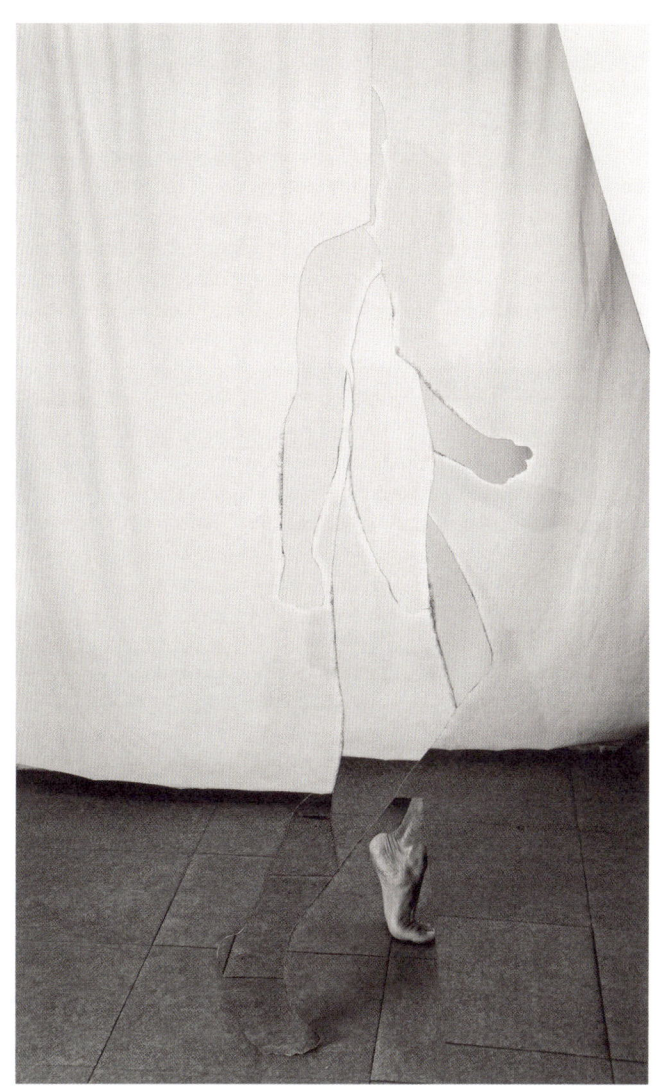

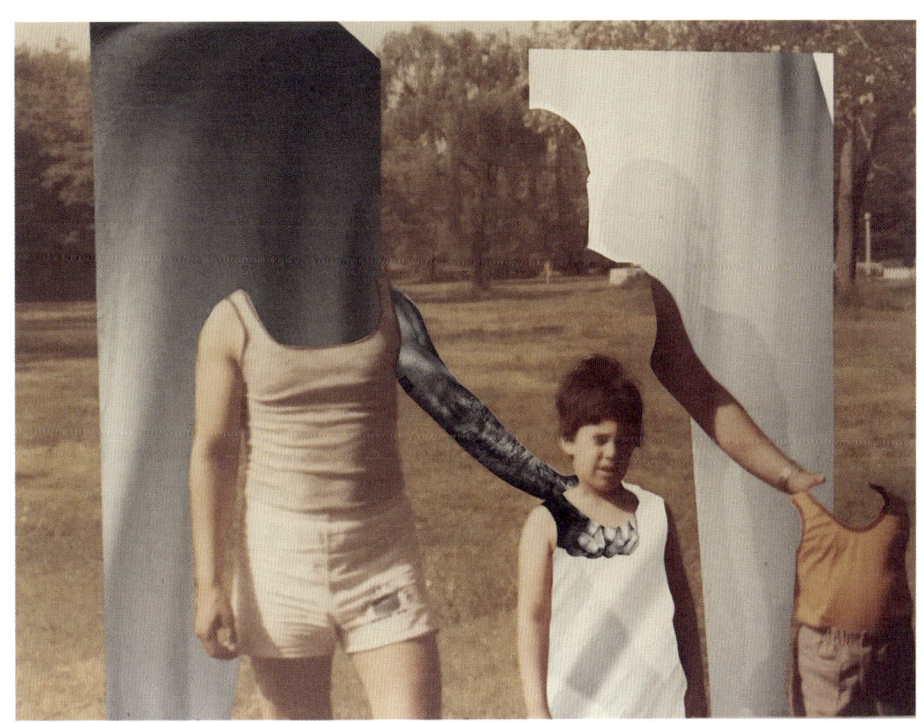

IBRAHIM AHMED

NJIDEKA AKUNYILI CROSBY

Njideka Akunyili Crosby has established an international reputation for her portrayal of quotidian scenes and domestic interiors as sites for conversations about culture, emphasizing their importance and role within larger socio-political contexts and narratives. Her imposing works on paper comprise collaged imagery drawn from magazines and other printed materials from her native Nigeria, along with elements that she paints and draws by hand. In these works, she aims to create a dialogue between her early years in Africa, where she lived until she was sixteen, and her life in North America. Her works can be read as a metaphor for hybridity and multiculturalism, reflecting on how, for manydiaspora communities, past experiences layer with the present in terms of cultural practices, language and relationships. Akunyili Crosby's process creates a visually textured yet flat surface. *As We See You: Dreams of Jand* (2017) depicts a corner of a room with a still life arrangement of every-day items. The closely cropped angle and sharp perspective draw the viewer into the composition. The 'Maltina' drinks can and the tin of 'Peak' evaporated milk are Nigerian products and the wall of collaged images – made in the artist's signature photographic transfer technique – also references Nigeria's history and pop culture. The willow pattern china plate and plastic kettle, however, reflect the legacy of British colonialism, as does the title: 'Jand' is Nigerian slang for 'London' or 'England'. In her interior scenes, the artist often incorporates thresholds, such as windows and doorways, to direct the viewers' eyes into the spaces, which are sites of accumulated memories, histories and personal anecdotes. In *Home: As You See Me* (2017) we look through turquoise curtains into a homely living room, complete with lace antimacassars on chairs and a television showing a vintage James Bond film. On the far wall is a motif of the artist's mother as seen in a medallion portrait printed on commemorative fabric from her senatorial campaign, which functions as wallpaper within this scene. The repeating phrase 'SERVICE TO THE PEOPLE' refers to both her mother's political role, but also her place within the family. Her smiling face can also be seen within the group portrait that hangs, significantly, on top of the wallpaper, demonstrating the power of collage to create hierarchies through layering. In contrast, *Potential, Displaced* (2021) offers no pictorial depth and no one image stands out above another. In another example of the layering of past and present, it relates to the history of Seneca Village, a nineteenth-century settlement of mostly African Americans within what would later become Central Park in Manhattan. It includes images of a survey map of the site, of artefacts discovered there by archaeologists, vintage photo-graphs of Black New Yorkers, and stylized silhouettes of an okra plant, which provide an alternative to the dense foliage of the park today.

MARITZA LACAYO

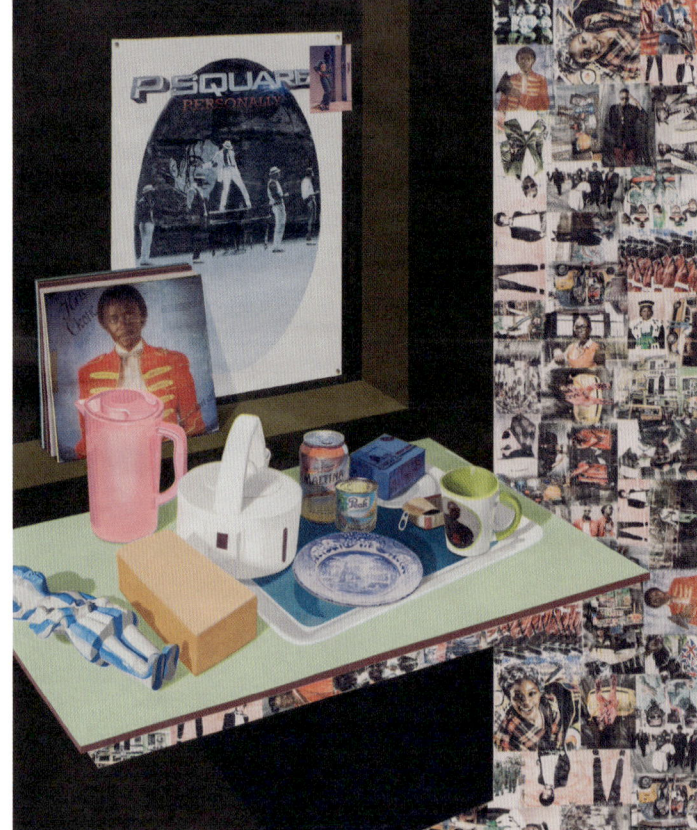

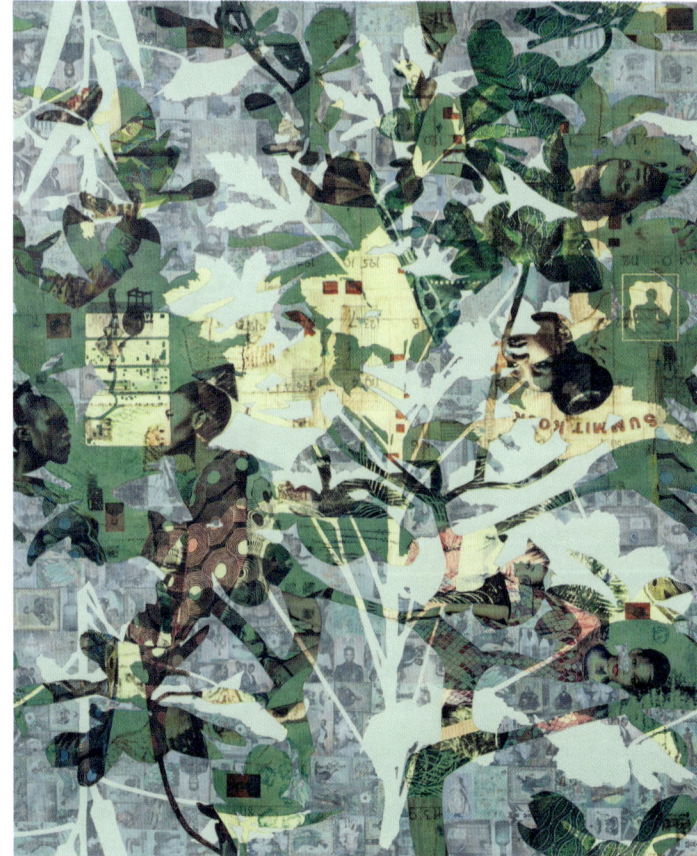

Born 1983, Enugu, Nigeria. Lives in Los Angeles, California, USA.

↑↑ **As We See You: Dreams of Jand**, 2017, acrylic, transfers, coloured pencil and collage on paper, 182.9 × 152.4 cm (72 × 60 in)

↑ **Potential, Displaced**, 2021, acrylic, transfers and coloured pencil on paper, 182.9 × 152.4 cm (72 × 60 in)

→ **Home: As You See Me**, 2017, acrylic, transfers, coloured pencil, charcoal, collage and commemorative fabric on paper, 213.4 × 211.5 cm (84 × 83¼ in)

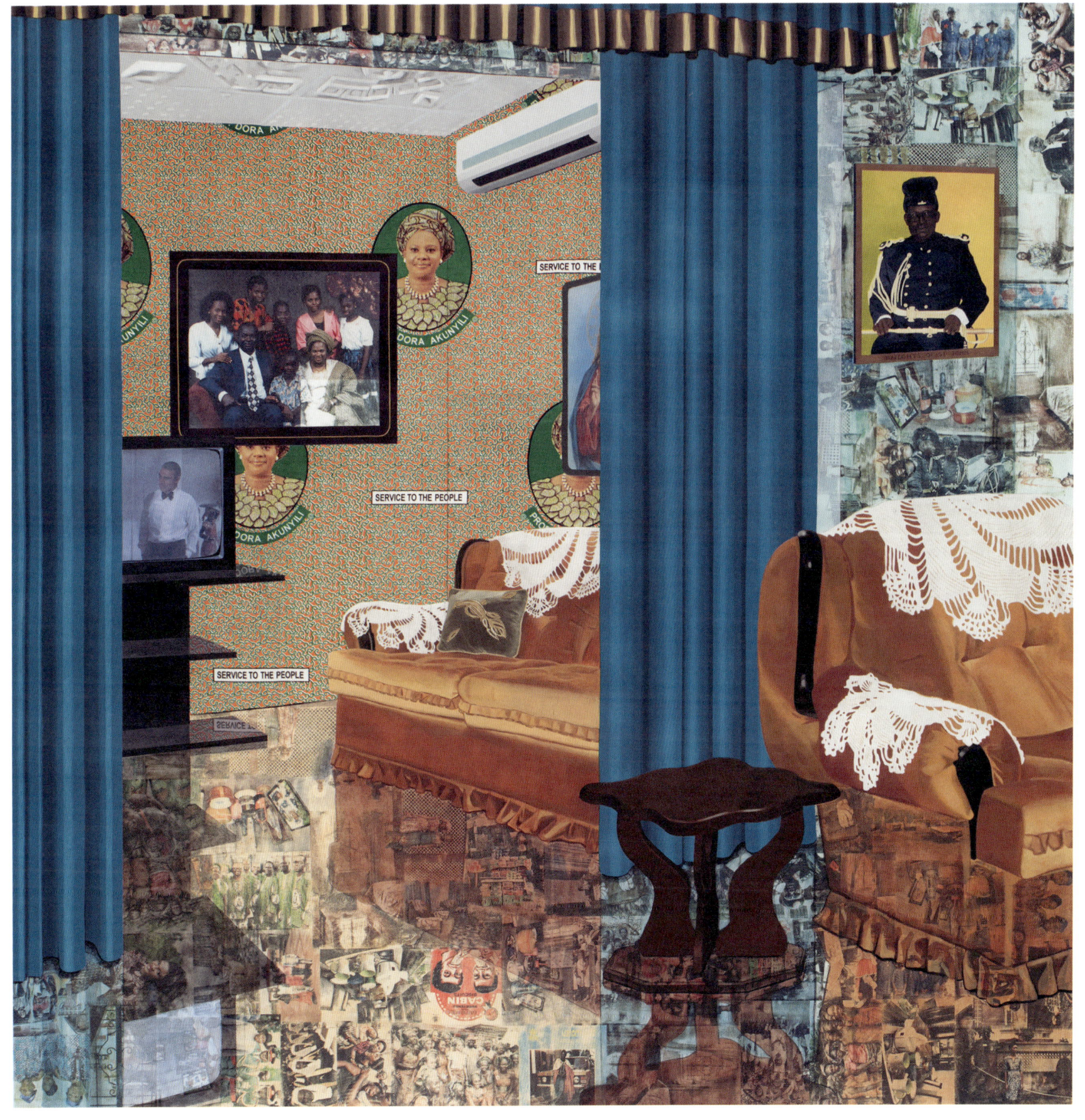

SERVICE TO THE PEOPLE

SERVICE TO THE PEOPLE

SERVICE TO THE PEOPLE

NJIDEKA
AKUNYILI CROSBY

TARIQ ALVI

Poised between the deliberate and happenstance, the precarious and permanent, Tariq Alvi's work plays with the transformative potential of collage. Alvi was first introduced to the art form as a postgraduate student at the Jan Van Eyck Academie in Maastricht in the Netherlands, when, struggling to find his medium, his tutor – the artist Avis Newman (b. 1946) – suggested he try collage. This, coupled with a fortuitous visit to an exhibition of the work of Hannah Höch (1889–1978) at LACMA, Los Angeles in 1997, began an enduring engagement with the medium, which he marries with other disciplines, including painting, sculpture, photography and performance. Alvi often uses found material, typically commercial ephemera like fliers and magazine adverts. In the works created for his solo exhibition 'Reaching for the Beginning' at Gallery Michael Benevento, Los Angeles, in 2017, the artist collected a range of such media, which he overlaid with tiny strips of paper that he had painstakingly guillotined, then meticulously glued, before photographing and printing them to poster size, reuniting the surface back into a glossy whole. The effect is a vortex of shape and colour that dazzles the eye while denying its attempts to make legible the work's contents. The collaged elements abstract and slyly subvert consumerist ideology. *The Jungle 2* (2017) was inspired by *Tiger in a Tropical Storm (Surprised!)*, the 1891 painting by Henri Rousseau, its verdant foliage replaced by slender snippets of greenery foraged from gardening magazines. These blades of grass punctuate an advertisement for beds selected, Alvi wryly recalled in a 2022 conversation with the author, because it reminded him of a crocodile ready to pounce on the woman delightedly examining underbed storage. Echoes of the white lashings of Rousseau's rain and the mark-making of Eric Ravilious's (1903–42) watercolour and woodcut depictions of the English countryside permeate the series, which Alvi made during an unseasonably rainy summer in East London. *Collage 41* (2017) shows an advert for luxury watches pummelled by diagonal strips of blank paper, obliterating the image and returning it to the pulp from whence it came. Time is a familiar trope in Alvi's work. In *Large Reality* (2016) the watches are almost completely obscured. An Op art riot of disco colours dances across the advert's surface creating an alternative, altogether kinkier version of the rainbow flag to better articulate the artist's queerness. The recurrent imagery of clocks hints towards the durational aspect of Alvi's practice. Each work is incredibly labour intensive, yet the artist's hand is erased through the ultimately slick print production. The poster, however, as well as being associated with mass media and commerce, is also a symbol of protest. Seemingly less overtly polemic than work made earlier in Alvi's career – for example *The Hanging* (2008), which centres on a homophobic execution – these works remain gently subversive, an oblique critique of the systems of capitalism and power that govern our lives.

SHAMITA SHARMACHARJA

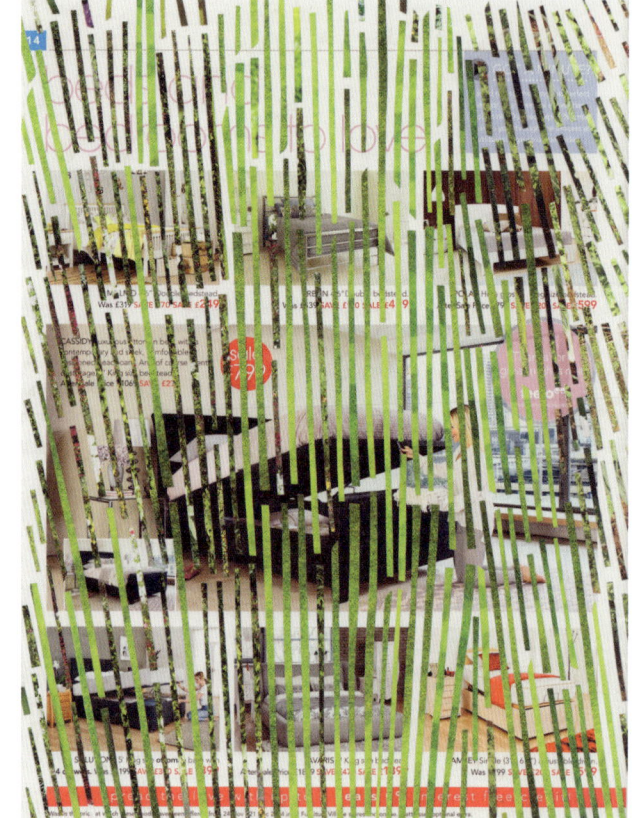

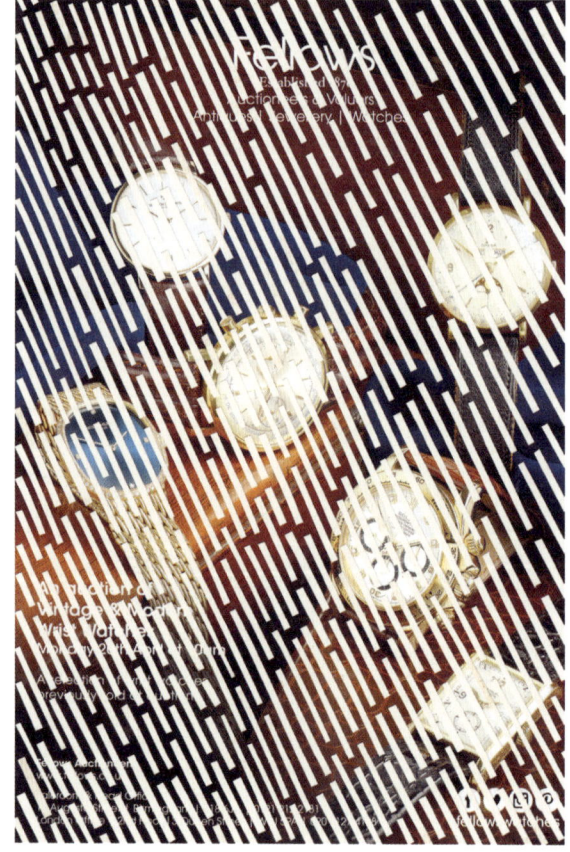

Born 1965, Newcastle upon Tyne, UK. Lives in London, UK.

↑↑ **The Jungle (2)**, 2017, C-print, 78.7 × 53.3 cm (31 × 21 in)

↑ **Collage 41**, 2017, C-print, 78.7 × 53.3 cm (31 × 21 in)

→ **Large Reality**, 2016, C-print, 78.7 × 53.3 cm (31 × 21 in)

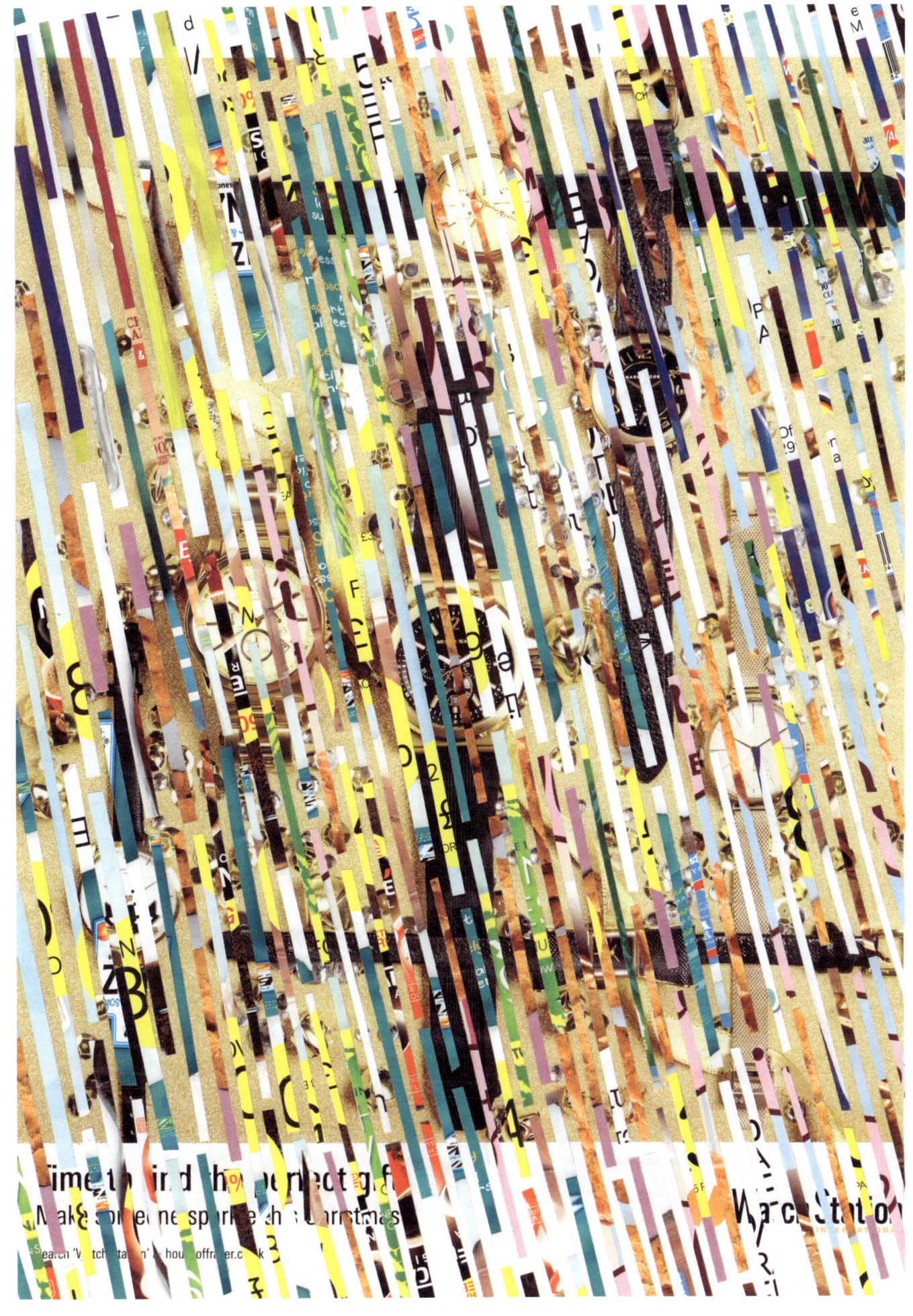

TARIQ ALVI

KADER ATTIA

Colonial legacies, exile and hybridization are just some of the themes Kader Attia explores through a reappropriation of historical images and artefacts. While his wider art practice is multidisciplinary and often involves sculptural installations, in his two-dimensional collages he cuts and edits found images to explore possibilities for disjunctions and connections. In his series 'Modern Architecture Genealogy' (2015), the French-Algerian artist reconstructs the architecture of housing projects in the *banlieues* of Paris like the one in which he grew up. As building blocks he uses squares of bold colour collaged alongside images of concrete high-rises and highways. In the empty spaces created between these, cut-outs of people appear alone or in small groups. Men walk along empty streets or socialize before entrances, juxtaposed with seemingly anachronistic figures and objects: a woman in traditional dress, a vintage television set, a twentieth-century jaguar sculpture, a snapshot of the modernist architect Le Corbusier. The genealogy Attia proposes here is less that of a family tree than a town square, with people occupying the same space even as they ignore one another. These works point towards unacknowledged histories: how social theories applied to French suburban housing projects of the 1970s were first developed in Algeria in the 1950s, just at the end of the colonial era. Or how elements of Le Corbusier's architecture and ideas were inspired by the terraced roofs and facades of Mzab houses in Ghardaia, an eleventh-century village located in the desert of Algeria. The connections Attia presents are just some among many, were his blocks to be rearranged in wholly different combinations.

Two untitled works from 2018 display a different collage strategy, one based less on amalgamation than on comparison and distinction. Portraits of disfigured First World War soldiers are placed on cardboard around black-and-white photographs of stylized African masks. The scars that marked these men out after the war are unsettlingly mirrored in the lopsided smiles carved in wood. Damaged white faces and the deliberately distorted Black faces of such artefacts are not often associated – and even in Attia's collages they do not overlap or even touch. But by placing them side by side, he highlights shared scars inflicted by trauma, whether bodily, psychological or historical. 'French society,' Attia told *Apollo* magazine in 2015, 'has a deep history of injuries generated by colonialism that have never been treated.' If brokenness suggests a lack, a weakness, or the locus of injury, then repair offers the possibility to recover what was once lost or taken away. Attia's collages point towards fractures in society, and while he offers no solutions, he leaves the spaces between the images open to the possibility for repair and reparation.

EDMÉE LEPERCQ

Born 1970, Dugny, France. Lives in Berlin, Germany and Paris, France.

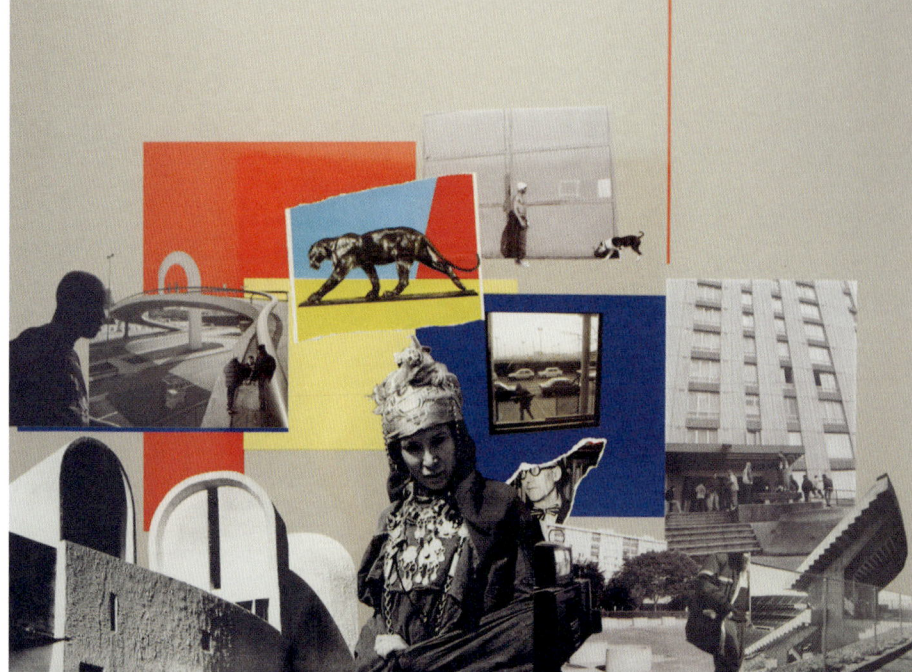

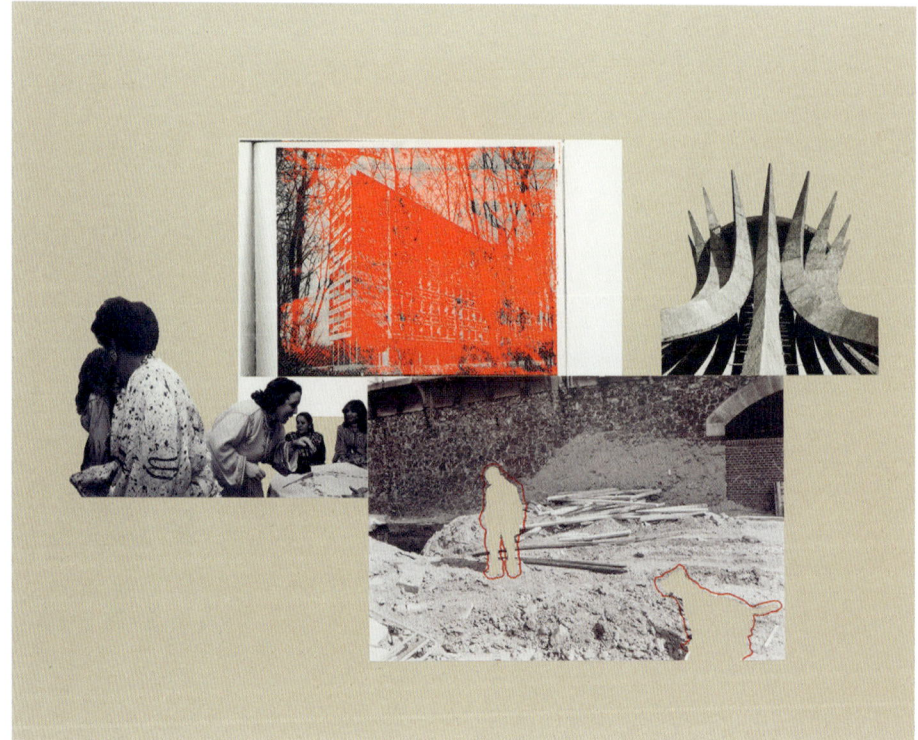

↑↑ Untitled, from the series '**Modern Architecture Genealogy**', 2015, collage on cardboard: silver gelatin prints and vintage documents, 80 × 120 cm (31½ × 47¼ in)

↑ Untitled, from the series '**Following the Modern Genealogy**', 2012–21, collage on cardboard: photographs, vintage documents, photocopies, 80 × 120 cm (31½ × 47¼ in)

↗ Untitled, 2018, collage on cardboard: photographs, vintage documents and photocopies, 52 × 38 cm (20½ × 15 in)

↗↗ Untitled, 2018, collage on cardboard: photographs, vintage documents and photocopies, 49 × 38 cm (19¼ × 15 in)

→ Untitled, from the series '**Hijras**', 2020, collage on paper: photographs, photocopies, vintage documents and ink, 50 × 65 cm (19¾ × 25⅝ in)

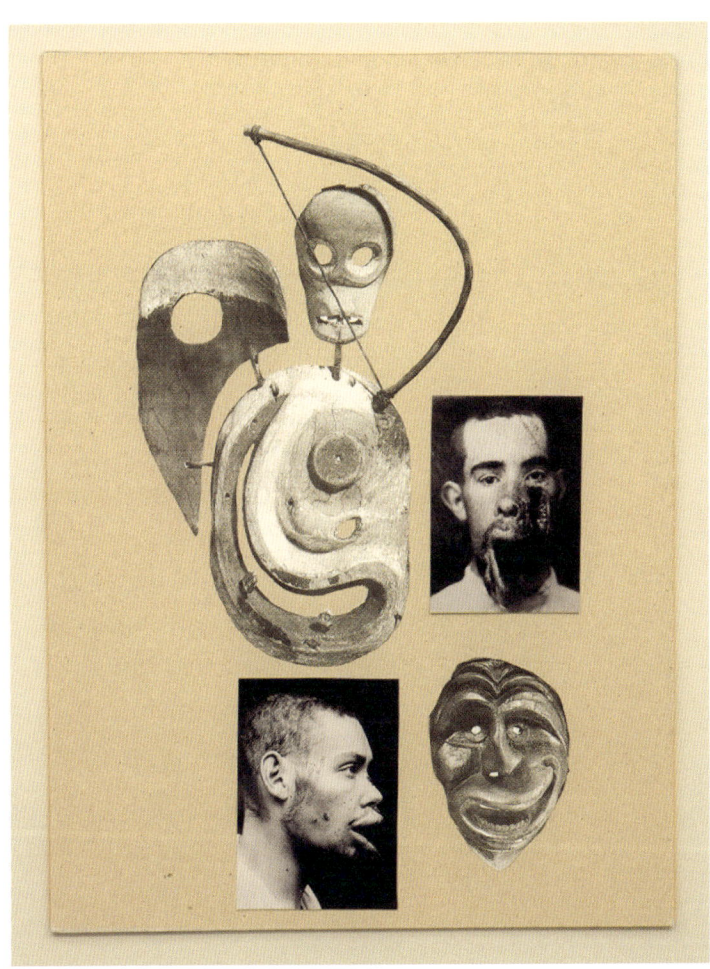

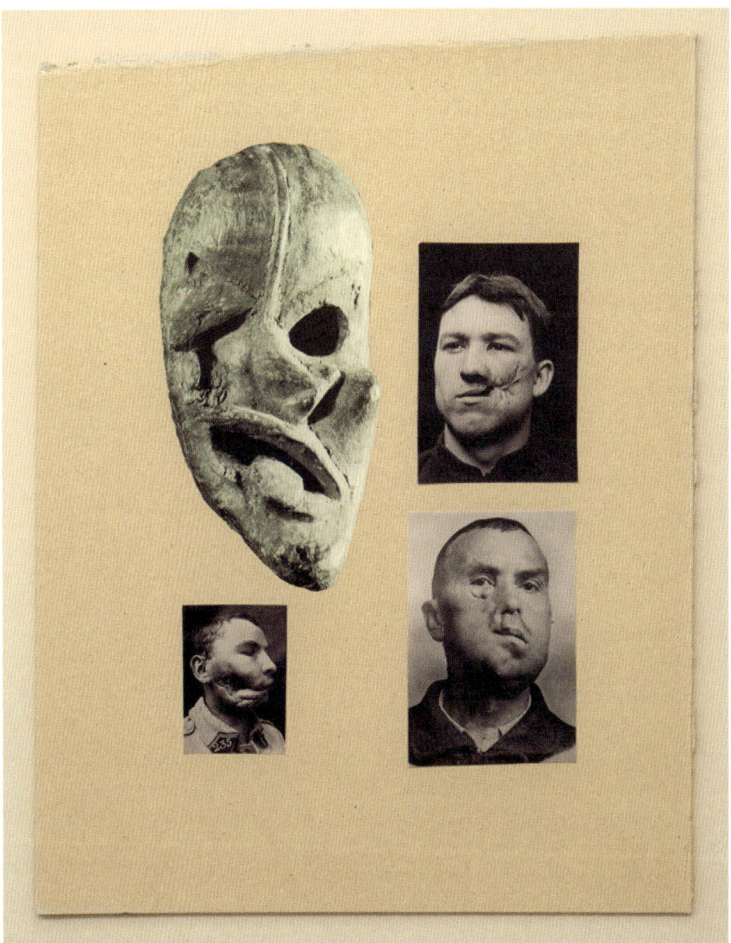

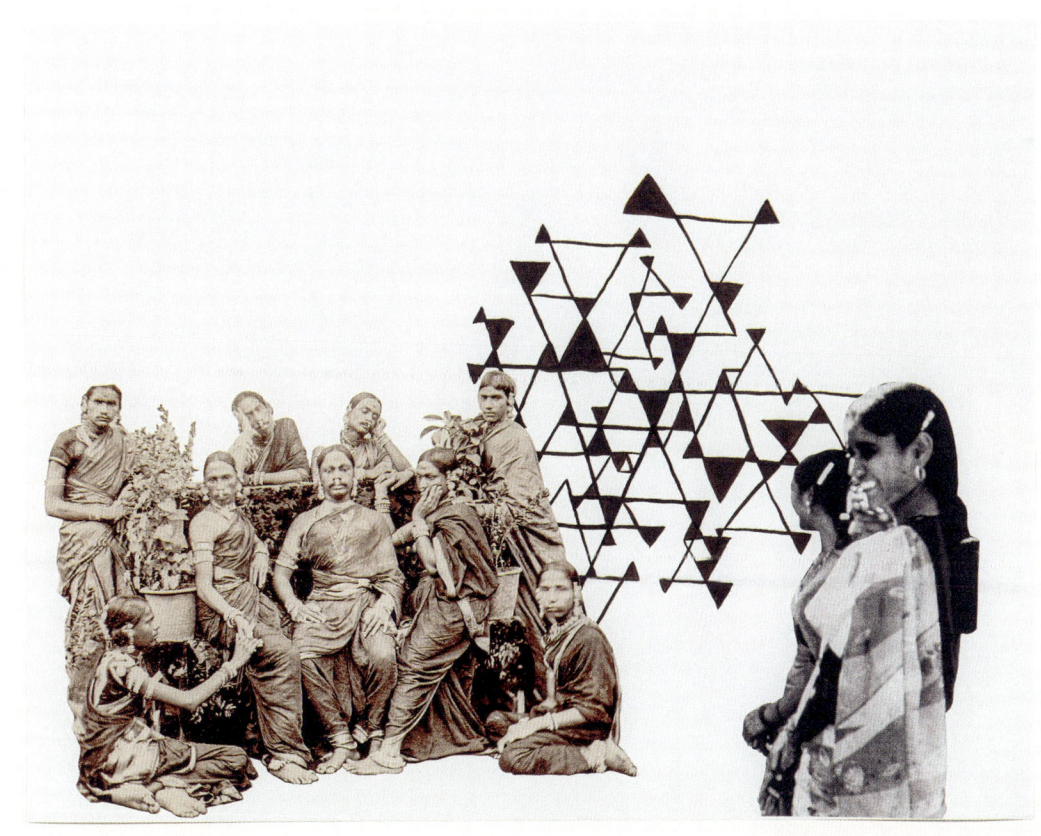

SAMMY BALOJI

Regardless of the medium employed, Sammy Baloji's work is fundamentally informed by the practice of collage, specifically centred around elements from the visual and material histories of the Democratic Republic of the Congo and Belgium – histories that are intertwined through colonial occupation and economic imperialism. This complex dynamic is the underlying subject of Baloji's films, sculptures, installations, photographs, performances and two-dimensional works, as well as his curatorial practice. Baloji first gained international recognition for his 'Mémoire' series (2004–6) in which he superimposed colonial-era photographic portraits of forced mine workers in the Katanga region upon his own landscape photographs of the same mines today. Rather than presenting a disjunction between past and present, these collages illustrated the continued economic subjugation of Congo. More recently, Baloji has developed a body of work drawing upon his own Luba culture and its understanding of history as oral and mutable, examining memory and contributing to contemporary discussions about restitution. It includes mirror-based collages that combine black-and-white archival photographs with colourful digital scans of minerals and of objects typically classed as ethnographic artefacts. The photographs were taken by German ethnographer Hans Himmelheber (1908–2003) at the moment of 'encounter', during collecting expeditions to Congo in 1938–9. The artefacts are now held by Museum Rietberg: Kunst der Welt in Zurich, Switzerland, which also houses Himmelheber's collection, while the minerals were found by the artist during his travels in Katanga. By scanning them, Baloji refers to the museographical practice of X-raying objects to prove their authenticity – and hence value – a practice that he considers to be an extension of colonial mining. By subjugating each object to technology, removing all intimacy or secrecy, it is ransacked to its very core. The composition of the mirror collages varies: some appear like the spread in a book, the archival photograph on the left 'page' and the scan on the right. Others work with superposition or inversion, which is further complicated by whatever else is present in the room and reflected in the mirrored surface, in a knowing nod to Michelangelo Pistoletto's (b.1933) 'Mirror Paintings' made since the early 1960s. The title of each piece includes Himmelheber's name, his description of his photograph, the name of the scanned object and the phrase 'and your reflection in the mirror' to reiterate that the artist considers the viewer an essential element that completes the work. Baloji was inspired by the close-ups in the 1953 art documentary film *Les Statues meurent aussi* (*Statues Also Die*) by Alain Resnais, Chris Marker and Ghislain Cloquet, in which the faces of museum visitors are reflected in the display cases containing objects separated from their original function and meaning. His collages underscore our implication as viewers in the interplay of collecting, representing and reflecting.

ZOË GRAY

Born 1978, Lubumbashi, Democratic Republic of the Congo.
Lives in Brussels, Belgium and Lubumbashi.

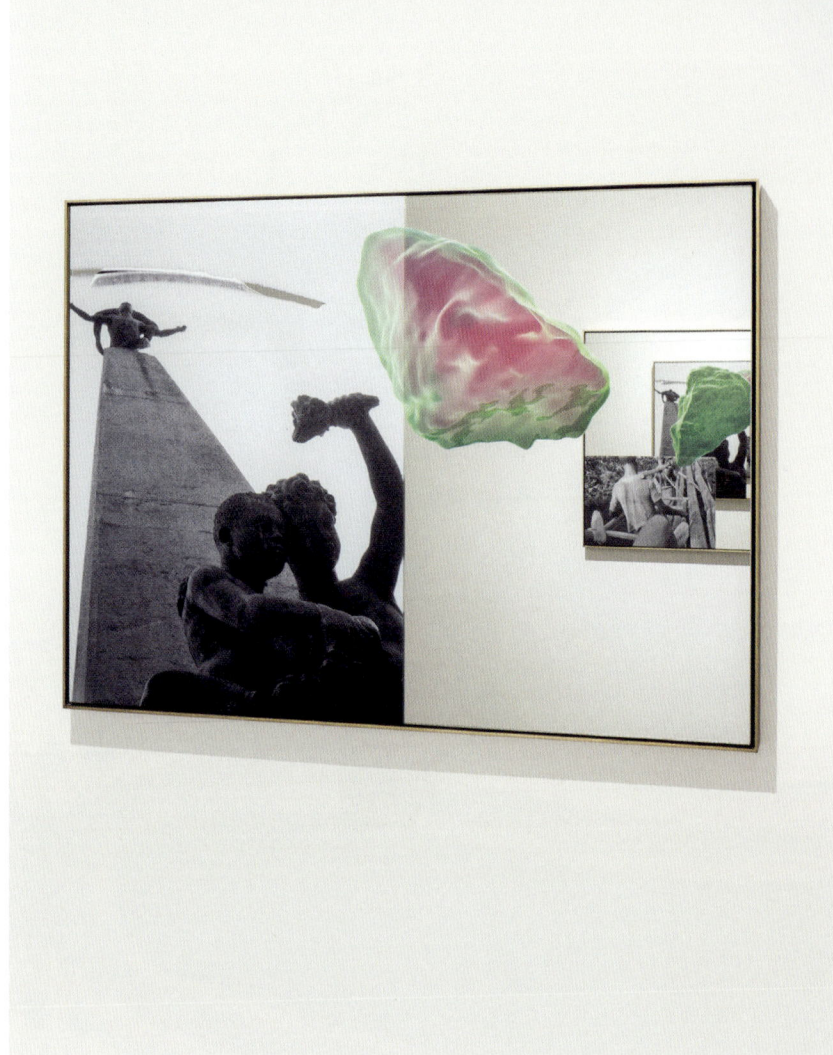

↑   Hans Himmelheber, Monument, DR Congo, Kinshasa, 1938, scan of a Chalcopyrite from Kipushi mine, and your reflection in the mirror, 2020, 2020, UV Print on mirror 4 mm, American case in polished brushed brass, 51 × 71 × 3 cm (20 × 28 × 1⅛ in), installation view, 'Kasala: The Slaughterhouse of Dreams or the First Human, Bende's Error', Imane Farès, Paris, 2020

↗   From top to bottom:
Hans Himmelheber, Performance of a mbuya mask with leaves and raffia costume, DR Congo, Pende region, 1939, scan of a Dioptase from Tantara mine, and your reflection in the mirror, 2020, 2020, 51 × 71 × 3 cm (20 × 28 × 1⅛ in)
Hans Himmelheber, Figure on the roof of Himmelheber's car, DR Congo, Luluwa region, 1939, scan of a Dioptase from Tantara mine, and your reflection in the mirror, 2020, 2020, 51 × 71 × 3 cm (20 × 28 × 1⅛ in)
Hans Himmelheber, Portrait of his shadow, DR Congo, Kingulu, June 18, 1938, scan of a Chalcopyrite from Kipushi mine, and your reflection in the mirror, 2020, 2020, 51 × 51 × 3 cm (20 × 20 × 1⅛ in)
All UV print on mirror 4 mm, American case in polished brushed brass, installation view, 'When I State that I Am an Anarchist', curated by Pierre Bal-Blanc, PLATO Ostrava, Czech Republic, 2022

↗↗ Hans Himmelheber, The long building of the circumcision camp can be seen behind the mask, DR Congo, Pende region, 1939, scan of the inside of a Songye power figure, and your reflection in the mirror, 2020, 2020, UV print on mirror 4 mm, American case in polished brushed brass, 205 × 85 × 3 cm (80¾ × 33⅜ × 1⅛ in), installation view, 'Kasala: The Slaughterhouse of Dreams or the First Human, Bende's Error', Imane Farès, Paris, France, 2020

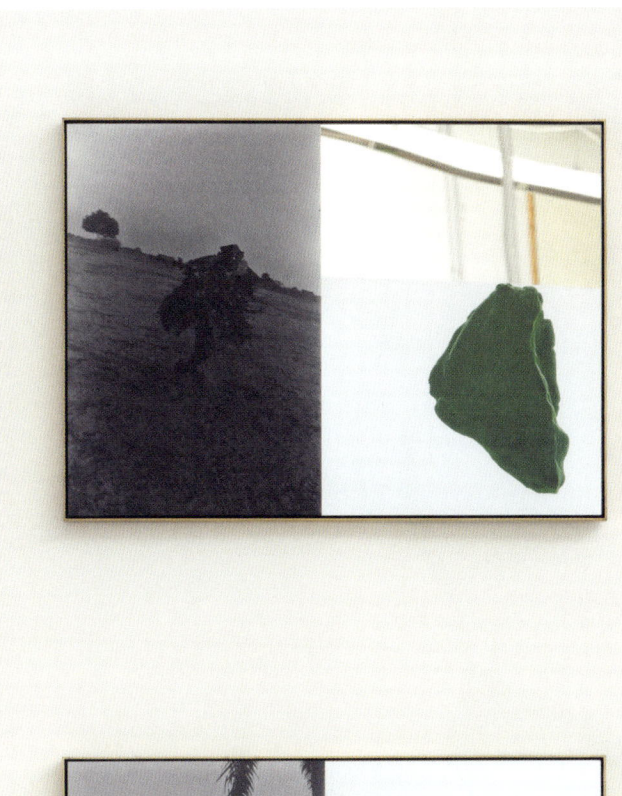

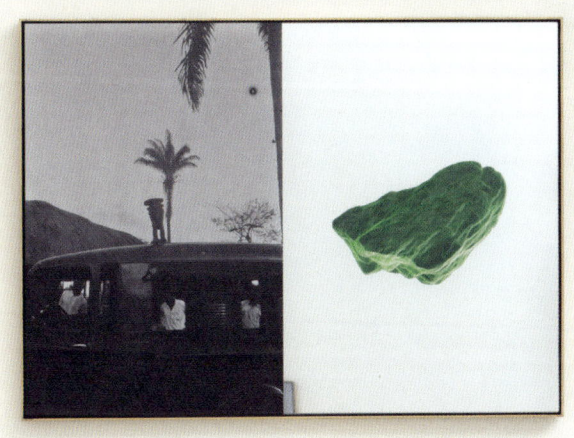

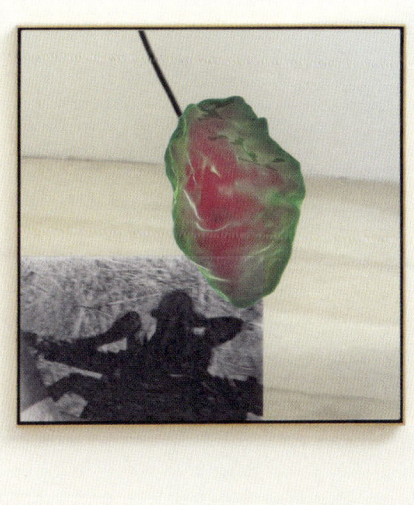

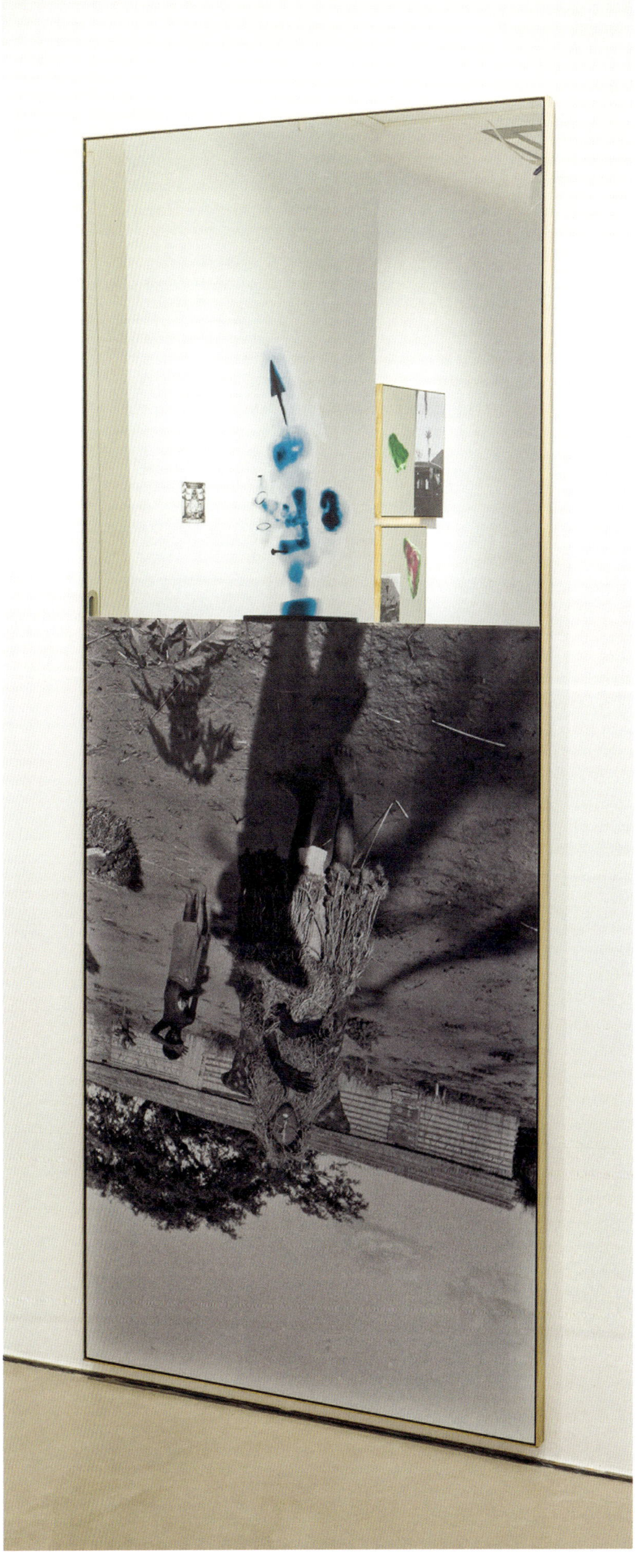

ALLAN BEALY

Following a long career as a graphic designer and art director, Allan Bealy has been creating handmade paper collages since the early 2010s. Made from the pages of old books, atlases, magazines, letters and envelopes, Bealy's highly aesthetic collages convey a romantic or nostalgic air, while nonetheless creating unexpected, and at times menacing, juxtapositions. He cites the Bauhaus, Russian Constructivist graphics, Dada and specifically Robert Rauschenberg (1925–2008) and Kurt Schwitters's (1887–1948) assemblages and collages as influences.

Having previously made works that incorporated imagery of 1950s and 1960s American culture and specifically vintage cars from hot rod magazines – itself a collagist approach to constructing vehicles – in more recent collages Bealy became submerged in the natural realms of botany and zoology, as a means of addressing more current affairs and environmental concerns. These later collages align found images of branches, twigs, trees and animals with drawings of bones and other medical or scientific illustrations. Some motifs are repeated across different works, such as the headless bird and black, amorphic shape seen in *The Visitation* (2022) and *Icarus* (2022). The black form may suggest a negativity, threating to consume the richness of the images, but may also function as an open starting point for the works' narrative, allowing multiple interpretations.

Icarus offers a contemporary interpretation of the Greek myth, and here the black shape functions as the plummeting figure's head, echoing the black smoke rising behind it with the density of an oil-spill fire. A concern with the impact of industrialization can also be seen in *Creator* (2022), which is inspired by the cyclonic twisting sculptures of American sculptor Alice Aycock (b. 1946). The collage is made of images of machinery and construction debris and presents a black-and-white post-apocalyptic rollercoaster that contrasts with a painterly blue sky.

Although these are austere subject matters, Bealy's collages are often whimsical and humorous, echoing their playful creation process in which layers and images are accumulated intuitively. In a 2022 interview in *Contemporary Collage Magazine*, Bealy stated that he likes his materials 'to be a bit mouldy', and often stains them before using them. The base layer for the works is itself a collage, composed like a two-dimensional sculpture from multiple layers of yellowish papers, in which traces of notes and doodles are visible, lending the works a vintage aesthetic, as well as a voluminous feel. Bealy is highly involved in the alternative collage artists' online community, which operates outside of the mainstream commercial art world. He often works collaboratively, creating collages through mail art correspondences. He also distributes his work independently, using social media as a gallery. Latterly, he resurrected *Benzene*, a literature and art magazine he co-edited in the 1980s, giving visibility to the works of his collage community. In this sense, his collagist approach manifests itself not only in a material and formal sense, but also plays a social role in bringing individuals together.

KEREN GOLDBERG

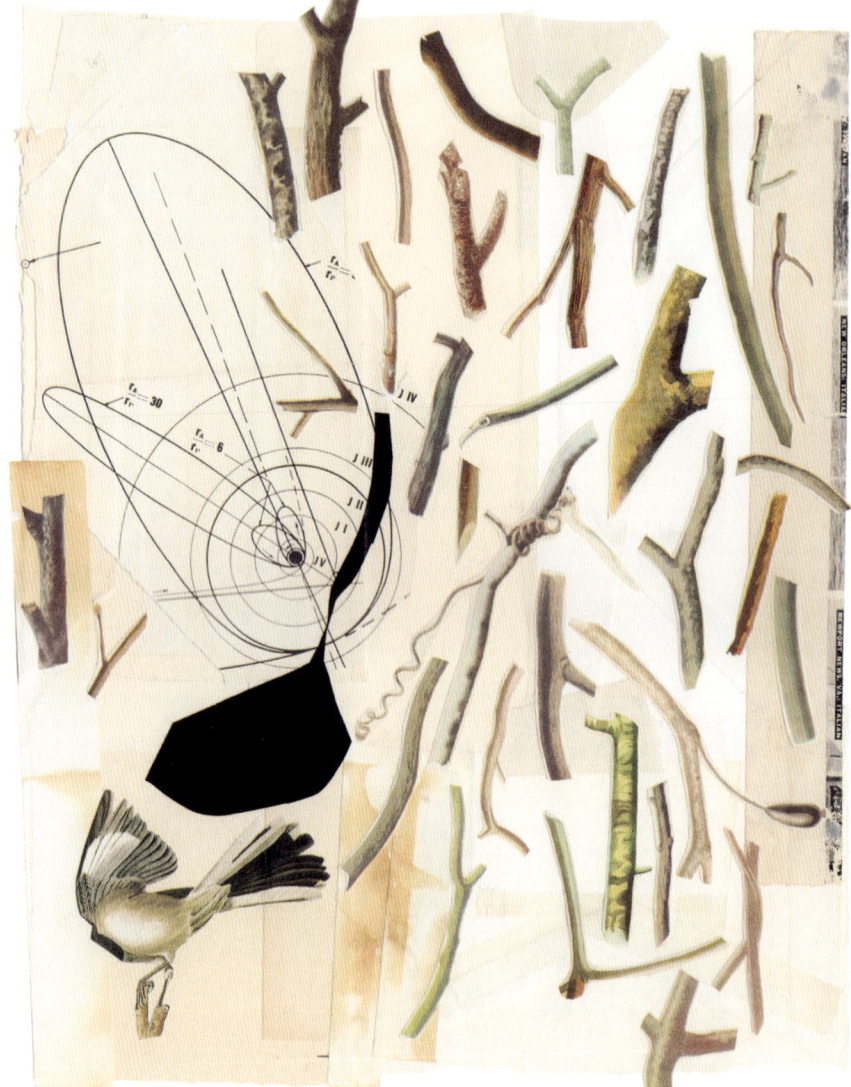

Born 1951, Montreal, Canada. Lives in Brooklyn, New York, USA.

↑ **The Visitation**, 2022, collage with vintage materials on card, 35.6 × 27.9 cm (14 × 11 in)

→ **Creator**, 2022, collage with vintage materials on card, 35.6 × 27.9 cm (14 × 11 in)

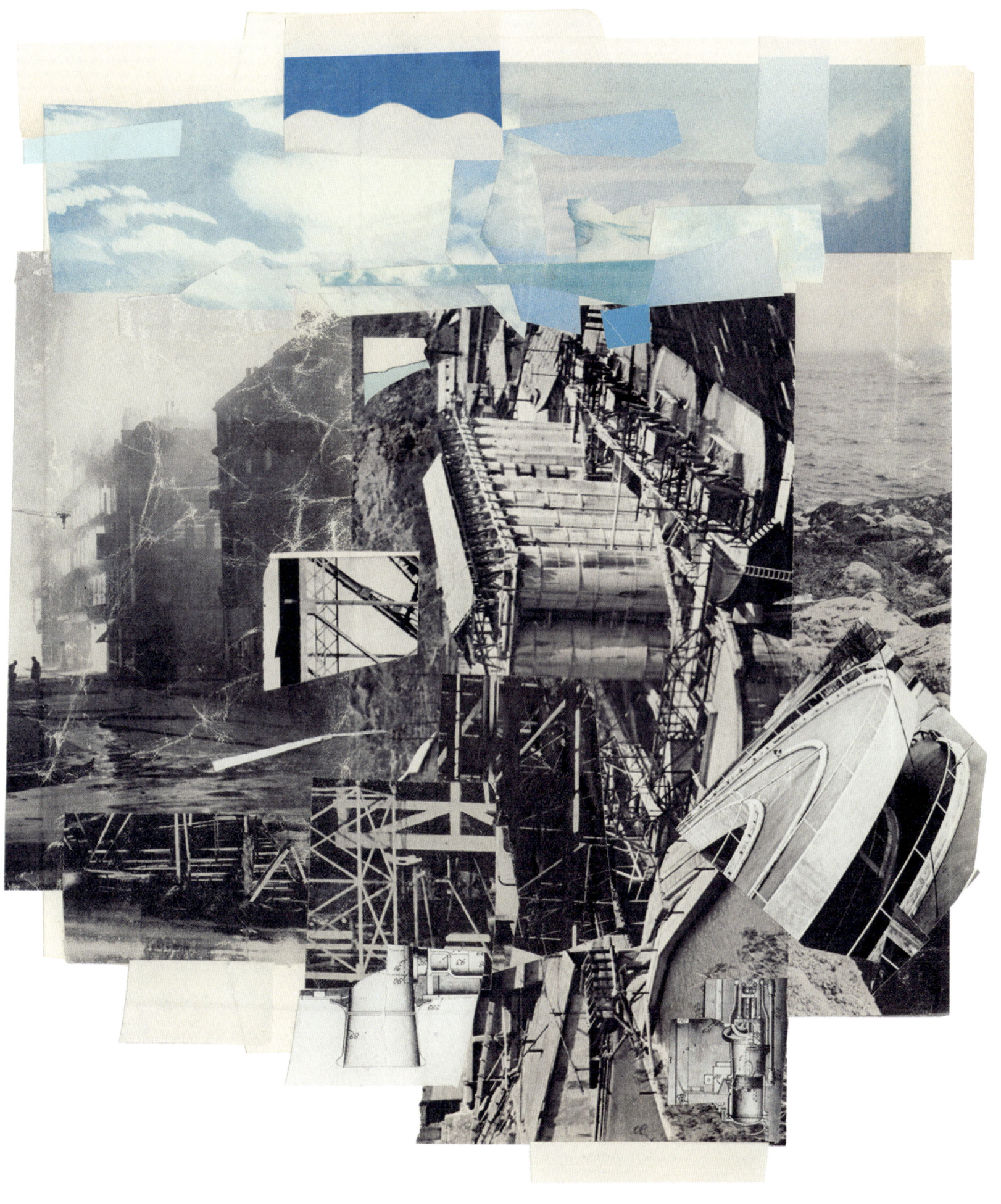

ALLAN
BEALY

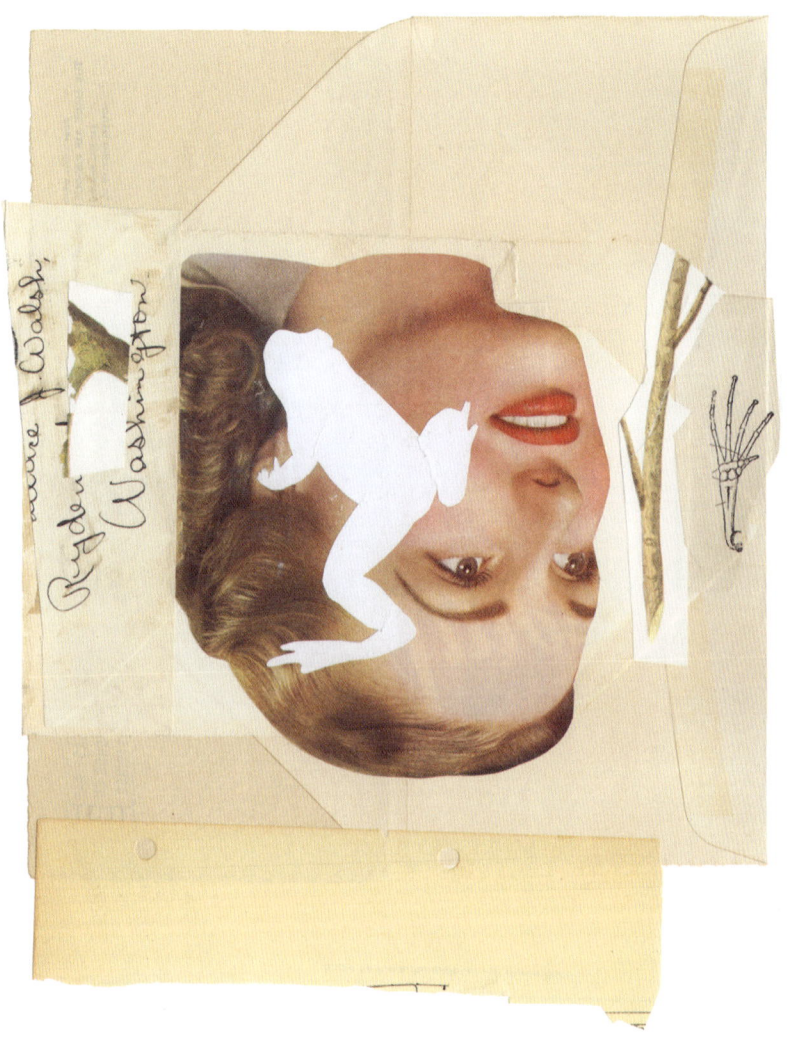

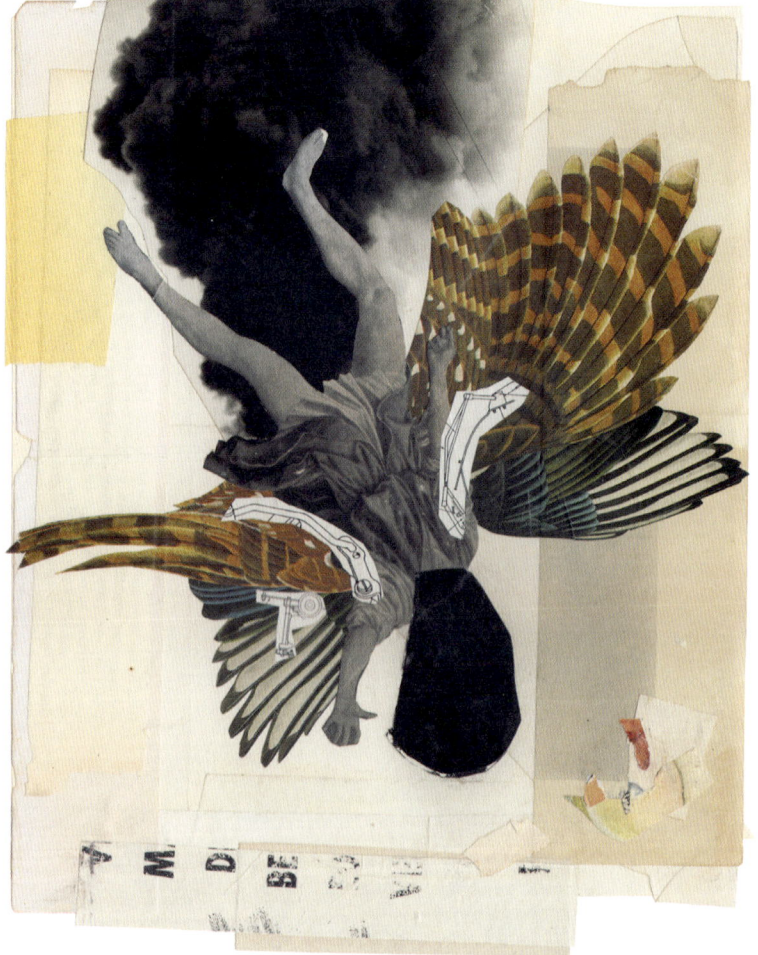

↖   **Natural Selection,** 2021, collage with vintage materials on card, 30.5 × 22.9 cm (12 × 9 in)

↑   **Icarus,** 2022, collage and image transfer with vintage materials on card, 30.5 × 22.9 cm (12 × 9 in)

↗   **Haunt,** 2021, collage and image transfer with vintage materials on card, 30.5 × 22.9 cm (12 × 9 in)

↗↗ **Demon,** 2019, collage with vintage materials and image transfer on card, 35.6 × 27.9 cm (14 × 11 in)

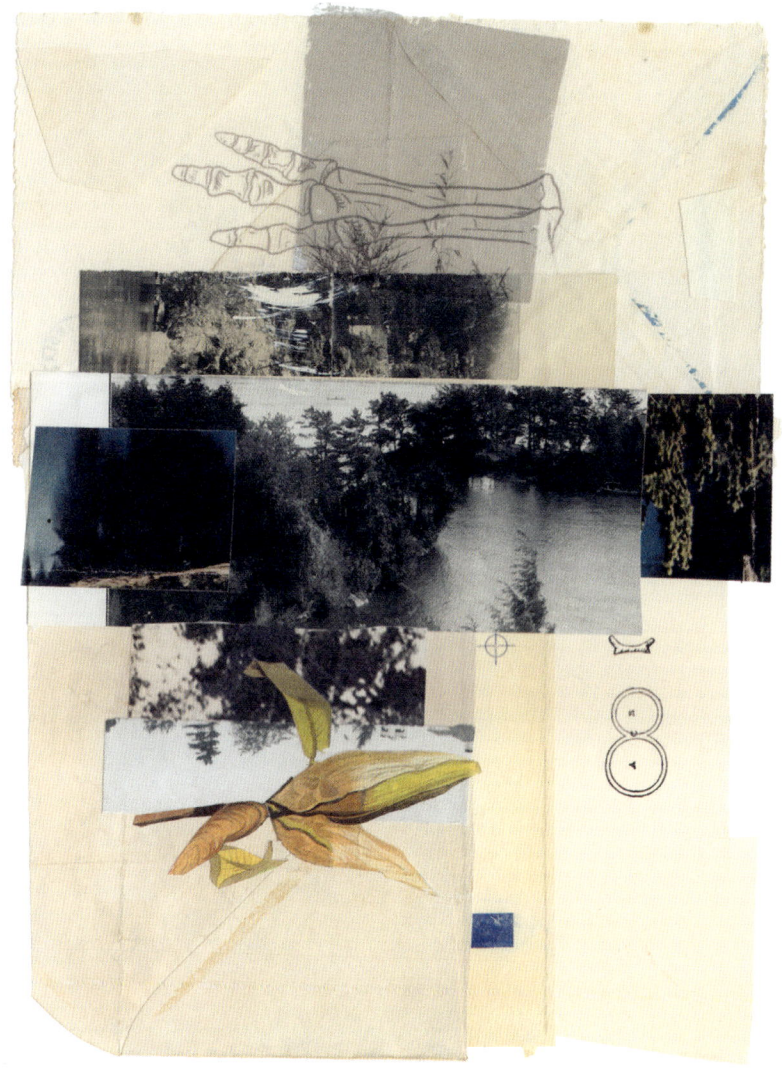

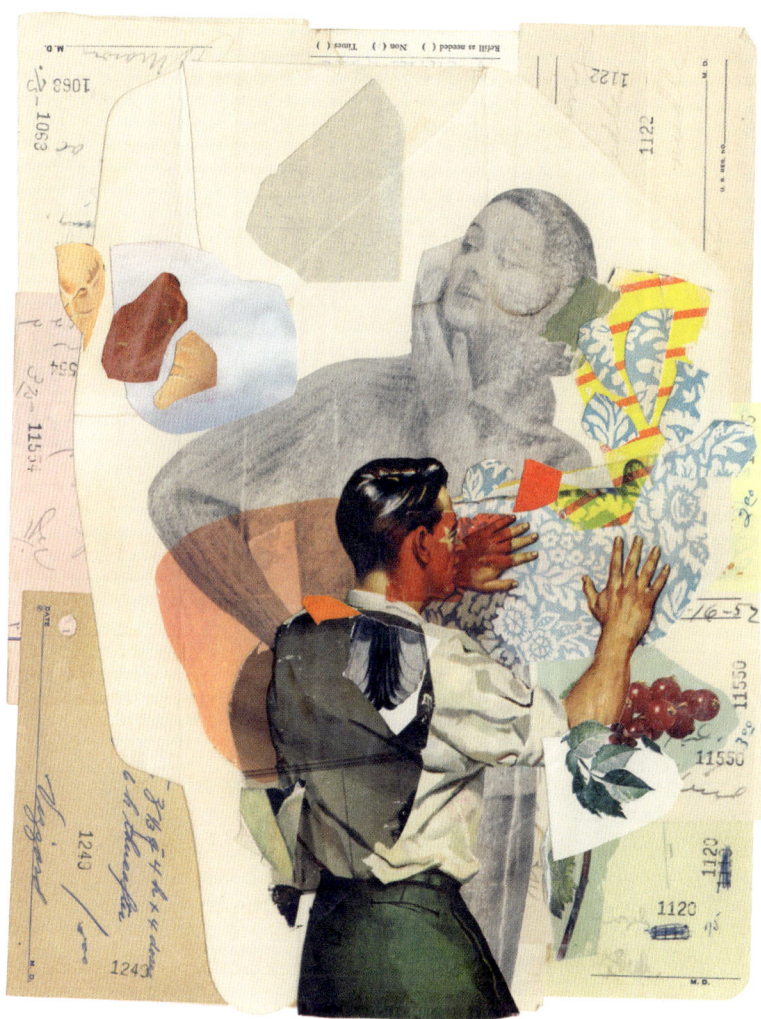

ALLAN BEALY

APRIL BEY

Merging photographic images with bold uses of colour, April Bey confronts issues relating to gender, race, sexuality and cultural identity. Working with a range of materials including paint, textiles, glitter and resin within an Afrofuturist style, Bey draws on imagery from American and Bahamian popular culture (she moved from the Bahamas to the United States in her early teens) to imagine Black futures and critique the ongoing ramifications of colonialism. In her 2021 exhibition 'Atlantica, The Gilda Region' at the California African American Museum in Los Angeles, she introduced a series of works imagining that Black people come from a fictional planet (Atlantica) and cast herself as an extra-terrestrial outsider observing Earth. The inspiration for this narrative stems back to Bey's childhood memories of her father using the metaphor of aliens to explain the mistreatment of Black people in North America. The role of the Atlantican aliens is to turn symbols of colonialism into beautiful objects that can be enjoyed by anyone. *COLONIAL SWAG: ALIENated in Palm Springs* (2021) depicts an elegantly posed woman in a flowing skirt, patterned jacket and large crown, with each garment created from a textile material sewn to the work's substrate. The figure's headpiece is a can of Royal Crown Hair Dressing that has been altered to take on a crown-like shape. The pomade is typically marketed as a Black haircare product, but the name and design of the brand allude to colonial histories and imagery. On the figure's skirt are a cluster of astronauts who have fists in place of their heads. A raised fist is a symbol associated with the 'Black Power' slogan and the fingernails of each hand are adorned with acrylic nails – an image that appears in several works in the series. This fashionable addition is a reference to Black people in this imaginary world having the time and freedom to pamper themselves. Bey frequently incorporates wax print fabric designs within her works. Often associated with West and Central African cultures, these fabrics tie in with Bey's exploration of colonial themes through their multicultural origins, having been brought from Indonesia to Africa in the nineteenth century by Dutch colonists. She uses one such hand-sewn material in the background of *And My Flames Stay Till You Get Out My Way* (2021), which incorporates images of riders from the real-life American rodeo team The Cowgirls of Color. In Bey's imagined universe, these Atlantican women are intergalactically famous for competing in rodeos. The images disrupt stereotypical notions of cowboys as white and male, and are made all the more impactful by the artist's use of real cowgirls as models. Bey's work explores a world where Black people can live unencumbered by racial injustice and enjoy lives full of colour and positivity.

FERREN GIPSON

Born 1987, New Providence, Bahamas. Lives in Los Angeles, California, USA.

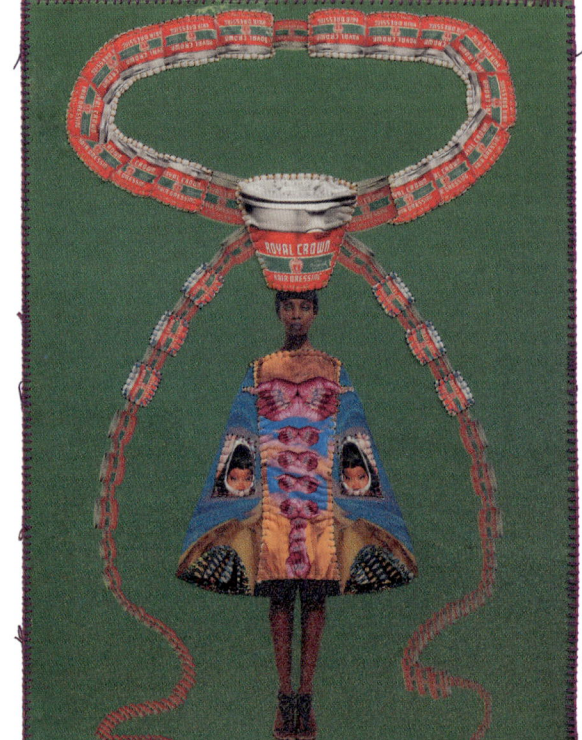

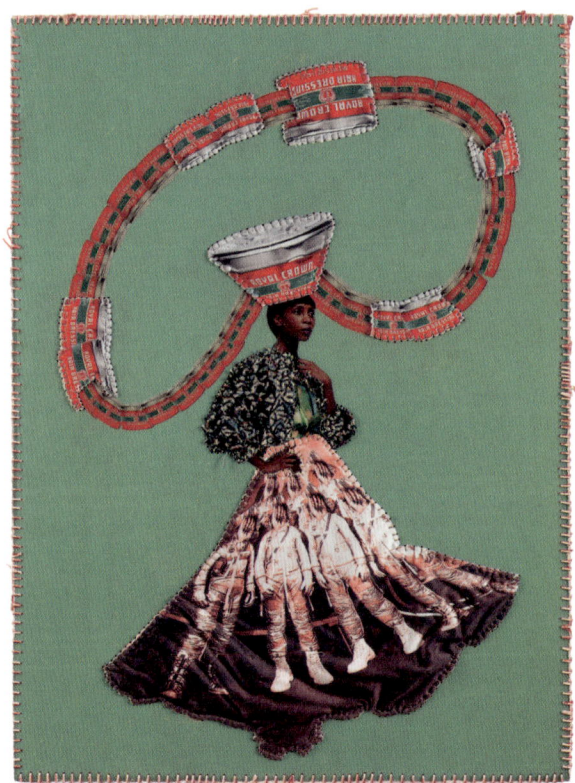

↑↑ COLONIAL SWAG: Dune, Not Palm Springs, 2021, canvas, sherpa and woven textile hand sewn into resin with acrylic paint, 121.8 × 91.4 cm (48 × 36 in)

↑ COLONIAL SWAG: ALIENated in Palm Springs, 2021, canvas, sherpa and woven textile hand sewn into resin with acrylic paint, 121.8 × 91.4 cm (48 × 36 in)

↗ And My Flames Stay Till You Get Out My Way, 2021, water-based latex paint, watercolour, hand-sewn fabric, glitter and sequins, 279.4 × 548.6 cm (110 × 216 in)

→ Carry Thy Cunny Yonder (IYKYK), 2022, woven textiles, sherpa, glitter, resin, metallic thread and acrylic paint on canvas, 121.9 × 91.4 cm (48 × 36 in)

→→ Fear No Man, 2022, digitally printed and woven blanket with hand-sewn 'African' Chinese knockoff wax fabric, 203.2 × 152.4 cm (80 × 60 in)

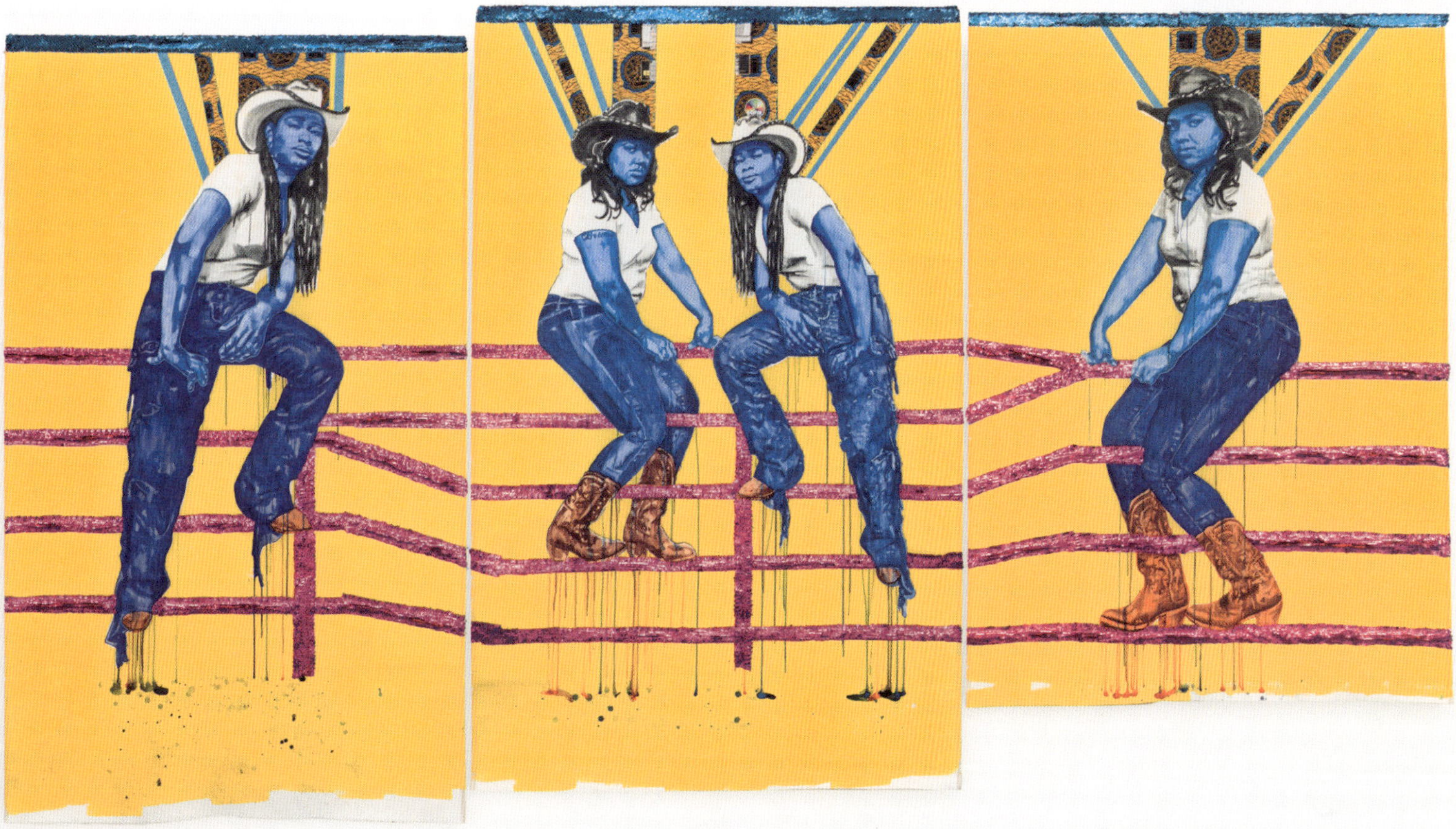

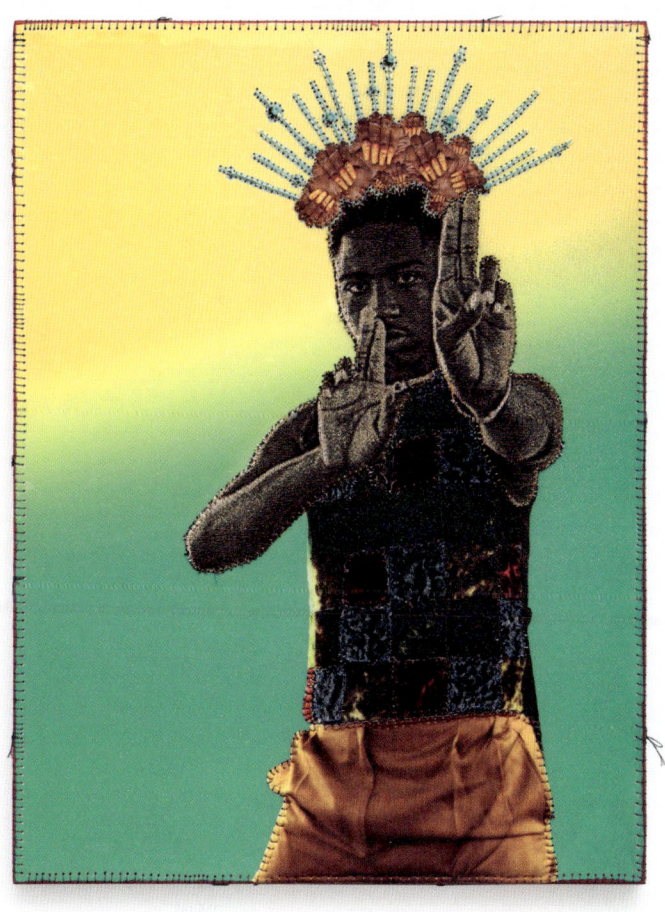
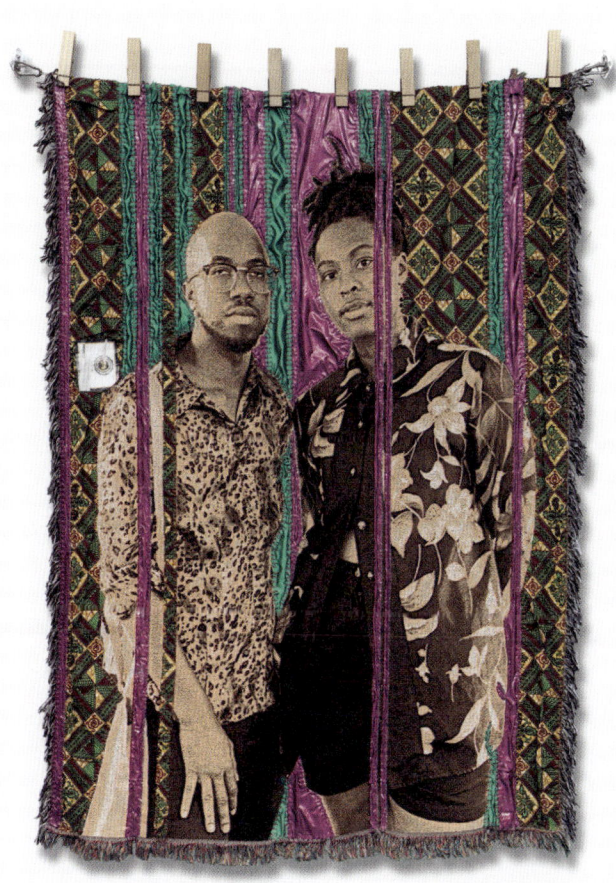

APRIL
BEY

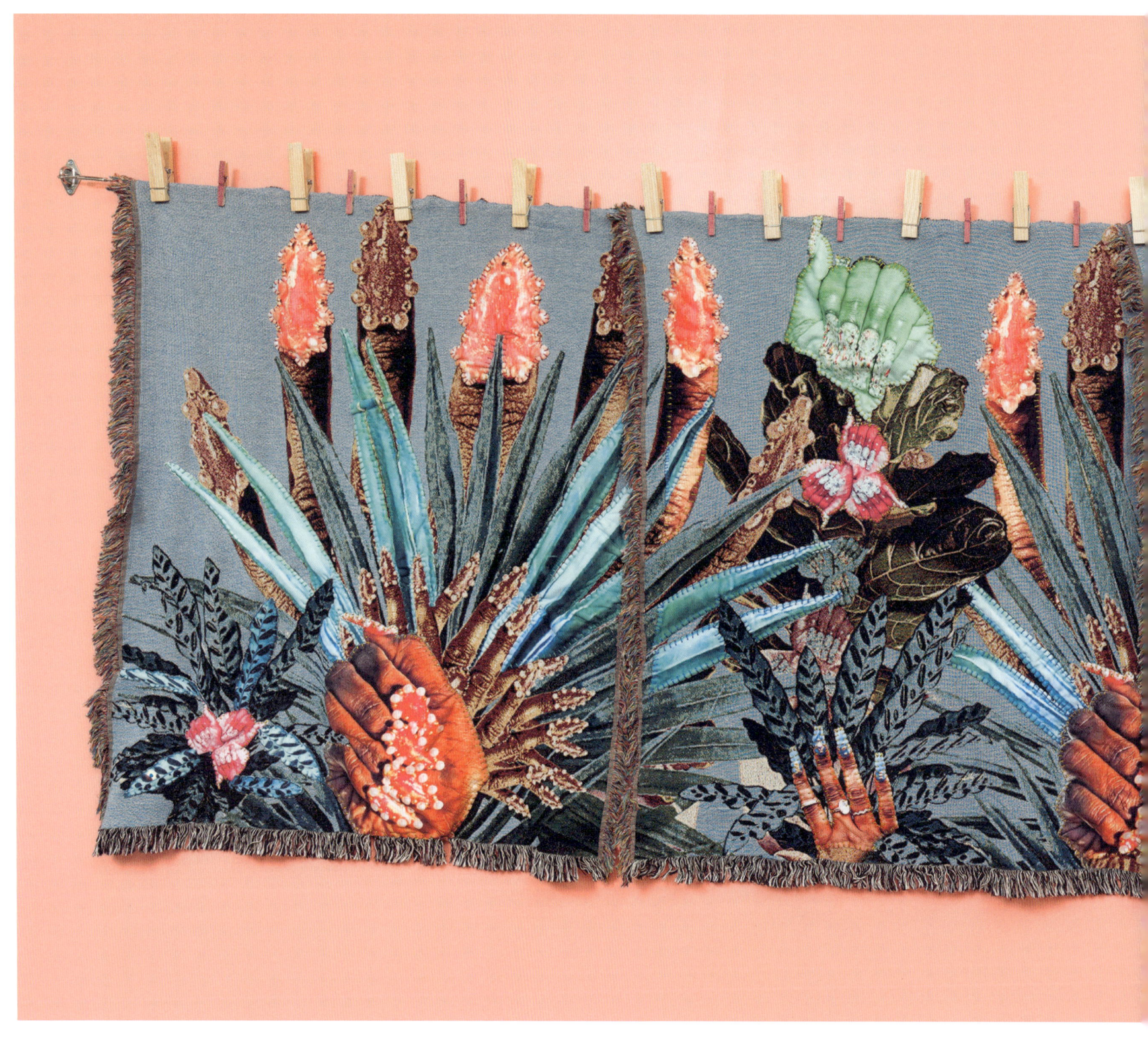

↑ **Oui Outside**, 2022, digitally woven blanket with hand-sewn fabric and glitter, 203.2 × 609.6 cm (80 × 240 in), installation view, 'April Bey: When You're On Another Planet And They Just Fly', GAVLAK Los Angeles, USA, 2022

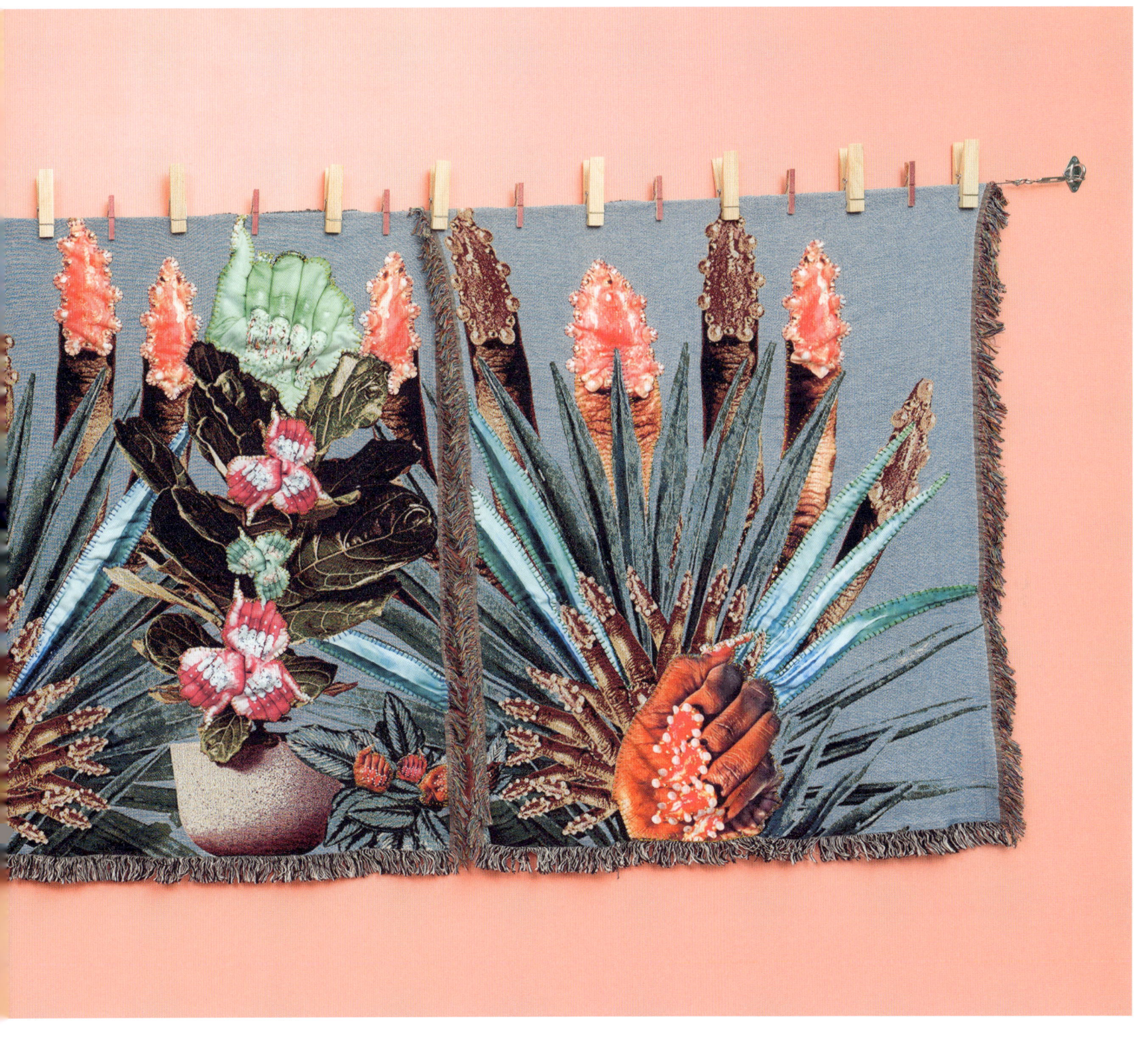

LUCAS

BLALOCK

Lucas Blalock's photographic images test the rationality of the image-based world, echoing moments within the medium's long history in a present mediated by the computer. That history is a multivalent chronicle of visions, rooted, for many of its practitioners, in properties of experimentation, technological possibility, illusion and material transformation. In the very earliest decades of the twentieth century, photographers throughout Europe and the United States registered the experiences of sweeping technological change – anxiety, desire, fear of the body's vulnerability – with artistic techniques such as photomontage, or trials with mirrors and double exposures, that unsettled the medium's most basic characteristics and reflected the increasingly fractured, machine-driven world. Now, at another distinct moment of rapid digital transformation, photographers such as Blalock are similarly recalibrating the processes of picture-making, creating humorous, Frankensteined images that are built through the camera, the scanner and the screen. ■ In a Blalock photograph, contorted figures, uncanny interior spaces or elements of still life scenes appear in tandem, at once suggestive of a type of collision between virtual and real dimensions and openly assertive of their ultimate artifice. The result of a process that the artist described in a 2016 interview with *Bomb* magazine as making 'a burlesque of commercial practice', Blalock's work often starts with staged studio set-ups that he captures on camera and then later splices together, layers or recomposes in post-production, with the aid of Photoshop's digital toolkit. Vibrating from the distortions of the programme's clone stamping, masking and painting tools, pictures such as *The House Guest* (2018) or *The Upstaters* (2019) propose alternative functions for the ubiquitous photo editing software: to enable a photograph to both look and act in a way that it isn't necessarily supposed to, or to expose the basic conditions under which such a photograph was made. (The former image, depicting a cartoonish dog-like figure, was constructed by placing two negatives on top of one another and exposing the bottom layer by drawing with the eraser tool; the latter makes use of a 3D photo editing tool that produces the effect of eccentric digital apparitions.) ■ Blalock's more recent photographs, including *Reverse Titanic / Hell is in the Air* (2019) – a picture of two decapitated fish-shaped beer can sleeves, making out, innards flying out in Brush tool dots – merges his spirited cut-and-paste ethos with increasingly autobiographical elements. The body of work recalls a freak accident that occurred on the 'Pirates of the Caribbean' ride at Disney World during which the then-ten-year-old artist irreparably damaged his right thumb and ultimately had it replaced in a novel surgical routine with one of his big toes. It is a story so apt that it almost feels prewritten: in Blalock's work, unstable physical and digital forms are spliced, grafted and layered with the psychic realm. ━

MADELINE WEISBURG

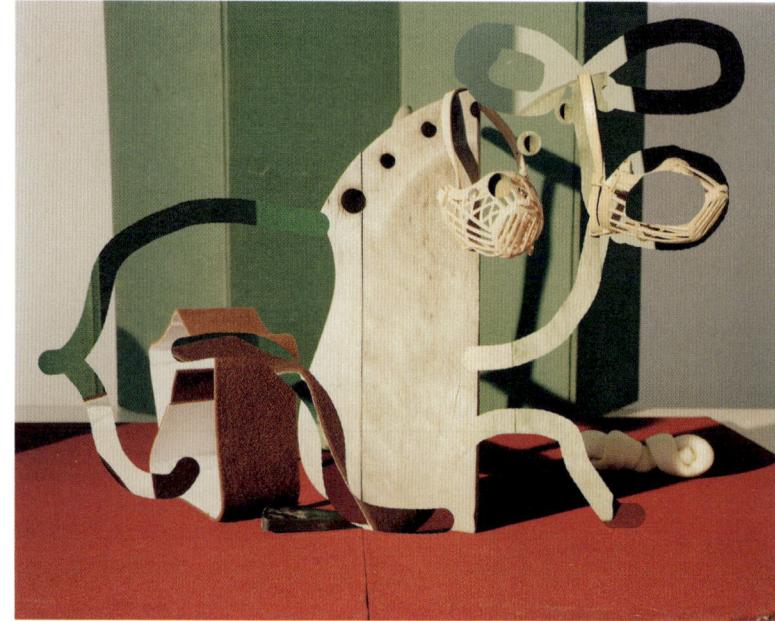

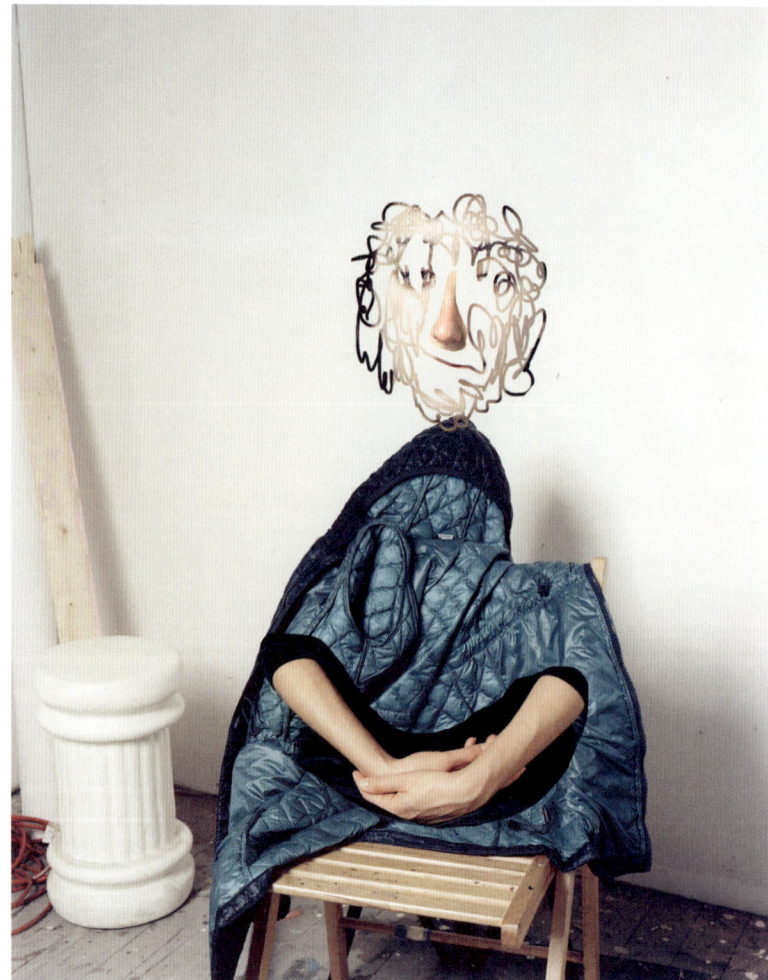

Born 1978, Asheville, North Carolina, USA. Lives in Brooklyn, New York, USA.

↑↑ **The House Guest**, 2018, archival inkjet print, 106.5 × 132 cm (42 × 52 in)

↑ **Tessa Sitting**, 2016, archival inkjet print, 131 × 105.5 cm (51½ × 41½ in)

↗ **Reverse Titanic / Hell is in the Air**, 2019, dye sublimation print on aluminium, 150 × 175 cm (59 × 69 in)

→ **The Upstaters**, 2019, archival inkjet print, 150 × 185.5 cm (59 × 73 in)

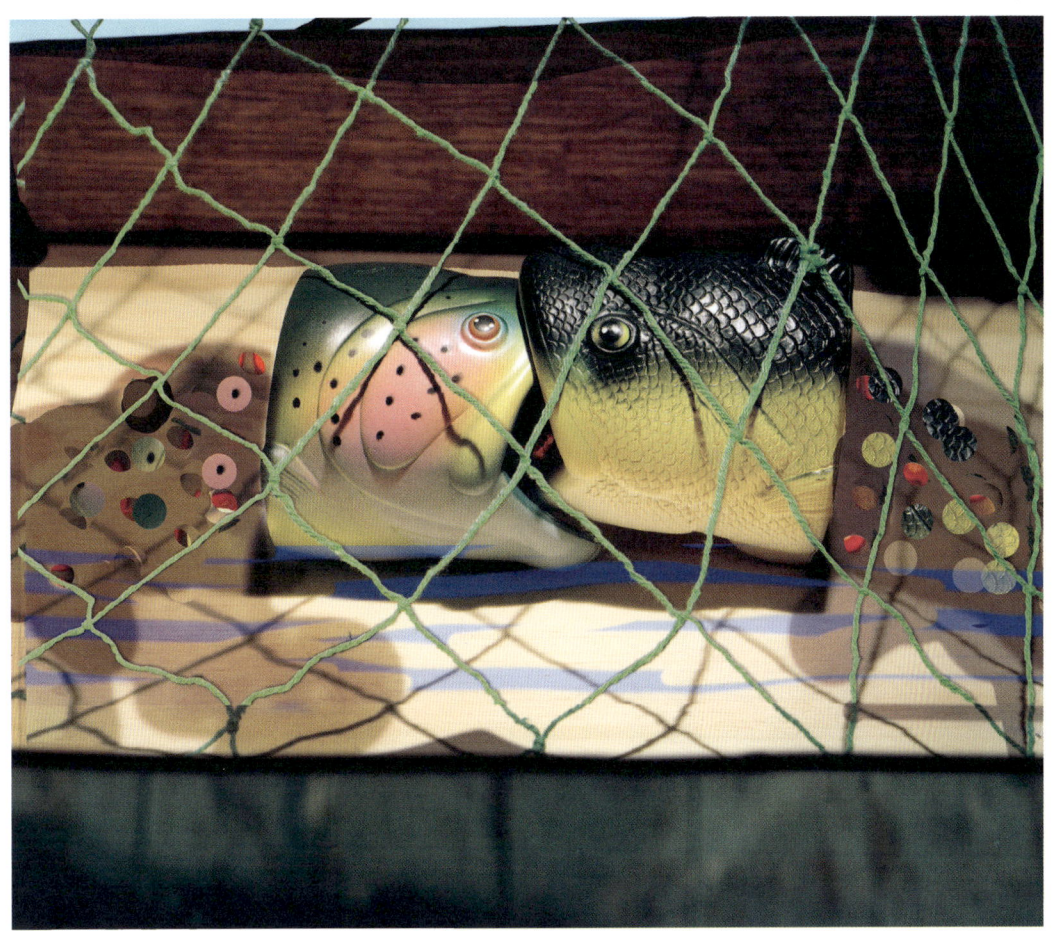

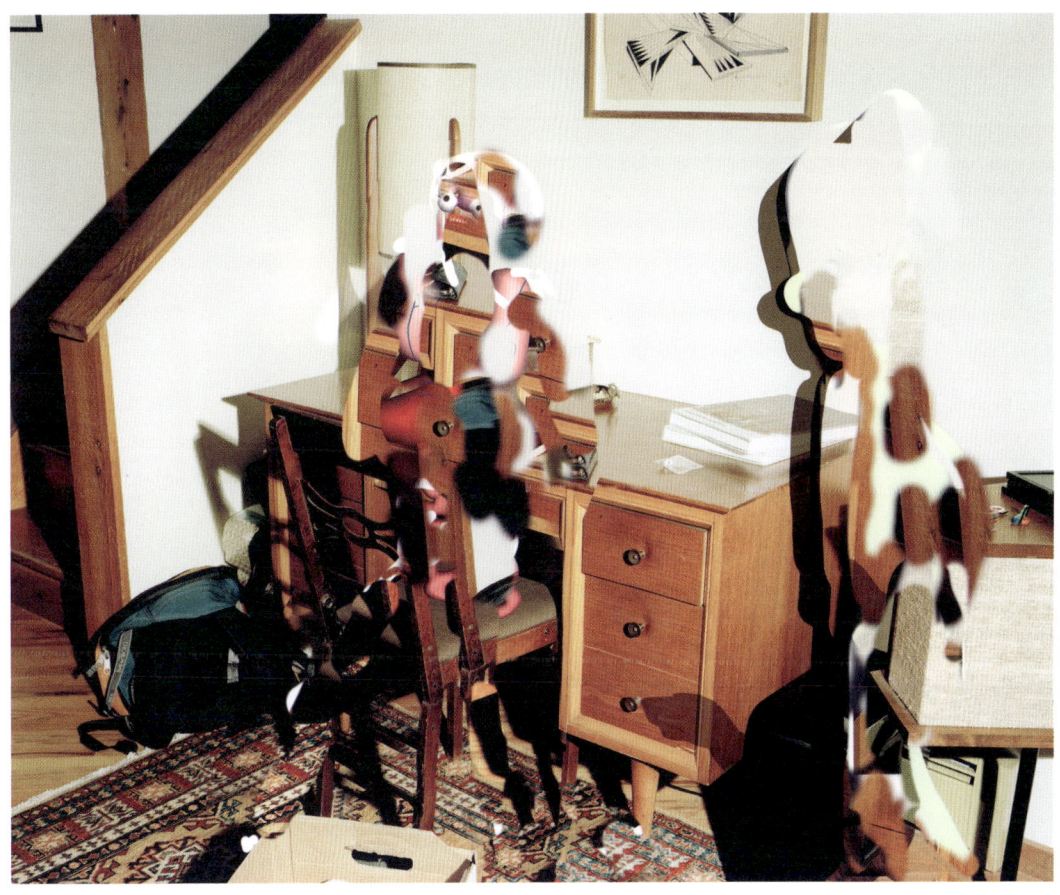

LUCAS
BLALOCK

IÑAKI BONILLAS

Iñaki Bonillas calls himself an 'attic photographer', attuned to working with dusty archives and found materials. This is apt for an artist who spent two decades responding to the photographic archive inherited from his maternal grandfather. Indeed, the trajectory of the artist's practice is inextricably linked to his family. In his youth he worked as an assistant's assistant in the studio of his uncle, the photographer Carlos Somonte (b. 1956), where despite helping to set up numerous shoots, Bonillas never took a single photograph. This experience of peripheral working informs Bonillas's approach to collage, which combines an interest in photography's grammar and materiality with the overlooked and marginal. Fascinated by the scribbled notes in his late father's book collection, Bonillas began musing on the nature of the sacrosanct margins in his own art books. These ignored spaces gave rise to the 'Marginalia' series, in which reproductions from the edges of pages are cropped and digitally reconfigured, creating new images in which snaking lines of white borders tease out unexpected associations. *Marginalia 1* (2019) focuses on nature's fecundity, incorporating fragments of paintings and photographs depicting trees, flowers, fruit and vegetables from across art history. Others in the series focus on hand gestures, faces, travel and domestic objects. By foregrounding information from the fringes, Bonillas encourages fresh ways of seeing. The act of looking is addressed in *Los ojos de Sol (The Eyes of Sol)* (2022), a collage reflecting on the unsettling experience of watching and being watched by others during video calls that took place when meetings had to move online during the COVID-19 pandemic. The photogravure borrows its formal structure from Sol LeWitt's *Fifteen Etchings: Straight Lines in Four Directions & All Their Possible Combinations* (1973), which reminded Bonillas of camera apertures opening and closing. Inserted into fifteen squares divided by lines are close-ups of eyes from the many classic films he enjoyed while confined at home in lockdown – threatened eyes from Alfred Hitchcock's *Psycho* (1960); startled eyes from Ingmar Bergman's *Persona* (1966) and so on. Some stare intently, others look askance; together they reenact the many emotions of a world facing an uncertain future. *Punto de Oro (Golden Point)* (2022) appropriates seven posed images of men playing tennis that Bonillas discovered among a suitcase of old negatives. The performers are set against a jet-black background with extreme chiaroscuro lighting, while gold leaf discs punctuate the scenes like stars at night. Referring to the golden point, a sudden-death overtime system used in sports to resolve drawn matches, its title evokes the conceptual link between photography and mortality. As Susan Sontag writes in *On Photography* (1977), 'all photographs are *memento mori*', reminders of the inevitable. Though photography's analogue era is dead, Bonillas's collages breathe new life into the residues of its past.

DAVID TRIGG

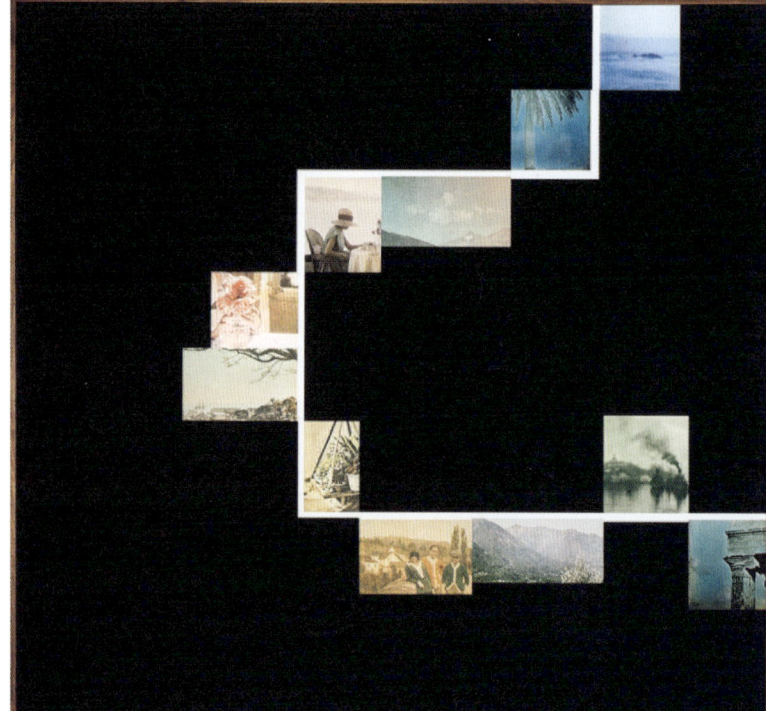

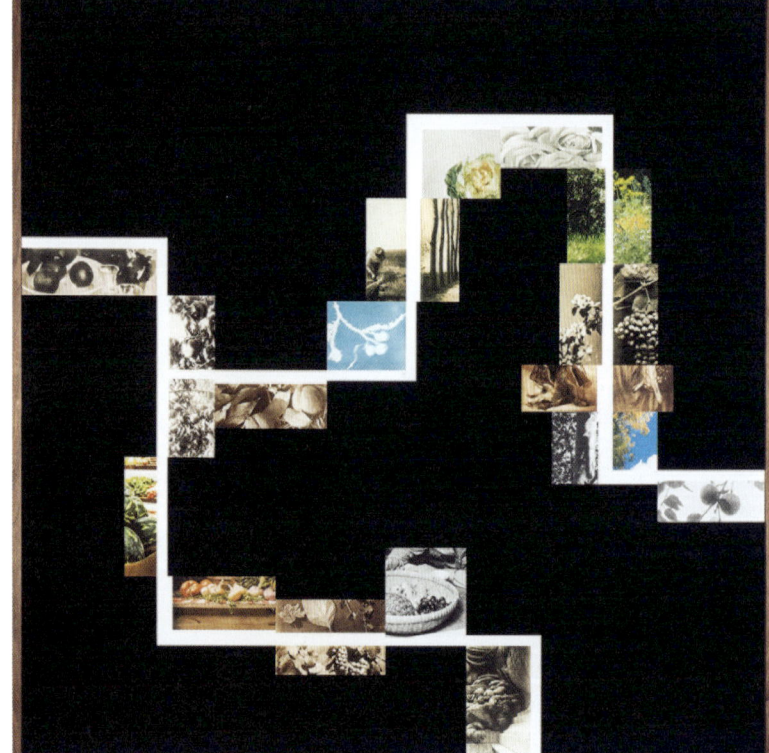

Born 1981, Mexico City, Mexico. Lives in Mexico City.

↑↑ **Marginalia 6**, 2019, pigment print on 308 gsm Hahnemühle Photo Rag, framed: 109.5 × 117.6 × 4.5 cm (43⅛ × 46⅓ × 1¾ in), edition of 3 + 1 AP

↑ **Marginalia 1**, 2019, pigment print on 308 gsm Hahnemühle Photo Rag, framed: 109 × 110 × 4.5 cm (42⅞ × 43¼ × 1¾ in), edition of 3 + 1 AP

→ **Los ojos de Sol (The Eyes of Sol)**, 2022, heliogravure on 350 gsm Hahnemühle cotton paper, set of 15, each 37 × 37 cm (14⅝ × 14⅝ in)

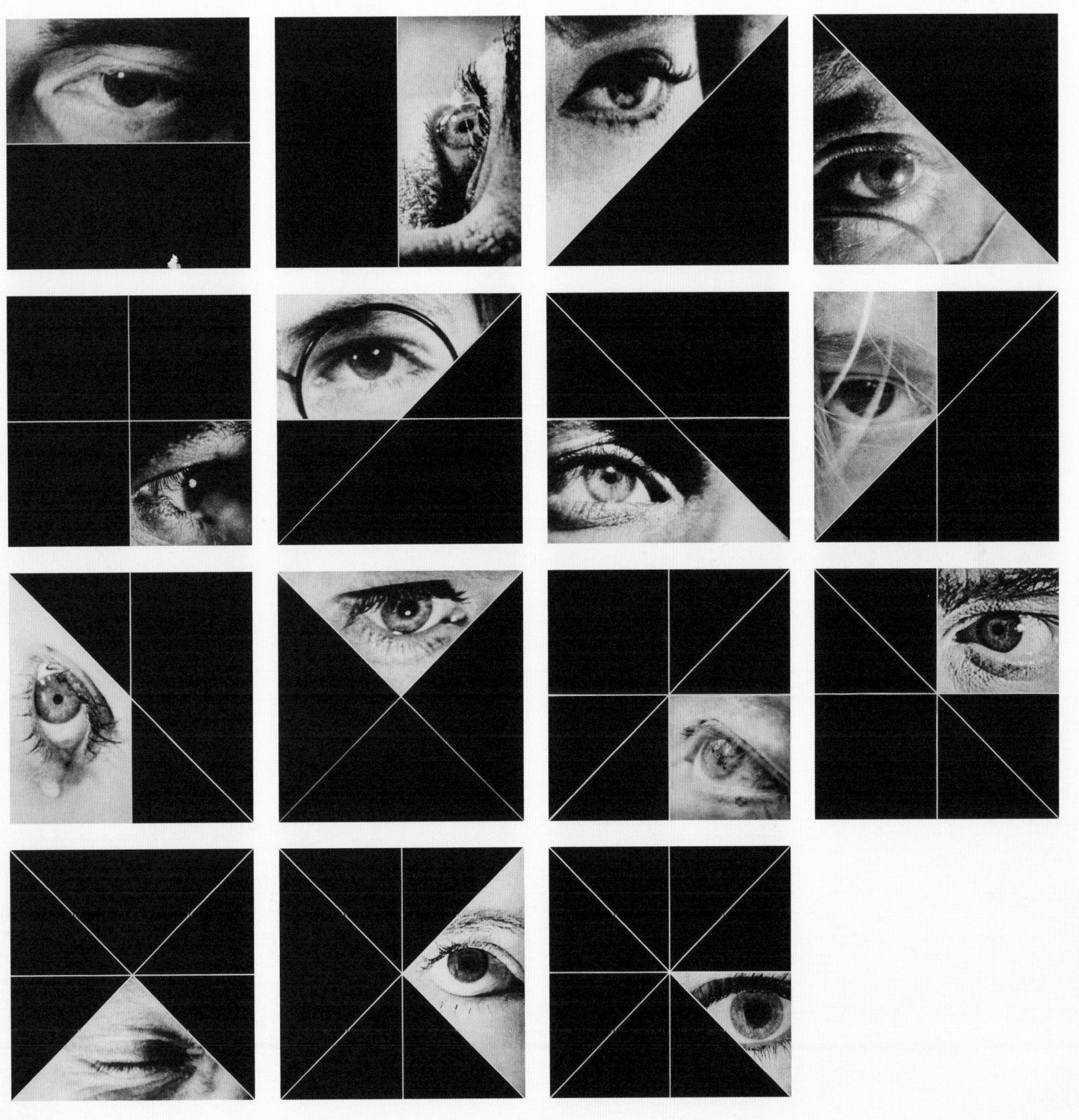

IÑAKI
BONILLAS

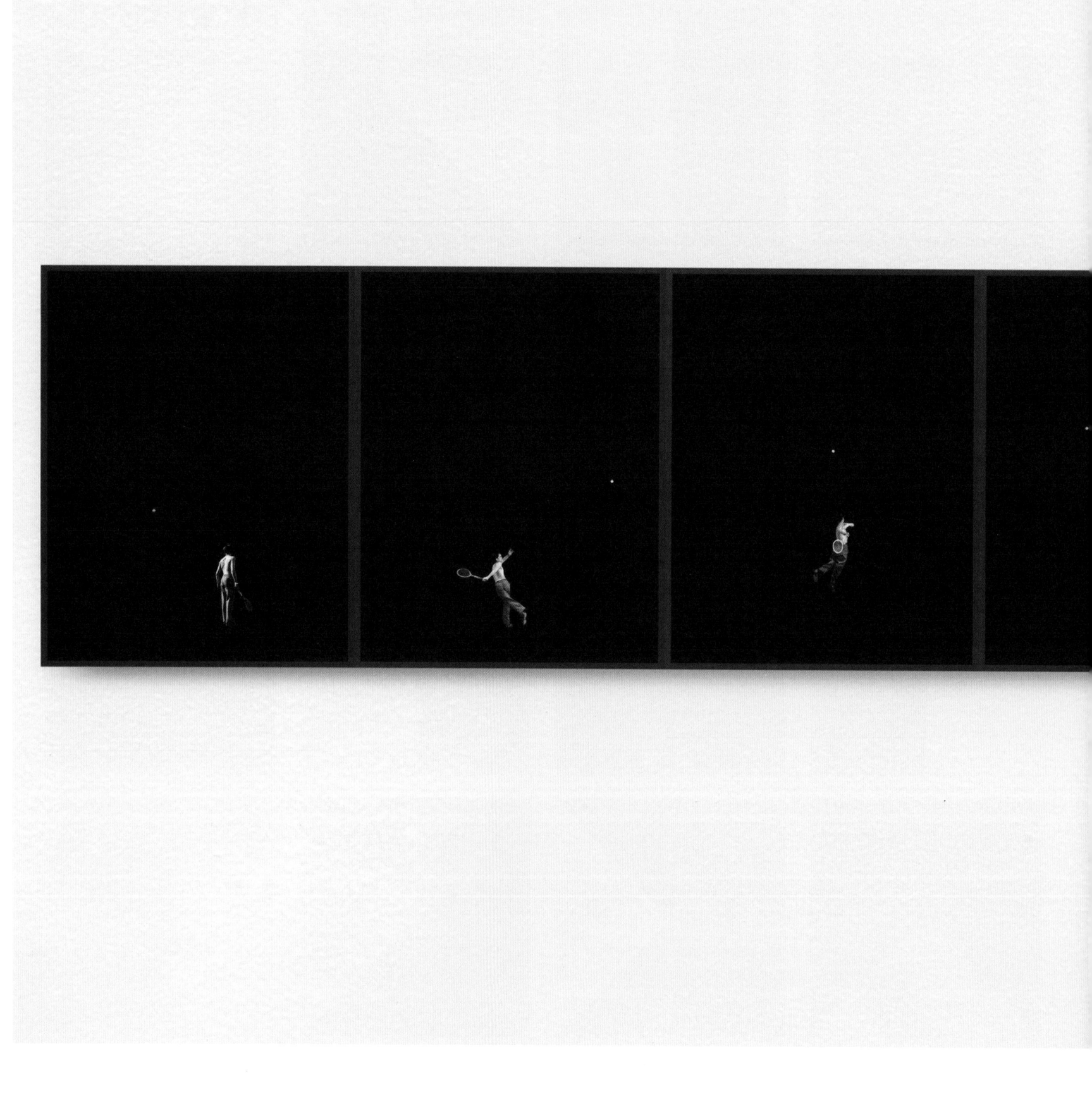

↑ **Punto de Oro (Golden Point)**, 2022, 24k gold leaf on pigmented print with carbon inks on 308 gsm Hahnemühle Photo Rag cotton paper, set of 7, framed, each 50 × 40 × 3.8 cm (19 ¾ × 15 ¾ × 1 ½ in)

MOHAMED BOUROUISSA

Committed to critiquing stereotypes of representation, Mohamed Bourouissa draws attention to the white Western biases that impact those on the margins of society. Through prolonged immersion with his subjects, he seeks to reveal the structural complexities of the often-disenfranchised communities he documents, traversing many art forms and media from photography, drawing and film to smartphone videos recorded in prison, sounds heard in the *banlieues* of Marseille in France and monumental collage-esque sculptures. Driven by a collaborative sensibility, he creates spaces that allow his subjects to be viewed on their own terms, as individuals rather than a demographic – a process informed by experiences relating to his French-Algerian identity. For the series 'Horse Day' (2013–17) Bourouissa explored the historical representation of cowboy culture in the United States – the romanticized and mythical mass-media image of the white John Wayne-type cowboy and the historic exclusion of minority groups from this narrative. Spending eight months with the African American horsemen of the Fletcher Street Urban Riding Club – a century-old, not-for-profit equestrian society in a working-class neighbourhood in North Philadelphia, USA –Bourouissa worked alongside the horsemen to plan and stage a celebratory 'Horse Day' in which the urban riders embellished their horses with shimmering, inexpensive materials such as CDs and tassels, a process akin to 'souping-up' a car.

Bourouissa documented the process of 'horse tuning' through eighty multi media works, including the expansive wall-mounted constructions *The ride* (2017) and smaller assemblages *Donnie* (2016) and *Untitled* (2016), in which the artist's photographs of the Fletcher Street urban riders are silkscreened directly onto jagged fragments of car parts. The photographs are reminiscent of tintypes –a common colonial-era printing process. They overlap with one another like a collage, to warped effect. Pieced together they reveal a new, distorted narrative, one that falls somewhere between myth and reality and reflects the complexity of representation. This metaphor is furthered by the artist's use of French car parts, through which he considers the commonality between his identity as an immigrant and that of the African American riders – both subcultures with a history of oppression and misrepresentation. Moreover, the leader of the American militant group The Black Panthers, Eldridge Cleaver, sought exile in Algiers following his arrest in the 1960s. The assemblages, in all their monumentality, recall the work of artist John Chamberlain (1927–2011), who regularly used fragmented and crushed car parts. However, Bourouissa's use of collaged documentary photography, elegant and richly layered over the metal reliefs, situates his work in a space of its own. These glimmering, wall-mounted, three-dimensional works break down traditional tropes and preconceptions, and reconstruct a new fragmentary world, while paying homage to a long overlooked African American legacy.

FRANKIE MOUTAFIS

Born 1978, Bilda, Algeria. Lives in Paris, France.

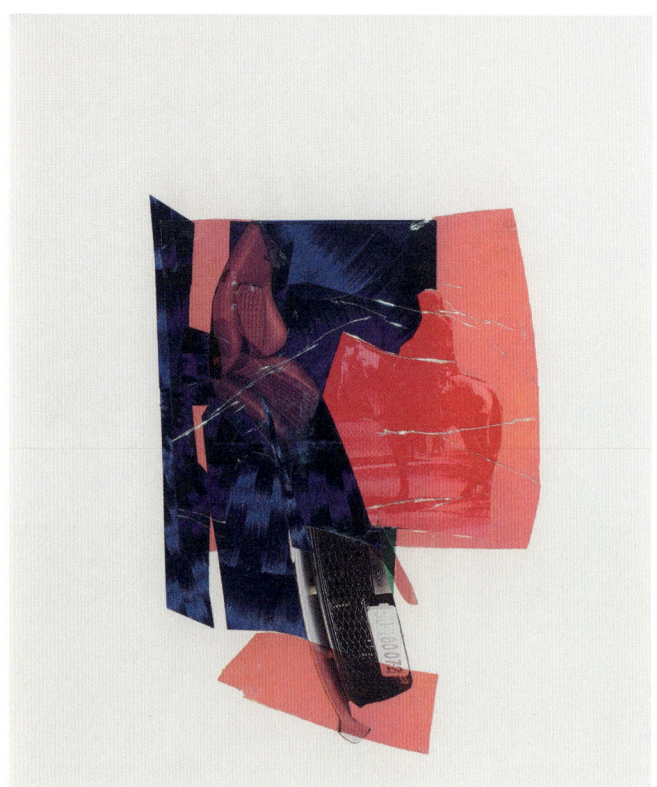

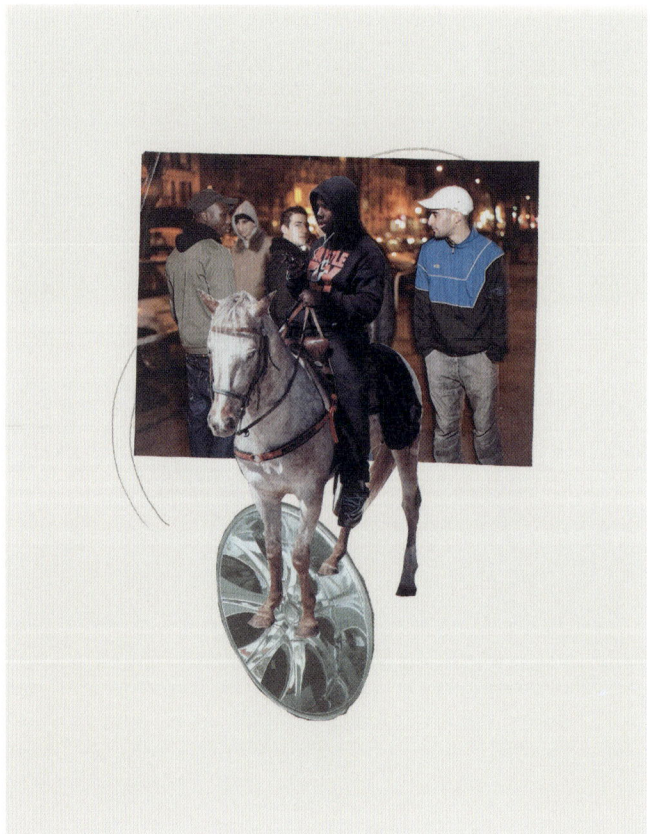

↑↑   **Untitled**, 2017, from the series '**Horse Day**', 2013–17, collage on paper, framed 43 × 35 cm (16⅞ × 13¾ in)

↑   **Untitled**, 2017, from the series '**Horse Day**', 2013–17, collage and pencil on paper, framed 43 × 35 cm (16⅞ × 13¾ in)

↗   **Untitled**, 2016, from the series '**The Hood**', 2016, black-and-white silver print (sublimation) on bodywork and metal plate, spray paint, varnish, 113 × 66 × 4 cm (944½ × 26 × 1⅝ in), private collection

↗↗   **Donnie**, 2016, black-and-white silver print on car body part, 193 × 112 × 21.5 cm (76 × 44⅛ × 8½ in), private collection§

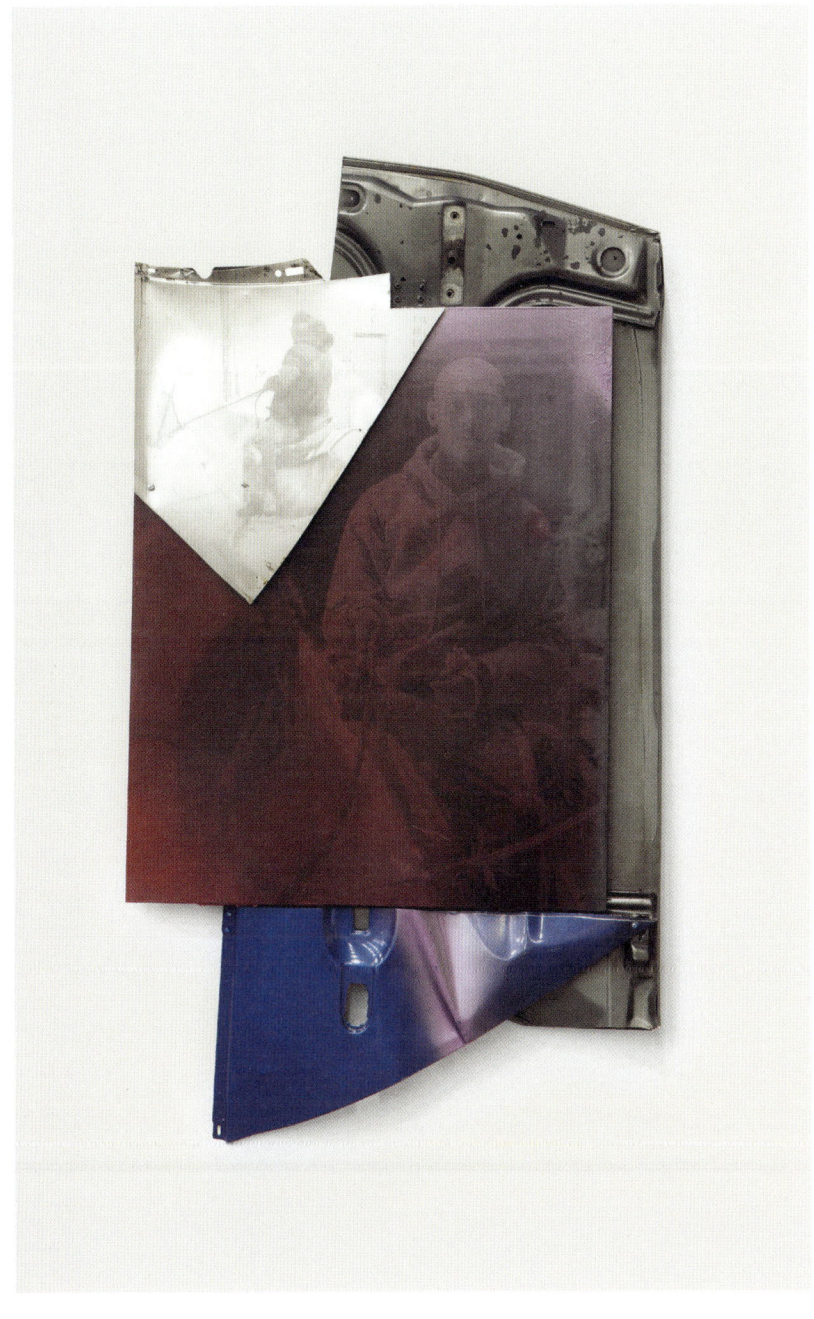
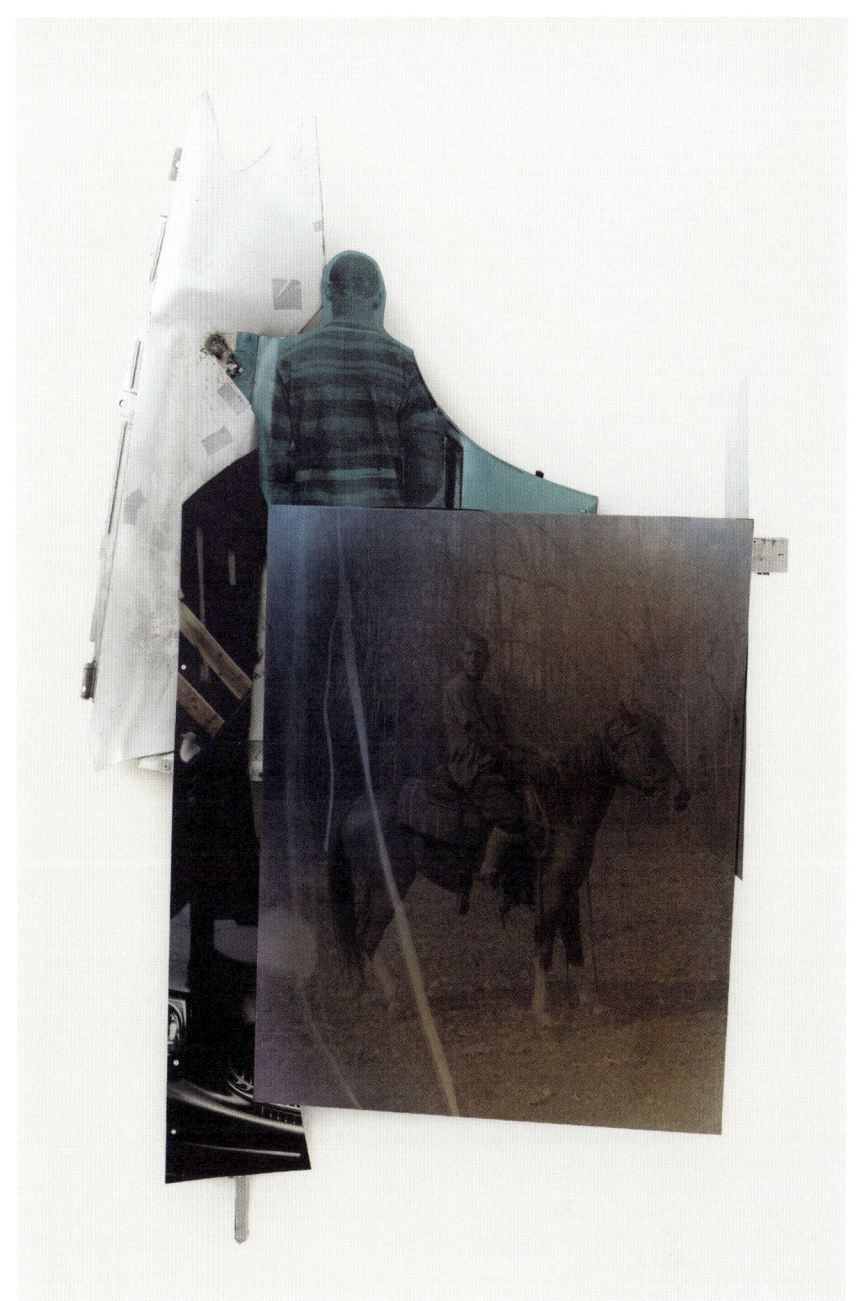

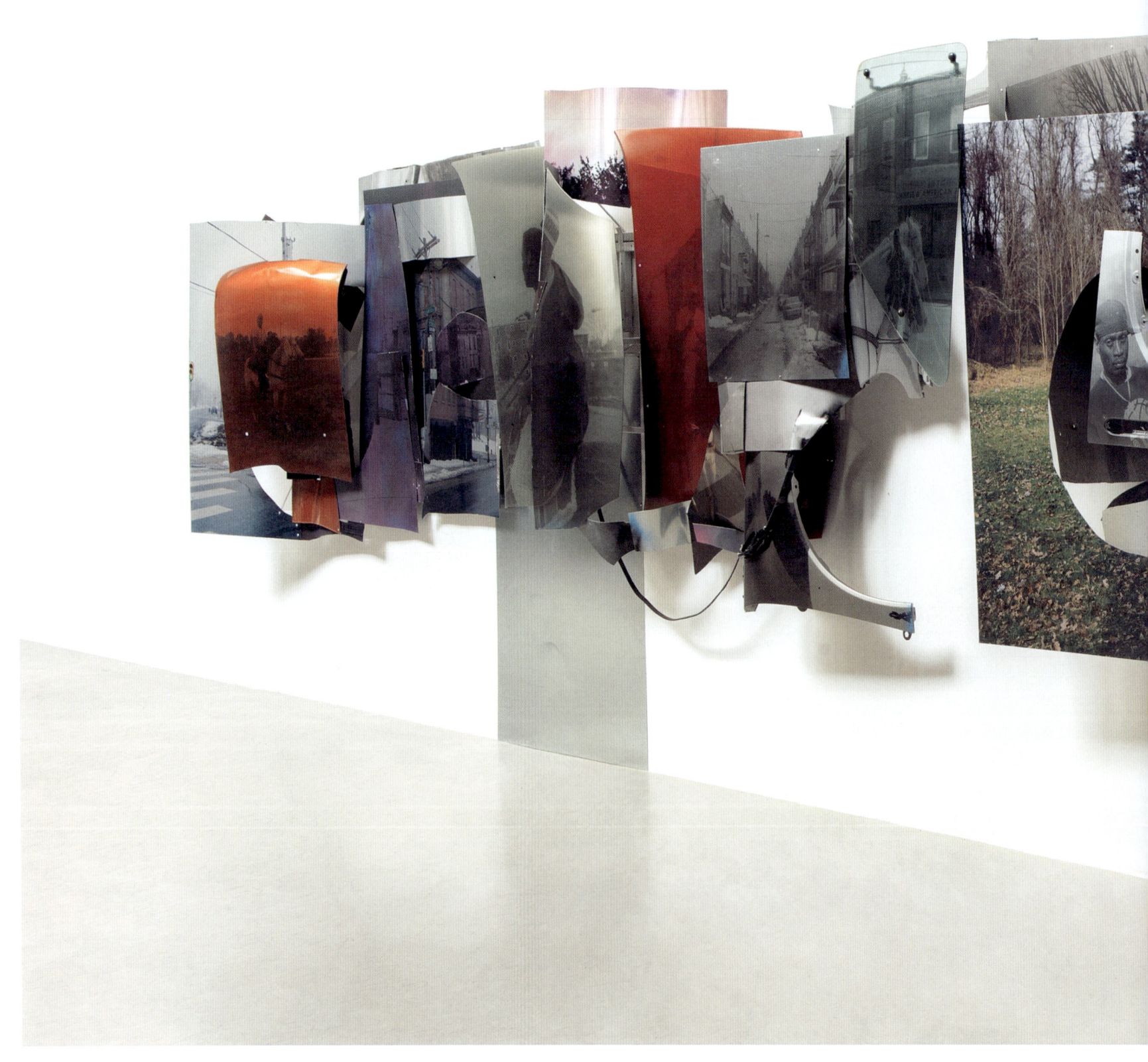

↑ **The ride**, 2017, colour and black-and-white silver print on car metal plate, body part, spray painting and lacquer, 235 × 800 cm (92½ × 315 in), installation view, 'Natures Mortes: Carte blanche à Anne Imhof', Palais de Tokyo, Paris, France, 2021, private collection

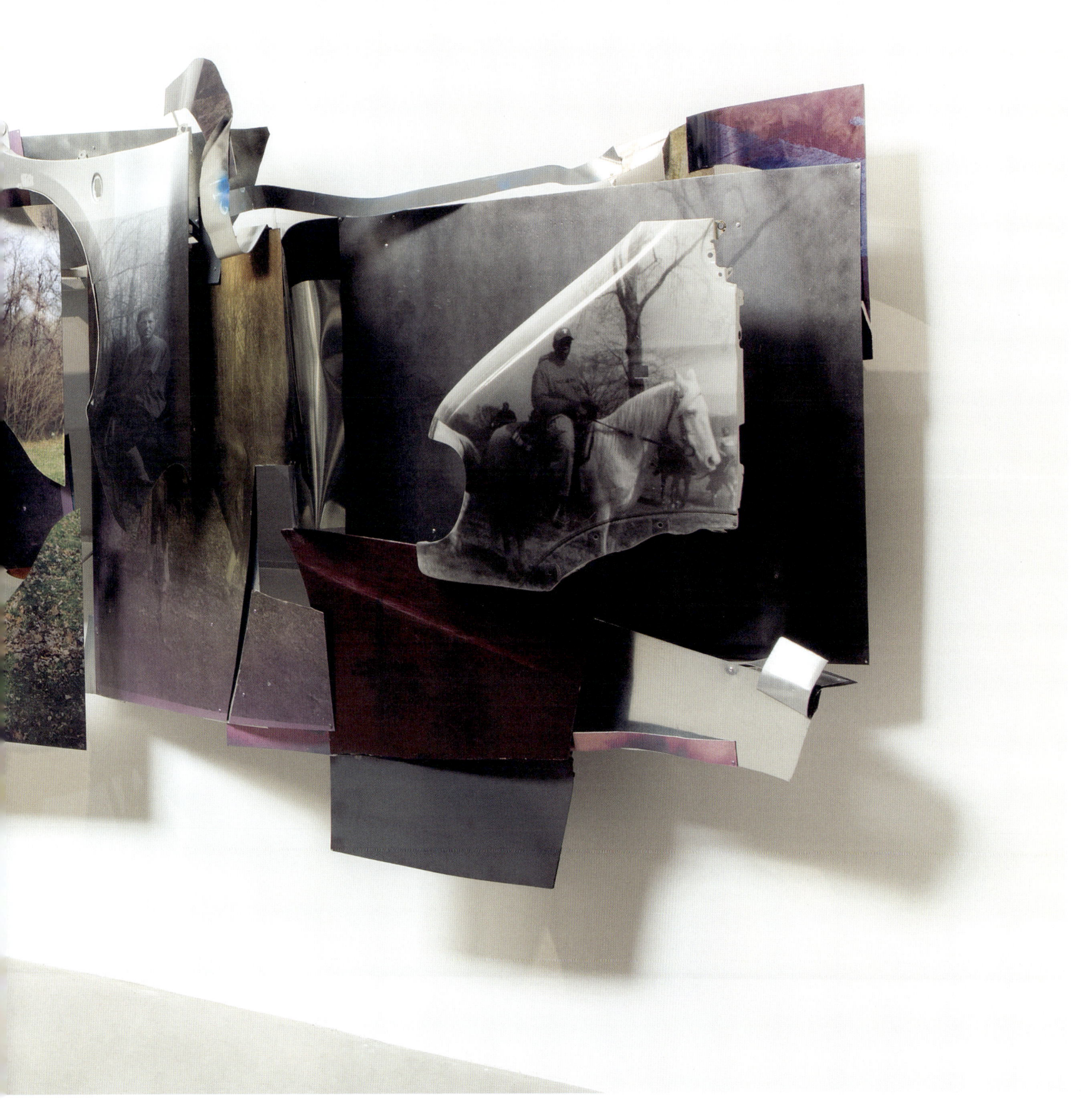

ADAM BROOMBERG

Dissatisfied with the limitations of photography, Adam Broomberg navigates the medium's shortcomings with a singular dexterity. His scepticism of the medium shapes his conceptual enquiries, as too does his discomfort with the intractable dynamics between photographer and subject. This ethical unease has informed not only his own work, but much of that made with fellow photographer Oliver Chanarin (b. 1971). Their prolific two-decade collaboration, which began in the late 1990s, shifted from an editorial approach aligned with photojournalism to a more conceptual bent – the pair pursuing a bricolage study of conflict and its images. In 2021 a death notice and 'posthumous' retrospective of their shared archive, 'The Late Estate of Broomberg & Chanarin', announced the end of their creative partnership. ▰ Striking out alone, Broomberg has since turned his attention to portraiture and its attendant failings. He applies both analogue methods and digital means to the genre, and offers an extended understanding of what might constitute the 'pictured self'. His collaborative works made with trans-activist and actress Gérsande 'Gigi' Spelsberg as subject consider identity's plurality across mediums – among them, one hundred near-identical portraits shot in medium format film, *Glitter in My Wounds* (2021), and an algorithm-generated video notating Gigi's transition, *Going. Full Time. 1* (2021). Such propositions of imaging identity are further explored in the artist's obscure self-portrait, *adam.baby* (2021), which bends AI learning to cryptic ends. Fed thirty years of Broomberg's internet search history and emails, the resulting neural network allows viewers to converse – by way of text – with a machine consciousness fashioned after the artist's own. ◀▰ If Broomberg is sceptical of photography, his sentiments regarding collage come closer to dismissal. But such disregard has proven productive. 'I think collage is to art what sarcasm is to humour. It's easy, not very smart or critical,' the artist said of his 'Blood in the cut' series (2020) in correspondence with the author in 2022. 'Maybe it's because I don't respect the medium that it allowed me to mess around and get dirty and personal for a change.' The series recounts a decade-long exchange between Broomberg and publisher Michael Mack, who sent the artist photobooks that were later returned, augmented or wholly undermined (the choice of words, the artist suggests, is a question of allegiance). To their pages, Broomberg applied squid ink, his own blood, the blade of a cutting knife, and images and texts both made and found. The resulting works – substantially enlarged digital reproductions of these collages – document discrete moments in this performative, time-based redaction – Broomberg working with and against the original photographs. They are, too, portraits after a fashion, however faceless – not of their sitters, rendered anonymous, but of the artist and his discontents. That the only likeness is a death mask, in *Blood in the cut #33*, is perhaps telling. ▰

LUCIENNE BESTALL

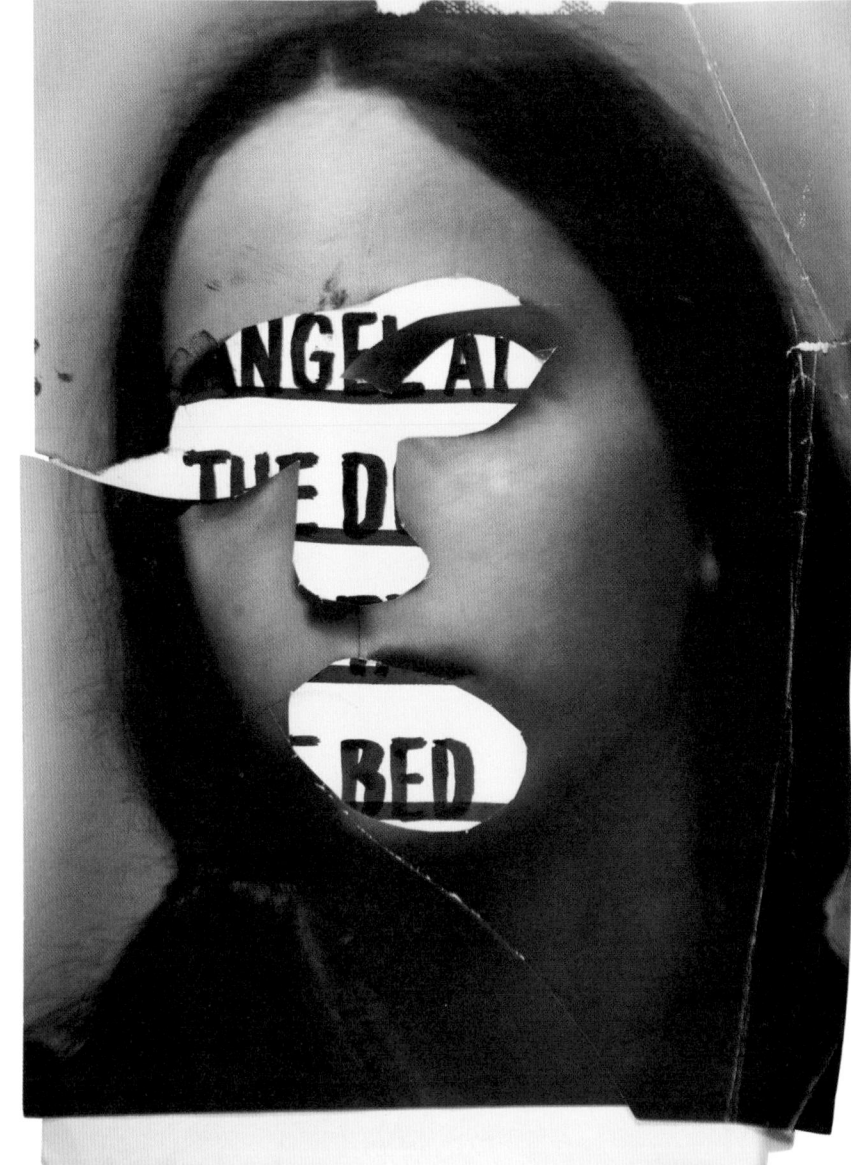

Born 1970, Johannesburg, South Africa. Lives in Berlin, Germany.

↑   **Blood in the cut #11**, 2020, C-type print, 150 × 105.5 cm (59 × 41½ in)

↗   **Blood in the cut #14**, 2020, C-type print, 150 × 105.5 cm (59 × 41½ in)

→   **Blood in the cut #33**, 2020, C-type print, 150 × 105.5 cm (59 × 41½ in)

→ →   **Blood in the cut #49**, 2020, C-type print, 150 × 105.5 cm (59 × 41½ in)

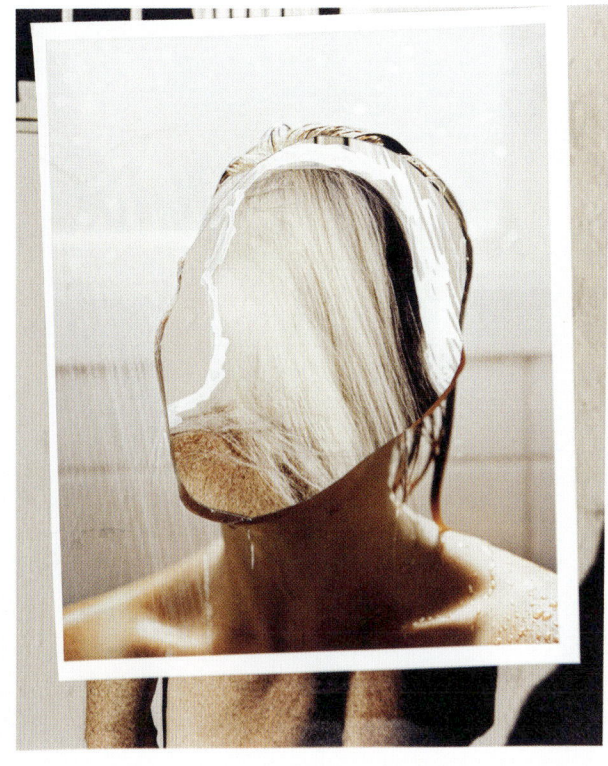

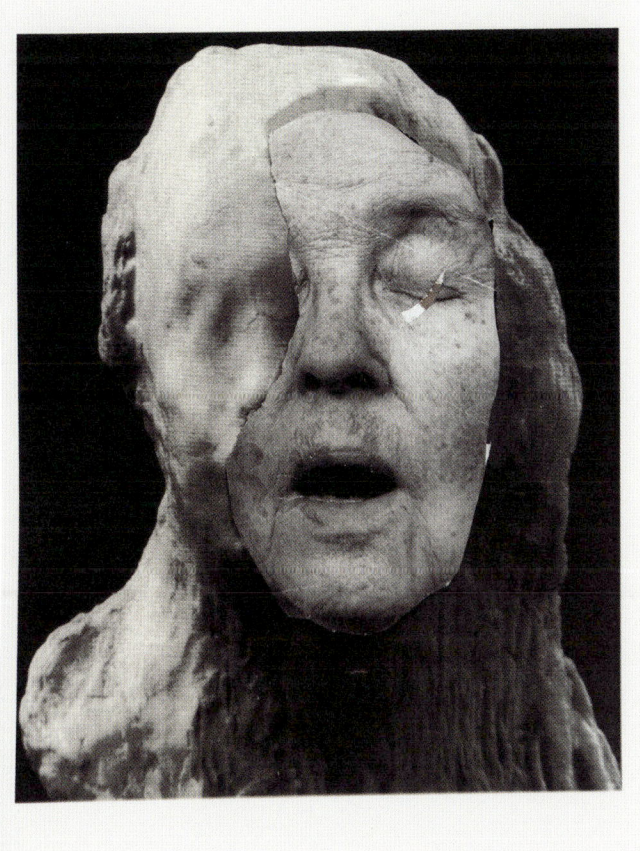

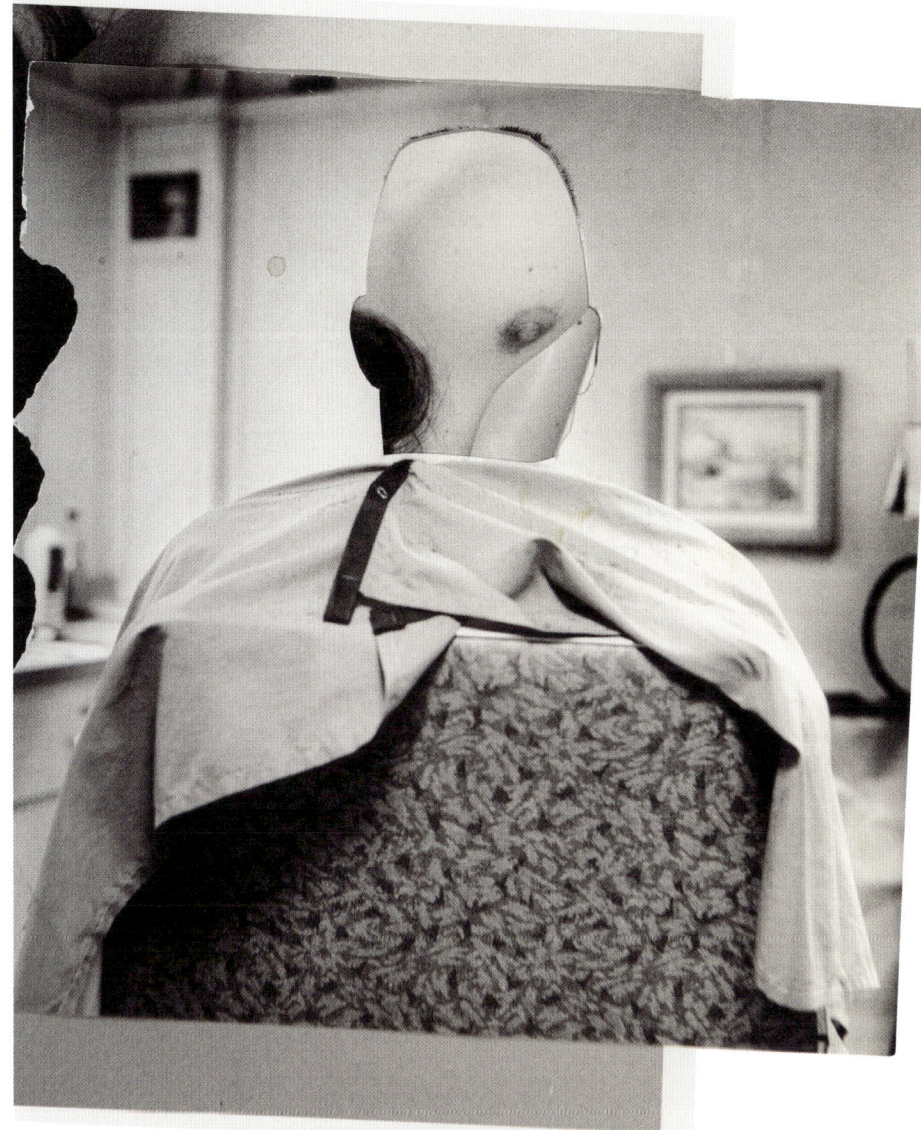

ADAM BROOMBERG

MUHANNED CADER

With their sinuous shapes, bright pops of colour and ample use of negative space, the collages of Muhanned Cader beguile as much as they draw in the viewer's gaze in a subtle balance of allusion and obfuscation. Constructed from found archival ephemera and Cader's own photography, often with flourishes of painted colour, the collages bring together the artist's keen observation of the flora and fauna of his native Sri Lanka, his careful study of the nation's colonial history and his personal experience of living through decades of its civil war. Though his work draws on the close observation and cataloguing of the changes – both physical and political, minute and catastrophic – to Sri Lanka's landscape, Cader frequently abstracts realities into impressionistic forms. *On the Island* (2016) is a photo-collage comprising two complementary outlines of nonrepresentational, slightly phallic shapes constructed from photographs of Sri Lanka's natural landscape found in contemporary art ephemera and corporate tourist advertisements. Scraps of blue sky and green leaves form the edges of these shapes and their hollowed-out centres reveal the gallery's white walls, underscoring the extractive procedures that fuel the Sri Lankan economy. While, initially, the two outlines appear to be mirror images, closer inspection reveals that the leftmost outline is slightly smaller than its complementary partner – suggesting, like the flora it depicts, that the image has been carved out and its original context warped. *Springtime in Paradise* (2015–16), an array of fifty resplendently hued collages of fantastical birds and insects set against stark white backgrounds, alludes to the developmental logic of the Sri Lankan state and its investment in soft power as a strategy to obscure violent domestic strife. The title of the series gestures to this irony, as well as to the ecological destruction wrought by the twin industries of tourism and contemporary art. When the series was displayed in the artist's solo exhibition 'Island' at the Talwar Gallery, New Delhi in 2016, the images were framed behind glass, but arranged salon-style in a compact, inverted pyramid – not unlike displays of exotic flora and fauna that were brought to the metropole from European colonies in South Asia beginning in the sixteenth century. *Disco-very* (2015) similarly draws from this legacy with collages in the shape of birds, dogs and other animals. Affixed directly to the white gallery walls, these works invert the colourful schema of the other collages, their compositions consisting largely of negative white space with coloured photo fragments of Sri Lanka's iconic beaches and verdant landscape. Here, the absence of the landscape is directly connected to the legacy of colonial destruction as it has morphed into new forms that continue to erode nature, now at an alarming pace. Cader's oscillation between foreground and background, history and presentism, forces the viewer to take in this erosion.

TAUSIF NOOR

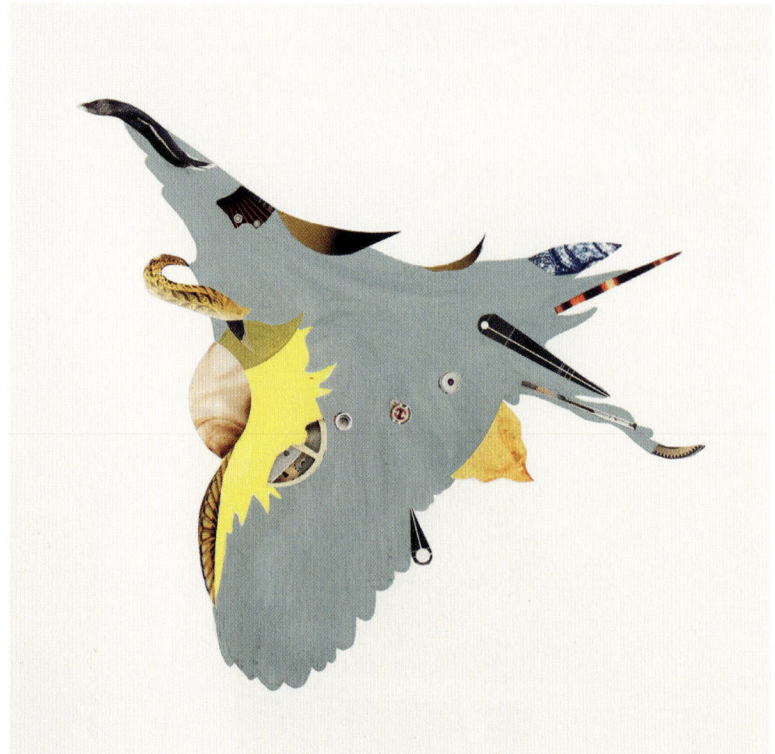

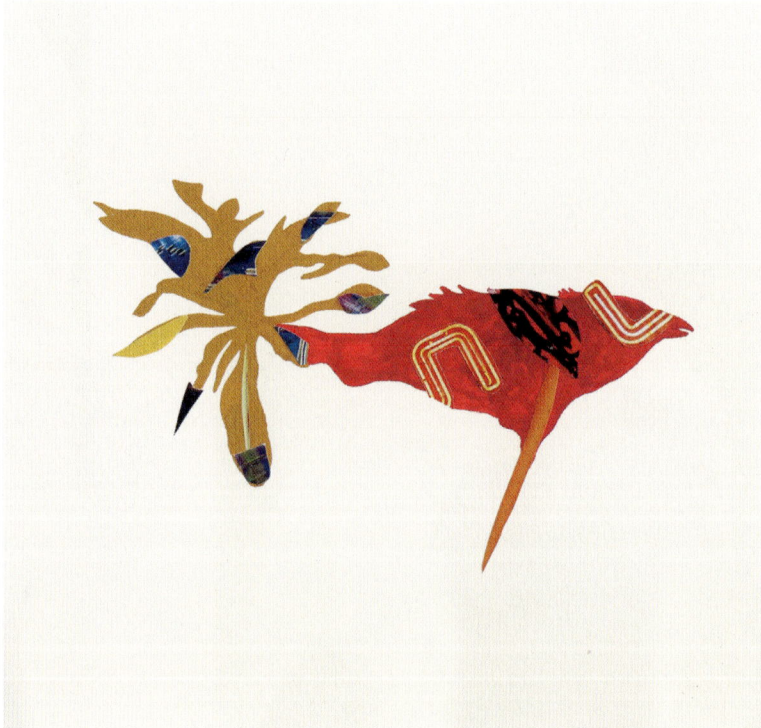

Born 1966, Colombo, Sri Lanka. Lives in Colombo.

↑ **Springtime in Paradise** (details), 2015–16, acrylic and collage on paper in 50 parts, each c.26.7 × 26.7 cm (c.10½ × 10½ in), Kiran Nadar Museum of Art, New Delhi, India

↗ **On the Island**, 2016, photo collage on paper in 2 parts, each 69.9 × 100.1 cm (27½ × 39⅜ in), installation view, 'Island', Talwar Gallery, New Delhi, India, 2016

→ **Disco-very** (details), 2015, photo collage on paper in 11 parts, each c.49.8 cm × 69.9 cm (c.19⅝ × 27½ in)

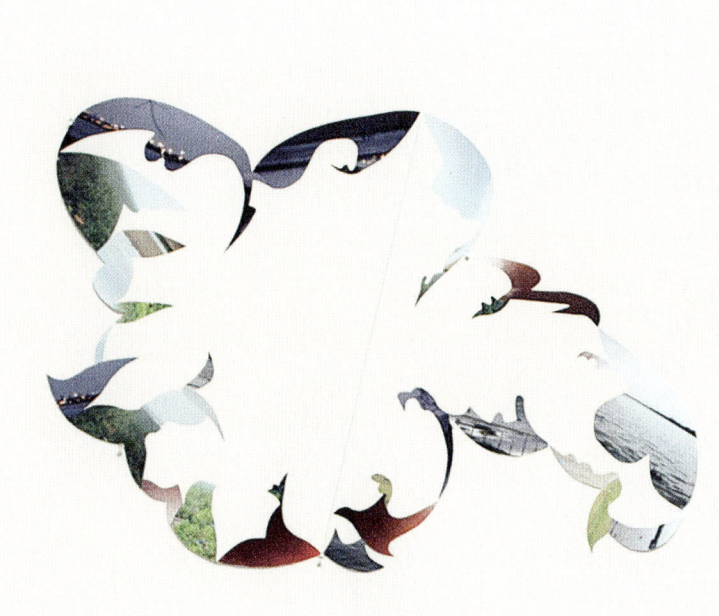
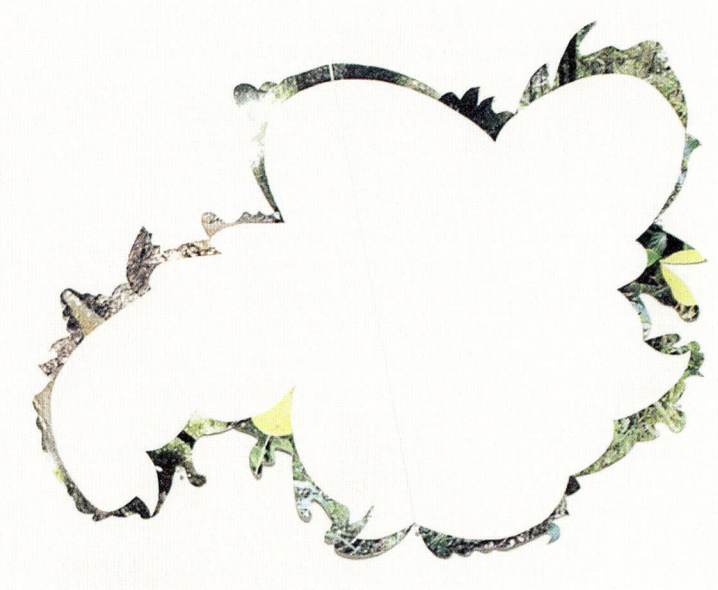
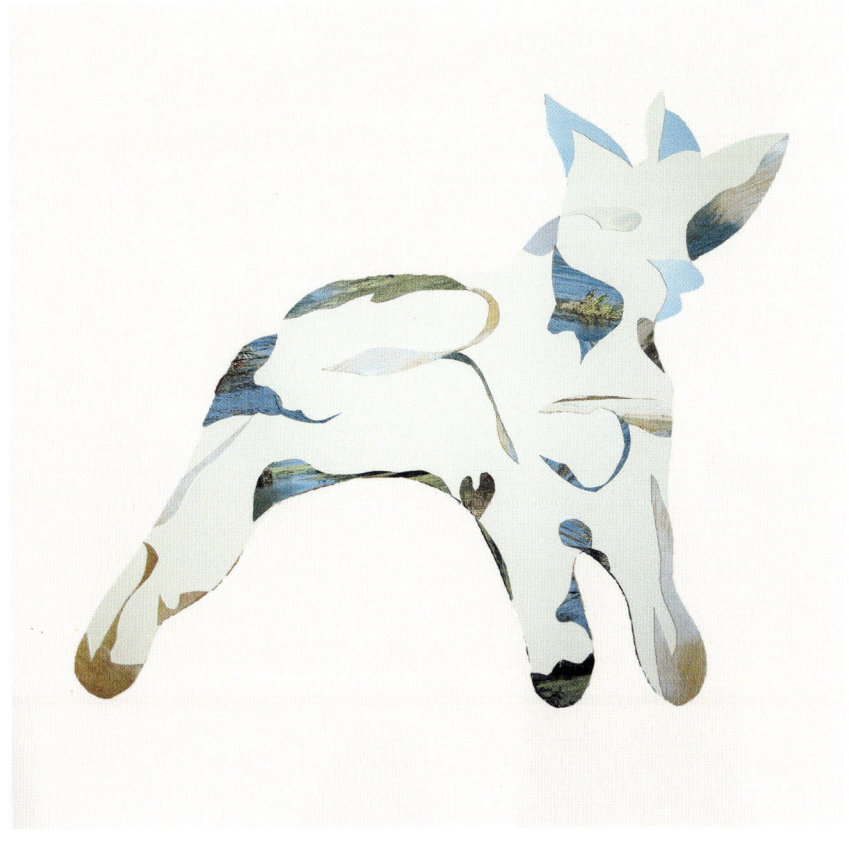
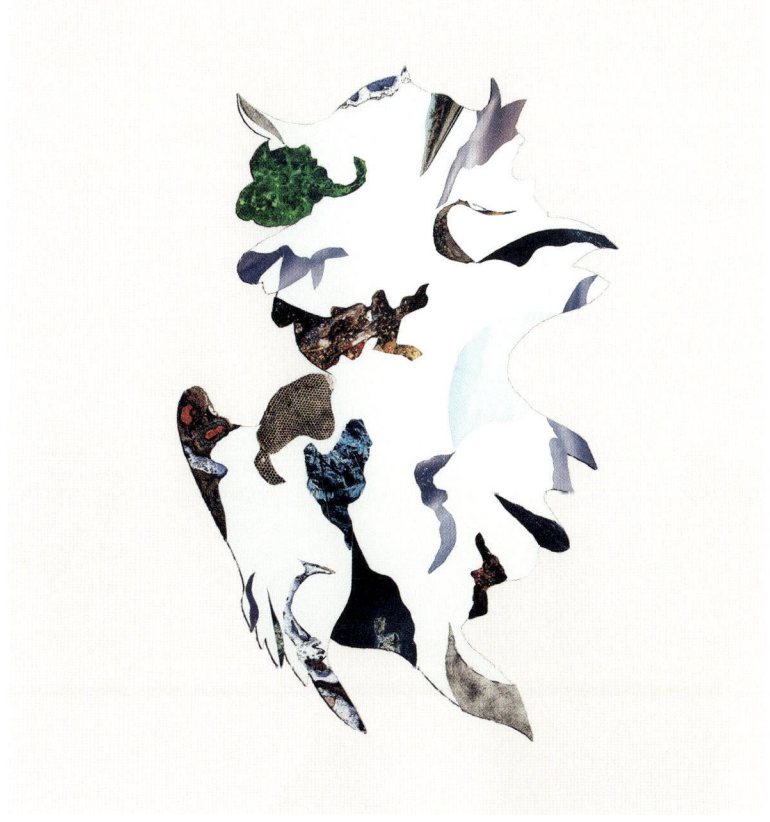

DAVIDE CASCIO

The mysteries of the natural world and the novels of the late, great Irish writer James Joyce are two cornerstones in Davide Cascio's practice. These two apparently disparate sources actually present a series of tight interrelations between them when viewed through the prism of Cascio's work, chief among them a perennial process of deconstruction and reconstruction that resonates within a bigger picture. If in the case of nature, this constitutes an essential trait in any life cycle, in Joyce's, it shows a predilection for non-linear narratives that convey a sense of perpetual movement – each sentence forming an etymological study in itself and a snapshot of fleeting moments aptly described through a multi-sensorial experience. Cascio is first and foremost a sculptor, but with such premises, it is hardly surprising to learn that he considers collage a foundational aspect of his work. Collage, after all, is an activity primarily founded on fragmentation that had lived one of its most pivotal moments in Zurich in the mid-1910s, when the Dadaists adopted it as a celebrational tool to regenerate the innocence and playful randomness lost to the drama of the First World War. Interestingly, this is also the same city where Joyce laid the basis for his ultimate masterpiece, *Ulysses* (1922), and when geometry – another tangible component in Cascio's work – was elevated to new heights in art and architecture during the twentieth century. Cascio's collages are both a sketching device and an extension of his three-dimensional pieces. Like most of his other works, they function autonomously while contributing an indispensable strand to his overall practice. *E.N. Esprit Nouveau* (2008), for example, refers to another unfinished opus – Le Corbusier's eponymous pavilion conceived for the 1925 International Exhibition of Modern Decorative and Industrial Arts in Paris. Frustrated by what they perceived as a discordant note with the extravagant attitude of the show, the organizers attempted to block the view of the Swiss architect's fragile and incomplete structure with a fence, only for the authorities to reopen it to the public a few days later following an intervention by the Ministry of Education. Presented on the occasion of an exhibition in Bologna, Italy, in 2008, where a group of Corbusier's admirers eventually built a second, more refined version of the pavilion thirty-one years before, Cascio's *E. N. Esprit Nouveau* is also an elegant, letter-shaped sculpture simultaneously acting as partition and point of passage – two facets that the collage reprises while reiterating the transitional quality of Le Corbusier's creation. The view of a deliberately ambiguous space as an asset rather than a setback is also masterfully illustrated in *E.N. Tree Diagram* (2008), a representation of independence and probability that shows how aspiration is not a step towards a goal but an existential condition that needs to be inhabited and explored.

MICHELE ROBECCHI

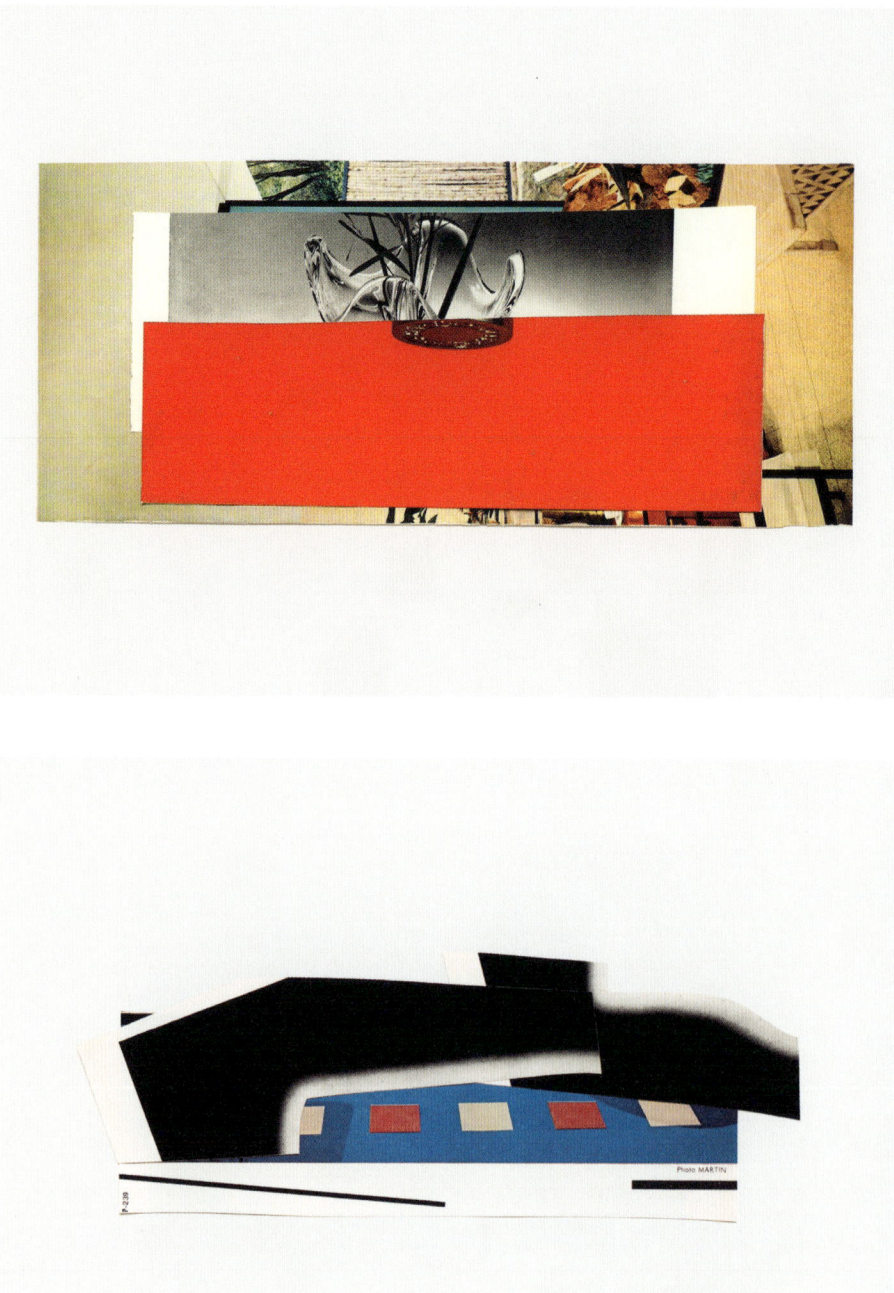

Born 1976, Lugano, Switzerland. Lives Paris, France and Lugano.

↑↑   Untitled, from the series '**Interiors landscapes**', 2020, collage on paper, 32.5 × 45 cm (12 ⅝ × 17 ¾ in)

↑   Untitled, from the series '**Interiors landscapes**', 2020, collage on paper, 32.5 × 45 cm (12 ⅝ × 17 ¾ in)

↗   E.N. Esprit Nouveau, 2008, collage on paper on MDF board, 70 × 50 cm (27 ½ × 19 ⅝ in)

→   E.N. Tree diagram, 2008, collage on paper on MDF board, 70 × 50 cm (27 ½ × 19 ⅝ in)

→→   Untitled, from the series '**Beside painting III**', 2020, collage and acrylic painting on paper, 45 × 32.5 cm (17 ¾ × 12 ⅝ in)

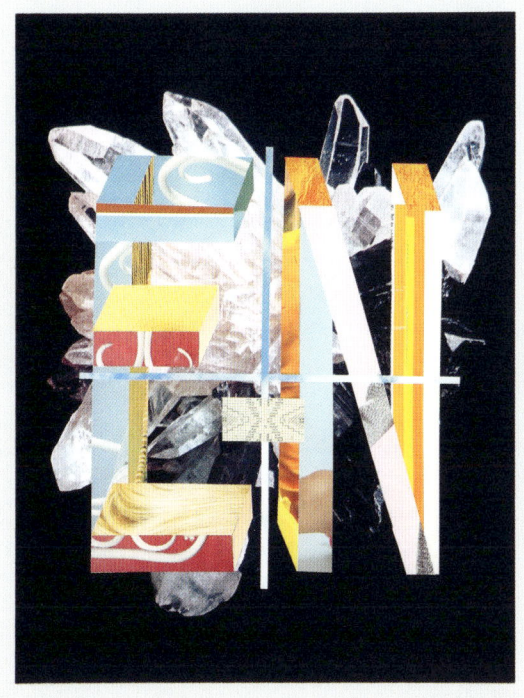

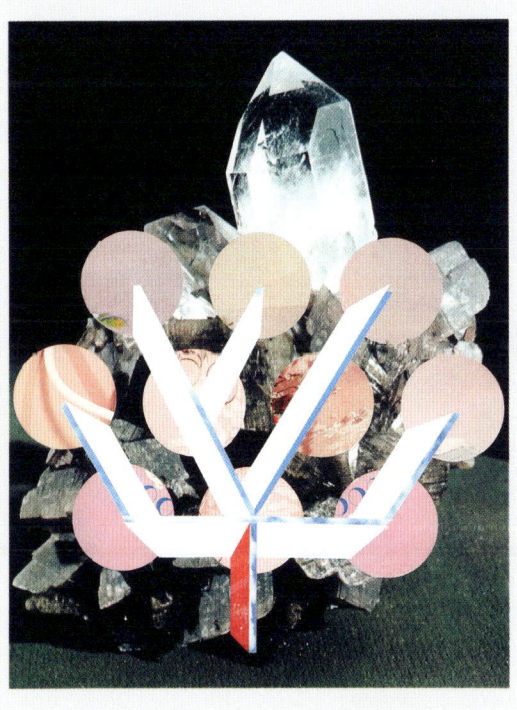

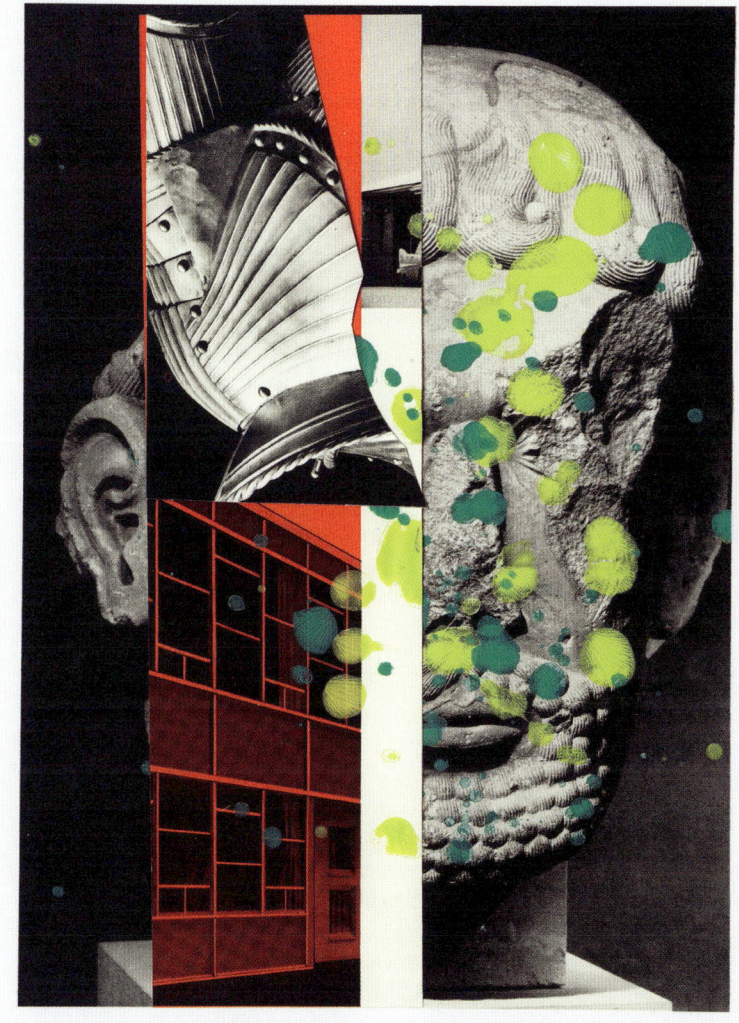

DAVIDE
CASCIO

NICHOLAS CHEVELDAVE

In an era when nearly everyone has a smartphone camera in their pocket and the minutiae of people's lives are shared online, Nicholas Cheveldave's work encapsulates the visual abundance of twenty-first-century visual culture. Amid this saturation of information, it can be difficult to absorb every image: users scroll and 'like' in a constant state of distraction. The personal and the corporate share the same online space, often becoming indistinguishable. Everyone seems to be selling something.

Cheveldave draws from personal and found photographs from online searches, flea markets, family albums, advertising and newspapers. He explores the ways in which images are circulated and received, extracting them from their context and placing them in new configurations to suggest enigmatic narratives. Combining a range of materials and approaches including digital and analogue printing, painting and drawing, he often includes unexpected items such as bandages, price stickers and glitter. Cheveldave grew up in suburban Vancouver with a father who worked in the movie industry. His art revels in a cinematic tradition that combines the dramatic and mundane, peeling away a suburban veneer. Take *The Ones Who Love Us Best* (2016), which is characteristic of the artist's earlier works. Photographs of smiling children are defaced with biro; their smiles become grimaces, eyes are black holes. Letters are cut from the newspaper recalling a ransom note. The work materializes the psychic underbelly of small-town life. In a recurrent motif, friendship bracelets are pasted across the image forming a web. The work's symbolism is manifold, hinting at the online commodification of relationships as well as the ubiquity of web-like internet metaphors. *Worm Hole pt. 7* (2019) incorporates laminated photographs of gardens, parks and allotments. Nature is contained and coiffured, a space of production, contemplation, ostentation and abandonment. What connects these images beyond their depictions of nature? Other works from this series combine banal imagery such as roof insulation, staircases, sofas, washing machines and refrigerators. What the pictures contain is less important than how they got there. The work makes physical the happenstance of a Google image search describing a world where choice – as a fundamentally creative act – is outsourced to algorithmic logic. In later works Cheveldave has pared back the number of his images and his use of colour. These stark monochromatic creations incorporate depictions of band posters, surfers and bridges. A sense of adolescent escape and transformation permeates the compositions. *Half Full* (2020) combines a shot of a watercooler containing a disposable glove with an inlaid image of a picket fence. Glitter is smeared across the surface. In this domestic scene, cheap glamour abuts the humdrum; imagination becomes a space of possibility. These images feel like half-remembered anecdotes refracted through time, concealing as much as they reveal. Like the best films, they thwart our desire for resolution, leaving us hanging on for the sequel.

GEORGE VASEY

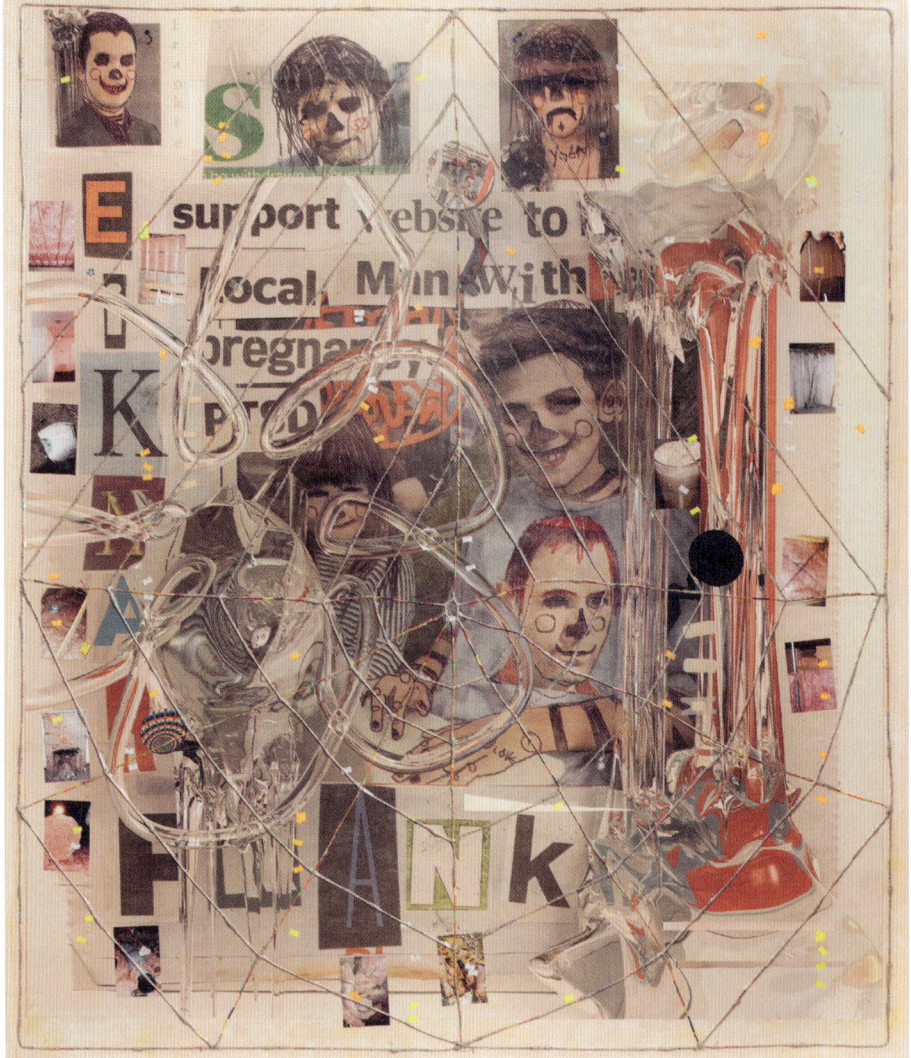

Born 1984, Victoria, Canada. Lives in London, UK.

↑   The Ones Who Love Us Best, 2016, photolaminate, acrylic, paper, friendship bracelets, hemp and metal on canvas, 230 × 200 cm (90½ × 78¾ in)

→   Half Full, 2020, paper, acrylic and glitter on canvas, 100 × 70 × 3.8 cm (39⅜ × 27½ × 1½ in)

↗↗ Worm Hole pt. 7, 2019, photolaminate and mixed media on Dibond, 180 × 122 × 3 cm (70⅞ × 48⅛ × 1⅛ in)

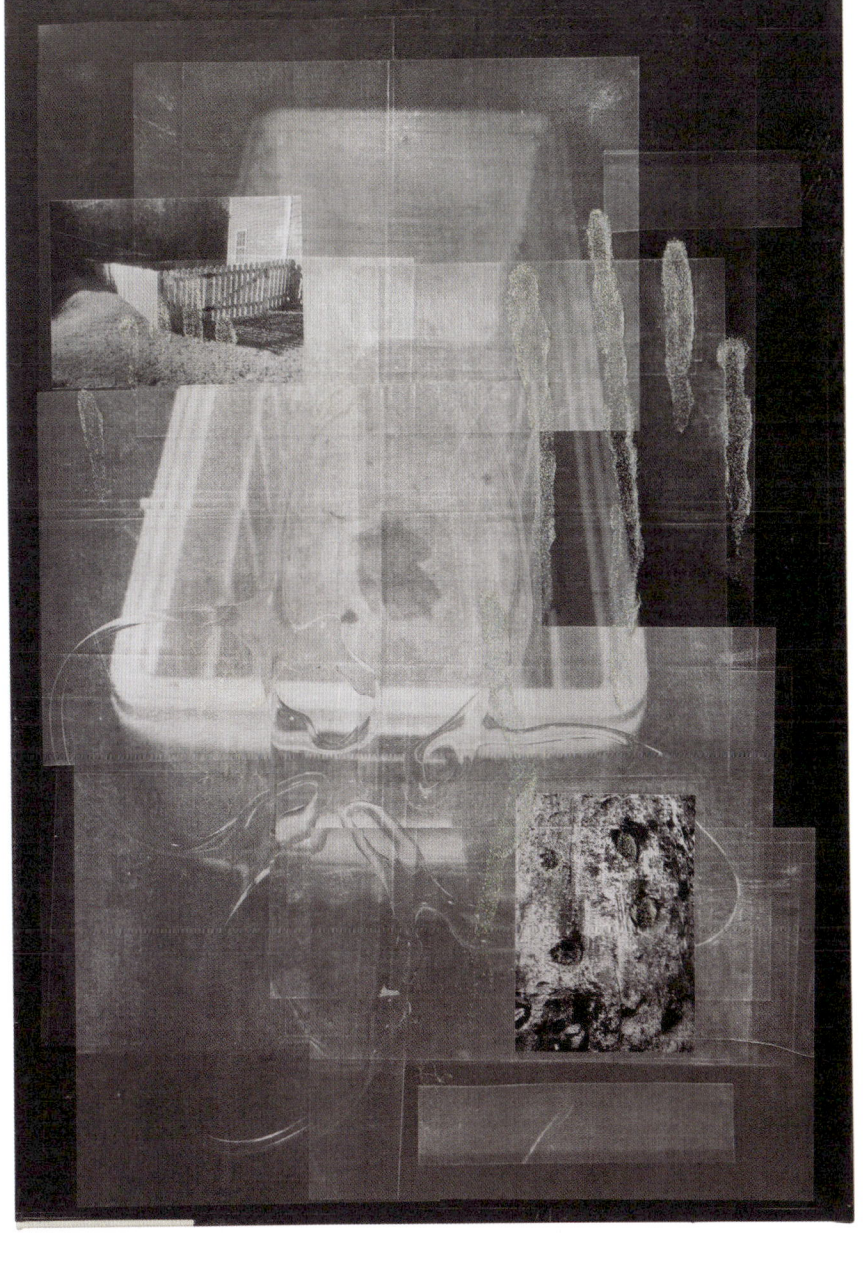

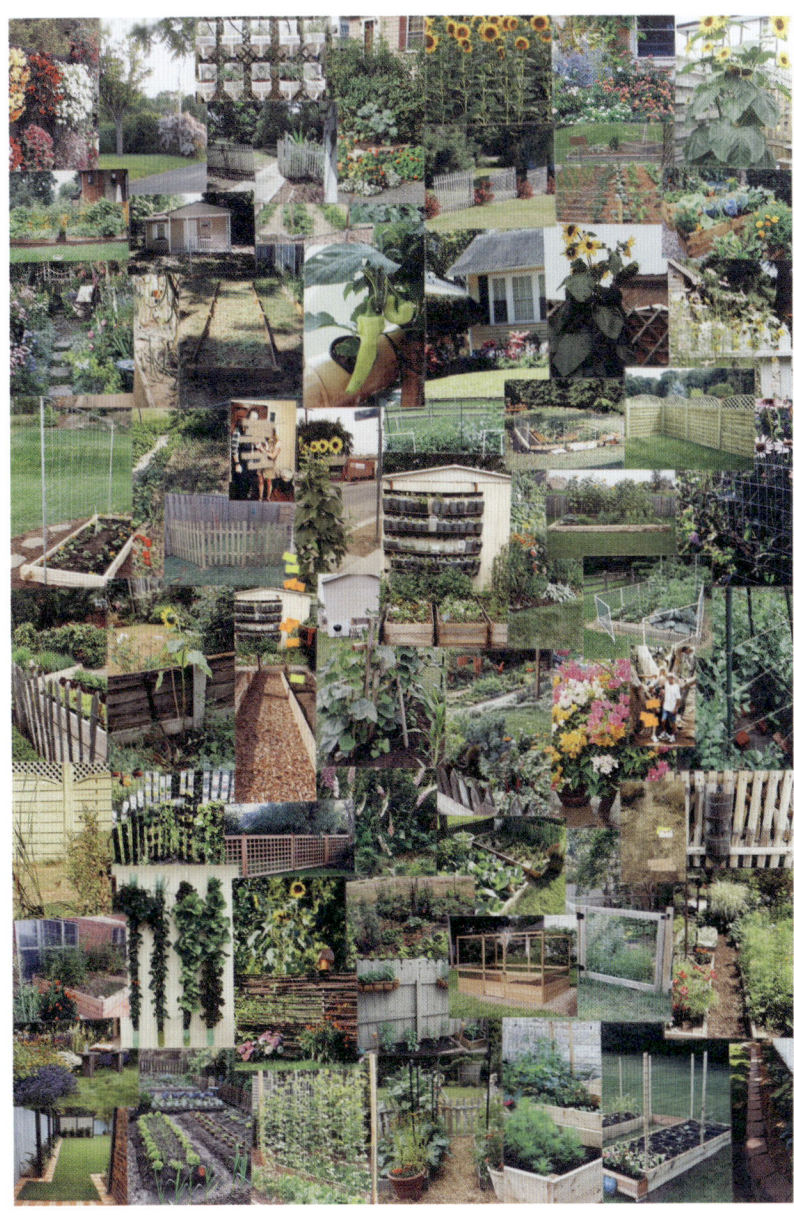

NICHOLAS CHEVELDAVE

SARA CWYNAR

Sara Cwynar's seductive visual universe revolves around questions of literacy in online communications. Her videos, installations and collages undermine distinctions between pictorial and textual language, as well as still and moving image, mimicking the way that on-screen media display information and encourage consumption. Contrasting an array of fabricated and found footage, real and simulated space, Cwynar's work is informed by a dense mix of theoretical texts as well as personal reflections on subjects as varied as advertising, phenomenology, feminist theory, psychology and art. 'My work involves hours, weeks, months of literary research and reference,' she explained in an interview at Luxembourg + Co, London, in 2021, 'and all of my images begin with references in writing and thinking about how language operates in the same way as images.' The results, however, do not always contain text or narration, but they consistently rely on a process of accumulation rather than juxtaposition of content. In *Jeff Koons Louis Vuitton Rubens bag* (2020), for example, she takes a photograph of Jeff Koons (b.1967) line of accessories for the French fashion brand Louis Vuitton in 2017, where Old Master painters were made into the subject of high street bags and purses – Peter Paul Rubens (1577–1640) in this instance – and adds multiple images in and around it. These include reproductions of paintings by Albrecht Dürer (1471–1528) and Jean-Auguste-Dominique Ingres (1780–1867), illustrations of fashion styles from encyclopedias, photographs of tongues, eyes, piercings and tattoos, and replicated portions from the bag itself, hereby offering an overwhelming experience of cultural pastiche in a bag. In other instances, as seen in *Tracey (Pantyhose)* (2017), Cwynar includes models (friends, dancers, or even herself) as the subjects of videos and photographs onto which she pastes layers of imagery in a manner that confuses real and artificial space. Yet what seems at first a playful process, executed using a mix of manual and digital methods of production, does not represent digital media as a platform for creative freedom. Rather, it indicates how the aesthetics of intuition and free choice, so commonly championed by advertisers and social media, is more often an indication of control, of guided taste, convention, and even law in certain periods and contexts. This is particularly noticeable in works where Cwynar examines advertising strategies using specific case studies, such as her photographic collage of *Formula 1 Racing Car from MoMA Collection*, 2020. An object recognized by a world-leading taste maker (Museum of Modern Art, New York) for its exceptional beauty and functionality, the red Ferrari is deconstructed in this work into a constellation of cut printouts and reproductions of itself and the brands it advertises, drowning in a series of associative images relating to the colour red, desire and mechanical reproduction.

YUVAL ETGAR

Born 1985, Vancouver, Canada. Lives in Brooklyn, New York, USA.

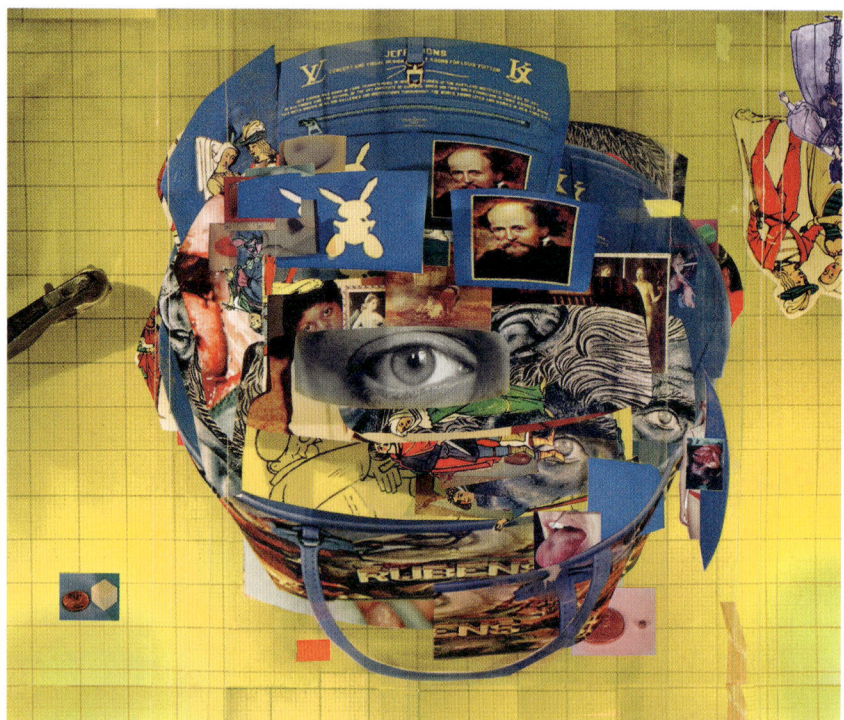

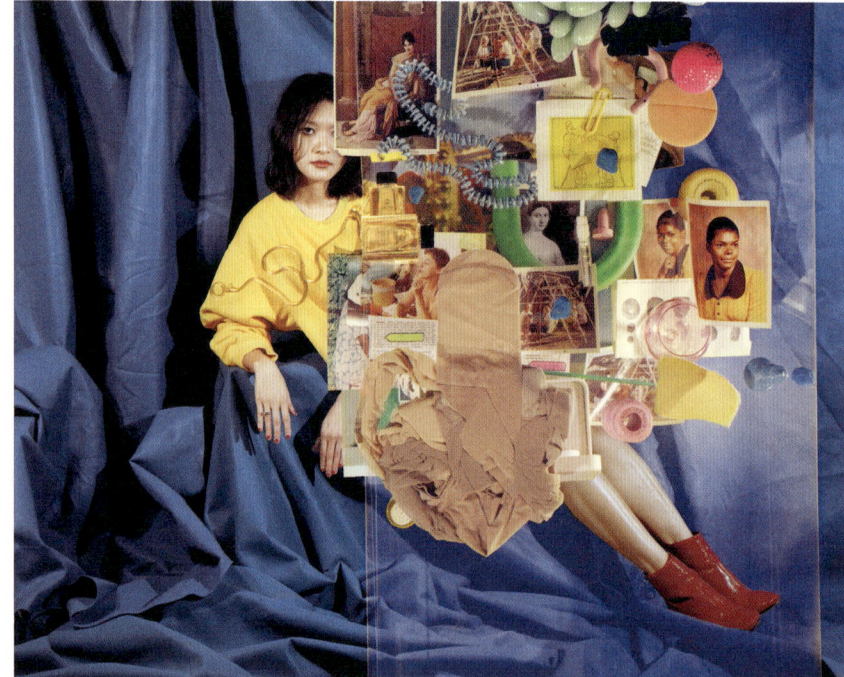

↑↑ Louis Vuitton Jeff Koons Rubens bag, 2020, archival pigment print mounted on Dibond, 76.2 × 91.4 cm (30 × 36 in), edition of 3 + 2 AP

↑ Tracy (Pantyhose), 2017, dye sublimation print on aluminium, 76.2 × 96.5 cm (30 × 38 in), edition of 3 + 2 AP

→ Ali from SSENSE.com (How to Marry a Millionaire), 2020, archival pigment print mounted on Dibond, 76.2 × 61 cm (30 × 24 in), edition of 3 + 2 AP

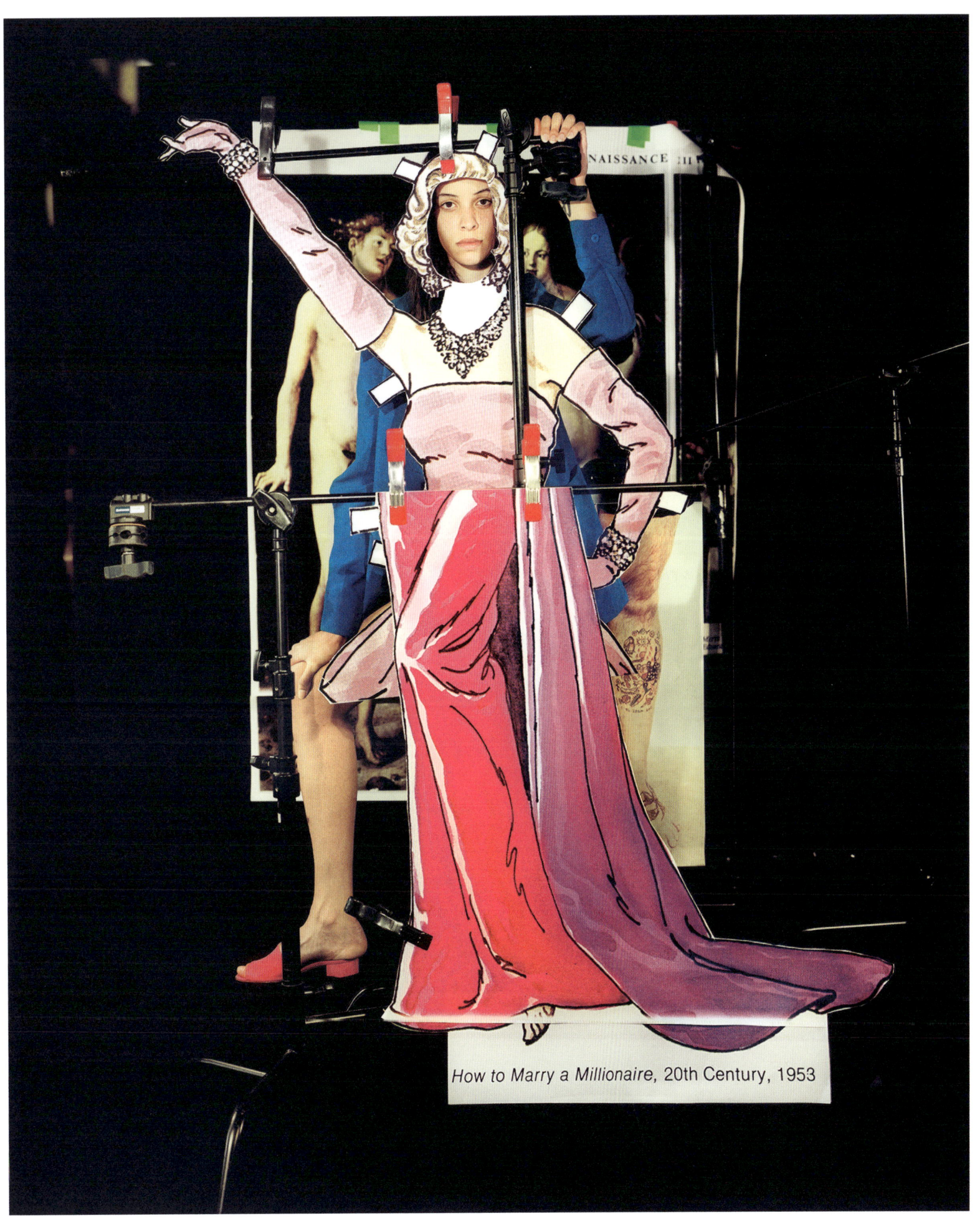

How to Marry a Millionaire, 20th Century, 1953

SARA CWYNAR

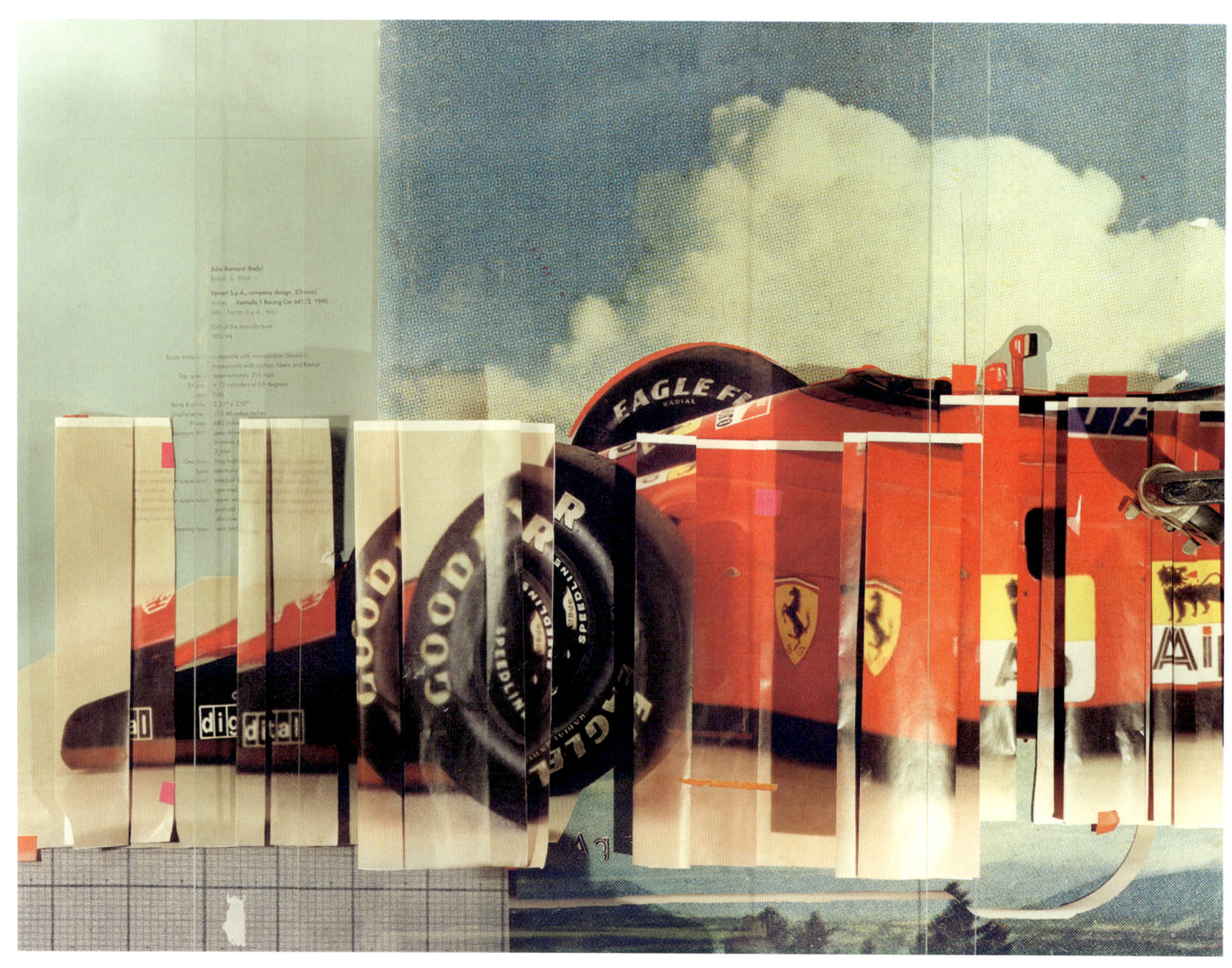

↑ **Formula 1 Racing Car from MoMA Collection**, 2020, archival pigment print mounted on Dibond, each: 76.2 × 101.6 cm (30 × 40 in), overall: 76.2 × 203.2 cm (30 × 80 in), edition of 3 + 2 AP

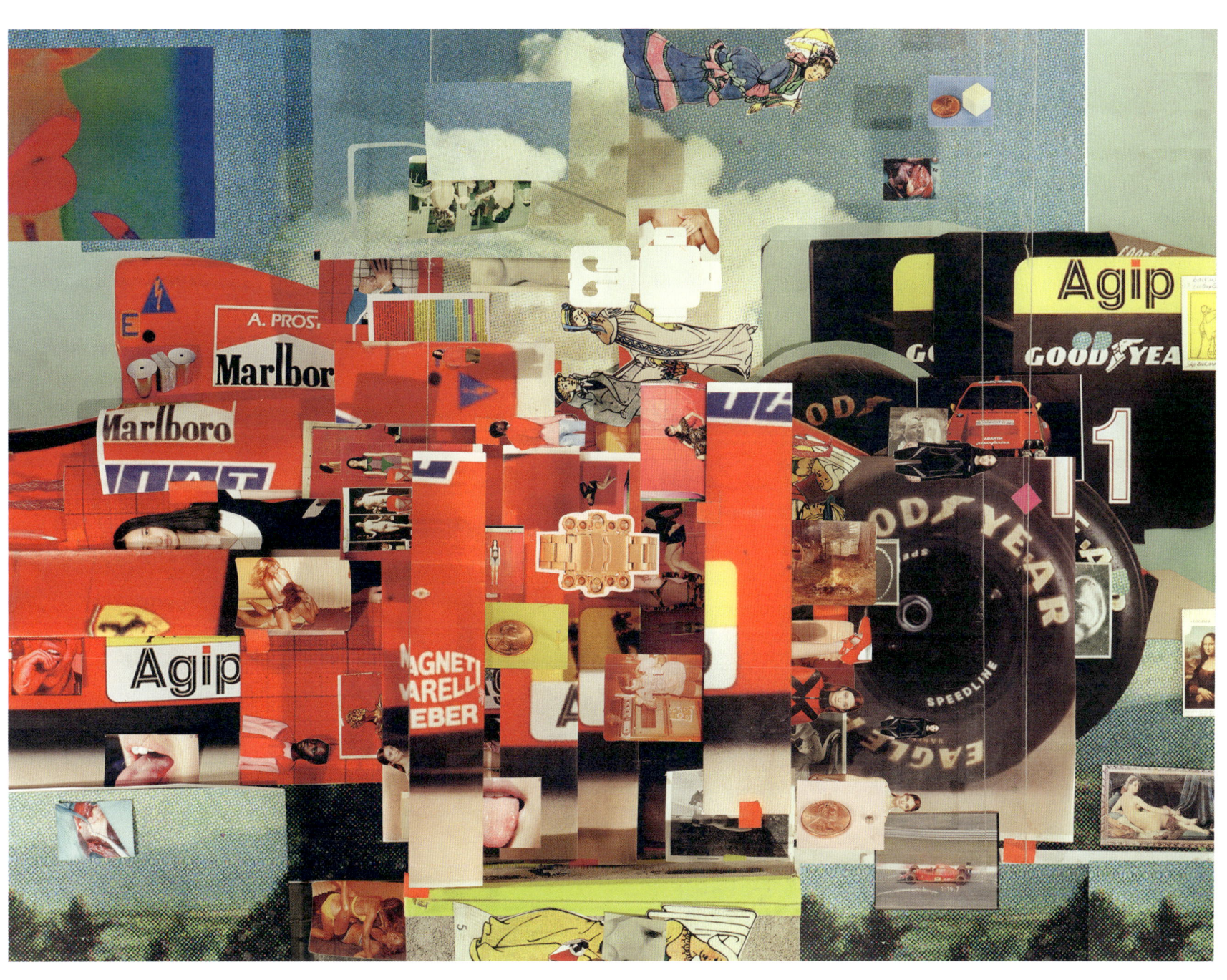

SARA CWYNAR

BADY DALLOUL

Born to Syrian parents, Bady Dalloul melds the real and the imaginary as a means of interrogating how histories, be they macro or local, are codified. In *King of the System* (2020) Dalloul has inked small drawings of men and women going about their daily routines atop a game board that he created; the work's origins can be traced to games Dalloul and his younger brother played growing up. Indeed, games underpin much of Dalloul's practice, though in his art they take on new, and theoretical, forms. *King of the System* – the title refers to a made-up play – weaves ideas around chance and risk, and the ways both can affect success. A similar intermingling of fact and fiction can be seen in the large installation *Bound Together* (2019–20), which traces the possible migration of Syrians resettling in West Africa. Dalloul was particularly interested in the possibility that he had family in Nigeria, an idea that turned out to be false. Nevertheless, friends of friends of Dalloul's parents undertook such a migration, and these journeys served as inspiration for the artist. How exactly, he asked in a short presentation for the interdisciplinary arts organization Kadist in 2022, 'do people change countries, and establish their new lives elsewhere?' To answer this question, *Bound Together* assembles colourful clothing, painted portraits, photographs, maps, postcards and books entitled *How to be Nigerian* and *History of Nigeria*, among others, into a large, multisensorial presentation. The mix of media and collage of imagery allow Dalloul to refract the world through a variety of lenses. Likewise, his scrapbook-like composition *Ordonator* (2020) narrates the history of an imaginary country, Dalloul having been obsessed with the idea of fictitious lands since adolescence. Alongside narrative annotations in blue ink are postage stamps, cut-out passenger jets and faceless portraits of the powerful and aristocratic, all set within a book's pages. As the book progresses, the country falls apart, and so the ephemera within serve as both an image and a record of a disintegrated past. To create *Ordonator*, Dalloul drew inspiration from Persian, Turkish, Indian and Arab manuscripts as well as Japanese *ukiyo-e* prints. With its relatively homogenous population, Japan, for the artist, functions as a powerful foil, offering an alternative to the ways in which the Arab diaspora is so often cast. 'It's extraordinary how, with time, what seem to be completely random acts become the purposeful historical realities we study in school,' he said in an undated interview with the Atassi Foundation. 'We imbue [them] with some kind of purpose... I am fascinated by this process of "writing" history – and how we, the people affected by it, are always witnesses, yet never actors in it.'

GRACE LINDEN

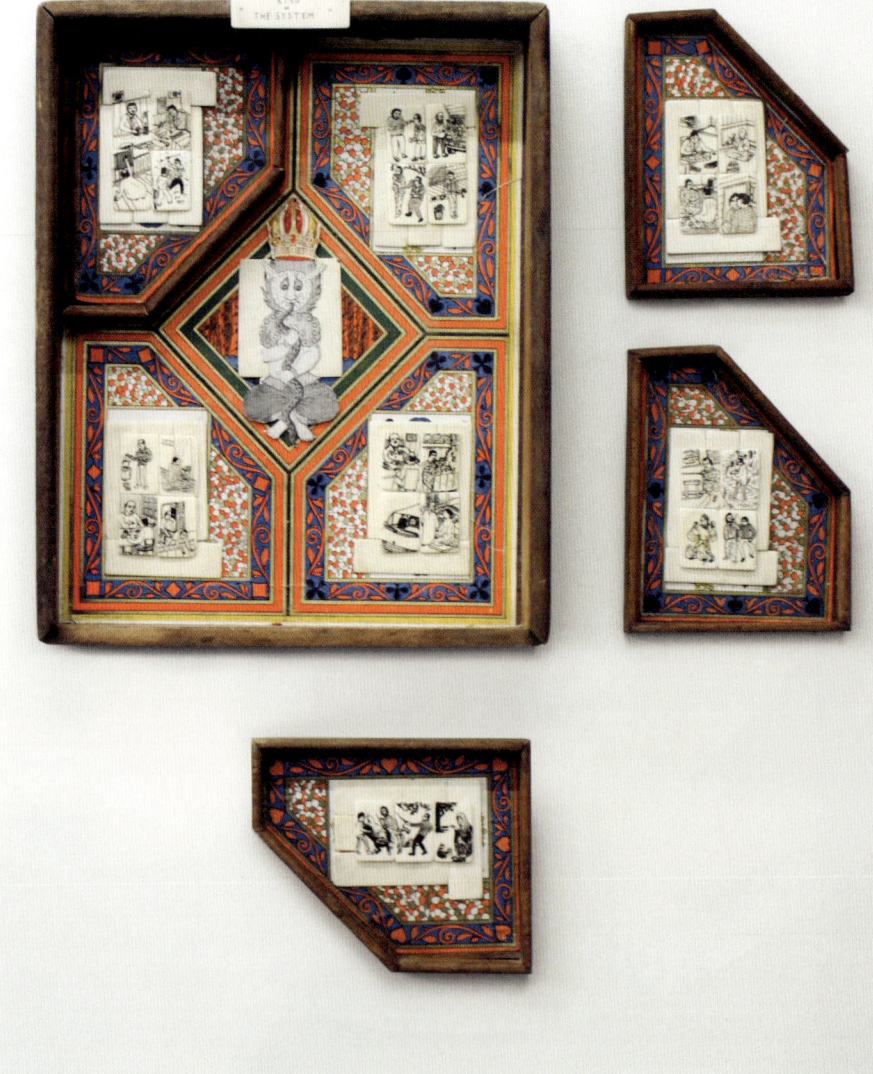

Born 1986, Paris, France. Lives in Paris.

↑ **King of the System**, 2020, ink on bone and collage on old gaming board, 26 × 30 × 5 cm (10¼ × 11¾ × 2 in)

↗ **Bound Together**, 2019–20, drawing printed on textile and sewn on native dresses, collage and drawing on frames, videos, dimensions variable, installation view, 'Diaspora at Home', Centre for Contemporary Art, Lagos, Nigeria, and Kadist Foundation, Paris, France, 2022

→ **Ordonator**, 2020, drawing and collage on vintage paper, 2 from book of 32 double pages, each page: 32 × 25 cm (13¾ × 9¾ in), installation view, 'The Equality of Possibility', Kunstverein Bielefeld, Germany, 2022, collection of the artist

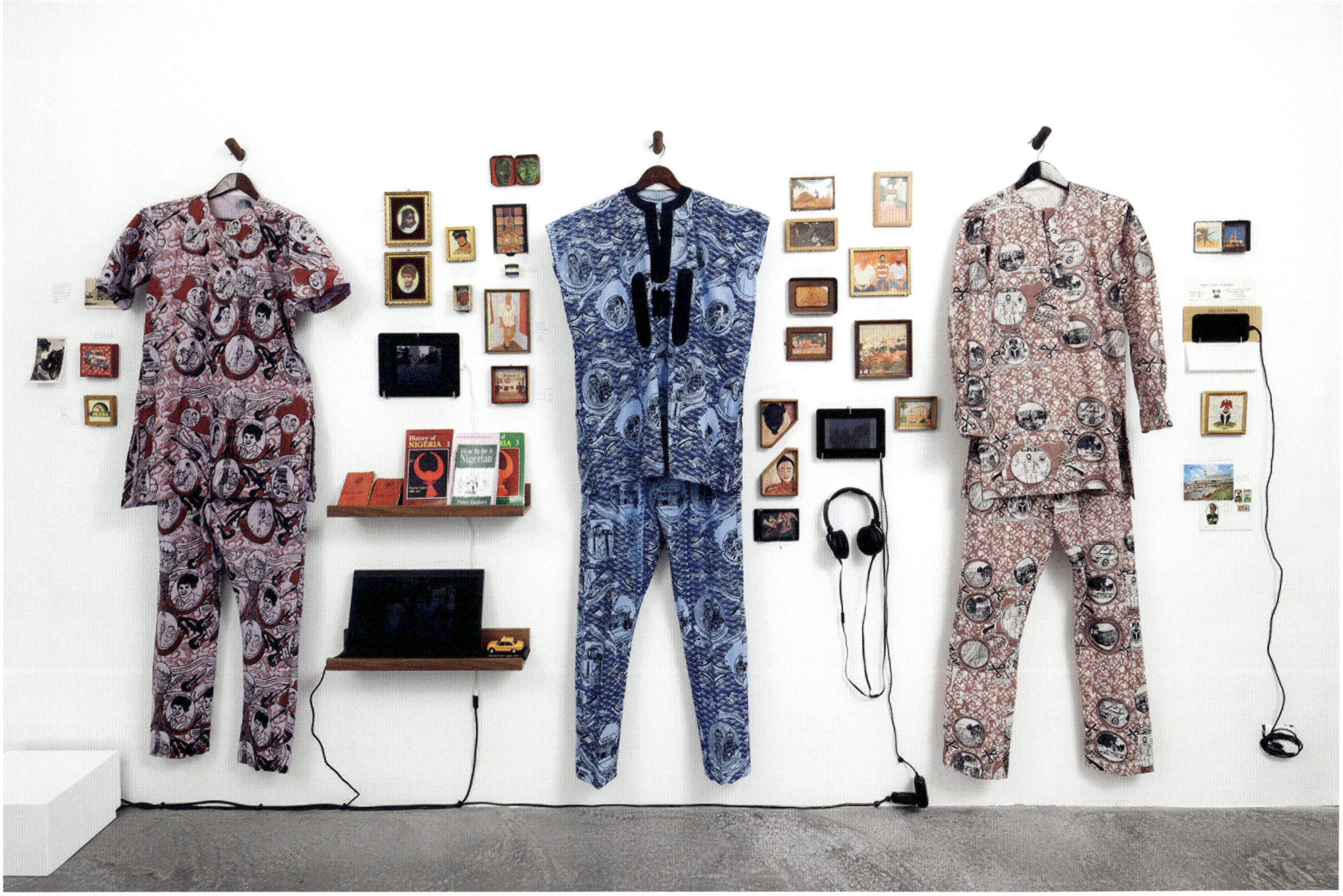

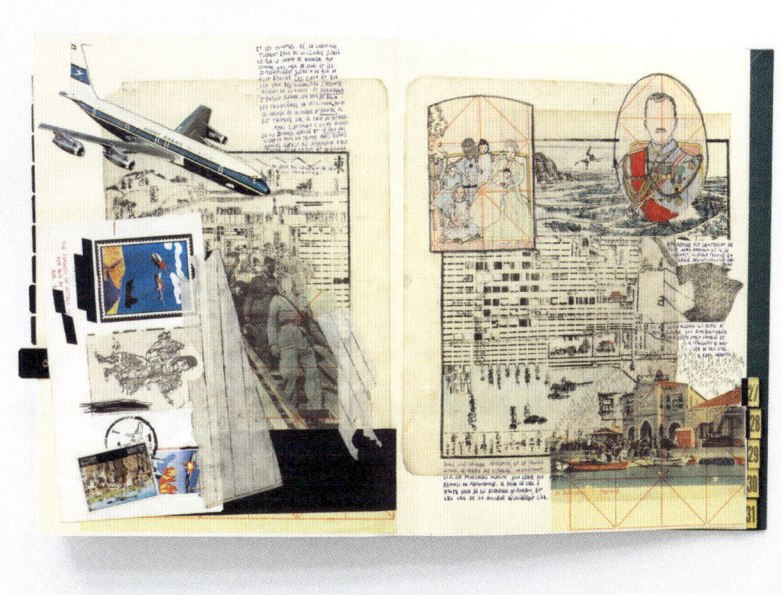

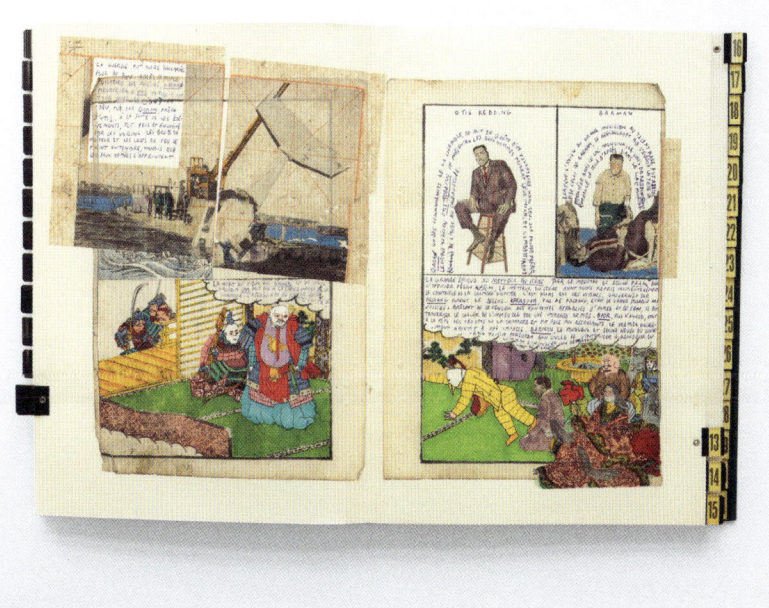

SAMIT DAS

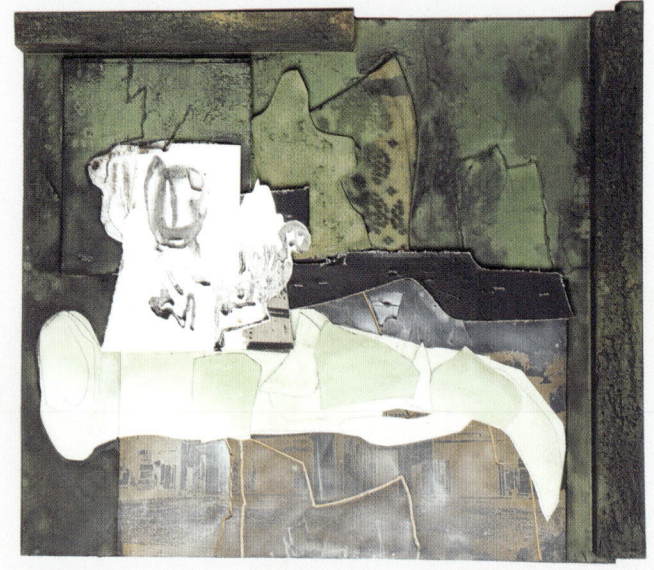

Spanning painting, photography, collage and artist books, Samit Das's eclectic practice is driven by an archival impulse. He excavates histories of architecture and visual traditions in India, producing scholarly and artistic work that expands the field of global modernism and challenges art history's Western biases. Das was educated at Santiniketan, the experimental school established in 1922 in rural West Bengal by celebrated polymath Rabindranath Tagore (1861–1941), aimed at providing alternative models of education than those introduced by British colonizers. By documenting key sites of modernist artistic development – such as the residence of the illustrious Tagore family, now a museum in Kolkata – and bringing such sites into conversation with European legacies and ancient South Asian traditions, Das demonstrates the interconnectedness of various artistic and cultural discourses across history. In his collage and mixed-media practice, Das layers various archival photographs – including many of Rabindranath Tagore and other significant figures – with spliced images of architectural fragments, sculptures and contemporary graffiti, placing snippets of literary texts in between these layers. This referential methodology demonstrates Das's deep understanding of history as constructed and subject to change by human agency. He also recognizes the contribution of the people of once-colonized nations to the modernist tradition and the ongoing relevance of their work. The 2003 exhibition 'Glue', curated by Peter Nagy at the Art Gallery of the Nehru Centre in New Delhi, for which Das designed the catalogue, articulated this balance of historic and contemporary references across a set of collage works by Indian artists including Vivan Sundaram (b. 1943), Jitish Kallat (b. 1974) and Bharti Kher (b. 1969). Combining die-cut windows and overlapping pages in a spiral-bound, non-linear arrangement, Das's catalogue eschews the rigid strictures of modernist history for a more fluid approach. 'Bibliography In Progress' (2014–17), a series of mixed-media collages, hones this fluidity. Exhibited in an eponymous show at Mumbai's TARQ gallery in collaboration with Clark House Initiative in 2017, the series consists of works made from an array of materials including sawdust, staples and wood, atop which are layered graphite drawings. The open-ended, sculptural forms of these collages resemble the shadow boxes of American artist Joseph Cornell (1903–72), but with their surfaces stained with dark, geometric compositions, they also reference the preoccupation with abstraction by artists of the subcontinent after India's independence in 1947. For the series 'Imagine the fluid empty rooms, but the sun is always there' (2021–2), Das continued to build on abstraction in collage, constructing diptychs with layers of glued watercolour, canvas and laserjet prints on board, over which he inscribed diagrammatic abstract shapes and linear forms. The quasi-cartographic nature of these assemblages speaks to Das's ongoing inquiries into how spatial understanding informs our progression in the world, and their enigmatic, unresolved quality underscores that much of this progress is yet to be charted.

TAUSIF NOOR

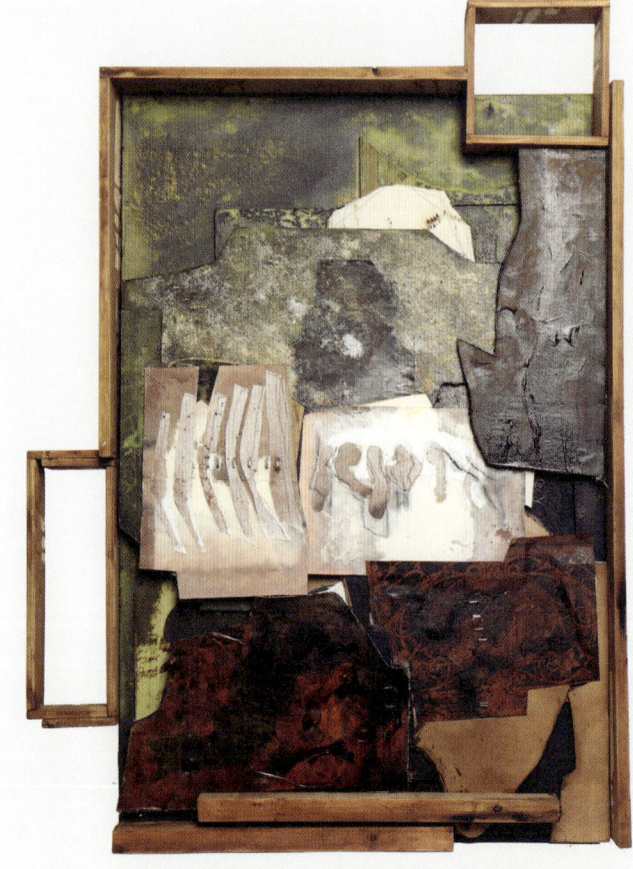

Born 1970, Jamshedpur, Jharkhand, India.
Lives in New Delhi, India.

↑↑ **Untitled**, from the series '**Bibliography In Progress (14)**', 2014–17, laser-engraved HDF and MDF board, watercolour on paper, acrylic colour, natural glue, sawdust, stapler pin coated with natural glue, graphite drawings, glass colour, canvas and pine wood, 28.5 × 33.5 × 8.1 cm (11¼ × 13¼ × 1¼ in)

↑ **Untitled**, from the series '**Bibliography In Progress (14)**', 2014–17, laser-engraved HDF and MDF board, watercolour on paper, acrylic colour, natural glue, sawdust, stapler pin coated with natural glue, graphite drawings, glass colour, canvas and pine wood, 101.6 × 73.7 × 8.9 cm (40 × 29 × 3½ in)

→ **Untitled**, from the series '**Imagine the fluid empty rooms, but the sun is always there**', 2021–2, acid-free board and paper, coated canvas, watercolour and Fuji Colour LaserJet multi-layered print on canvas and coated with natural glue, graphite and ink pen drawing, embossed surface, each 27 × 39 cm (10⅜ × 15⅜ in)

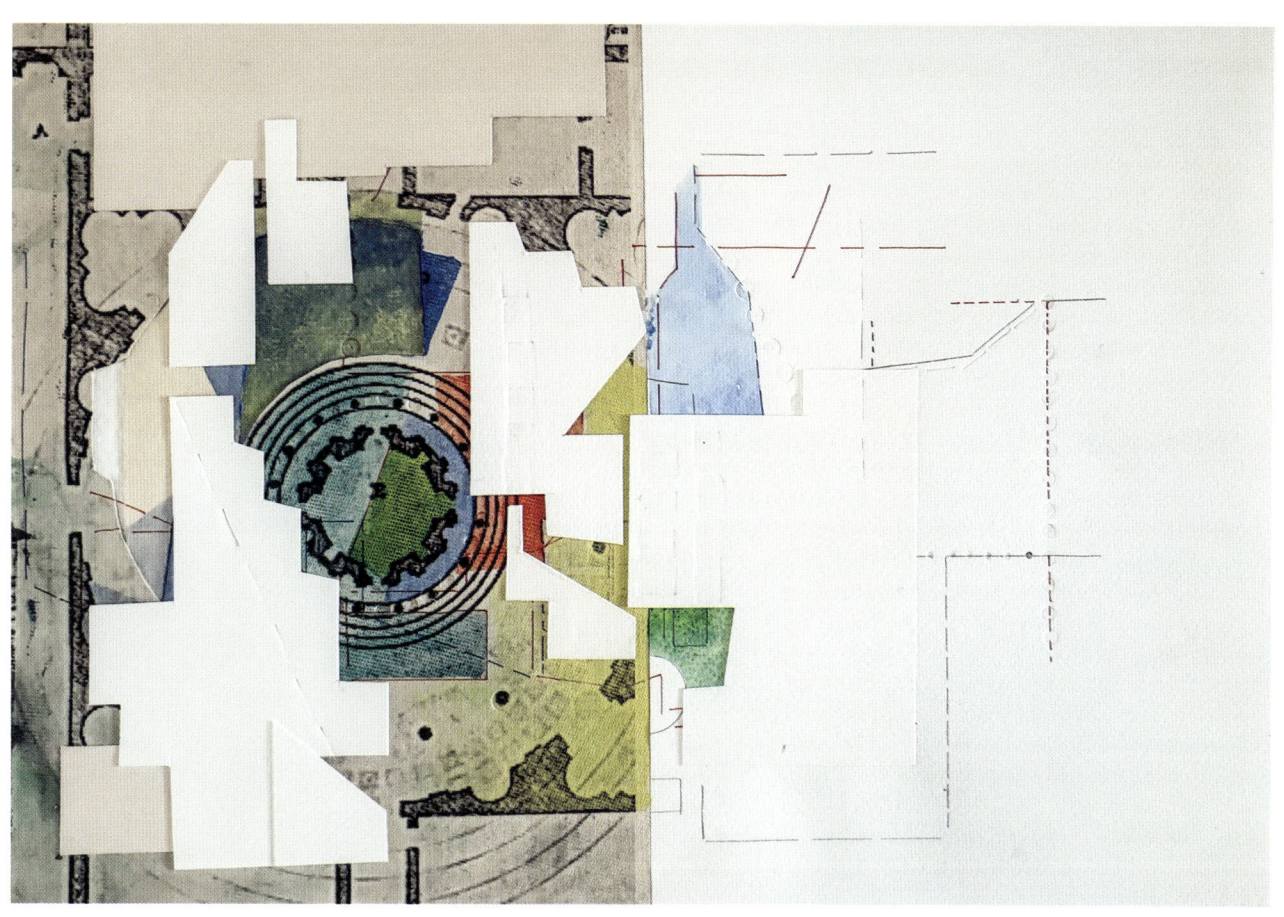

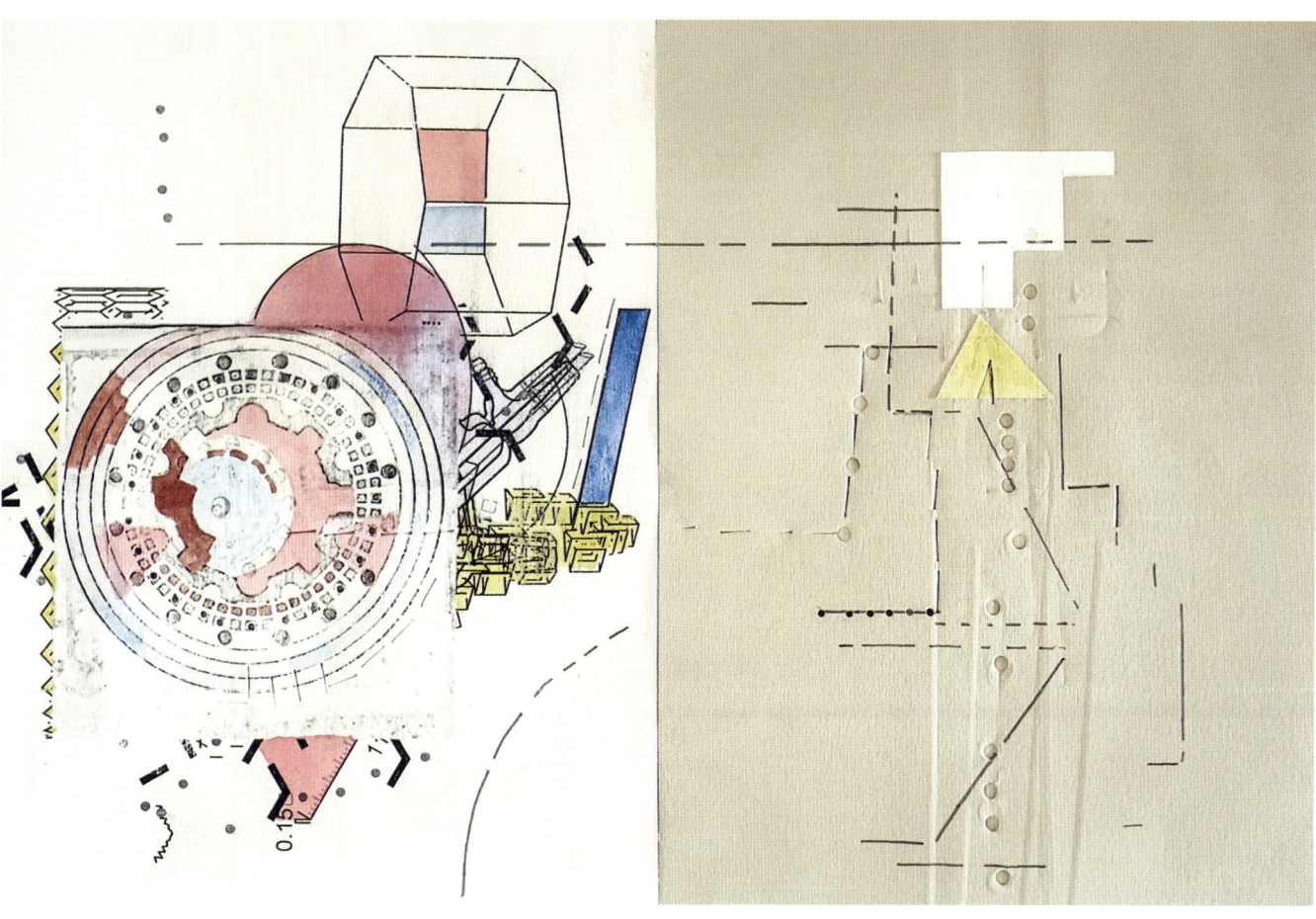

SAMIT
DAS

DEXTER DAVIS

Dexter Davis has experienced physical and emotional trauma from living in the often violent, crime-ridden heartland of America, where he has encountered death on several occasions, including being hit by a stray bullet (now lodged in his lower back) in 2020. Such senseless brutality is obliquely depicted in his collages, which capture the essence of improvisation and layered, reconstructed content, performatively functioning to help process his – and, by extension, his community's – sometimes lethal circumstances. Marks that reference violence, injustice and extreme poverty prevail in Davis's visual vocabulary of bold, abstracted collages that also focus on a shamanistic spirit of healing. In *The Clown* (2016) tensions are made visible through Davis's abrasively scored linoleum-cut printing technique. He then cuts and tears his prints up, fragmenting them to be reassembled as intensely chaotic images that oscillate between figuration and abstraction. Perhaps we see a dreadlocked head, with three or more eyes, bloodshot and spiralling. Maybe there are claws or fangs drawn in charcoal in black and white phalanxes. A visible handprint is a recurring motif – is it signalling extended arms, perhaps responding to the police demand of 'hands up'? All these fragments are suggestive of the historical crisis of displacement and inequality experienced by African Americans. It is worth remembering that clowns or jesters allude to a disruption of the norm, symbolizing those who see a truth that might destabilize order. Using an array of sources, Davis summons autobiographical memories to the densely textured surfaces of his multifaceted and accumulative collages. *Dream Box* (2016) is also an assemblage of fragments, with kente cloth patterns that infuse the work with an African spirit. Again, a skull is implied by the clenched teeth at the centre of the image, surrounded as if by a coiling gyre of energy. Disembodied eyes, rough-hewn bodies and references to the flash of a gun in the dark each contribute to a sense of anxiety. Physical and psychic pain are palpable, especially at the frayed edges of *Untitled* (2021), wilfully left as an uneven piece of scrap. Bursts of colour highlight the urgent, energetic images, evocative of a moment of quick assessment as one might experience in a fight-or-flight reaction. Since the early 1990s Davis has worked as a security guard at the Cleveland Museum of Art, where he has had the unique privilege of guarding one of his own works, *Black Heads* (2010), acquired in 2012 by the museum for its permanent collection and installed in galleries alongside works by giants of twentieth-century art history including Lee Krasner (1908–84), Jackson Pollock (1912–56) and Andy Warhol (1928–87) – a triumphal indication of his joyful spirit of resilience and capacity to exorcize his struggles through his skill as an artist.

KATHLEEN MADDEN

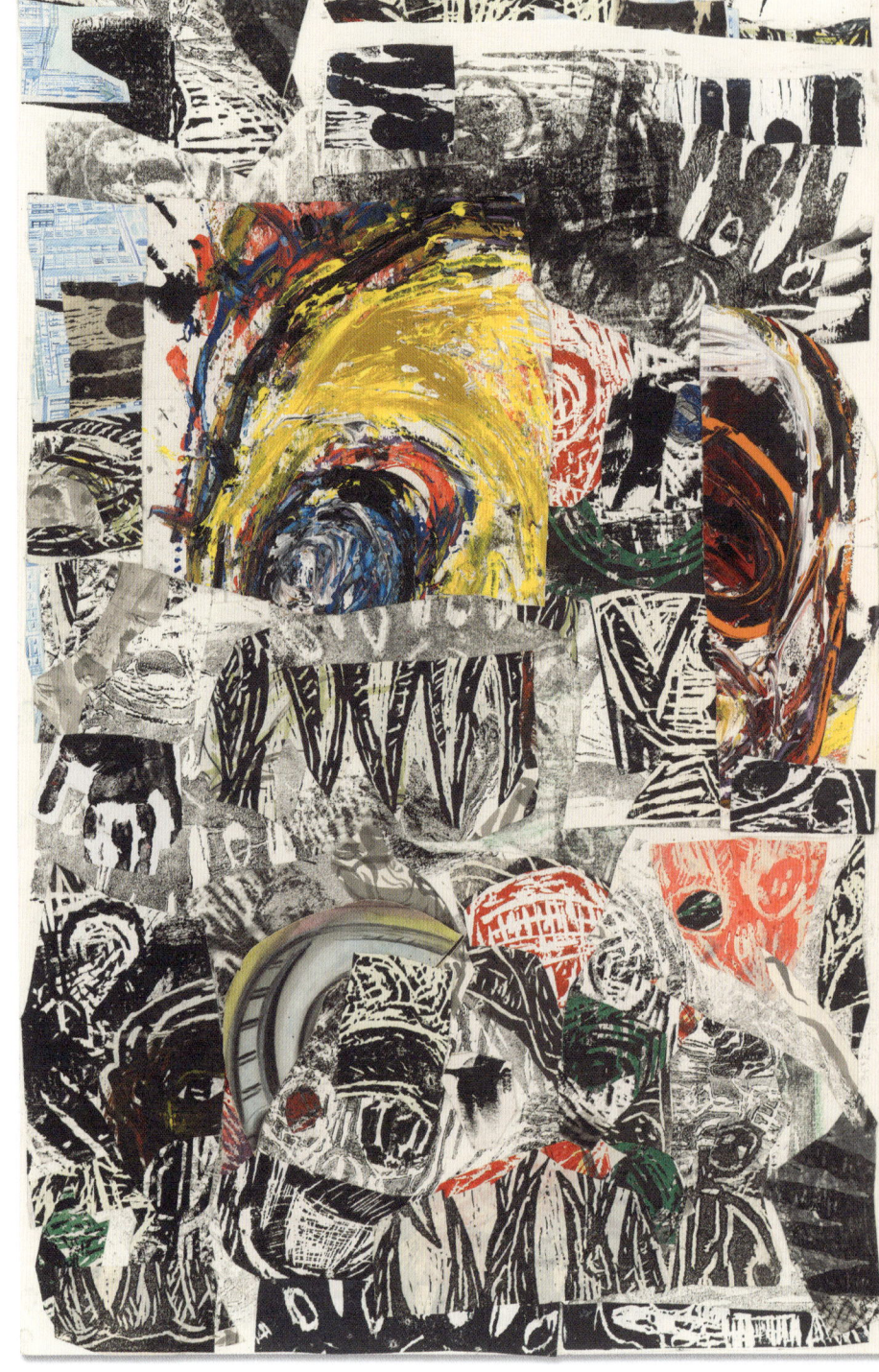

Born 1965, Cleveland, Ohio, USA. Lives in Cleveland.

↑   **The Clown**, 2016, collage with relief printed elements, watercolour and charcoal, 101.9 × 66.4 cm (40⅛ × 26⅛ in)

→   **Dream Box**, 2016, relief and mixed-media collage, 35.6 × 27.9 cm (14 × 11 in)

↗   **Untitled**, 2021, relief and mixed-media collage, 43.5 × 31.1 cm (17⅛ × 12¼ in)

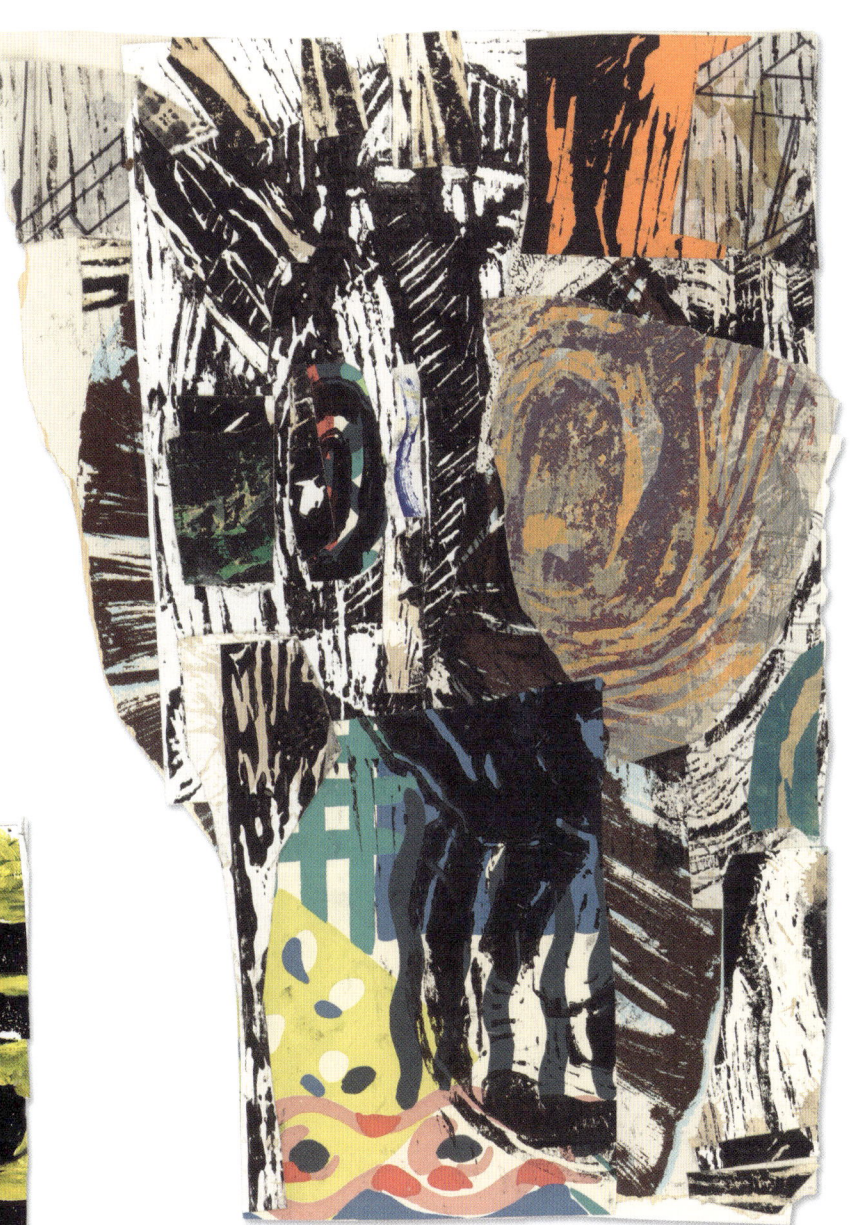

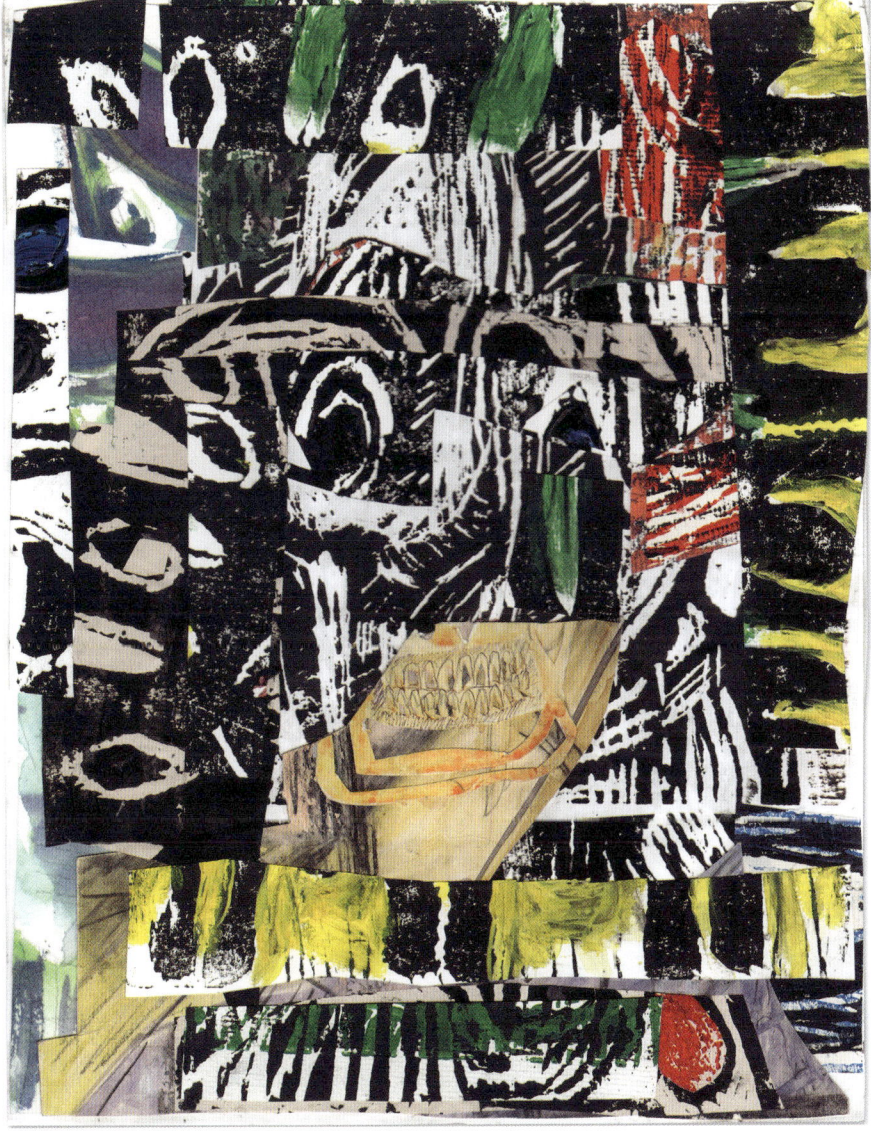

DEXTER DAVIS

GODFRIED DONKOR

From an early age – his family moved from Ghana to the UK in 1972 – Godfried Donkor has been fascinated by accounts of the relationship between Africa and its European colonizers. He has spent his artistic career researching visual and textual sources, from nineteenth-century photographic prints to pages of the *Financial Times*, which he remixes or recreates in his work. For Donkor, art is a form of history-making, with the same sources often recurring across multiple projects. As he explained in a 2018 interview for *Africanah*, 'History can be used over and over again to tell many different stories.' Of particular interest to Donkor is what he refers to as 'creolization': moments of cultural interaction that generate creativity, complicating familiar narratives of enslavement and subjugation. His subjects include the transatlantic migrations of the production of lace, glamour girls and boxing. But his approach is far from straight-forwardly celebratory – making repeated reference to the dehumanizing logic of commodification on which the slave trade was built. Donkor's relationship to the figure of the Black boxer is particularly complex. In *Apollo* magazine in 2019 referring to Muhammad Ali, Jack Johnson and others, he explained how 'the boxer represents the closest I can get to a superhero-type figure, someone larger than life'. But he also describes the troubling, racialized history of boxing: 'There are descriptions of crowds of white men in southern America watching a group of black men beat themselves up.' This account unpins *BATTLE ROYALE, last man standing* (2019). Donkor's works, which also include painting, sculpture and video, can themselves be considered a kind of creolization: a creative force that emerges from the encounters he stages between his source materials. This is especially evident in Donkor's use of collage on paper, a practice that originated with the scrapbooks he produced while studying fashion and then later painting at Central St Martin's in London in the 1990s. In his collaged compositions the artist brings together images and texts from different times and contexts – dream interpretations colliding with stock market pages; an etching of a Black figure emerging from a shell, an echo of Botticelli's iconic *The Birth of Venus* (1485–6) – in order to draw out alternate perspectives and construct new mythologies. Donkor's collages are usually components in wider bodies of work. *The oldest Ashantee and Warsaw air* and *mosee air* (both 2017) are part of Za project inspired by the travelogue of British explorer Thomas Edward Bowdich, who visited the Asante court at Donkor's hometown of Kumasi in 1817. The dancers and umbrellas are extracted from Donkor's large painted replica of the explorer's aquatint illustration of the annual Ashanti Yam Festival, while the musical annotations were featured in Bowdich's written account of the event. Here, figures stand out against the white background, radiating shards of colour like religious icons – a significant departure from the anonymous crowd in the historical source material. The sense of radical transformation is central to the meaning of the work. In Donkor's art, we are invited to see the past anew.

GABRIELLE SCHWARZ

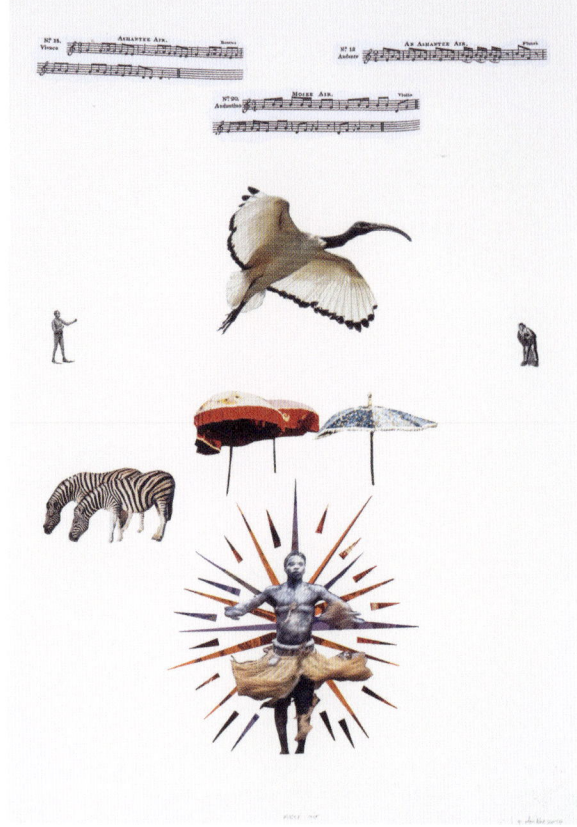

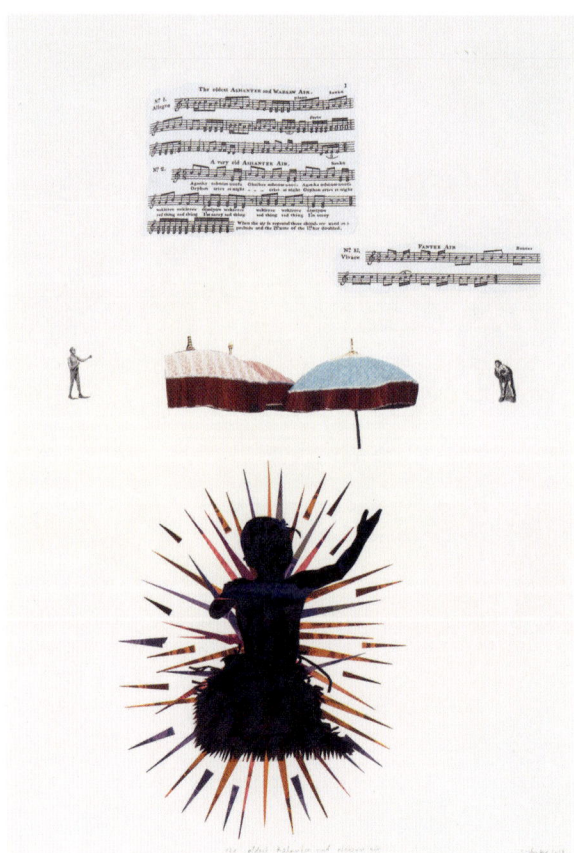

Born 1964, Kumasi, Ghana. Lives in London, UK and Accra, Ghana.

↑↑ **Mosee Air**, 2017, acrylic ink and collage on paper, 100 × 70 cm (39 × 28 in)

↑ **The Oldest Ashantee and Warsaw air**, 2017, oil and collage on paper, 100 × 70 cm (39 × 28 in)

↗ **Ebony Lagos Edition**, 2017, collage on paper, 100 × 70 cm (39 × 28 in)

→ **BATTLE ROYALE, last man standing**, 2019, collage on paper, 100 × 70 cm (39 × 28 in)

→ → **Birth of Venus**, 2017, collage on paper, 100 × 70 cm (39 × 28 in)

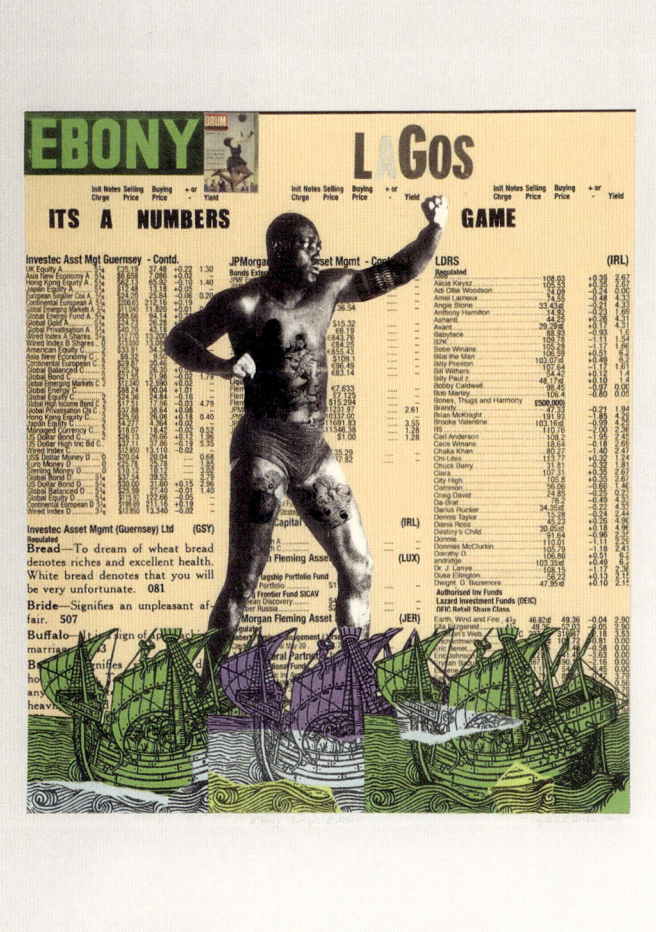

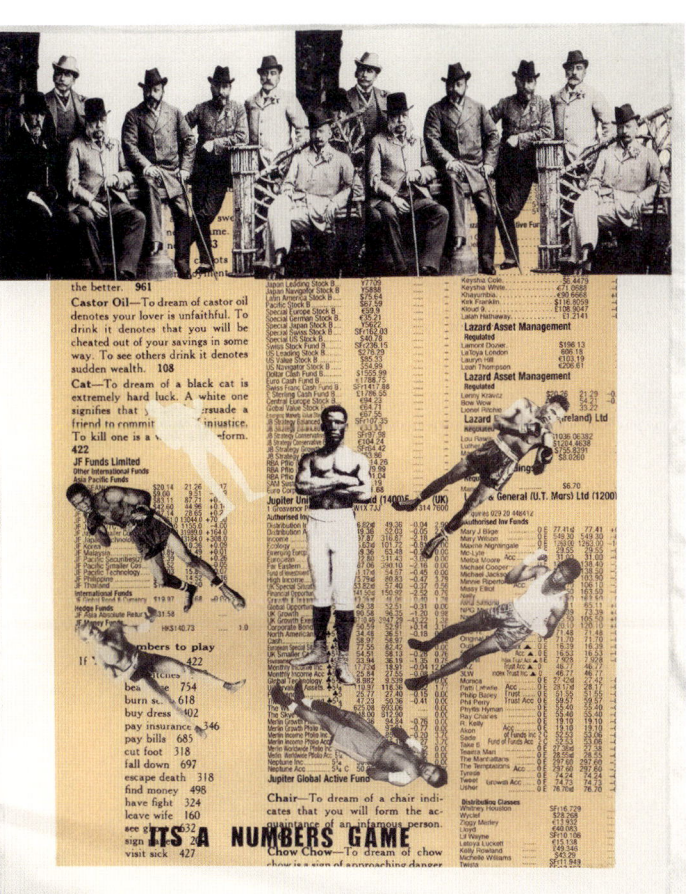

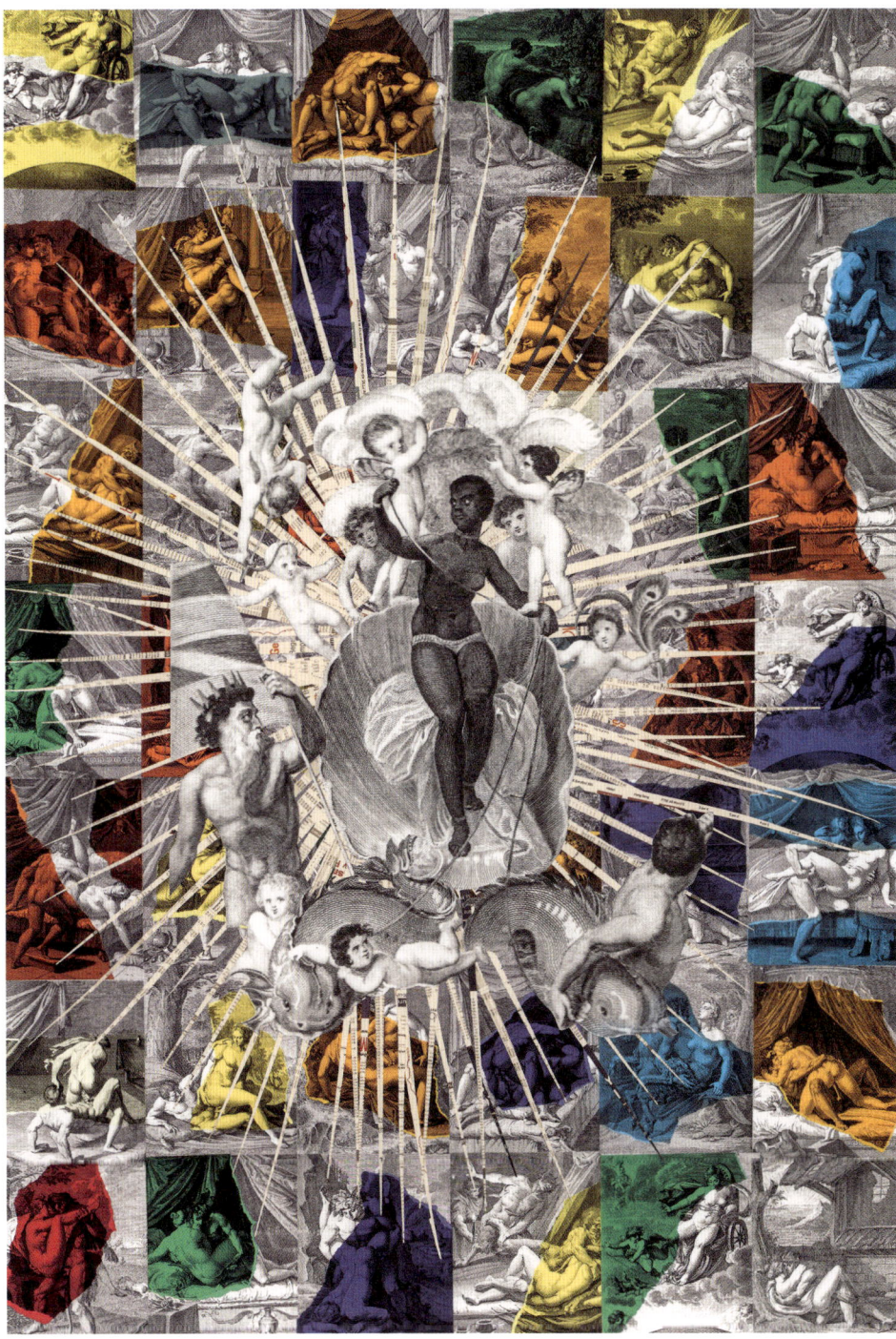

IPEK DUBEN

The work of Ipek Duben deals in big themes: identity, migration, culture, memory. Her deeply researched and sharply political projects take a range of forms, from early artist books to more recent multimedia video installations, but she has returned to collage continuously throughout her career. It is a fitting technique for an artist whose practice regularly draws together different perspectives, weaving her own history together with the stories of strangers from across the globe. ◢ Duben's creative vision is rooted in her own education and experience, moving between disciplines (art and politics) and cultures (the Islamic and Western worlds). She left her home country to study in the United States, where she undertook an undergraduate degree in philosophy and art history in Atlanta followed by a Master's in political science in Chicago and subsequent training in drawing and anatomy in New York. She returned to Istanbul for her PhD in Turkish painting and criticism, which involved the close study of Islamic miniatures, before another stint in New York from 1991 to 2001. During this time she used her work to question what she has described in an undated artist statement for the British Museum as 'my identity as a modern woman in relation and in opposition to Islamic morality and codes of being'. ◢ Reflecting this personal exploration, photographic images of the artist's body appear as collage elements in many of her works, including the 'Suspended' series (2012–18). Flattened and layered, the outlines of her figure here become a kind of decorative pattern – the kind that might border a traditional miniature painting. For Duben, her abstracted body has come to represent not just her own identity as a woman caught or *suspended* between cultures but also the universal condition of humanity. What does it mean to be a person of a particular gender, nationality or ethnicity, at a particular place or moment in time? This question is explored more literally in other works by the artist such as her 2003 postcard installation *What Is a Turk?* ◢ Duben returns to the medium of the postcard in *Istanbul II #7* (2020) and *Gods I #4* (2020), both from her series 'Angels and Clowns'. Here, postcards collected by the artist on her travels are layered with paint and stickers to offer a commentary on the ills of contemporary society. 'I watch with tears and smiles the condition of humanity in the post-truth, post-fact, post-faith era,' she wrote for an exhibition of the series at Pi Artworks in Istanbul. The red-nosed clowns are her 'smiles' – irony and humour in the face of economic, geopolitical and environmental crisis – while the pudgy cherubs may represent her 'tears': the artist's profound moral seriousness as she surveys the state of humanity today. ◢

GABRIELLE SCHWARZ

Born 1941, Istanbul, Turkey. Lives in Istanbul.

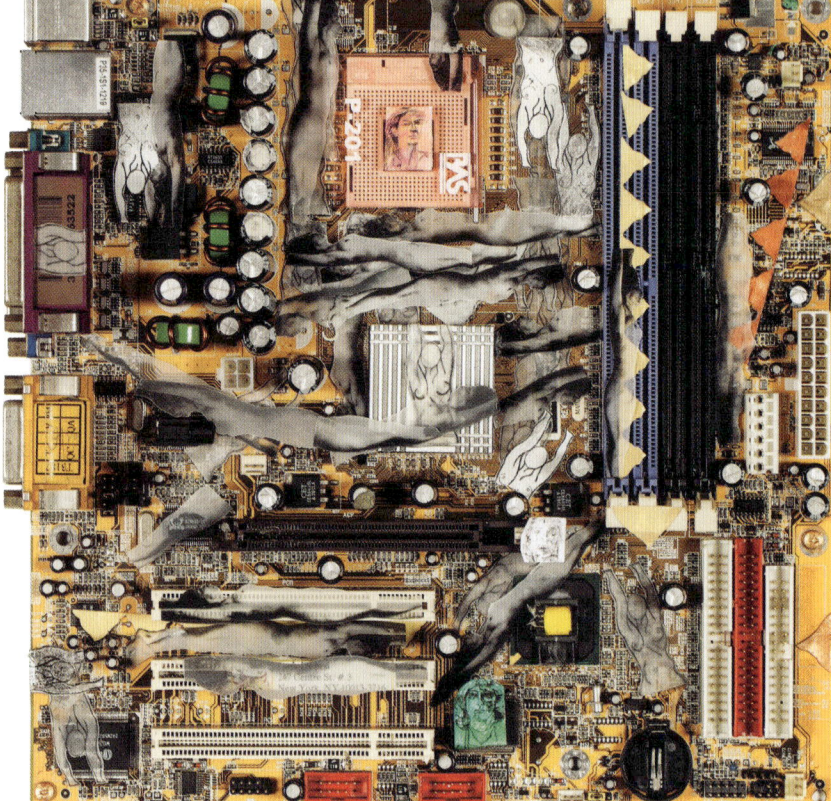

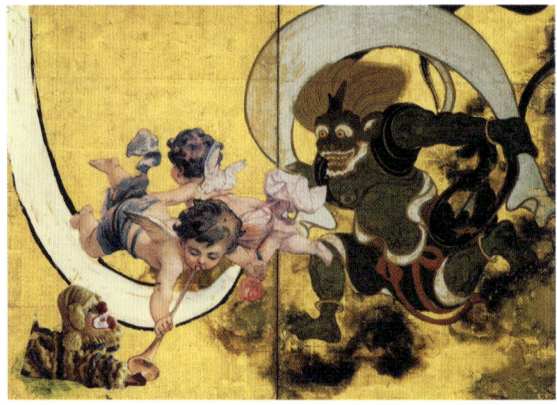

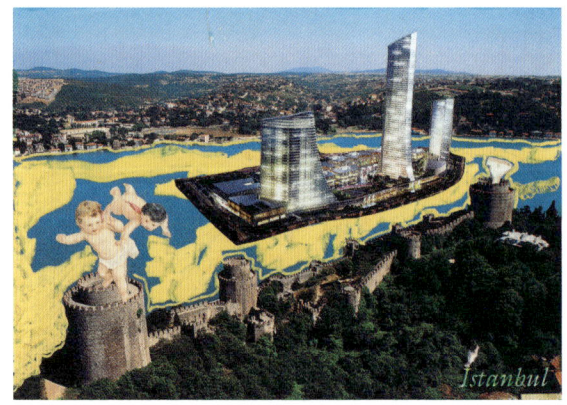

↑↑↑ **Memory Chip/Hafiza Karti #3**, 2011, photo print on paper, photo print on vellum paper, acrylic paint on paper and Plexiglas on computer parts, 35.7 × 36.6 × 6 cm (14 × 14⅜ × 2⅜ in)

↑↑ **Gods I #4**, 2020, postcard of *Wind God and Thunder God* (showing right panel only) by Tawaraya Sōtatsu, Edo period (17th century), Kennin-ji, Kyoto, stickers and acrylic paint, 10.5 × 15 cm (4⅛ × 5⅞ in)

↑ **Istanbul II #7**, 2020, postcard of Rumelihisarı and the Bosphorus, Istanbul, Keskin Color Ltd. Şti., Istanbul, stickers and acrylic paint, 11.5 × 16.5 cm (4½ × 6½ in), private collection

→ **Muallak #9**, from the series '**Suspended**', 2012–18, photo print on vellum paper, paper, acrylic paint, moulding paste on canvas and aluminium, 180 × 160 × 3.5 cm (70⅞ × 63 × 1⅜ in), private collection

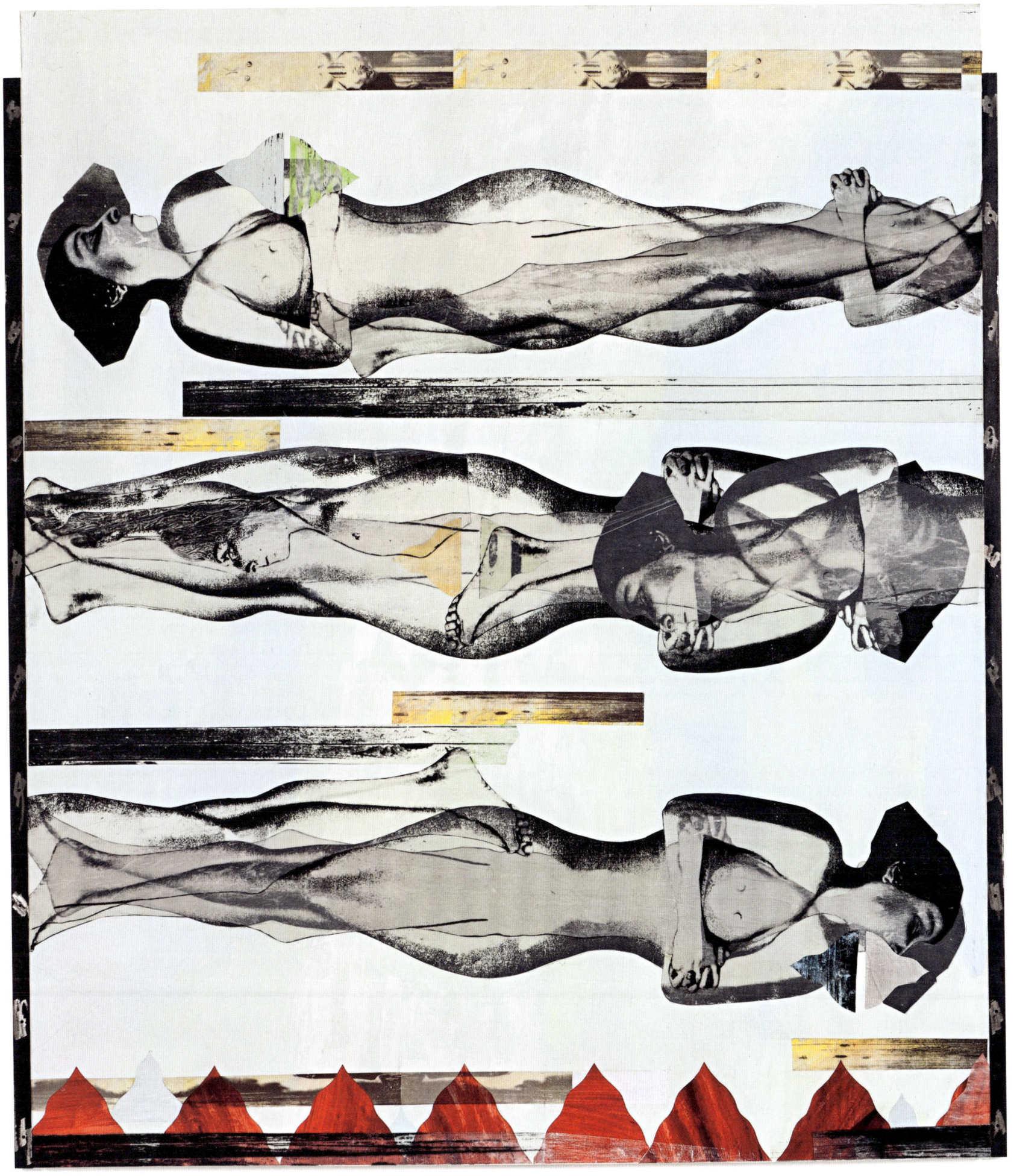

IPEK

DUBEN

MANDY
EL-SAYEGH

Part of a wider practice that includes film and performance, Mandy El-Sayegh's intensely immersive, collaged paintings and installations sit in an art tradition where the dynamic process of making is imbued into the work itself. In El-Sayegh's case, her physically embodied movements are driven by an aesthetic response to the material and an automatic impulse. She often works on the ground, and has a studio full of collected detritus from which elements are taken and assembled onto her canvases. The resulting collages can be viewed as flayed bodies laid bare for surgical inspection. Their fragments are lost historical remnants, recontextualized in new bodies. Sculptural forms that resist narration, they remain accumulations rather than compositions.

El-Sayegh's pieces combine recognizable artistic techniques – drawing, painting and screenprinting – with everyday ephemera including image- and text-based print material, sweet wrappers, anatomy books and her father's Arabic calligraphy. Their fluctuating visibility and legibility is orchestrated by the artist. The grid is a recurrent motif, most notably in the 'Net-Grid' works, where it is given a primacy through the titling of this ongoing series. El-Sayegh responds to, and critiques, the use of the grid as a pure form of containment and repetitive structure by also foregrounding an interest in the natural affective qualities of her materials, thereby allowing both order and disorder to coexist. This is further registered by the fact that El Sayegh's grids are hand-drawn and screenprinted, their visibility shifting in and out of focus. They act as a skeleton of sorts, with the artist often referring to her works as bodies. This relationship to the corporeal is continued in the tonal range of colours that are built into the works through both hand application and collaged elements. In *protection* (2021) hues of brown and red as well as pink permeate the canvas, flowing like bodily fluids that congeal into deeply chromatic areas, like bruises or clots. Brief passages of other colours add to a sense that, as with the bodily processes of healing and disintegration, nothing remains stable. The accumulation of meaning through excessive layering in works such as *The Face* (2021) is organized to critique systems (of categorization and dissemination) and hierarchies of visual and textual information, whether by the news media or art galleries. El-Sayegh's fragments have a Dadaist sensibility and engender difficult questions about society and politics, as well as the role of the artist and the purpose of art. El-Sayegh creates intricate palimpsests that pulsate with societal information, art history and corporeal processes to upend meaning and allow the beholder space to create their own.

HABDA RASHID

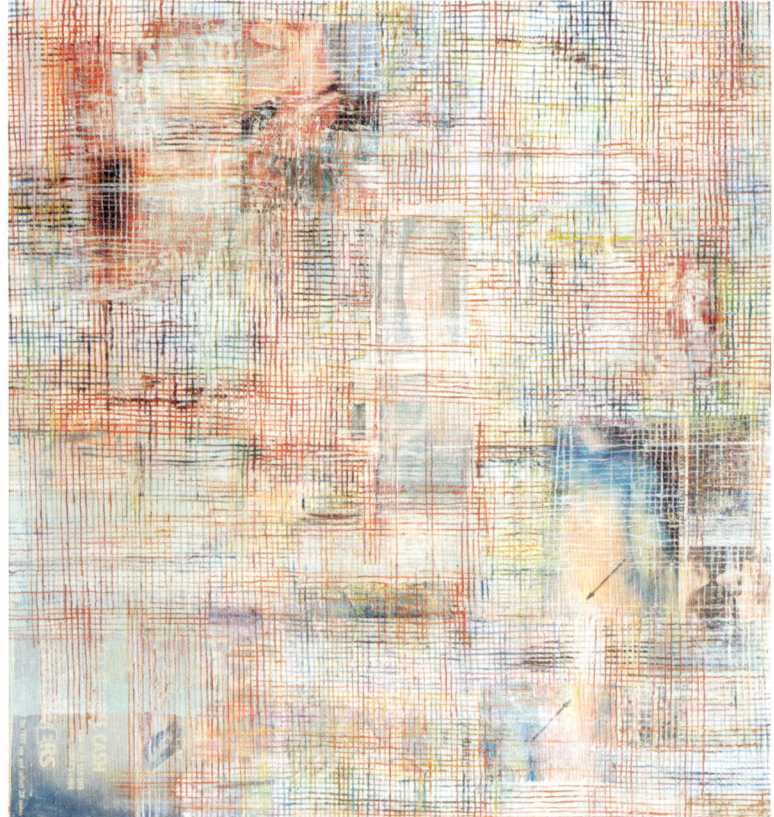

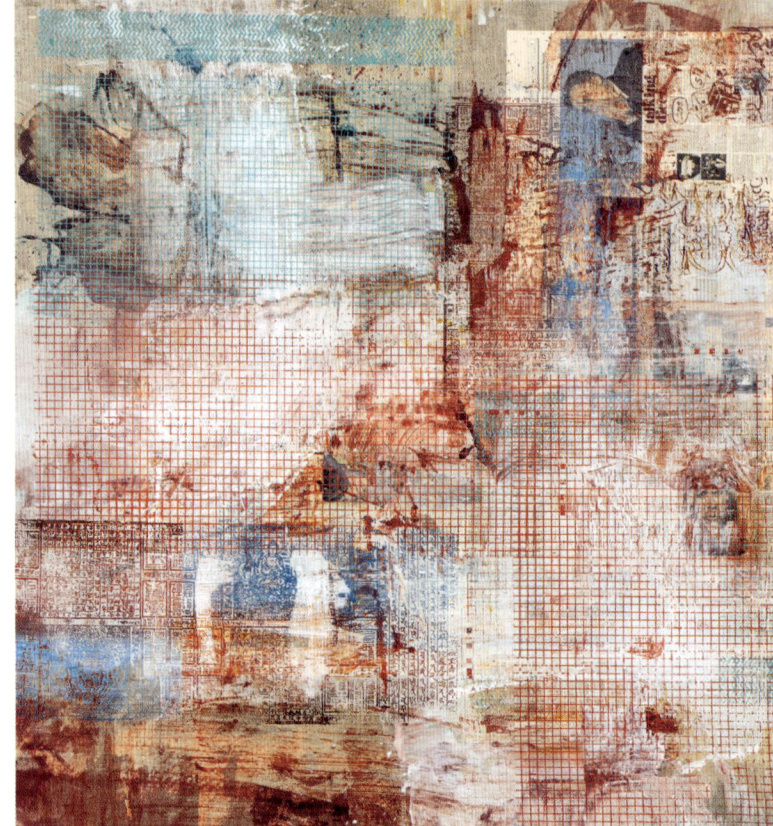

Born 1985, Selangor, Malaysia. Lives in London, UK.

↑↑ **Net-Grid (Lucky Fiver)**, 2021, oil and mixed media on linen with silkscreened collaged elements, 235 × 225 cm (92½ × 88⅝ in)

↑ **protection**, 2021, oil and mixed media on silkscreened linen, 156 × 146 cm (61⅜ × 57⅜ in)

→ **The Face**, 2021, silkscreened oil and acrylic on linen with collaged elements, 218 × 144 cm (85⅞ × 56¾ in)

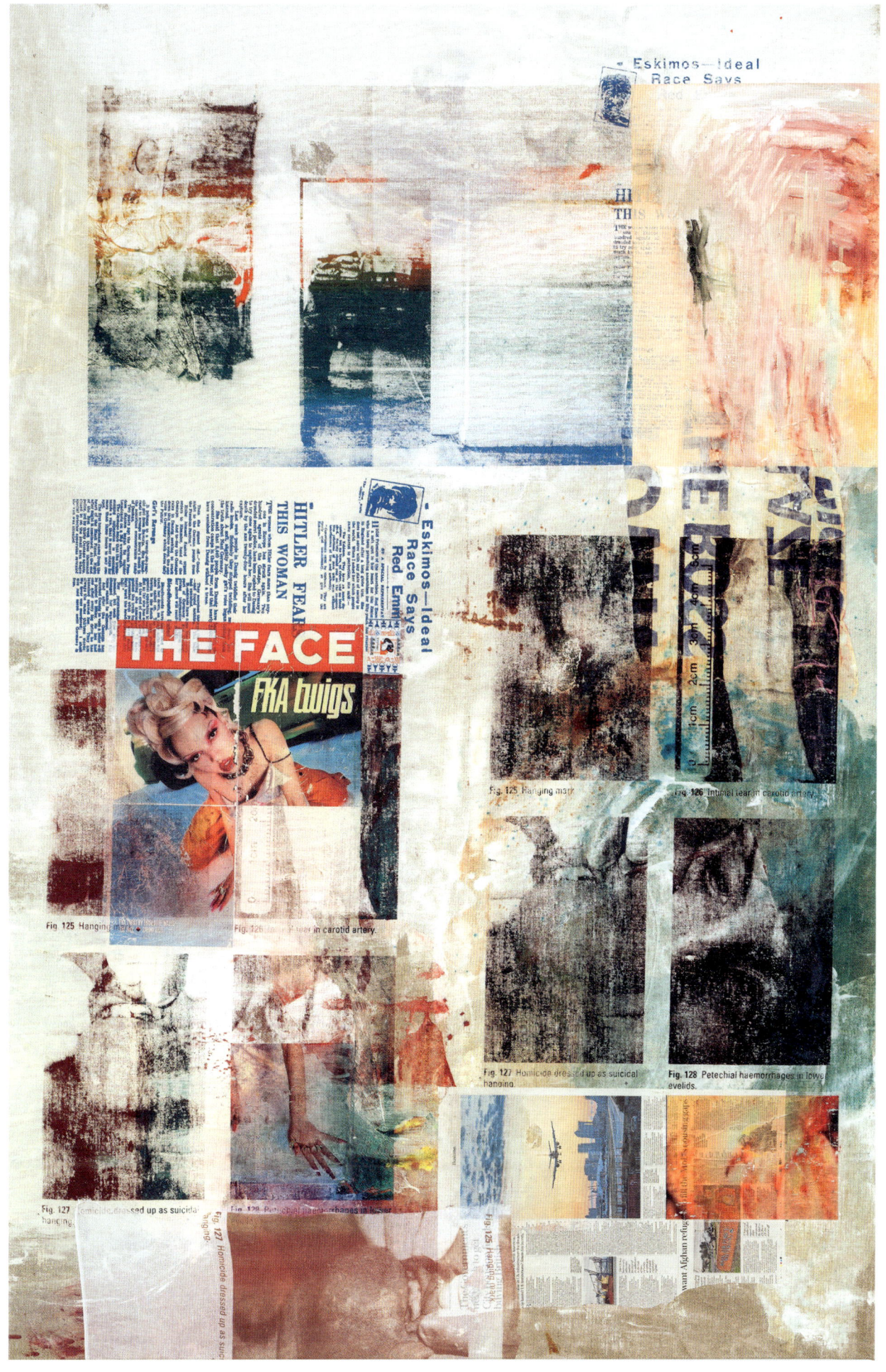

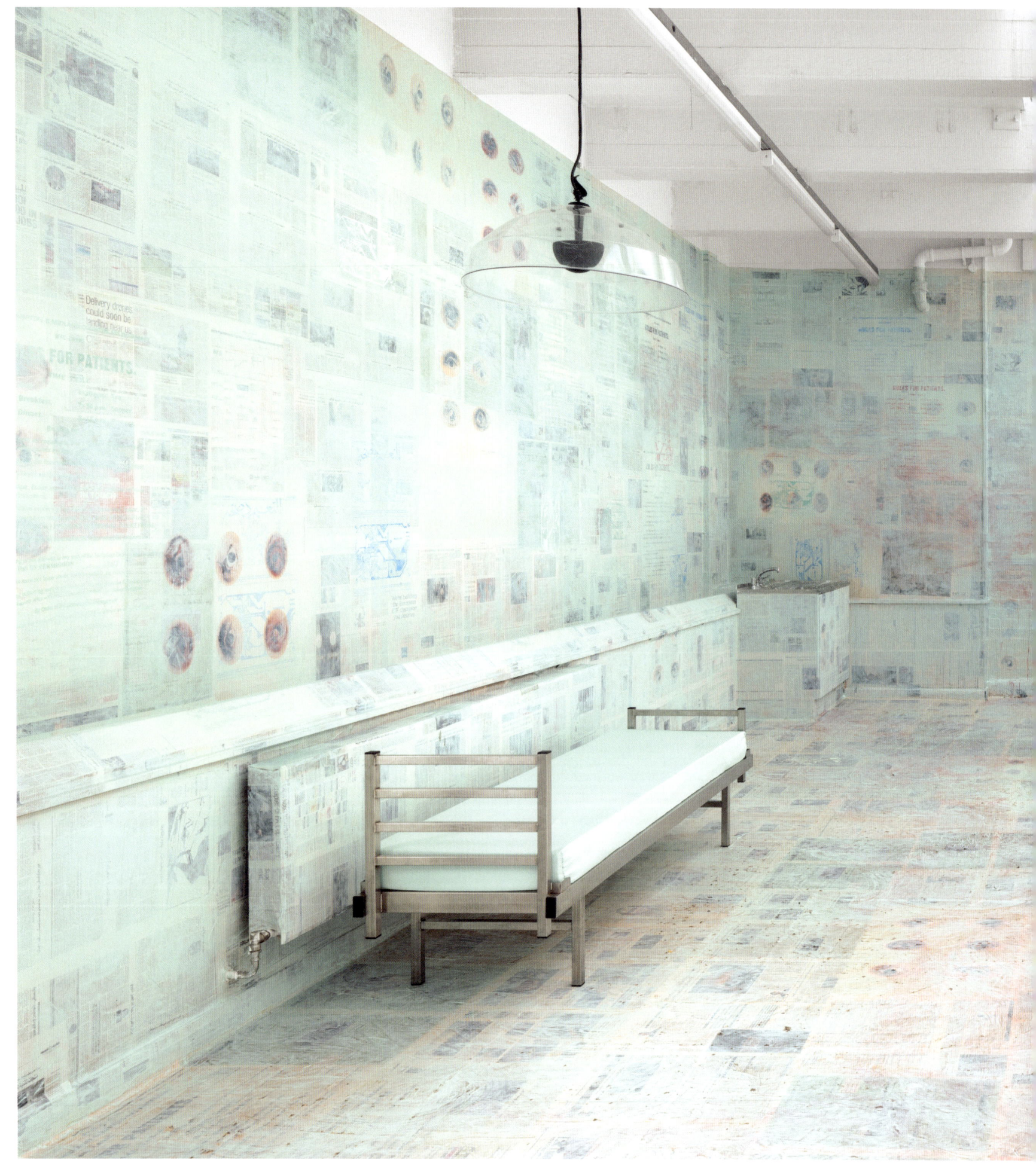

↑ **blank verse blanket man**, 2022, immersive installation with original score by Lily Oakes, dimensions variable, installation view, 'British Art Show 9', Wolverhampton School of Art, UK, 2022

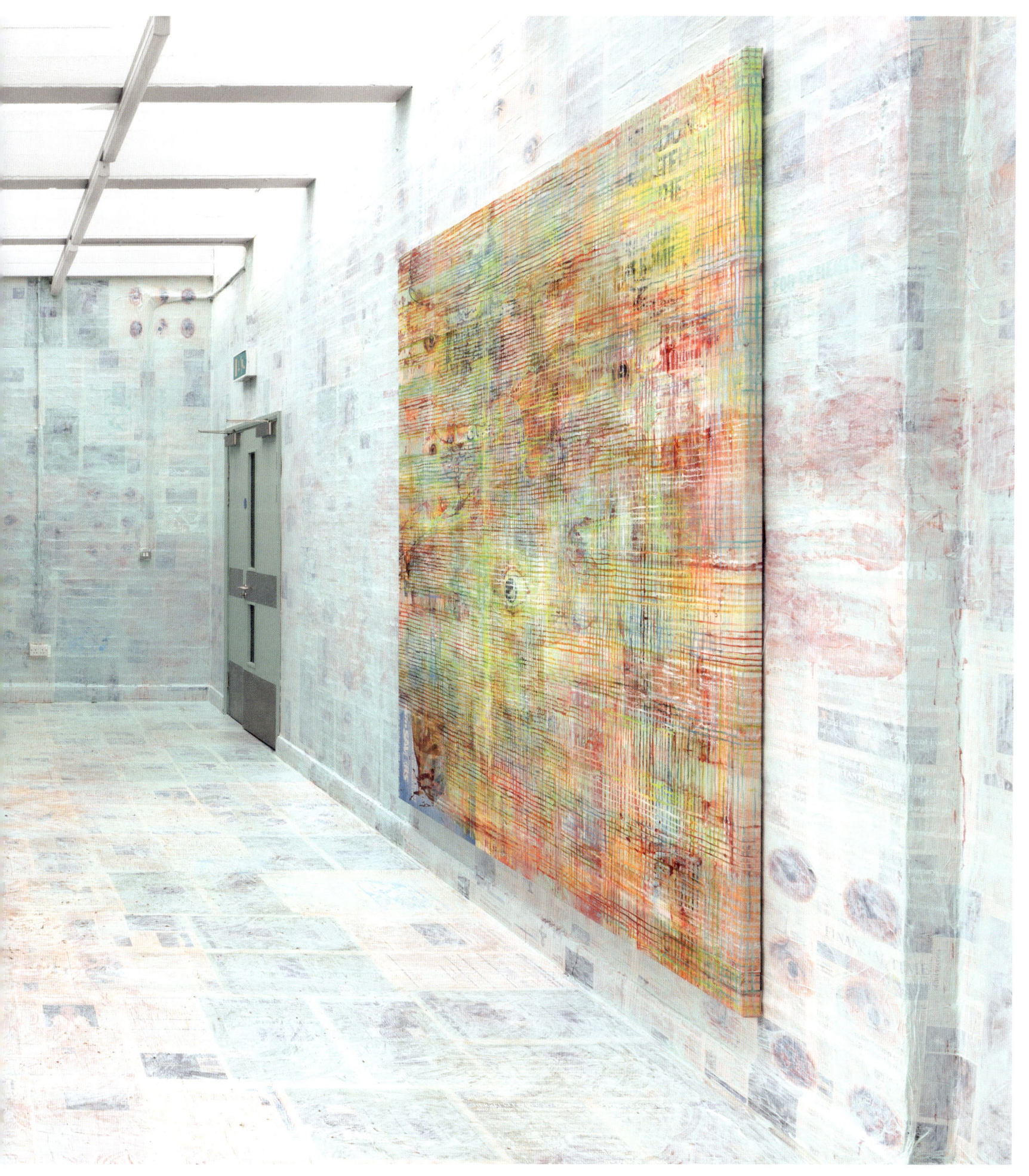

HARIS
EPAMINONDA

'A master of understatement,' as one critic from *The New Yorker* described her in 2016, Haris Epaminonda creates and collects historical and traditional objects and artefacts as well as depictions of these through film and photography. Using collage and installation as methods to activate these objects, Epaminonda's work crosses geopolitical as well as historical borders. ◢ Her imaginative conglomerations can take the shape of a photographic collage based on found images, such as *Untitled #02 b/h*, *#05 b/h*, *#11 b/h* and *#19 b/h* (all from 2015–16), in which ancient sculptural objects, such as the foot of a *Drunken Hercules* from the first century BC, become a pedestal or part of an Ikebana plant arrangement, paradoxically supporting and undermining its delicate balance at the same time. In fact, much of Epaminonda's photographic collage work depicts historical sculptures and engages with questions concerning balance, scale and volume, as is the case in *Untitled #011 c/g* (2007), where added lines transform the spear of a Greek soldier's heroic sculpture into something like a gymnastics bar. ◢ Indeed collage, for Epaminonda, is a method that also expands to other media. In her architectural installations, for example, she often creates arrangements of sculptures, photographs and found objects to create composite images. This was the case with *VOL. XXVII* (2019), which earned the artist the Silver Lion for Promising Young Participant in the 58th edition of the Venice Biennale in 2019. In this multi-part presentation a found image of a Greek vase, a sculpture of a bird, a bonsai tree, a *trompe l'oeil* marble sphere, a reproduction of a horse head from the Parthenon in Athens by the Classical sculptor Phidias and other objects were positioned among a series of fabricated columns alluding to conflicting historical styles, against an abstract geometric backdrop resembling a theatrical setting. The work confirmed Epaminonda's continuous efforts to create imaginary scenarios that rely on the historical relics of a past turned eclectic by the legacy of colonialism and the impact of globalization. Her filmic work, in turn, is also connected with the notion of collage, usually exhibited as a constellation of short films depicting still or moving subjects associated with archaeology, nature or cultural heritage. ◢ In parallel to her multimedia work, over the years Epaminonda has formed an archive of images and books that informs her practice and examples of which have found their way into an ongoing project developed in collaboration with the artist Daniel Gustav Cramer (b. 1975) since 2007 and known as *The Infinite Library*. The Library is an exercise in recontextualizing images, symbols and textual narratives, by rearranging pages from books, adding formal elements to some and binding these together according to formal or conceptual interests. Like Epaminonda's installations, sculptures, films and collages, it relies on displaced cultural artefacts as a way to travel through time and place into an imagined elsewhere that is nevertheless composed of accumulated concrete realities. ◢

YUVAL ETGAR

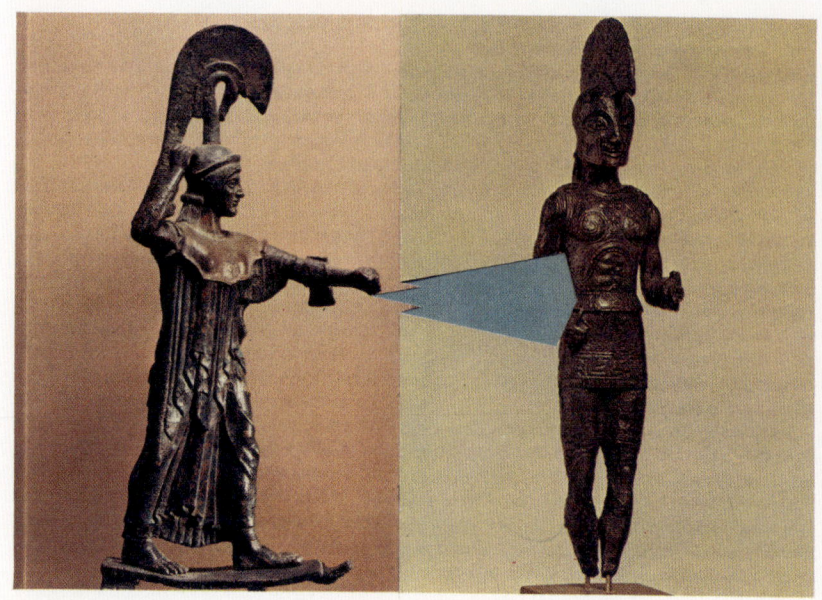

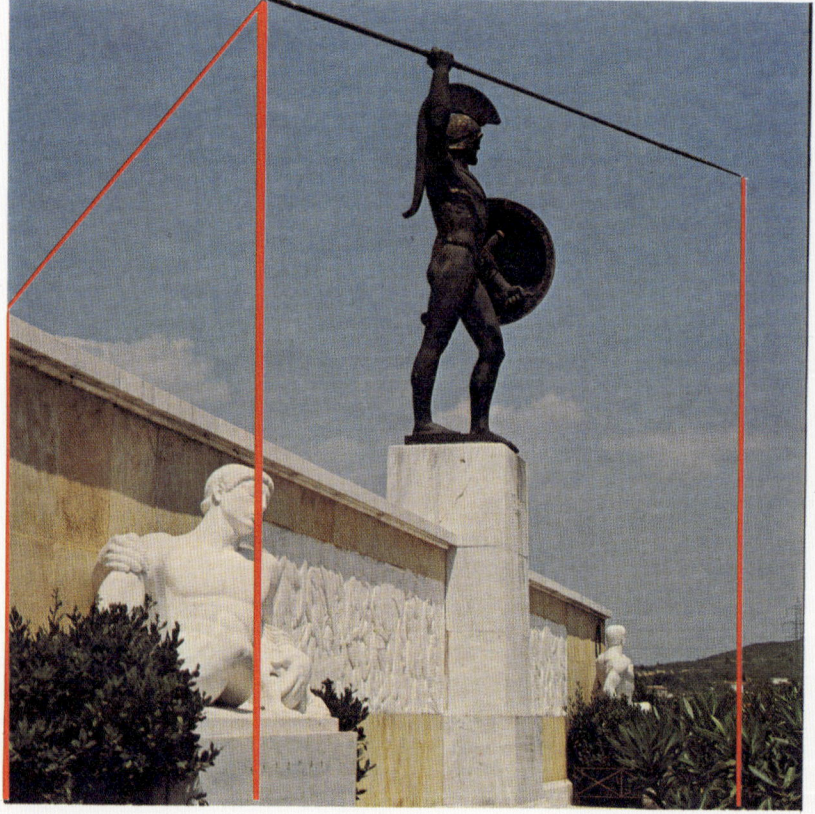

Born 1980, Nicosia, Cyprus. Lives in Berlin, Germany.

↑↑ Untitled #012 c/g, 2007, paper collage, 11.6 × 16.5 cm (4½ × 6½ in), private collection

↑ Untitled #011 c/g, 2007, paper collage, 17.5 × 17 cm (6⅞ × 6¾ in), private collection

↗ Untitled #02 b/h, 2015, paper collage, 27 × 20 cm (10⅝ × 7⅞ in), private collection

↗↗ Untitled #19 b/h, 2016, paper collage, 27 × 20 cm (10⅝ × 7⅞ in)

→ Untitled #11 b/h, 2015, paper collage, 27 × 20 cm (10⅝ × 7⅞ in)

→→ Untitled #05 b/h, 2015, paper collage, 27 × 20 cm (10⅝ × 7⅞ in), private collection

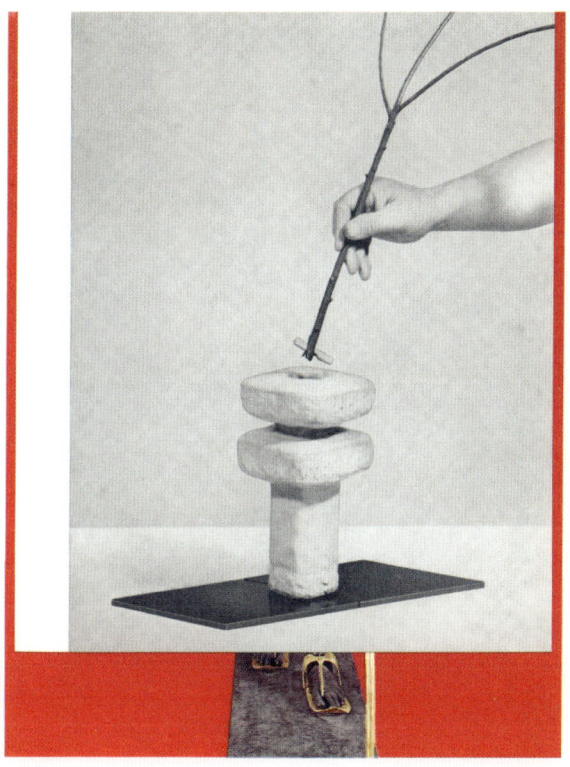

XVI. O «KA» DO REI (cerca de 1342 a. C.).
Túmulo de Tutankhamon. Entrada da câmara funerária.
Estátua em madeira vermelha, betumada e dourada sobre gesso.

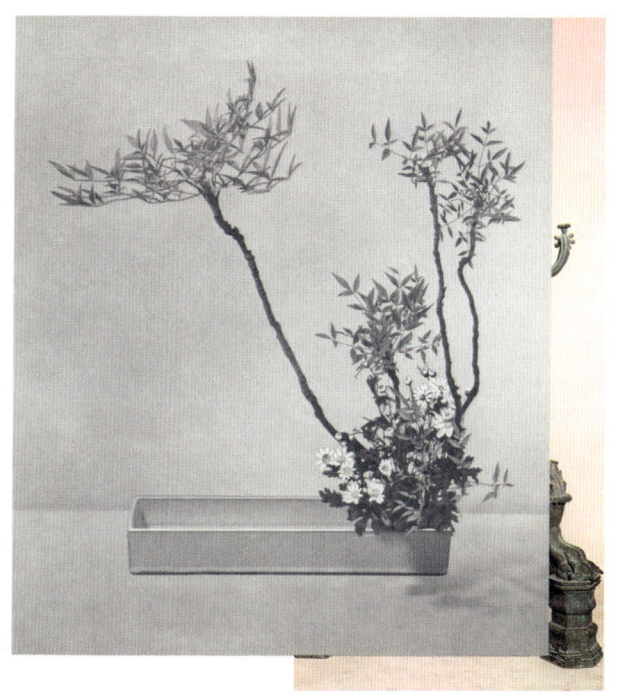

XXVI. AQUECEDOR DE ÁGUA E FOGÃO DE BRONZE TRABALHADO. *Pompeia*

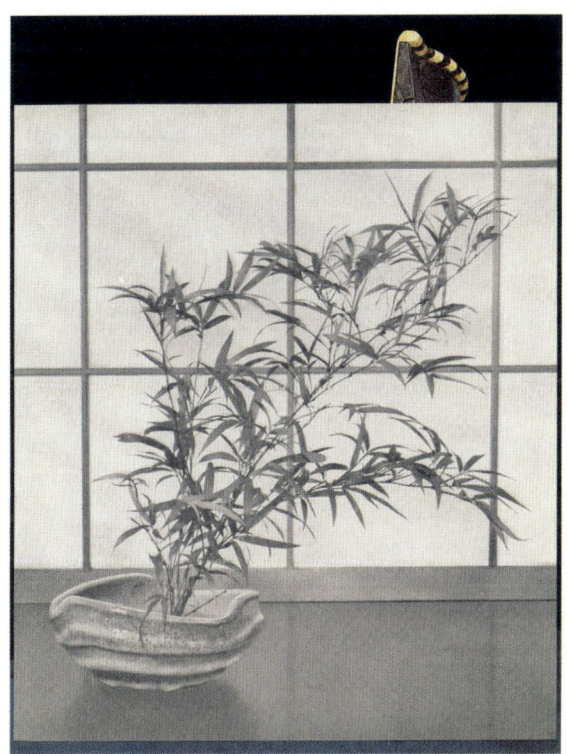

XII. CADEIRÃO DO PRINCIPEZINHO
Visto de lado.

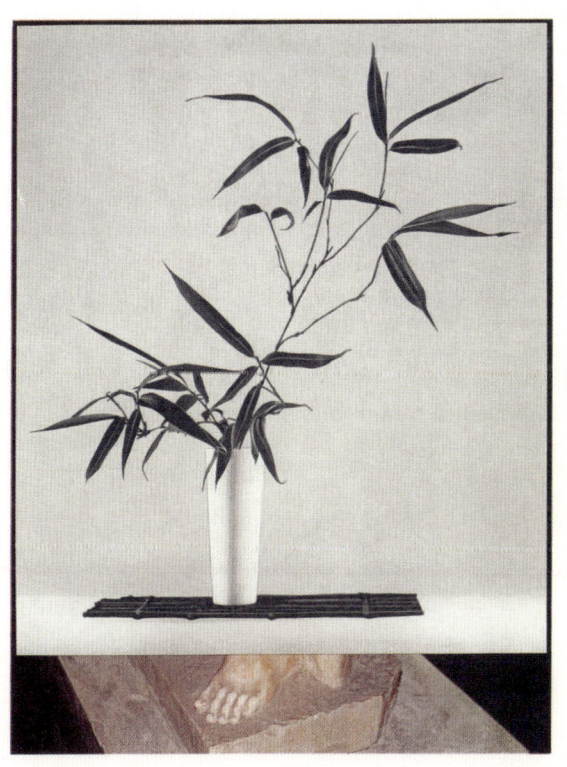

XXXVIII. HÉRCULES ÉBRIO. CASA DOS VEADOS. *Herculano*

HARIS
EPAMINONDA

SIMON EVANS™

Simon Evans™ is the faux-corporate moniker of duo Simon Evans and Sarah Lannan. Their collages are made from prosaic materials such as Post-it notes, discarded wrappers, tape and pencil shavings. Traversing different styles – abstract formalism, figuration, graffiti – the art historical references in these works belie their function as taxonomies, diaries and idiosyncratic infographics. What binds all these visually disparate pieces together, however, is a principal concern for the role language plays in the construction of meaning. As both a graphic component of the work and as conceptual device, the inclusion of handwritten, found or printed text always appears as a fundamentally embedded material. ◢ Works can be approached from three distinct perspectives. From a distance they are images. Closer, their materiality becomes evident, often at odds with the viewer's first impression. Once at close quarters, their surface must literally be read. The dishevelled patinas and scratchy compositions seen from afar are revealed as densely annotated notes and writing. At this moment, the intricacy of their construction is understood and a complex interplay between form, materiality and direct communication is revealed. ◢ In *Black Magic Capitalism* (2016), the word 'SPORT' has been hastily applied in bubble-writing, the letters like water balloons, choked into shape and squeezed into the frame of a grey, rectangular panel – its surface like a concrete wall, the vernacular of early graffiti writers deliberate. But, on closer inspection, the wall is dense with written notes and scribbles in various coloured inks. The layers of textual information – from the graphic depiction of the word 'sport' to the intensity of annotation, and even the title itself – exposes the mechanics of how meaning is made. The resultant provocation is tantalizing: that capitalism might be best understood as a kind of dark alchemy. When individuals are pitted against one another, their efforts and prowess are ruthlessly transformed into profit. Sport as the ultimate expression of the individual inside a performance economy. But what of us that are excluded from such opportunity? In what ways are disenfranchised bodies exploited? How do we stake a claim to our environment, ensuring our voices are heard and experiences understood? ◣ *Insecurity Card* (2020) remakes the familiar US Social Security card as a talisman of precarity. 'I am still just a thing in someone else's story' can be read beneath the card's 'insecurity number'. Evidence of a life is here mapped and tracked inside a nation state that renders some, if not most, vulnerable and without agency. Across all of Simon Evans™'s work, the interplay between the subjective experience and humanity of the individual, the environmental conditions imposed upon them and the violent inequities of the world finds expression in how form and content come together in text and image. ◤

HANA NOORALI AND LYNTON TALBOT

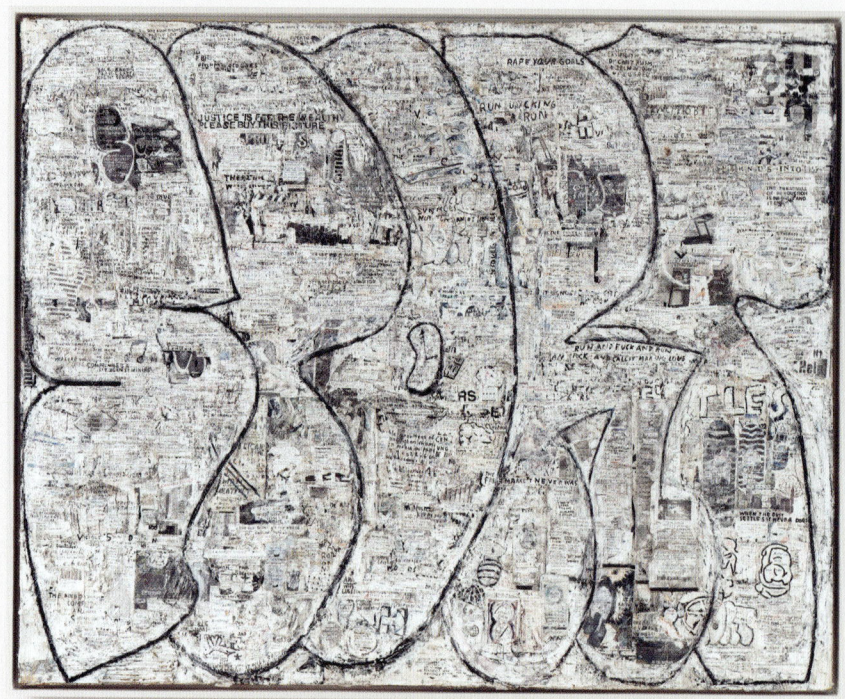

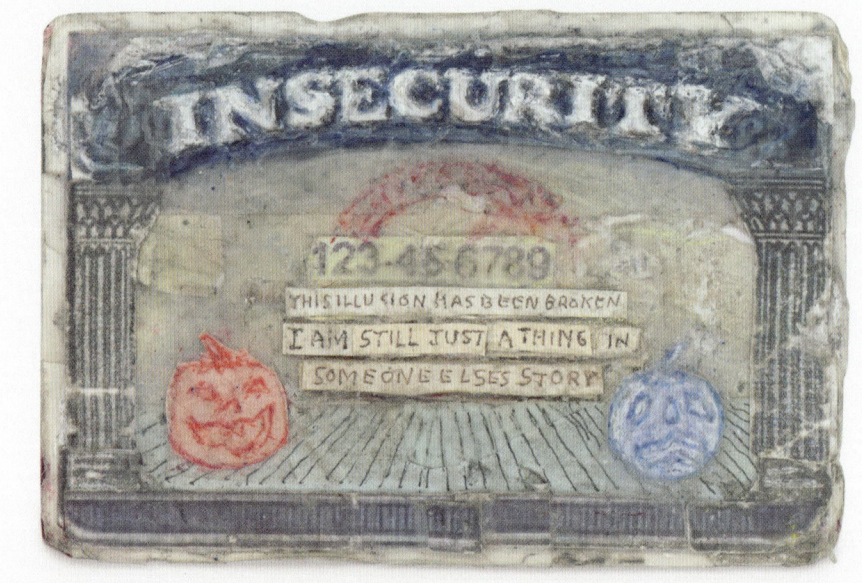

Simon Evans: Born 1972, London, UK. Sarah Lannan: Born 1984, Arizona, USA. Both live in Brooklyn, New York, USA.

↑↑   **Black Magic Capitalism**, 2016, mixed media, 121.9 × 152.4 cm (48 × 60 in)
↑   **Insecurity Card**, 2020, paper, pen and tape, 5.1 × 7.6 cm (2 × 3 in)
→   **This American Dollhouse**, 2021, mixed media, 101.8 × 76.4 cm (40⅛ × 30⅛ in)

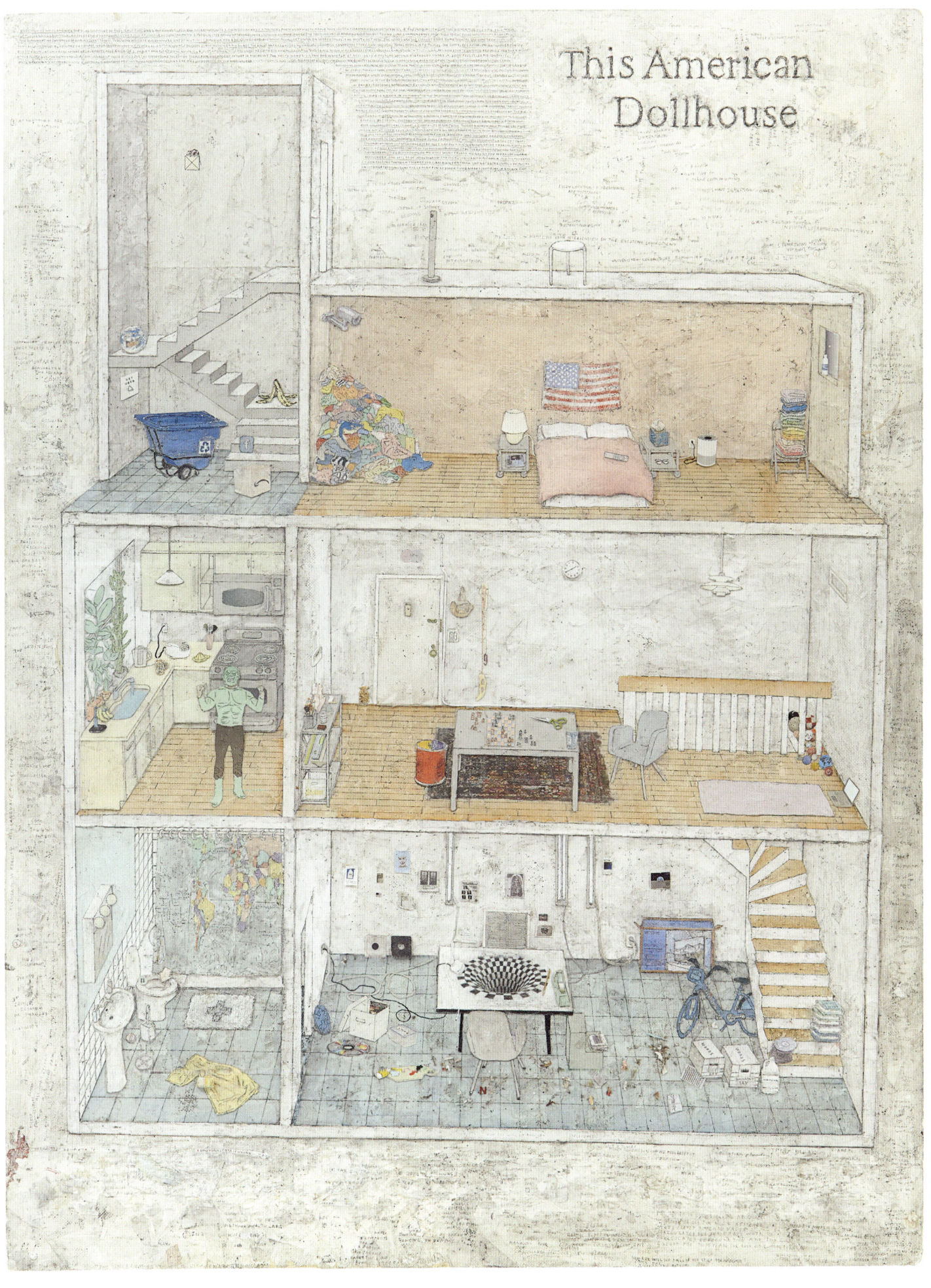

The Land that Time Reshot

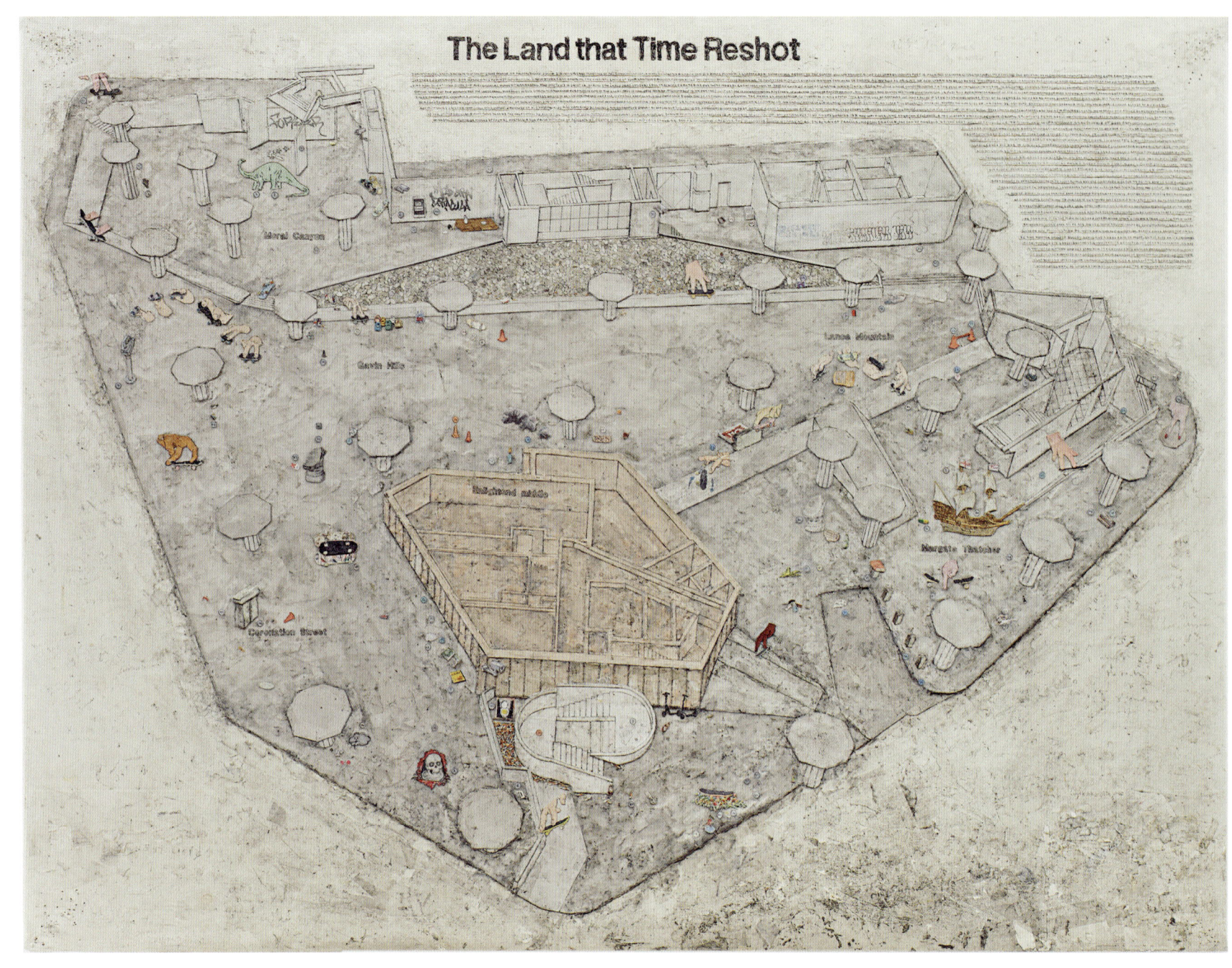

↑   **The Land that Time Reshot**, 2021, mixed media, 76.2 × 101.6 cm (30 × 40 in)

→   **Savings**, 2019, mixed media, 51.8 × 52.5 cm (20⅜ × 20⅝ in)

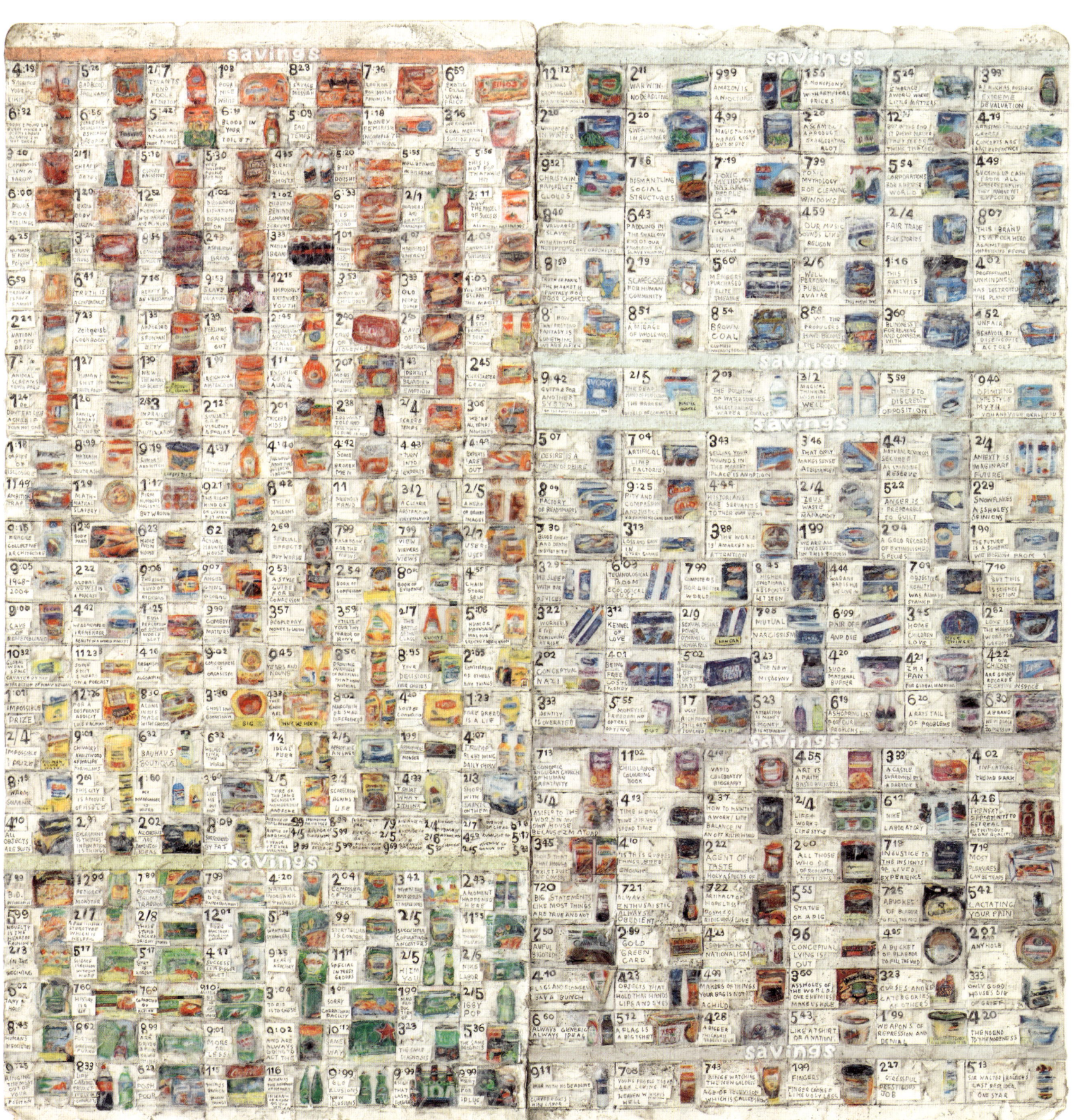

SIMON EVANS™

MOYNA FLANNIGAN

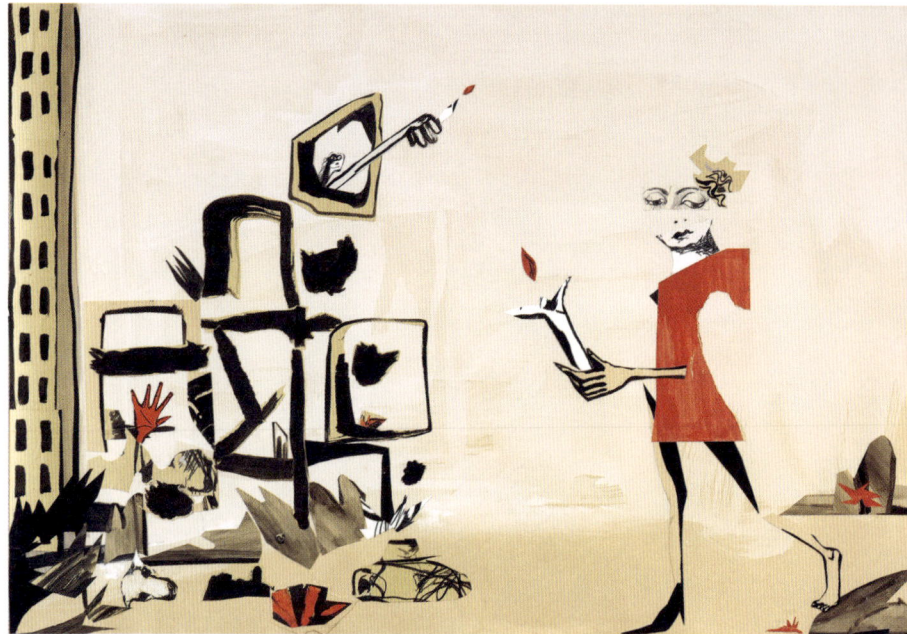

Since the beginning of her career Moyna Flannigan has placed the female figure at the centre of her paintings and works on paper. In 2016 a new body of work based on collage principles emerged when she tore and cut up a cache of ink-and-gouache drawings that had dissatisfied her. The combination of analogue heads and limbs with digital source material from Flannigan's personal memory and interests, as well as mythology and popular culture, generates new connections within an only fragmentarily understandable world. The differences in scale between fragments, as well as the nature of fragments themselves as expressions of the essence of things, have proved fertile for the artist's practice. The methods of collage, as the artist explained in the 2020 documentary film *Moyna Flannigan in the Studio*, 'change the meaning and the impact of the original material'.

The works from the 'Tear' series, begun in 2016, depict women in various poses, sometimes with dismembered limbs floating nearby, as in *Tear 42* (2018), where the figure seemingly levitates against a vast night sky. The three upturned hooves to the left of an indicated mountain range conjure the Greek myth of Europa, who was abducted by Zeus disguised as a bull, with the falling yellow stars representing the violated princess's teardrops. Playing with the double meaning of the series' title, the composite faces of Flannigan's figures appear both wistful and forlorn. The features of classic beauty ideals – big eyes, long hair, wasp waist, spindly legs – are exaggerated to the point of caricature in *Tear 22* (2016): objectified beings perform destructive concepts of femininity on a stage. Flannigan is critical of how society raises women to popular idol status, then violently tears them down from such pedestals, with Marilyn Monroe as the most poignant example appearing in her works. The collages sometimes lead the artist to execute a painting of the composition, although the two versions sit so independently from each other that they are sometimes displayed together. In the 2021 exhibition 'MATTER' at Ingleby Gallery in Edinburgh, for example, Flannigan exhibited both versions of *Reel Time Women* (2021), for which she drew on multiple references related to the year of her birth, 1963: this was the year after Monroe's death, but also when Federico Fellini made the avant-garde film *8½*; when feminist activist Gloria Steinem exposed the world of Playboy bunny clubs; and when Betty Friedan published the influential book *The Feminine Mystique*. One of the film frames behind Flannigan's three women shows a reverse image of Saint Cecilia, a Baroque sculpture by Stefano Maderno (c.1576–1636) of the Roman martyr who convinced her husband to let her remain a virgin and whose 'incorrupt' body was supposedly found in this recumbent position in 1599.

PIA GOTTSCHALLER

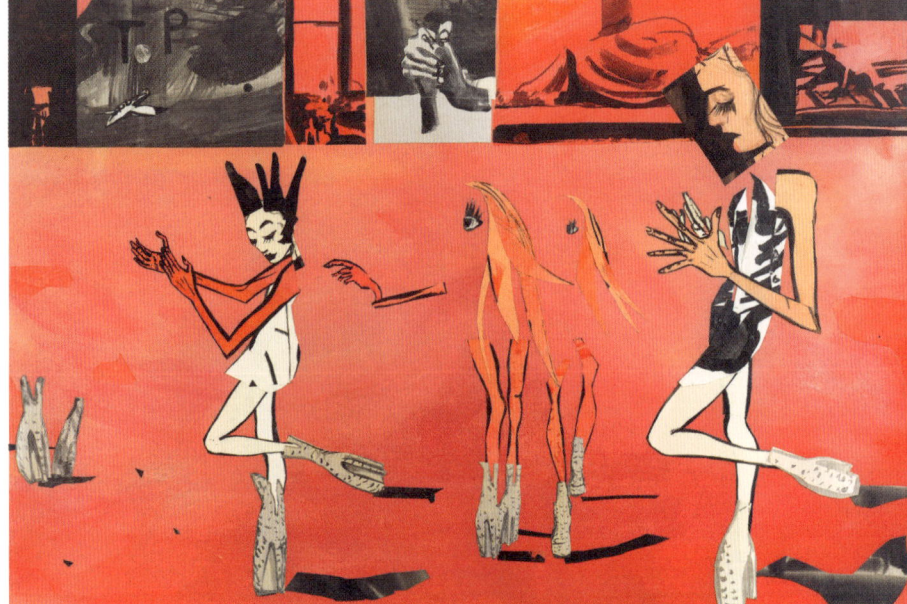

Born 1963, Kirkcaldy, Scotland, UK. Lives in Edinburgh, Scotland, UK.

↑↑   **Tear 20**, 2016, ink, gouache and collage on paper, 97.5 × 145 cm (38 ⅜ × 57 ⅛ in)

↑   **Reel Time Women**, 2021, ink, gouache and collage on paper, 97.5 × 145.5 cm (38 ⅜ × 57 ⅛ in)

↗   **Tear 22**, 2016, ink, gouache and collage on paper, 92 × 76 cm (36 ¼ × 29 ⅞ in)

→   **Tear 56**, 2019, ink, gouache and collage on paper, 98.5 × 76.6 cm (38 ¾ × 30 ⅛ in)

→→   **Tear 42**, 2018, ink, gouache and collage on paper, 145 × 97.5 cm (57 ⅛ × 38 ⅜ in)

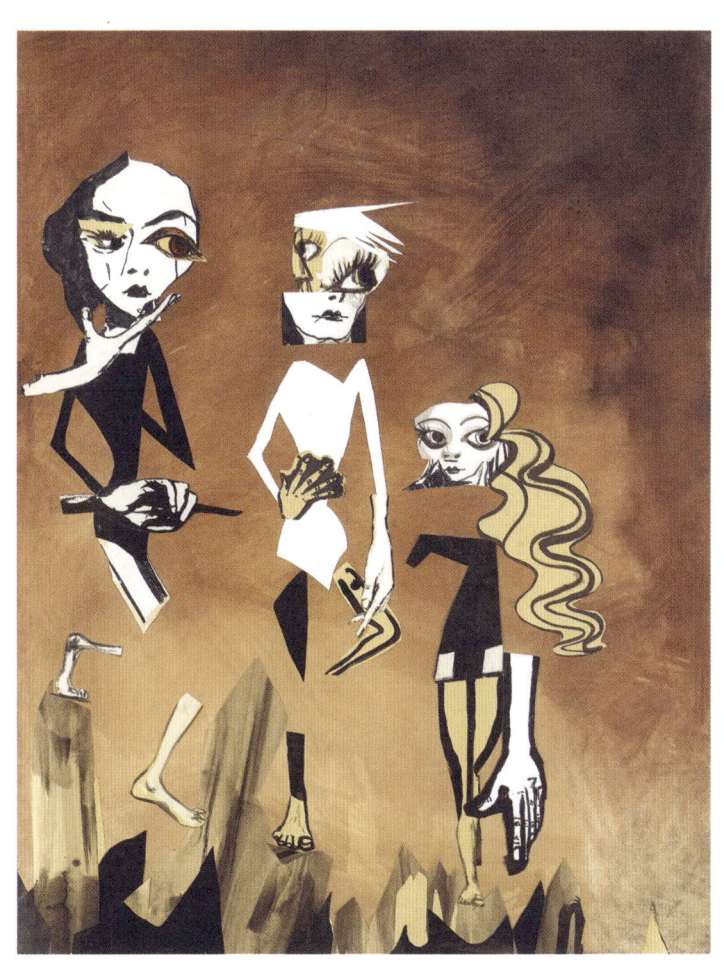

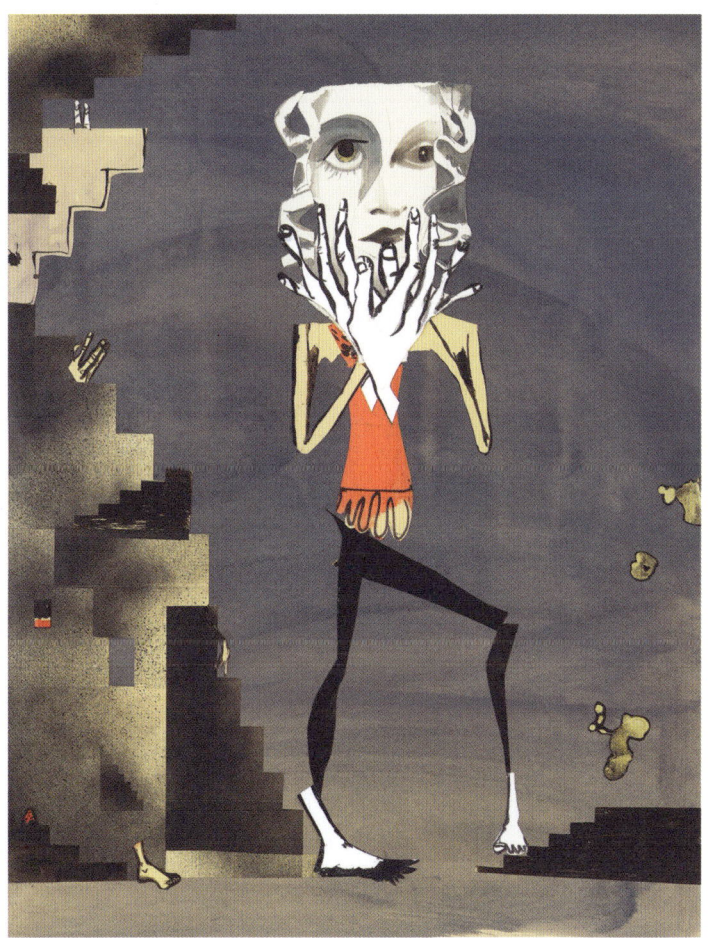

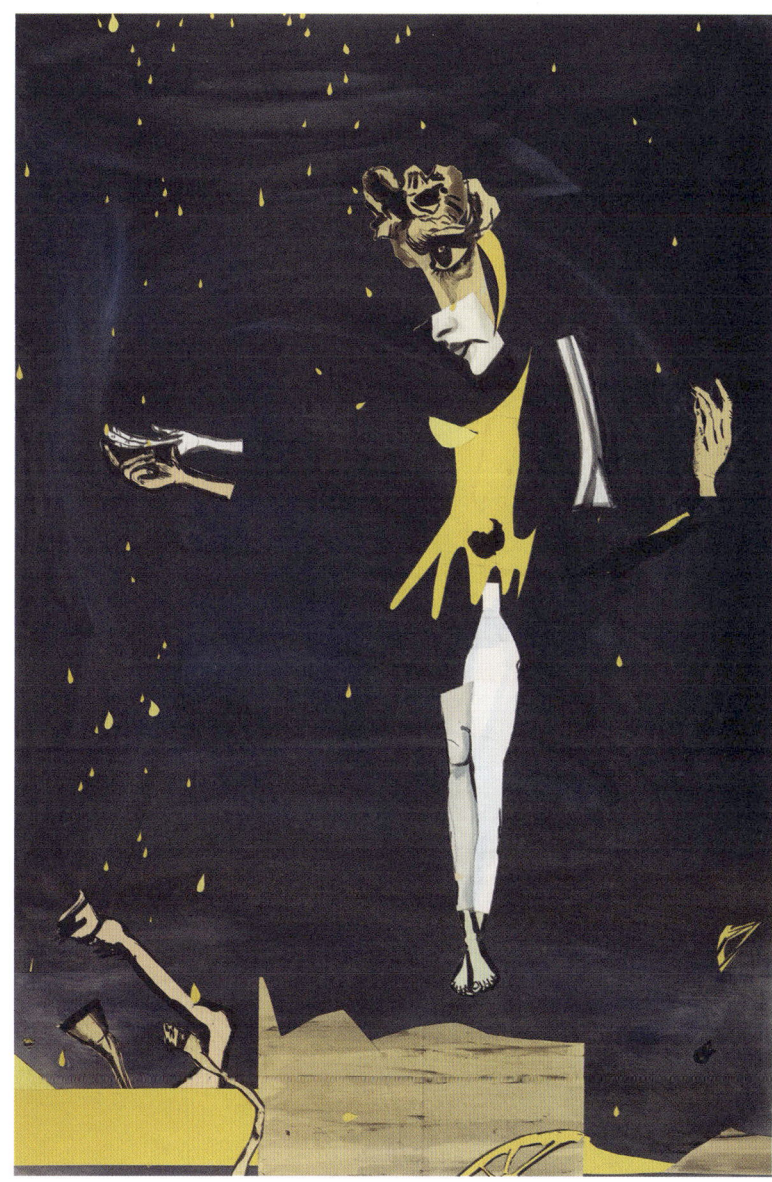

ELLEN GALLAGHER

Collage has been fundamental to Ellen Gallagher's work from the outset. The literal basis of her paintings is an irregular grid of lined pages of the kind used to instruct children in penmanship, which she glues onto the canvas support. This forms the ground on which her compositions are meticulously built up in ways that have varied over the years. In her earliest works the canonical forms of the grid and the monochrome were repeatedly colonized by swarms of tiny painted motifs derived from the tradition of blackface minstrelsy, pointedly registering the historical occlusions and violent undertow of Western modernism. This signature lexicon was subsequently augmented with images excised from the pages of mid-twentieth-century magazines aimed at an African American readership. Initially focusing on the headshots in hair-product advertisements, submitting them to vivid disfigurations, Gallagher has also deployed the accompanying ad-copy in works such as *Esirn Coaler* (2007), influenced by the linguistic experimentalism of such acknowledged modernist forebears as Gertrude Stein and the Bahamian-American Vaudevillian Bert Williams. Collage is a productive resource for work that addresses a cluster of interrelated issues – identity, race, displacement, ecology – while drawing on a range of sources including natural history and oceanography, the speculative fictions of Afrofuturism and the traumatic legacy of the African slave trade. Unpicking the web of allusions in a work like *Abu Simbel* (2005), is both challenging and rewarding. Composed for a solo exhibition at London's Freud Museum, this is a mash-up of a photogravure displayed in Sigmund Freud's library of the Great Temple of Rameses II – an ancient example of what Gallagher terms 'Black technologies' – and a cartoon rendition of Afrofuturist pioneer Sun Ra's spaceship from the 1974 film *Space is the Place*. The disembodied heads of numerous Black men have been dashed against the temple's stone figures, evidently lured by the siren-song of two uniformed nurses, an allusion to Eunice Rivers, who participated in the notorious Tuskegee Experiment (1932–72), which caused unnecessary suffering to hundreds of syphilitic Black men in rural Alabama. Informed by research undertaken during time spent in Belgium, *Elephantine* (2019) comprises a threadbare wall map of pre-independence Africa hung between two wooden dowels painted in the colours of the Belgian national flag. While the upper portion of the map remains legible, Southern Africa is largely obscured by a spectral figure with gaping eye sockets and an elongated trunk whose sinuous form is echoed by the decorative silver clasps attached at the map's four corners. These forms evoke the 'Congo style' of Belgian Art Nouveau, whose ornamental grammar has recently been shown to be inextricably linked to the brute realities of extractive colonialism through its recurring motifs of the vine, the lash and the elephant. Gallagher's is an art consistently animated by such troubling revenants and disconcerting revelations.

CAOIMHÍN MAC GIOLLA LÉITH

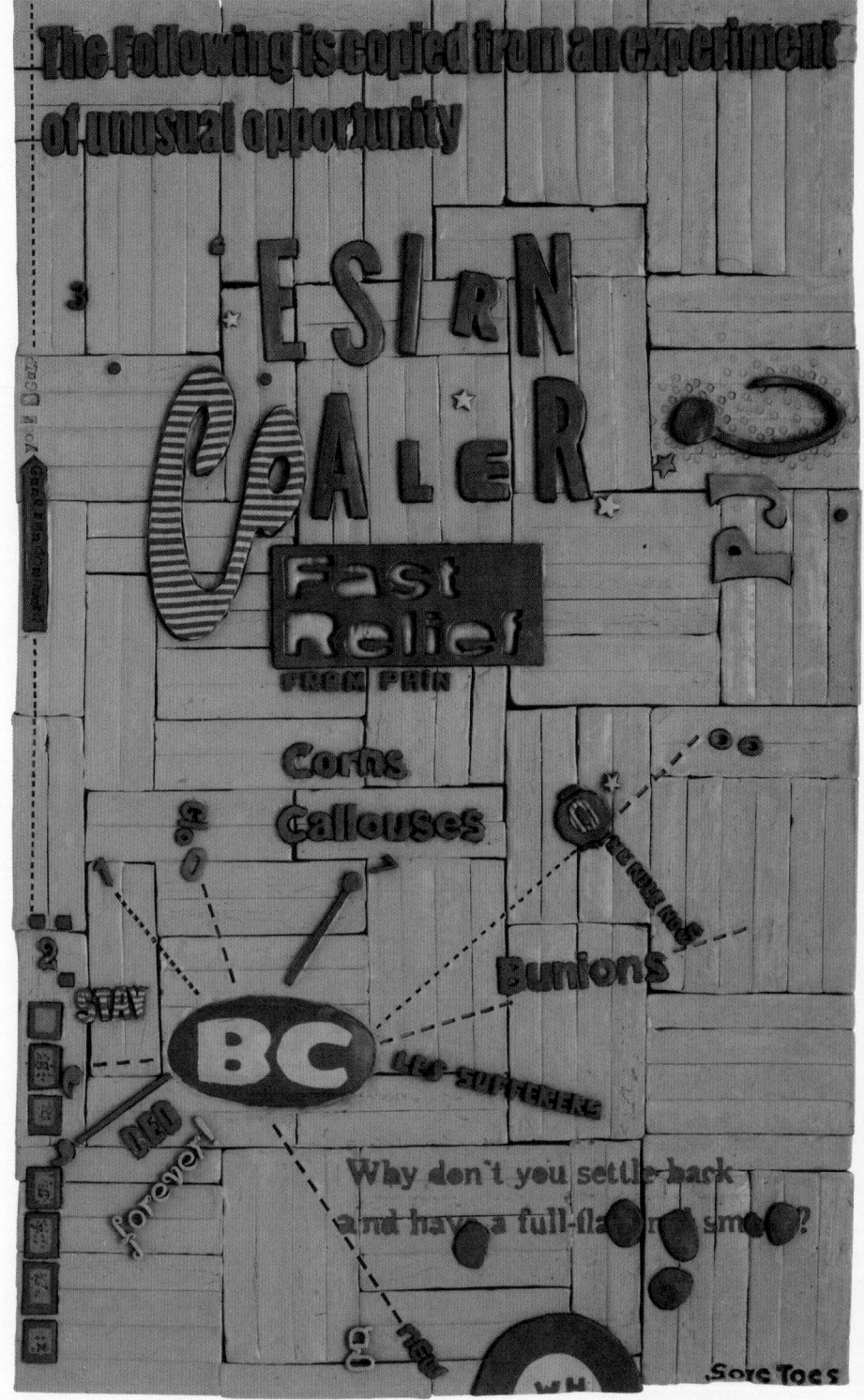

Born 1965, Providence, Rhode Island, USA. Lives in Rotterdam, Netherlands and New York, USA.

↑ **Esirn Coaler**, 2007, plasticine and aluminium, 89.4 × 55.2 × 4.5 cm (35¼ × 21¾ × 1¾ in), Tate, London, UK

↗ **Elephantine**, 2019, linen on paper hung between 2 wooden dowels, 119 × 106.5 × 4 cm (46⅞ × 41⅞ × 1⅝ in)

→ **Abu Simbel**, 2005, photogravure, watercolour, coloured pencil, varnish, pomade, plasticine, blue fur, gold leaf and crystals, 62 × 90 cm (24⅜ × 35⅜ in)

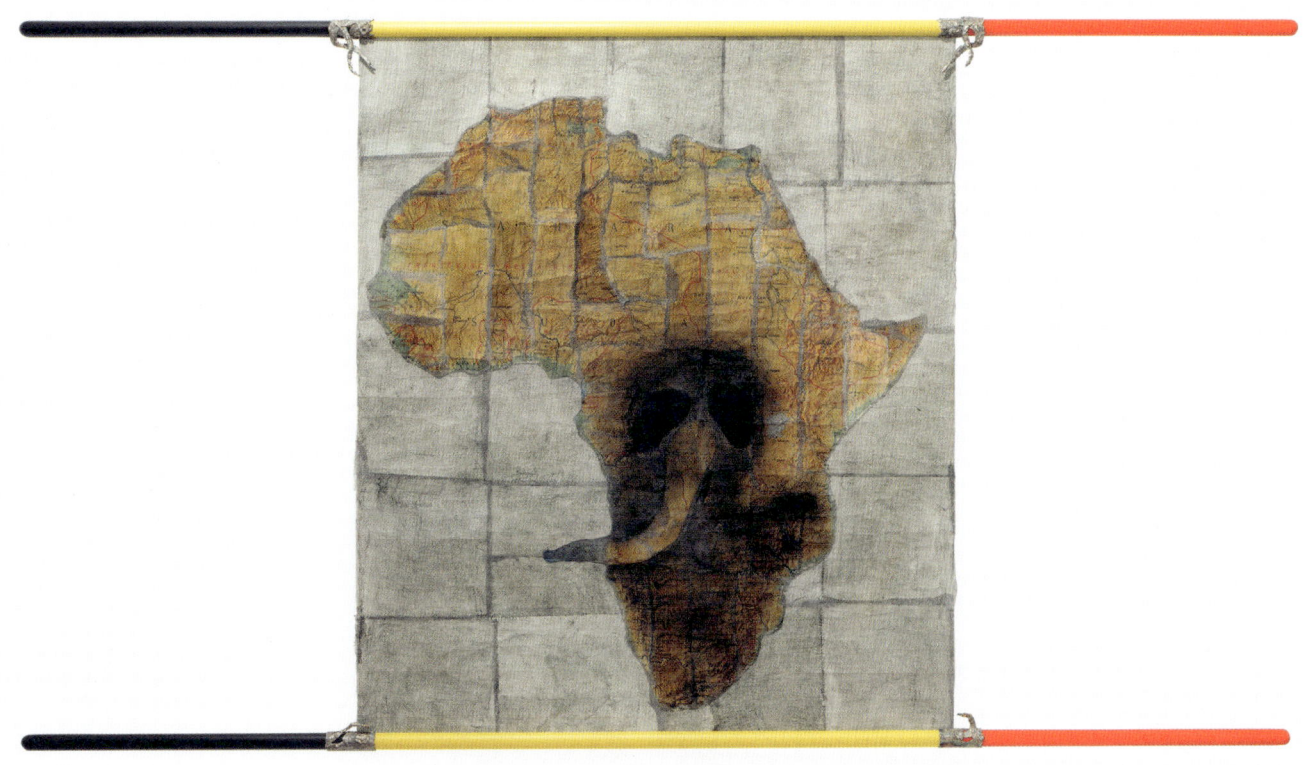

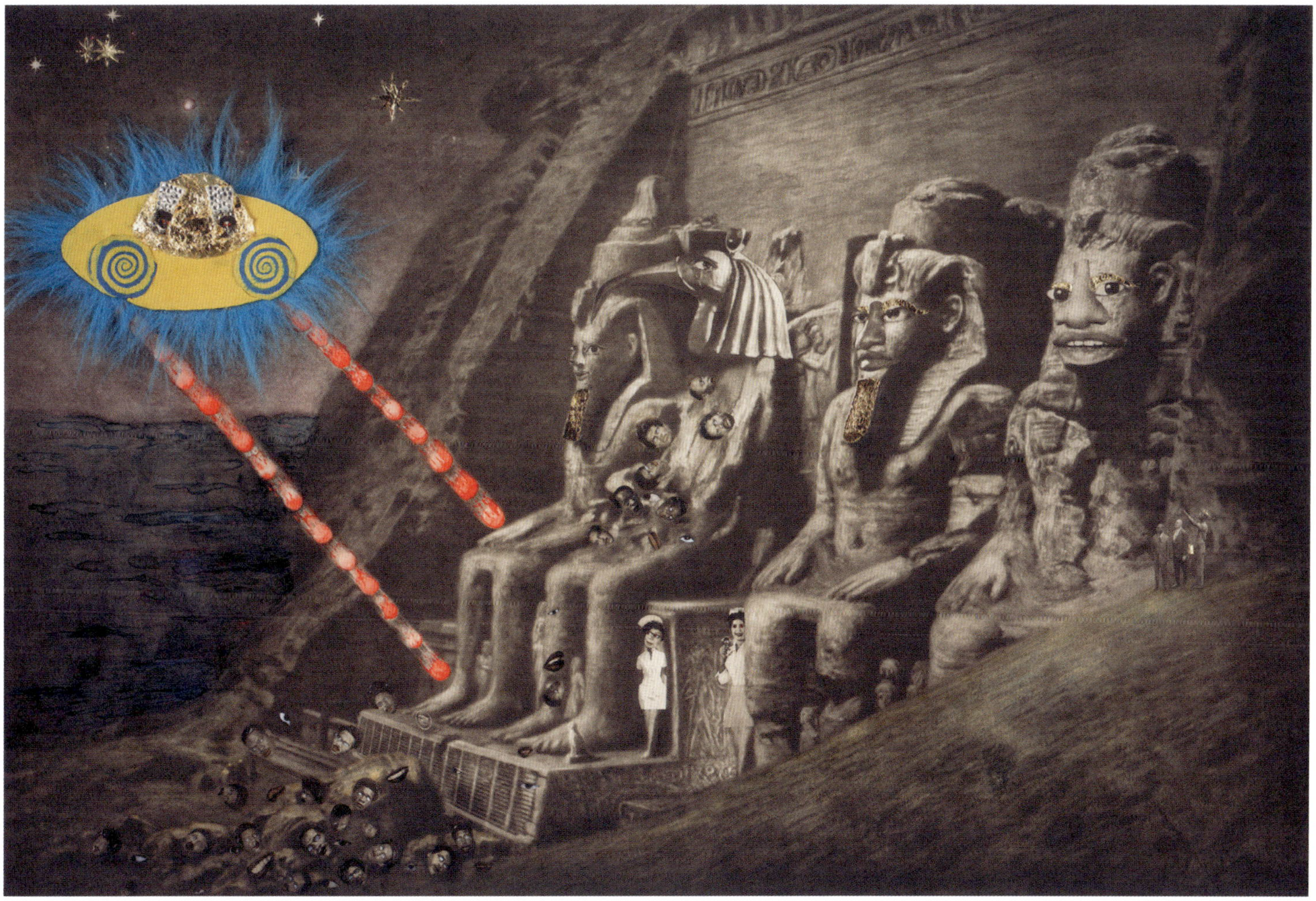

ELLEN
GALLAGHER

DANIEL GORDON

Vibrant and dazzling, Daniel Gordon's works not only vividly reinterpret the still life painting genre of Western art but also blur the boundaries between photography, painting and sculpture. Mixing his own digital and analogue photographic material with found images, Gordon invites the viewer to reconsider what a photograph or indeed a collage might be. Cut-out elements are carefully glued and arranged into rich tableaux in which foliage, food and objects intersect and overlap. These are then lit and rephotographed by the artist. The result is a deceptive hybrid – a sculptural collage flattened once again by the camera lens; photographs of photographs, folded, spliced and juxtaposed to complicate the relationship between image and time, past and present. This conceptual approach slows down the encounter with the photographic image in order to question perception and materiality. While the artist has explored many different subjects in his career, including portraiture and landscape, it is in his still life compositions that his approach to collage manifests more pronouncedly. The still life genre in painting first gained popularity in seventeenth-century Europe. These paintings – often called *vanitas* for reminding viewers that beauty and earthly pleasures are only temporary – were an important methodological precursor to collage. While their detail and accuracy made it appear that the artist had gathered and arranged all the depicted objects, these works were rarely painted directly from life. In a pre-photographic world, it was common for artists to copy from botanical treatises, anatomical atlases and other artist's paintings. Many of the flowers and fruits in still life paintings bloom and ripen at different times of the year and, furthermore, it would have been impossible to keep the flowers fresh or the food from rotting long enough to complete the painting. One of the most important skills was therefore to use light and shadows to harmonize a composition that never was.

Gordon's conglomerations, however, forsake the deceit. The shadows in *Still Life with Eggs and Avocado* (2018) are outlined with a contrasting neon hue that adds to the artifice of the image and heightens the emotional charge, while in *Summer Still Life with Lobsters and Fern* (2020), several items of fruit are shaded an unnatural electric blue, so that even among the visual overload of colourful, zig-zag and check patterns, they appear jarring to the eye and stand out. Gordon's work also proudly owns the fragmentation and construction of the image, embracing the quintessential ability of collage to materialize the impossible. This conceptual anchoring is further enriched by the influence of Fauvist and Cubist approaches to perception. Objects, such as the jugs in *Fern and Fruit* (2021) and *Lobsters and Blue Pitcher* (2021), are repeatedly layered, to indicate different perspectives at once. All these techniques further distance the photographic image from the reality it originally represented. To Gordon, photographs never provide an objective record of reality, but instead offer the opportunity to transform it.

GIOVANNI ALOI

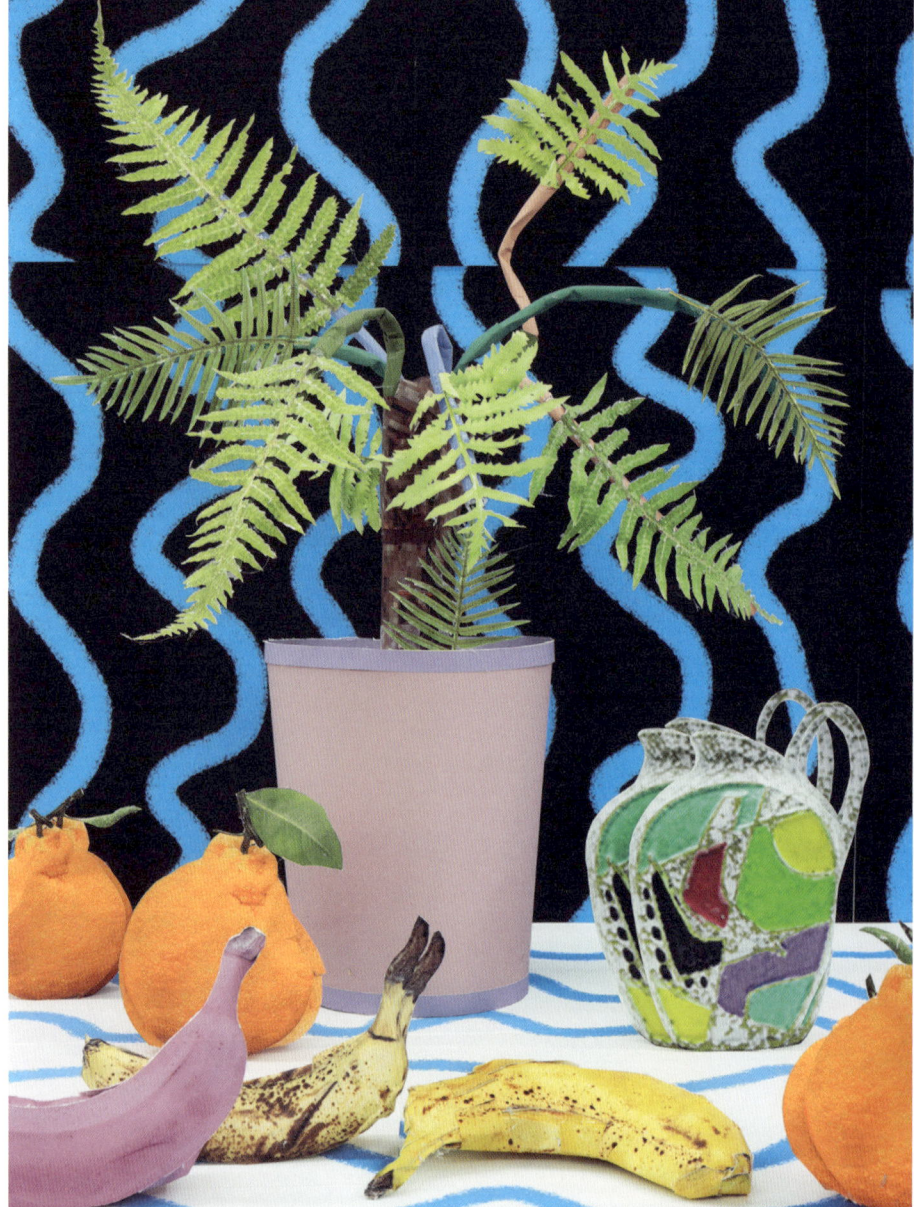

Born 1980, Boston, Massachusetts, USA. Lives in Brooklyn, New York, USA.

↑ **Fern and Fruit**, 2021, pigment print with UV lamination, 71.1 × 53.3 cm (28 × 21 in), edition of 3 + 1 AP

→ **Lobsters and Blue Pitcher**, 2021, pigment print with UV lamination, 53.3 × 71.1 cm (21 × 28 in), edition of 3 + 1 AP

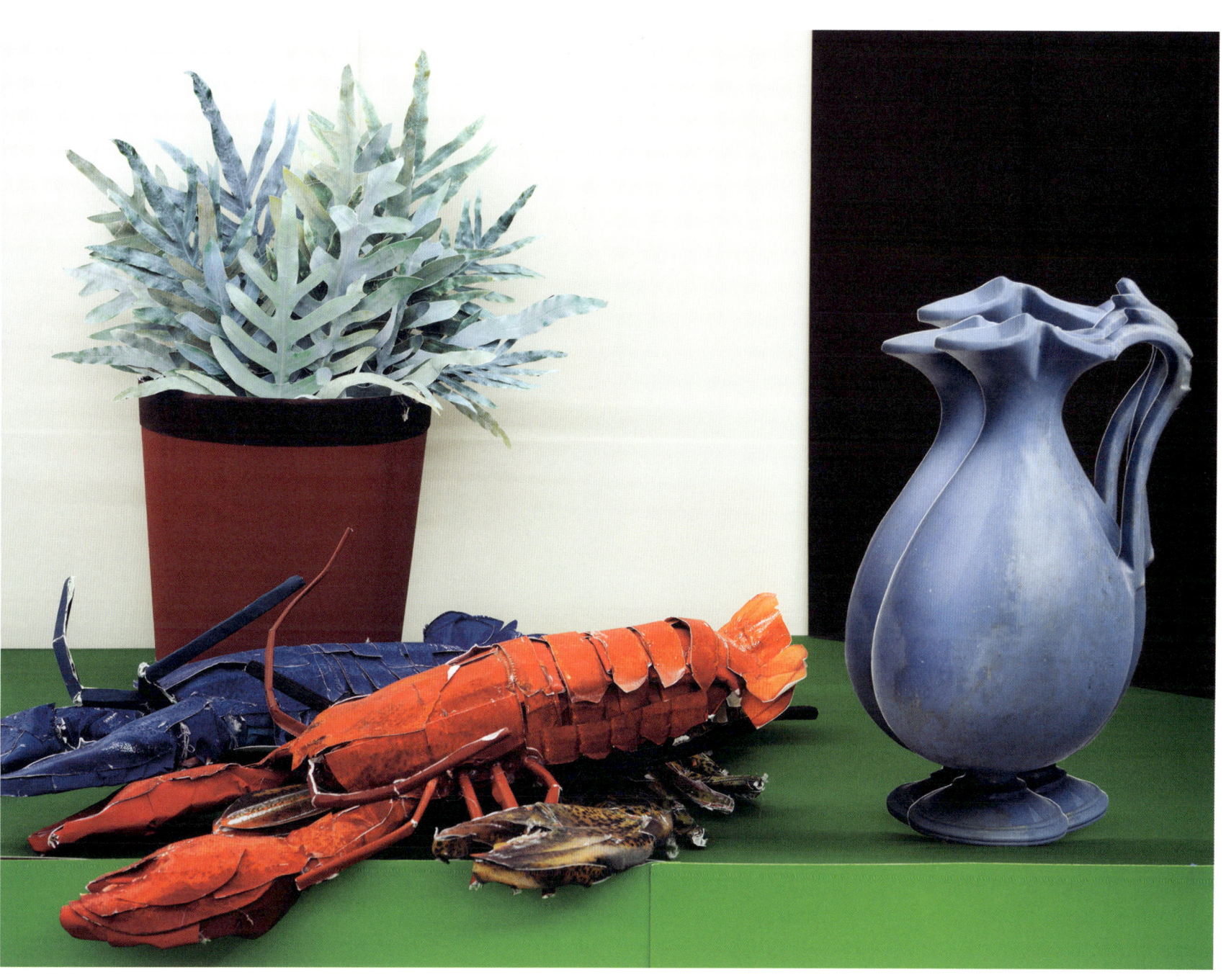

DANIEL
GORDON

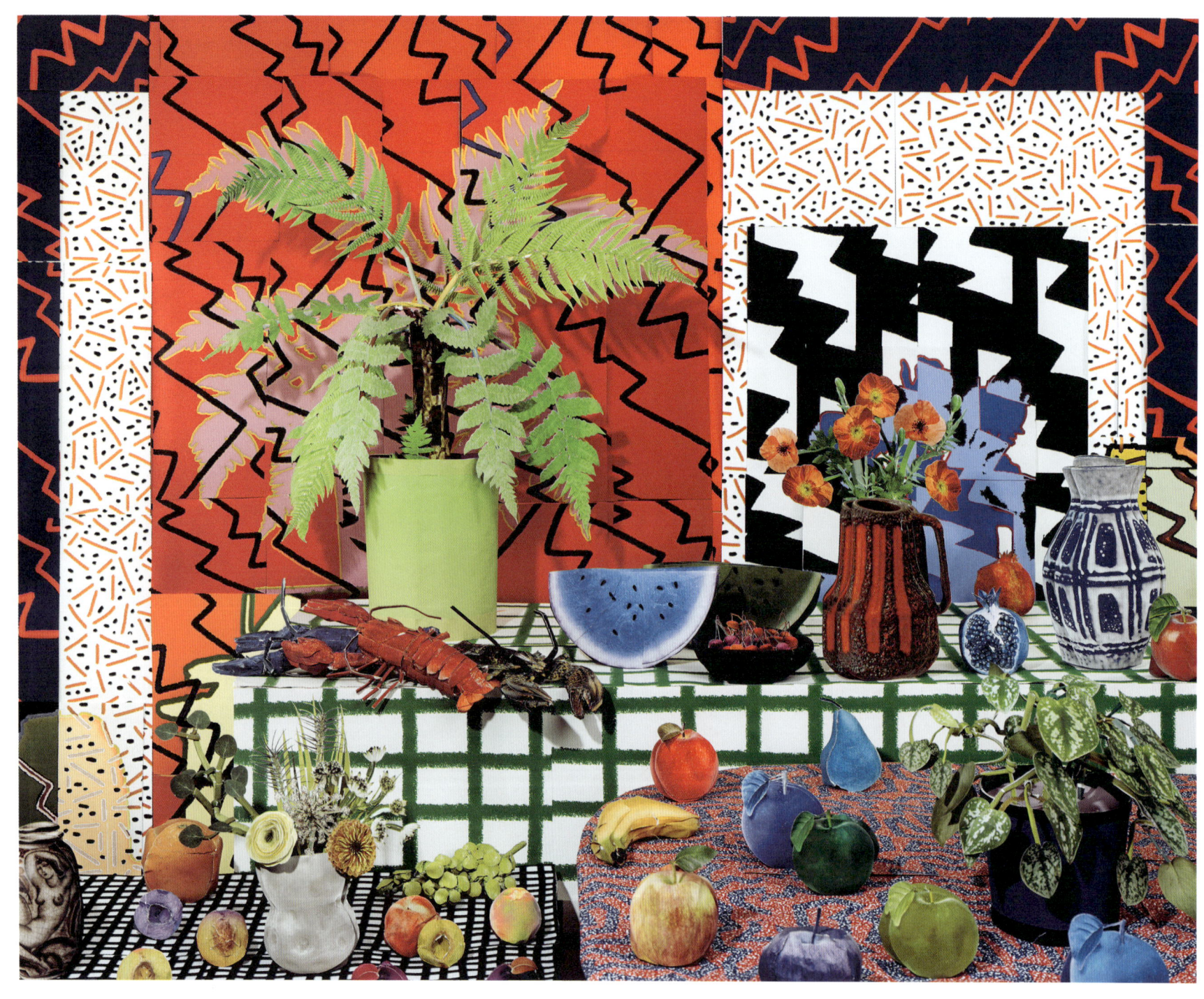

↑   **Summer Still Life with Lobsters and Fern**, 2020, pigment print with UV lamination, 150.5 × 190.5 cm
(59¼ × 75 in), edition of 3 + 1 AP

→   **Still Life with Eggs and Avocado**, 2018, pigment print with UV lamination, 126.4 × 101 cm
(49¾ × 39¾ in), edition of 3 + 1 AP

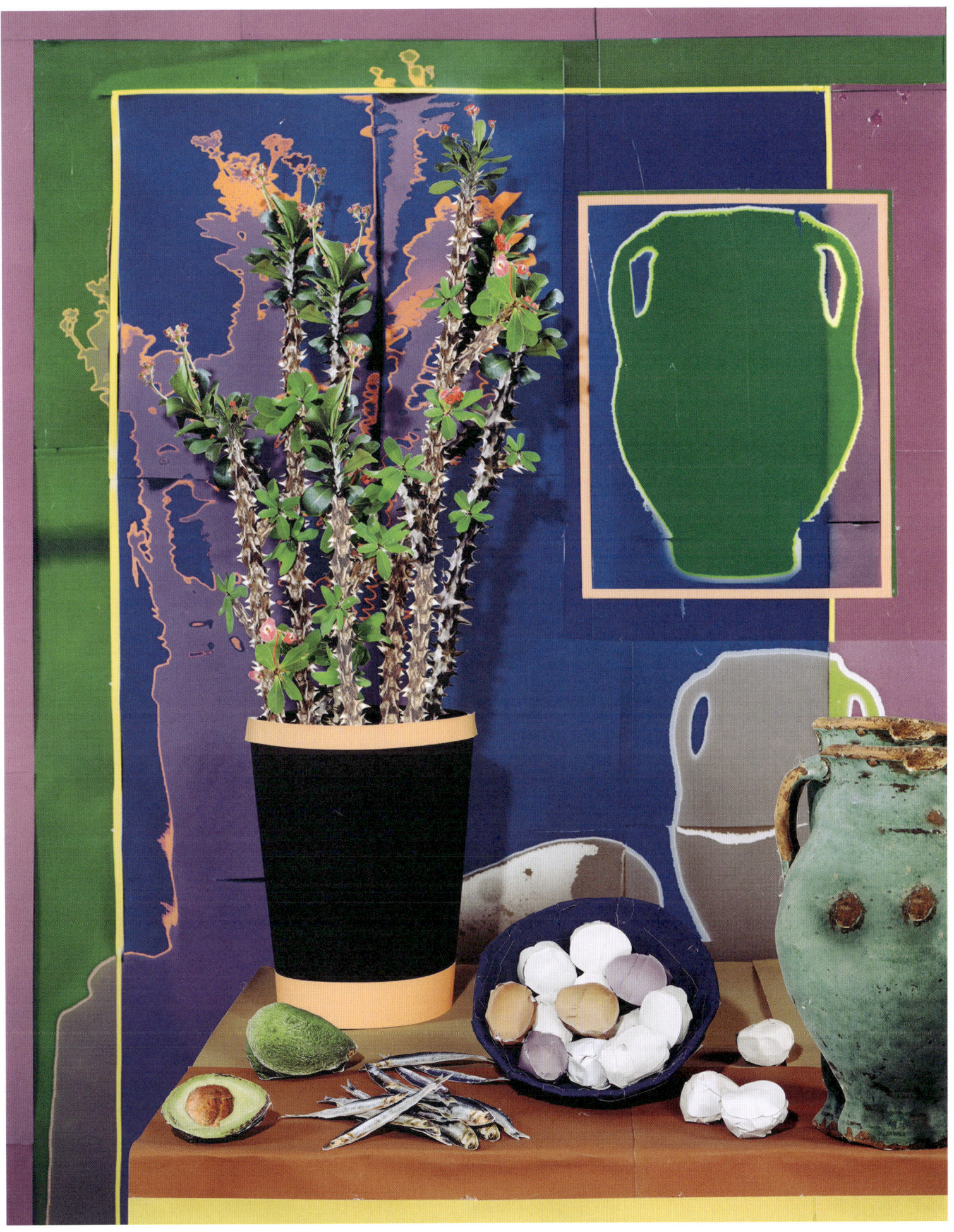

DANIEL
GORDON

NOÉMIE GOUDAL

Since 2010 Noémie Goudal has staged quietly sublime photographs tinged with an undercurrent of dread. She often introduces surreal constructions to otherwise virginal environments, questioning our perception of Earth's history and our place within it. Look closely at her sublime landscapes, though, and the illusion will begin to unravel: paper clips will appear, revealing threadbare systems holding together the scene, while creases and smudges will dirty what at first appeared pristine. *Phoenix IV* (2021) depicts a species of palm trees (named *Phoenix atlantica*) found only in South America and Western Africa. Their existence is considered one example of proof that the two continents once formed a single landmass two billion years ago. To create *Phoenix IV*, Goudal used a monumental printer to print lifesize photographs of the trees standing before her. She then sliced these images into strips and arranged them in front of the original scene through a discrete system of strings and clips and rephotographed the result, creating this collage not on a computer, or on paper, but in situ. Yet the resulting work looks digital, like a glitched image. *Station VI* (2015) similarly undercuts an aesthetic of the sublime through small details that reveal modest materials and processes. The work belongs to a series on the cosmos in which Goudal transformed large paper discs into sinister celestial bodies by placing them against the sky. 'We feel that we know the universe,' the artist told the *Guardian* newspaper in 2022. 'We know the moon, we know our bodies, we know our viruses, we know everything. But actually we need to be a lot more humble.' The edges of the disc are wobbly rather than perfectly geometrical, creating a sense of intimacy with a fragile material that at first glance appeared alien and other. All of Goudal's landscapes are unpeopled, yet some series address the impact of humankind more directly than others. *Observatoire III* (2013) shows a concrete structure lost amid a placid grey landscape, like a ruin from the future. The composition evokes the familiar tropes of Bernd (1931–2007) and Hilla Becher's (1934–2015) architectural typology. The influential German couple systematically used a seemingly objective frame to photograph the disappearing industrial architecture that fired up the modern era – furnaces, grain silos, gas tanks and wind towers. The function of Goudal's structure, however, is less clear. The title suggests it is an observatory – a building for meditation rather than production. Close inspection reveals folds and creases in the surface, as the structure is not concrete but composed instead of images of buildings collaged together onto cardboard cut-outs. The small markings in Goudal's work highlight the transience of her gestures and of the structures and landscapes she captures.

EDMÉE LEPERCQ

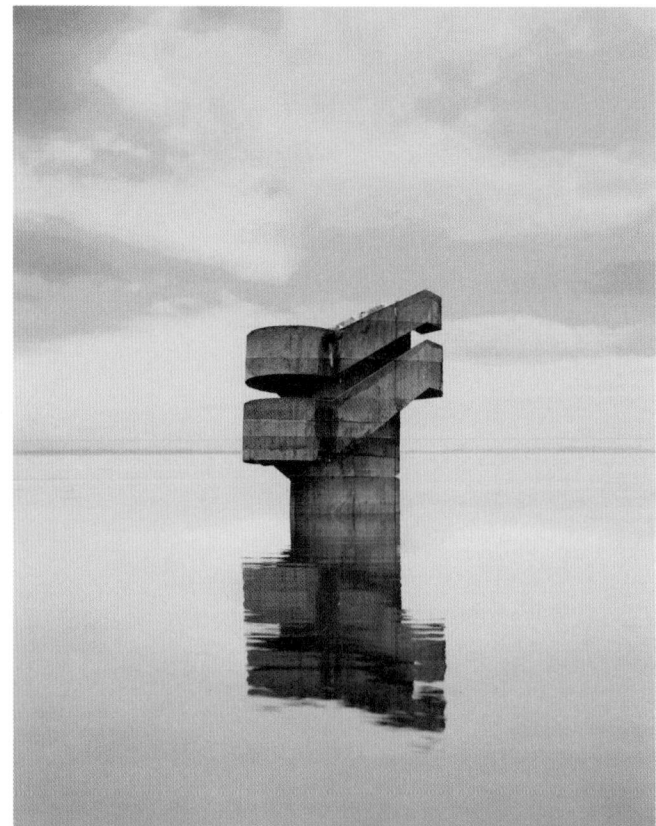

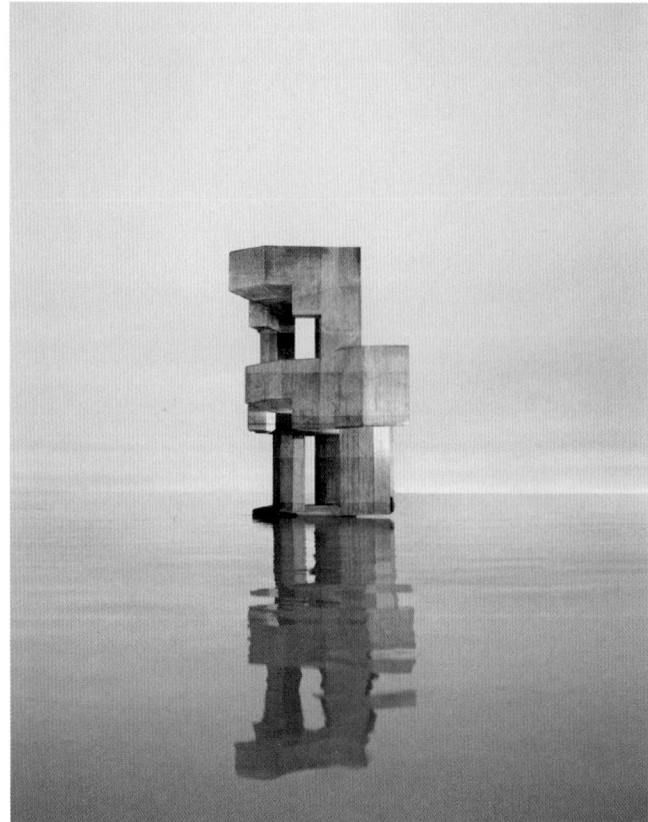

Born 1984, Paris, France. Lives in Paris.

↑↑ **Observatoire III**, 2013, C-print, 150 × 120 cm (59⅛ × 47¼ in) and 60 × 48 cm (23⅝ × 18⅞ in), each in an edition of 5 + 2 AP

↑ **Observatoire VIII**, 2014, C-print, 150 × 120 cm (59⅛ × 47¼ in) and 60 × 48 cm (23⅝ × 18⅞ in), each in an edition of 5 + 2 AP

↗ **Station II**, 2015, C-print, 168 × 214 cm (66⅛ × 84¼ in) and 111 × 147 cm (43¾ × 57⅞ in), each in an edition of 5 + 2 AP

→ **Station VI**, 2015, C-print, 168 × 214 cm (66⅛ × 84¼ in) and 111 × 147 cm (43¾ × 57⅞ in), each in an edition of 5 + 2 AP

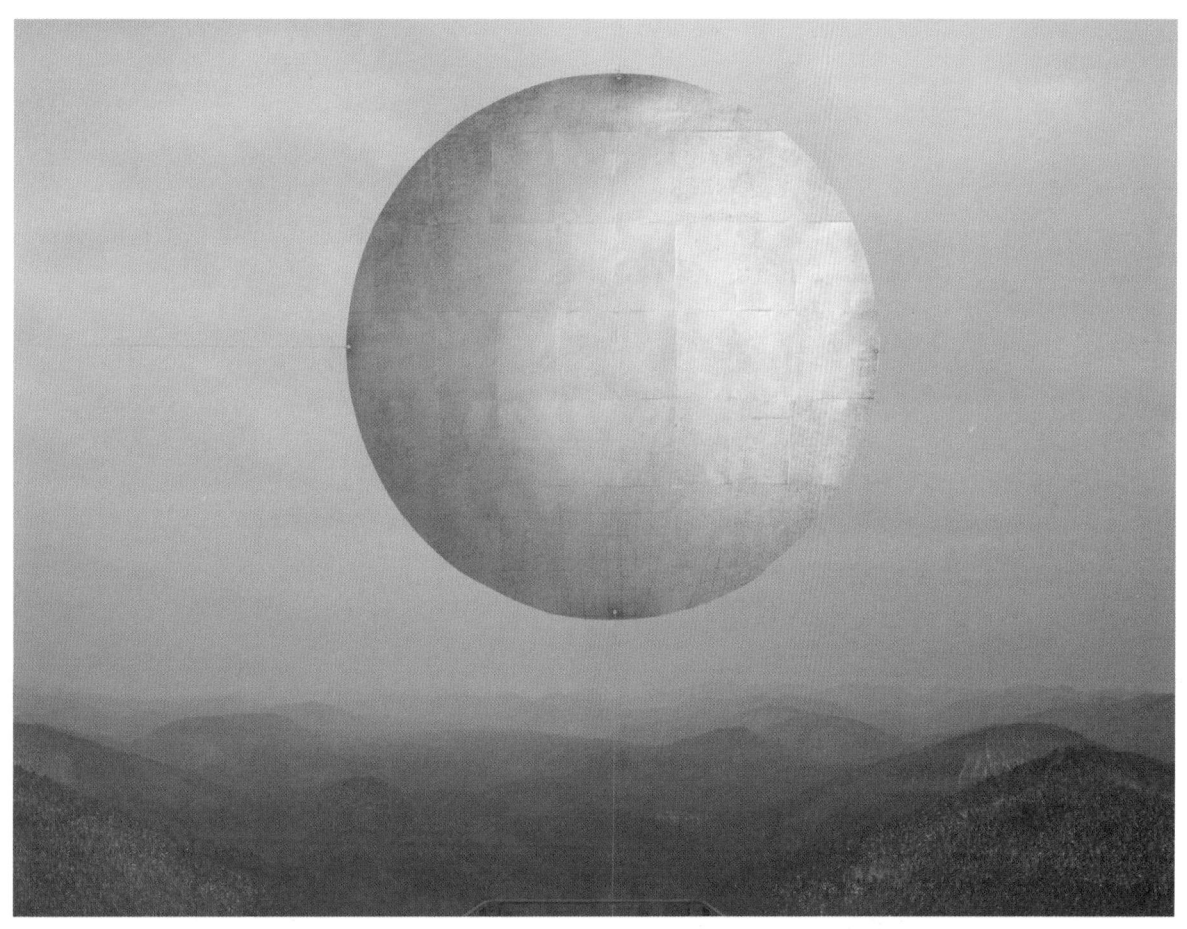

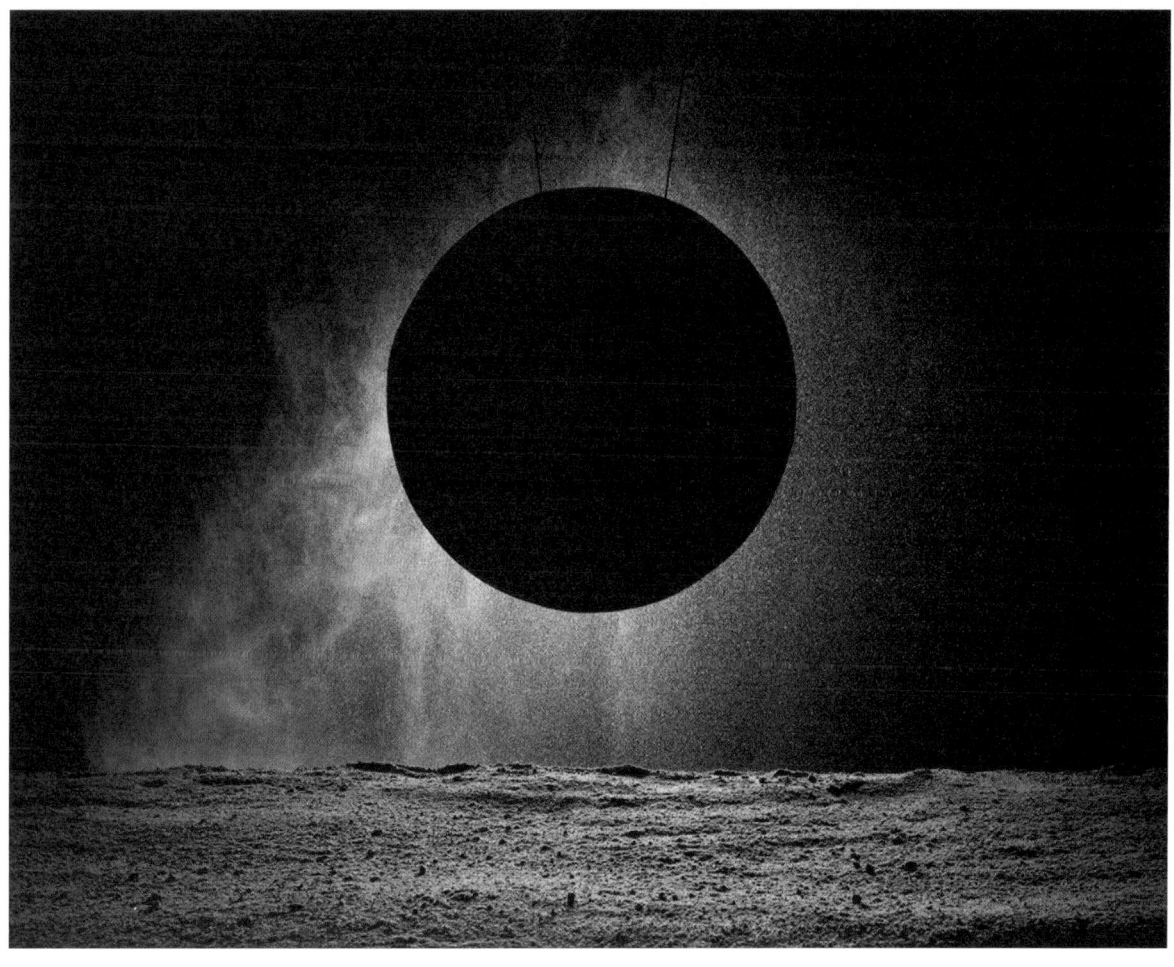

NOÉMIE GOUDAL

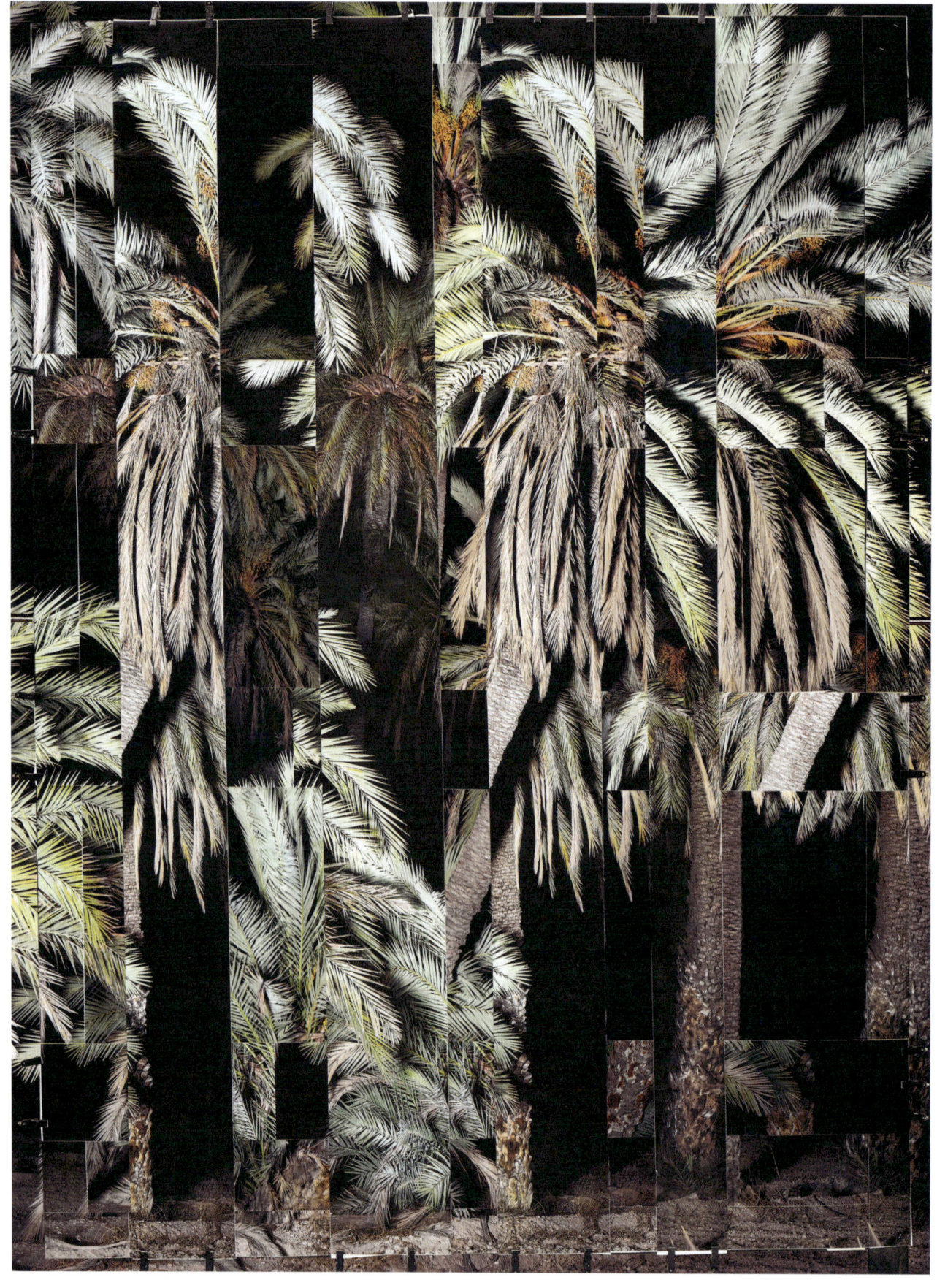

↑   **Phoenix VI**, 2021, C-print, 200 × 149 cm (78 ¾ × 58 ⅝ in) and 148.5 × 111 cm (58 ½ × 43 ¾ in), each in an edition of 5 + 2 AP

→   **Phoenix IV**, 2021, C-print, 200 × 149 cm (78 ¾ × 58 ⅝ in) and 148.5 × 111 cm (58 ½ × 43 ¾ in), each in an edition of 5 + 2 AP

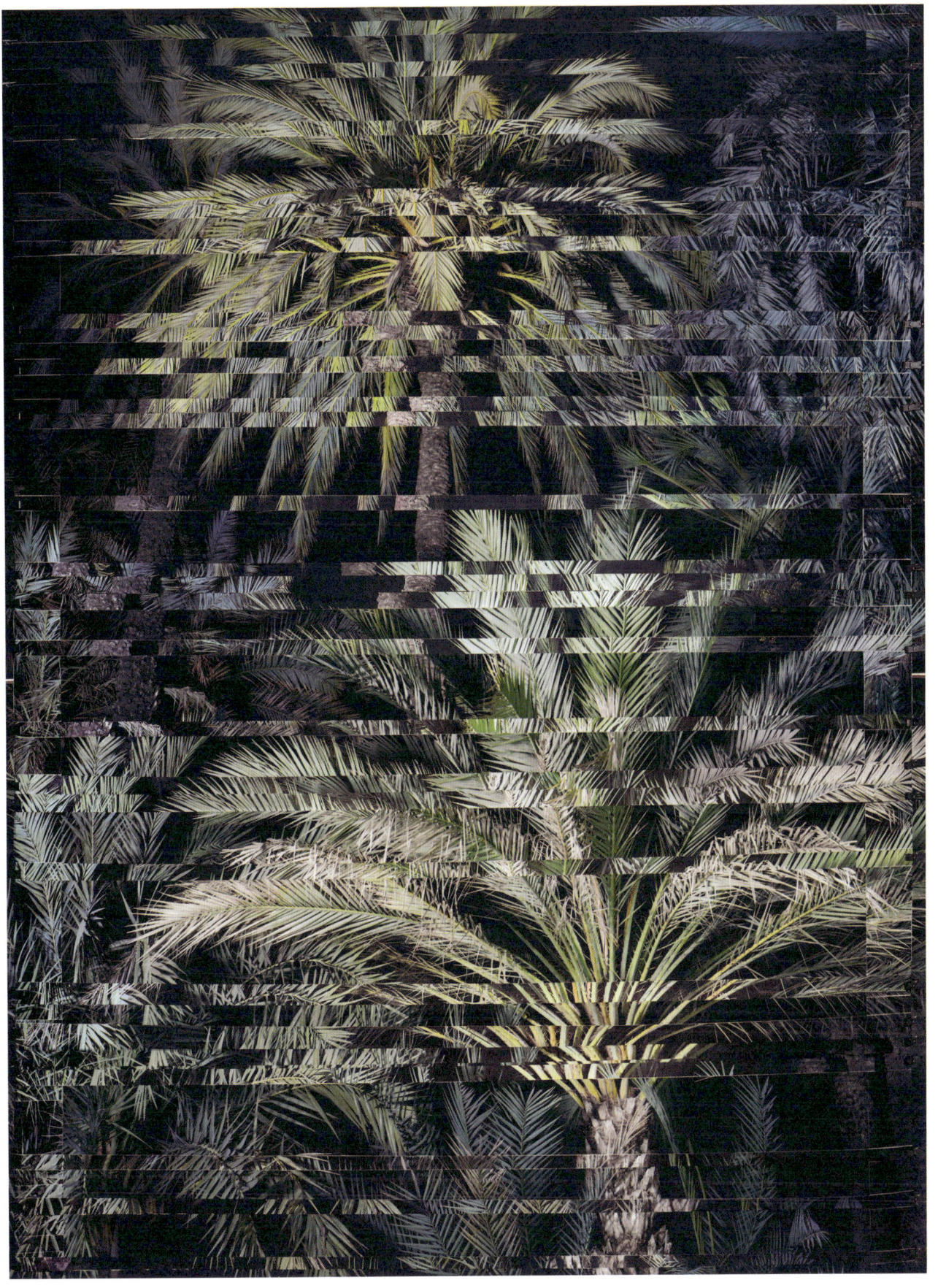

LAUREN HALSEY

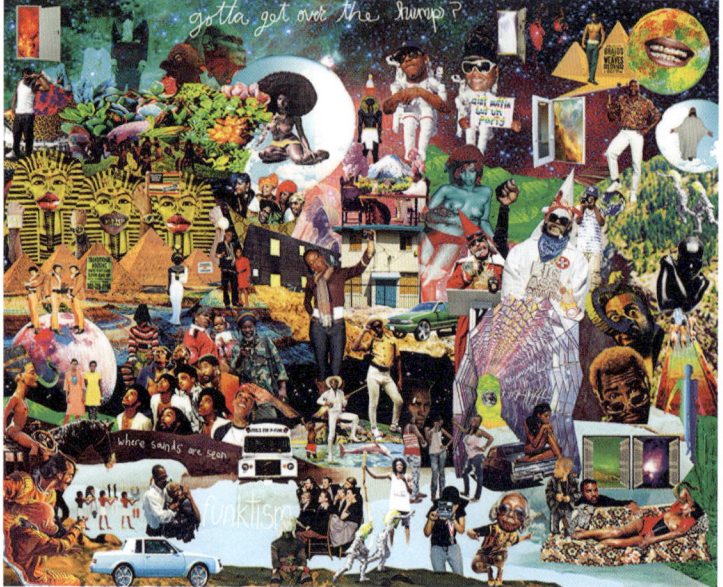

WE ARE STILL HERE. These are the words Lauren Halsey asserts to evoke permanence for South Central, a Los Angeles neighbourhood in constant flux, syncretized by shared stories of migration and settlement. Halsey's work enters a long history of local artisans speaking through layers upon layers of information via the practice of collage. The medium reflects the determination of the community, addressing their presence despite redevelopment and asks new questions. Halsey situates the idea of 'home' in juxtaposed iconography, albeit one full of extreme familiarity to anyone of a shared upbringing. Among a dense montage of cultural references, *We Still Here* (2020) includes Thomas 'Tommy the Clown' Johnson, who, like Halsey, is deeply committed to future generations of South Central youth and their creative practices. Tommy the Clown pioneered a competitive and complex improv dance battle style called Krumping, wherein the goal is to best your opponent, receive affirmation from onlookers and create in others an echo of spirituality. Halsey's extensive use of collage complements this inventive style, giving new context to even the inflatable bouncy castle as source material, a traditional component of a child's birthday party that offers a carefree weightlessness often associated with the astronauts and space travel that populate her work. Halsey's digital collages are a database of memory; she recalls and collects residential signs and ephemera and compiles them as they would be seen in public spaces. The signage amplifies businesses and services for personal expressions, such as hair and nails to parties and dances. Relics of Black-owned businesses, family photos and flea markets collide and find new meaning in her neighbourhood assemblages. In an interview with curator Erin Christovale in connection with receiving the 2018 Mohn Award at the Hammer Museum, Los Angeles, Halsey reflected on this source material, calling it 'cool moments in Black LA that I would otherwise have no access to just from moving into my grandmother's garage', remixed and overlapped across her work into sculpture and installation. Repetition and working on a grand scale aid Halsey in this curiosity, as she replays and reproduces familiar items and noteworthy personas. For example, the late American rapper Nipsey Hussle is often monumental and centred, speaking to his ever-present significance both in the artist's work and in their community. In *gotta get over the hump?* (2010), Halsey repeats the Egyptian King Tutankhamen three times, a rhythm carried over to other iterations of work in the following years. Bringing together hieroglyphics and graffiti, those forgotten and those remembered, in their radiance of expressive colour – especially neons – these collages help to illuminate the harmony and cohesion found across time and place. Images of hands in agreement, golden smiles and proud residents all combine to signal to the viewer a joy beyond the surface and a continuity of presence.

AJ GIRARD

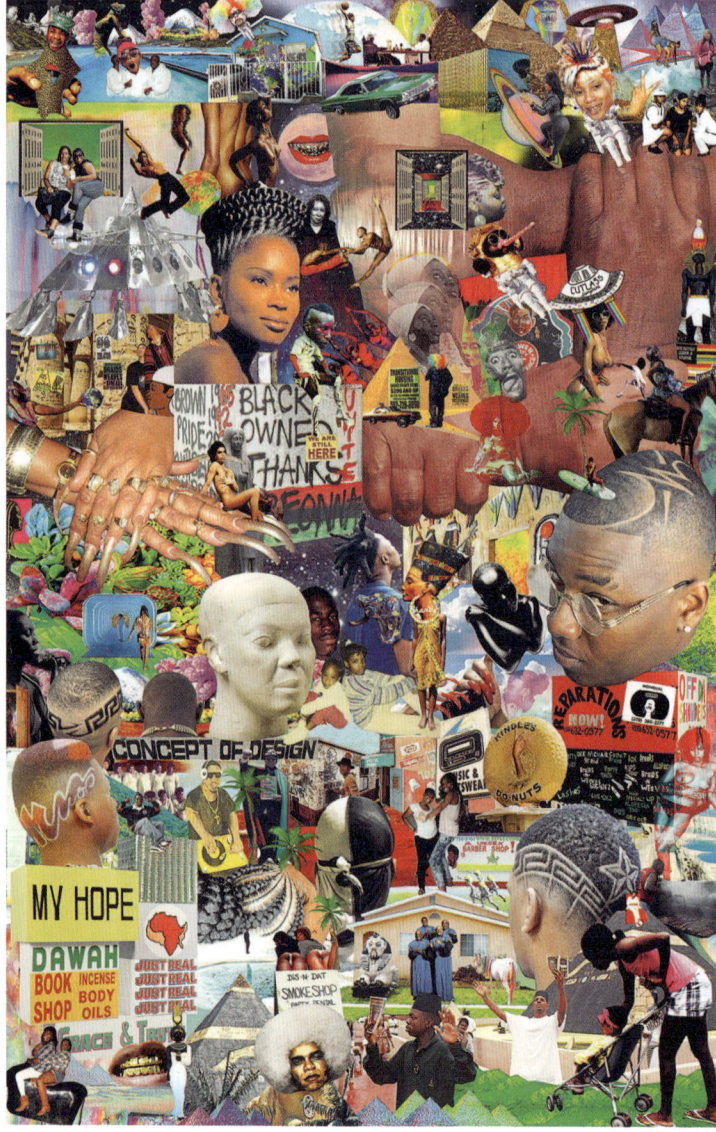

Born 1987, Los Angeles, California, USA. Lives in Los Angeles.

↑↑   gotta get over the hump?, 2010, digital collage

↑   bah bah black sheep, 2021, inkjet print on paper, 243.8 × 158.8 cm (96 × 62½ in), edition of 6 + 2 AP

→   We Still Here, 2020, downloadable digital collage

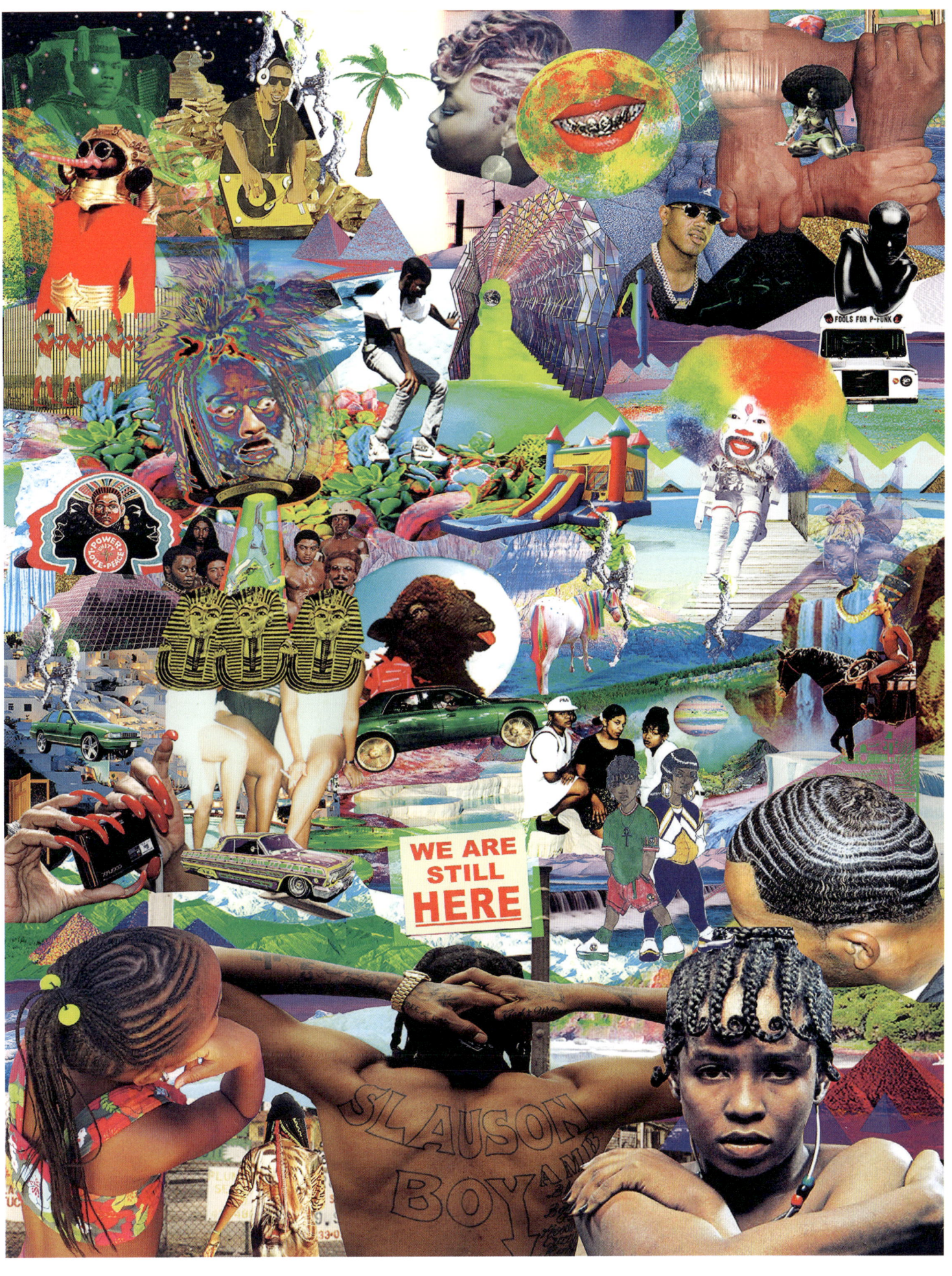

WE ARE
STILL
HERE

LAUREN
HALSEY

HAZEM HARB

Born in Gaza and now splitting his time between Dubai and Rome, this displacement from his homeland fuels Hazem Harb's interrogation of Palestinian history and the construction of heritage through the built environment. Working with images sourced from the internet and physical archives, he uses a range of collage techniques including cropping, cutting and rearranging, adding abstract elements that fragment and partially obscure photographs of cities, buildings and landscapes. By intervening in these sites, Harb destabilizes their freighted histories. Much of his work explores pre-Nakba Palestine, a time before the 1948 displacement of the majority of Palestinian Arabs. In contrasting historic depictions with later examples of architectural expansion, Harb is interested in how architecture can reveal and obscure histories.

1-2 *Bauhaus as imperialism* (2019) depicts a modernist civic building next to an historic fortification in Jerusalem. The image is interrupted by geometric and abstract shapes. To fully grasp Harb's work it helps to understand its context. Jerusalem is one of the oldest cities in the world and is considered holy in Judaism, Christianity and Islam. It has been partially destroyed multiple times and its architecture documents histories of occupation and migration. Bauhaus design was brought to the city by Jewish designers emigrating from Europe after the Second World War. This time saw rapid expansion and Harb subtly merges the iconography of this new architecture with abstraction, a style synonymous with progress. In Harb's work these touchstones suggest something malevolent. Abstraction hides parts of the image, creating a form of erasure. In works like this, Harb foregrounds how architecture is an instrument of ideology, frequently used to naturalize identities and histories. In *Map of land, Series #01* (2019) an historic image of Palestine is superimposed with a drawing of concentric circles that recall a tree's growth rings. The drawing hovers over the image, impossible to ignore. Harb's practice can be seen as a form of archaeology, digging into histories and pealing back the layers. He visualizes the ways in which land is formed incrementally as well as instantly, territories shaped over time by natural, as well as human-made, events. *PERMANENT MONUMENTS* (2021) incorporates photographs of an environmentally degraded and desolate River Jordan, framing a healthier looking Lake Tiberias (also known as the Sea of Galilee). The River Jordan is a Jewish and Christian holy site that flows through Lake Tiberias. In the middle of the image the two stretches of water merge, seen through a blue Plexiglas circle that reflects the viewer's profile. Harb's work is full of these moments, peeling back the sedimented histories of these two sites, asking the viewer to understand what might connezt them. He takes what is hidden in plain sight and makes it centre stage.

GEORGE VASEY

Born 1980, Gaza, Palestine. Lives in Rome, Italy and Dubai, UAE.

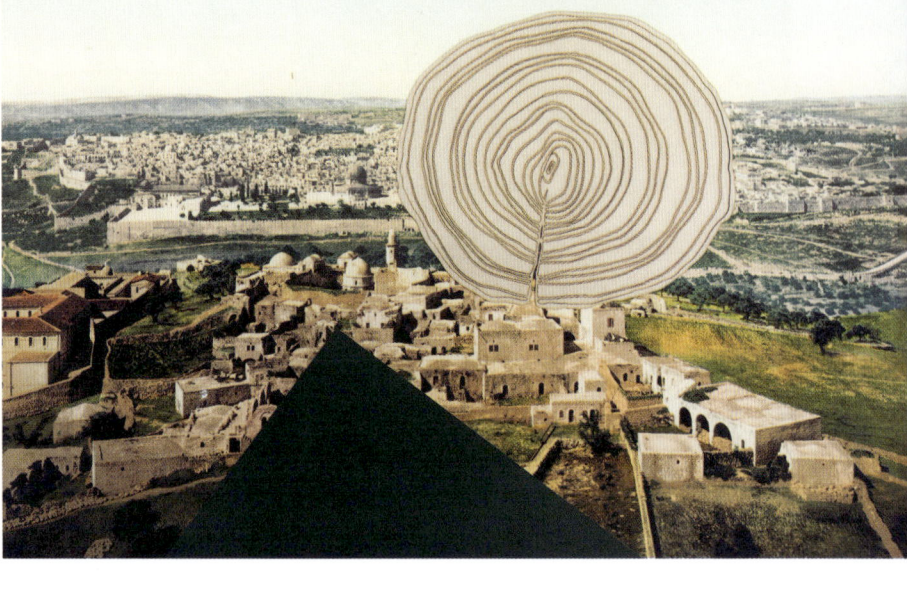

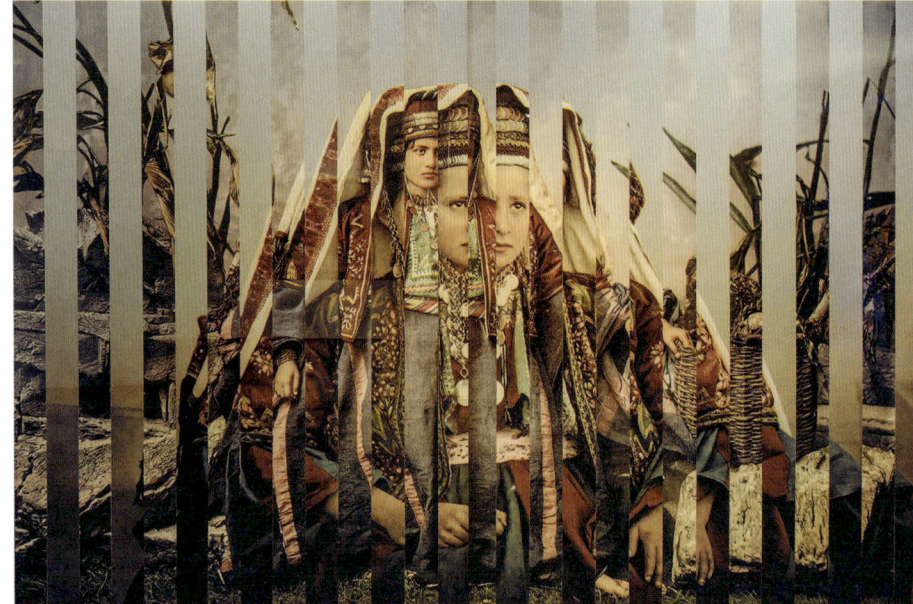

↑↑ **Map of land, Series #01**, 2019, C-P archival photography print and collage on fine art paper mounted on wood, 200 × 120 cm (78¾ × 47¼ in), Contemporary Art Platform (CAP), Kuwait

↑ **The Silk Line of Identity**, 2020, layers of collage of archival fine art C-P photography on MDF wood, diptych, overall 200 × 300 × 5 cm (28¾ × 118⅛ × 2 in), private collection of Rula Khadra

↗ **PERMANENT MONUMENTS**, 2021, prints on pigmented Plexiglas and collage on wood, 230 × 150 cm (94⅛ × 60 in)

→ **1-2 Bauhaus as imperialism**, 2019, analogue collage of archival fine art photography print mounted wood, diptych 200 × 110 cm (78¾ × 43¼ in)

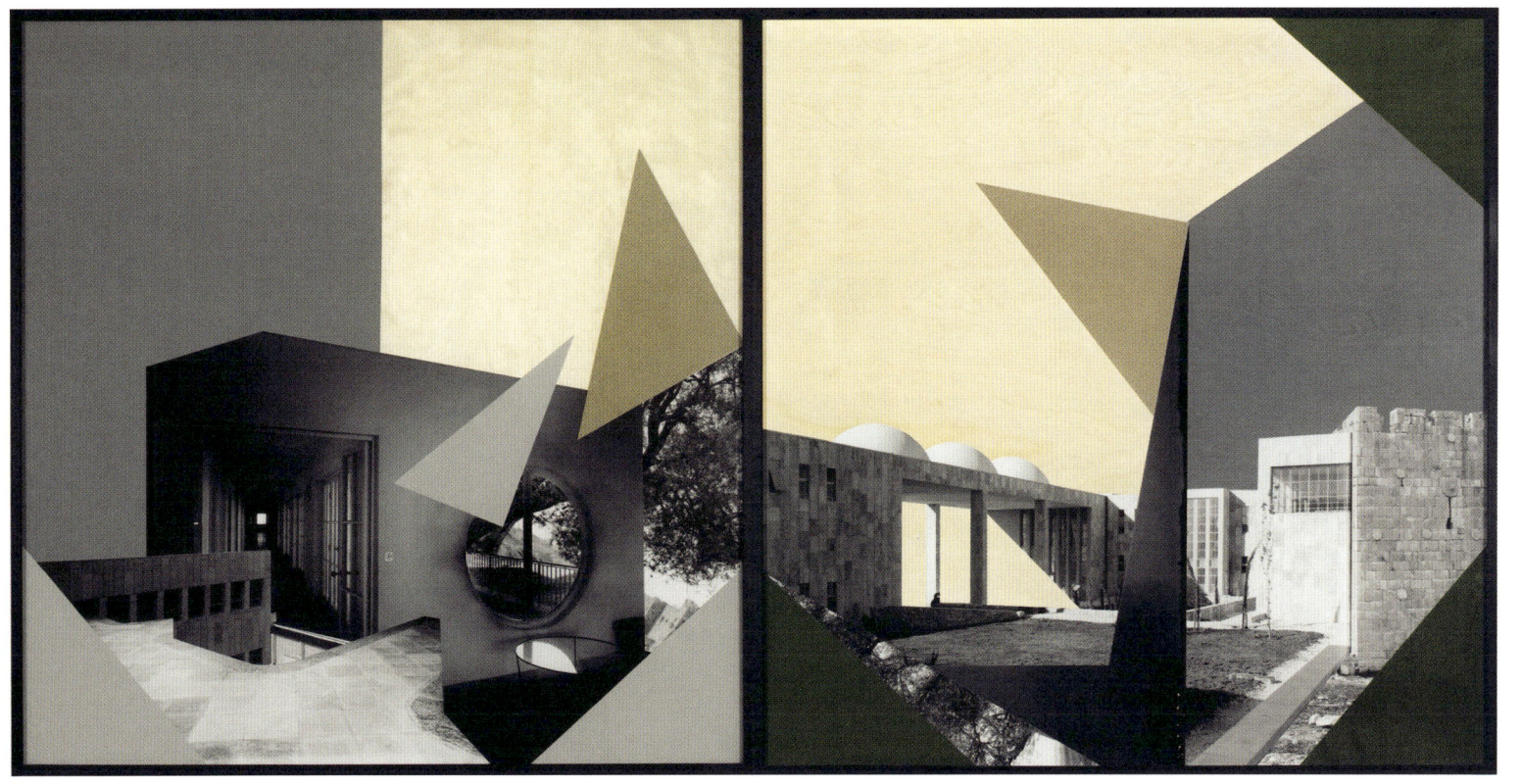

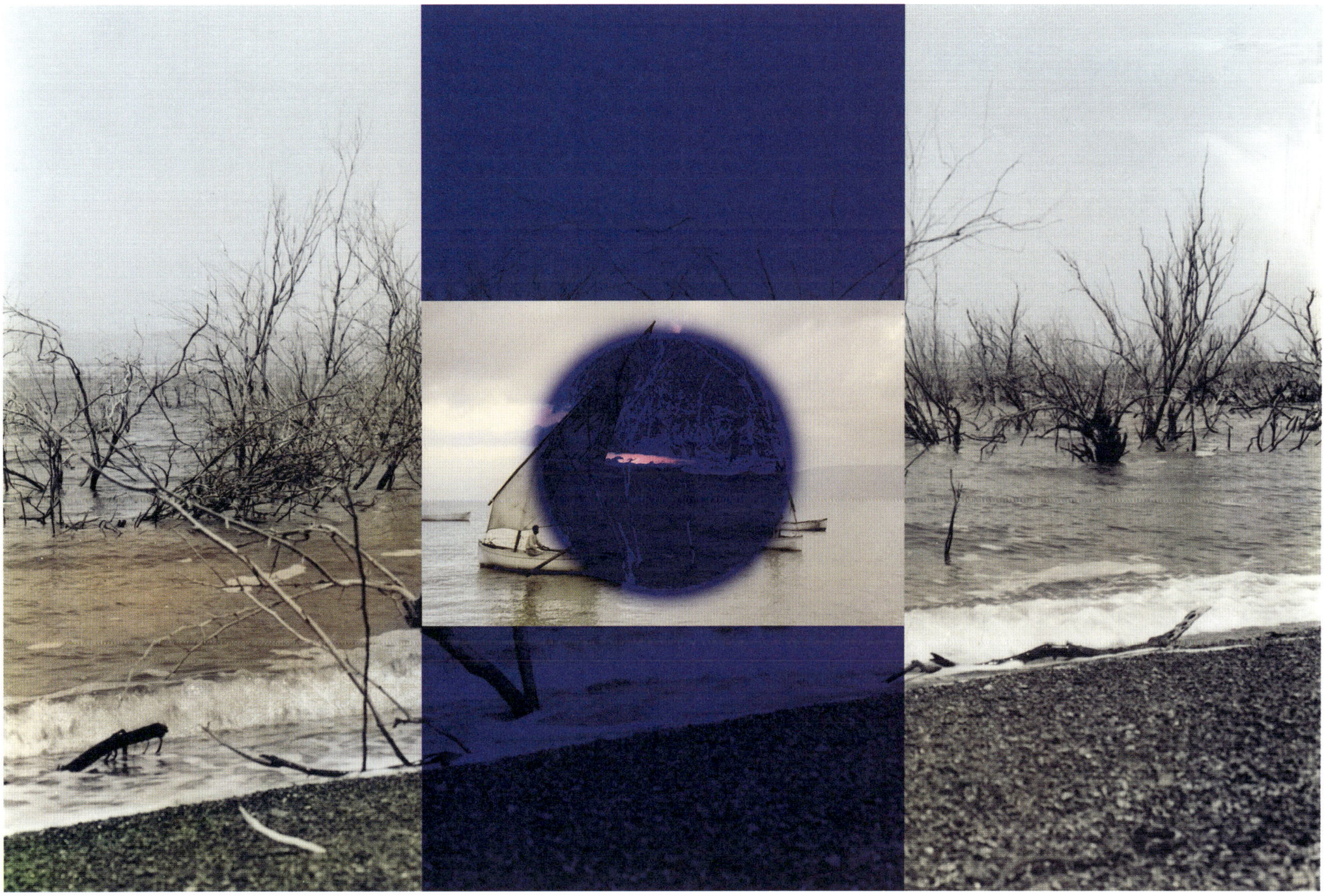

HAZEM
HARB

LYLE ASHTON
HARRIS

Collage is just one of many artistic mediums used by Lyle Ashton Harris to make works 'that explore intersections between the personal and the political, examining the impact of ethnicity, gender, and desire on the contemporary social and cultural dynamic', as he explains on his website. Harris has travelled regularly to Ghana since 2005 as a professor at New York University's Global Program in Accra, and Ghana has been a frequent presence in his work. *Oracle* (2020) is from the series 'Shadow Works' (2017–ongoing), in which Harris assembles dye sublimation prints of monochromatically photographed collages, and brings these together on patterned fabric panels made of West African cloth. Using acrylic-sprayed stencil lettering and mementos from his own archives, Harris slips personal affects into a political history with simple, sweeping juxtapositions.

Untitled (DAD) (2018) is a meticulous assembly of two-dimensional images, held together by magnets, tape and pins. What is collaged here spans decades of popular culture, archival photography and the artist's personal history. Elements include several types of photographic print, such as tintypes – direct positives taken on thin sheets of metal and coated with dark enamel or lacquer – and dye diffusion prints, commonly known as Polaroids. Harris's interest in photography was influenced by his economist grandfather, an amateur photographer who shot over 10,000 slides of family, friends and the local community. The vast collection of images in *Untitled (DAD)* is tied at its centre by a letter printed on fabric addressed to 'Thomas AKA Daddy'. It is a kind of epistolary monologue that mediates on absence, health and grief. In an expanded version of this work, which premiered at Participant Inc., New York, in 2018 and included a multi-channel video and performance, Harris presented a hybrid reimagining of the rituals of mourning and loss. The 'Blow Up' series encompasses several mixed-media and often site-specific installations, beginning in 2001 while Harris was in residence as a fellow at the American Academy in Rome, Italy. It was sparked by Harris chancing upon an advertisement for Adidas shoes that resembled Édouard Manet's *Olympia* (1863) and featured a young man of African descent giving a pedicure to the Algerian-French footballer Zinedine Zidane. Painted renditions of the exchange often feature in works from the series. For *Blow Up (Verso)* (2010–19), Harris collaborated with Ghanaian painter Nicholas Wayo (b.1976) to make an acrylic painting on wheat-flour bags, which are traditionally stitched together to make sunshades by Ghanaian fisherman. The paint seeps through the coarse, porous fabric, and inverts the image. Alongside the recurring central duo is a collation of smaller paintings of flags, portraits and team photos. In the midst of this, a small version of Manet's *Olympia* is seen blurred and floating – a tense citation. While the work is fundamentally a painting, it maintains the compositional qualities of Harris's literal collages, and reveals his ongoing interest in how images gain meaning through juxtaposition.

SKYE ARUNDHATI THOMAS

Born 1965, Bronx, New York, USA. Lives in New York.

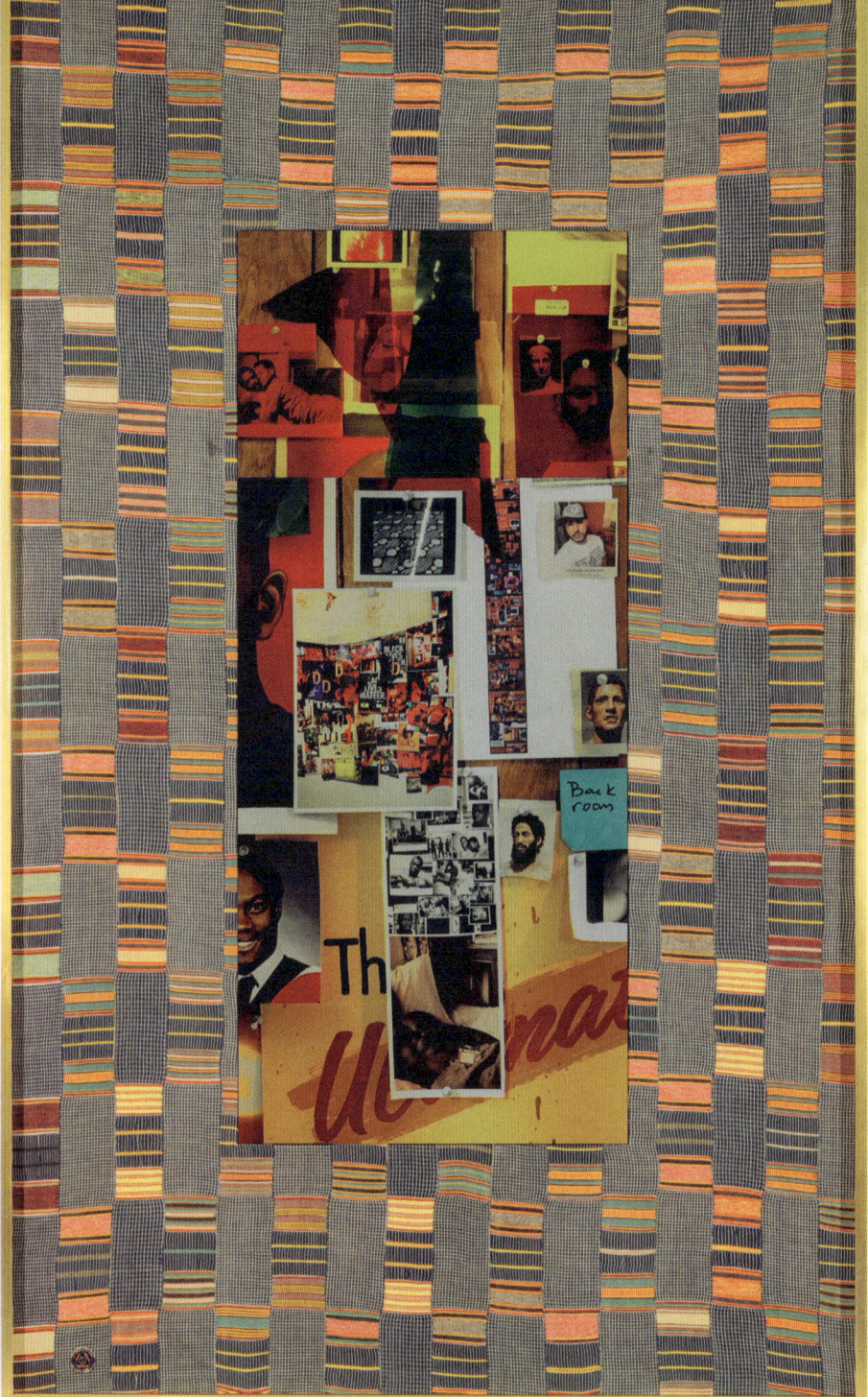

↑   Oracle, 2020, unique assemblage: Ghanaian cloth and two-dye sublimation prints, 191 × 118 × 7 cm (75¼ × 46¾ × 3 in)

→   Untitled (DAD), 2018, inkjet prints on paper, acetate and silk; and chromogenic prints, photocopies, dye diffusion transfer prints (Polaroids), newspapers, magazine covers, paper, acrylic paint, ink, gouache, record cover, tintype, magnet, tape and push-pins, c.264.2 × 254 cm (c.104 × 100 in)

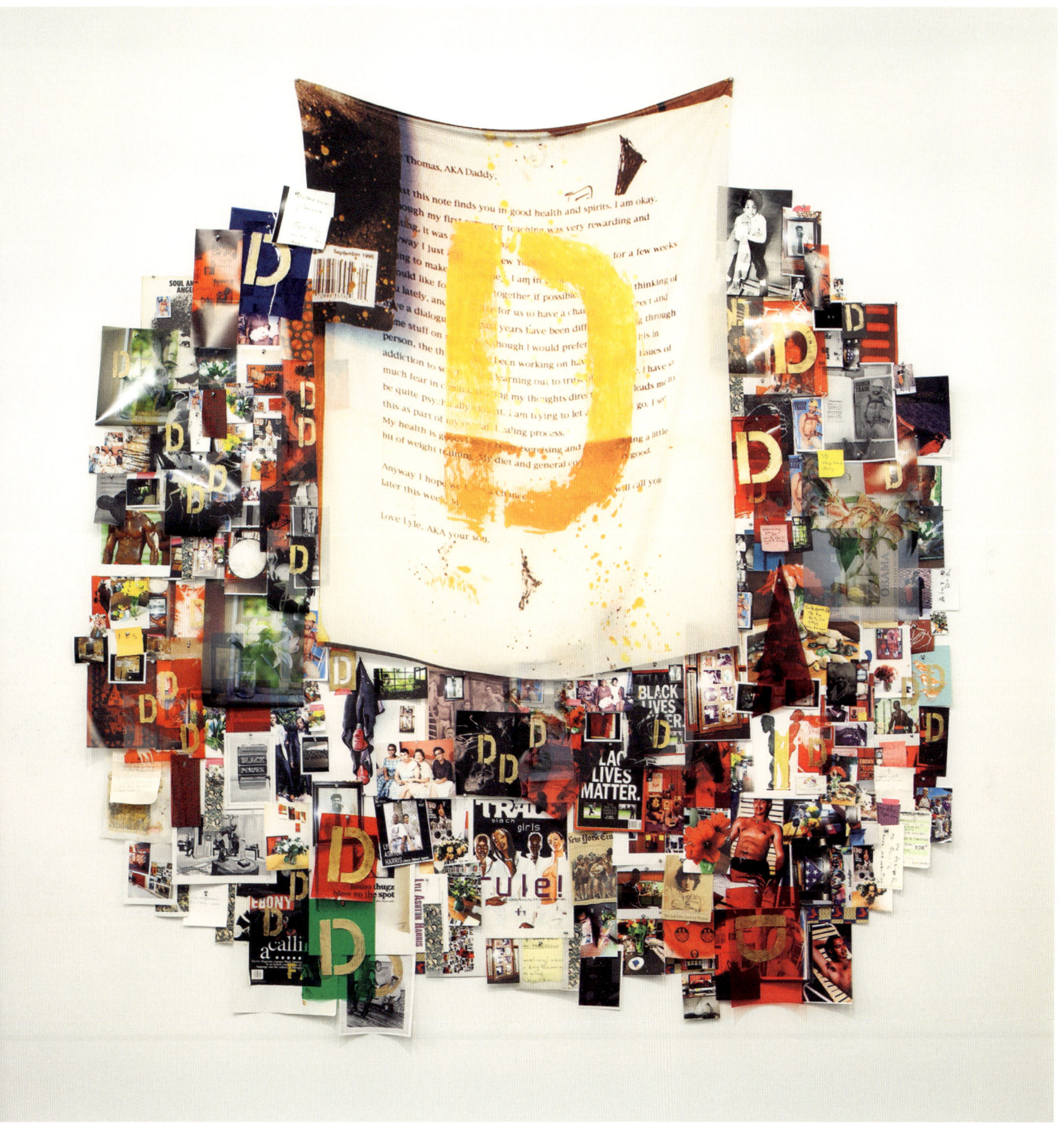

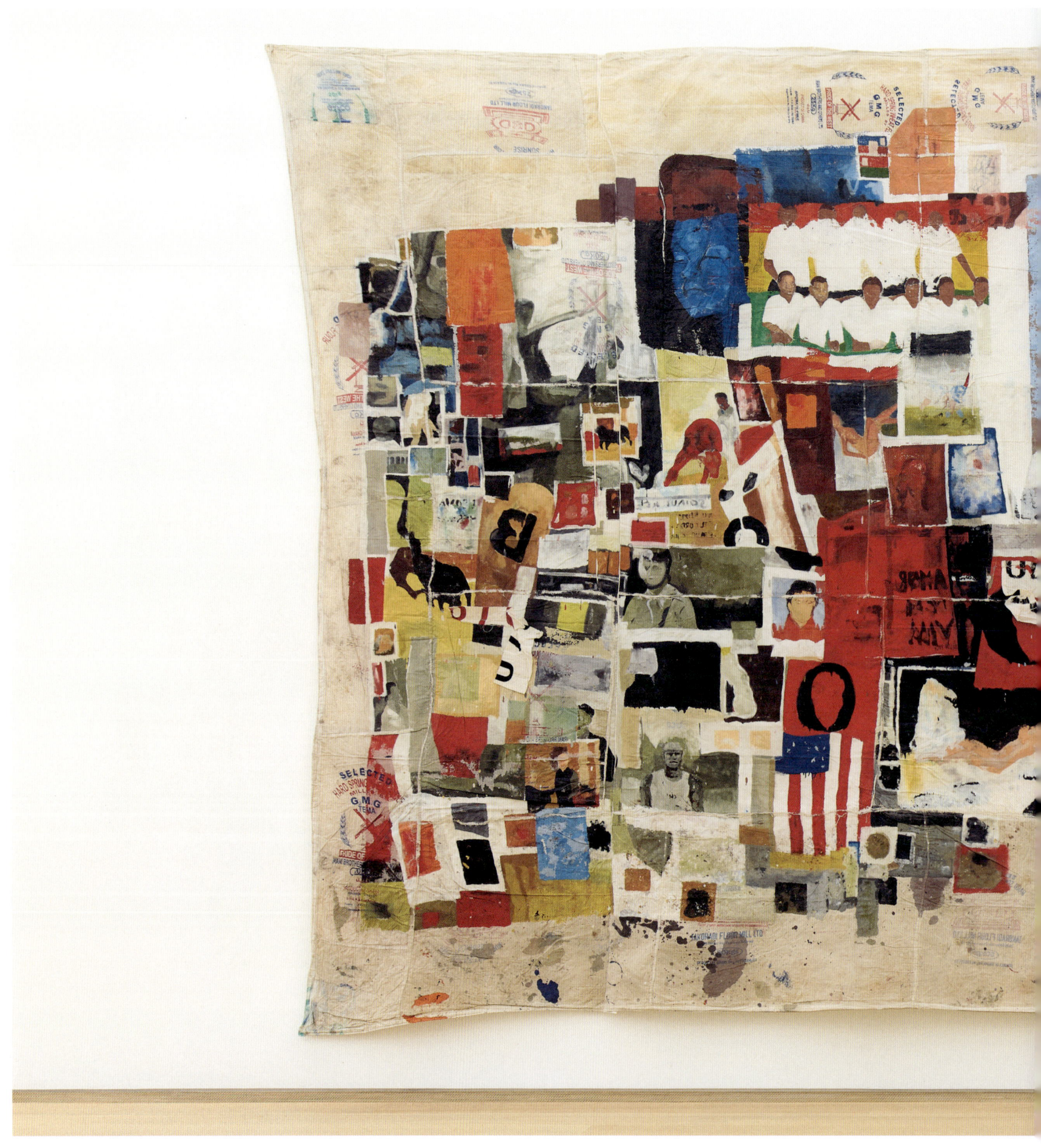

↑ **Blow Up (Verso)**, 2010–19, acrylic paint on found printed cotton cloth with muslin backing, 414 × 594.4 cm (169 × 295 in), Collection of Voorlinden Museum, Wassenaar, the Netherlands

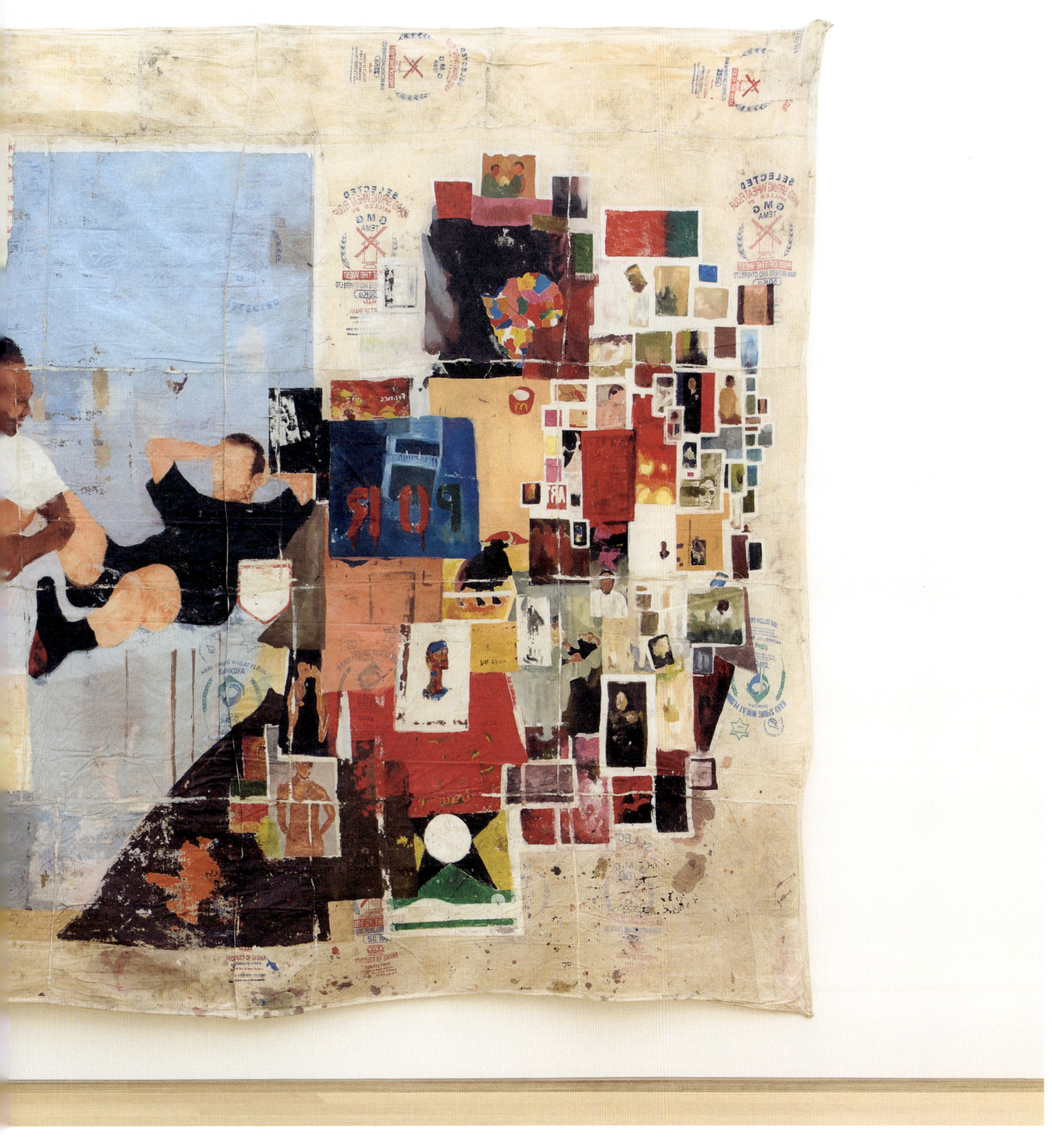

LYLE ASHTON
HARRIS

RICHARD HAWKINS

Yes, the unusually far-flung art of Richard Hawkins encompasses painting and sculpture – terms that for him, in any case, seem loosely defined – but his heart belongs to collage. His aesthetic seems to be based on the idea that anything can go with anything, if only you're obsessive enough to figure out how to make it work. The subject can be Greek statuary, gay porn, serial killers, whatever, and might be taken from mass culture, high art or esoterica. From the beginning, Hawkins's work has been unapologetically queer, both in the specific sense that it has focused on same-sex desire, and in the broader sense of being counter-normative and reading sources against the grain. Often based on deep, one might even say fanatical research, his work is typically produced in series but bears no trace of the dryness and didacticism of what is usually classified as 'research-based practice'. This is because, as the artist-critic Michelle Grabner observed in her *Artforum* review of Hawkins's exhibition at De Appel in Amsterdam in 2007, 'the artist's libido and intellectual curiosity are the actual and enthralling subjects of his work'. He has plumbed the work of left-field predecessors like visionary writer and director Antonin Artaud (1896–1948), self-taught painter/fisherman Forrest Bess (1911–77) and Butoh choreographer Tatsumi Hijikata (1928–86) with a passion.

Ankoku 124 (Bacon Branches) (2014) is titled for the designation Hijikata gave his innovative and transgressive style of dance theatre, *ankoku butoh*, or 'dance of darkness'; for Hawkins, *ankoku* 'alludes to extreme ideas of abjection, darkness and eroticism' as he explained in a 2014 interview in *The Double Negative*. The work's presentation in the form of a group of colour-coded folders conveys the artist's earnestness of intent towards his subject even while mockingly parodying that same self-seriousness. But the specific image that is repeated seven times (once partly obscured) at different scales, sometimes in monochrome and sometimes in colour, is Francis Bacon's (1909–92) works the English artist based on an 1888 Vincent van Gogh self-portrait that had been destroyed in the Second World War and which he therefore knew only in reproduction – an artist's attempt to reach across time to a precursor who had cast a spell on him. This is exactly what Hawkins attempts to do in return. Inspired by the scrapbooks in which Hijikata recorded his sometimes perverse reflections, often inspired, in turn, by Western painting, Hawkins assembled images and handwritten texts in similar fashion – Hijikata's books were paired with Hawkins's own work in a 2014 exhibition at Tate Liverpool, UK – Hawkins assembled images and handwritten texts in similar fashion. The free-associative results of the artist's immersion in his subject matter place his work in unconstrained dialogue with a ramifying network of imagined interlocutors. As Hawkins himself observed in the same 2014 interview, 'There are so many rabbit holes in here to fall down, if you're interested enough.'

BARRY SCHWABSKY

Born 1961, Mexia, Texas, USA. Lives in Los Angeles, California, USA.

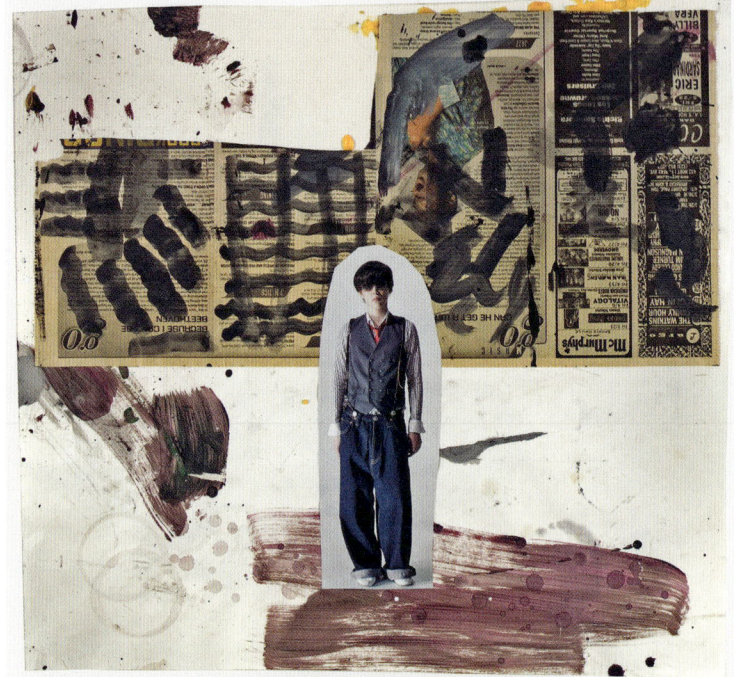

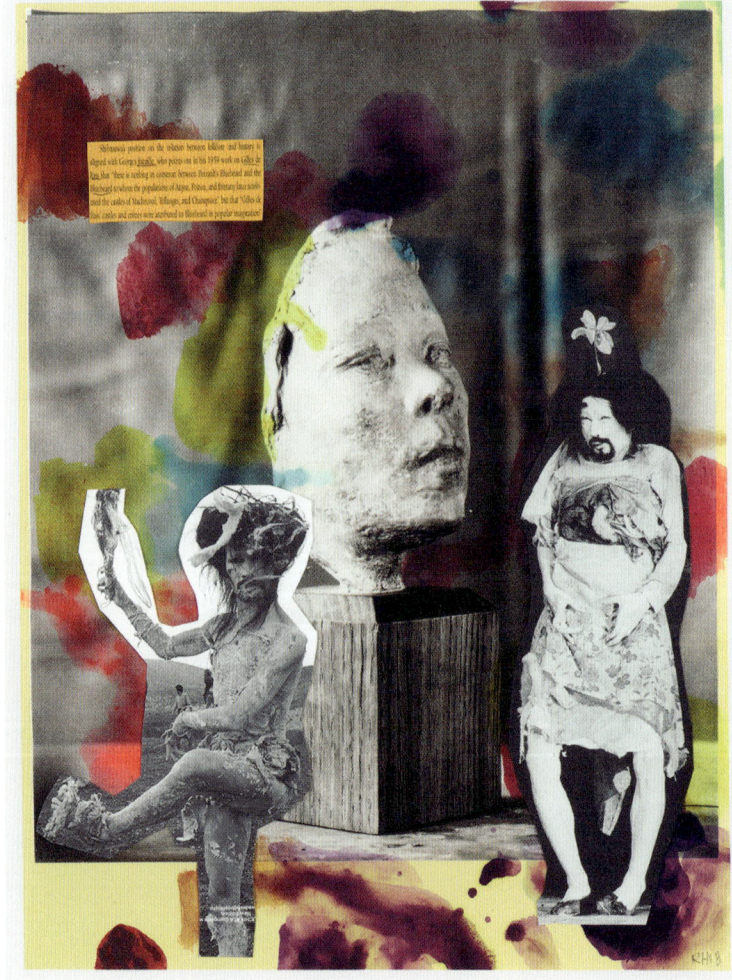

↑↑   **Shinjuku Boy (#3)**, 2008, collage, 51 × 57 cm (31⅛ × 22½ in)

↑   **Gilles de Rais**, 2018, collage, 42.5 × 32 cm (16¾ × 12⅝ in)

→   **Ankoku 124 (Bacon Branches)**, 2014, collage, 68.7 × 79 cm (27 × 31⅛ in)

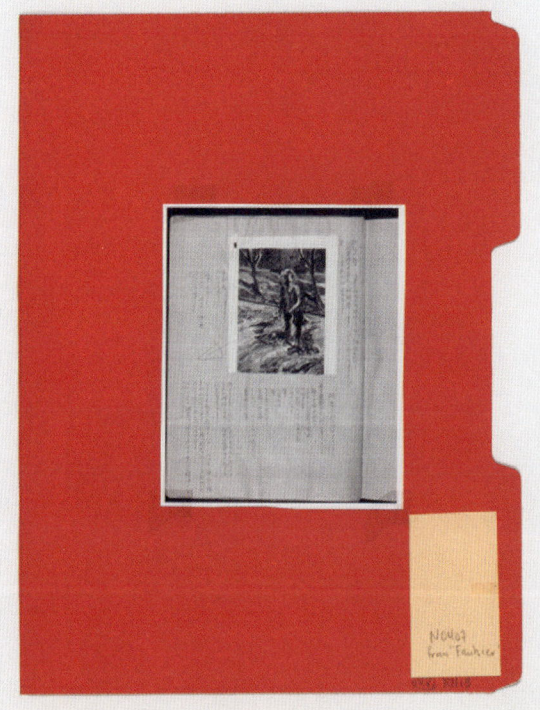

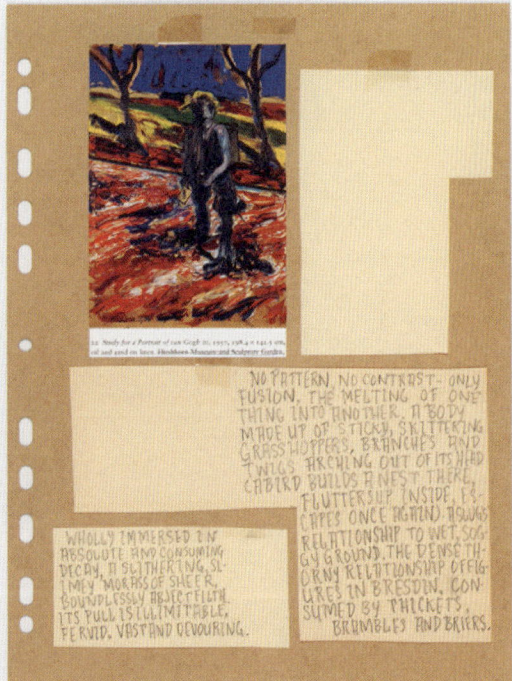

NO PATTERN, NO CONTRAST- ONLY THING INTO ANOTHER. A BODY MADE UP OF STICKS, SKITTERING GRASSHOPPERS, BRANCHES AND TWIGS ARCHING OUT OF ITS HEAD A BIRD BUILDS A NEST THERE, FLUTTERS UP INSIDE, ES-CAPES ONCE AGAIN) ALWAYS RELATIONSHIP TO WET, SOG-GY GROUND. THE DENSE THORNY RELATIONSHIP OF FIG-URES IN BRESDIN, CON-SUMED BY THICKETS, BRAMBLES AND BRIERS.

WHOLLY IMMERSED IN ABSOLUTE AND CONSUMING DECAY, A SLITHERING, SLIMEY MORASS OF SHEER, BOUNDLESSLY ABJECT FILTH. ITS PULL IS ILLIMITABLE, FERVID, VAST AND DEVOURING.

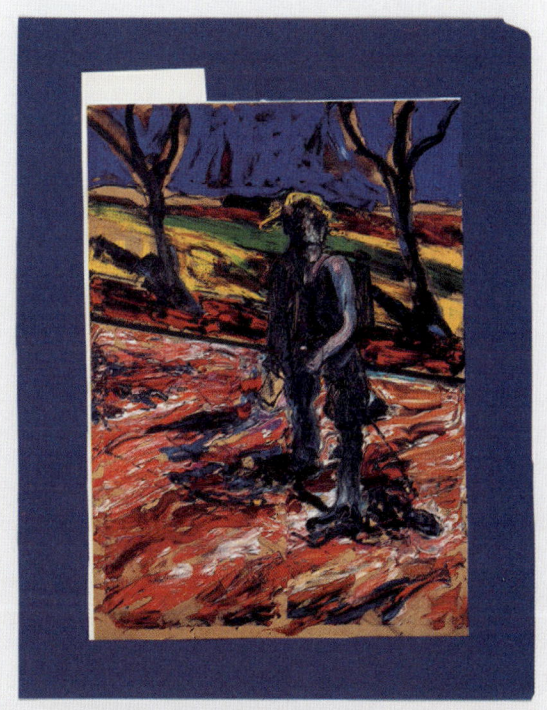

On Material II Fautrier[1]

Hijikata Tatsumi

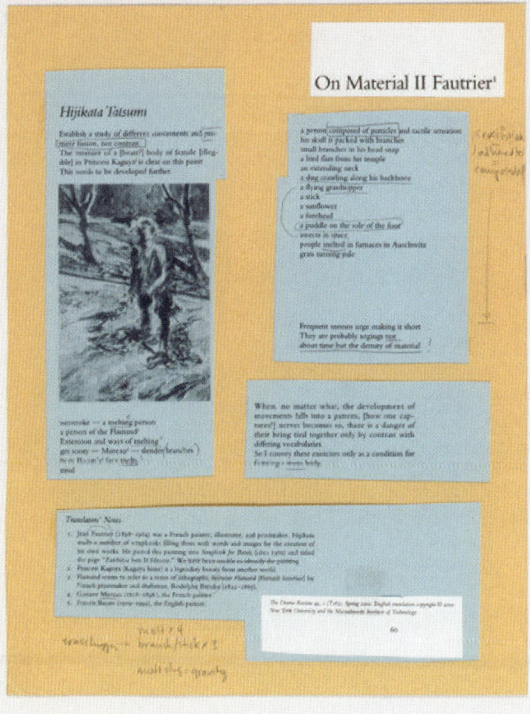

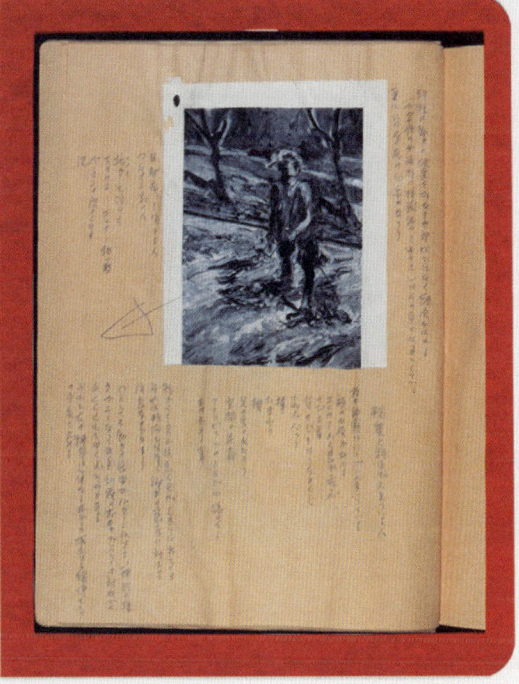

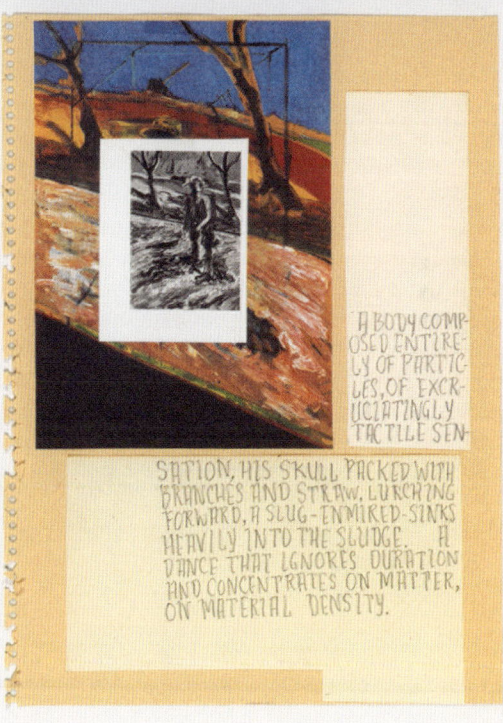

A BODY COMP-OSED ENTIRE-LY OF PARTIC-LES, OF EXCR-UCIATINGLY TACTILE SEN-SATION, HIS SKULL PACKED WITH BRANCHES AND STRAW, LURCHING FORWARD, A SLUG-ENMIRED-SINKS HEAVILY INTO THE SLUDGE. A DANCE THAT IGNORES DURATION AND CONCENTRATES ON MATTER, ON MATERIAL DENSITY.

ARTURO HERRERA

Born in Venezuela, educated in the United States and based in Germany, Arturo Herrera began to work with paper collage soon after he received his MFA from the University of Illinois at Chicago in 1992. It was a choice made out of sheer need as he initially could not afford oil and canvas and had to work on a modest scale in a shared living space. Growing up in Caracas, a city full of prime examples of modernist art and architecture, had imbued Herrera with a deep reverence for the abstract tradition, especially the biomorphic sculptures of Jean Arp (1886–1966), the filigree nets in the sculptures of Gego (1912–94), Gio Ponti's *Villa Planchart* (1953–7) in Caracas and kinetic art. But this exposure also sensitized him to the flawed promises of mid-century Latin American modernism , which disappointed hopes for a more stable democratic and just social order. Among Herrera's earliest source material was a children's colouring book that he bought at a charity shop in 1995 and from which he cut and combined two figurative elements to form a fantastical creature. A recurring starting point for his compositions are fragments of line-drawn Disney characters, with favourites being Bambi, Snow White and the Seven Dwarves: they are 'ready-made, contaminated modernist shapes,' the artist explained in a lecture at the Pérez Art Museum Miami, Florida, in 2016. Enlarging these sections beyond recognition into organic shapes – see, for example, the red line drawing of the middle layer of the work on page 106 – allows him to approach abstraction and non-linear narration. In the left-hand image on page 105, Herrera flattened a book cover and sandwiched it between a turquoise and white screenprint as well as more printed and painted paper and canvas elements, with motifs such as the Wicked Queen's castle. Herrera's main tool is the utility knife, with which he sliced the positive-negative spaces from the blue paper mask of the right-hand image on page 105. The materials and techniques that he harnesses range from found bits of paper to repurposed photographs, photocopies and ink drawings, from relief, etching, digital pigment printing, collagraphy, pochoir, aquatint and cyanotype to brushed oil, airbrushed acrylic and silkscreened gouache. A photocopy might show an earlier work of his, and a duo-tone print might be based on a book page that he had drawn on. The viewer is not expected to recognize a particular technique or reference, but is invited to engage with the multiple steps of translation between media and mark-making. When in 2014 Herrera finally began to paint in earnest, he returned to his first principle of working with what was around him in the studio: he has brushed onto, silkscreened and airbrushed supports such as felt sheets, but most recently also the kinds of cloth shopping bags that are ubiquitous in his hometown of Berlin (page 107).

PIA GOTTSCHALLER

Born 1959, Caracas, Venezuela. Lives in Berlin, Germany.

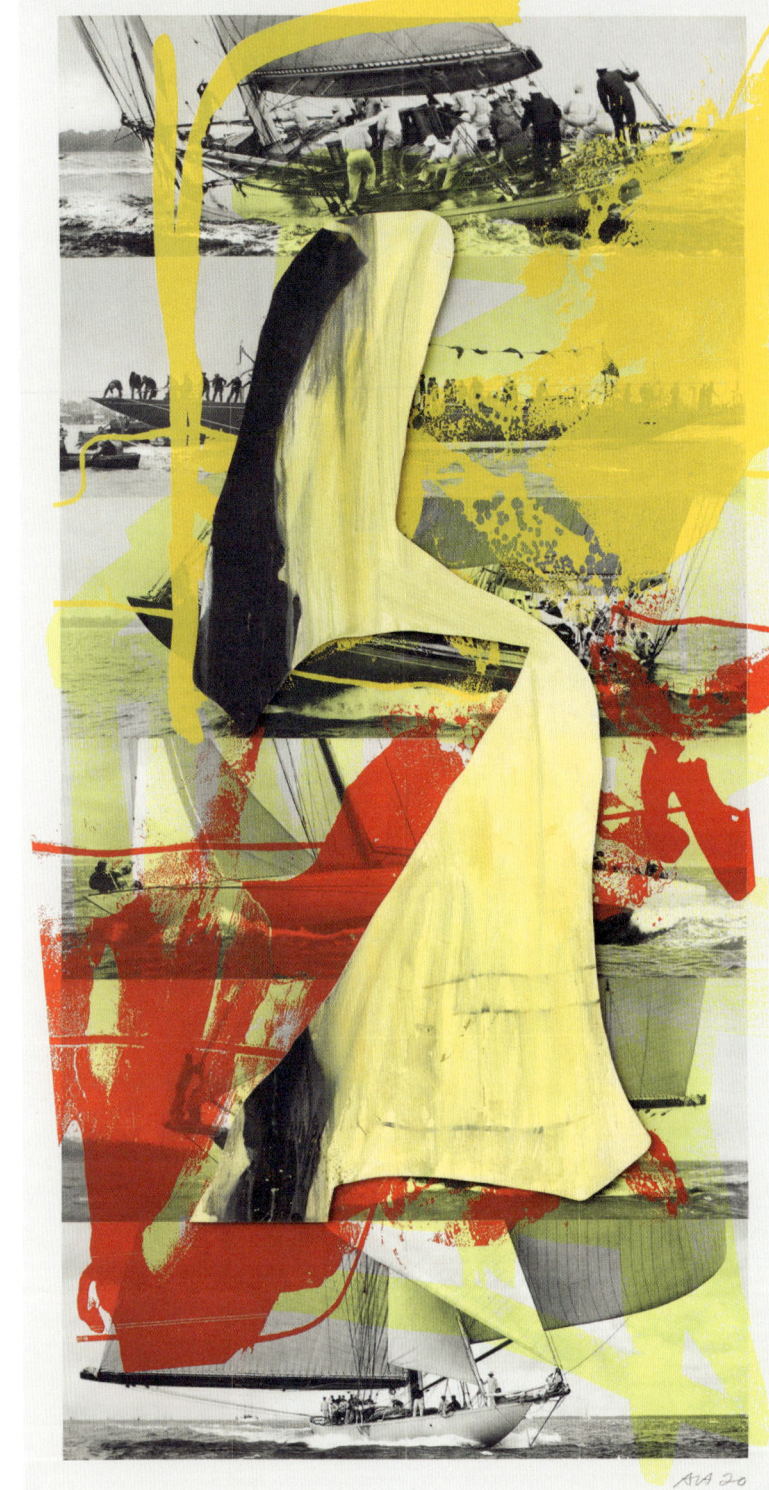

↑ **Untitled**, 2020, collage, mixed media and wood on board, 182 × 93 cm (71⅝ × 36⅝ in)

→ **Untitled**, 2020, collage and mixed media on silkscreen print, 56 × 39.5 cm (22 × 15½ in)

→→ **Untitled**, 2020, collage, mixed media and felt on board, 182 × 93 cm (71⅝ × 36⅝ in)

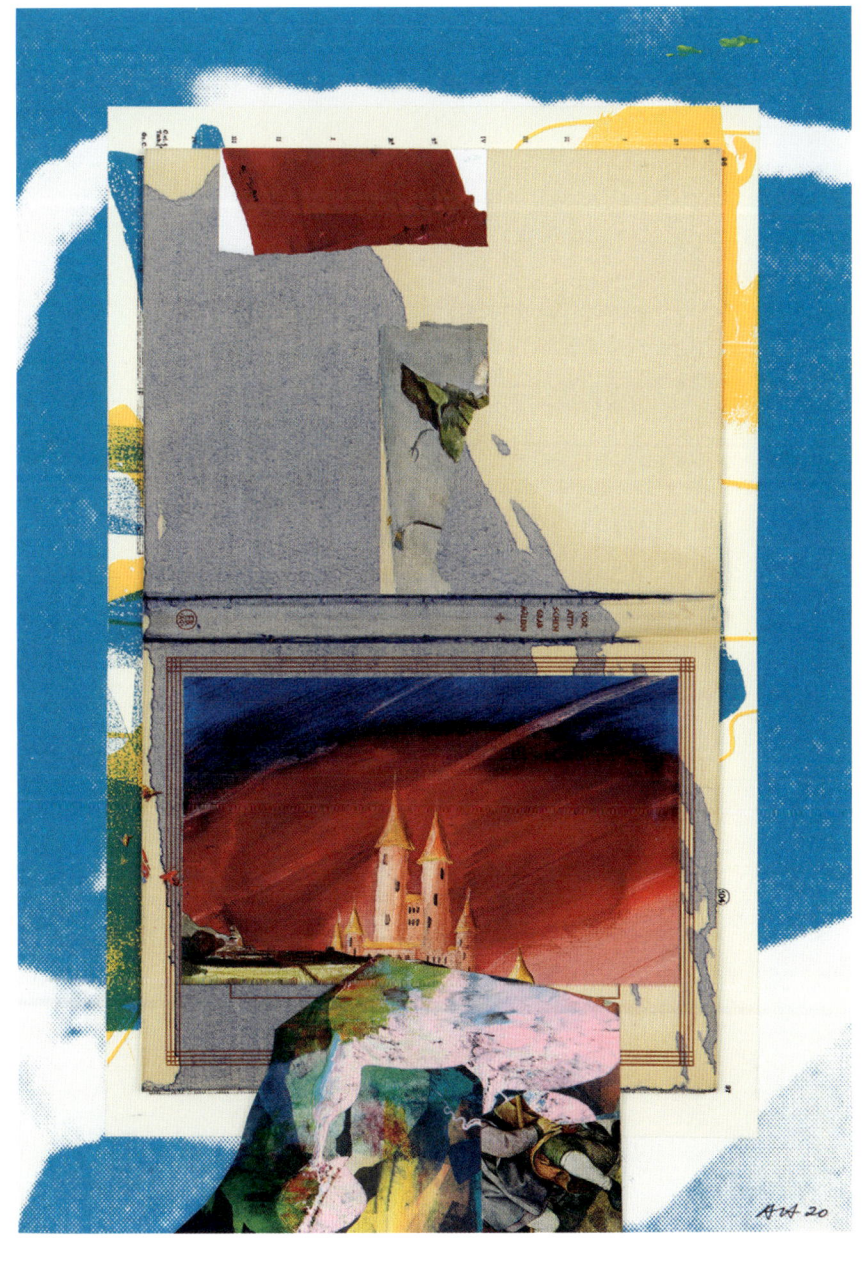

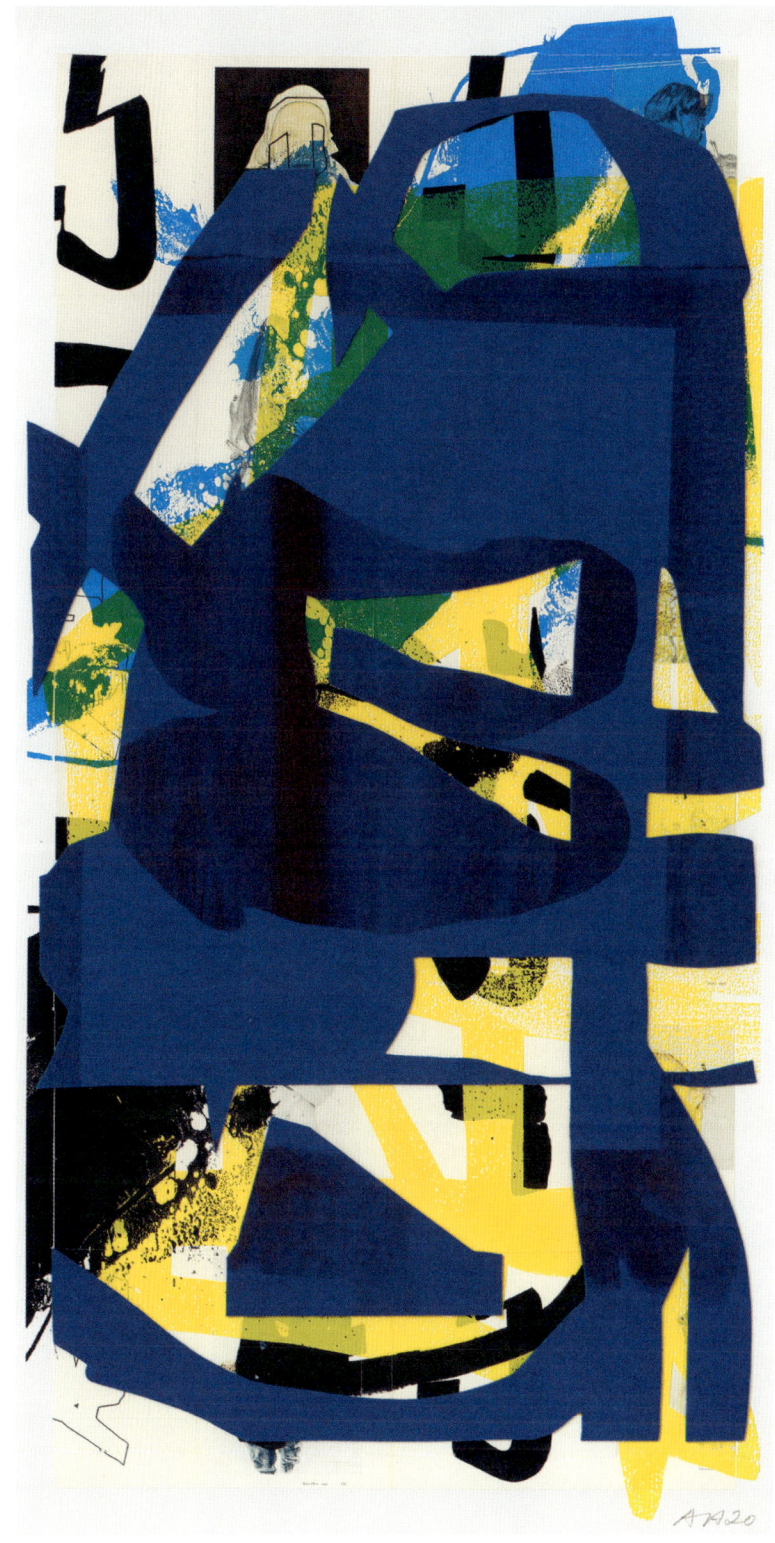

ARTURO HERRERA

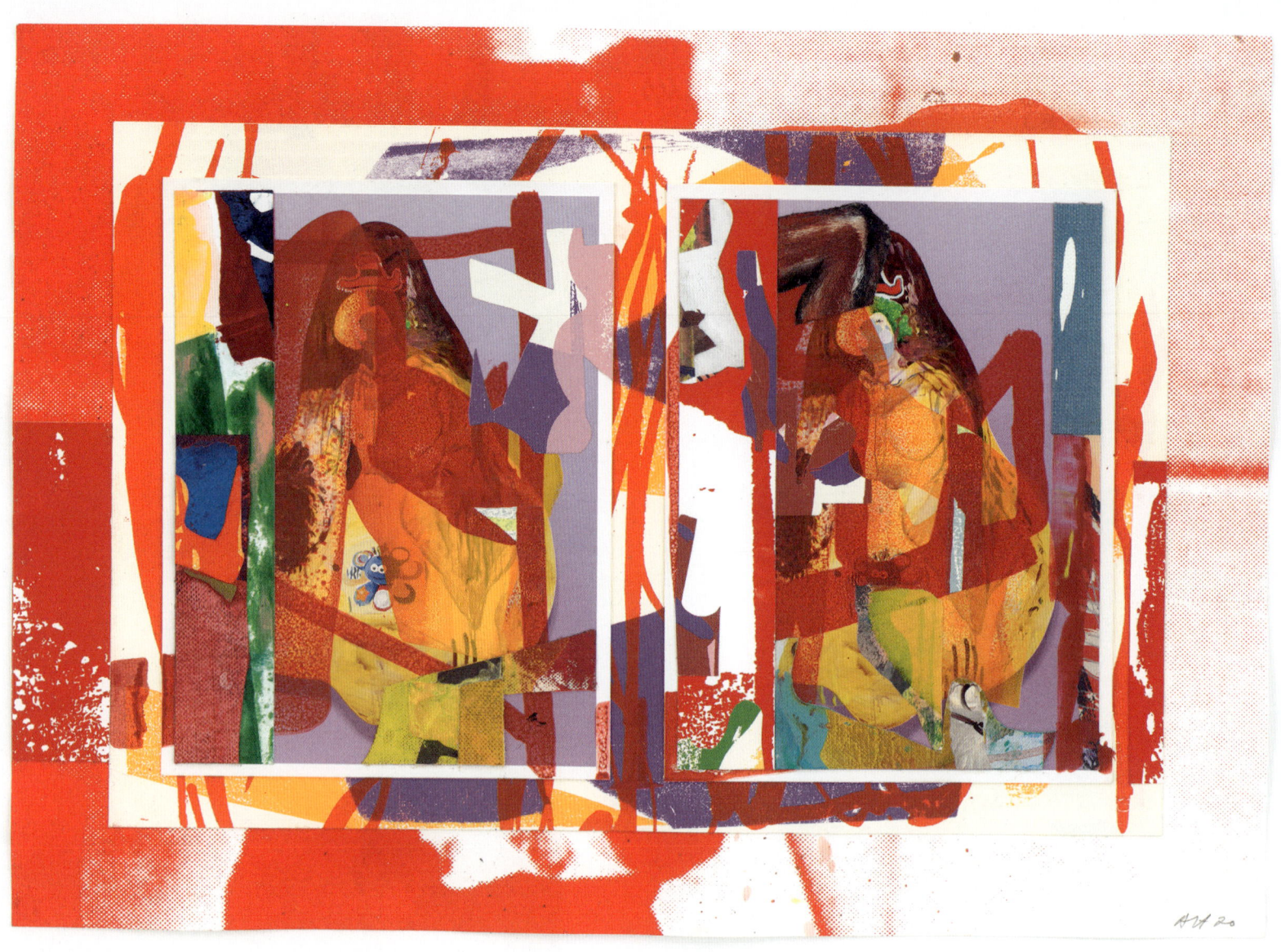

↑   **Untitled**, 2020, collage and mixed media on silkscreen print, 39.5 × 56 cm (15½ × 22 in)

→   **Untitled**, 2020, collage and mixed media on cotton bag, 72 × 38 cm (28⅜ × 15 in)

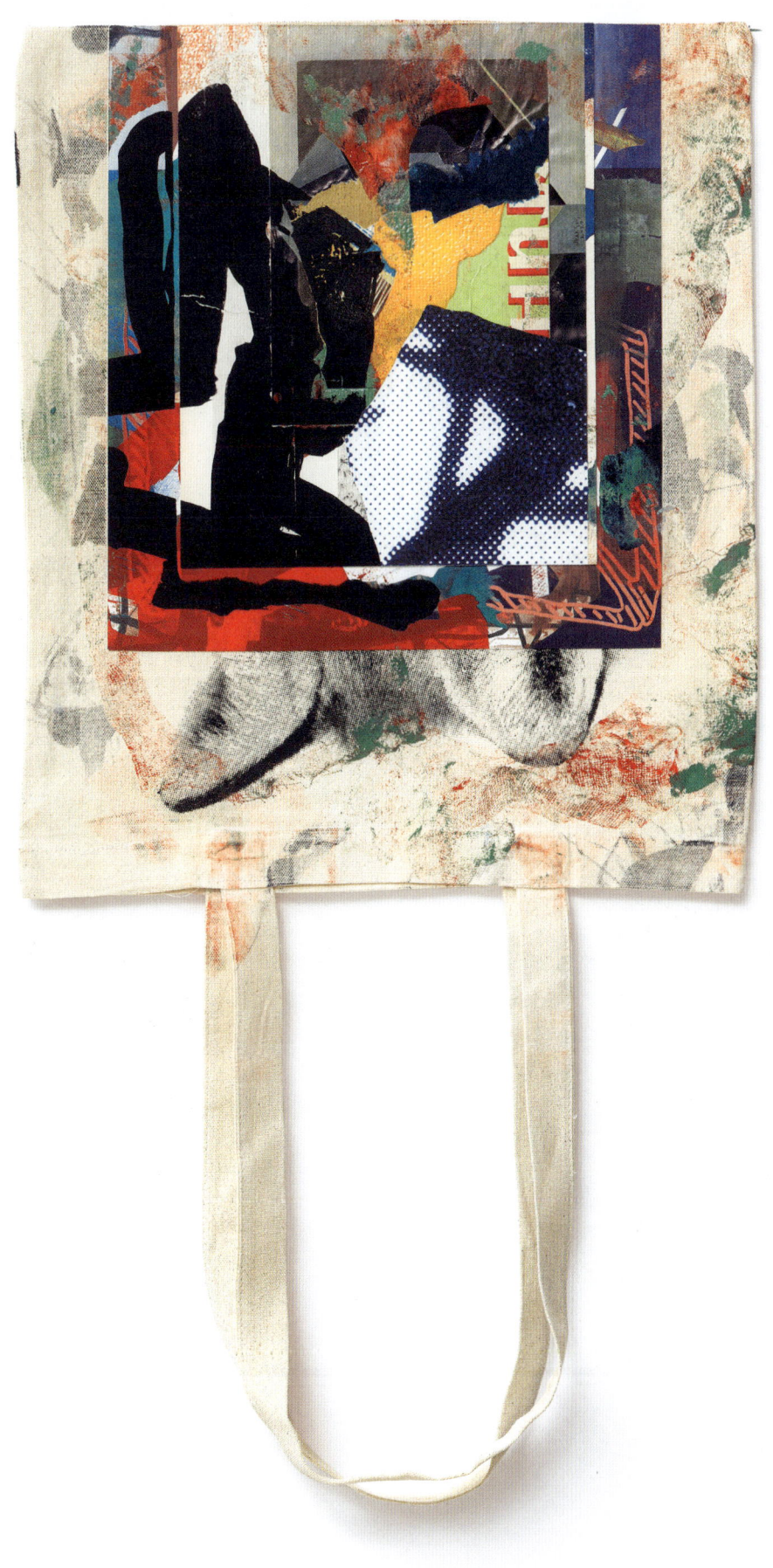

ARTURO
HERRERA

THOMAS HIRSCHHORN

'Making a collage means pasting together existing elements of reality to create a new world that did not exist before,' Thomas Hirschhorn stated in his text 'New Pixel-Collage' in 2016. 'A collage requires at least two different elements brought together, but can be made with more,' he continued. And with Hirschhorn, more is usually the answer. The artist has been producing his signature sprawling and information-loaded sculptures since the 1990s. His most minimal gesture consists of the act of placing a single object, easily confused with refuse, into a random urban environment, as in his 1992 project *Jemand kümmert sich um Meine Arbeit (Somebody takes care of my work)*. His maximal (and more common) gestures are exemplified in the series of temporary monuments, such as *Gramsci Monument* (2013), that take over vast outdoor spaces and essentially function as commemorative event hubs, replete with radio, newspaper, theatre stage, museum, art school, community-sourced employees and more. Most of Hirschhorn's works would qualify as collage, according to his own definition. For in sculptural as well as two-dimensional form he often repurposes existing images, objects and texts. Duct tape, plastic, cardboard, aluminium foil and permanent markers – common and effective materials – act as the glue that ties the various elements together, usually in excessive measure. 'Quality = No! Energy = Yes!', as his dictum confirms. For Hirschhorn, politics and aesthetics are inherently tied, and the way we make, circulate and consume images deeply informs our way of being in the world. The series 'Pixel-Collage' (2015–17) includes photographs of war casualties taken and circulated by civilians. The disfigured corpses are overlaid with more quotidian imagery, which in turn has been partially pixelated, signalling a kind of reversal of the censorship that normally prevents such portrayal of war from circulating in public. We should dare to confront the reality of the world we are living in, the collages seem to say, without words. The political commitment, and the material and verbal excessiveness which permeates Hirschhorn's practice, channels the early twentieth-century Dada movement and the photomontages of artists such as Raoul Hausmann (1886–1971) and Hannah Höch (1889–1978), sometimes quite directly as in the tongue-in-cheek *I-nfluencer-Poster (#Collage)* (2021), where Höch's famous 1924 collage *Mischling (Half Caste)*, which packs its own political punch, is reproduced on a poster-sized blow-up of a social media feed. 'A collage owns the capacity of non-exclusion, a collage always remains suspicious, and a collage is not taken seriously' reads the final handwritten post. Through this performative materialization of the digital feed, Hirschhorn reflects on the construction and circulation of images, highlighting the subversive potential that the practice of collage has always held.

MARGRETHE TROENSEGAARD

Born 1957, Bern, Switzerland. Lives in Paris, France.

↑ **Gravity and Grace (Chat-Poster)**, 2020, cardboard, wood, prints, felt pen, adhesive tape and crystals, 240 × 123 cm (94½ × 48⅜ in)

↗ **Pixel-Collage n°19**, 2015, prints, tape and plastic foil, 40 × 51 cm (15¾ × 20⅛ in), private collection

→ **Pixel-Collage n°12**, 2015, prints, tape and plastic foil, 28 × 46 cm (11 × 18⅛ in)

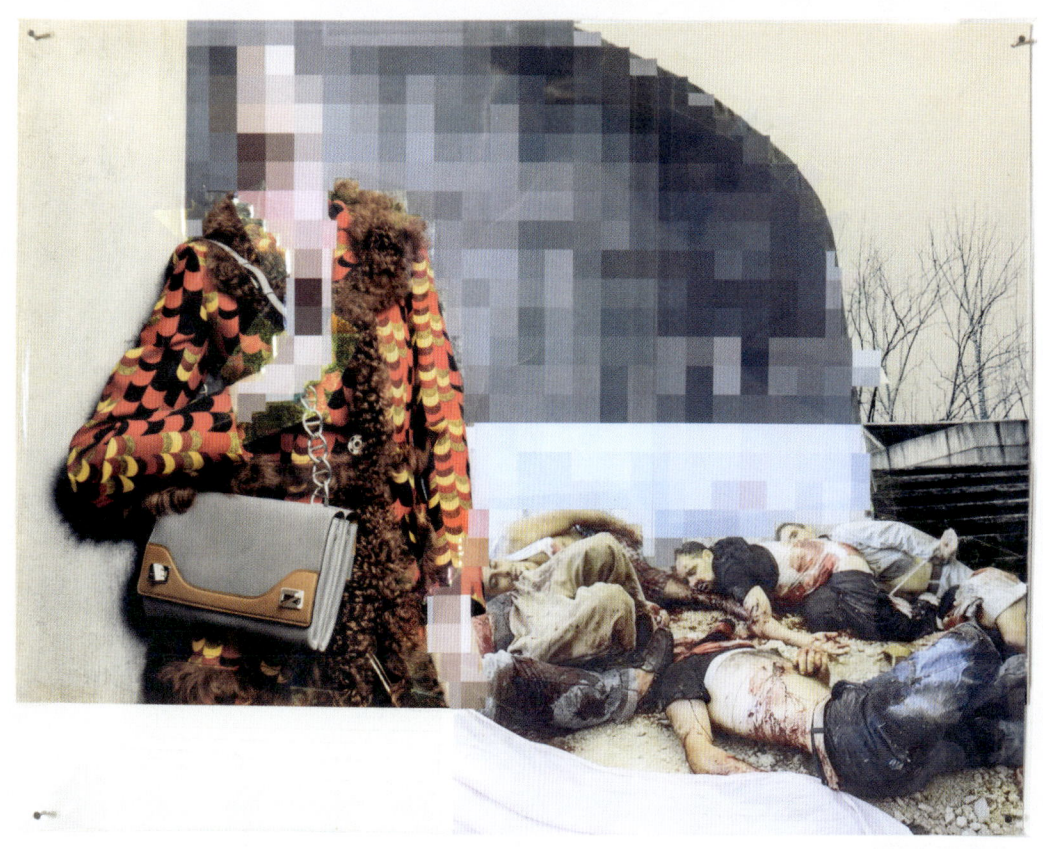

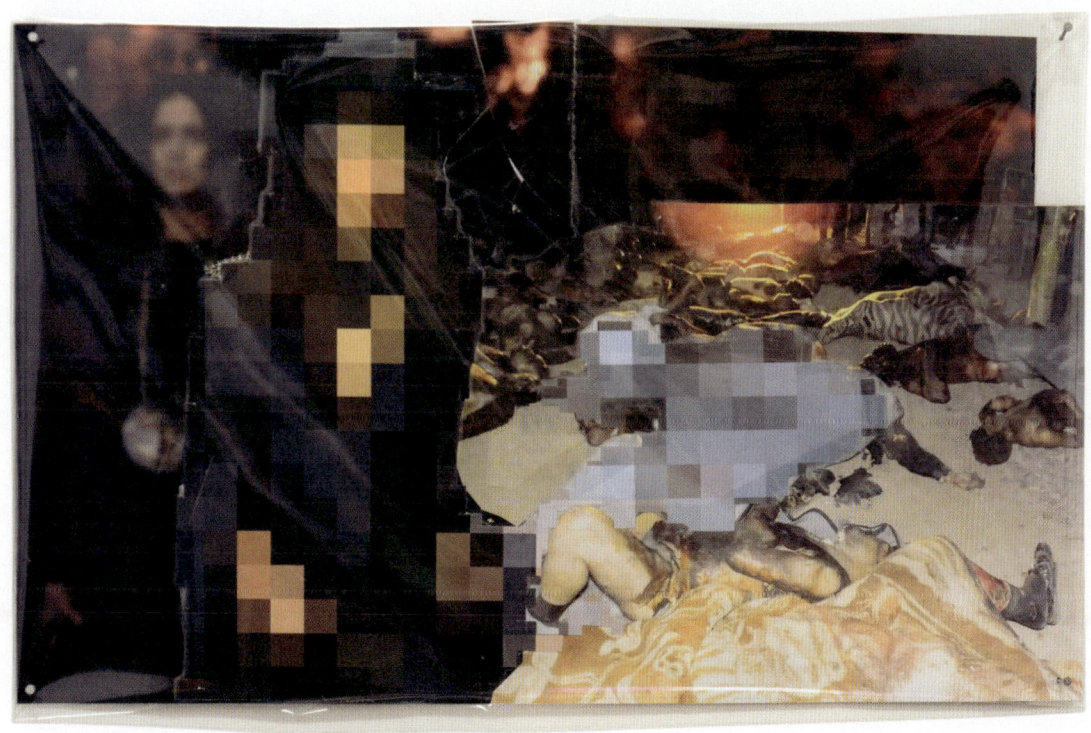

THOMAS HIRSCHHORN

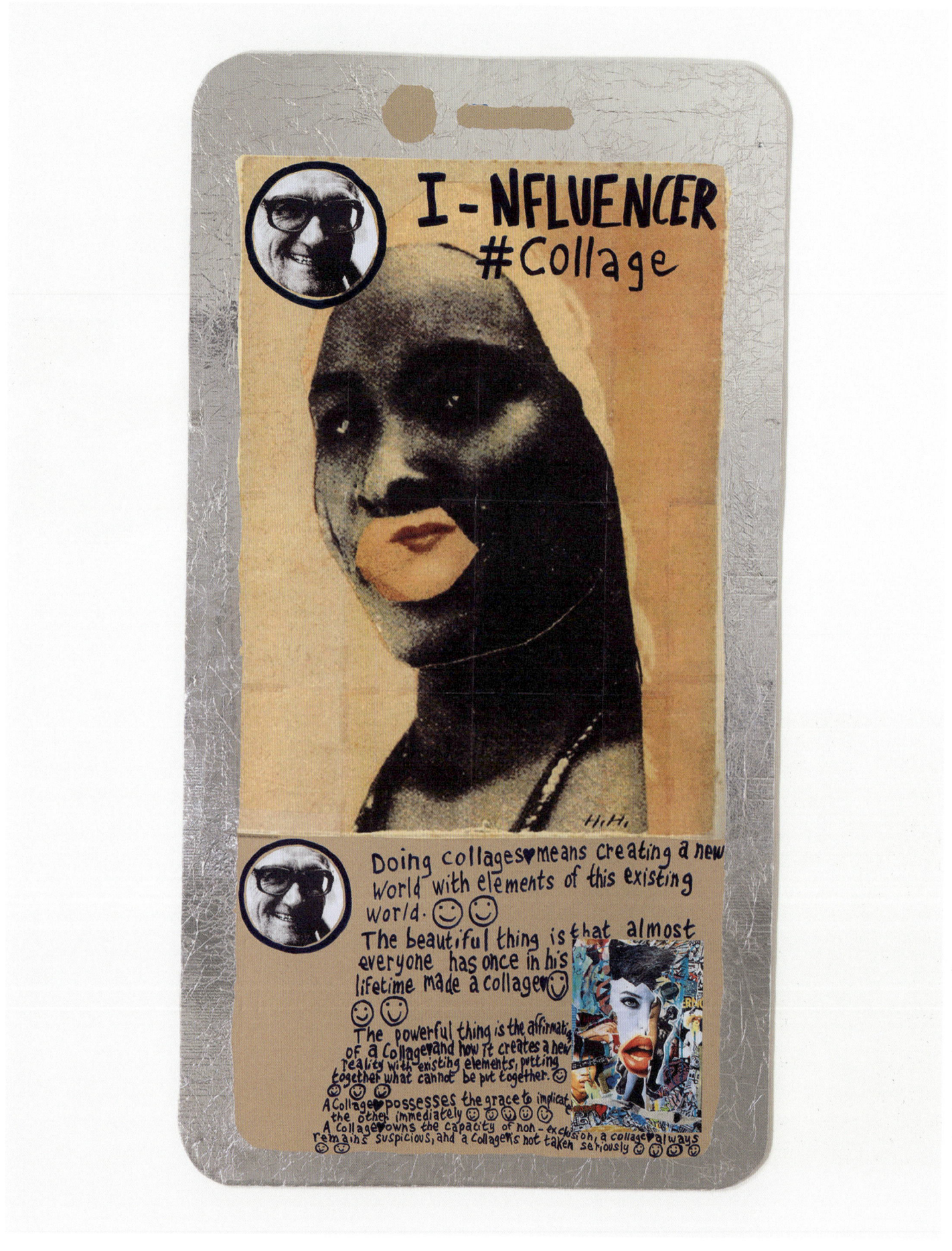

↑   I-nfluencer-Poster (#Collage), 2021, wood, cardboard, prints, felt pen, aluminium foil and adhesive tape, 240 × 130 cm (94½ × 51⅛ in)

→   I-nfluencer-Poster (#Monument), 2021, wood, cardboard, prints, felt pen, aluminium foil and adhesive tape, 240 × 130 cm (94½ × 51⅛ in)

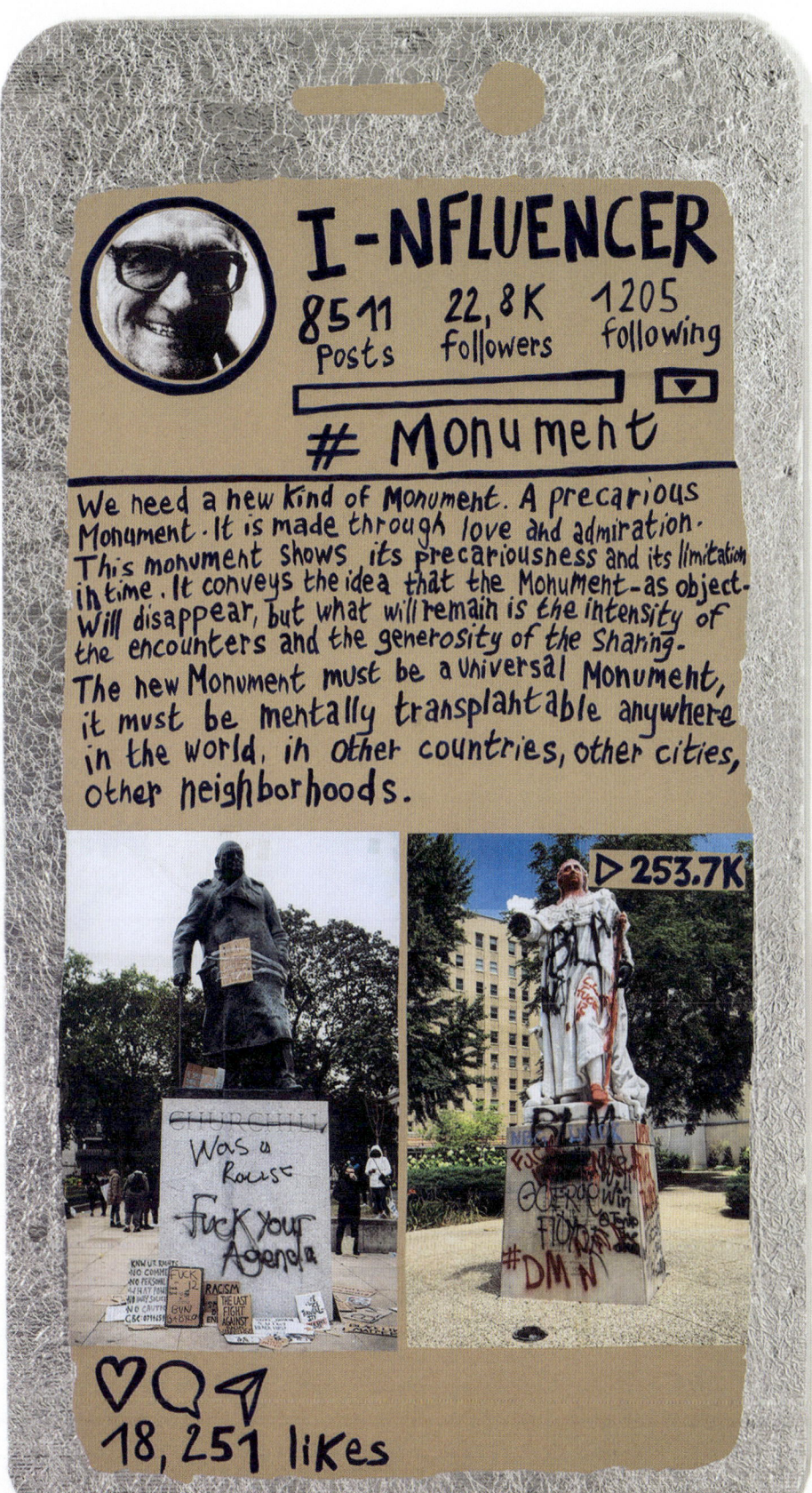

I-NFLUENCER

8511 Posts **22,8K** followers **1205** following

Monument

We need a new kind of Monument. A precarious Monument. It is made through love and admiration. This monument shows its precariousness and its limitation in time. It conveys the idea that the Monument-as object- Will disappear, but what will remain is the intensity of the encounters and the generosity of the Sharing. The new Monument must be a universal Monument, it must be mentally transplantable anywhere in the world, in other countries, other cities, other neighborhoods.

▷ **253.7K**

♡ ⬭ ⏵
18,251 likes

GEORGIE
HOPTON

Georgie Hopton's multimedia practice spans collage, textiles, printmaking and photography to create images inspired by nature. Her work is largely informed by experiences tending her own garden, from which she harvests flowers, vegetables and fruits that inspire – and at times are incorporated into – her work. Hopton's collages are abstract interpretations of familiar themes, such as still life and portraiture, but her use of contrasting patterns and textures adds greater density to the images and reflects a lifetime of amassing a wide range of materials. 'This long-term love of richly detailed surfaces is given full throttle in the exuberant and surprising encounters within her collages,' as critic Louisa Buck wrote in a catalogue essay to accompany Hopton's 2019 solo exhibition at Lyndsey Ingram Gallery, London. In *Parliament* (2019) the shapes of the paper cut-outs create the outlines of flowers, yet Hopton's use of floral designs turns each blossom into its own bouquet, enriching the work with further layers and complexity. The multiplicity of motifs in this work also challenges the viewer's sense of scale, where we could be looking at a close-up of one flower or a meadow full of blooms in varying sizes and colours. This is a common quality of Hopton's work, with the artist often using a blend of large and small prints that are dynamic and pleasantly disorienting. For *Geisha* (2021) Hopton has created an interpretation of the fabric flowers and hair ornaments (*kanzashi*) worn in some traditional Japanese hairstyles. These accessories sometimes include hanging blossoms associated with different seasons, such as cherry blossoms worn in April. The larger flower shapes of Hopton's work are fashioned with a warm-toned leaf pattern, suggesting the collage is set in the autumn. She creates the effect of trailing flowers with loose lengths of wool in the pink and purple tones traditionally observed at that time of year. This awareness of seasonality connects to Hopton's experience of splitting her time between London and Upstate New York, according to planting and harvesting times. Her dual lifestyles in the country and the city can be interpreted through the way she combines patterns and materials. In *Untitled* (2020) a knitted wool section in earthy shades of brown and gold is juxtaposed with a large brick pattern – the two parts contrast ideas of rural and urban, organic and human-made. Similarly, in *Bo Peep* (2020) Hopton pairs a blue toile fabric that evokes vintage aesthetics with its intricate images of the French countryside with a graphic dot motif that is bolder and more modern. Hopton's work offers a personal view into her passions in a style that combines tradition and ingenuity. It is informed as much by her appreciation for historic movements like Arts and Crafts as it is by her love of nature and command of working with strong graphics. She has increasingly extended her practice to include fabric, rug and wallpaper designs, merging art with the everyday.

FERREN GIPSON

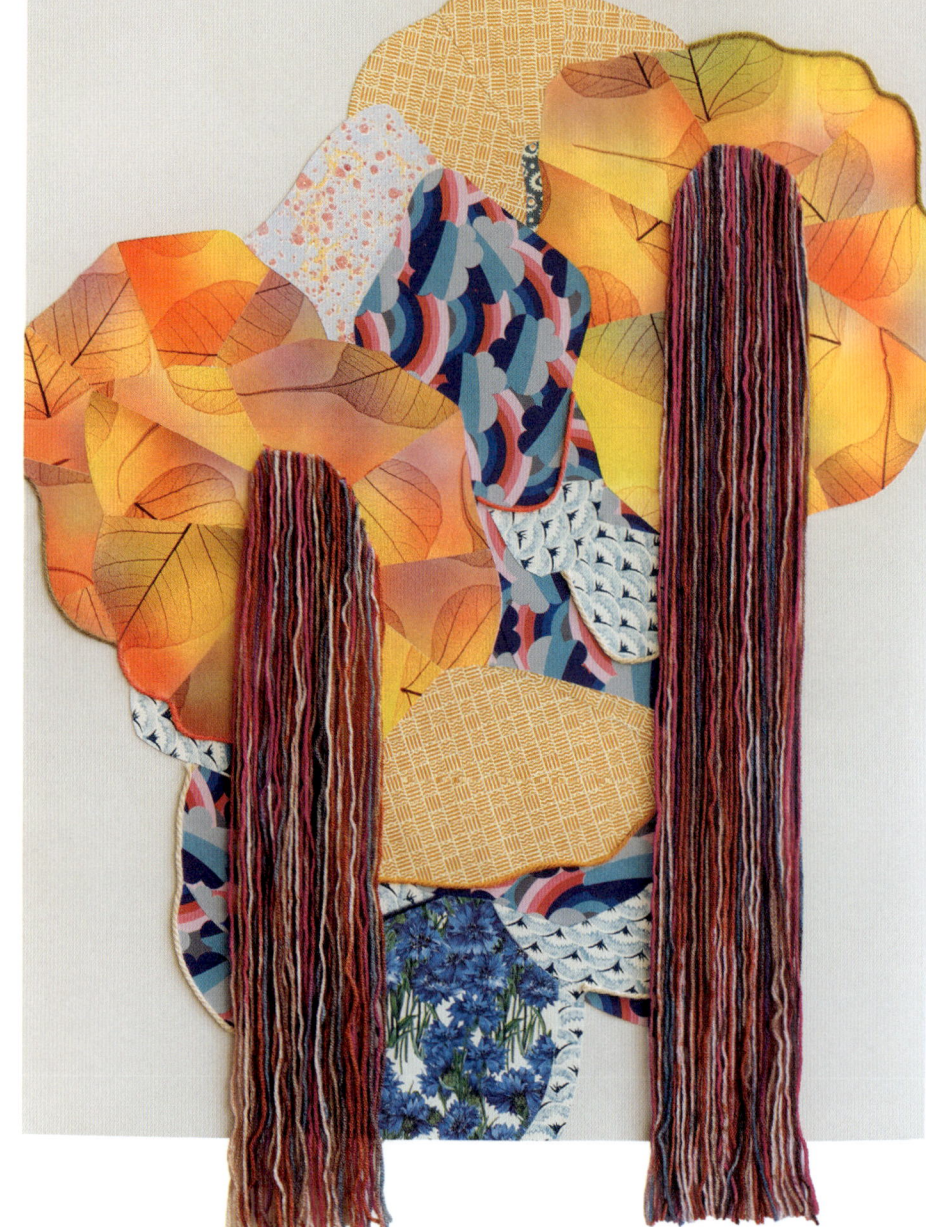

Born 1967, North Yorkshire, UK. Lives in London, UK and New York, USA.

↑   **Geisha**, 2021, collage and wool on paper, 69.5 × 52.5 cm (27 ⅜ × 20 ⅝ in)

↗   **Parliament**, 2019, collage and wool on painted paper, 129 × 143.7 cm (50 ¾ × 56 ⅝ in)

→   **Untitled**, 2020, collage, wool and painted paper, 45.8 × 37.6 cm (18 × 14 ¾ in)

→ →   **Bo Peep**, 2020, collage and wool on paper, 44.8 × 38.4 cm (17 ⅝ × 15 ⅛ in)

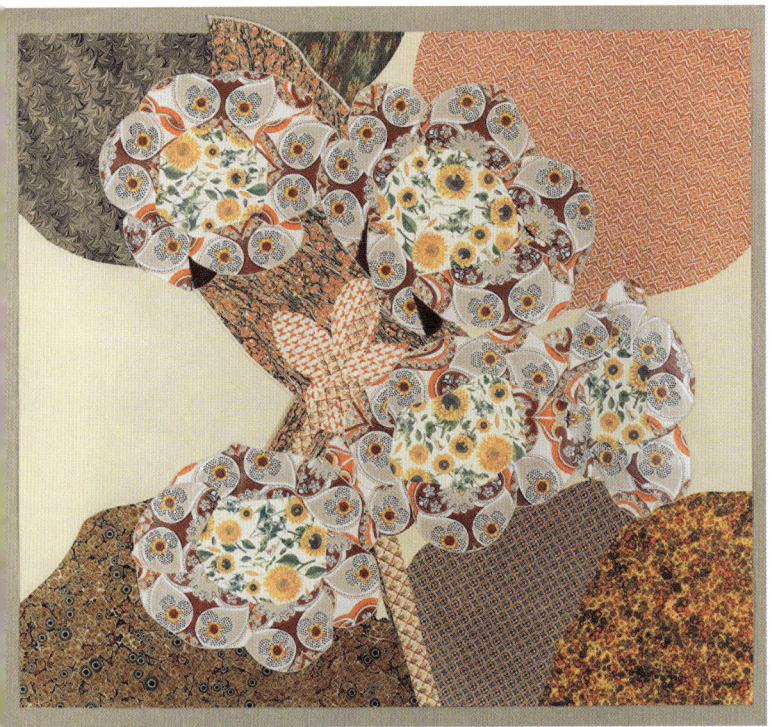

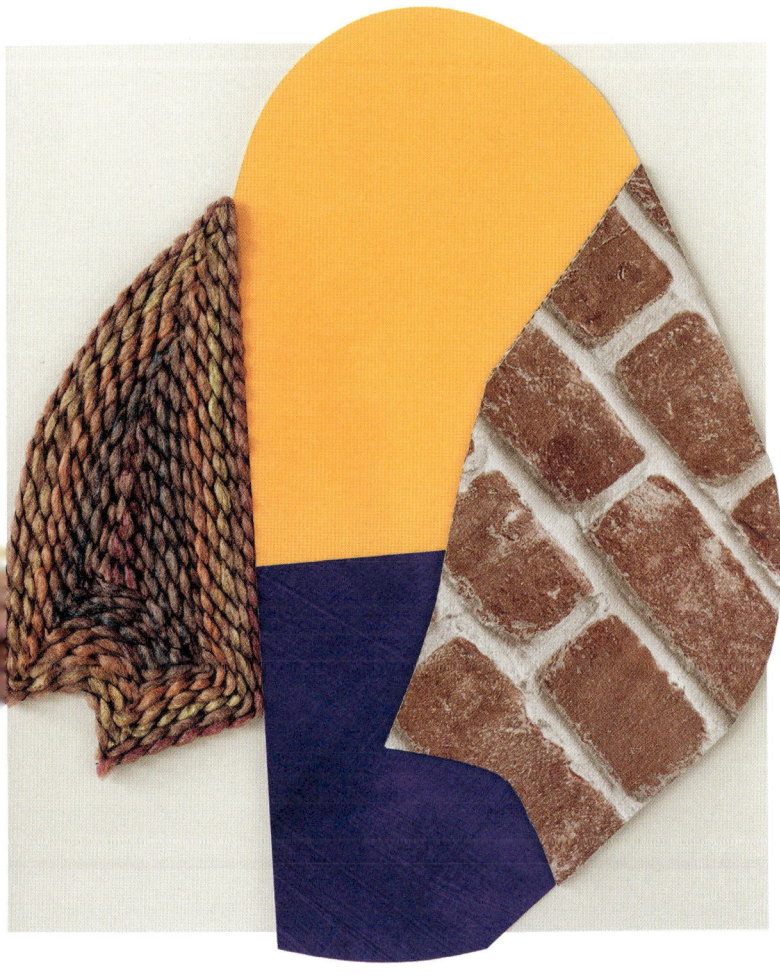

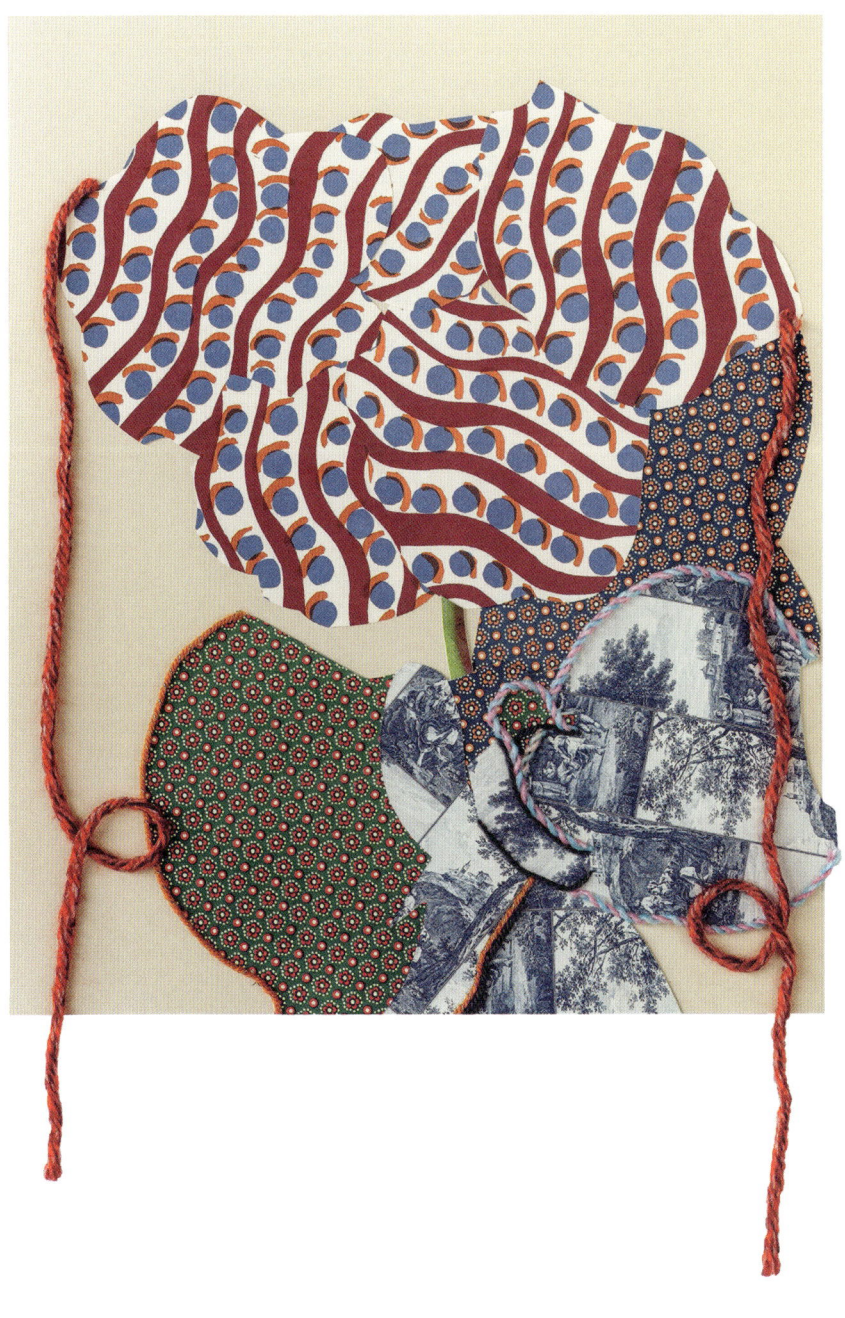

SHEREE HOVSEPIAN

Although trained in photography, Sheree Hovsepian is not concerned with capturing images, but rather with creating bodily forms from abstract images. She uses photography as a point of departure to arrive at synthetic compositions characterized by multiple materials, often contained within custom-built frames. The 1990s brought rapid advancements in digital photography, rewriting the ways in which many artists work with images. In Hovsepian's hands, however, the seemingly old-fashioned silver gelatin print becomes a petri dish for the subsequent conception of figurative assemblages: the embryo that develops into a multifaceted body through the combination of various abstract fragments. Hovsepian's process often starts with the creation of an analogue photograph in which different effects of light, shade and tone are achieved by varying exposure times. The resulting prints become a sensuous recording of the artist's performance in the darkroom. Sometimes human body parts appear, with the artist's sister acting as her stand-in in front of the camera. Their shared physicality allows Hovsepian to appear present as the subject of her works while still directing proceedings from behind the lens. Such identity and kinship are never explicitly spelt out in the artist's work, but lurk in anonymity below the surface. In *Poser* (2020), for example, a stretching body is pieced together by three components in distinct materials, veiled behind a dense network of overlapping string. The curved shape of the female torso in the photographic print is extended by wood and ceramic panels to create a biomorphic form. A recurring material in Hovsepian's work, ceramic alludes to the chemical transformation that occurs when clay is fired, with its inherent threat of failure. This underlying fragility echoes the alchemical and essentially unpredictable nature of the darkroom process. The erratic crisscrossing of the strings disrupts the delicate counterbalance of the forms lying beneath, their tension and linearity contrasting with the hard smoothness of the organic materials. Hovsepian's use of string has established a new constant in her practice, becoming a meditative activity adopted by the artist during the COVID-19 pandemic. A childhood memory of her mother's repetitive string crafting, knitting and crocheting – popular activities in the 1970s when the artist was growing up – imbue the material with both a personal and a feminine legacy. But the mapping quality of string also opens up a new sense of spatial politics in Hovsepian's work. In *Magical Thinking* (2021) monochromatic photographs of a female's arm, a leaf and a ball of string, as well as two pieces of differently textured walnut wood, combine like a puzzle to create a statue-like figure. Two arrow-like diamonds of string overlay the image, setting up a play of spatial illusion and tension between body and non-body, real and fabricated. Manufactured objects are removed from their historical associations in Hovsepian's work – a gentle call, perhaps, for a return to the very essence of materials and of life.

POPPY DONGXUE WU

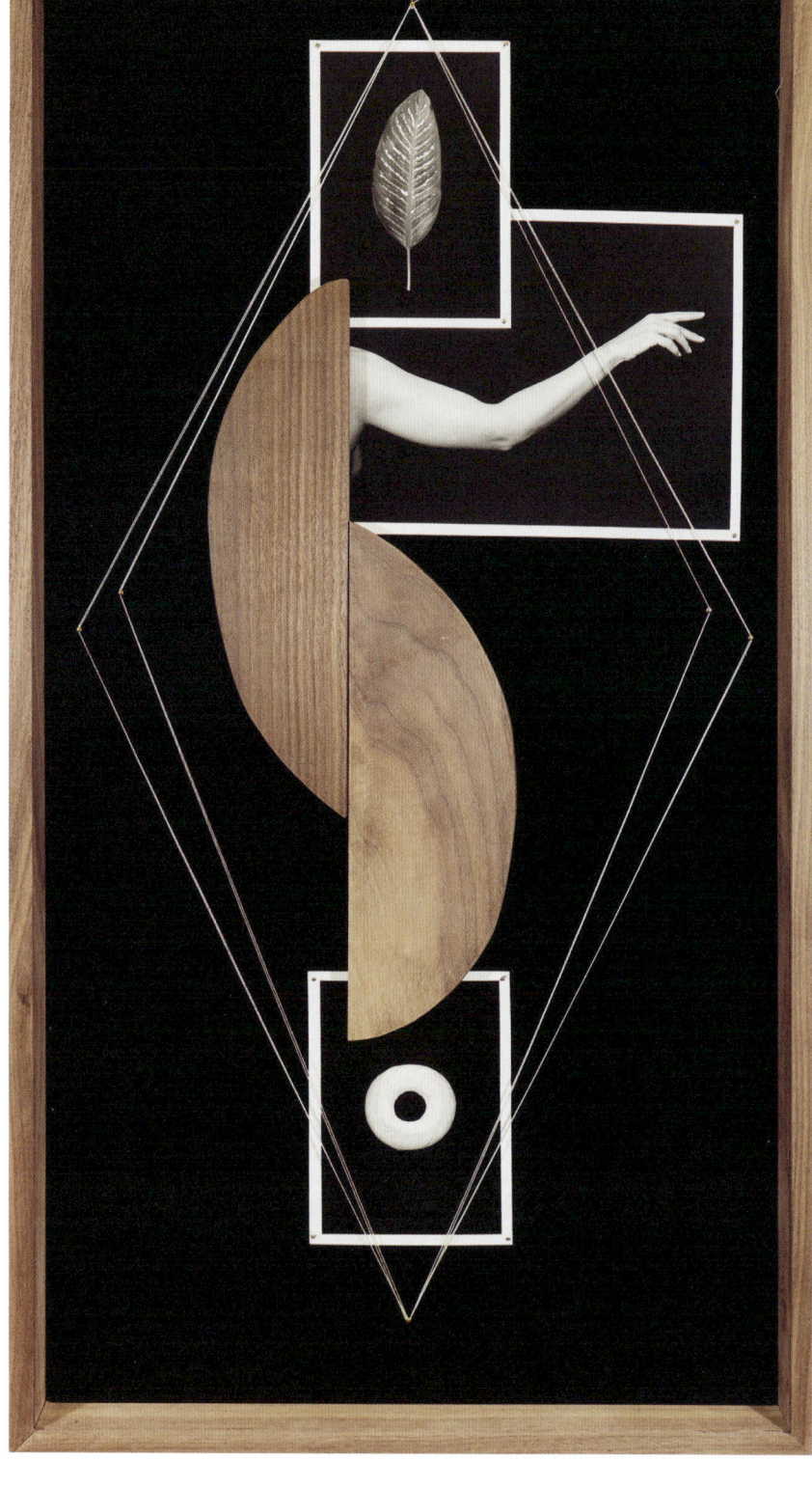

Born 1974, Isfahan, Iran. Lives in New York, USA.

↑ **Magical Thinking**, 2021, silver gelatin photographs, wood, nails, velvet and walnut artist frame, 95.3 × 49.5 × 8.9 cm (37½ × 19½ × 3½ in)

↗ **Poser**, 2020, silver gelatin photograph, ceramic, string, nails, walnut wood and walnut artist frame, 54.6 × 44.5 × 8.9 cm (21½ × 17½ × 3½ in)

↗↗ **Self Care**, 2019, silver gelatin prints, ceramic, wood, string, nails and artist frame, 63.5 × 48.9 × 10.2 cm (25 × 19¼ × 4 in)

→ **The State of Nature**, 2015, archival dye transfer print, graphite, acrylic, silver gelatin prints, brass nails and string, 101.6 × 76.2 × 5 cm (40 × 30 × 2 in)

→→ **Reveries of a Solitary Walker**, 2015, archival dye transfer print, graphite, acrylic, silver gelatin prints, wood, ink drawing on paper, brass nails and string, 129.5 × 104.1 × 6.3 cm (51 × 41 × 2½ in)

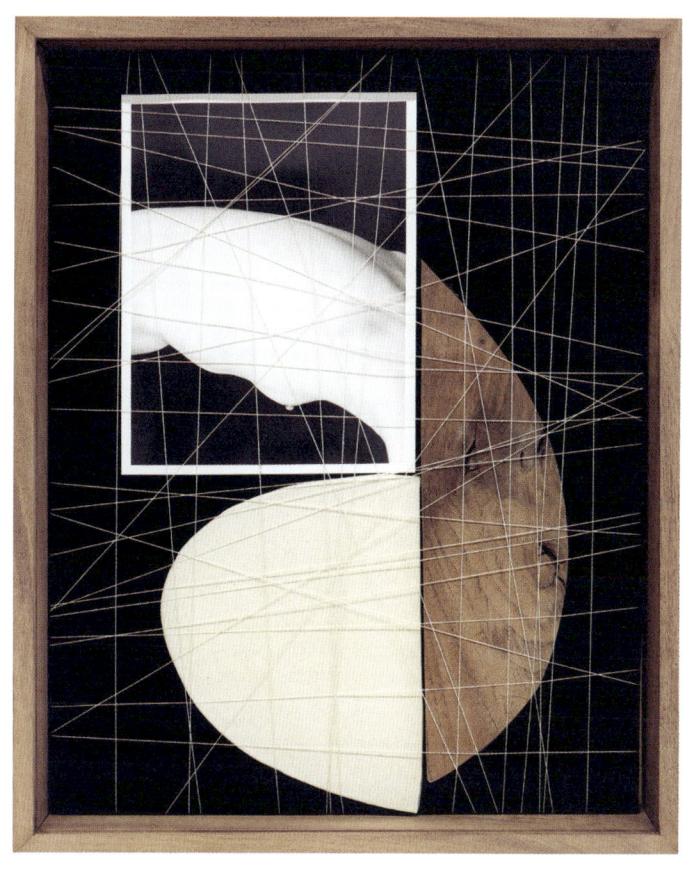

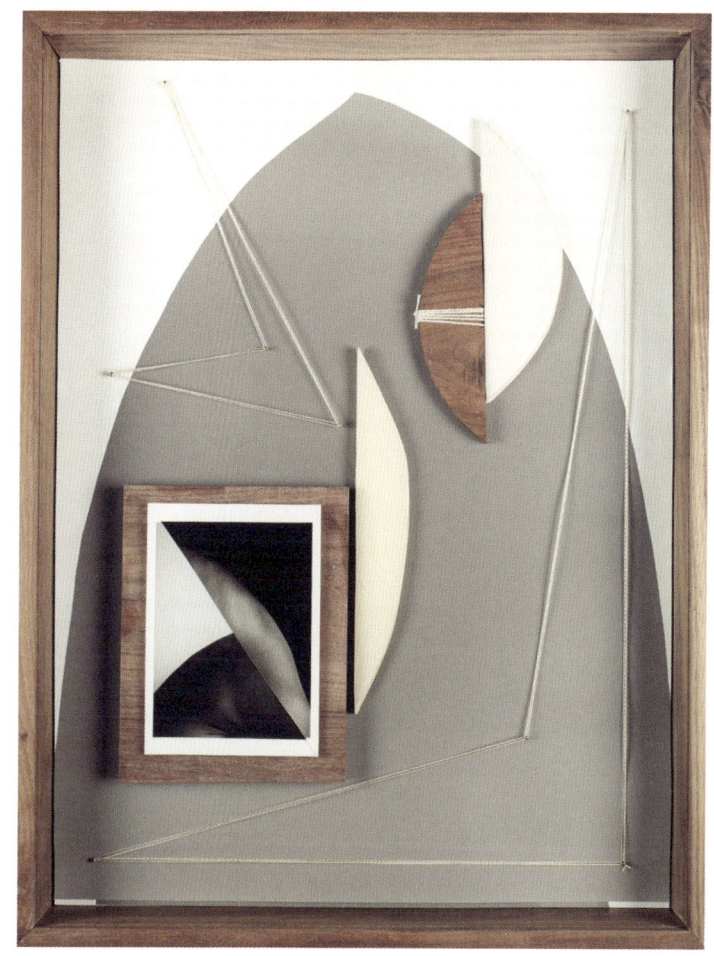

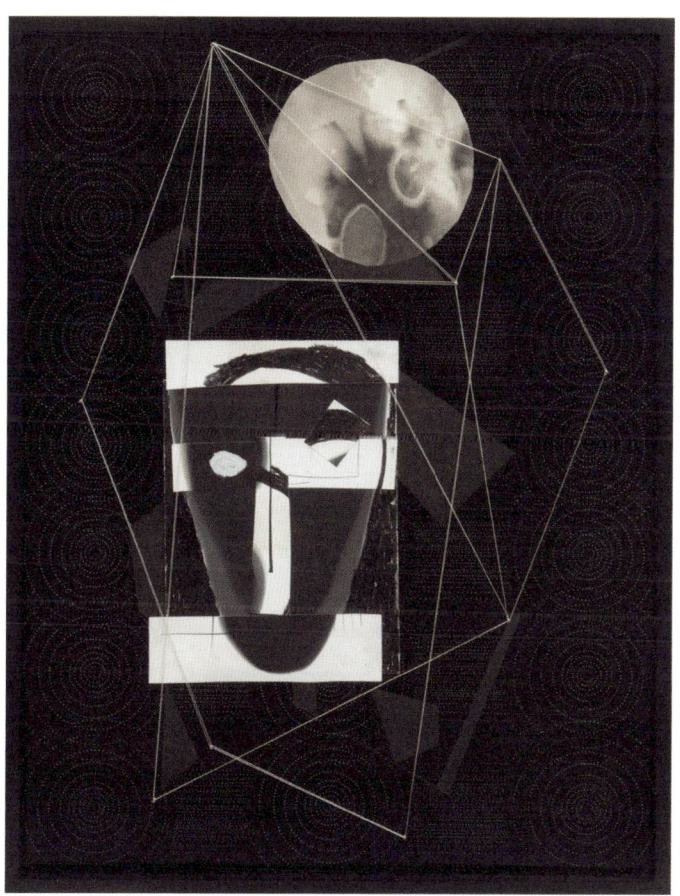

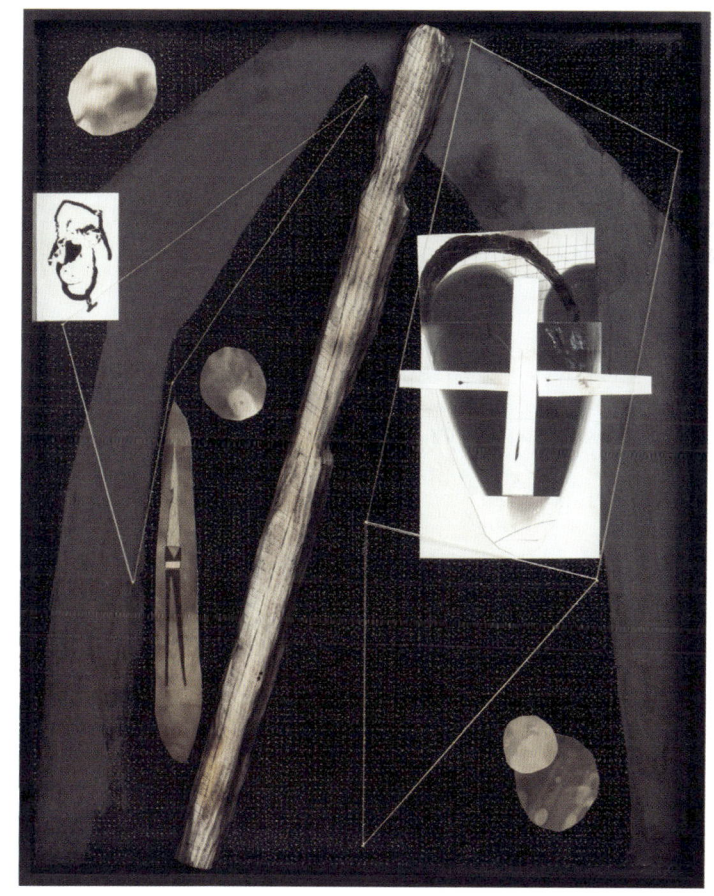

SHEREE
HOVSEPIAN

KAHLIL ROBERT IRVING

Colliding ancient and modern technologies, Kahlil Robert Irving's complex ceramic and digital assemblages probe Black experience in the United States, exploring the ways in which historical events reverberate in the present. This is most overt in his eye-popping digitally made collages, in which blizzards of social media posts, film stills, internet memes, screenshots of video chats, scanned ephemera, hip-hop album covers and his own photographs commingle to dizzying effect as he examines the legacies of colonial violence and oppression. Drawing from a growing archive of visual material amassed since 2013, these images suggest computer screens cluttered with multiple open windows, conflating different events and experiences across time. Presented as prints and installed as wallpapers – as in his 2021 presentation at New York's Museum of Modern Art – each one drips with personal and political resonances. ◣ Irving became enamoured with clay's possibilities at an early age and the medium remains central to his practice. Increasingly collage-like, his small ceramic sculptures combine representational and abstract forms with glazed elements, sparkling lustres and layers of decal transfers in conglomerate forms that hover between figurative sculptures, vessels and lumpen amassments. Appearing like a mutated teapot, *Construct-ING(MASS_withedges&Chimney) ManyMEEN'INGS+/Remnants=Black* (2021) features spout-like forms protruding from a mass of material resembling brick, concrete and strewn garbage. Adorned with a dense collage of fragmented images, including drinks logos, a tattered US flag, FaceTime screenshots and references to protests, it evokes the abandoned smokestacks and decaying industrial architecture in the artist's hometown of St. Louis, Missouri and other Midwest cities, where the exploitation of Black labour has left legacies of racial tension and social unrest. Together, the forms and images poetically lament the negative psychological effects that such crumbling urban environments can have on their inhabitants. ◣ Meditating on cultural appropriation and racial injustice, the digital collage *Screen Shot Charts: {from Ming to Ebay and google scrolls (mixedmicro Messages (DMs)*1}* (2018) connects the dots between the history of ceramic production, international trade and white supremacy. Images referencing the way that Chinese Ming and Qing dynasty porcelain designs have been purloined and exploited by Western producers are combined with myriad scans, screenshots, Instagram posts and Google searches relating to racist incidents, including the case of a white police officer acquitted in 2017 for the murder of a young African American man from St. Louis. Acknowledging that the significance of such juxtapositions speaks clearly to some viewers while eluding others, Irving points to the fragmented and idiosyncratic nature of our contemporary media landscape. That is not to say that these works need deciphering to be appreciated. 'That's one of the beautiful things about collage,' he said, in correspondence with the author in 2022, 'that references and forms can oscillate between ambiguity and legibility.' ◣

DAVID TRIGG

Born 1992, San Diego, California, USA. Lives in St. Louis, Missouri, USA.

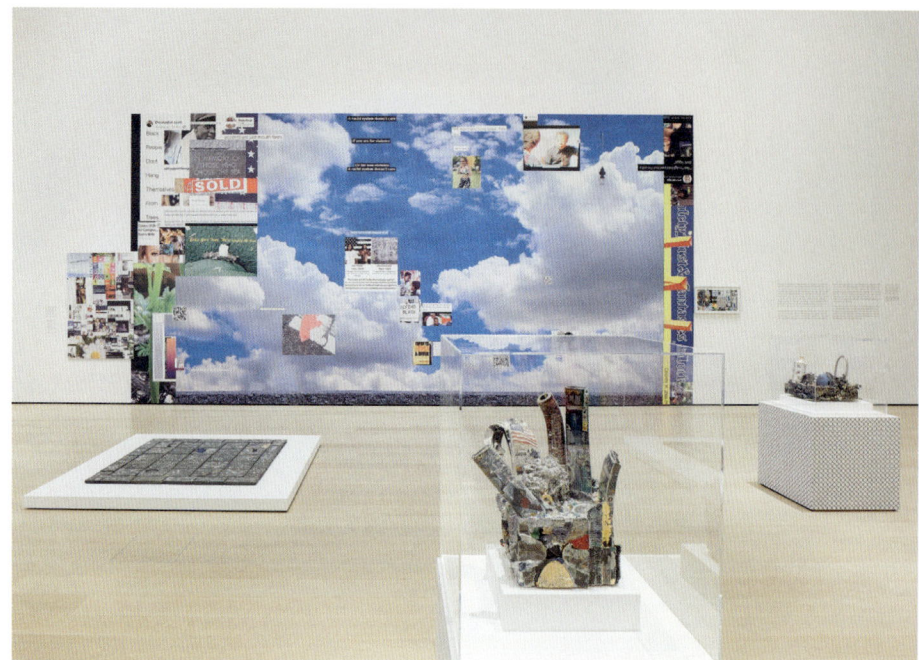

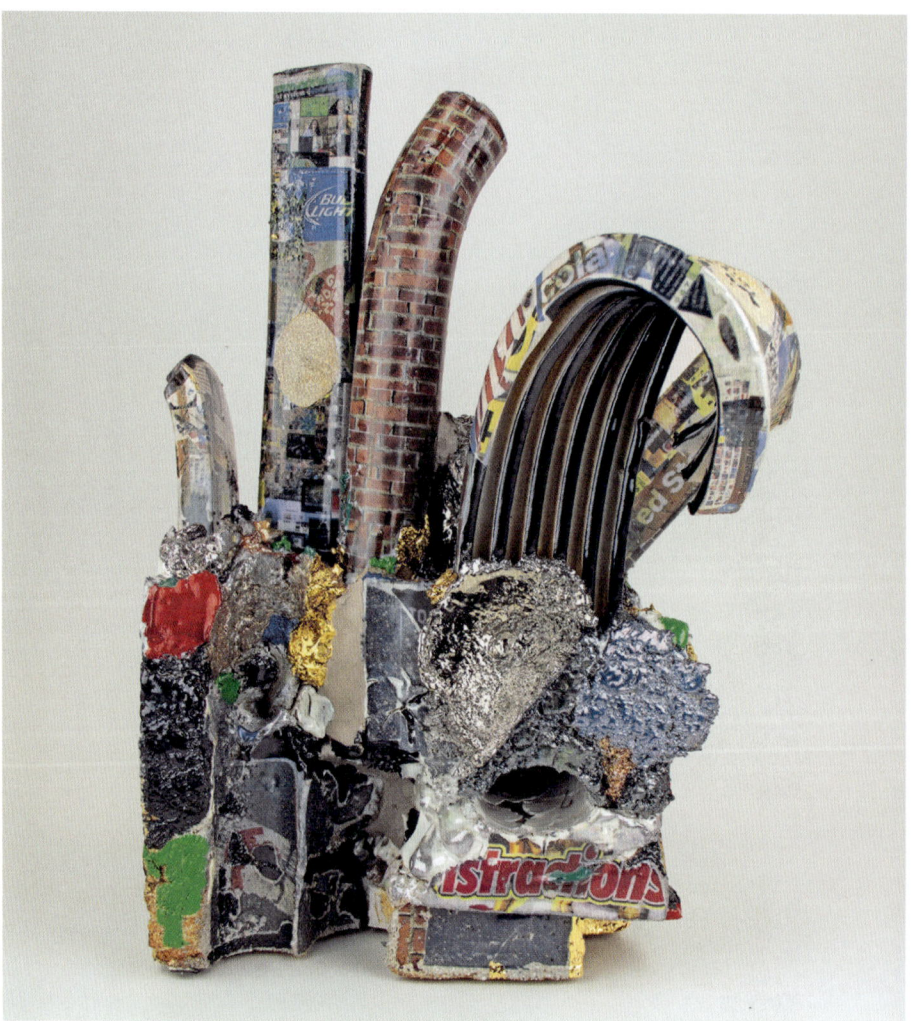

↑↑ Installation view, 'Projects: Kahlil Robert Irving', Museum of Modern Art, New York, USA, 2021–2

↑ Construct-ING(MASS_withedges&Chimney) ManyMEEN'INGS+/Remnants=Black, 2021, glazed and unglazed ceramic, lustre, found and personally constructed decals, 55.9 × 44.5 × 38.1 cm (22 × 17½ × 15 in)

↗ Screen Shot Charts: {from Ming to Ebay and google scrolls (mixedmicro Messages (DMs)*1}, 2018, digitally sourced and constructed collage, digital print, 30.5 × 61 cm (12 × 24 in)

→ Mixed Messages (Streets & Screens) AOL + Lottery, 2020, lightbox: aluminium, mylar and digital print, 91.4 × 152.4 × 10.2 cm (36 × 60 × 4 in)

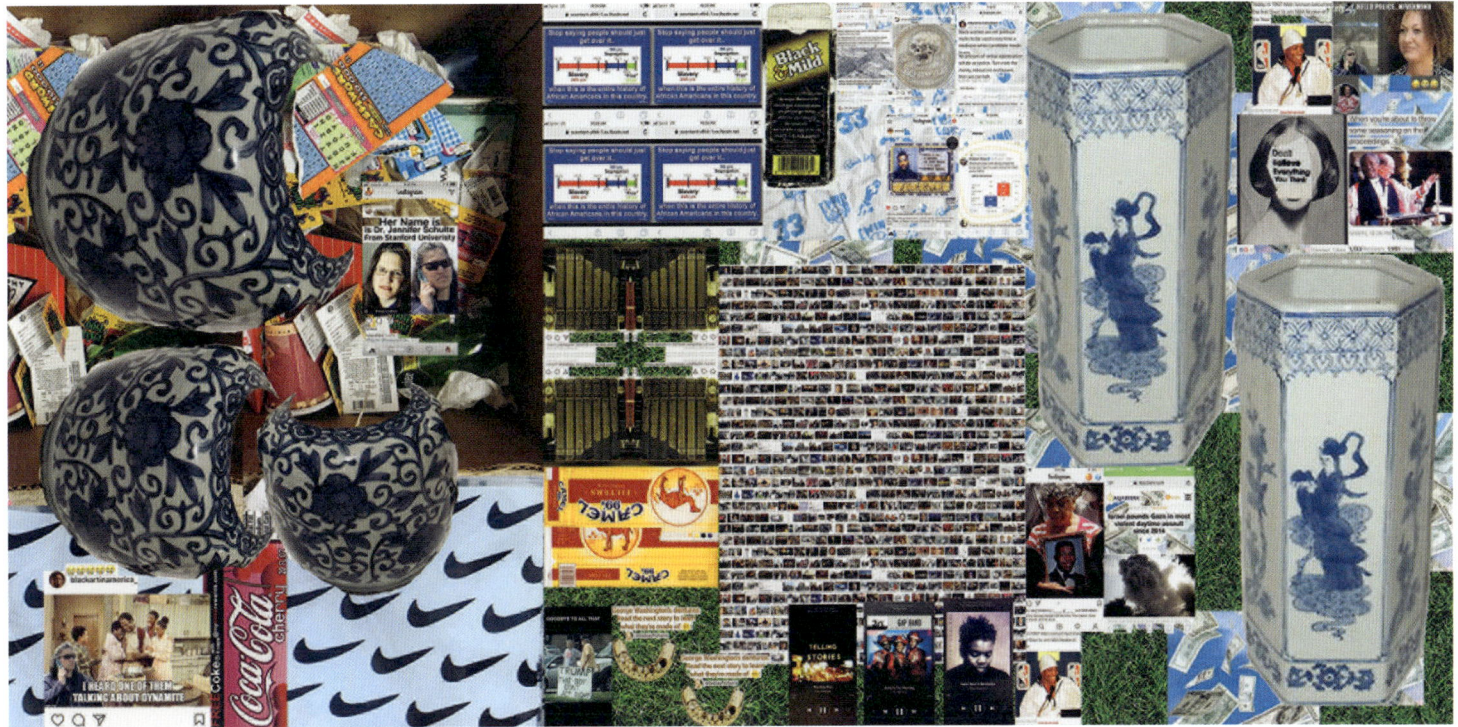

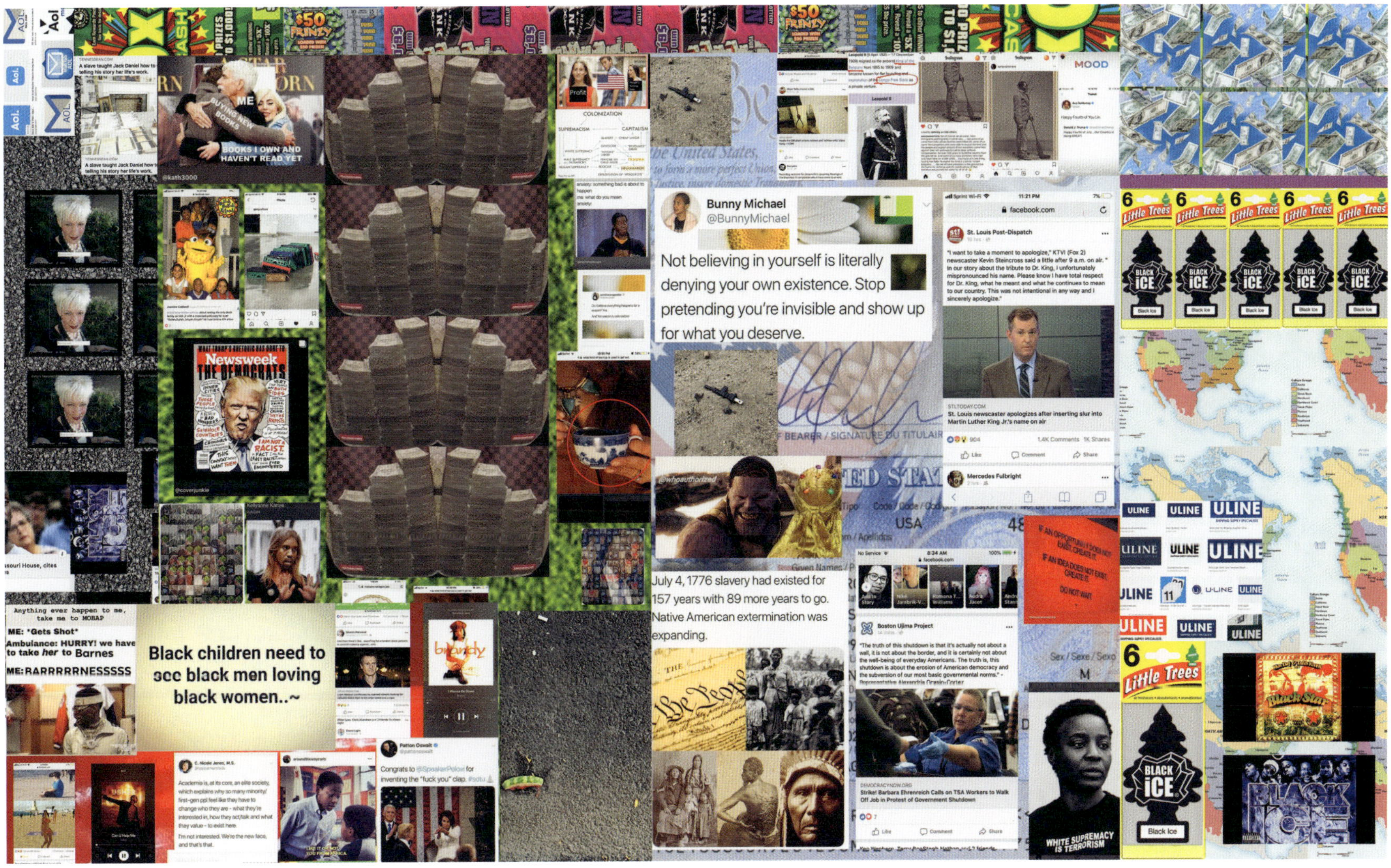

KAHLIL ROBERT
IRVING

CLOTILDE JIMÉNEZ

In collages that draw subject matter from autobiographical occurrences in his own life, Clotilde Jiménez incorporates found materials including clothes, magazine cuttings, wallpaper and charcoal to create work that is situated at the intersection of discourses around race, gender and sexuality. By adopting ubiquitous and prosaic materials, the collages foreground and universalize the narratives of those who have been marginalized or ignored. Formally, the work emerges from a lineage of artists such as Faith Ringgold (b. 1930), Jacob Lawrence (1917–2000) and Romare Bearden (1911–88), all of whom employed collage in their work to document African American experience. For Jiménez, the collages become an exploration of his own experiences and identity as a Black Hispanic and Queer person.

In *Beso Inesperado* (*Unexpected Kiss*) (2021) a patchwork of facial features comprised of magazine cut-outs, geometric patterned fabrics and other, more colourful materials produces the effect of two faces in uneasy proximity. Their long-lashed eyes are imbued with sadness, yet their red and orange lips are ardently poised in anticipation of an apparently unexpected embrace. Disavowed of their bodies, these collaged heads simultaneously depict different viewpoints and the singularity of their three-dimensional form. In doing so, both dimensions are emphasized and yet the formally Cubist preoccupation belies the work's additional critique: that perspective is cultural and psycho-political as well as spatial and temporal. This multi-dimensional quality of the image is also emphasized in *Birth in Flower Garden* (2021). A figure wearing a dress and high-heeled shoes can be seen hunched into the shape of a question mark, knees pulled to their chest with their hands. Surrounded by rudimentary-shaped flowers with blue, yellow and purple petals, we bear witness to an event that is both intimate and strange. The figure is ostensibly giving birth, yet both the mother and child's faces are an amalgam of black-and-white magazine cut-outs of adult bodies. They clearly depict sadness, rage and surprise yet produce a peculiarly singular expression that speaks of the violence of certain forms of cultural reproduction. *La Guapa* (*The Beautiful*) (2021) is a reference to the Asafo flags of the Fante – an Akan people who live to the west of Accra in Ghana. Traditionally ,the flags, called *Frankaa*, are embroidered by warrior groups (Asafo) and frequently depict visual metaphors using people, spirits and animals. Each animal relates to an Akan proverb and is used to signify the Fante's strength, solidarity and the power they hold over their enemies. The adoption of the flag as a powerful marker of identity and carrier of cultural history is significant. In Jiménez's collage the picture plane does the work of a flag, yet its multi-faceted imagery seems at odds with the flattening hegemony of a national symbol.

HANA NOORALI AND LYNTON TALBOT

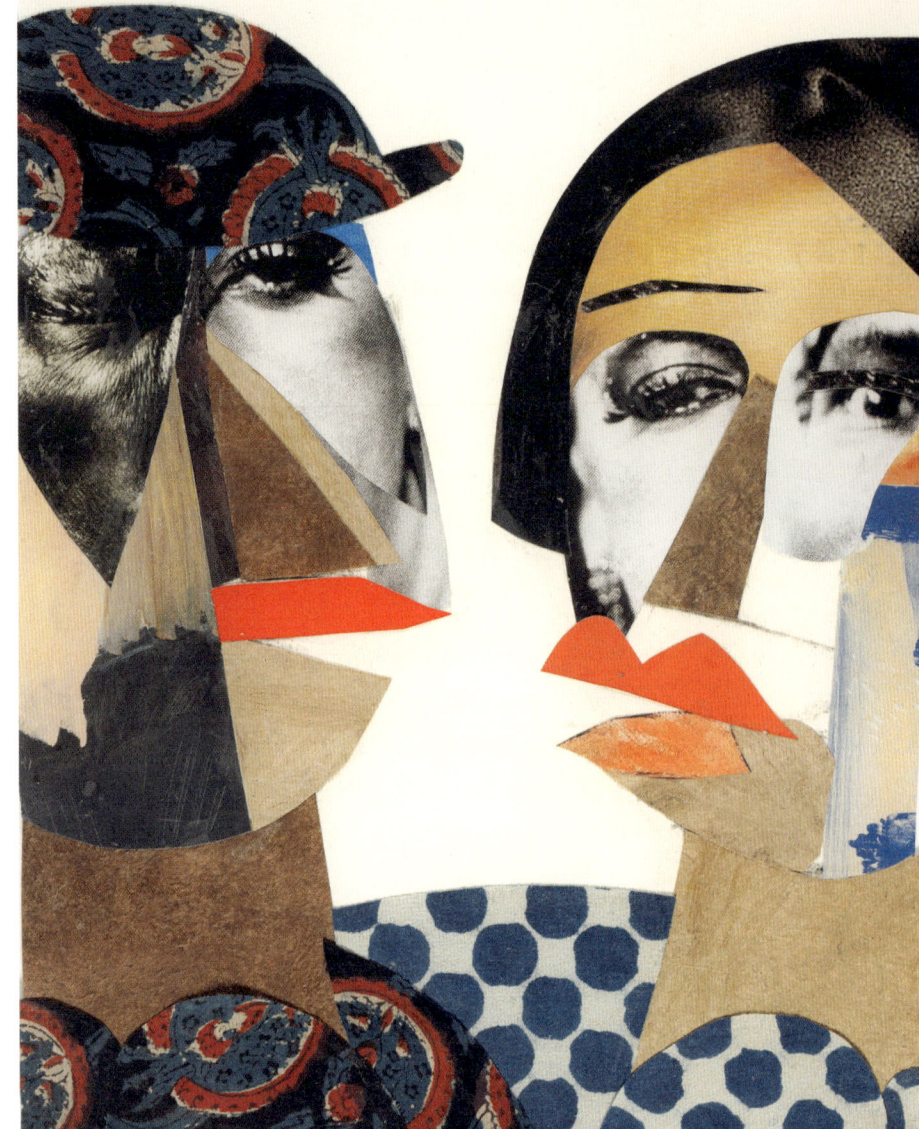

Born 1990, Honolulu, Hawaii, USA. Lives in Mexico City, Mexico.

↑ Beso Inesperado (Unexpected Kiss), 2021, mixed-media collage on paper, 40.6 × 33 cm (16 × 13 in)

→ Baptism, 2021, acrylic, charcoal and mixed-media collage on paper, 90 × 78 cm (35⅜ × 30¾ in)

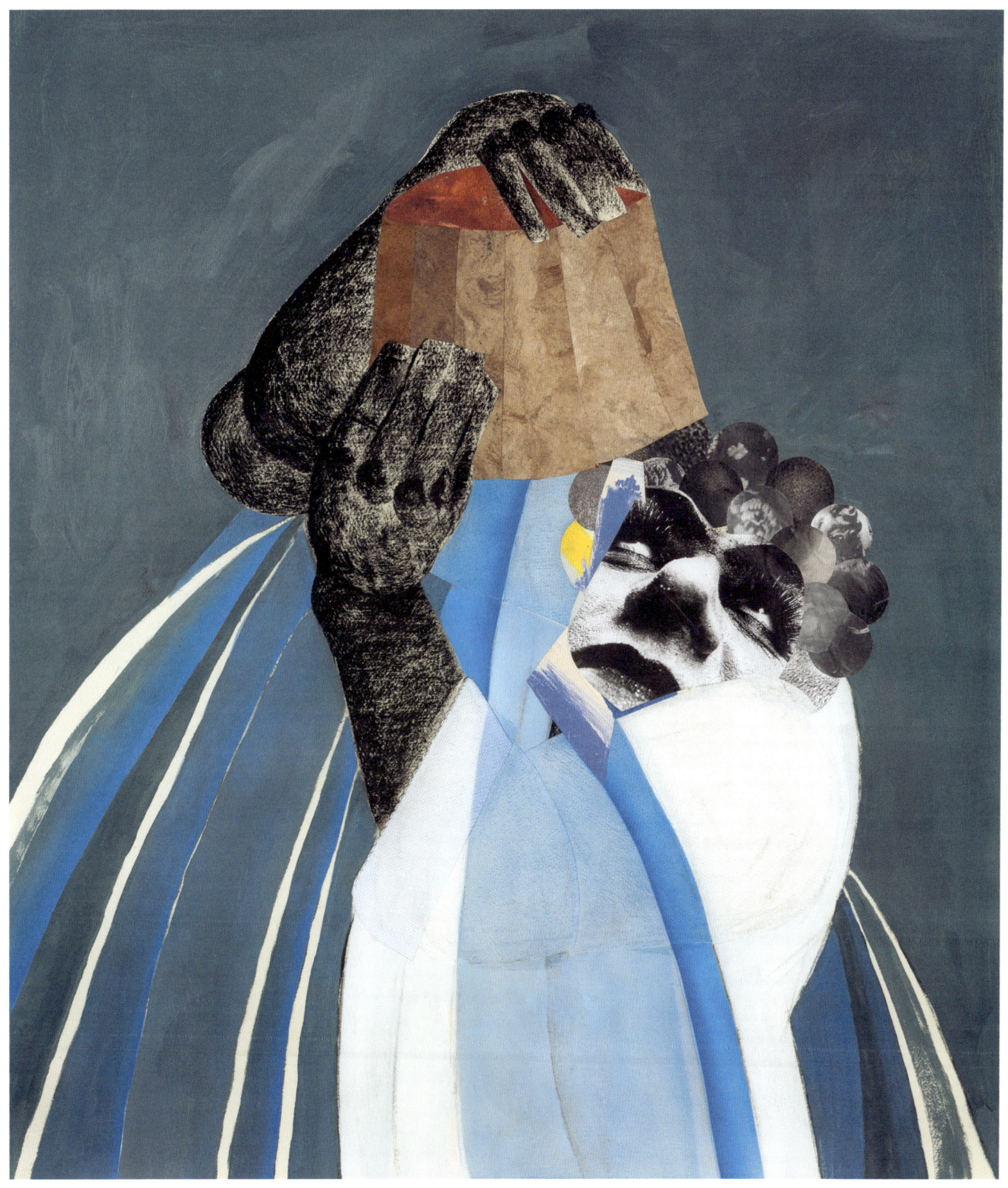

CLOTILDE
JIMÉNEZ

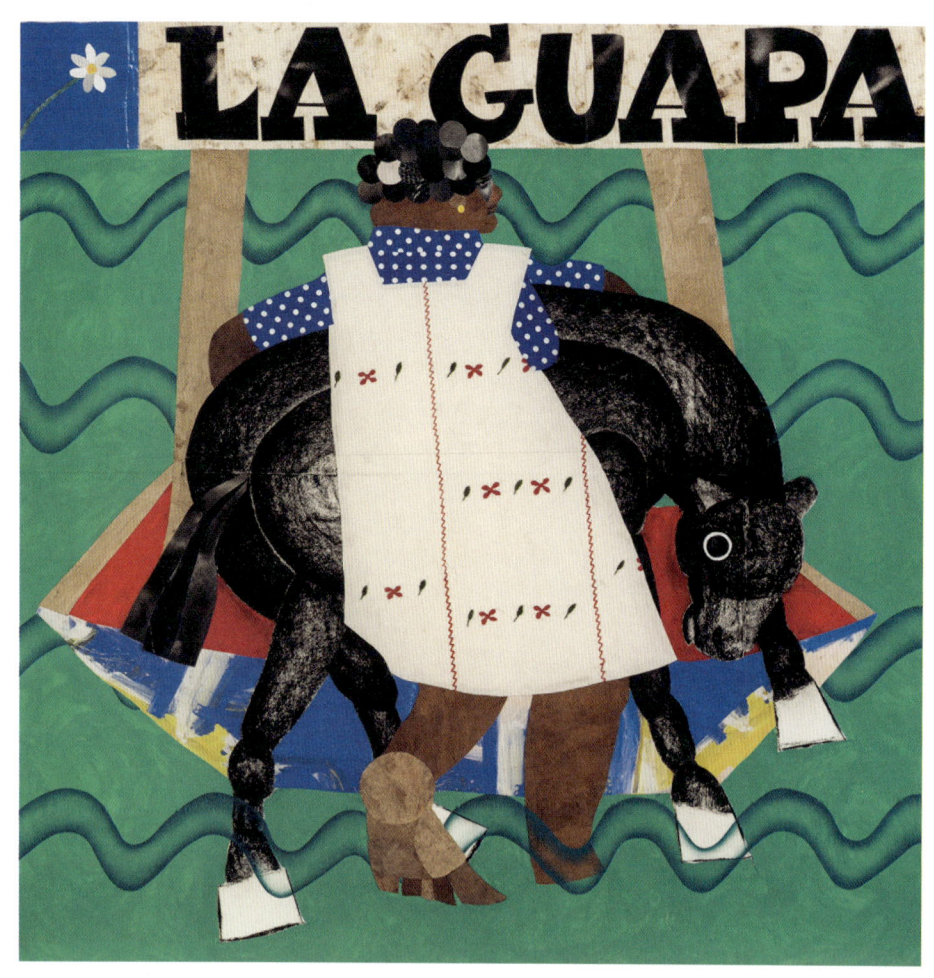

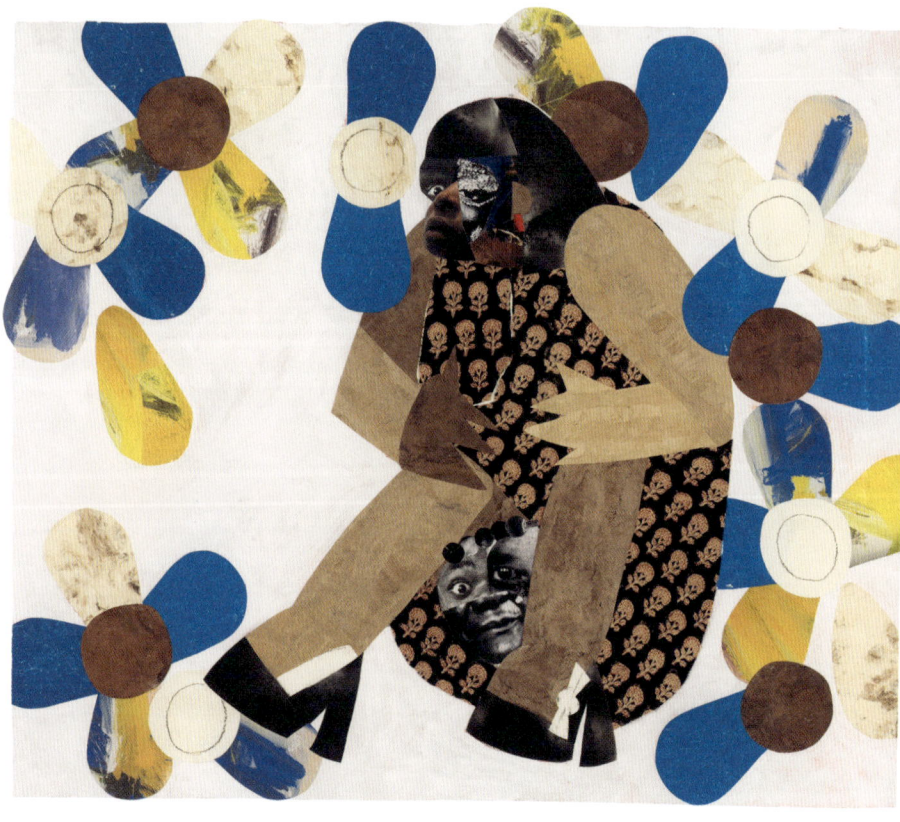

↖ **La Guapa (The Beautiful)**, 2021, acrylic, charcoal and mixed-media collage on paper, 152.4 × 152.4 cm (60 × 60 in)

↑ **Birth in Flower Garden**, 2021, acrylic, charcoal and mixed-media collage on paper, 106.7 × 127 cm (43 × 50½ in)

↗ **Tête à la fleur (Autoportrait) (Flower Head (Self-Portrait))**, 2021, charcoal and mixed-media collage on paper, 47 × 31.8 cm (18½ × 12½ in)

→ **Ruby Earrings**, 2021, charcoal and mixed-media collage on paper, 47 × 30.5 cm (18½ × 12 in)

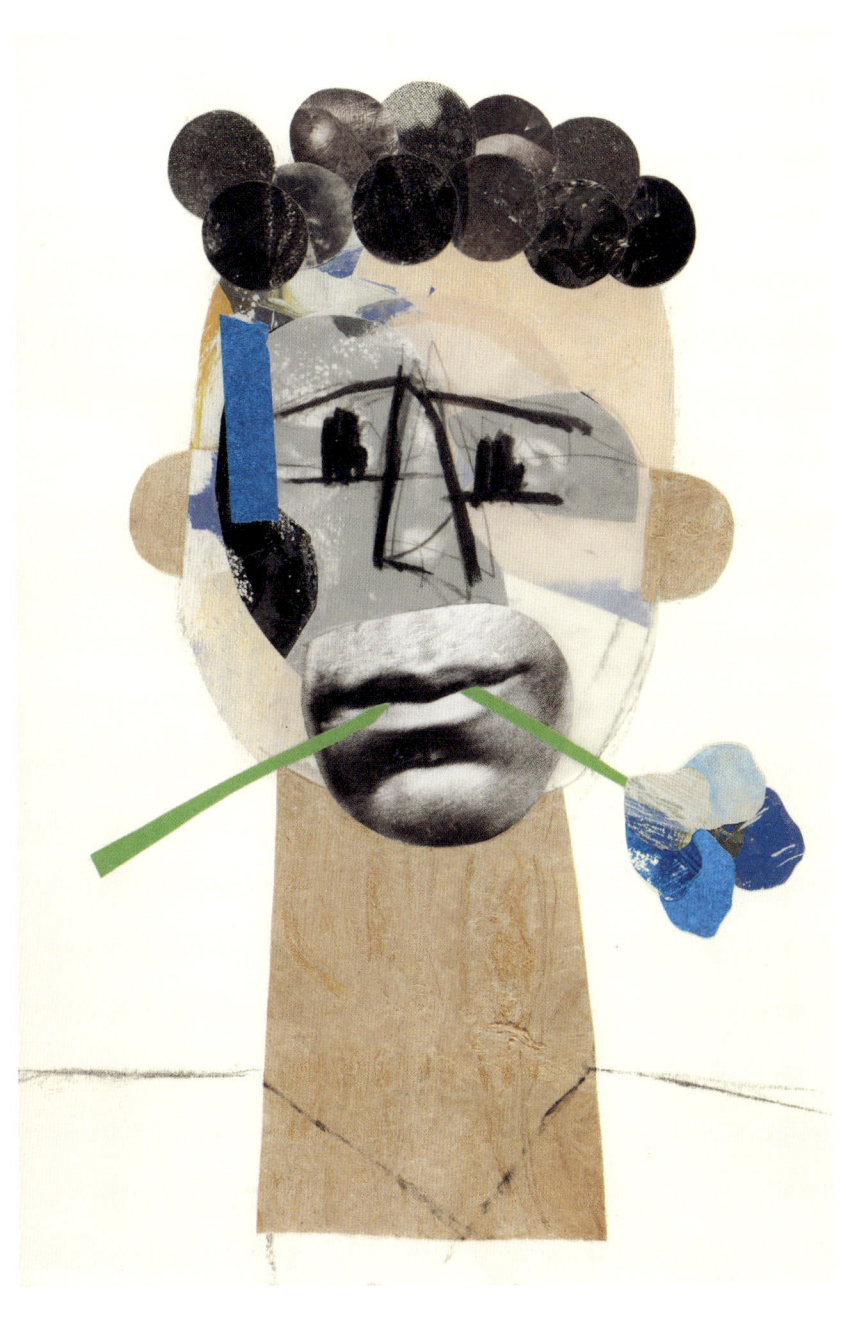
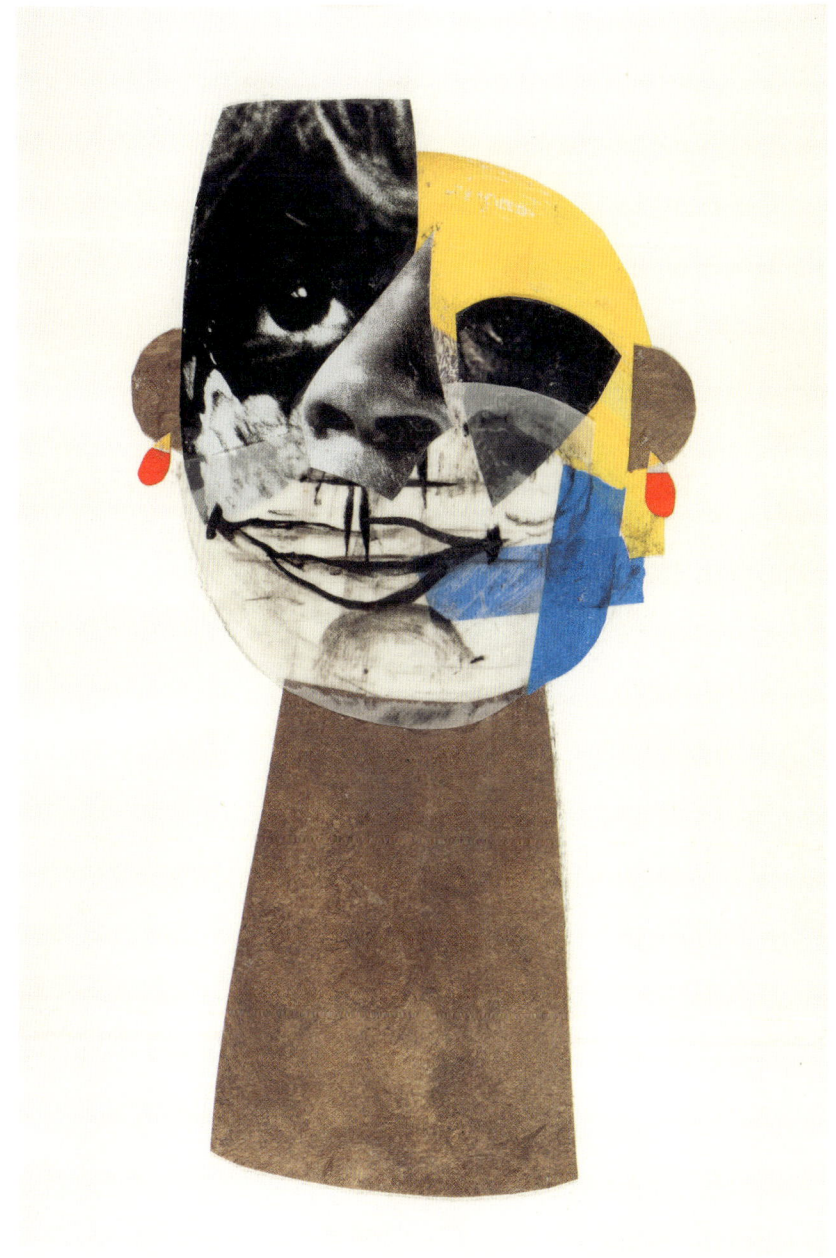

AARON JONES

Aaron Jones uses collage to reimagine forms, bodies and identities. In a 2022 interview with the author he described these as 'non-persons, non-humans, colours, shapes, trees, mushrooms, rocks and water'. His characters are neither quite one thing nor another, moving in-between the recognizable and the abstract, rendering them otherworldly and unknowable. ■ Studying photography at OCAD University in Toronto (2018), Jones was initially interested in manipulating the camera and exploring what it could do. However, he soon realized that, for him, adding to the existing surfeit of photographs already in existence was not a way forward. Seeing the work of artist Wangechi Mutu (pp.176–7) was a revelatory experience, her complex, science fiction-like collages striking a unique chord with him compared to the other photographs that he was encountering at the time. Jones began sourcing images from printed matter found in his own home, ranging from copies of magazines like *Ebony* and *Essence*, which foreground the worlds of Black people in America, to encyclopedias and books on space, nature and exotic birds. Cut up into fragments, they come together as new characters that hint at aspects of Jones's life, while also entering new terrain. Playing with pasts and futures, his collages act as an archive of their everyday sources, while also envisaging entirely new beings and ways of being. ■ Take, for example, *Miner in Brobdingnagian* (2021), in which a creature stands amid a rocky outcrop, its rust-orange body a composite of animal, human and machine. It seems born of the land and able to traverse its barrenness; upending any potential for isolation or loneliness, it proudly surveys its sandy kingdom. In contrast, the lush forest depicted in *Sitting on the sky in the woods* (2021) is home to a many-armed figure resting in nirvana beneath a canopy of trees. In the same 2022 interview, Jones described how 'recently the natural landscape has been my biggest influence. I feel my best and my work feels its best after I've been bathed in the forest.' From evergreen environments to the ochre dust of the desert, Jones's settings hint at personal moments from his own life, creating an intimacy that feels both vulnerable and bold. ■ An earlier, larger collage, *Sweet Country* (2018), takes the form of an installation, with figures hanging suspended by fishing lines in front of a verdant background landscape. It speaks to how Jones's whole family is from Jamaica yet have come from different places with different experiences. *Sweet Country* became a way of showing characters from diverse origins inhabiting a new place. Each family member is made up of fragmented imagery, which includes people – such as the Black figure from Édouard Manet's iconic painting *Olympia* (1863) – but also planets, feathers and other more abstract elements. Together, these become innovative bodies claiming their own space and evading objectification. ◀

LOUISA ELDERTON

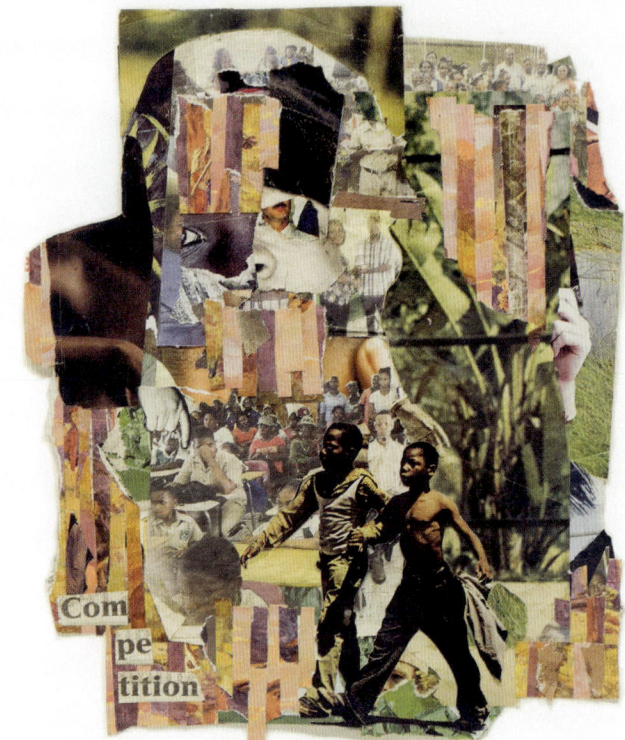

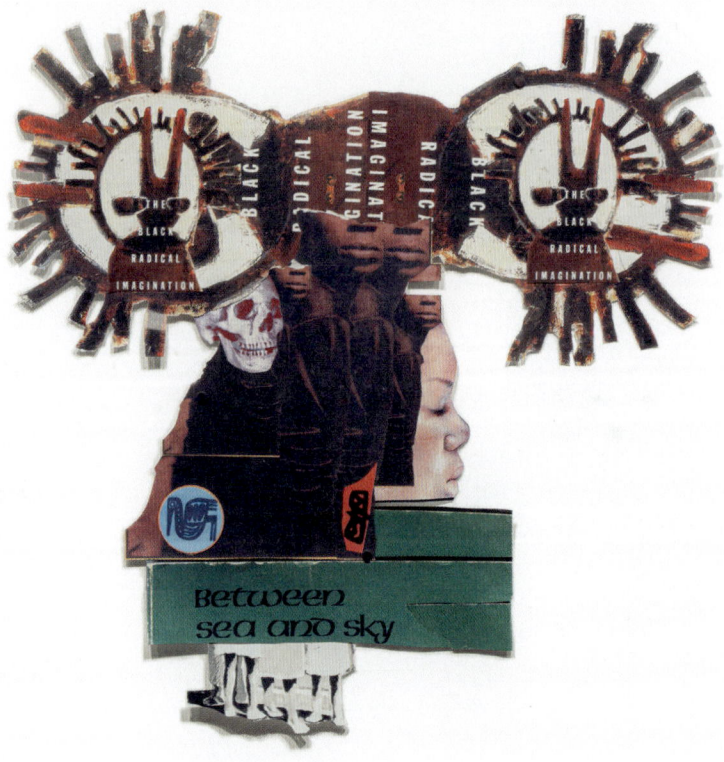

Born 1993, Toronto, Canada. Lives in Toronto.

↑↑ **No competition**, 2019, paper collage, 35 × 28 cm (14 × 11 in)

↑ **A posteriori**, 2020, paper collage, 38 × 59 cm (15 × 22 in)

↗ **Sweet Country**, 2018, paper on wall, paper collage, wooden dowels and fishing line, 122 × 367 cm (48 × 144 in), installation view, 'Ragga NYC', Mercer Union, Toronto, Canada 2018

→ **Miner in Brobdingnagian**, 2021, C-print, 83 × 124 cm (75 × 48¾ in)

→→ **Sitting on the sky in the woods**, 2021, C-print, 83 × 124 cm (32¾ × 48¾ in)

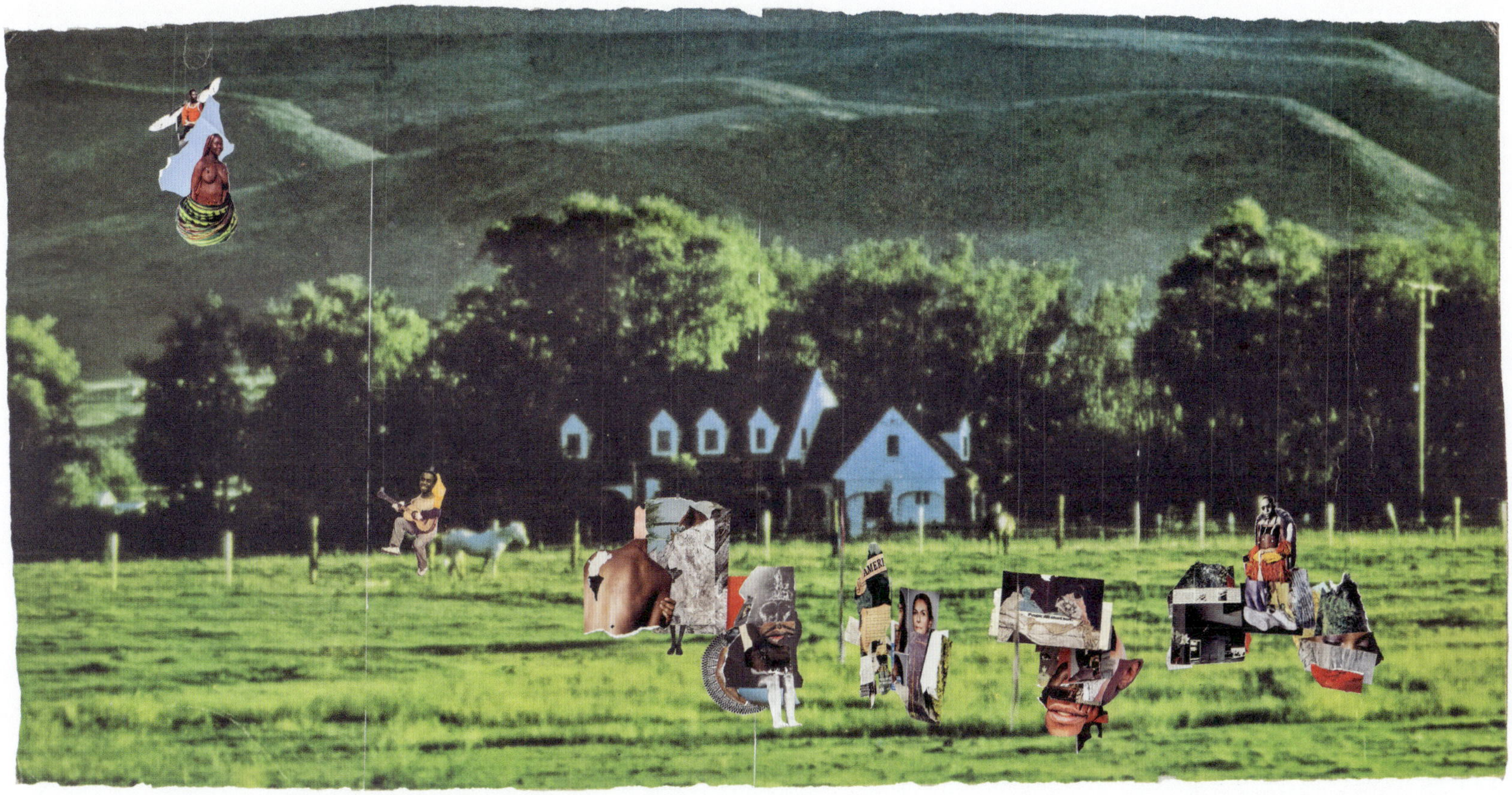

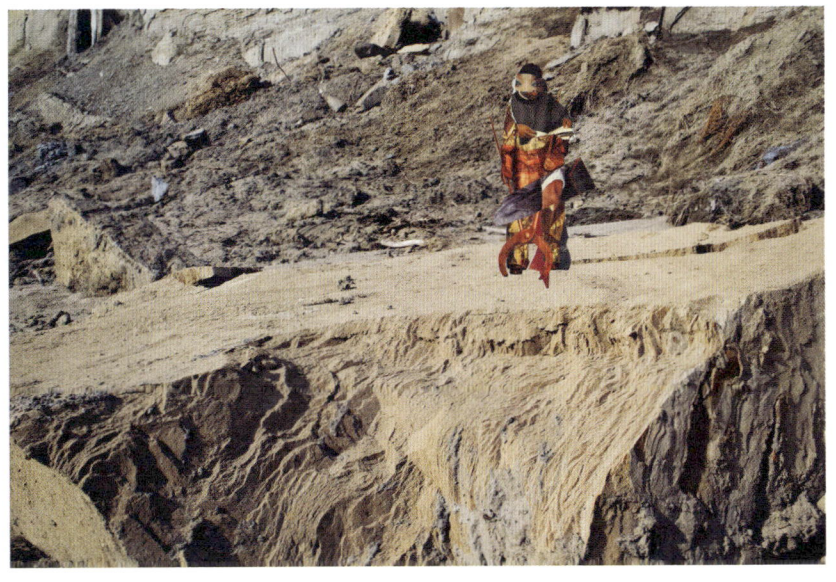

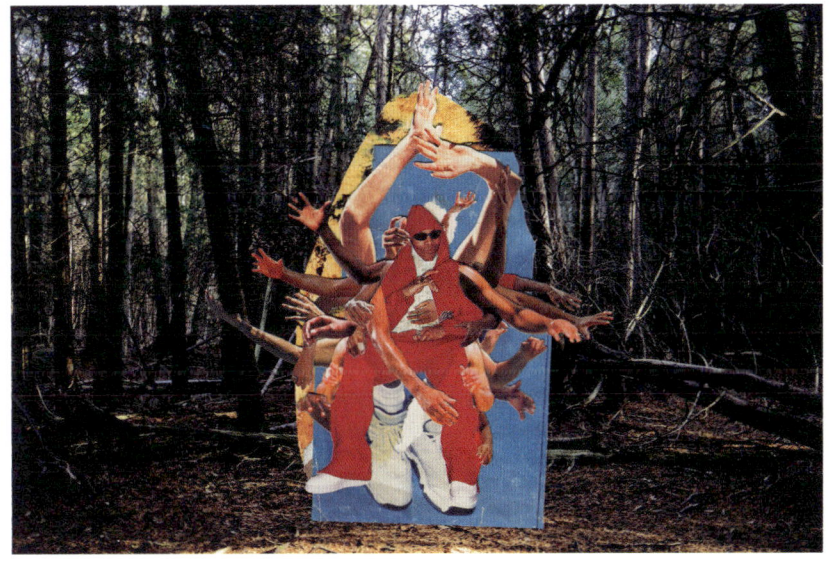

AARON
JONES

HARRI KALHA

Harri Kalha describes himself as a university-educated folk artist, a statement that suggests a peripheral relationship with the mainstream art world. For many years, the artist was better known as an art historian and writer. Despite training at the University of Helsinki's drawing school and studying art at the Académie d'Art Roederer in Paris, France, in the late 1980s, he moved on to pursue a scholarly career for more than two decades. Collage was always a fascination, but it was the emotional impact of his mother's death in 2005 that stirred him to start cutting and pasting. As he told the online journal *Toombes* in 2021, 'there was this whole visual universe inside me that beckoned to come out'. However, it would be another fifteen years until he felt able to exhibit his works publicly. ◢◤ Working on a modest scale and predominantly in black and white, Kalha sources his imagery from encyclopedias, art books and other vintage publications. He works intuitively, choosing images that resonate on a visceral rather than intellectual level. Sometimes a narrative emerges as elements are added, but most compositions are about striking a mood or conveying a state of mind. Each one is meticulously hand-cut without the use of computers. It is a painstaking, time-consuming approach, but one he finds relaxing, even meditative. ◢◤ As a young man, Kalha loved life drawing and cherished precise linearity. This sensibility is evident in the delightfully surreal *Getting Set* (2021), in which an athlete's contour is carefully traced to clothe him with a swarm of bees and a horrifying appendage. It is a masterclass in how to merge two elements to unsettling effect and reflects the artist's fascination with the push-pull of beauty and ugliness, of desire and disavowal. The human form, especially the face, recurs throughout Kalha's work, and his long-standing engagement with theories of the gaze accounts for his fondness for eyes, which he considers to be the most expressive and directly engaging part of the body. ◢◤ Kalha works thematically in several ongoing series. Some, such as 'Minun Taidehistoriani' ('My Art History') playfully interrogate his love/hate relationship with his scholarly discipline. Others hang on technique, such as works from the series 'Rollaaseja', inspired by Czech collagist Jiří Kolář (1914–2002) who spliced different images by interpolating them in even, vertica,l strips. Kalha's title is a play on words that uses 'roll' in place of 'coll' in collage, to create a new word that roughly translates as 'rollage'. The technique is used in *Luonnotar / Nature Empowered* (2020), which combines vintage images of an unusual lactating mermaid fountain and a woman suggestively rolling her tongue to create a striking composition that supplants sexist connotations with suggestions of power and sexual agency. As with all of Kalha's works, the combination is significantly more than the sum of its parts. ◢◤

DAVID TRIGG

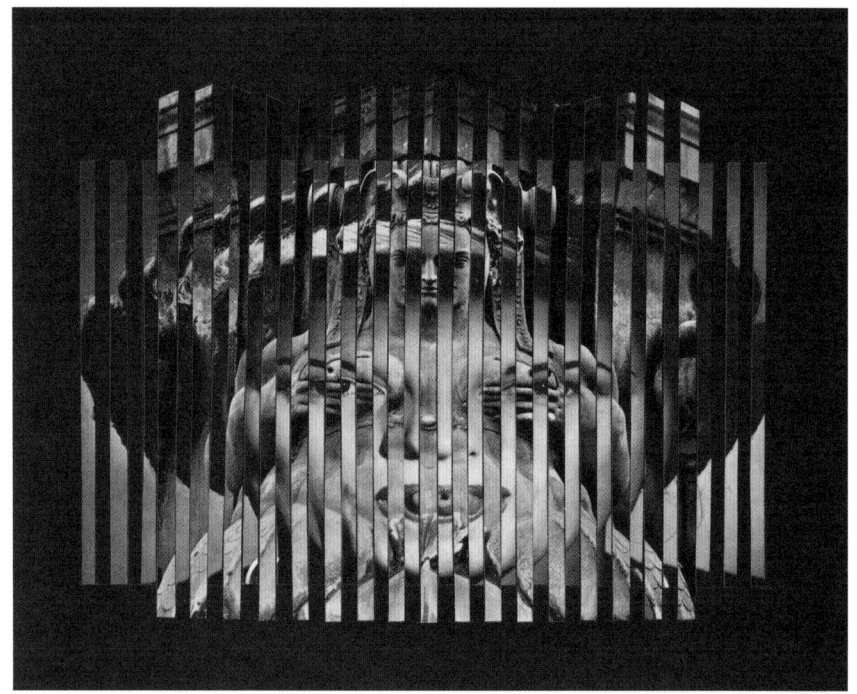

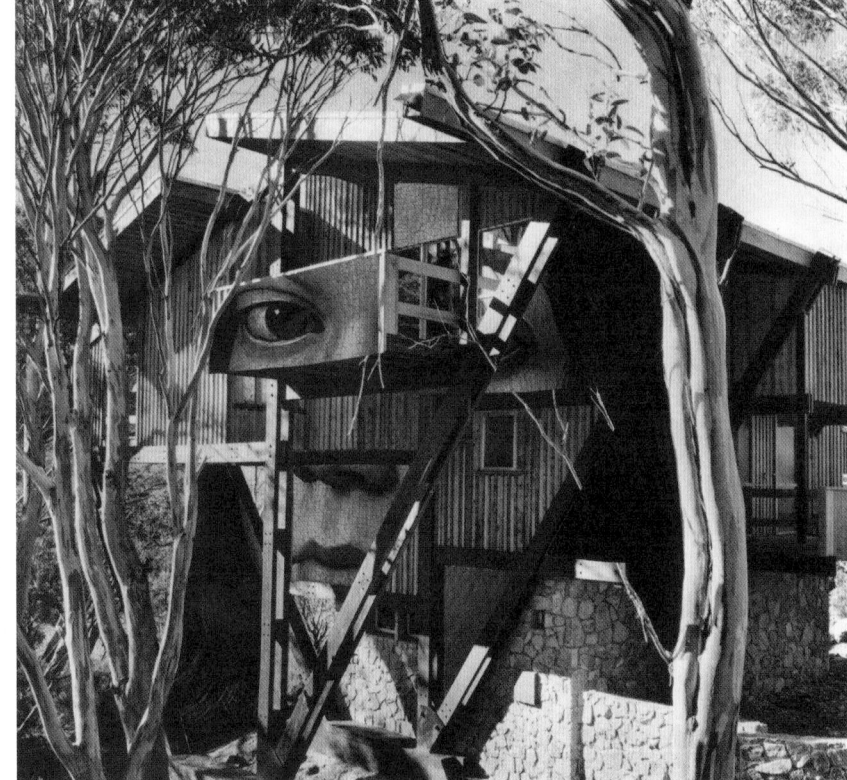

Born 1962, Geneva, Switzerland. Lives in Helsinki, Finland.

↑↑ **Luonnotar / Nature Empowered**, 2020, analogue collage combining hand-cut strips from vintage source images, c. 35 × 40 cm (c.13¾ × 15¾ in), private collection

↑ **Hidey-Hole**, 2020, hand-cut analogue collage combining vintage papers, c.26 × 29 cm (c.10¼ × 11⅜ in)

↗ **Getting Set**, 2021, hand-cut analogue collage on vintage illustration of a sculpture by Wäinö Aaltonen, c.34 × 23 cm (c.13⅜ × 9 in), Turku Art Museum/Lars Göran Johnsson collection, Finland

↗↗ **The First Cut is the Deepest**, 2020, hand-cut analogue collage combining vintage art historical illustrations, c.29 × 24 cm (c.11⅜ × 9⅜ in), private collection

→ **Untuvikko / Downy**, 2021, hand-cut analogue collage combining vintage papers, c.21 × 30 cm (c.8¼ × 11¾ in)

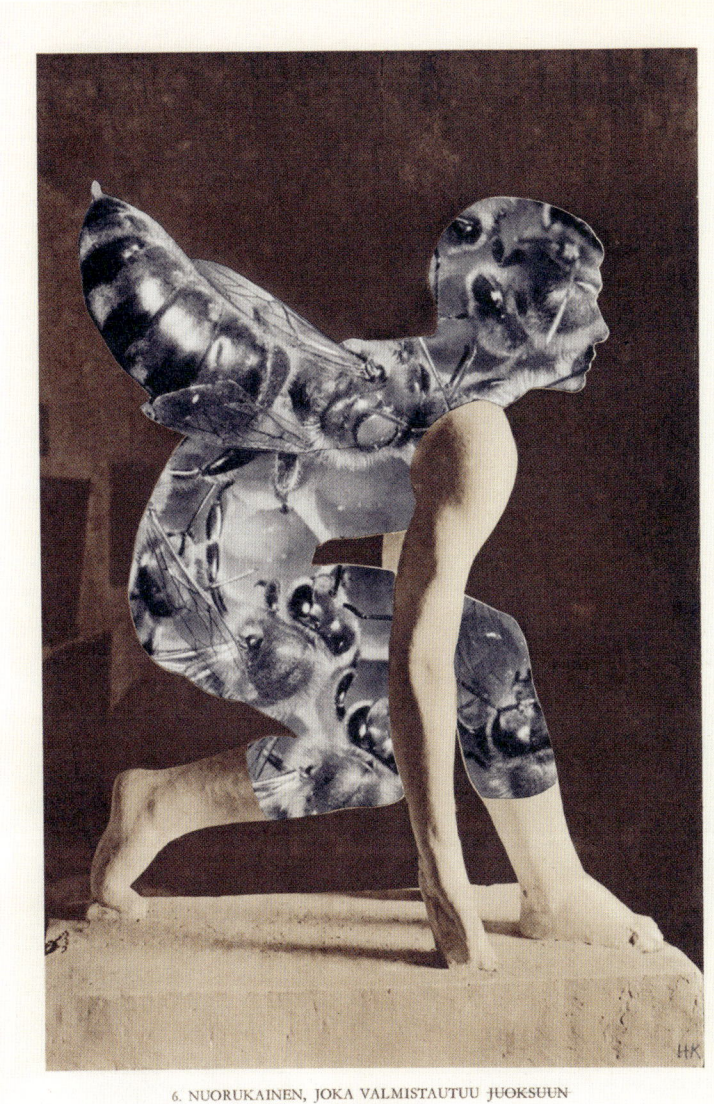

6. NUORUKAINEN, JOKA VALMISTAUTUU JUOKSUUN
Kipsiä, 1917

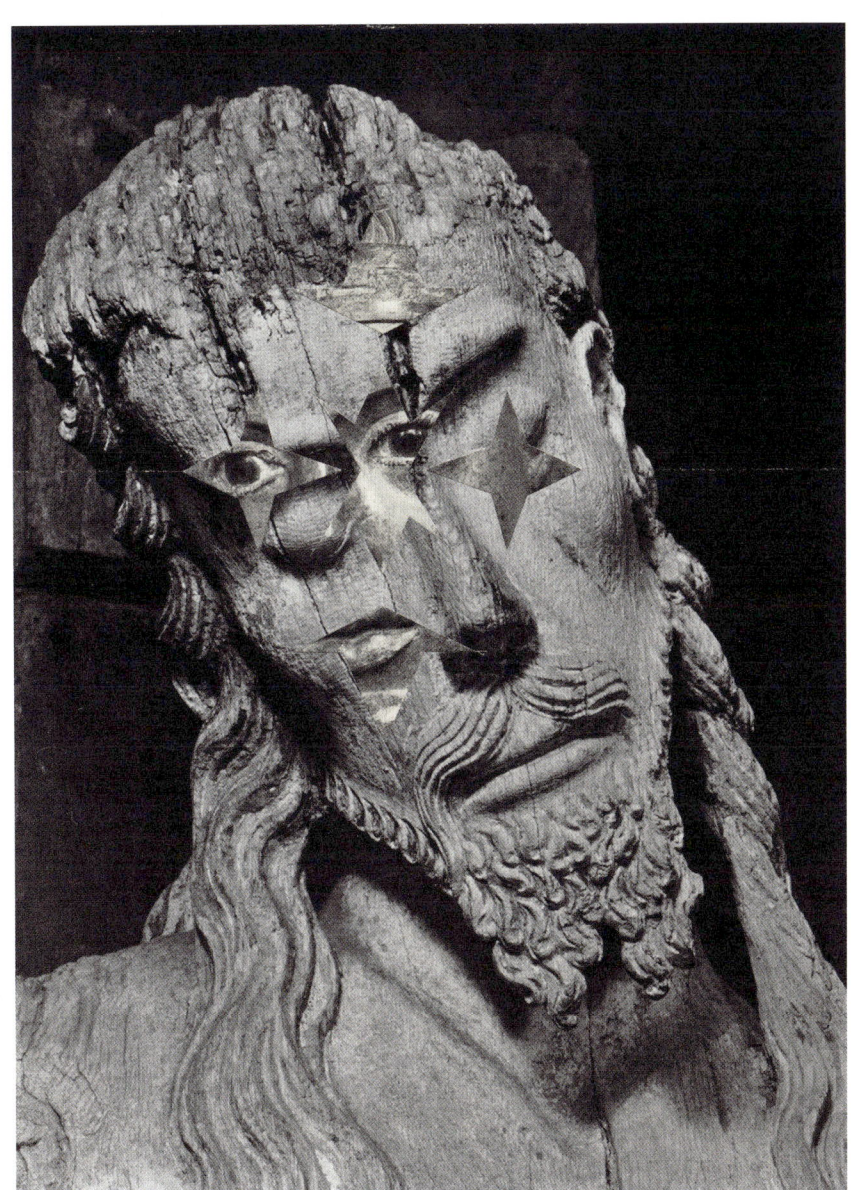

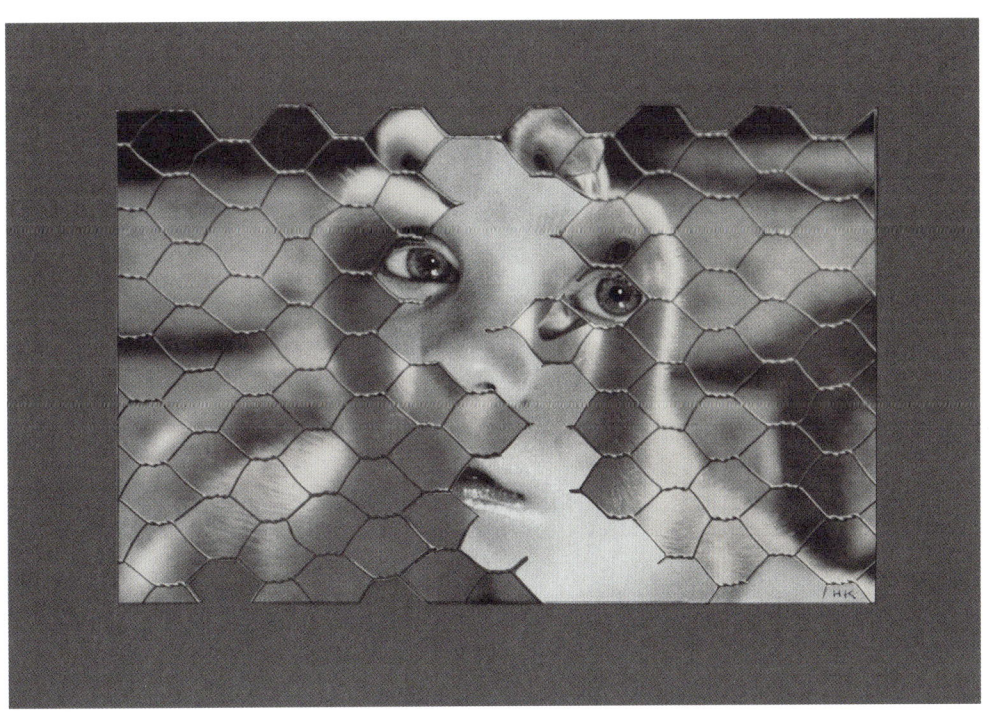

GÜLSÜN

KARAMUSTAFA

If one had to choose a single word to describe Gülsün Karamustafa's concerns, it might be 'hybridization'. Her home city of Istanbul, poised between East and West, is full of religious, political and cultural contrasts that reflect successive waves of migration from within Turkey to the predominant cities of Istanbul and Ankara (where Karamustafa was born), as well as from Turkey to Eastern Europe and between Greece and Turkey, much of it involuntary. Add the political and economic changes associated with the military coups of 1960, 1971 and 1980 and the failed attempt of 2016, together with the consequent stop-go periods of liberalization and repression, and the outcome is a context for the mixing and formation of identities that has shifted continually. Karamustafa has responded over the past five decades with installations, paintings and textiles tackling such highly charged subjects as the life of women in prison (where she and her husband spent six months in 1971 for assisting anti-government protesters), gender roles and femininity, and the conditions of displaced people. The still all-too-topical *Mystic Transports* (1992), which brought Karamustafa fame at that year's Istanbul Biennale, saw viewers walk between steel baskets in which she had placed embroidered survival blankets. Karamustafa's personal history ties in: for example, her grandmother was among the thousands of Ottoman Turks who were forced to migrate from Bulgaria to Turkey in 1893. The artist has recently turned to collage as a naturally hybrid form for relating Turkey's diverse cultures and collective histories to her established themes. As she explained in her proposal for the solo exhibition 'Peculiar Song' at Nitra Gallery, Athens, Greece, in 2019, the body of work she presented was 'about a city that has grown into 20 million in less than a quarter of a century' – from just six million in 1990 – 'covering all the history and memory under heavy dust where one has to dig so deep to find the traces of what once had been lived there…'. *Monthly Illustrated I* (2016) is one of a series combining prints on the underside of glass with paper collages drawn from the covers of popular magazines aimed at Ottoman women in the 1920s – a time when paintings under glass would have been found at the coffeehouses that acted as the centre of male socializing. This, then, is a twenty-first-century view of disparate aspects of the scene a century earlier, setting up a conversation between generations. In the series of twelve 'Instanbulites' (2019) historic photographs of former inhabitants of the city are pasted onto a dual backdrop: on the one hand a monochrome wall that might stand for modernity and minimalism (the Western influence); on the other hand more traditional decorative patterns, again making thematic use of the layering of collage to suggest the contrasting formative influences buried in the city's past.

PAUL CAREY-KENT

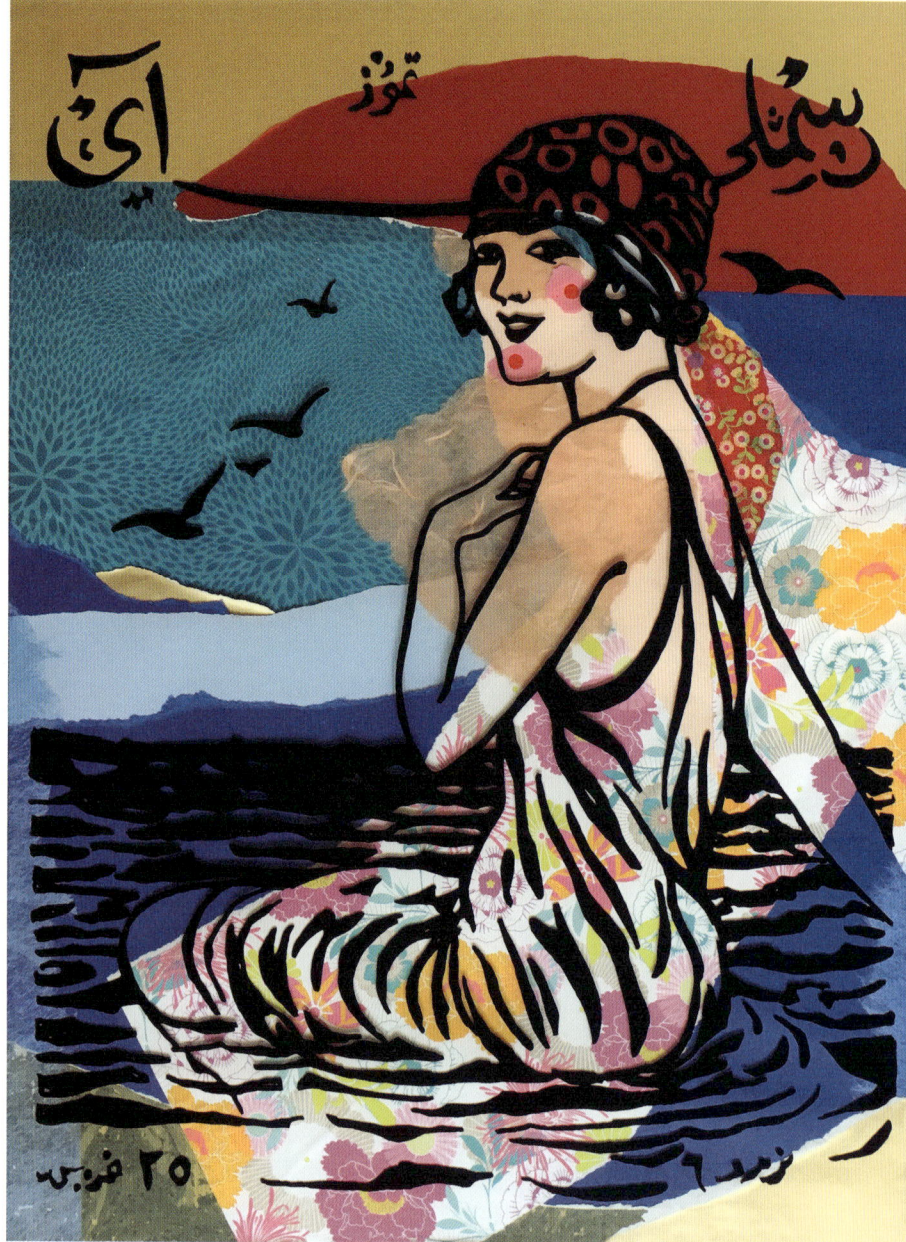

Born 1946, Ankara, Turkey. Lives in Istanbul, Turkey.

↑   Monthly Illustrated I, 2016, paper collage under glass print, 80 × 60 cm (31½ × 32⅝ in)
↗   Obsession Dada (A Must-See), 2016, paper collage, 21 × 30 cm (8¼ × 11¾ in)
↗↗ Istanbulites II, 2019, paper collage, 21 × 29 cm (8¾ × 11⅜ in)
→   Istanbulites I, 2019, paper collage, 21 × 29 cm (8¾ × 11⅜ in)

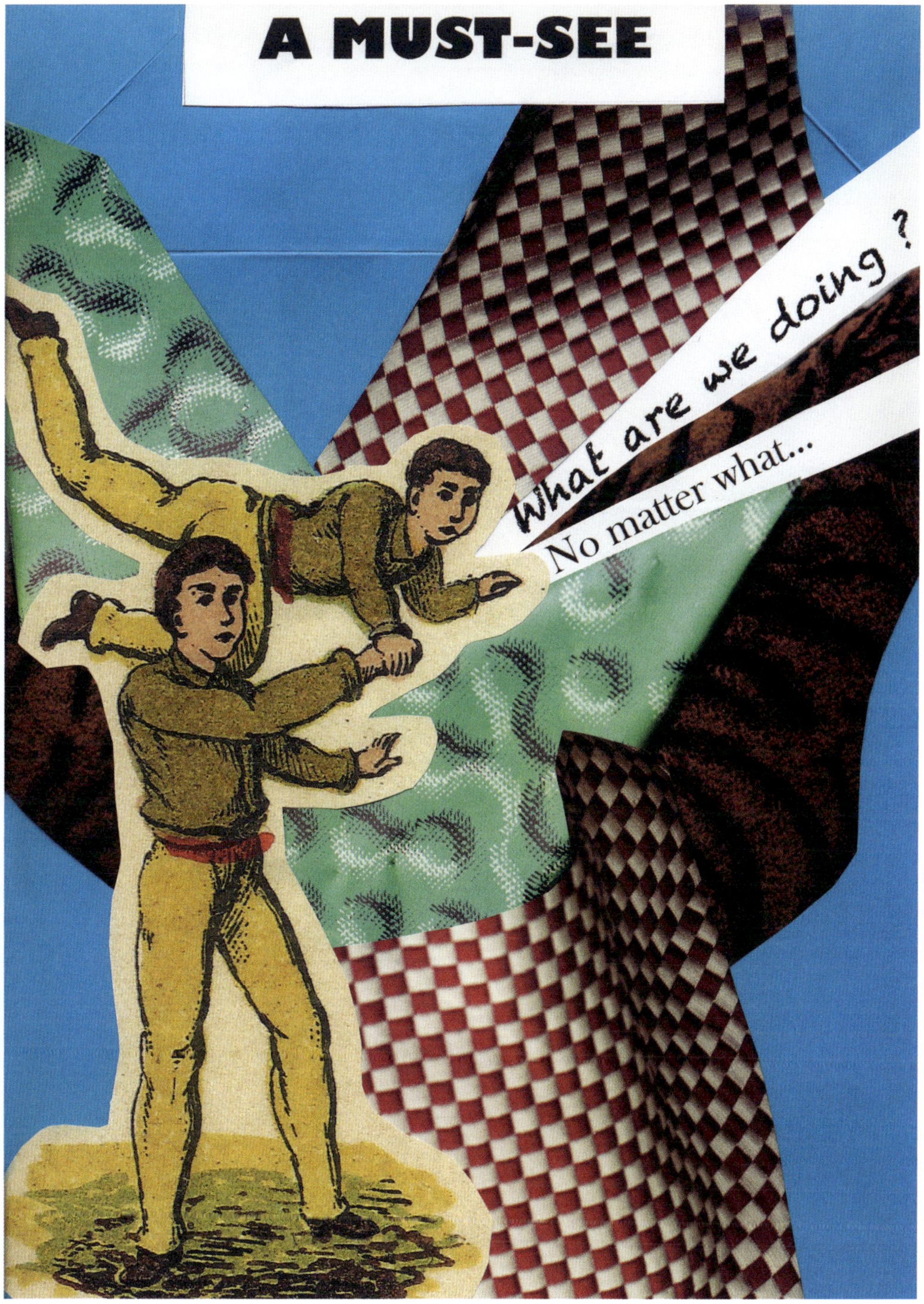

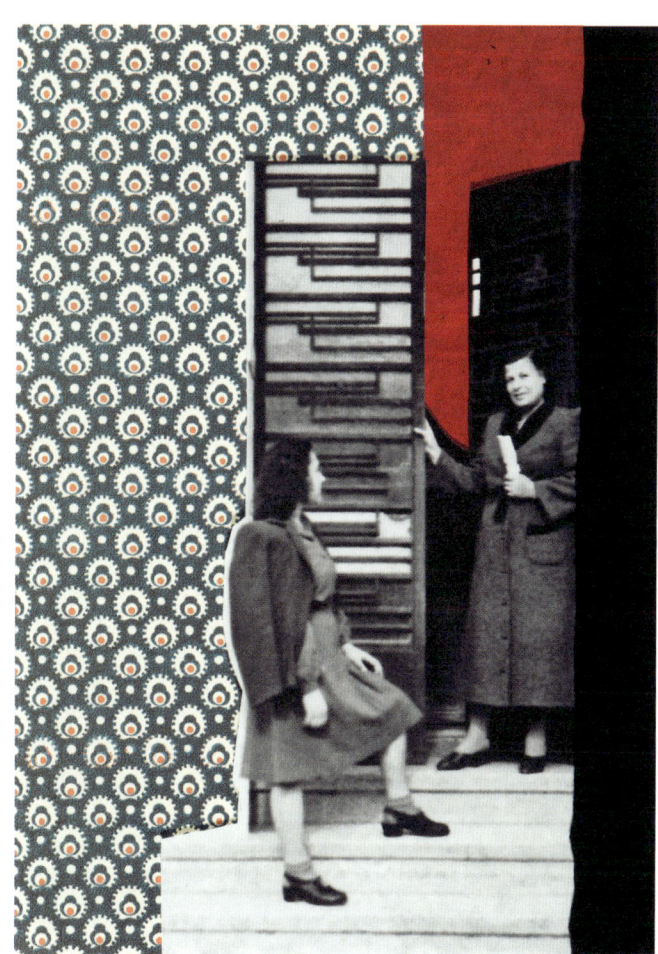

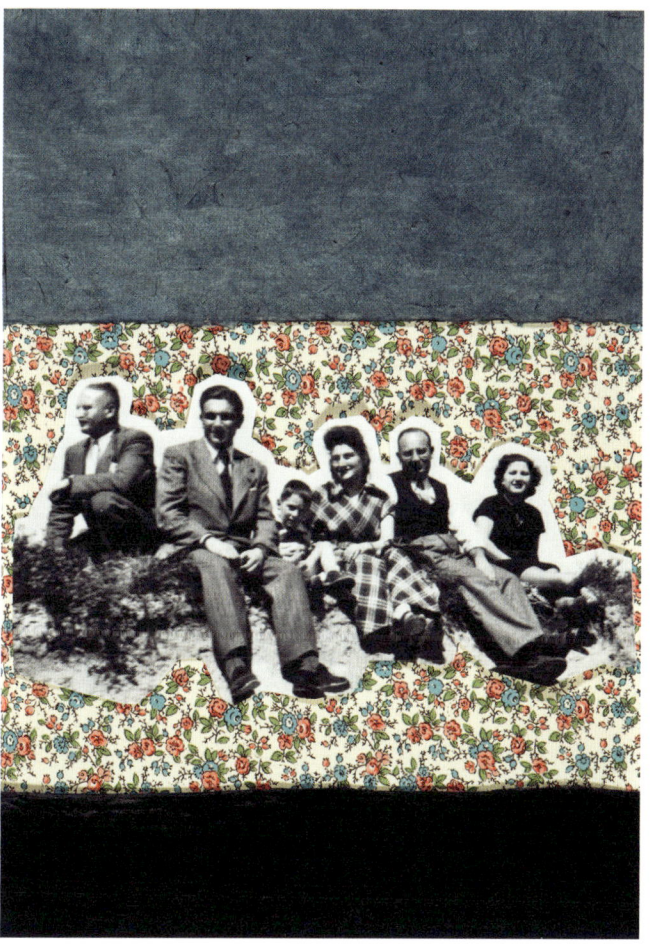

GÜLSÜN KARAMUSTAFA

IRINI
KARAYANNOPOULOU

Described by the artist as 'collage paintings', the phantasmagorical works of Irini Karayannopoulou are fuelled by an abiding interest in women's bodies and the way they are visually represented. Using archival materials, be they vintage erotica, postcards or women's magazines, Karayannopoulou's process unfolds intuitively, and often late at night: she prefers to work after midnight when the dark and quiet liberate her unconscious and imbue her images with the intoxicating and strange atmosphere of the dark. ◣ Karayannopoulou's female subjects are found in printed matter but their identity is erased by the application of oil paint over their collaged paper surfaces, concealing their individual traits. In doing so, the artist attempts to reclaim their agency and to transform their objectified, sexualized womanhood by forging mysterious, darkly comic and nuanced narratives that are open-ended and left for the viewer to unravel. ◣ In *Be drunk* (2022), which takes its title from an 1869 poem by Charles Baudelaire and belongs to the artist's 'After Hours' series, we encounter two such forms of unidentifiable and anonymous women: one whose face is covered with a mask of serpentine brushstrokes of paint, the other represented in the small headless nude form that dangles like an earring from the larger figure. One clothed, one naked, they seem perhaps to represent two versions of the same woman. Other symbols are coded into the ambivalent image: the gilded cage could serve as a visual metaphor for the woman's own circumstances. Her elegant clothing suggests she is wealthy, but she is depicted alone, a solitary figure who may not be free to act. In Baudelaire's poem, the writer expounds the pleasure of being drunk, whether it's on 'wine, poetry or virtue', as the only form of escape from the doom of one's mortal existence.

◣ In other works, Karayannopoulou employs a playful language to comment on feminine stereotypes and social constraints around women's behaviour and place in society; as the artist explained in correspondence with the author in 2022, 'I like to mess with preconceptions and stereotypes, test the boundaries of image, see how far it can go – or how close it can come.' In *Insomniac* (2020) the artist humorously exploits the collaging together of two images from opposing sides of the pop culture sphere: in the original context of a 1960s advertisement, the glamorized household sponge was originally intended to tempt women – the assumed consumers and dishwashers – to purchase it. With the addition of a pair of sensuous red lips, however, in Karayannopoulou's rendition the anthropomorphized sponge seems to take on an absurd life of its own. Karayannopoulou also reinstates red lipstick as an expression of self-empowerment and subversion for women (rather than its stereotypical associations with seduction and sexualization) – in the Dark Ages, dark red lips were thought to represent the devil, while the Suffragettes wore it as part of their uniform to communicate power and strength. ◣

CHARLOTTE JANSEN

Born 1973, Thessaloniki, Greece. Lives in Athens, Greece.

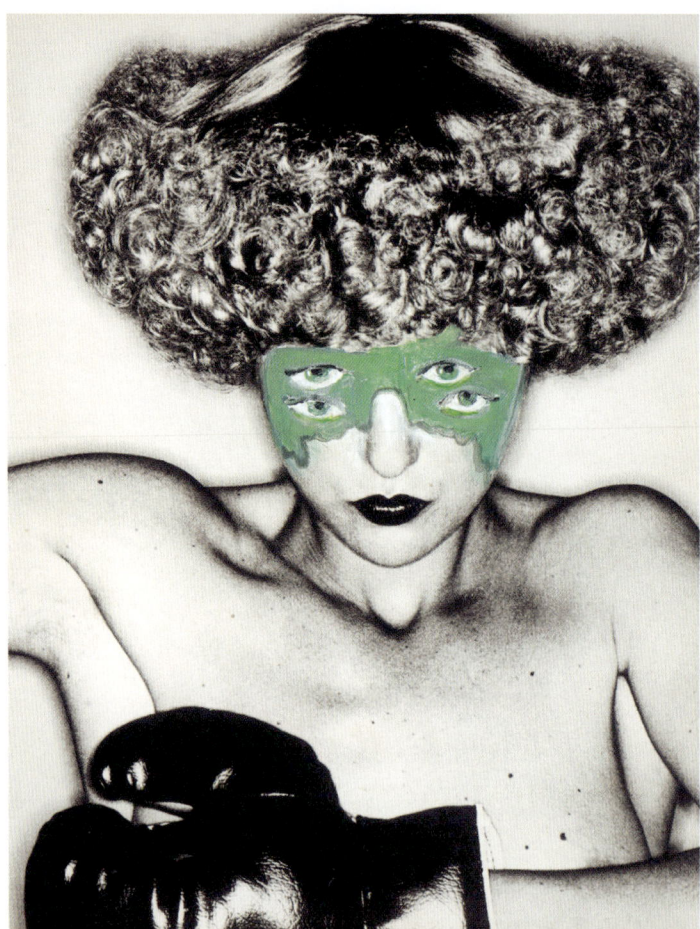

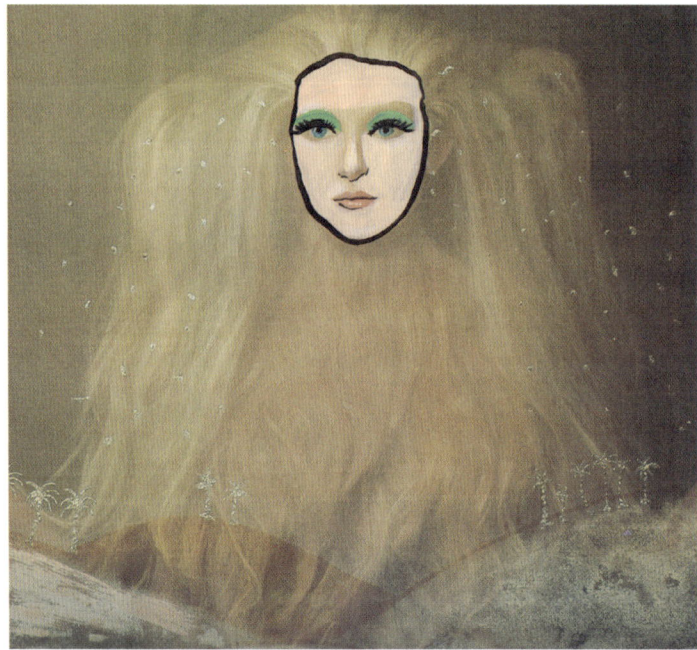

↑↑ **Aureole**, 2019, acrylic, ink and paper cuts on giclée printed fine art paper, 107 × 82 cm (42⅛ × 32¼ in), private collection

↑ **The Pearl Maiden**, 2020, acrylic, pearl pigment and collage on giclée printed fine art paper, 116 × 105 cm (45⅝ × 41 in)

↗ **Be drunk**, 2022, acrylic, metal powders and collage on giclée printed fine art paper, 160 × 115 cm (62⅞ × 45¼ in)

↗↗ **Tyche, a capricious dispenser of good and ill fortune**, 2022, acrylic, pearl pigment and collage on giclée printed fine art paper, 140 × 105 cm (55 × 41 in)

→ **Insomniac**, 2020, collage on offset print, 20 × 22 cm (7¾ × 8⅝ in)

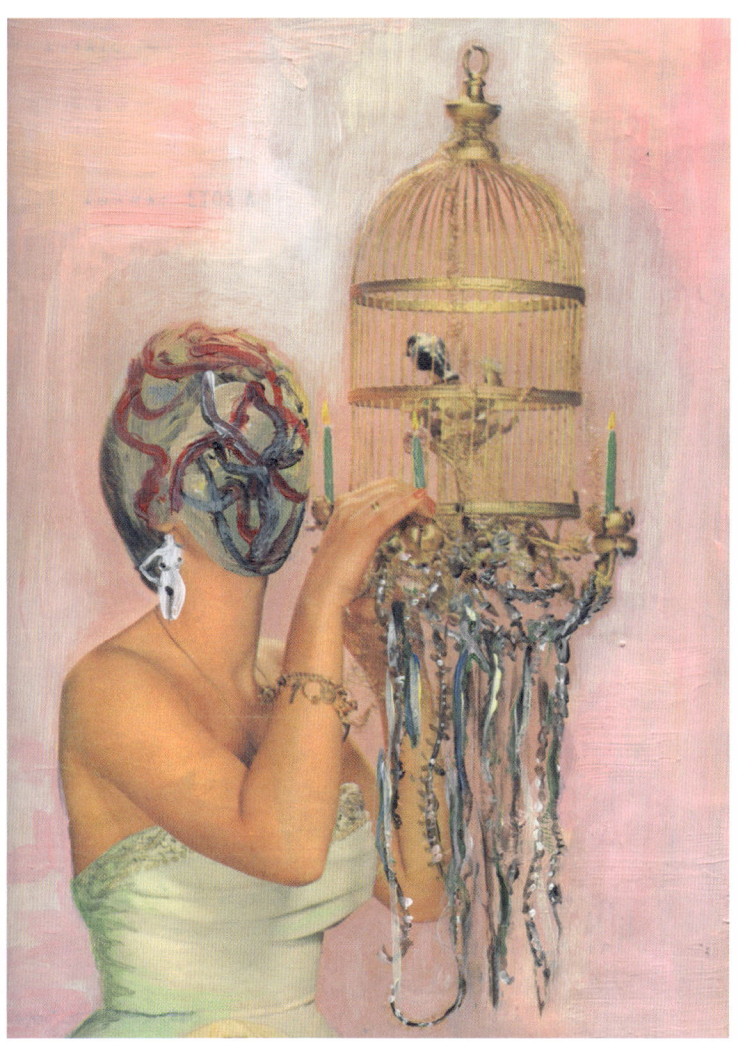

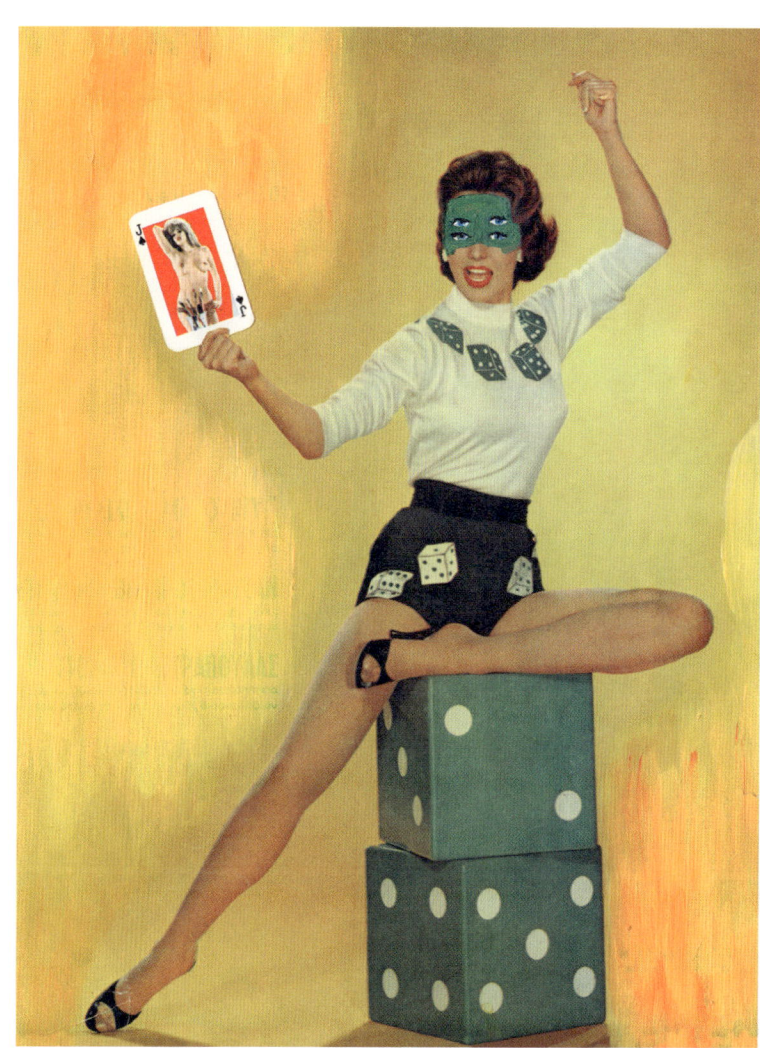

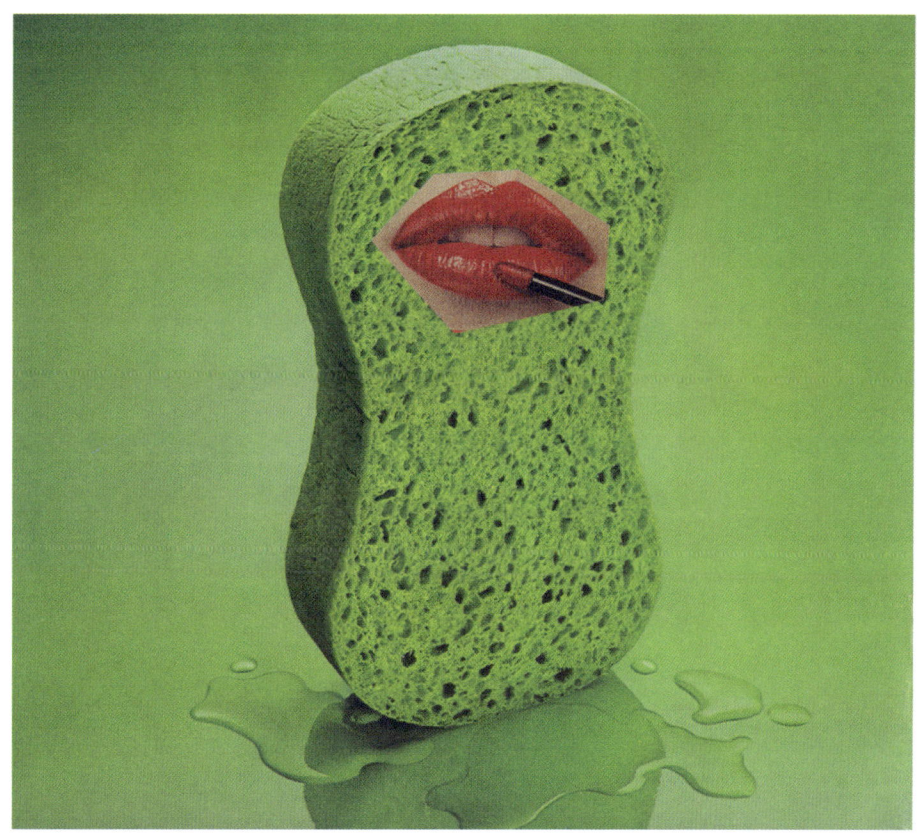

IRINI
KARAYANNOPOULOU

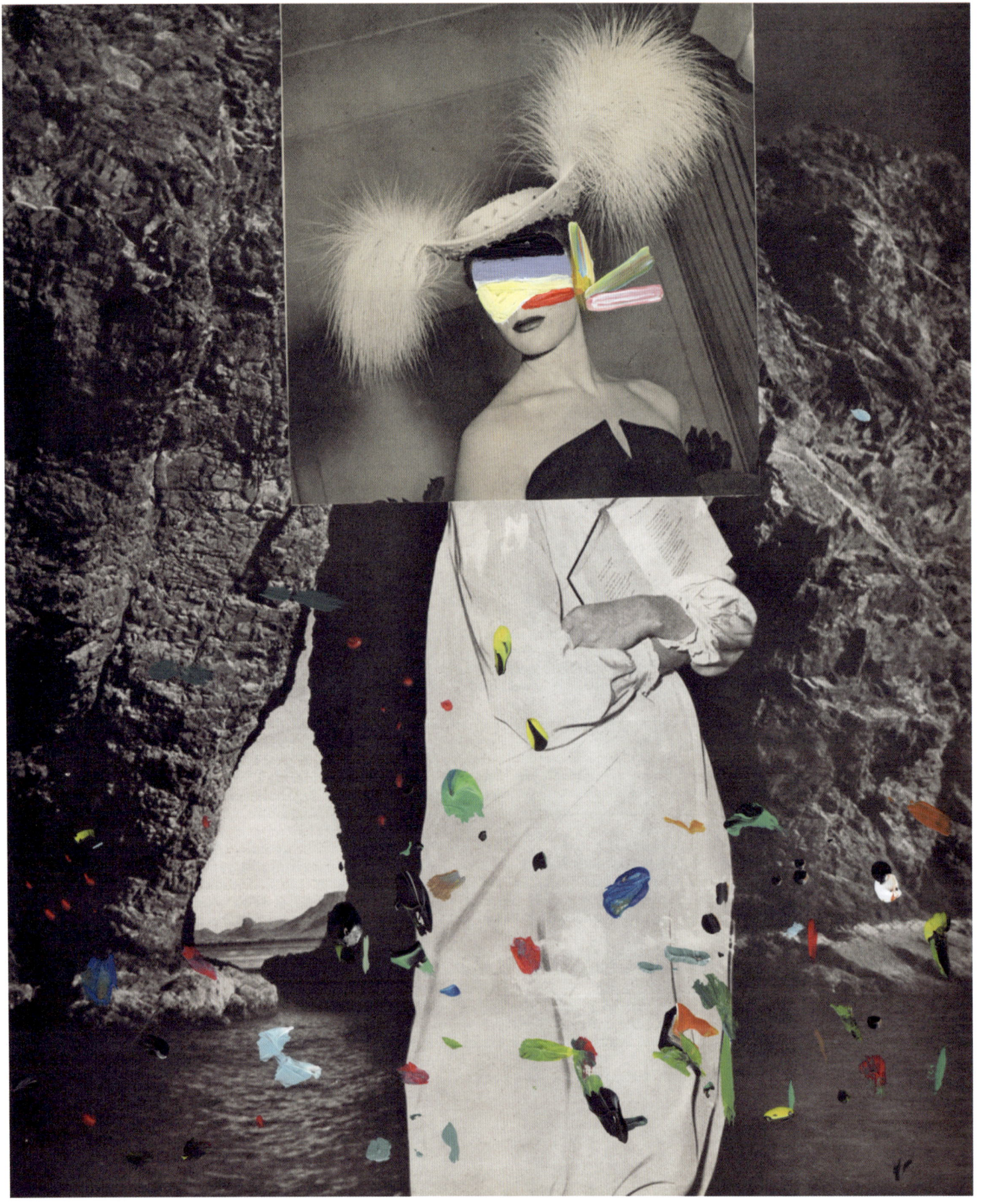

↑   **The meaning of caves in a dream**, 2022, acrylic and collage on giclée printed fine art paper,
140 × 115 cm (55 × 45¼ in)

→   **The Atlantist**, 2022, acrylic, sticker and collage on giclée printed fine art paper, 155 × 115 cm
(61 × 45¼ in)

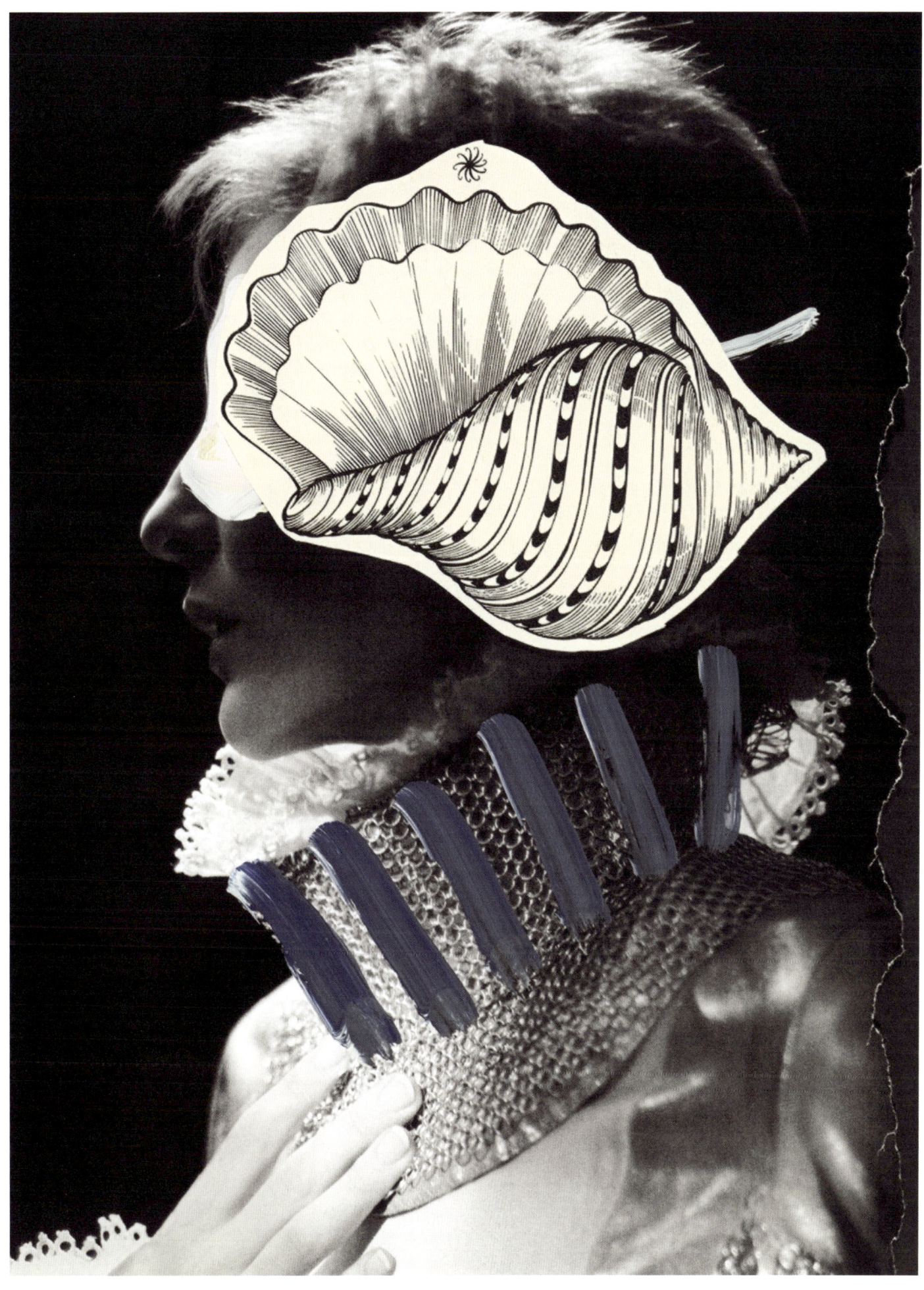

IRINI
KARAYANNOPOULOU

PETER KENNARD

Tony Blair taking a selfie in front of a burning Iraq oil field. A peace symbol severing a bomb. John Constable's *The Hay Wain* (1821) redecorated with surface to air missiles. Peter Kennard's iconic and polemic photomontages have been part of Britain's visual culture for over fifty years. Kennard is a master of straight-to-the-point picture-making, splicing incongruent images together to create powerful visual messages. Appearing on billboards and notebooks, newspaper front-pages and placards, Kennard's work has significant reach, speaking far beyond the art world. Starting his career as a painter before becoming politicized by the protests against the Vietnam War, Kennard made work for left-wing newspapers and collaborated with activist organizations, including CND (Campaign for Nuclear Disarmament). He has raised awareness on topics such as environmentalism, nuclear war, racism and apartheid. In a world of mixed messages, his is loud and clear: where inequality and oppression exist, we shouldn't look away. Kennard belongs to a rich heritage of montage artists, such as the German pioneers of the medium Hannah Höch (1889–1978) and John Heartfield (1891–1968). For them, cutting is a political as well as a physical gesture, rupturing the dominant media image and using it against itself. In *Sub-Trump* (2018) Kennard tackles one of the big topics of our age. The work combines an image of former US president Donald Trump and a nuclear submarine. To many, Trump was a figure of political derision, yet his proud military triumphalism and regressive nationalism found broad public support. While others have attempted to deflate Trump's egotism with humour, Kennard returns him to the world of terror, reminding us that, while in office, Trump had the power to launch nuclear war. These images are warnings from history asking us not to make the same mistakes. *Ukraine 1* (2022) incorporates the Ukrainian flag partially obscured by a stark image of someone holding a smartphone that shows a portrait of an injured screaming face. The contrasting monochromatic figure is placed in front of the bright blue and yellow flag, amplifying the polarized aspect of the conflict following Russia's invasion of Ukraine in 2022. While the image highlights the huge suffering reported in the press and across social media, it also offers a sense of hope and resilience as well as international solidarity. In *Syria* (2018) Kennard tackles conflict through a more poetic tenor. A destroyed street frames a desolate tree fashioned from barbed wire. If the tree symbolizes continuity and longevity, the wire reminds us of people bombed out of their homes and forced to seek refuge in other countries. As in other works, the piece juxtaposes an image of pain with a sense of defiance. Kennard's compositions remind us of the importance of art in speaking through the noise and giving form to our collective feelings.

GEORGE VASEY

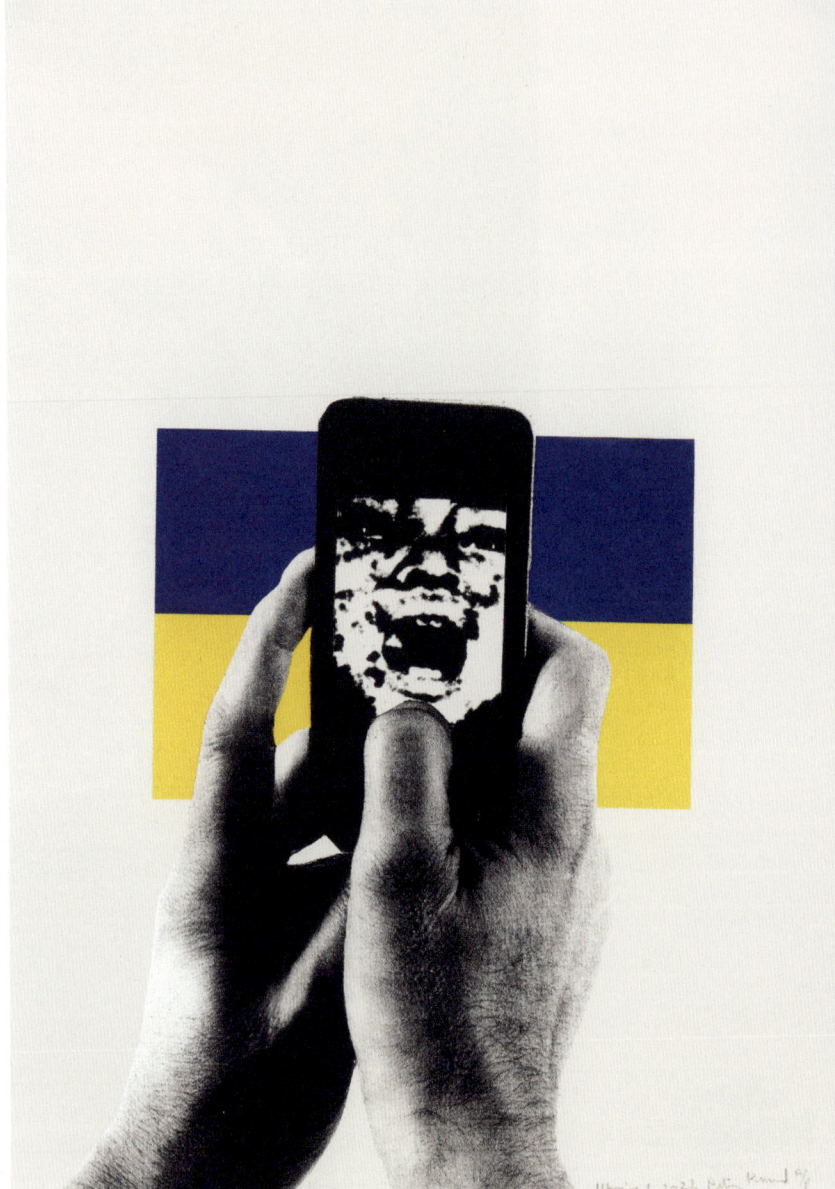

Born 1949, London, UK. Lives in London.

↑   **Ukraine 1**, 2022, pigment print on 255 gsm Somerset Archival paper, 59 × 42 cm (23¼ × 16½ in), edition of 50

↗   **Sub-Trump**, 2018, photomontage: pigment prints and ink on card, 50 × 42 cm (19½ × 16½ in)

↗↗ **Syria**, 2018, photomontage: pigment print, graphite, pastel and gouache on card, 55 × 39.5 cm (21½ × 15½ in)

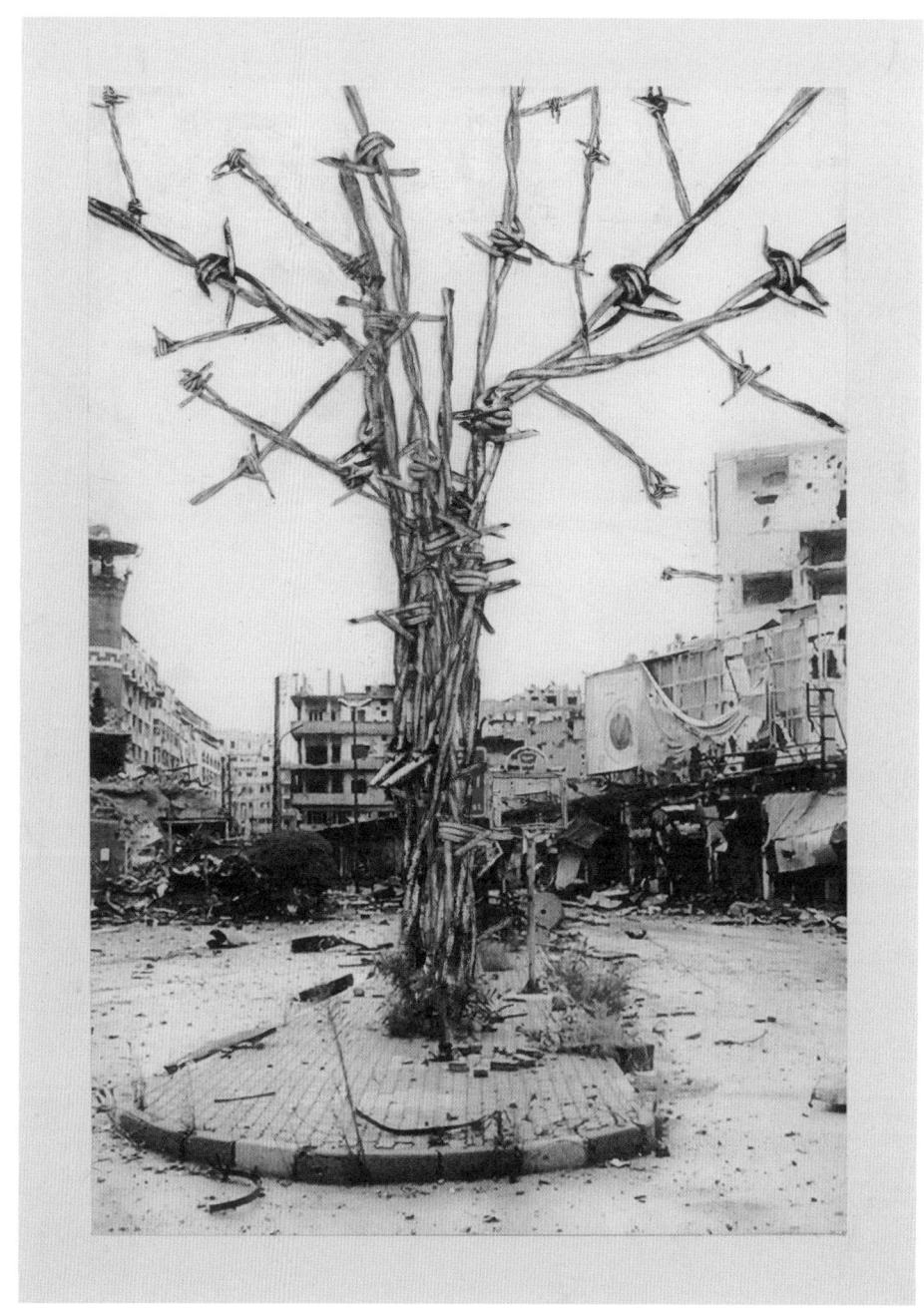

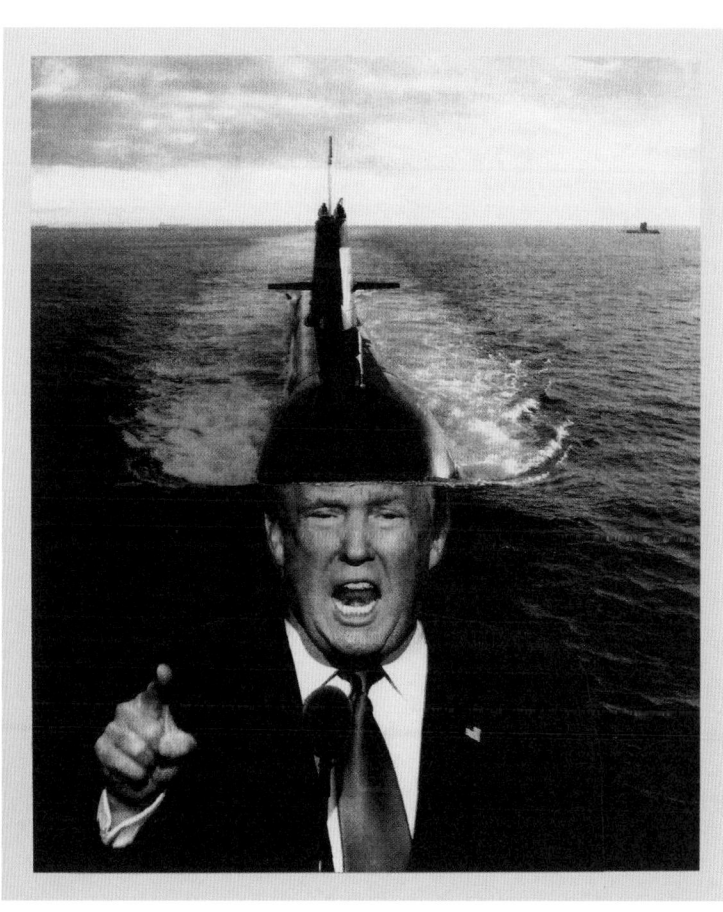

RADHIKA KHIMJI

Building up images, layer by layer, using photographic imagery, drawing and painting on a plywood or MDF base, Radhika Khimji creates dense accumulations that are caught between flat image and relief sculpture. The artist seeks to evade the easy categorization so often applied to specific mediums. Instead, her approach is process-oriented, and she lets the materials guide the work. As Khimji explained to curator Reem Fadda in *Ocula* in 2021, 'As soon as the work stops, it almost feels like a lie to explain and describe what it is, because they are so process-based and come out of a compulsion to make.' A twisting headless and armless figure leaps playfully in *Lick the sky* (2021). As with many of Khimji's figures, it is genderless. The origins of these biomorphic forms can be traced to the artist's childhood, when she often made sketches for her aunt, a fashion designer, of curvaceous figures with large thighs and breasts. Less a representation of any specific person than an exploration of the corporeal, *Lick the sky* endeavours to represent bodily consciousness – what it means to inhabit a body and to move through space. Khimji was inspired, in part, by *The Mind is a Muscle* (1968), an iconic performance for seven dancers created by Yvonne Rainer (b. 1934), which stripped away gestural conventions of narrative. Rainer's choreography offered Khimji both a language to diagram a body's movements and a framework for considering repetition and ritual. Indeed, in many of Khimji's compositions, pulsating recurring dots dapple the background and the figures' bodies. In *Lick the sky* a swarm of muscular crimson marks swells over the thigh and knee of the prancing figure. As Khimji explained in the same interview, 'I've been fascinated with watching a mark cover up an area to veil and reveal it at the same time. There's a physical hovering over a zone… which feels like an energy zone, or a portal to another space.' This signature motif has been noted by critics as echoing a number of art historical precedents, from seventeenth- and eighteenth-century Nathdwara miniature paintings in India, to Australian Aboriginal art, to the rasterbilder dots used to create gradation and form by the German artist Sigmar Polke (1941–2010). In the aperture-like *Mechanical eye* (2021) sight and space collapse into one another. Over an abstracted landscape filled with black oblongs are hundreds of dots. Together these white pinpricks form the titular eye, a giant, isolated entity that operates as both a screen and a portal onto this terrain. Unsettling and surreal, *Mechanical eye* recalls the fantastical close-up painting of a human eye, *The False Mirror* (1929), by René Magritte. Khimji captures bodily sensation rather than simply depicting a likeness: though recognizably an eye, the work also questions what it means both to see and be seen. ∎

GRACE LINDEN

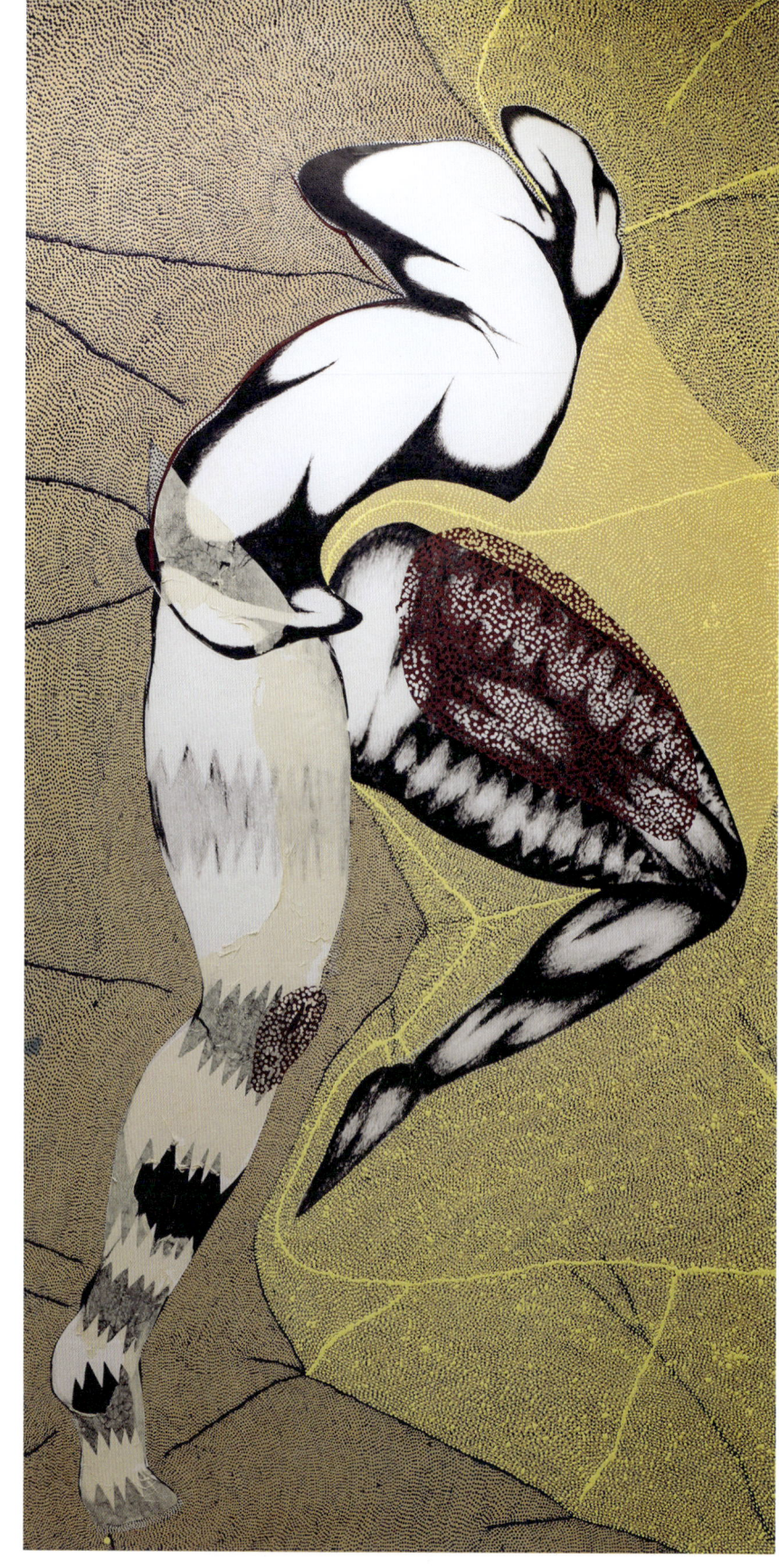

Born 1979, Muscat, Oman. Lives in London, UK.

↑   **Lick the sky**, 2021, acrylic and glue on digital print on paper and MDF, 243.8 × 121.9 × 0.5 cm (96 × 48 × ¼ in)

↗   **Mechanical eye**, 2021, oil and photo transfer on birch plywood, 100 × 120 cm (39⅜ × 47¼ in)

→   **There's a black splash coming**, 2021, oil on photo transfer on paper, canvas, wood and glass, 150 × 190 cm (59⅛ × 74 ¾ in)

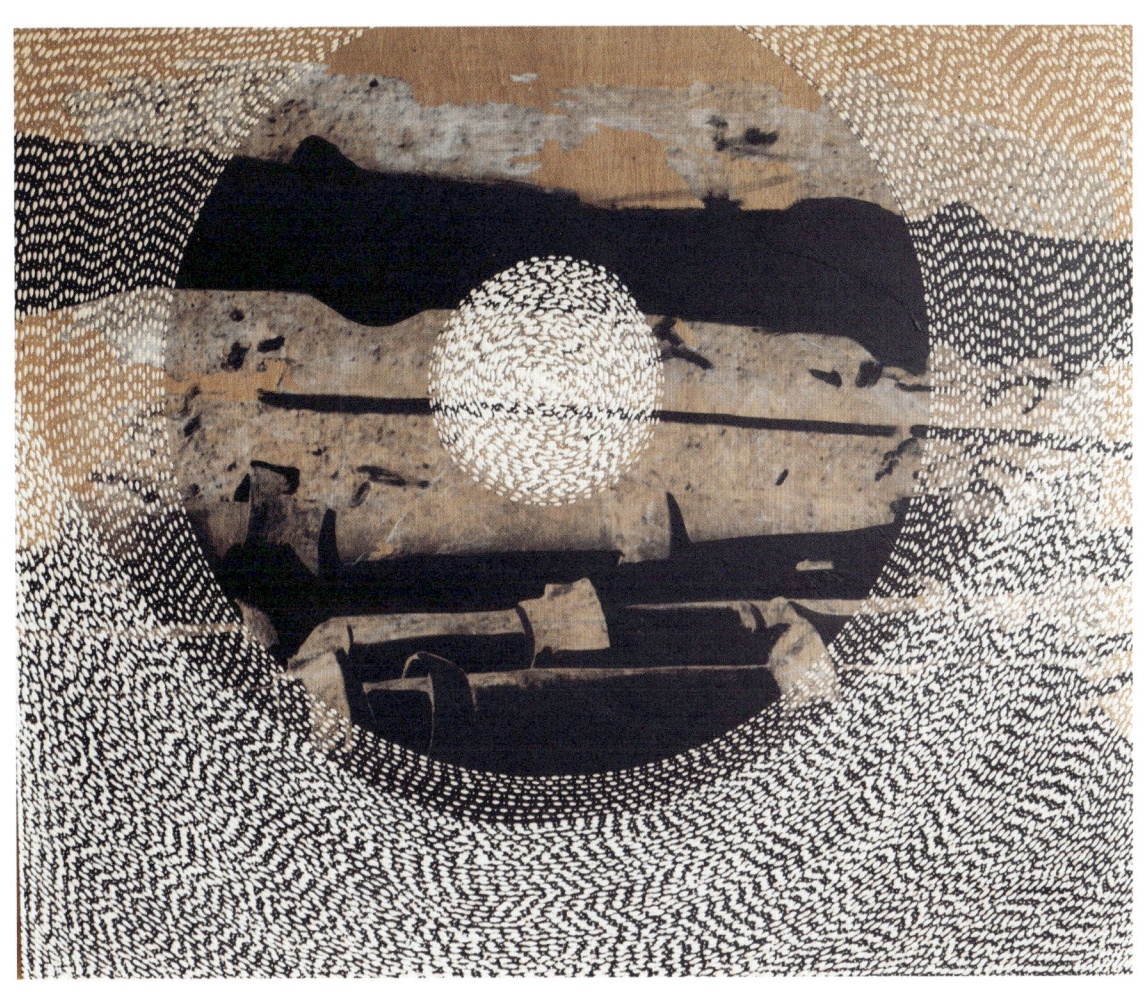

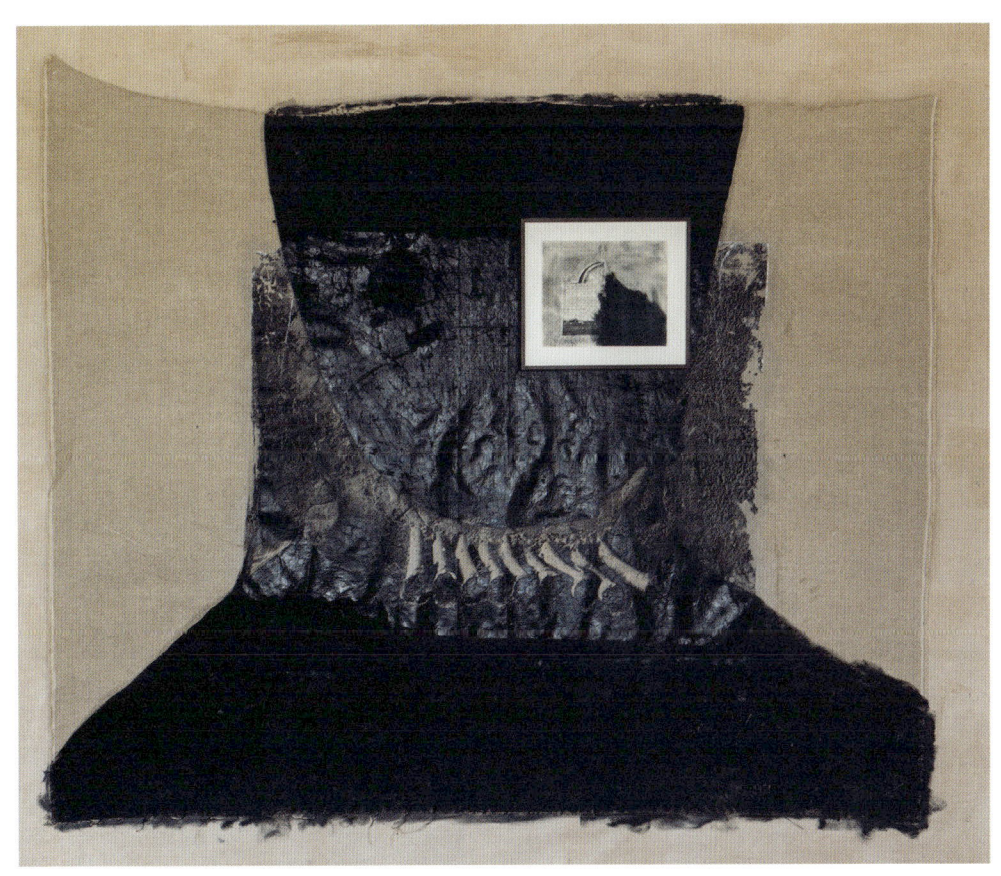

RADHIKA
KHIMJI

YASHUA KLOS

In the multi-layered works of Yashua Klos, collage becomes a metaphor for the fragmentation and reconstruction of Black identity in America. Taking his cue from the printmaking of twentieth-century African American artist-activists Charles White (1918–79) and Elizabeth Catlett (1915–2012), and the explosive graphics produced by Emory Douglas (b.1943) for the Black Panther Party in the 1960s, Klos uses the raw and direct medium of woodblock to carve and print reams of original source material, from which he selects patterns, shapes and textures to build figurative collages addressing the interrelations of race, class and community. This involved and time-consuming process results in bold, fragmented images characterized by rich detail, sensitive mark-making and restricted palettes. At a time when the spotlight is again being shone on racial inequalities in America and around the world, Klos's work of the early 2020s stands as a testament to the strengths and vulnerabilities of communities of colour. Their resilience is sometimes symbolized in Klos's collages by plant motifs. In *Flower Father* (2021) a pair of hands cradles a blue flower from which fragments of wood, concrete and brick are exploding. Signifying hope for the disenfranchised and marginalized in post-industrial urban centres, the collage also relates to the artist's unexpected discovery in 2018 of numerous biological family members on his estranged father's side. Some of these newfound relatives had worked at the Ford Motor Company assembly plant in Detroit, a city that prospered from the exodus of Black labour from the rural Southern United States in the early twentieth century, but which spiralled into decline as deindustrialization, unemployment and social unrest took hold. Klos's flower hints at the vitality associated with the subsequent urban renewal, but also questions the long-term benefits to that community – this is, after all, a flower without roots. A stoic fortitude energizes many of Klos's collages, an attitude he witnessed among African Americans living in Chicago's South Side, where he was raised by his white single mother. Marked by a deliberate ambiguity, works such as *You See Through It All* and *You Stand As Still As Stars* (both 2021) feature chiselled heads intersected by partially constructed walls of wood, brick and concrete that could equally be in the process of disintegrating. Caught in a liminal state, these defiant, anonymous faces embody empowerment and survival amid oppression and injustice, while the fragmenting building materials suggest both urban decay and the resourcefulness of those who reclaim and rebuild a racial identity for themselves. As Klos said in a 2016 interview in online journal *Newfound*: 'I'm seeing the Black body as a state in flux. The survival of Black life in America is reliant upon ingenuity – knowing when to adapt, transform, or stand your ground.'

DAVID TRIGG

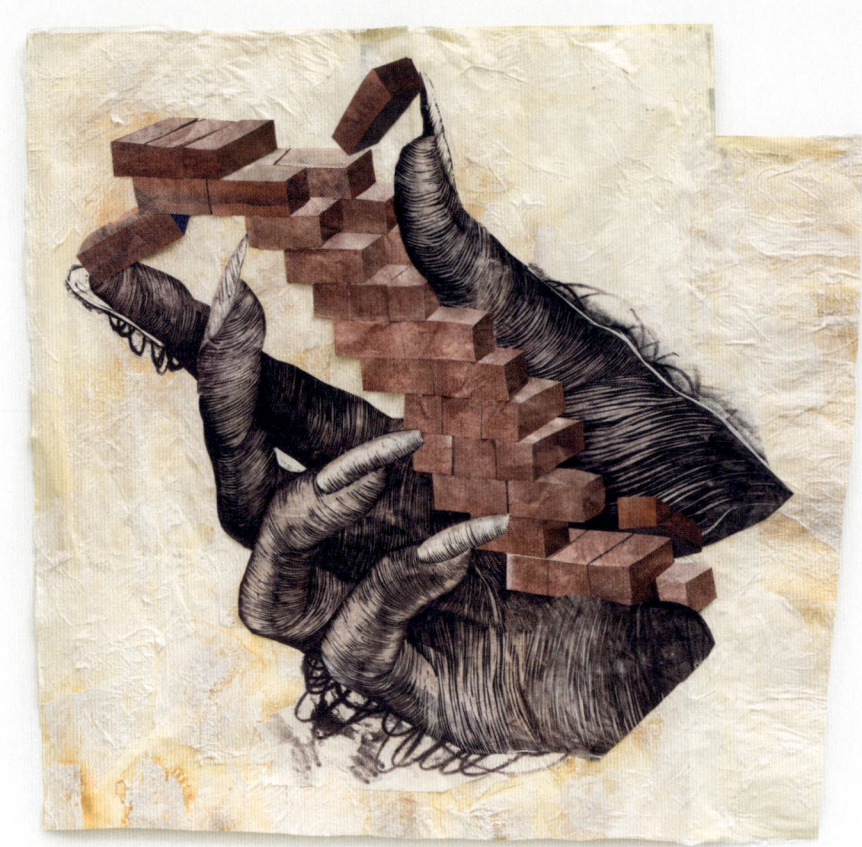

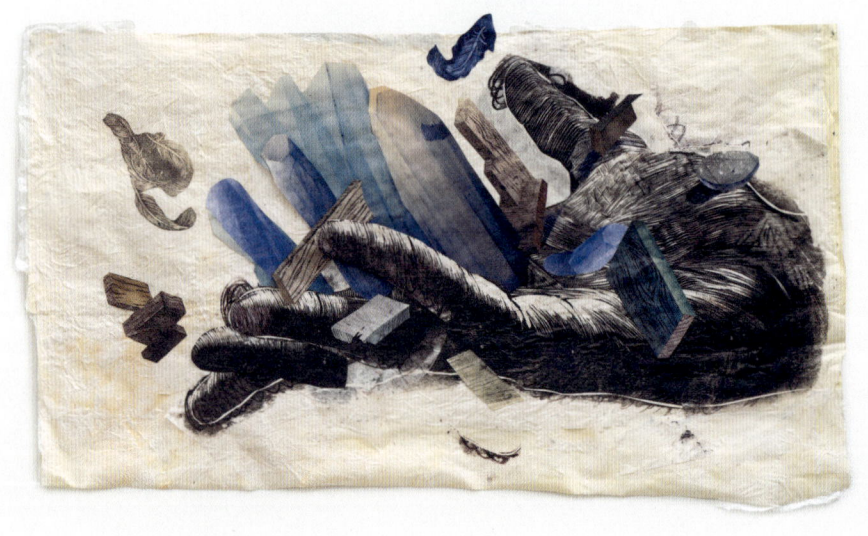

Born 1977, Chicago, Illinois, USA. Lives in New York, USA.

↑↑ **Diagram of How She Hold It All Together**, 2021, paper construction of woodblock prints and graphite on archival paper, 132 × 134.6 cm (52 × 53 in)

↑ **All This Black Shit Valuable**, 2021, paper construction of woodblock prints and graphite on archival paper, 106.7 × 188 × cm (42 × 74 in)

↗ **You See Through It All**, 2021, paper construction of woodblock prints and graphite on archival paper, 138.4 × 104.1 cm (54½ × 41 in)

↗↗ **You Stand As Still As Stars**, 2021, paper construction of woodblock prints and graphite on archival paper, 213.4 × 166.4 cm (84 × 65½ in)

→ **Flower Father**, 2021, paper construction of woodblock prints and graphite on archival paper, 121.9 × 215.9 cm (48 × 85 in)

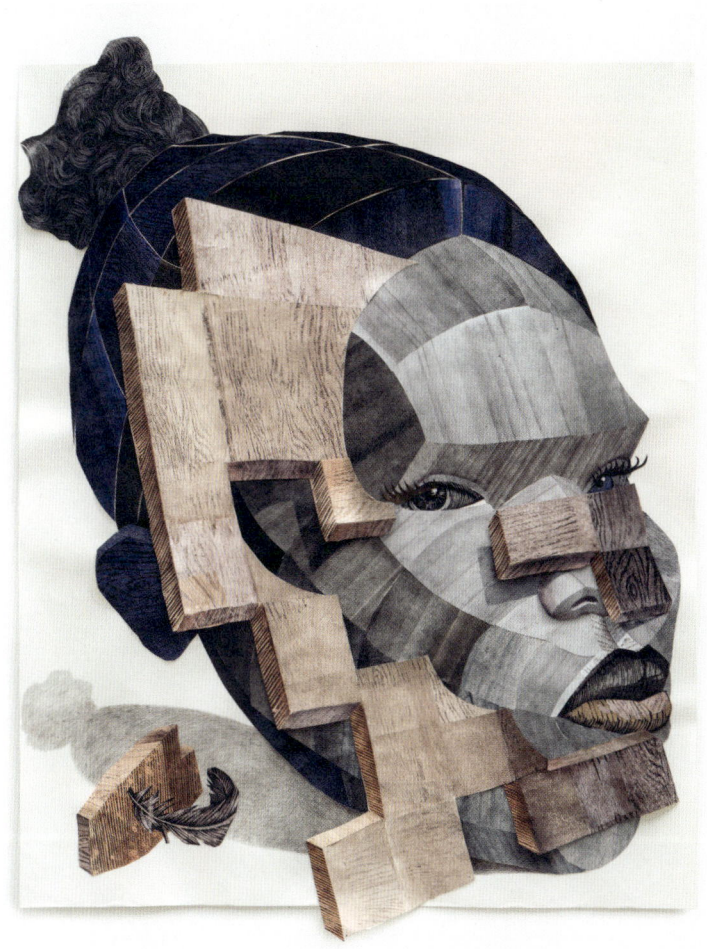

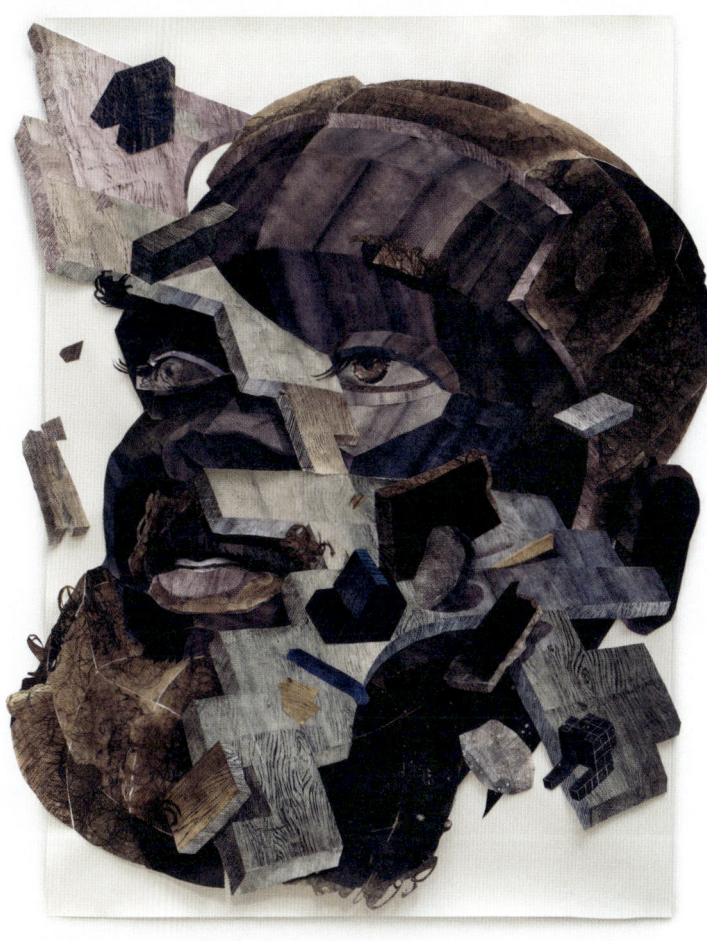

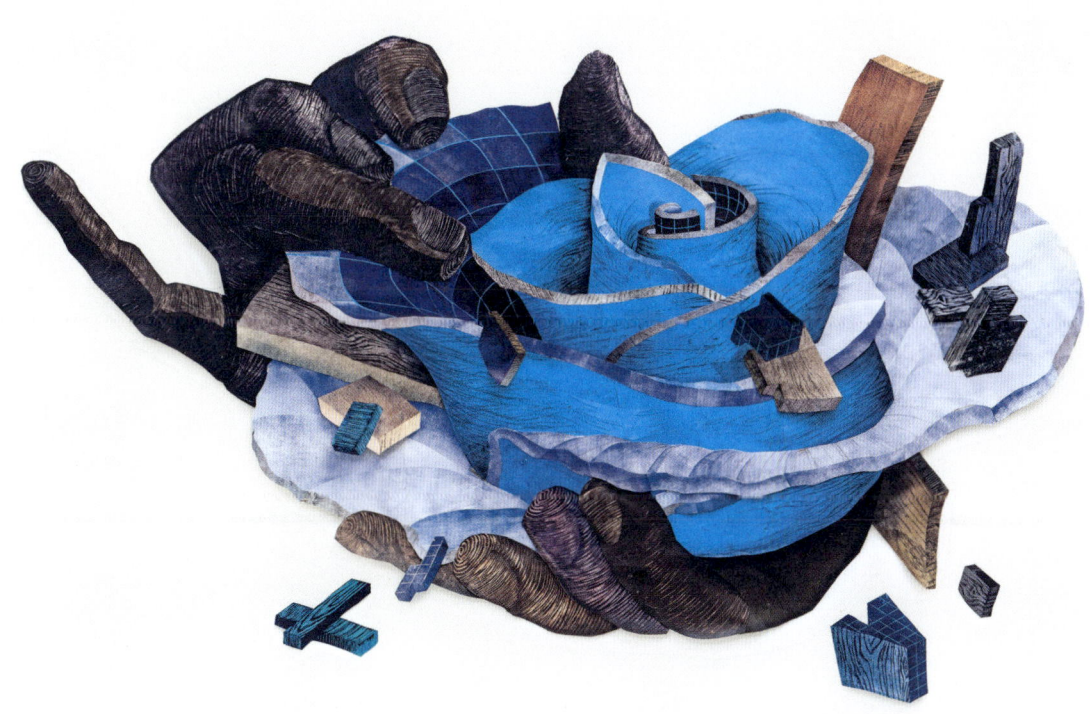

YASHUA
KLOS

JAKOB KOLDING

In the works of Jakob Kolding, collage is used as a spatial practice, both in form and content, while reframing references from art history, literature, architecture and the history of modernism at large. Kolding's practice has developed from an interest in the social space of the built environment, and from questions of class and gentrification, to include a more general exploration of space as an abstract, while nonetheless subjective, notion, constructed from constantly changing interrelations. The two-metre (six-and-a-half feet) wide digital collage *Folds* (2022) reveals Kolding's interest in the subversive possibilities of carving alternative enclaves in an already planned environment. Its urban landscape incorporates multiple elements including a rendition of Minimalist artist Sol LeWitt's *Untitled (Fold Drawing)* (1973), buildings by the Chilean-based and social housing-focused architect company Elemental, and a ramp for skate-boarding. The different patterns and surfaces, emphasized by the magnification of the images, indicate the variety of photographic sources. At the same time, the black masks of the foreground figures that dominate the scene disturbingly anonymize and unite them, perhaps suggesting some kind of resistance movement within the folded space. Alongside his paper-cut and digital collages, Kolding also creates room-sized installations that resemble nineteenth-century dioramas or theatre sets. In *The Outside or the Inside of Internalised Externalised* (2017) a space is populated by a collection of lifesize cut-out figures and over-sized headshots, all made from digital prints on birch veneer. These included major tenants of modernism, such as Sigmund Freud, together with the creatives who have influenced Kolding's practice – choreographer Yvonne Rainer, artists Édouard Manet, Carl Andre and Lygia Clark, and writers Virginia Woolf, Jorge Luis Borges and Adolfo Bioy Casares. Abstract-geometric floating forms in the shape of black hanging walls add to the modernist aesthetic, while distorting the space into a three-dimensional collage. Small paper collages, whose colourful surreal scenes seemed to animate the ideas of the black-and-white modernist thinkers dominating the space, are interspersed throughout. They attain the mythical qualities of symbols, while allowing multiple subjective entry points to the scene encompassing them. When first exhibited at the Centre d'édition Contemporaine, Geneva, and viewed through the exhibition space's glass-fronted facade, the installation functioned as a public artwork, while any spectators moving inside joined the cut-out figures in a spontaneous, performative scenography. Upon entering the show, viewers would discover the exposed structural supports of the individual elements, a 'behind the scenes' effect that revealed the theatrical illusion. As a whole, the dream-like installation drew from the modernist desire to uncover the inner spaces hidden beneath the surface, and employed collage's historical urge to delve reflexively into the image in a spatial manner. It intersected not only internal and outer formal, aesthetic, psychological and cultural spaces, but also various modes of spectatorship.
KEREN GOLDBERG

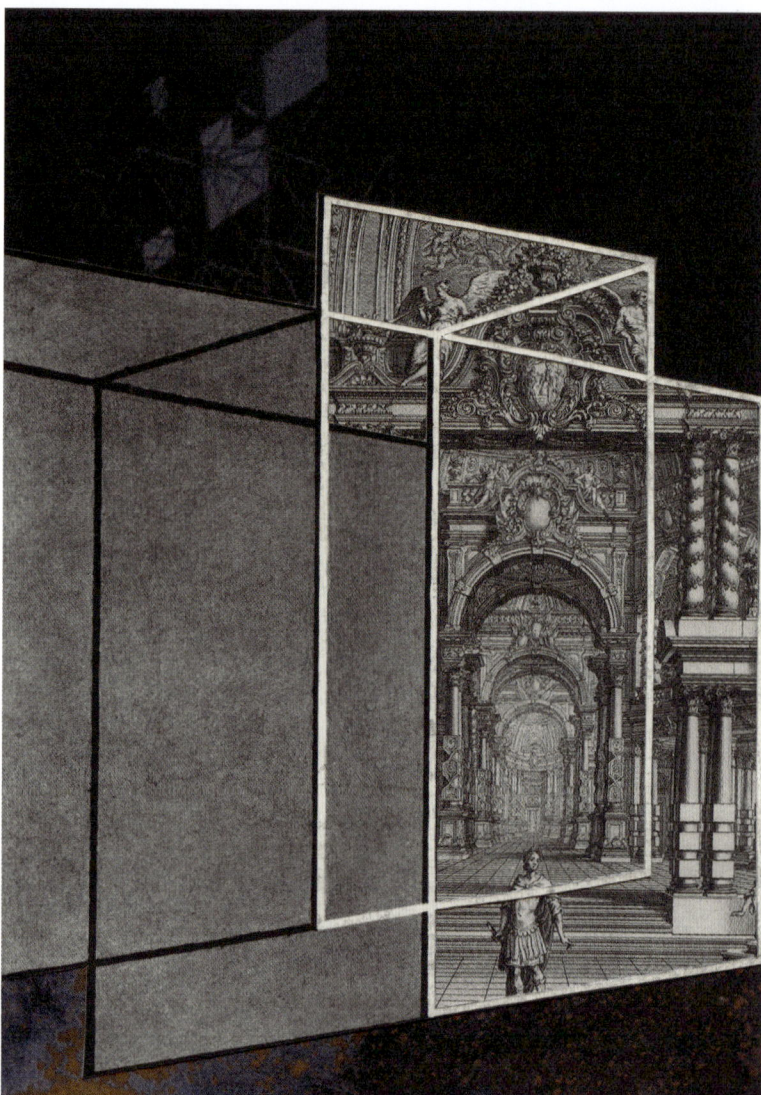

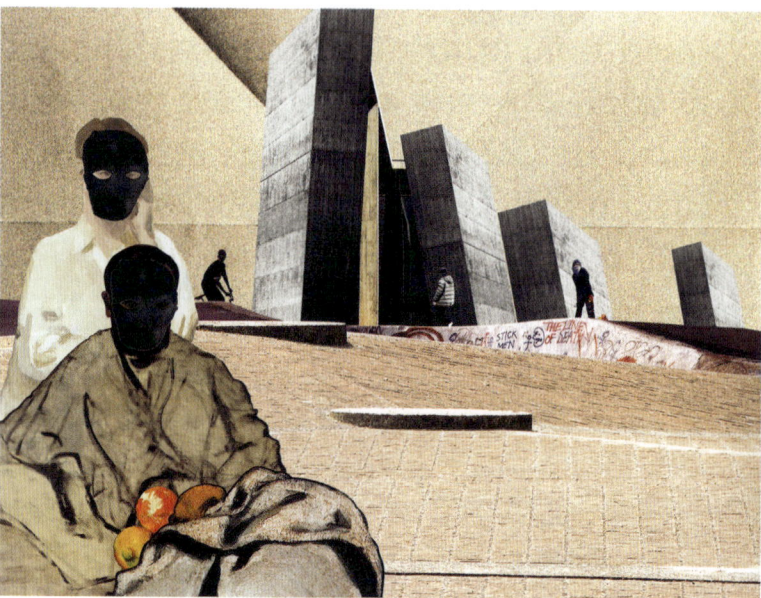

Born 1971, Albertslund, Denmark. Lives in Berlin, Germany.

↑↑ Spaceman, 2019, collage on paper, 24 × 17 cm (9½ × 6¾)

↑ Folds, 2022, laserchrome colour print mounted on 4mm aluminium with 8mm Plexiglas, 150 × 200 cm (59 × 78¾ in)

↗ World With Difficulties, 2015, digital prints on birch veneer, dimensions variable, installation view, 'World With Difficulties', Team Gallery, New York, USA, 2015

→ The Outside or the Inside of the Internalised Externalised, 2017, digital prints on birch veneer, hanging walls, collages on paper, dimensions variable, installation view, 'The Outside or the Inside of the Internalised Externalised', Centre d'édition Contemporaine, Geneva, Switzerland, 2017

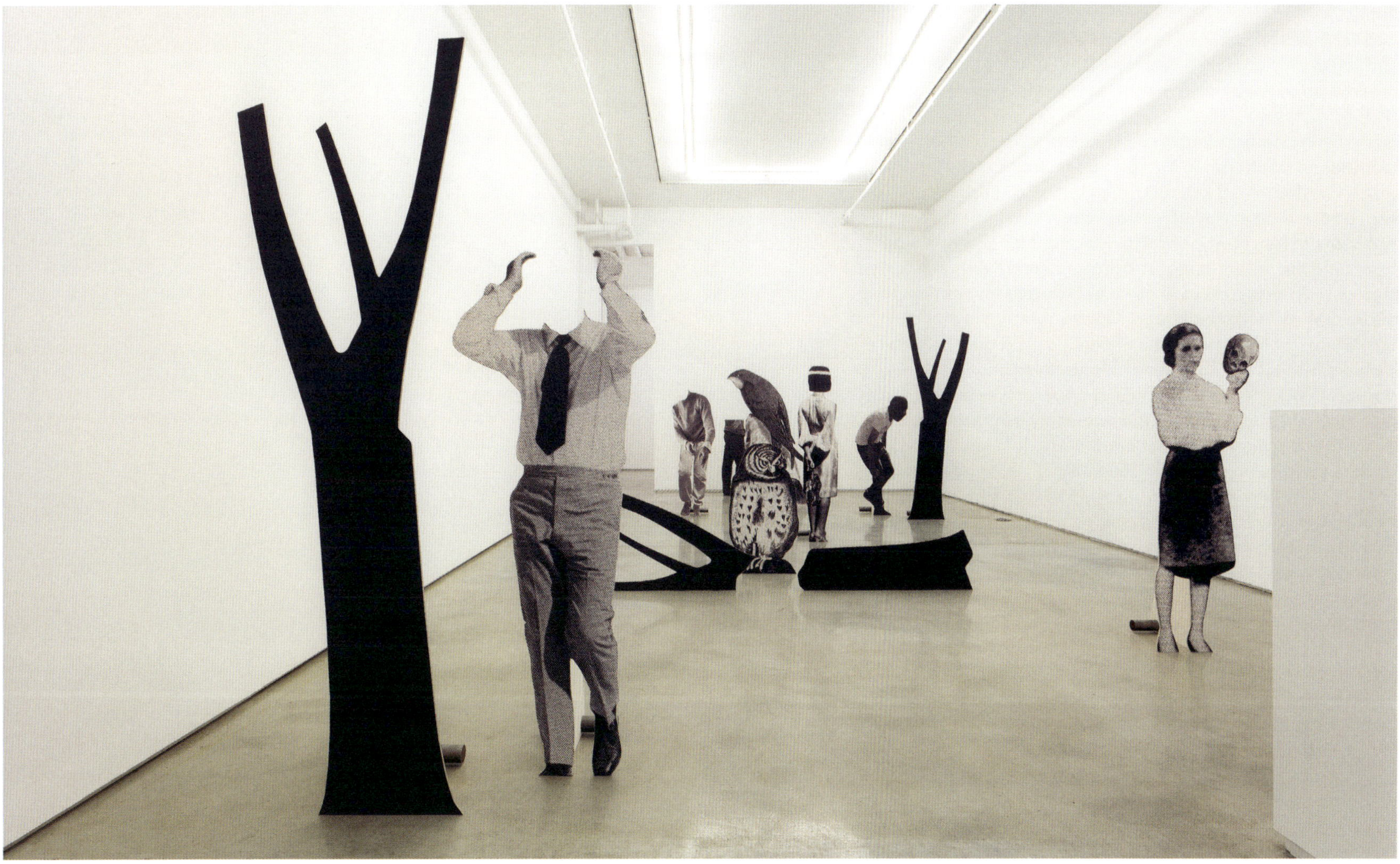

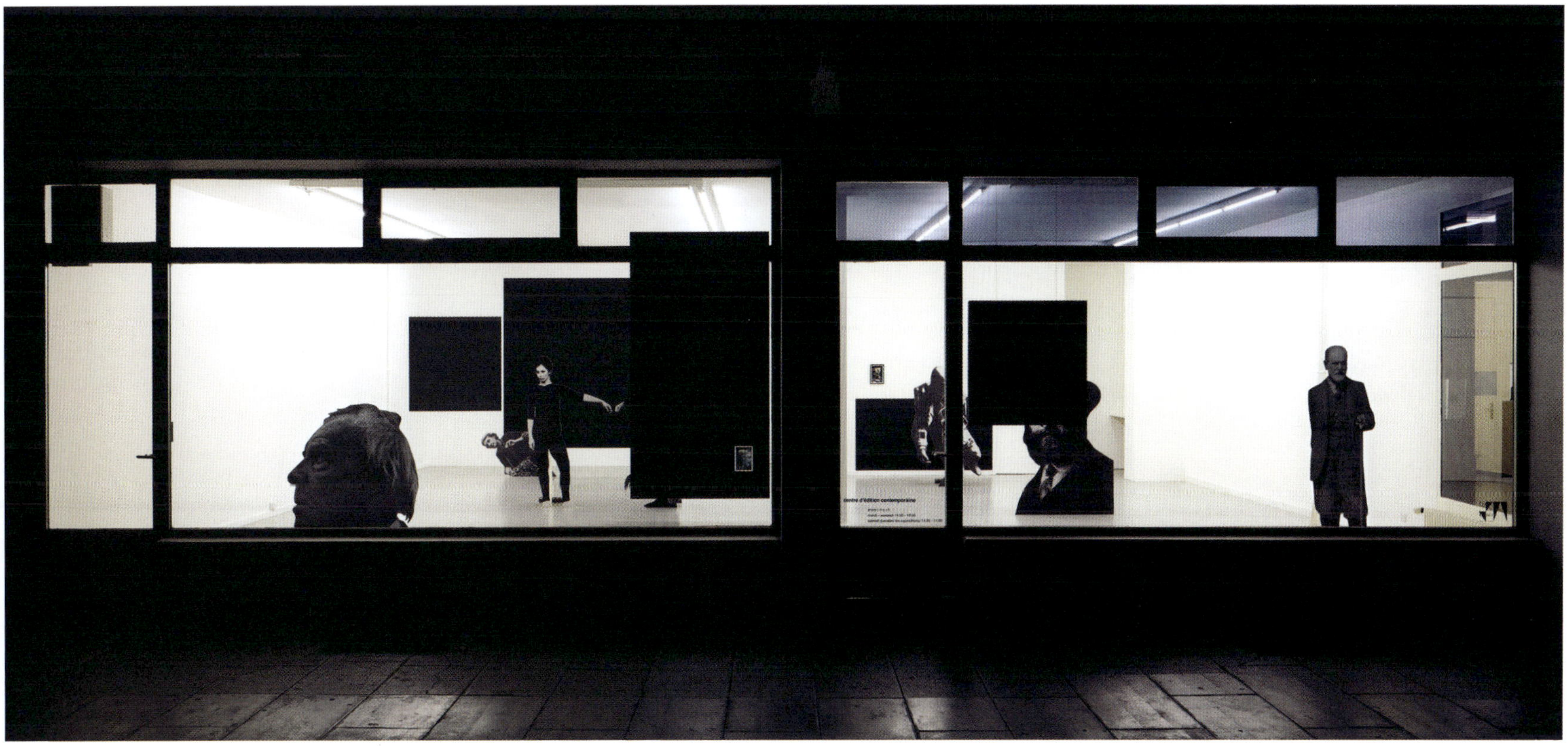

JAKOB KOLDING

NICO KRIJNO

'Photography' is an imperfect designation for Nico Krijno's process-orientated practice. While his works' final form is indeed photographic, the process of their making traverses the plastic and performing arts, finding a momentary balance between the material and gestural. To Krijno, the camera's frame becomes a stage – a window not onto the world but onto constructed scenes. That he has a background in theatre and experimental film is apparent in his set-like environments and makeshift props. Extending the still life to more abstracted ends, Krijno more often creates sculptural compositions from discarded household objects and materials, which he photographs against purpose-built backdrops. To these images, he applies post-production tools with a painter's sensibility, attending to form, contrast and colour, both augmenting the image and making apparent his manipulation of it. The final photograph is the coincidence of these physical and digital constructions, an 'electro bricolage' – to use the artist's term – of the real and invented. ▬▬▬ In a visual language that is boldly graphic and bright, Krijno explores what the photograph might offer our image-saturated culture as art object. The post-truth information age has released the medium from any prior responsibilities to veracity allowing for playful engagements with photography's formal qualities. To this end, there is an insistent flatness in his images, with their hard flash and lack of depth – a confused, composite perspective that renders them all surface. Here, his experiments in sculptural forms – in *object-ness* – enter into pictorial tension, rendered not as constructions in-the-round but as incidents of pattern, texture and rhythm. ▬ While such compositions make evident use of digital manipulation, his 'Lockdown' series (2020), created in the first uncertain months of a global pandemic, pursues a more immediate image-making: 'cameraless work, without any editing – no cropping, no Photoshop: instant photographs,' as he said in a 2020 feature for *1854. photography*. The resulting collages are the collision of two time registers: the slow accumulation of found images, reprinted and resized, and the mere minutes taken to create a composition on his home scanner. The making of each collage (its 'performance', if you will) lasts only as long as it takes the scanner's bulb to travel the length of the glass plate against which Krijno presses his chosen images in quick succession. The resulting compositions – vertical arrangements of these picture fragments – feature horizontal glitches reminiscent of now-obsolete media: a VHS on rewind, an untuned cathode-ray tube television. While each of the hundreds of found images holds significance to the artist, to the viewer, they appear as an encyclopaedic chorus of referents lent a novel unity – the reimagined parts of a new whole. Notating the lockdown in seven-minute intervals – the time taken for the scanner to record the artist's gestures – Krijno's collages offer a choreography of image and movement. ▬▬

LUCIENNE BESTALL

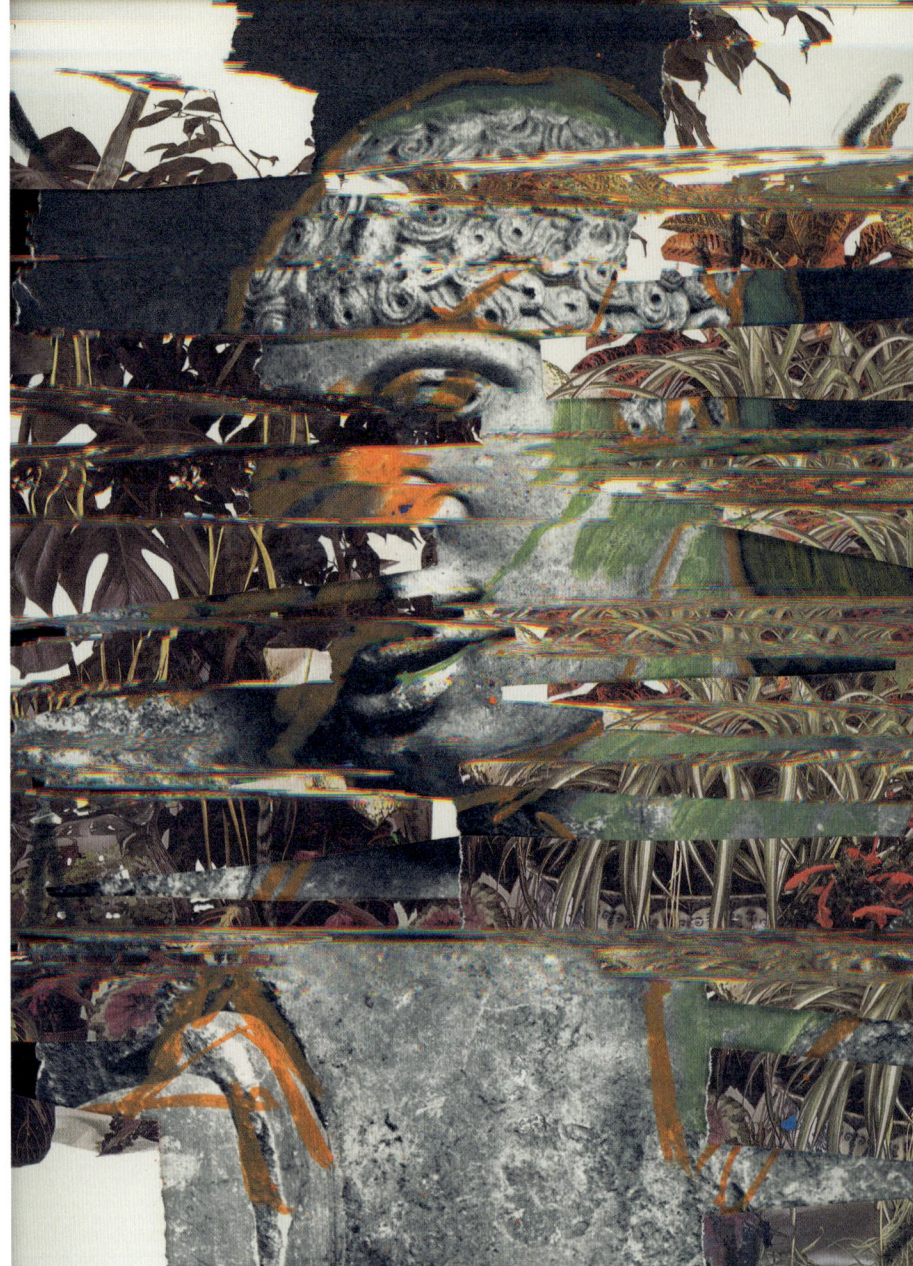

Born 1981, Cape Town, South Africa. Lives in Stanford, South Africa.

↑ Lockdown Collage #2, 2020, archival inkjet print, 120 × 87.5 cm (47¼ × 34½ in)

↗ Lockdown Collage #236, 2020, archival inkjet print, 120 × 87.5 cm (47¼ × 34½ in)

↗↗ Lockdown Collage #51, 2020, archival inkjet print, 120 × 87.5 cm (47¼ × 34½ in)

→ Lockdown Collage #9, 2020, archival inkjet print, 120 × 87.5 cm (47¼ × 34½ in)

→→ Lockdown Collage #66, 2020, archival inkjet print, 120 × 87.5 cm (47¼ × 34½ in)

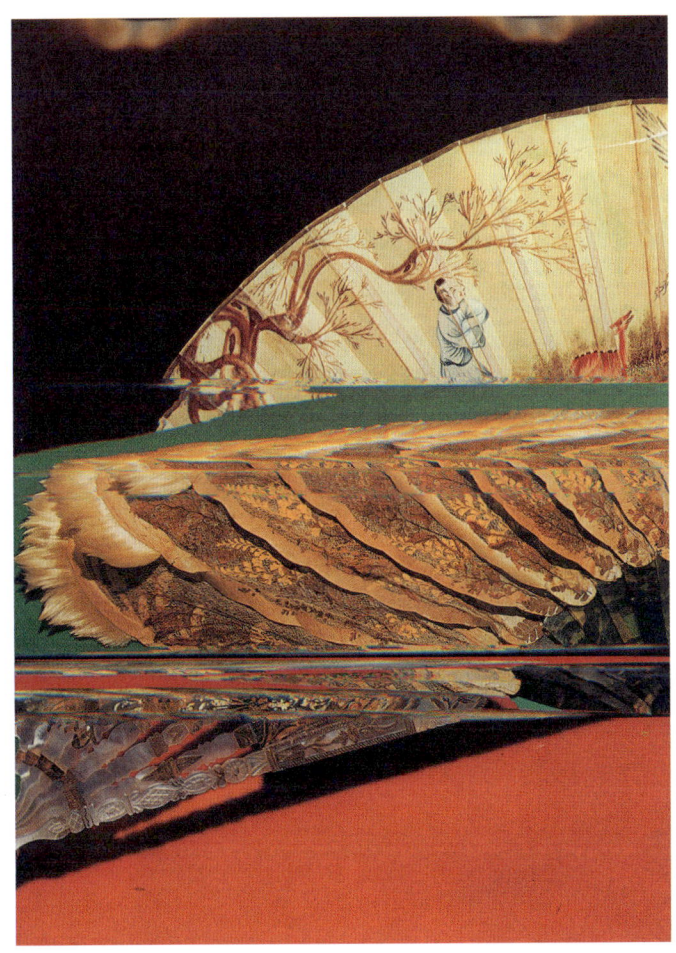
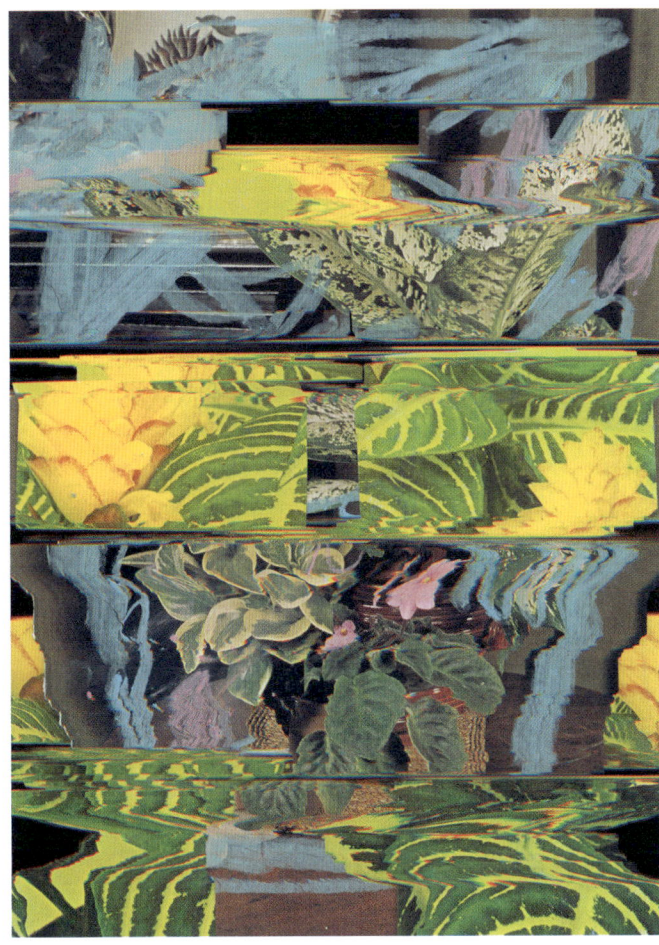
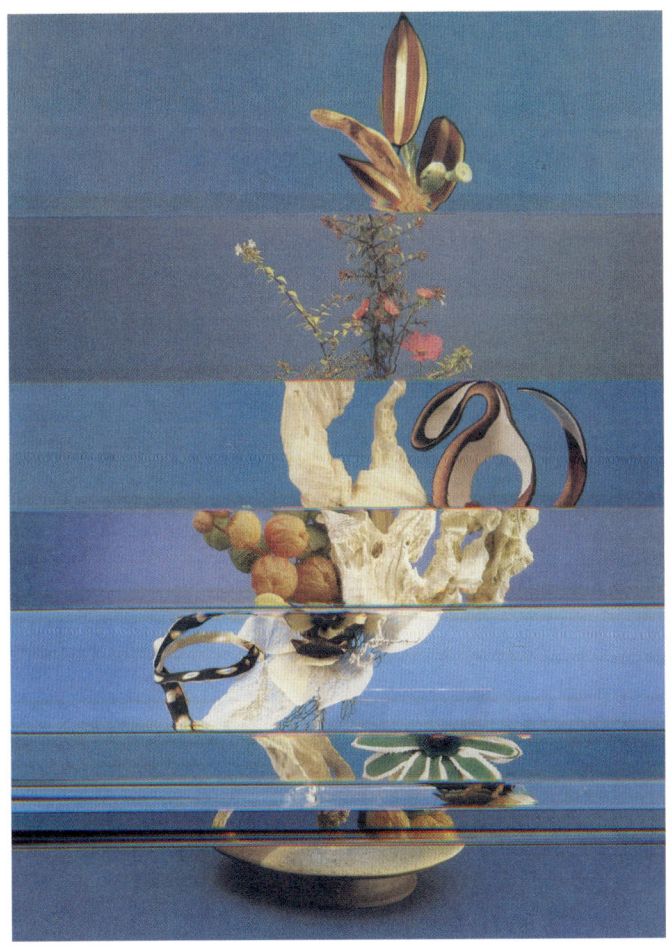
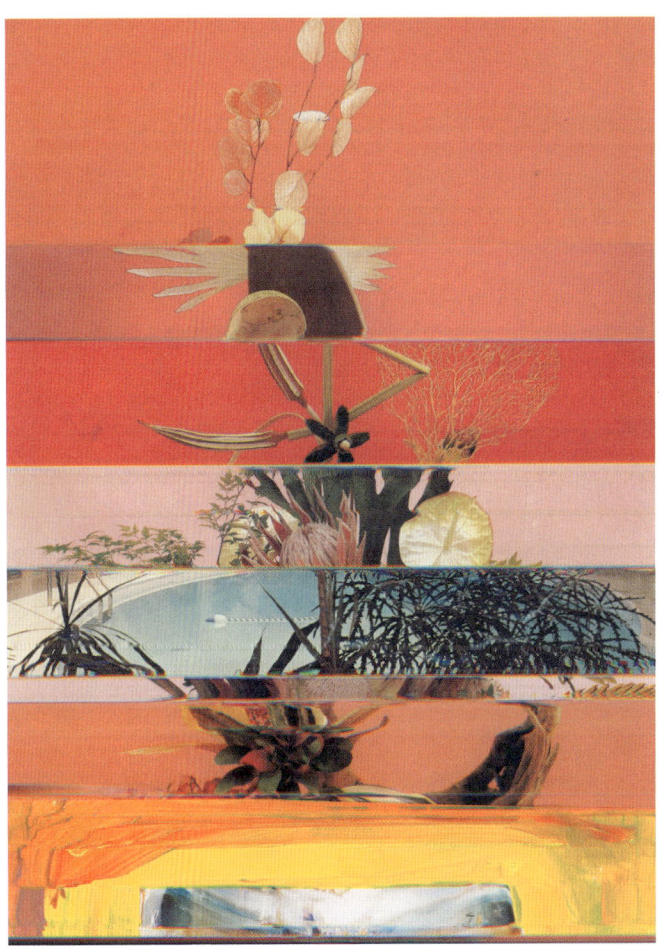

NICO KRIJNO

JUSTINE KURLAND

Over the years, Justine Kurland has cut up and reassembled images found in over 150 photobooks. She targets those with a canonical reputation, and those authored by white, cis male photographers. *Passing Through Eden* (2020), for example, draws material from Tod Papageorge's (b.1940) 2007 volume of the same name. His book features images from New York's Central Park taken in the 1970s with medium-format cameras: moody black-and-white settings of bodies lounging in tall grass, sometimes melancholic, sometimes jubilant. In Kurland's reassembly we see a thick cluster of folded limbs and spaces, densely stuck together as though reshaping the many into a single corps. There is no gender here, and the garden of the title is abstracted across a blue-coloured plane. There is none of the implied biblical moralism of Eden, but rather hedonism: bodies melt, orgy-like, pooled in an almost never-ending twist. Kurland isn't only directing her critique at Papageorge. 'It's about systems and structures of power not individuals,' she said in a 2022 interview with the *Guardian*. 'Though I have to say, some of these guys have been taking up too much room for too long.' ◤ In a response to the hyper-visibility and dominance of white male photographers, Kurland has artfully, and wittily, remade their celebrated works – jolting them with a freshly layered charge. The series is brought together under the title of 'SCUMB', adding the word 'Books' to feminist Valerie Solanas's (1936–88) original S.C.U.M. – Society for Cutting Up Men – and in 2022 Kurland published it as a photobook itself, entitled *SCUMB Manifesto*. ◤ As well as bodies, Kurland also tackles the use of landscape and objects in photography. *What We Bought: The New World* (2021) is a redressal of Robert Adams's (b.1937) eponymous book of 1995, a survey of the post-industrial American West, in particular the mountain-lined city of Denver, with its trailer lots and emptied shopping malls. If Adams's project is considered weighty because of its reluctance to engage with sentimentality, Kurland turns the footage into something fantastical, even theatrical – an intricate tableau of mannequins and shop windows, free-floating highways, speedy motorcars, houseplants and trees, and the emptied interior of homes. If Adams's work is intentionally emptied of whimsy, Kurland brings it back in, making the campness of object and aspiration the protagonists of her work. ◤ Yet Kurland's collages are about process as much as subject matter. 'I started out thinking it would be a purely punk act of destruction, but really it's the most delicate, fussy medium,' Kurland explained in the same interview. 'It's about the glue as well as the scissors… it is a reparative act rather than a destructive one.' *Women Are Beautiful* (2021), used by the artist for the endpapers of her photobook *SCUMB Manifesto*, demonstrates this delicacy. Unlike the collages that she pastes onto endpapers attached to hardback book covers, this is a two-sided, self-supporting work – collage in its purest form. ◤

SKYE ARUNDHATI THOMAS

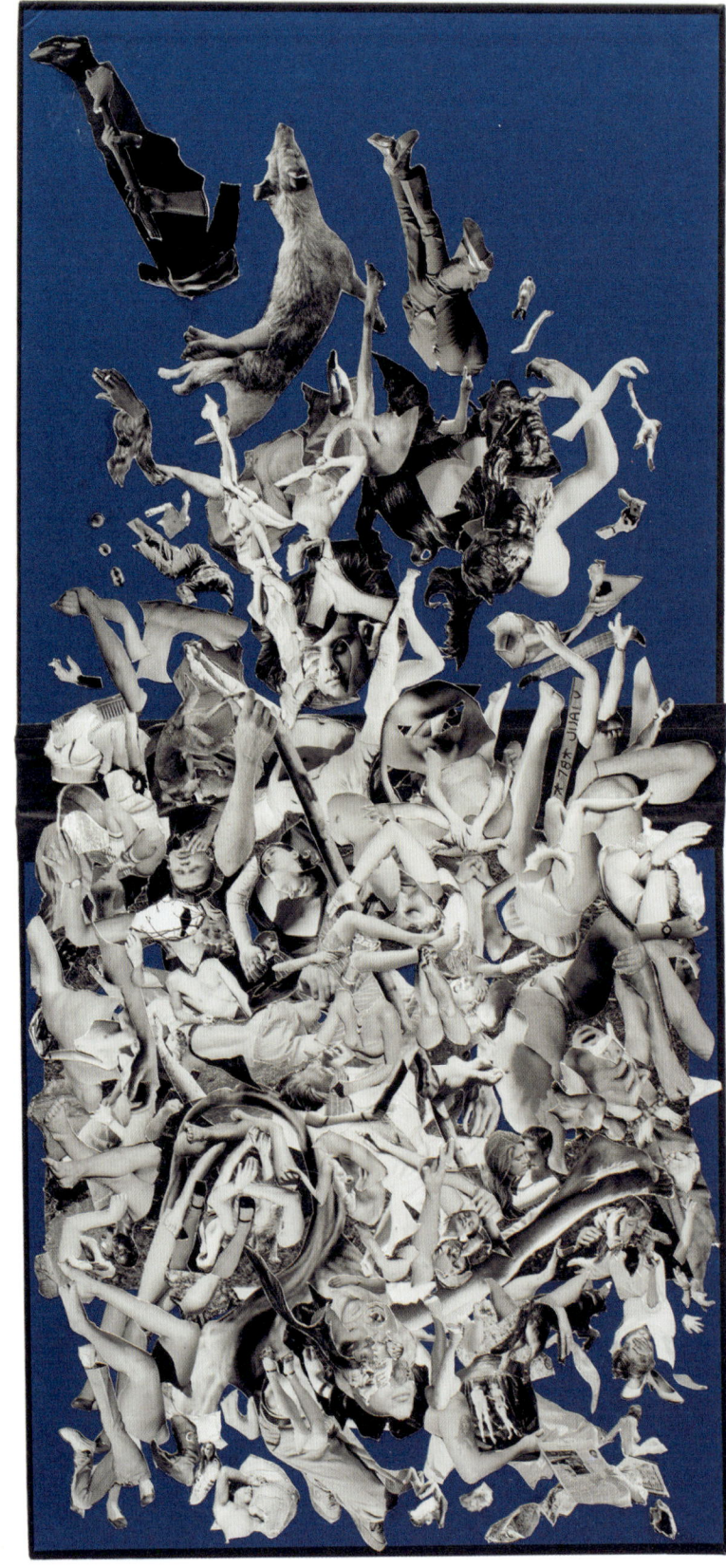

Born 1969, Warsaw, New York, USA. Lives in New York, USA.

142.143

↑　Passing Through Eden, 2020, collage (hardcover), 61.9 × 29.2 cm (24⅜ × 11½ in)

↗　Women Are Beautiful (verso and recto), 2021, collage (excerpt), each 28.6 × 31.6 cm (11¼ × 12½ in)

→　What We Bought: The New World, 2021, collage (hardcover), 20.3 × 48.6 cm (8 × 19⅛ in)

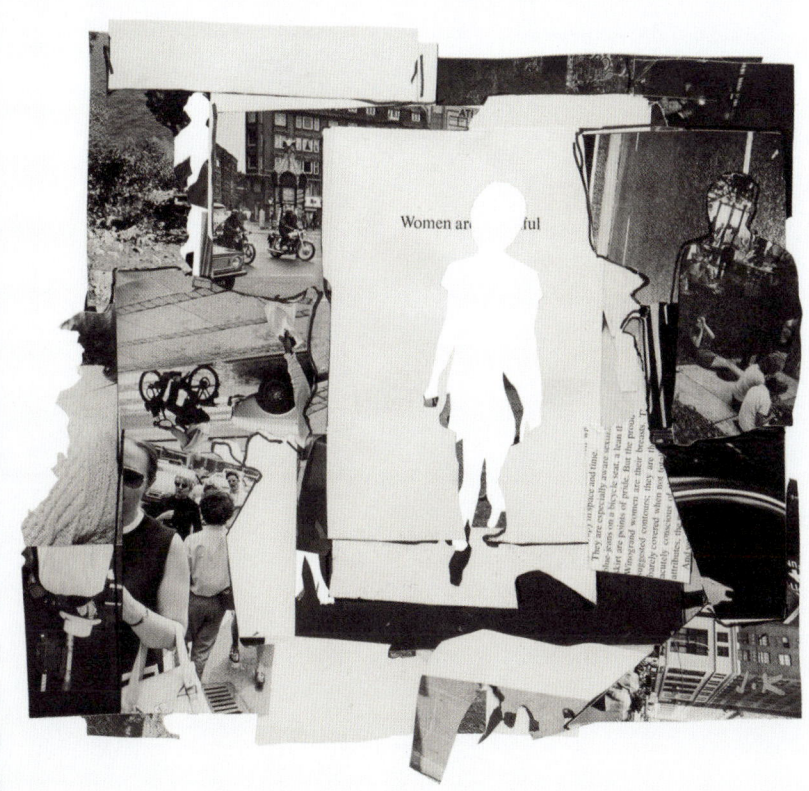

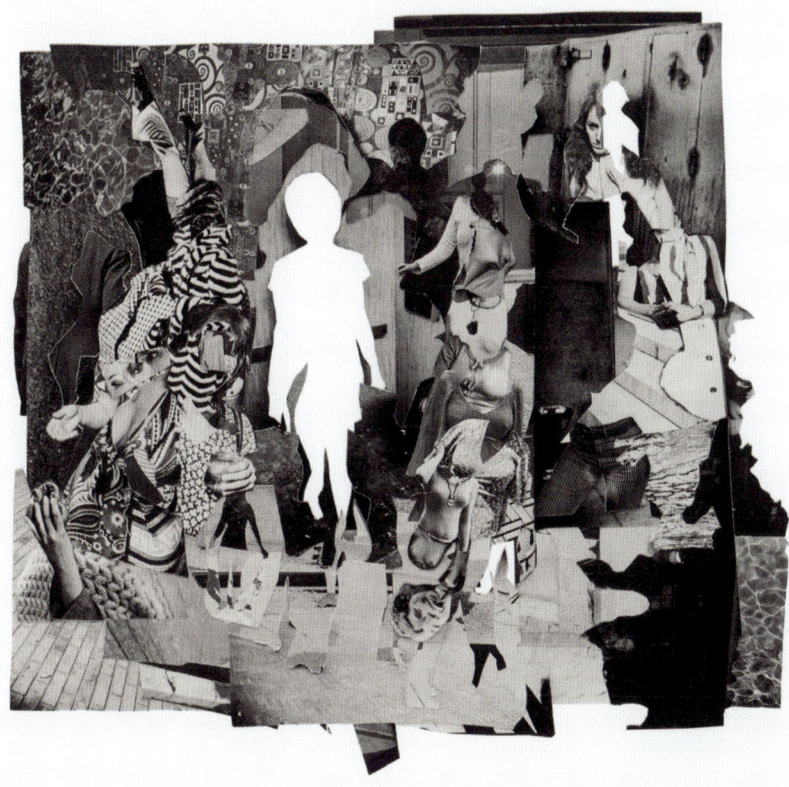

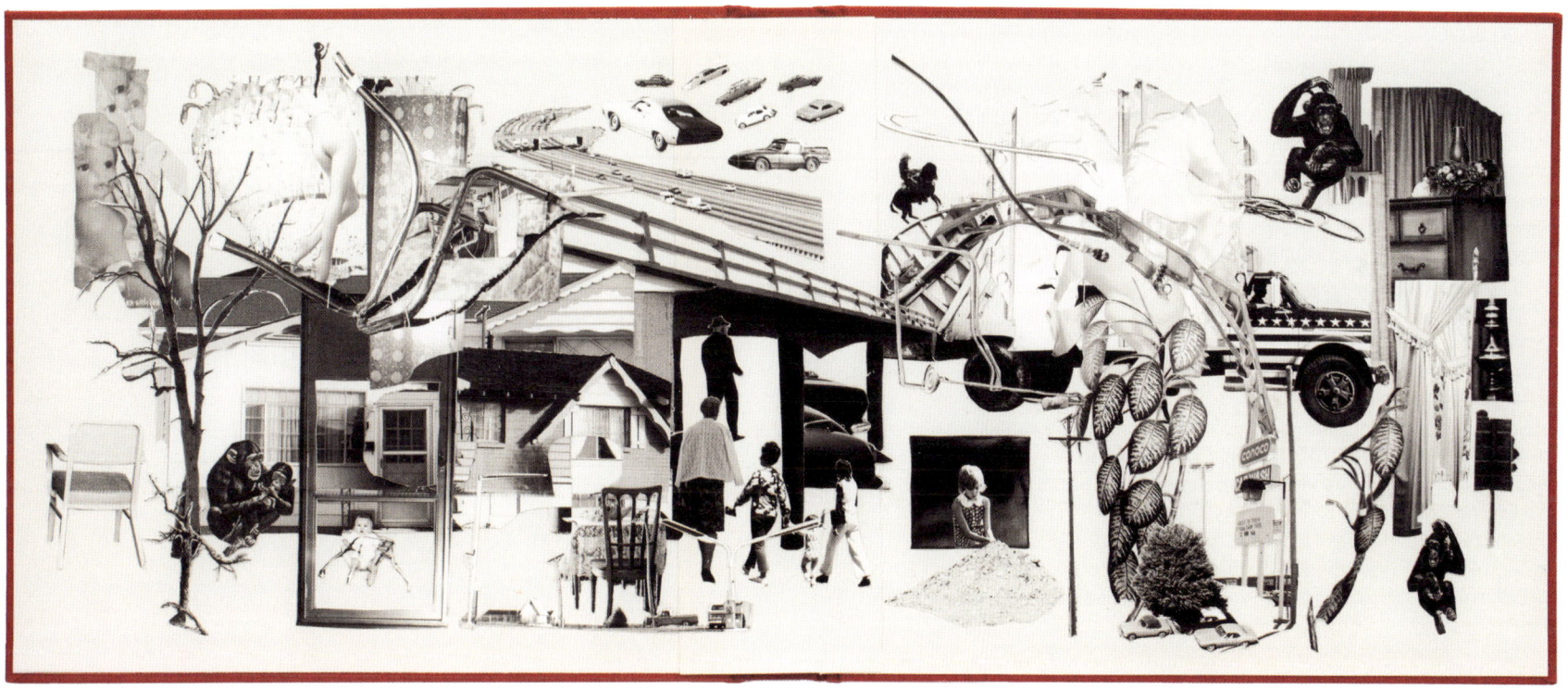

MOSHEKWA LANGA

'Biography is, essentially, a methodology for Langa,' wrote critic Tracy Murinik in the catalogue accompanying Moshekwa Langa's 2002 exhibition at the South African National Gallery, Cape Town. Langa once had aspirations to be a biographical writer but gave up his prose aspirations when he realized his talents lay in more visual pursuits, translating the drive to minutely detail his experiences into his art practice. 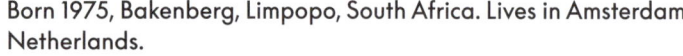 Langa has a polymorphic approach to art-making and effortlessly transitions between collage, drawing, painting, photography, video and installation. An understanding of method is important to an appreciation of his collages. His improvisatory process of working with whatever is at hand has culminated in an output characterized by raw materialism and makeshift aesthetics. His impressionistic way of combining found media purposefully tests these materials' capacity as viable carriers of biography, identity and history. It is a method grounded in self-discovery. After finishing boarding school in Pretoria in 1993, Langa spent eighteen months working on artistic experiments at his mother's home in KwaMhlanga, a segregated settlement further north. Langa did not create these works for exhibition; rather, they acted as intricate, visual 'notes to self'. The first phase of his public career began in 1995 with a debut solo exhibition in Johannesburg, a mesmeric showcase of distinctive collages and paper constructions. This emergent phase extended up until the artist's major solo presentation at the Kunsthalle Bern, Switzerland in 2011. The early 2010s were a difficult and transformative period in Langa's life. He had resettled in Johannesburg after living in Amsterdam since he started his studies at the Rijksakademie van Beeldende Kunsten in 1997. Back in South Africa, Langa made frequent trips to rural Bakenberg, where he had spent his first eleven years. Its location in the country's rapidly transforming and socially volatile platinum belt had changed the area. His extended family viewed him with suspicion and community members labelled him a foreigner. As a result, Langa relocated permanently to the Netherlands around 2014. The second phase of Langa's artistic career commenced with a solo exhibition at ifa-Galerie in Stuttgart, Germany, in 2014. It included a new style of collages, featuring photocopied images of archetypal African subjects floating in liquid colour, which have been central to Langa's practice ever since. These elements may be drawn from the natural world, as in the acacia trees and tiger seen in *Cat on a hot tin roof (as if)* (2014–17), or material culture such as the patterned beadwork, ceramics and cave paintings of *'Tonsils'/Manwe uwe Buela bitseng [Verbal cure]* (2017). Produced in Paris and Amsterdam, these collages recall the visual landscapes and emotional geographies of a forsaken home. The haunted quality of *Metseng ya batho* (2016), which translates as 'in the villages of the people', was amplified further when it was first exhibited in Johannesburg in 2017. It was displayed opposite canvases stained with iron oxide that had been dragged along a gravel road near Langa's first home.

SEAN O'TOOLE

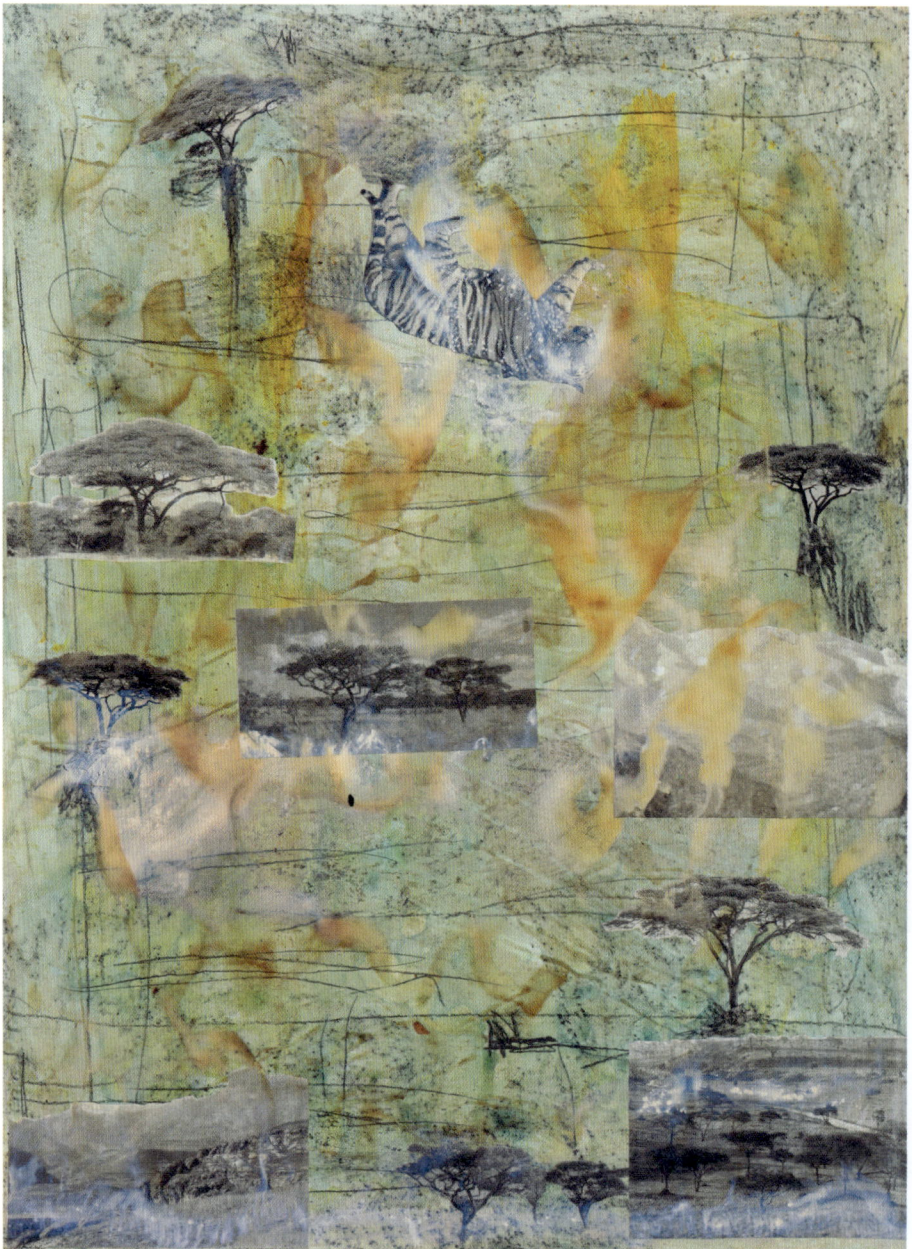

Born 1975, Bakenberg, Limpopo, South Africa. Lives in Amsterdam, Netherlands.

↑   Cat on a hot tin roof (as if), 2014–17, mixed media on paper, 162 × 122 cm (63¾ × 48 in)

↗   Metseng ya batho (In the Villages of the People), 2016, mixed media on paper, 140 × 100 cm (55⅛ × 39⅜ in)

→   Sobhuza III, 2018–19, mixed media on paper, 162 × 122 cm (63¾ × 48 in)

→ →   'Tonsils'/Manwe uwe Buela bitseng [Verbal cure], 2017, mixed media on paper, 162 × 122 cm (63¾ × 48 in)

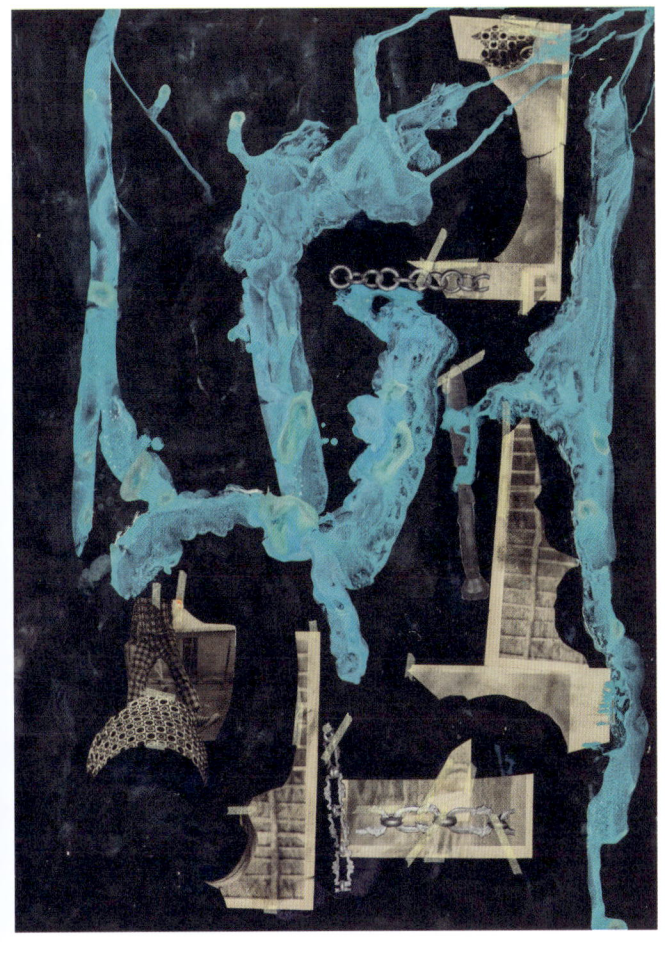

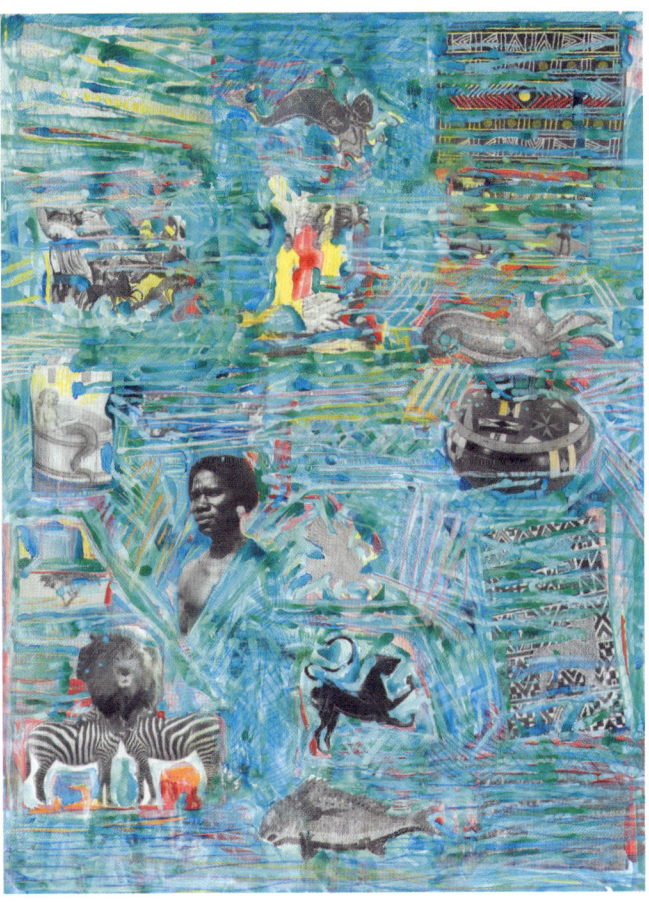

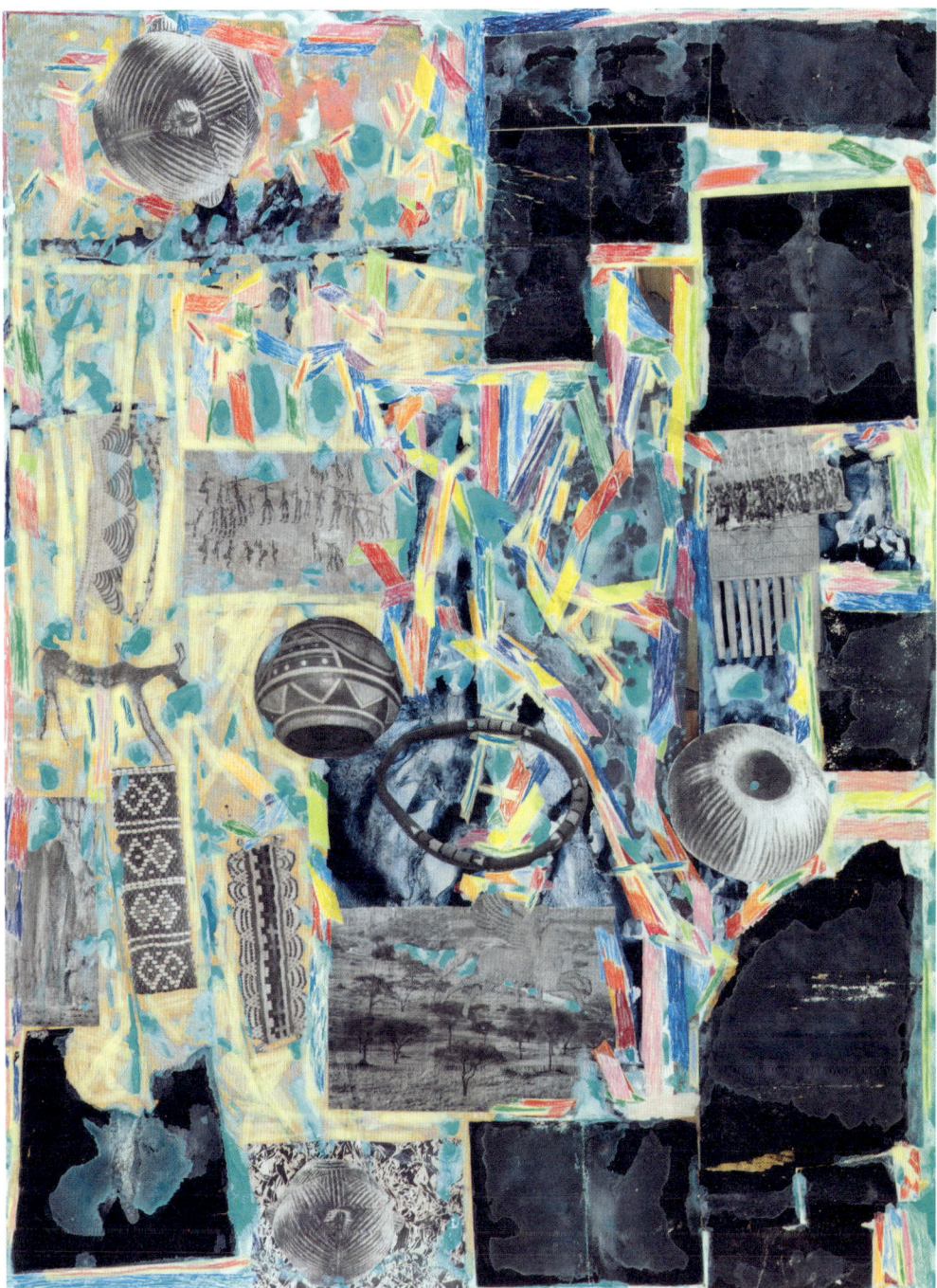

MOSHEKWA
LANGA

DIONNE LEE

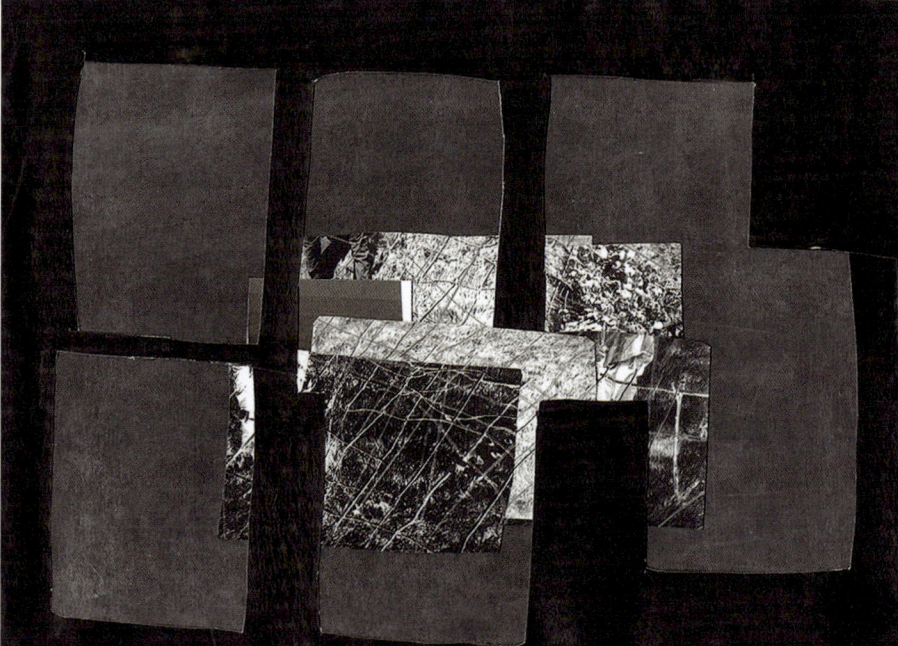

In complex and deeply personal collage work, rendered almost exclusively in black and white with frenetic graphite markings, Dionne Lee interrogates the racialized histories of the American landscape. Exploring the profound structural inequalities laid down by a long legacy of unequal power relationships in the United States, particularly in relation to the land, climate justice, environmental racism and memory, Lee's work asks the critical question: who is best placed to survive ecological destruction? Climate change and racism are two of the biggest challenges of the twenty-first century – they are also inextricably intertwined. There is a stark divide between who has caused climate change and who most suffers its effects, and it is in this interstitial space that Lee locates her practice. After relocating to northern California, where she experienced first-hand the ferocious wildfires that decimated large swathes of land, survival skills assumed a new urgency in Lee's life and art practice. Created through repetition and mirroring – and deploying double exposures, scanning and collage – her work is populated with images from survival manuals. In *AA O KK* (2019) fire-making tools and roundels of rope are juxtaposed against Lee's own prints of hand gestures. Her carefully orchestrated images not only explore the tradition of American landscape photography but also question *who* has historically taken such images and with what underlying agenda. In doing so, Lee contributes to delegitimizing the colonial project. Lee often inserts her own body into the landscape, referencing the histories of her ancestors who toiled the land for centuries but whose knowledge of the environment has been lost due to a lack of access and migration. Hands are a recurring motif in her work: whether as a tool for navigating the land by searching the sky for the North Star, tearing or folding found images of meandering rivers, vivid sunsets and glaciers, as in Lee's 2016 film *Drafts*, or clearing leaves on the ground to create a fire bed. These bodily gestures serve to reclaim her ancestors' wisdom and can be read as an act of resistance against institutional and environmental racism. Combining found imagery from wilderness survival manuals with Lee's own silver gelatin prints, *Contact (A Muscle Memory)* (2020) presents two roughly cut-out hands occupying the centre of the frame, superimposed upon which are a series of images of a sparse forest tree, a simple hut-like shelter and a hunting-related tool. The implication here is that human survival is intimately woven into the survival of the trees, the forest and the wider ecosystem that supports all life. Lee's work pays homage to the land as not only a site of trauma but also a space of potential refuge, emancipation and inter-connectedness with an other-than-human world.

ALONA PARDO

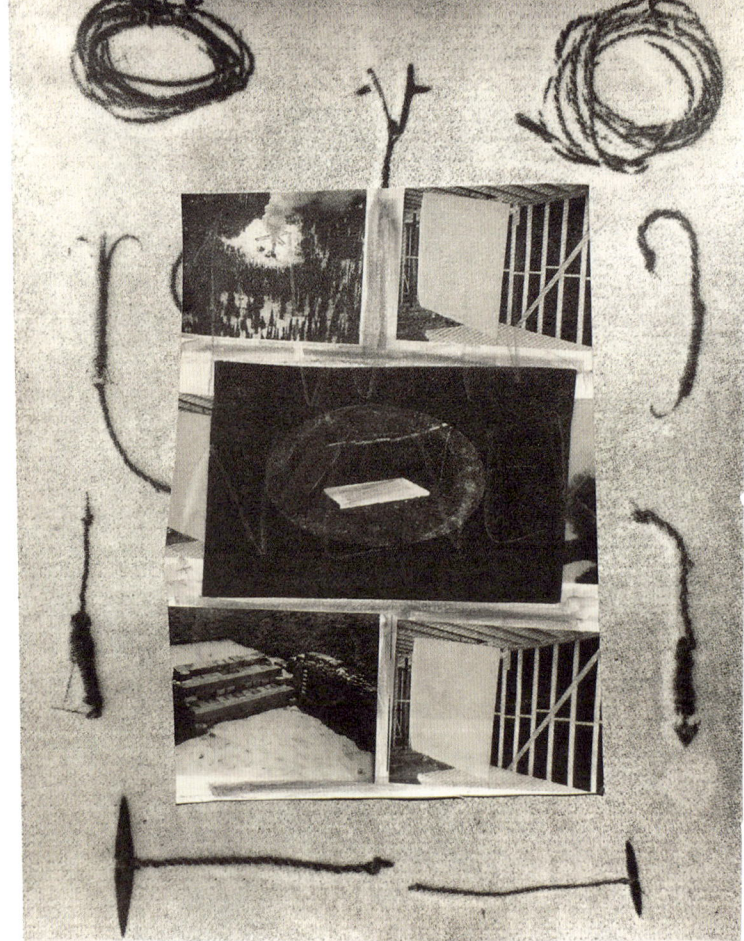

Born 1988, New York, USA. Lives in Columbus, Ohio, USA.

↑↑ **Leaning to and Against**, 2019, silver gelatin print and collage with graphite, 30.5 40.6 cm (12 × 16 in)

↑ **Warnings (II)**, 2020, silver gelatin print, cut paper and collage with graphite, 35.6 × 27.9 cm (14 × 11 in)

↗ **Netting**, 2019, silver gelatin print and collage with graphite, 35.6 × 27.9 cm (14 × 11 in)

↗↗ **Contact (A Muscle Memory)**, 2020, silver gelatin print, cut paper and collage with graphite, 40.6 × 30.5 cm (16 × 12 in)

→ **AA O KK**, 2019, silver gelatin prints and collage with graphite, each 40.6 × 30.5 cm (16 × 12 in), Museum of Modern Art, New York, USA

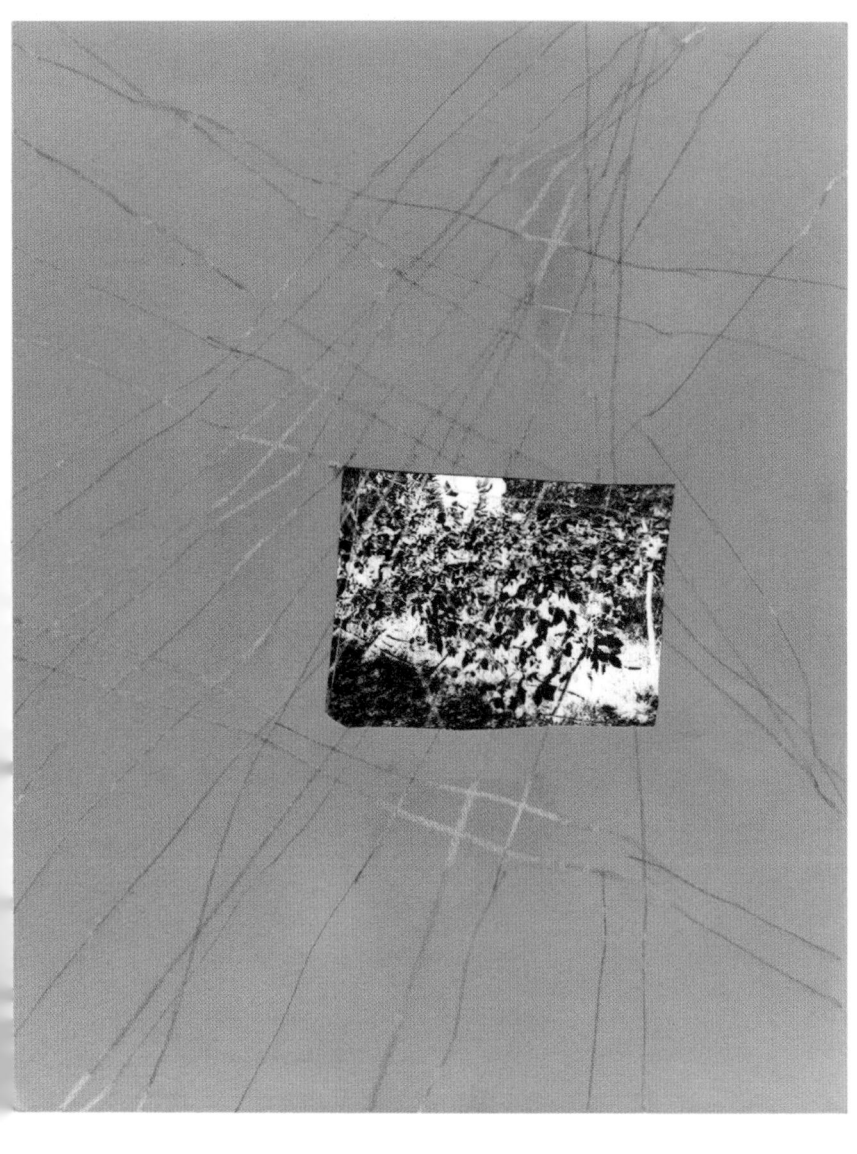

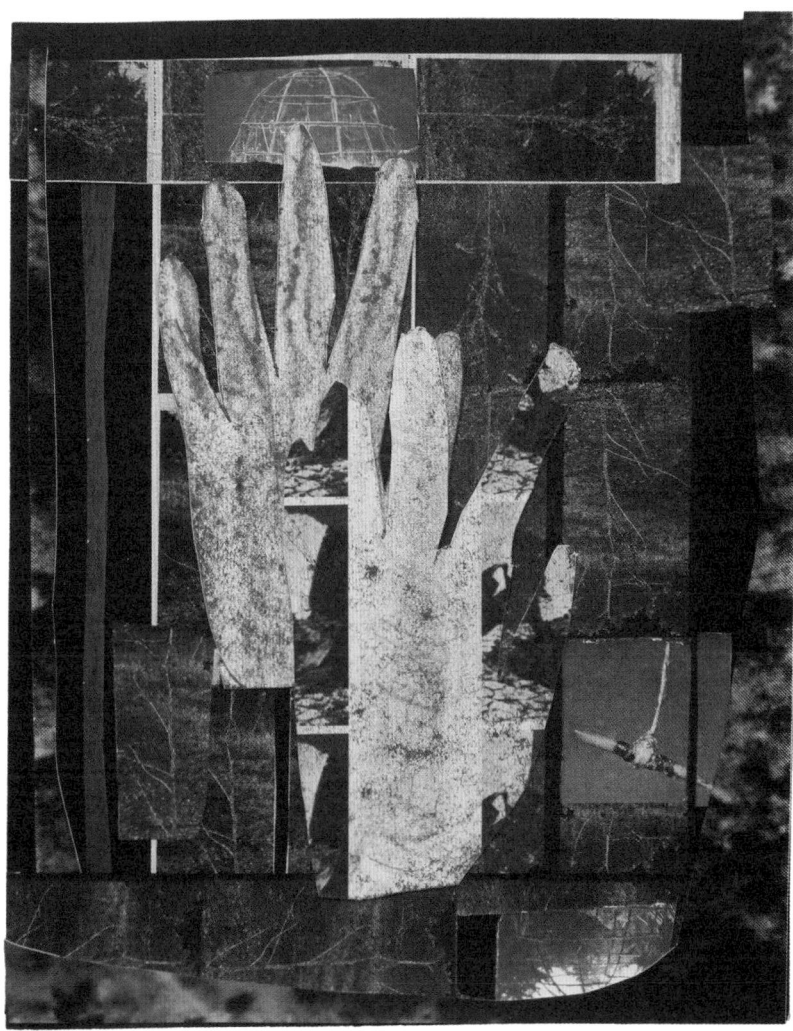

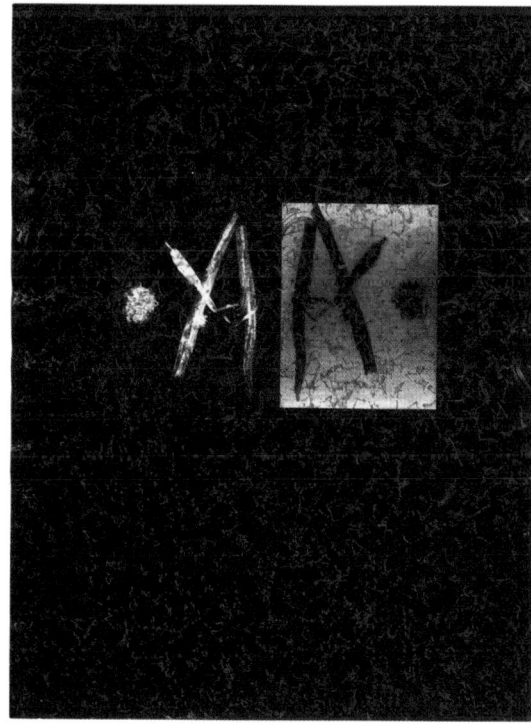

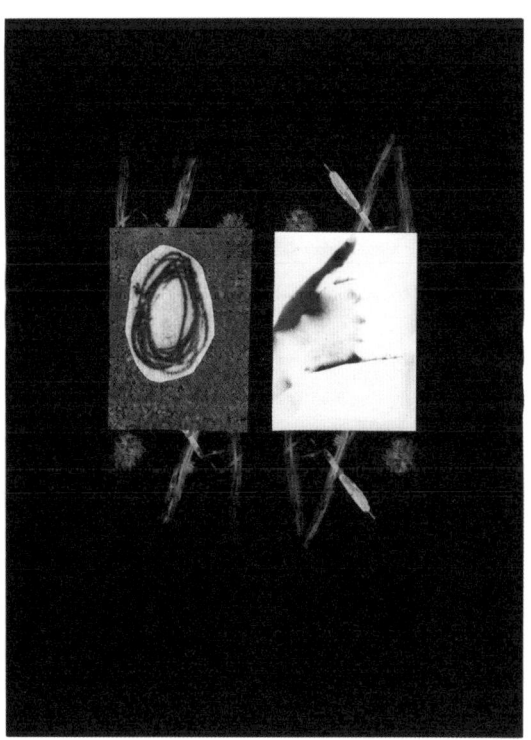

DIONNE LEE

RACHEL LIBESKIND

Leveraging the unique potential of collage to juxtapose and recontextualize, Rachel Libeskind is interested in 'remaking' images to reveal social patterns, hidden truths and unexpected parallels. She translates pre-existing photographic reproductions through enlarging, highlighting, inverting colours, cutting up or piecing together hundreds of images from diverse sources – historical documentation, public and private archives, vernacular Pop photographs, magazine clippings and scientific illustrations. She is particularly intent on exposing the sentiment and emotional feelings embedded within an image, and believes that innate meanings can be used as her raw material. She obsessively researches and accumulates 'stuff', with all its attendant emotional baggage. ◢ History doesn't have many bright spots; Libeskind's family experienced the traumas of the Holocaust and several upheavals from war, so she sees too many regressions in culture. Having been gifted the 1940s British board game Physogs, where play revolves around image-cards to interpret physiognomy – the discredited pseudoscience of determining an individual's character based on traits of facial recognition – Libeskind enlivened the game's rather stern, stereotyped facial cards by placing them on colourful backgrounds to make them look stoned or drunk. With works like *Easily Embarrassed* and *Tenacity of Purpose* (both 2019), she inserted levity through joyful appropriation, creating tie-dyed rainbow-coloured backdrops on which to assemble the various facial features, humorously with too many noses and sometimes on an arched-shaped sheet that echoes sacred space. Libeskind sees excess, especially within consumer-culture, as reflective of interior and existential baggage to be considered within the cycles of life and death. For her, objects gain status like relics, reifying a spiritual potential. ◢ Replete with body fragments, *Hand in Hand* (2020) instils a sense of care, of human touch across disparate generations. Ripped tape visibly holds together classical and contemporary depictions of touching and handling. Tape is also conspicuous in *Scriptorium I* (2020), where eyes from the reproductions of two different paintings are placed over the photograph of a sculpted classical head, dismembered perhaps in an iconoclastic era, now bestowed with new features. Libeskind feels there is always a contest of meaning, of mining archival images to merge intellectual and visual arrangements – one thing next to another in a seemingly random way, taking meaning from it, while projecting narratives and histories. More seamlessly, *Over the Moon* (2021) reflects Libeskind's progression to using a scanner to capture two images, one literally on top of the other, in what she describes as a more expansive method, one that is less handled. Unlike her celebrated architect father, Daniel, who had to grapple in post-war Europe with the vestiges of a lost world in which certain totems were immutable, Rachel's pursuit of creativity has exploded into many possibilities and great opportunity.

KATHLEEN MADDEN

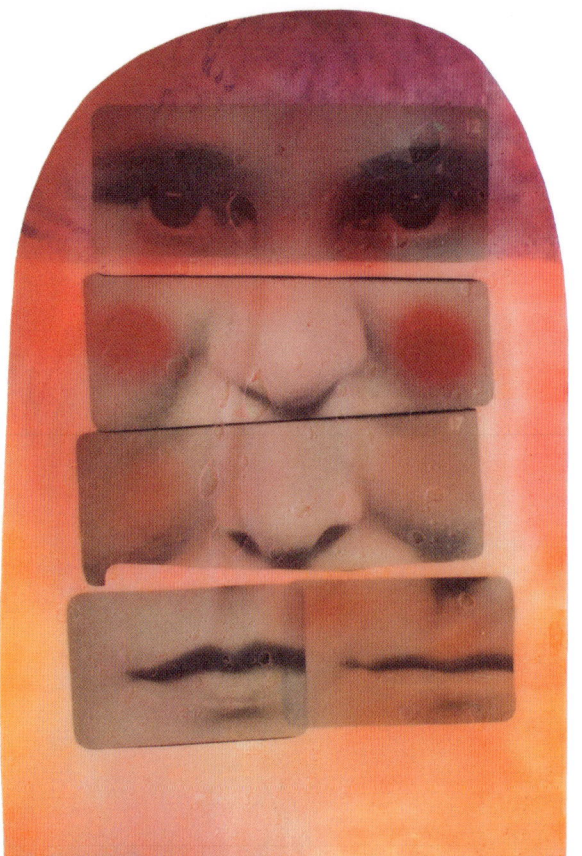

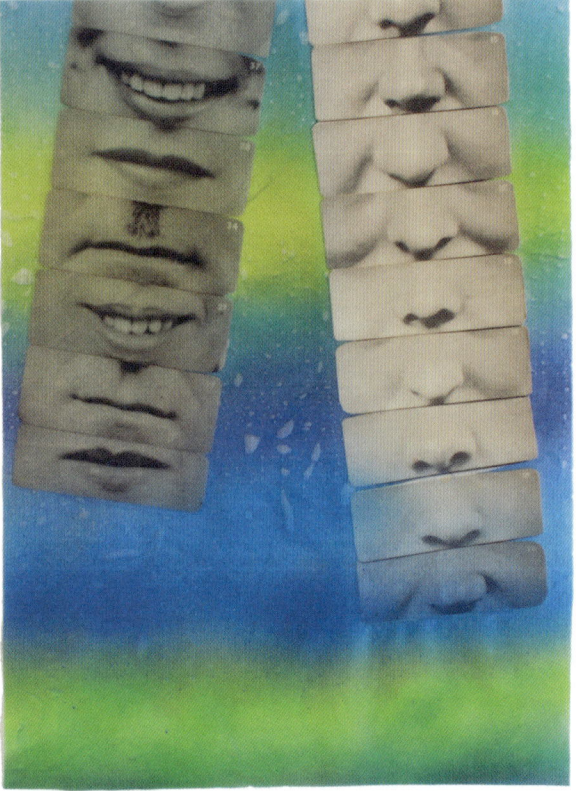

Born 1989, Milan, Italy. Lives in New York, USA and Berlin, Germany.

↑↑ **Easily Embarrassed**, 2019, collage on Japanese paper with fabric hardener and acrylic airbrush pigment, 61 × 40.6 cm (24 × 16 in), private collection, New York, USA

↑ **Tenacity of Purpose**, 2019, collage on Japanese paper with fabric hardener and acrylic airbrush pigment, 41.9 × 30.5 cm (16½ × 12 in), , New York, USA

↗ **Hand in Hand**, 2020, giclée print with found and cut images and tape, 50.8 × 21.6 cm (20 × 8½ in)

↗↗ **Scriptorium I**, 2020, giclée print with found and cut images and tape, 36.8 × 30.5 cm (14½ × 12 in), private collection, Denver, Colorado, USA

→ **Over The Moon**, 2021, found pages taped together, 27.9 × 21.6 cm (11 × 8½ in)

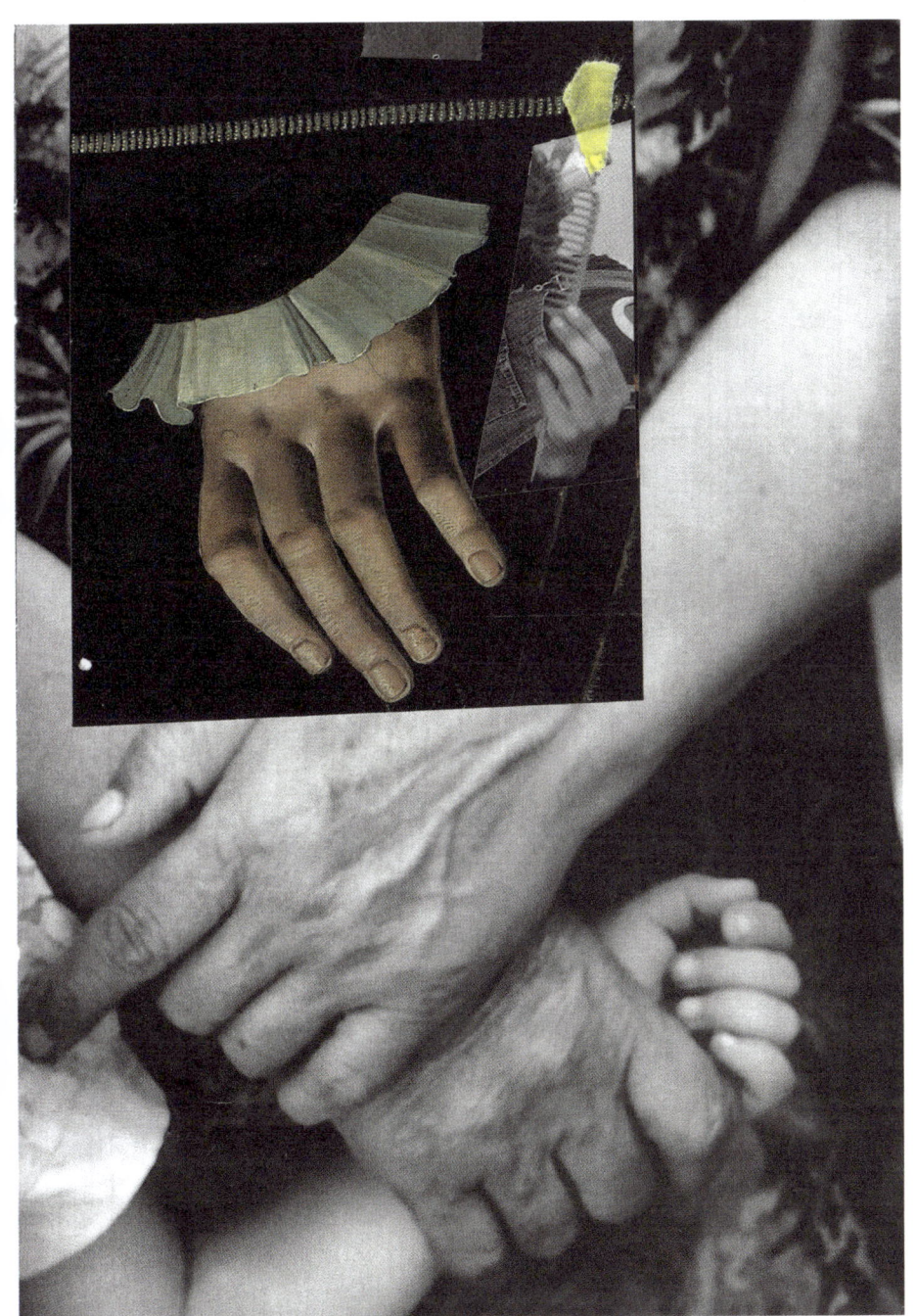

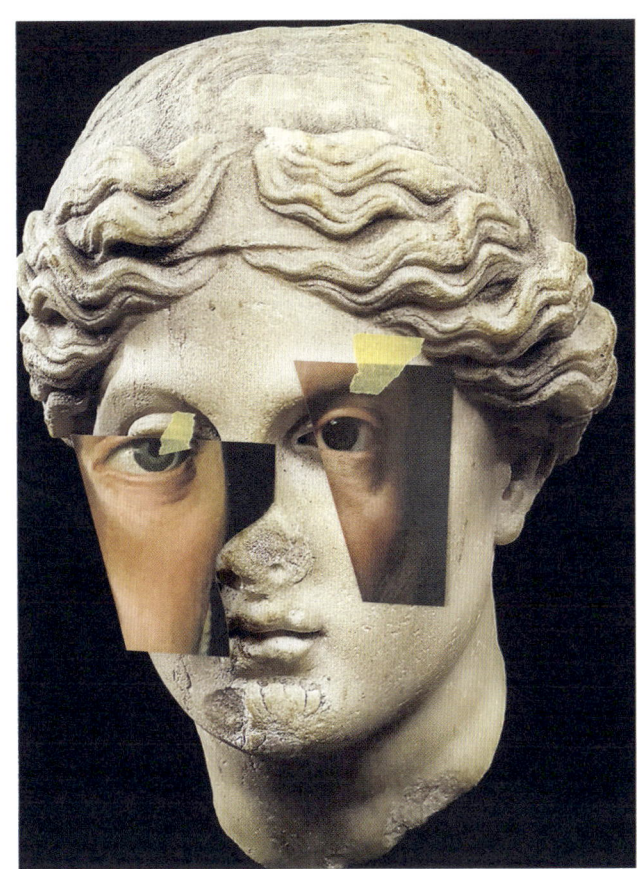

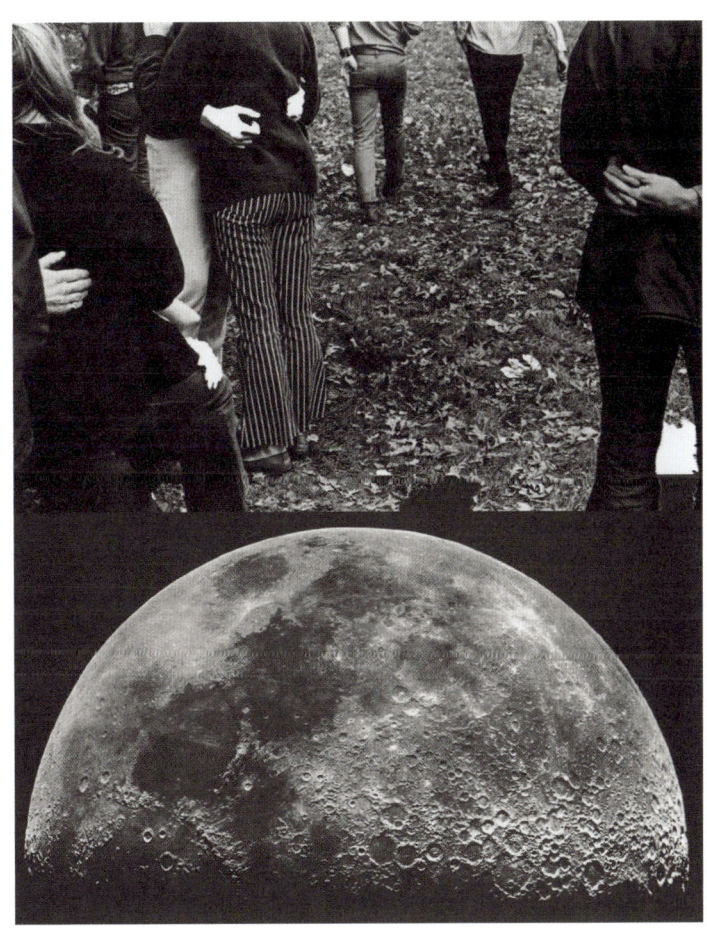

RACHEL LIBESKIND

LINDER

'We never talk about the sticky stuff,' announced Linder in a public lecture in 2017 before going on to admit that she uses ordinary Pritt stick glue as the binding agent for her photomontages. Linder's interest in 'sticky stuff', however, extends beyond technical terms. It is a way to stir a debate about tabooed desires and to expose links between bodies of living and inanimate objects in exciting as well as uncomfortable ways. Linder began her artistic career in the late 1970s, initially doubling as the lead singer for the post-punk music band, Ludus, and as a visual artist making photomontages. Her early work was primarily distributed through alternative channels associated with the music industry rather than the art world. Most notable among these are her zine publication *The Secret Public* (1978) and a series of album covers for music bands, including for the Buzzcocks' 1977 single 'Orgasm Addict'. In this photomontage, she replaced the head of a naked model with an iron and covered her nipples with two smiling mouths to create a dystopian male fantasy where the female body is nothing more than an expression of the functions imposed on it by patriarchal conventions. Today, the crossover between the performing and visual arts continues to be at the heart of Linder's practice and it informs her interest in the politics of the body and its representations through culture. In the field of photomontage, this comes into expression in her reliance on found imagery where sex, humour and symbols of luxury are used to define desires and encourage consumption. Her sources include specialized literature and magazines – pornography, design, gastronomy, botany, zoology and art – visual worlds that serve Linder's fascination with linguistic and visual puns, and associations between technology, knowledge and intimacy. Consider, for example, *Mayniel Relief* (2017) and *Bardot Relief (ii)* (2018), two photomontages where Linder conceals parts of famous French actresses from the 1950s and 1960s with photographs of designed furniture, emphasizing similarities between the human figure and the mechanisms designed to support it: cushions, back rests and table legs. In other works, a more complex arrangement of found images is employed to create a theatrical scenario with multiple elements. In *Origin of the World* (2016) Adam and Eve are presented in the Garden of Eden, except that in Linder's pictorial universe the garden is filled with traces of human presence: bits of furniture, urban landscape and artificial flower arrangements. The mythological couple, in turn, are two models cut out from the pages of erotic magazines. Their genitals are concealed, his by a caterpillar and hers by a flower, gendered symbols that continue to echo in nature's patterns all around, referencing the 'sticky stuff' that links bodily organs, sexuality and nature.

YUVAL ETGAR

Born 1954, Liverpool, UK. Lives in London, UK.

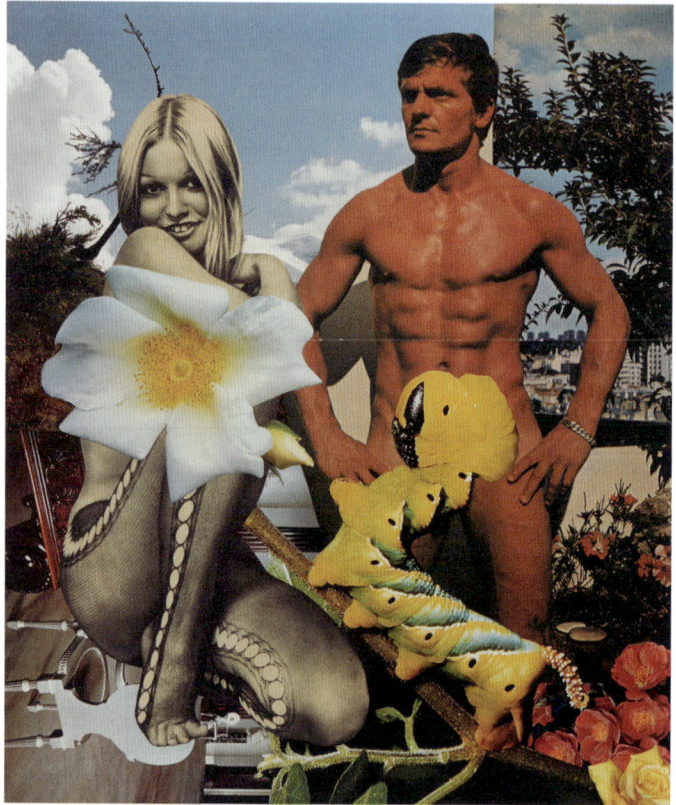

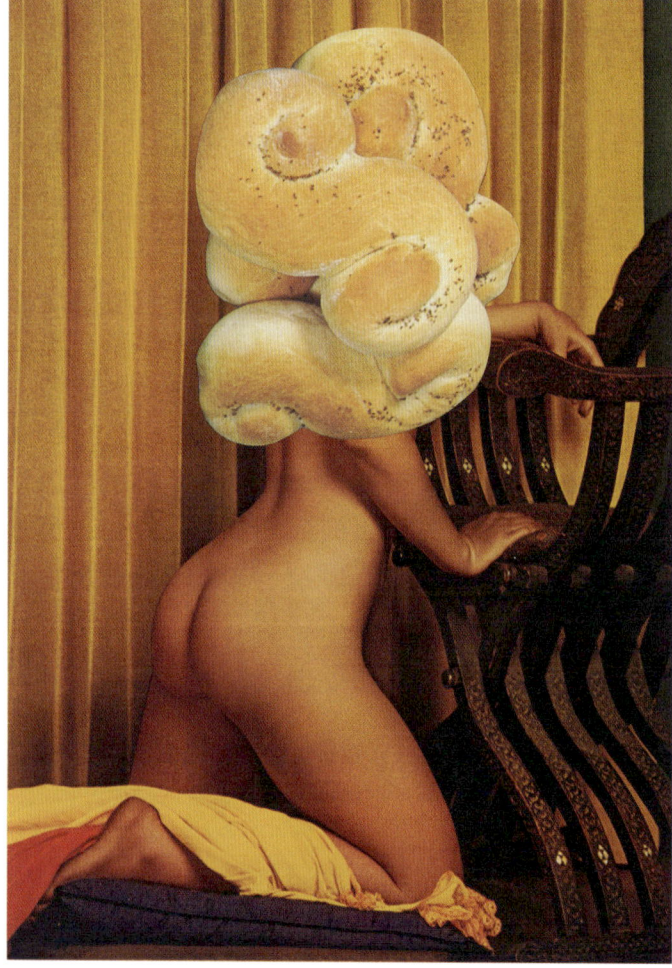

↑↑ Origin of the World, 2016, photomontage, 49.1 × 42.1 cm (19 ⅜ × 16 ⅝ in)
↑ The Still Unravished Bride, 2020, photomontage, 30.5 × 21.8 cm (12 ⅛ × 8 ⅝ in)
→ The Sphinx, 2021, photomontage, 35.5 × 34.5 cm (14 × 13 ⅝ in)

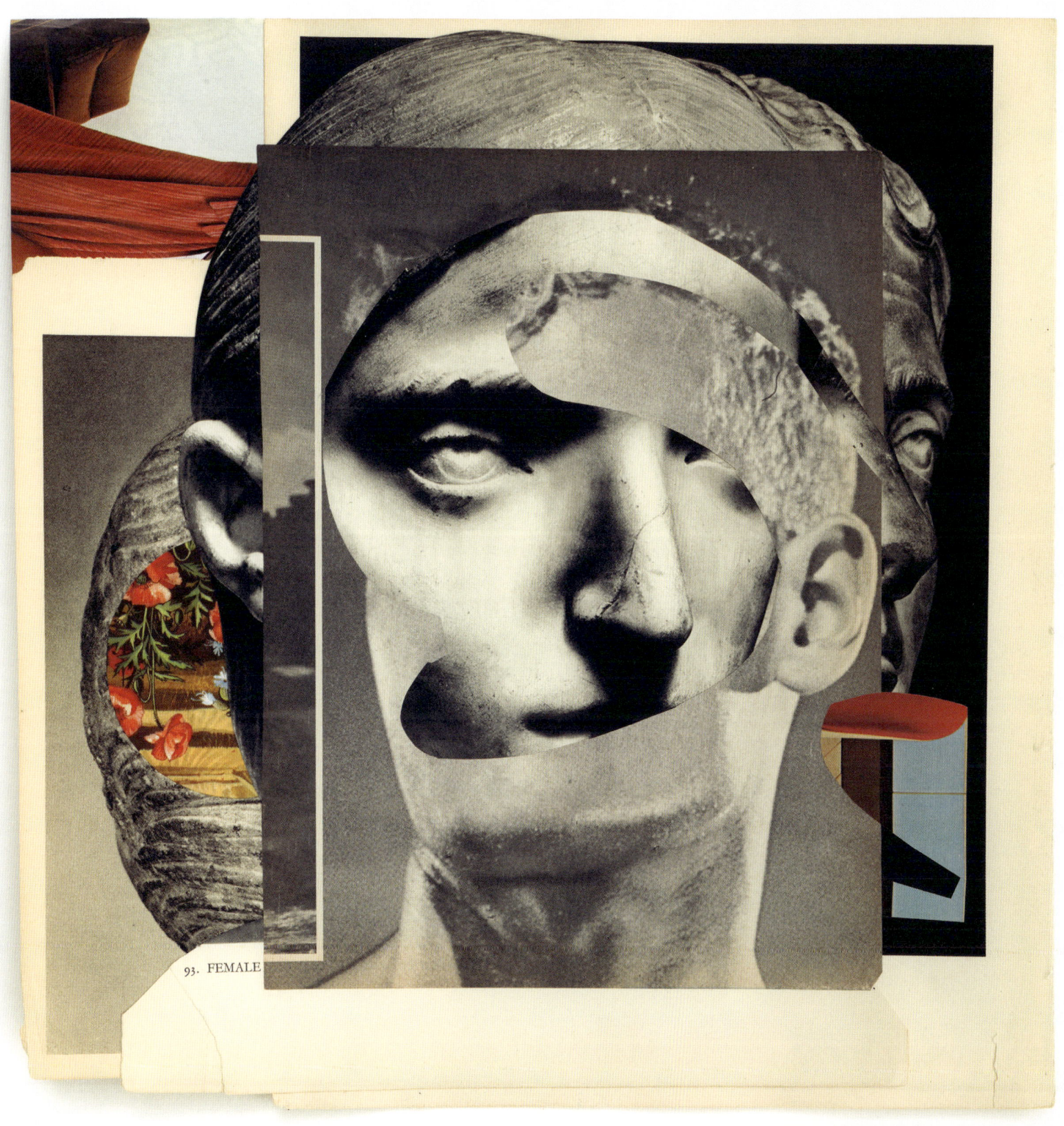

93. FEMALE

LINDER

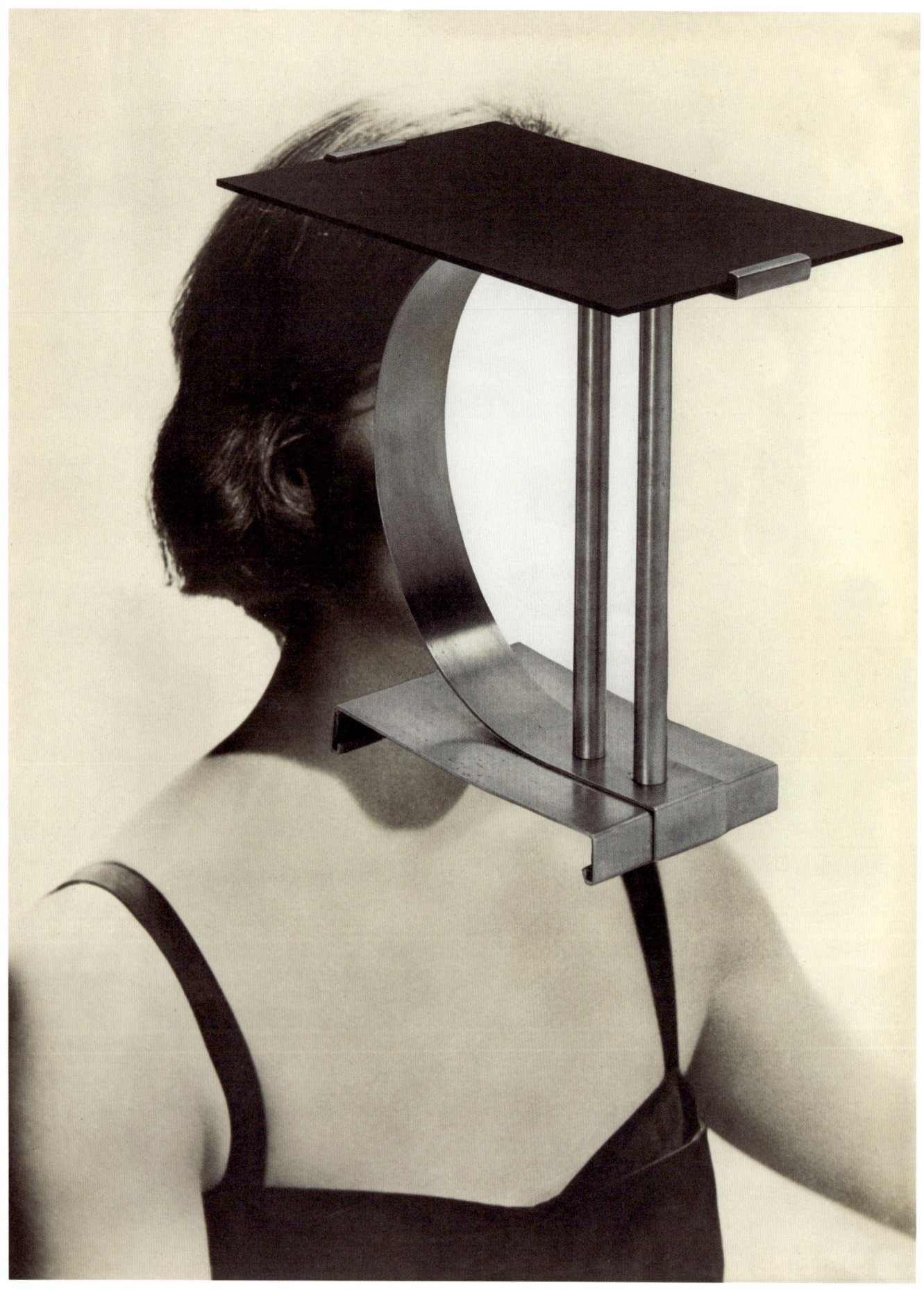

↑   **Mayniel Relief**, 2017, photomontage, 22.7 × 16.8 cm (9 × 6 ⅝ in)

→   **Bardot Relief (ii)**, 2018, photomontage, 22.6 × 17 cm (8 ⅞ × 6 ¾ in)

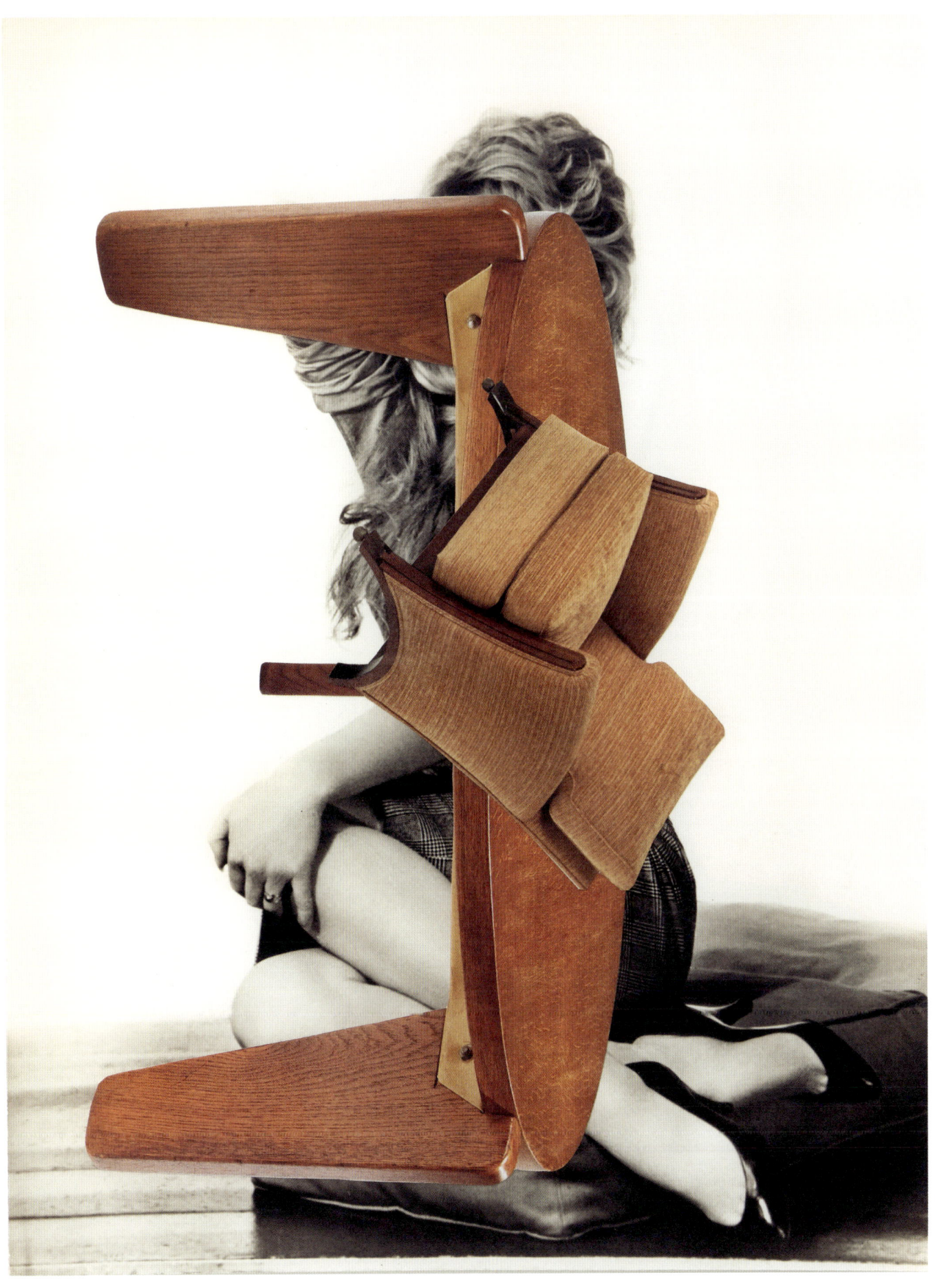

LINDER

MARY LUM

Comprising a wide range of coalescing materials, the work of Mary Lum finds acrylic, watercolour, found materials and text sharing the same plane as the artist's own photographs. The juxtaposition of materials and viewpoints formally references Cubism, the influential modern art movement that first presented different views in the same fractured plane. Lum's work also draws on a Russian Constructivist aesthetic – another early twentieth-century abstract art movement, which sought to reflect and shape urban geographies and the socialist industrial society within which it gained momentum after the October Revolution of 1917. Both these movements rejected the traditional, illustrative arts that preceded them and offered a graphically and technologically progressive critique; both are also useful frames of reference through which to understand the critical impulse of Lum's practice. In *Informations Pratiques* (French for 'useful information') (2021) a slice of a cityscape is visible through the several different perspectives and multiple layers of graphic information. Black and white fragmented text, geometric shapes and architectural plans overlay a rendering of a building, itself composed of deceptive perspectives. With its multi-coloured facade panels and supporting piloti, it is reminiscent of Le Corbusier's *Unité d'habitation de Marseille* (1947–52), another canonical touchstone of mid-century technology, design and its attendant ideology. The subject matter is perhaps a homage to modernism, yet conceptually at odds with the rationality of the work's title. This is not so much 'useful information' as it is productive problematization. It is not an evocation of the modernist desire to find signal in the noise, but an evocation of the noise itself. How are we to contend with the mess of history and make sense of the technological developments of our own moment? *Pont Marie* (2021) takes its title from a bridge that crosses the River Seine in Paris, or from the eponymous Metro station nearby. Two-thirds of the image is taken up with found paper elements that include bold cut-outs of letters and block shapes. These are latticed together to create the familiar effect and texture of fly-posted city walls or poster advertisements that have been repeatedly layered and partially removed. On the remaining third is a photograph of a train in a Metro station, its view framed by shapes painted in acrylic. *Pont Marie* illustrates Lum's interest in psychogeography by bringing to the fore forgotten aspects of the urban environment. Read in the context of our digital age in particular, Lum's collages are unapologetically ambiguous. They are clearly analogue in construction, yet reference the digital renderings that precede the building of all our contemporary infrastructure. In a world that prioritizes smoothness of experience, Lum's collages take us behind the glossy contemporary surface. Too frequently, the neo-liberal operations of capital are rendered invisible behind a constant shower of information. By problematizing this interface, Lum lifts the veil as her predecessors did in their own time.

HANA NOORALI AND LYNTON TALBOT

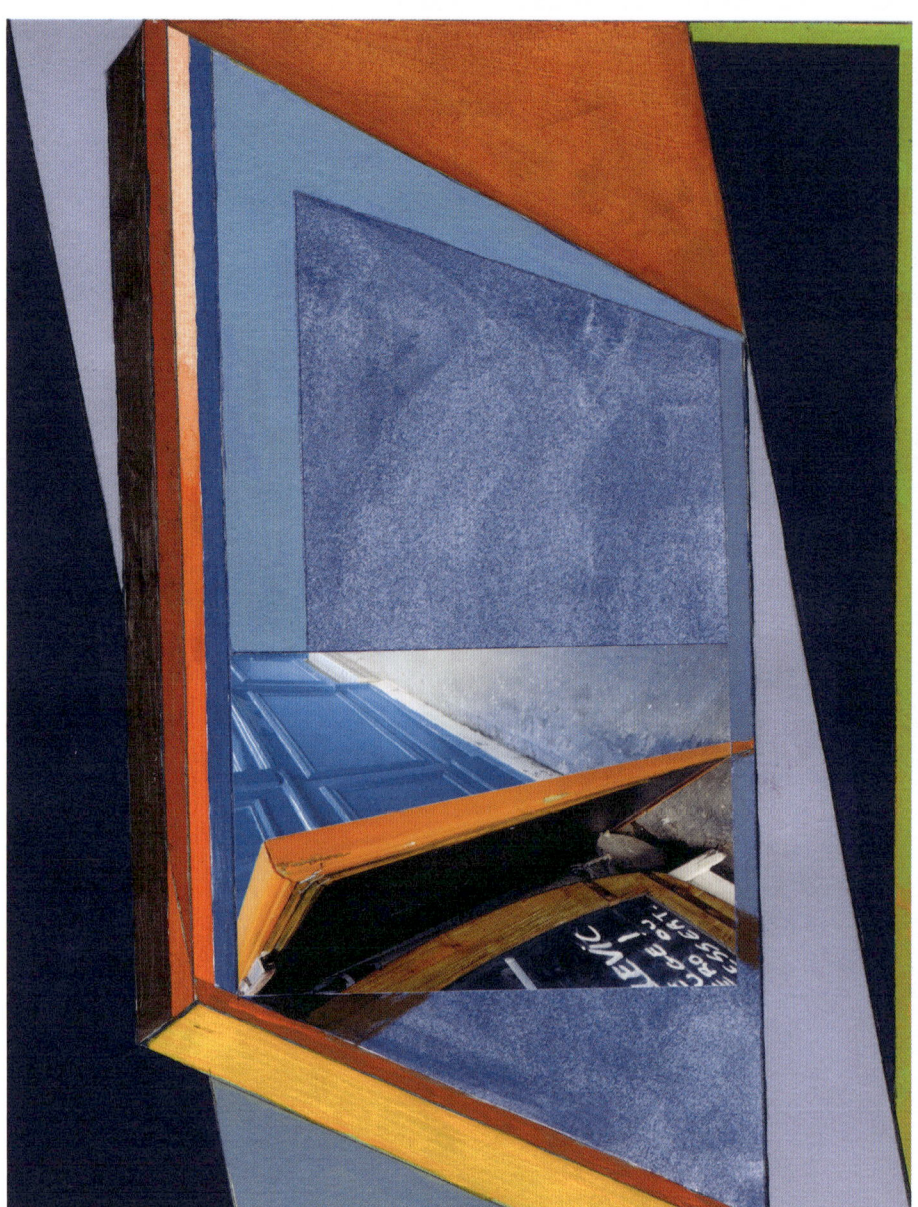

Born 1951, St. Cloud, Minnesota, USA. Lives in North Adams, Massachusetts, USA.

↑ **Menu**, 2021, acrylic, watercolour and photo-collage on paper, 45.1 × 37.2 cm (17 ¾ × 14 ⅝ in)

→ **Informations Pratiques**, 2021, acrylic and photo-collage on paper, 184.2 × 125.7 cm (72½ × 49½ in)

↗ **Poster**, 2021, acrylic, found paper and photo-collage on paper, 86.4 × 67.3 cm (34 × 26½ in)

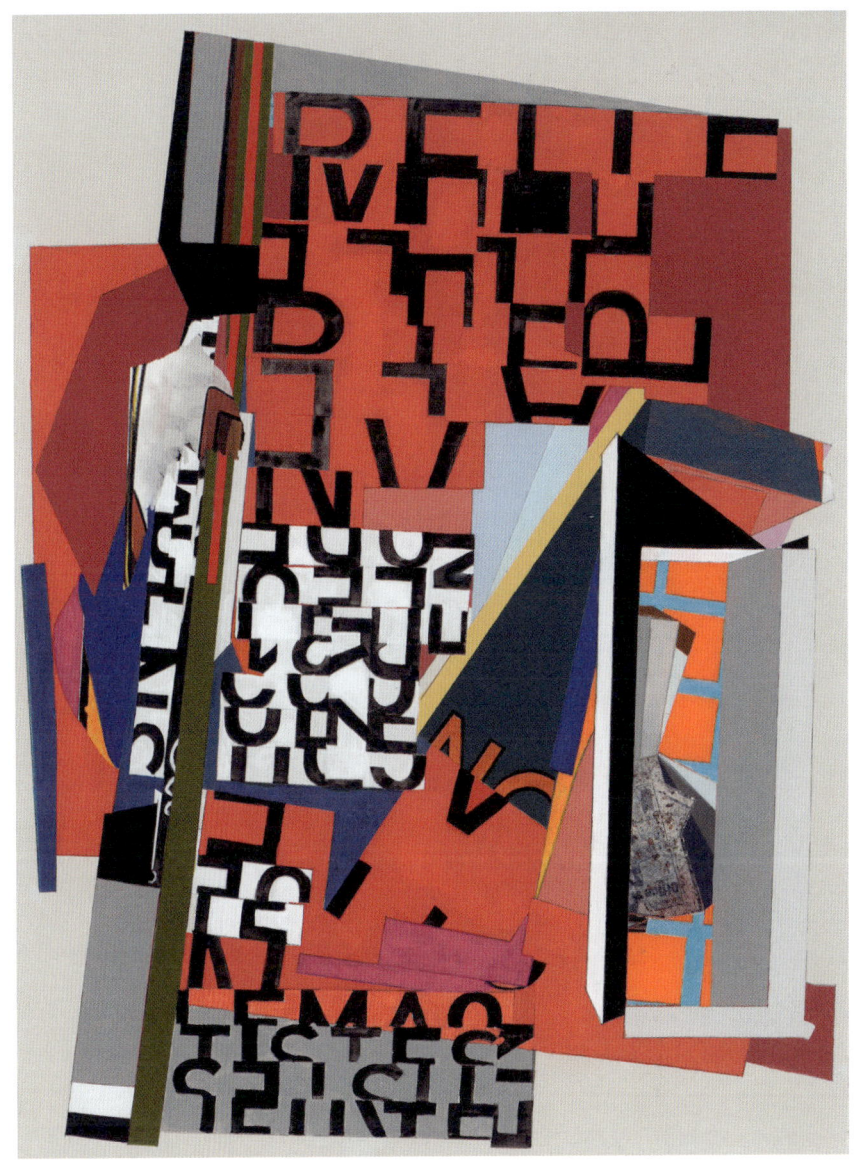

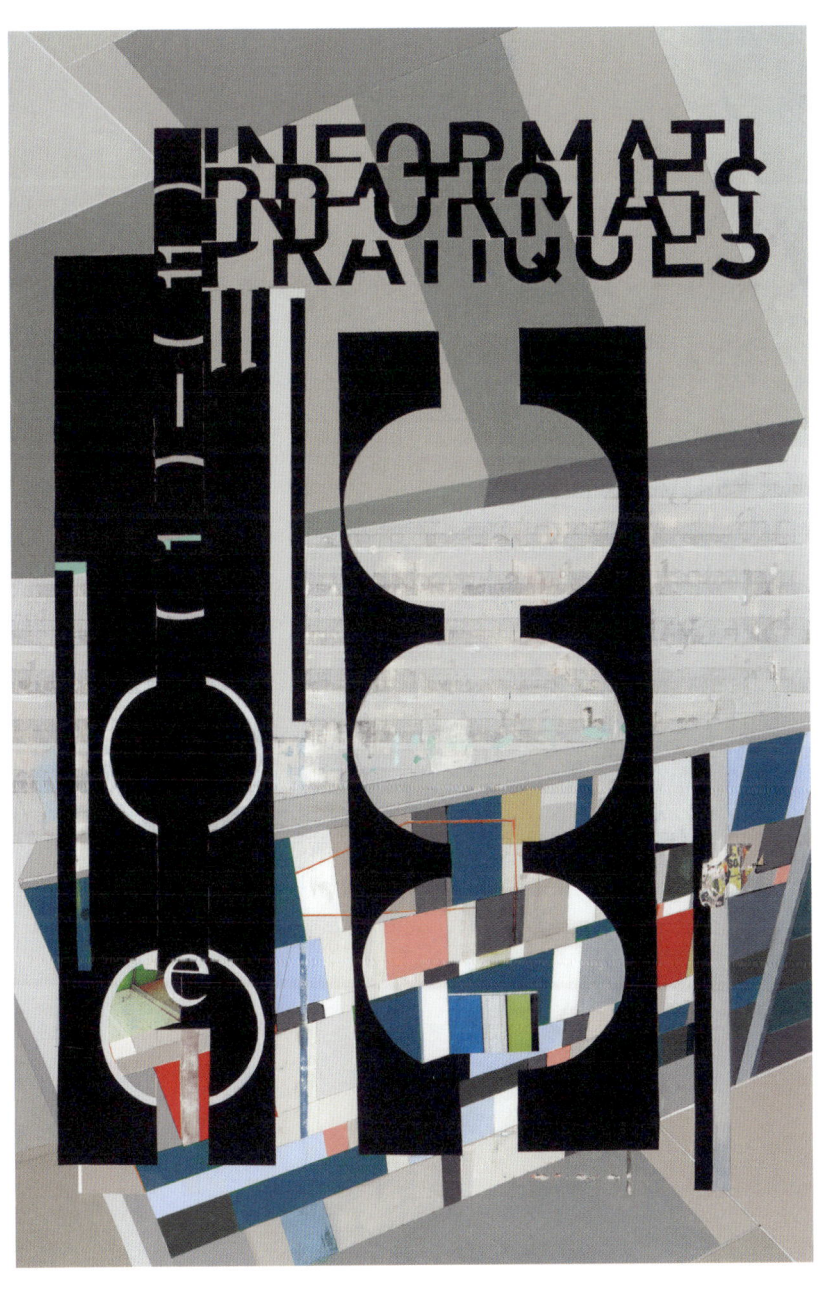

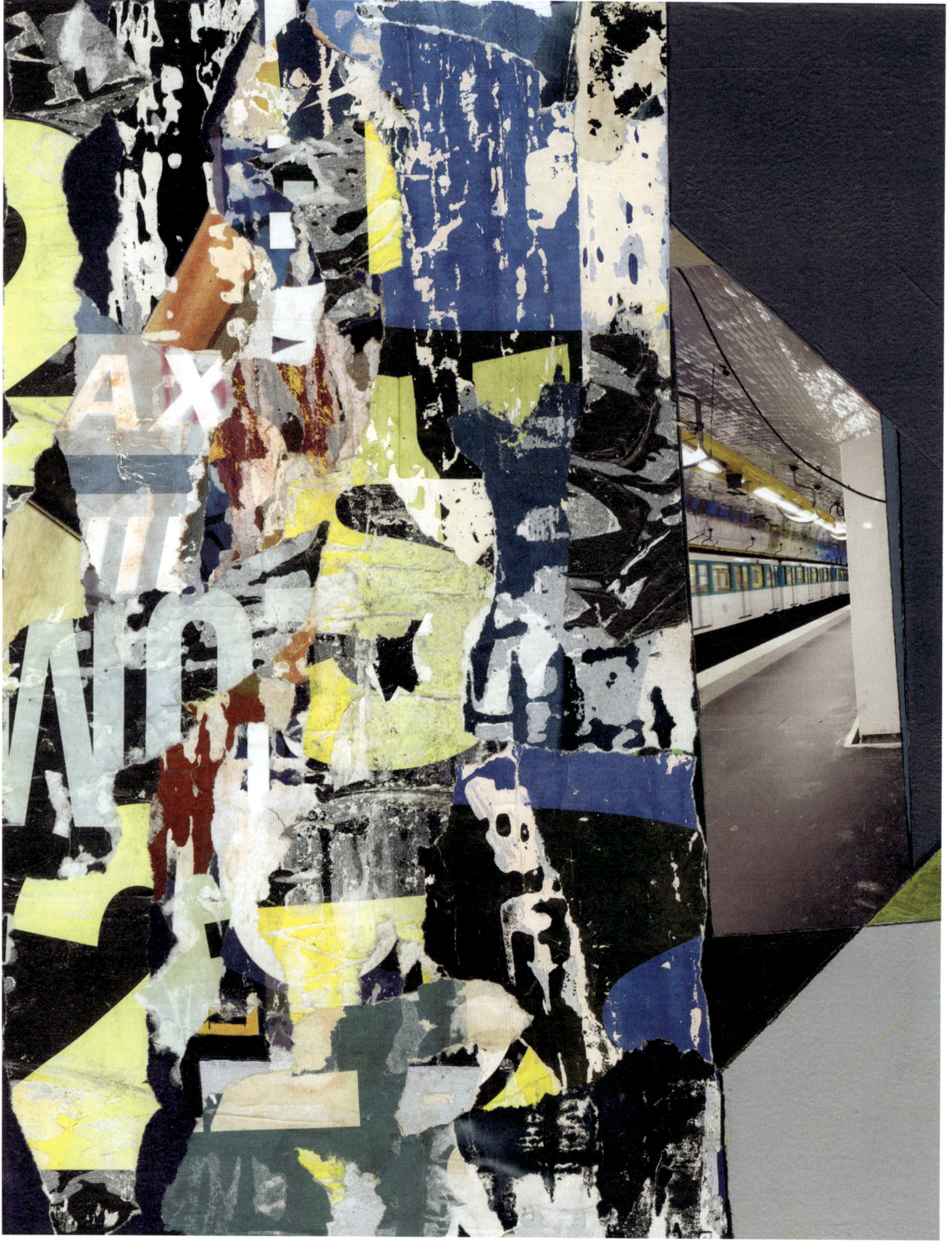

↑ **Pont Marie**, 2021, photo and found paper collage, acrylic on paper, 38.1 × 27.9 cm (15 × 11 in)

→ **Reflection**, 2021, acrylic and photo-collage on paper, 45.1 × 37.2 cm (17 ¾ × 14 ⅝ in)

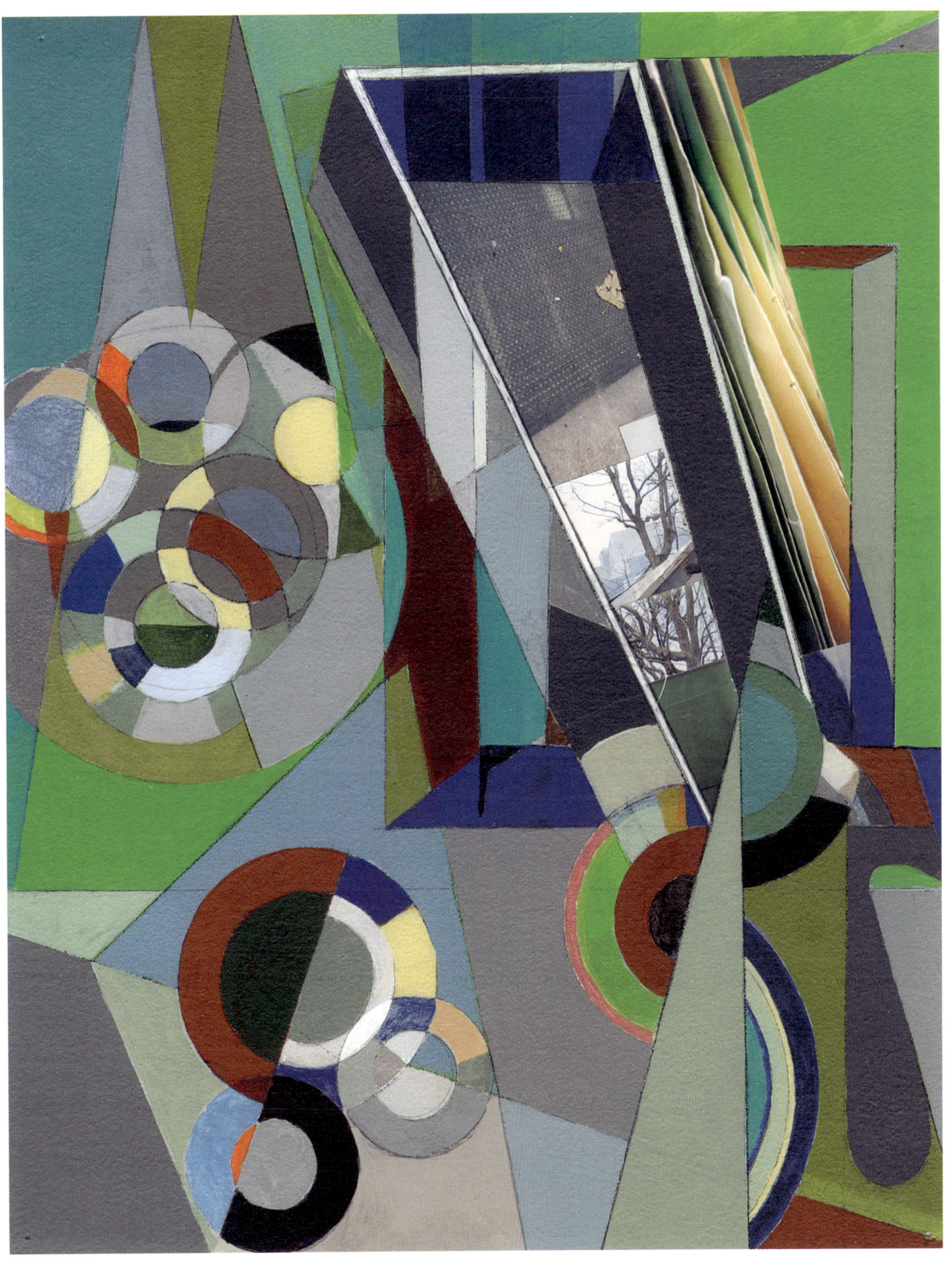

MARY LUM

DAVID MALJKOVIC

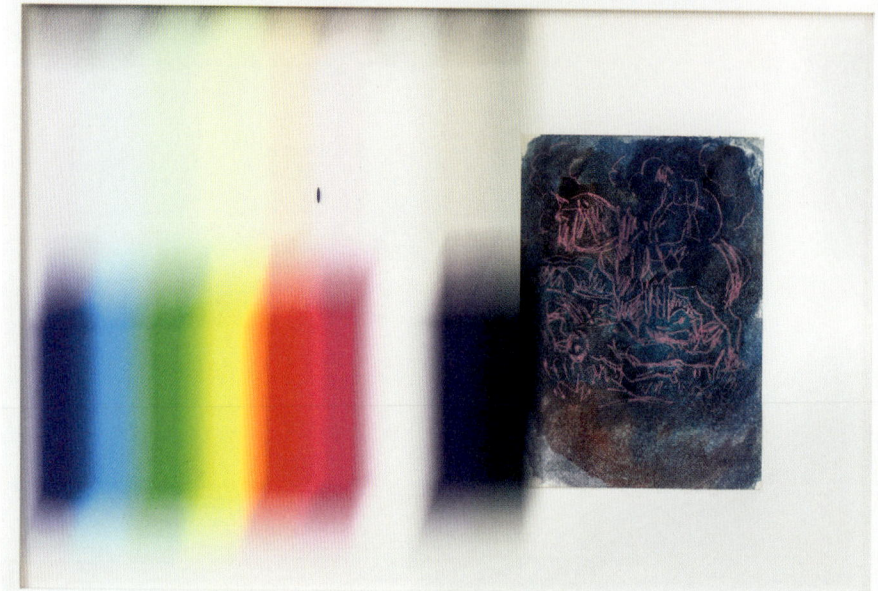

Vision in David Maljkovic's work is an emotional construct conditioned by a range of circumstances, memories and historical context, and thus inevitably presented as fantasy or illusion. Brutalist architecture becomes a sci-fi image, experimental car models are used as ordinary means of transport and shiny crystal-like shapes are placed in the middle of the ocean as monuments for an unspecified occasion, where humour, nostalgia and imagination are enmeshed into one. Maljkovic works in film, sculpture, photography and installation, but his strategy relies on the principles of collage-making, where different elements function in relation to one another and expose the very mechanisms of display that enable their visibility. Every work in Maljkovic's world is at once a depiction of something concrete and a meditation about how its image was made. Consider his series of elaborate digital collages, 'New Reproductions' (2014–15), in which the artist piles several photographs one on top of the other, each referring to some artistic experiment associated with a formal or technological vision of the future. Some of the photographs are then subjected to light filters, others to digital editing, manual tearing, cutting or pasting. The result, however, is a printed (albeit unique) enlargement of the accumulated sources, framed by a typical Kodak colour-control strip as used to proof colour photographs. According to Caroline Douglas in her Contemporary Art Society Friday Dispatch in 2015, these visual metaphors are meant to offer 'some sense of objective reality, of fixity of material and meaning'. However, in Maljkovic's case, the premise of an objective quantifiable source is a paradoxical one, and the collapse of intimacy, emotion and fact are recurring themes. The works titled *All Day All Year* (2016) are another potent example of Maljkovic's distinctive sensibility to image-making. They are part of a series of collages in which deconstruction of intimate and familiar objects takes place by way of sectioning parts of photographs depicting a chair, a desk or a plant, and processing the demarcated areas in different light conditions. In these works, the artist undermines the status of the photograph – as well as the object it depicts – as something fixed that can be viewed from an ideal point of view. But for Maljkovic collage is more than a technical procedure or a formal device. It is a question of the artificial nature of ideology, which comes into expression in his choice of imagery that infiltrates the works as a reflection on personal experience – in his case, having grown up in socialist former Yugoslavia, where visions of a modernized society were imposed as a substitute for an oppressing political reality. Collage, as his gallery's website explains, is a way of merging together 'unredeemed promises of the past and what they offer for our present'.

YUVAL ETGAR

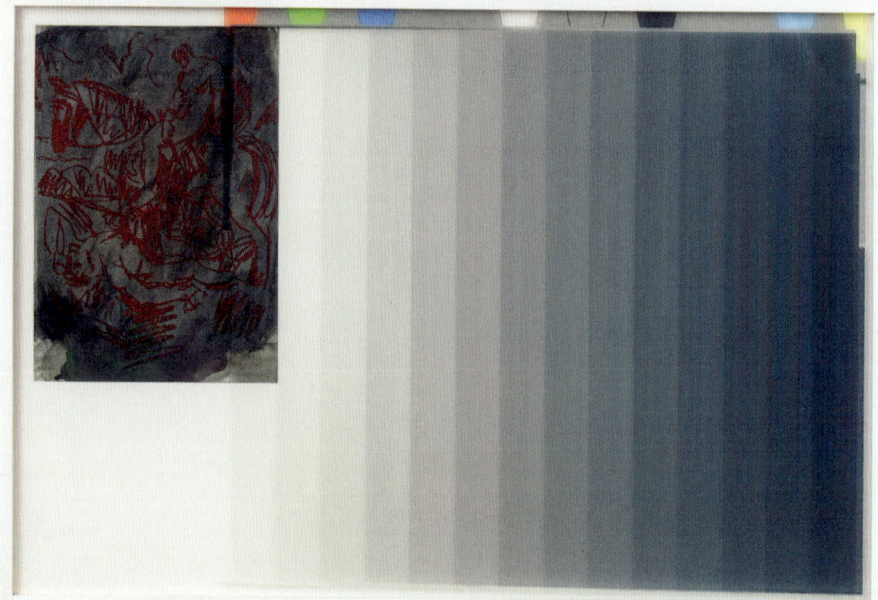

Born 1973, Rijeka, Croatia. Lives in Zagreb, Croatia.

↑↑ **PART 7: EXHIBITION**, 2020, watercolour and oil pastel on paper with print on glass, 70 × 100 cm (27 ½ × 39 ⅜ in)

↑ **PART 7: EXHIBITION**, 2020, watercolour and oil pastel on paper with print on glass, 70 × 100 cm (27 ½ × 39 ⅜ in)

↗ **All Day All Year**, 2016, inkjet on canvas painted with oil colours mounted on aluminium composite panel and inkjet print on archival paper mounted on archival cardboard, 150 × 100 cm (59 × 39 ⅜ in)

↗↗ **New Reproduction**, 2015, collage on brass sheet, 150 × 100 cm (59 × 39 ⅜ in)

→ **All Day All Year**, 2016, inkjet on canvas painted with oil colours mounted on aluminium composite panel and inkjet print on archival paper mounted on archival cardboard, 150 × 100 cm (59 × 39 ⅜ in)

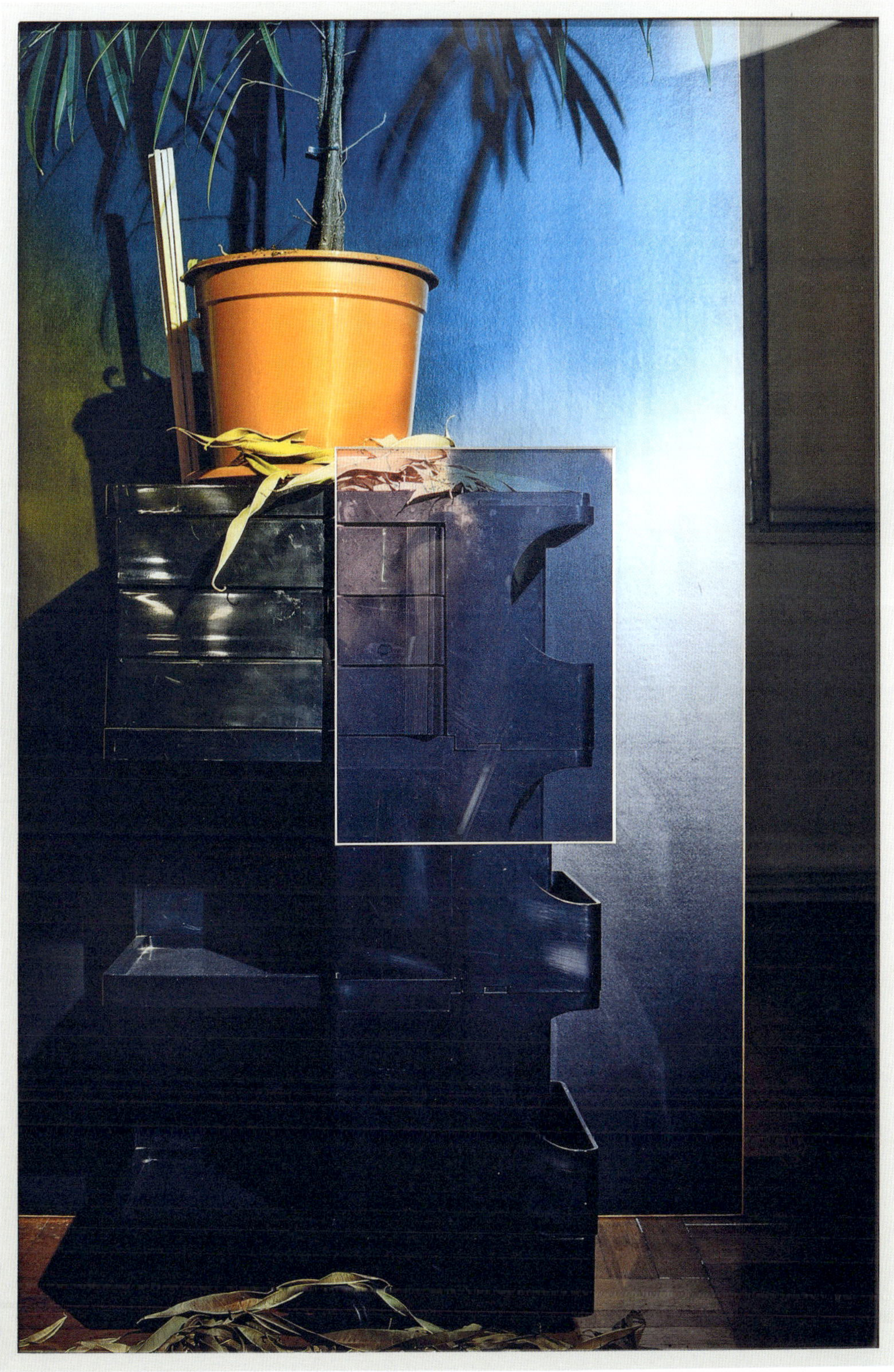

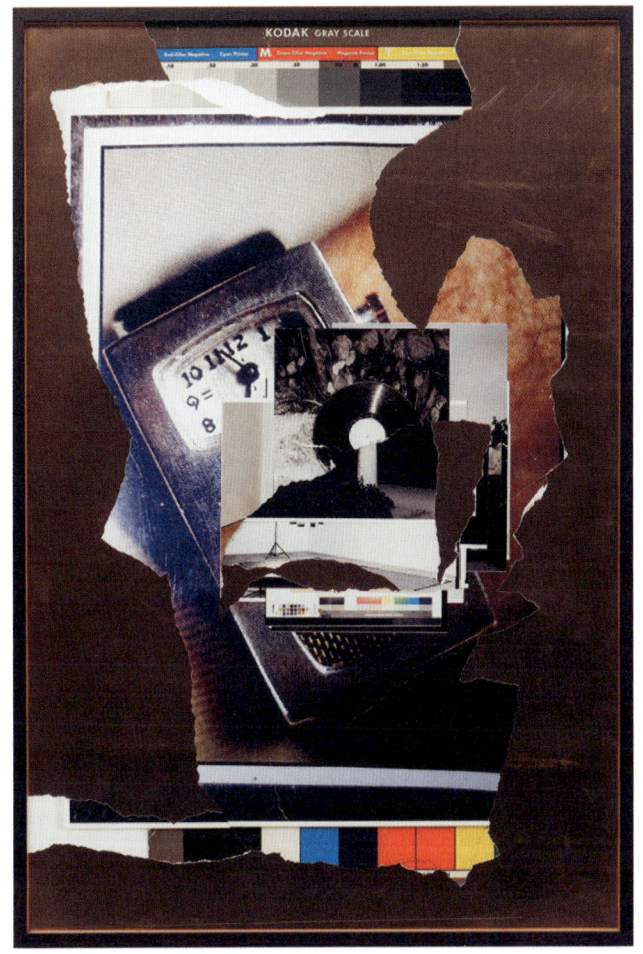

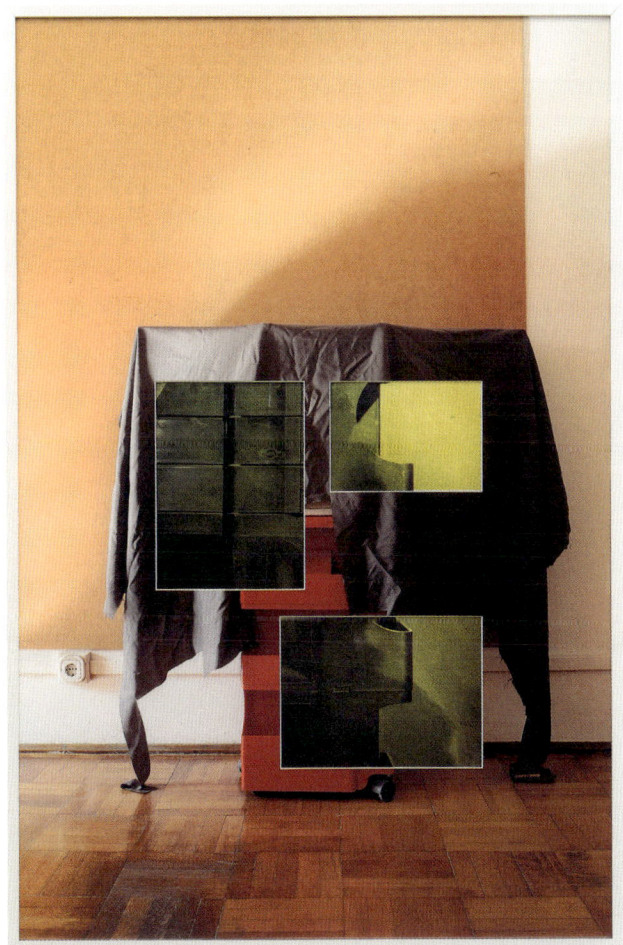

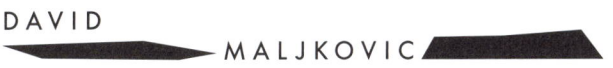

DAVID MALJKOVIC

CHRISTIAN MARCLAY

'I suppose my work is constantly a process of taking advantage of different technologies of communication,' explained Christian Marclay in an interview with the author in 2021, 'embracing their disadvantages, and turning them into a strength'. Marclay's practice occupies a distinctive place in the crossover between sound, word and image production. At the end of the 1970s, when he was still an art student, Marclay began to perform as a DJ and a musician, playing turntables, sampling audio and producing live music, while also exploring sculptural strategies as part of his auditory creations. By joining fragments of vinyl records into hybrid objects, his early series of 'Recycled Records' (1980–6) confirms the potential of making collages whose broken aesthetics are not only expressed in the fragmented appearance of the objects but also in the abrupt leaps in sound that they produce when played. ◢ Over the years, Marclay's work also extended to include moving image, primarily as a means of addressing the rhythmic and auditory aspects of technological appliances common to popular culture. *Telephones* (1995), for example, is a filmic montage based on scenes from recognizable television series and movies arranged according to the order of rituals associated with making a telephone call – dialling, picking up, talking, listening and hanging up. Similar strategies of narrative deconstruction associated with audio-visual experience also extend to Marclay's multi-channel installations, such as *Video Quartet* (2002) and *Crossfire* (2007), and to other filmic montage works, such as *The Clock* (2010), where scenes representing specific times of the day are synchronized with real time to create a twenty-four-hour-long looped film in which fiction and reality are united. ◢ Marclay's fascination with the overlap between different technologies and registers of performative communication is equally manifested in his studies of notation and language systems through text, printmaking and collage. This is clearly expressed in his collages based on comic strips, of which the 'Face' (2020) series is an example. In these works, he questions the interpretative scope of onomatopoeic language, composing portraits of grotesque figures whose emotional or expressive state is manifested through a cacophony of sound words that cover or rather compose these portraits. Each is made of dozens of sound words that extend into every part of the countenance, leaving only the eyes, mouths and ears exposed. As Marclay further explained in his 2021 interview, 'consider the way movement is represented, for example, and time, when you have such a poor medium at your disposal as comics, it's brilliant. Since you cannot have a description narrative that tells you there is wind or darkness, that a place is cold or wet, you get these vocal iterations instead: "Brrrrr...", "Thwip", "Aaaargh", "Fwoooosh".'

YUVAL ETGAR

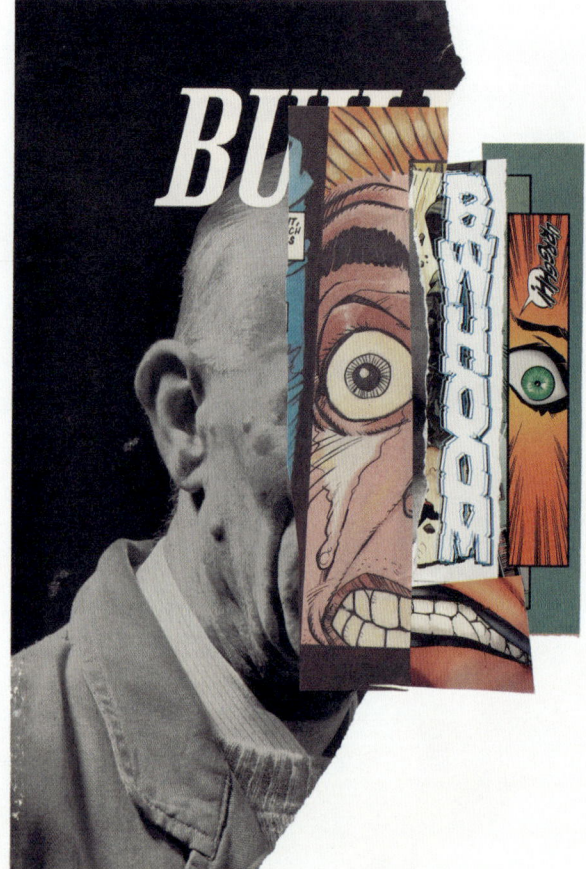

Born 1955, San Rafael, California, USA. Lives in London, UK.

↑   Tragic Mask, 2020, collage on paper, 41.8 × 29.5 cm (16 7/16 × 11 5/8 in)

↗   Face (Anger), 2020, collage on paper, 30.3 × 30.3 cm (11 15/16 × 11 15/16 in)

↗↗ Face (Blinded), 2020, collage on paper, 30 × 30 cm (11 13/16 × 11 13/16 in)

→   Face (Green), 2020, collage on paper, 30 × 30.3 cm (11 13/16 × 11 15/16 in)

→ → Face (Fear), 2020, collage on paper, 30.2 × 30.3 cm (11 7/8 × 11 15/16 in), private collection

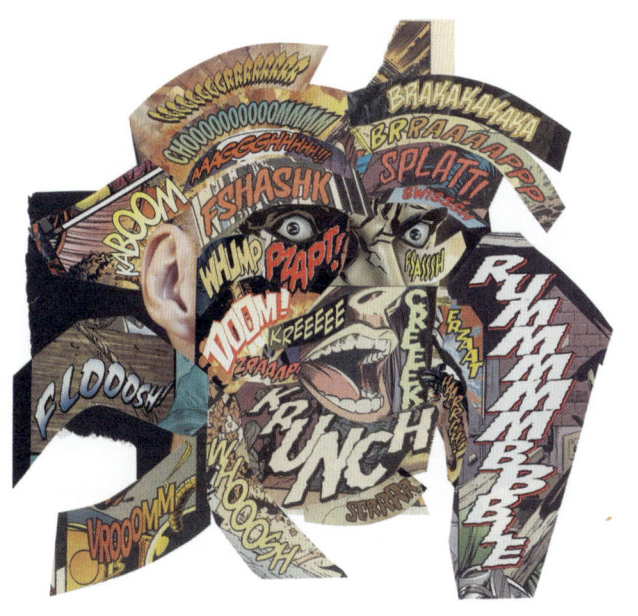

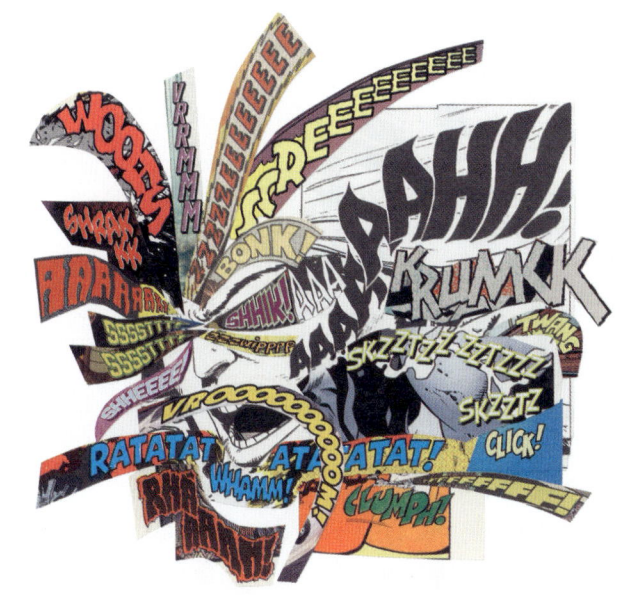

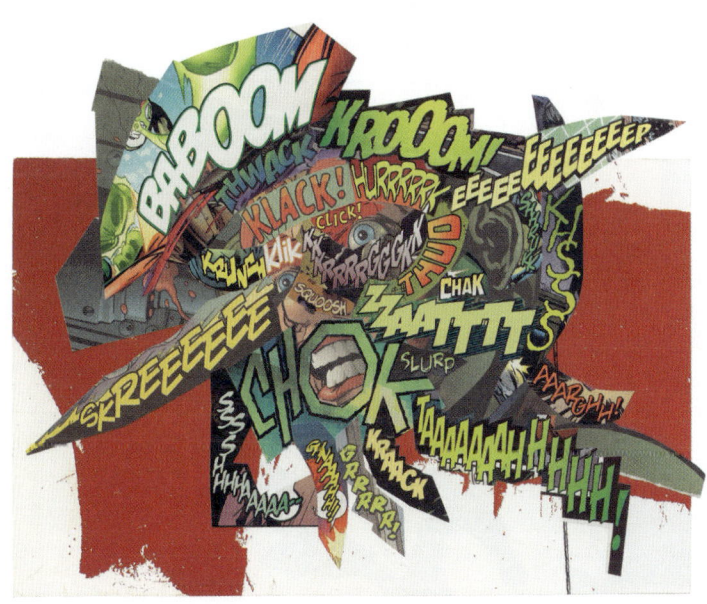

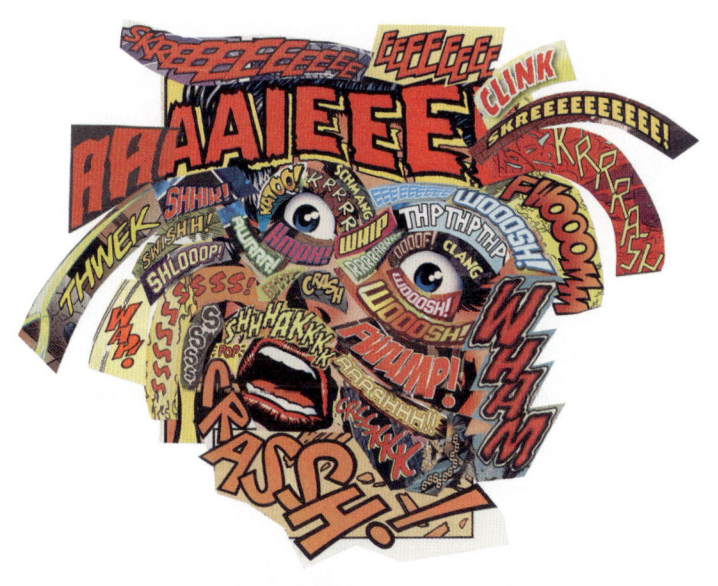

NEO MATLOGA

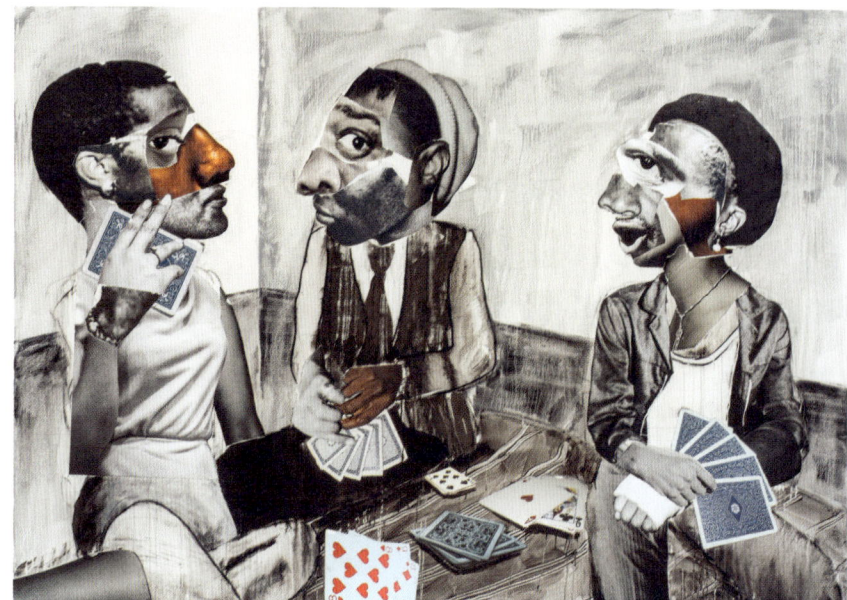

Like others of the Millennial generation, Neo Matloga has been deeply affected by the dominating, globalized mass media, submerging himself in events happening close to home and far away. Family albums, TV and radio programmes, and magazines are his primary sources of inspiration, facilitating his constant scouting for images and situations to use in his works. In a 2020 interview for *Culture Type*, he explains how radio, in particular, influenced his imagination, when as a child the television was broken and he listened to his parents' radio choices: 'We listened to news, as well as captivating local dramas that highlighted family conflicts, relationships, love affairs and daily trials. There was room for dreaming and also, in a way, radio made us story-tellers.' ◢ Matloga represents groups of people in authentic yet imagined scenarios: a couple deep in conversation nesting under a baroque headboard, as in *Bare gao ntswaneli* (*They say you don't suit me*), (2021); dancing and drinking in a modernist living room embellished with tribal art in *Bo papa Mapula, ba na le masela* (*Mapula's dad, dresses sartorially*) (2021); and a local Sunday service gathering in *Sontaga* (*Sunday*) (2021). Fascinated with difference, the artist unites people from all areas of life within his works, from celebrities and politicians to housewives and queer fashionistas. These figures are captured in various domestic settings of the post-apartheid era, immersed in love, intimacy and temptation. The collaged photographic elements contrast with a blend of drawing and painting materials. Distinct from overt racial discourses, Matloga's monochromatic, theatrical scenes and uplifting characters counter the often dominant agenda in contemporary African art, which is rooted in ethnic politics and immigration histories. ◢◣ In Matloga's earliest works, faces are collaged from multiple sources to intensify the human emo-tions – infatuation, desperation, apathy, desire – plotted within one frame. While the compositions appear to be capturing an instant, the artist's scenes extend beyond this moment in time, introducing a sense of malleability in their evocation of a sequence of events, of what happened before and what happened after. The process of collage permits the artist to implement new situations and contexts that deconstruct the existing image, allowing a displacement of time and space to contribute to an alternative reality. The way Matloga represents bodies and limbs becomes another field for his experiments in interruption and reconstruction. ◢ *Sontaga* is a lifesize picture that, unusually for the artist, has characters featured in an outdoor space. Its sheer scale contributes to the construction of pictorial depth, creating a three-layered space of the building and the exterior areas behind and in front of the diamond-pattern wire fence. Rich details such as stripes and checks on clothing, disproportionate facial features and hands, grasped Bibles and an unpaired sock render a quirky and grotesque scene. In Matloga's hands this medley of visual elements is assembled into a solemn farce. ◢

POPPY DONGXUE WU

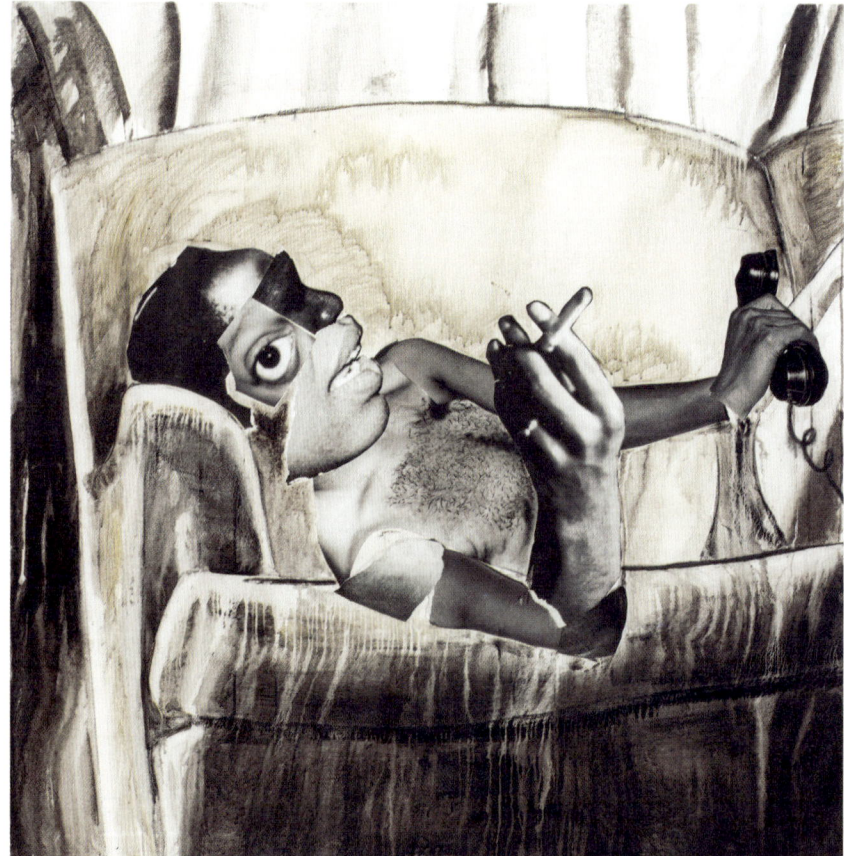

Born 1993, Mamaila, Limpopo, South Africa. Lives in Mamaila and Amsterdam, Netherlands.

↑↑ Dikarata (Cards), 2021, collage, charcoal, liquid charcoal, ink, soft pastel and acrylic on canvas, 175 × 250 cm (68⅞ × 98⅜ in)

↑ Petunia, 2021, collage, charcoal and ink on canvas, 150 × 150 cm (59 × 59 in)

↗ Bare gao ntswaneli (They say you don't suit me), 2021, collage, charcoal, liquid charcoal, ink, soft pastel and acrylic on canvas, 200 × 200 cm (78¾ × 78¾ in)

→ Bo papa Mapula, ba na le masela, (Mapula's dad, dresses sartorially), 2021, collage, charcoal, ink and oil stick on canvas, 250 × 375 cm (98⅜ × 147⅝ in)

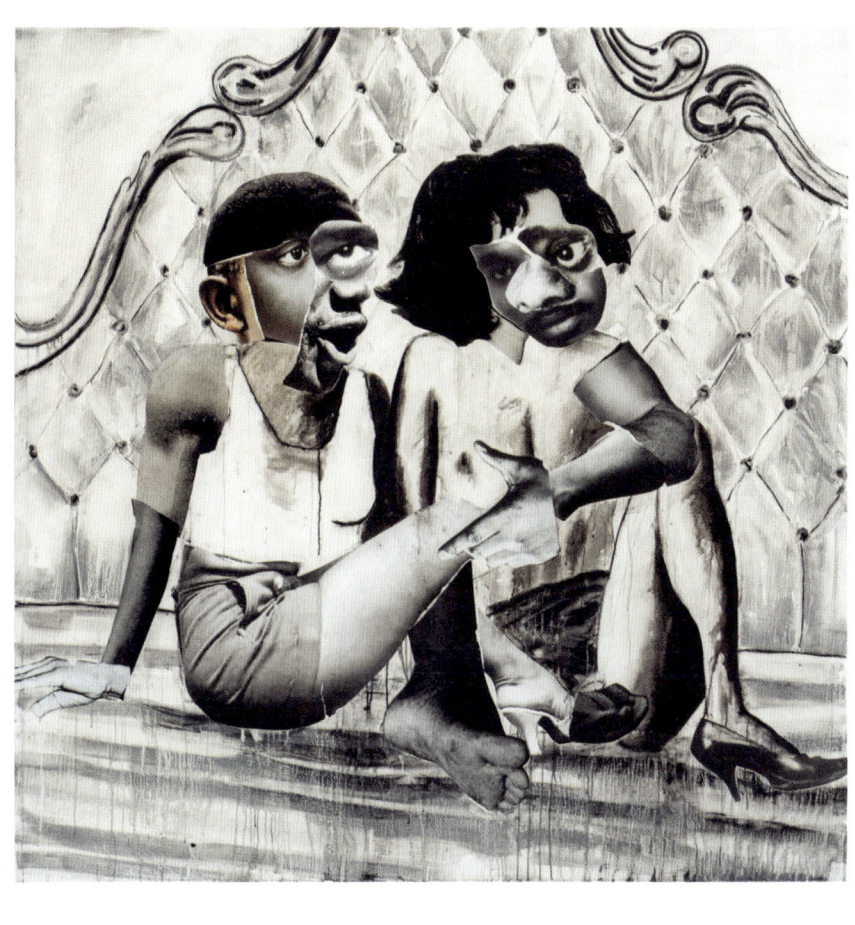

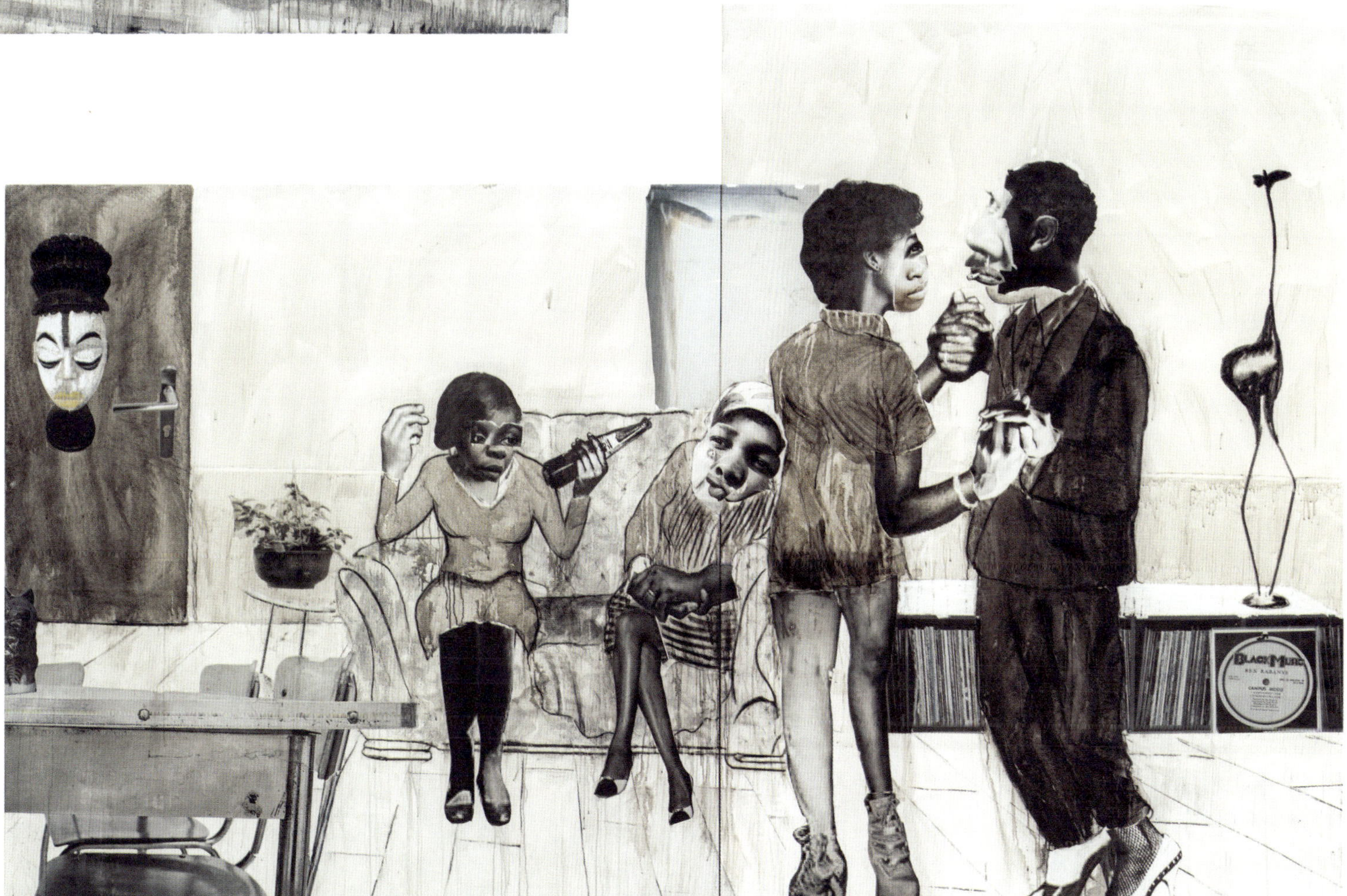

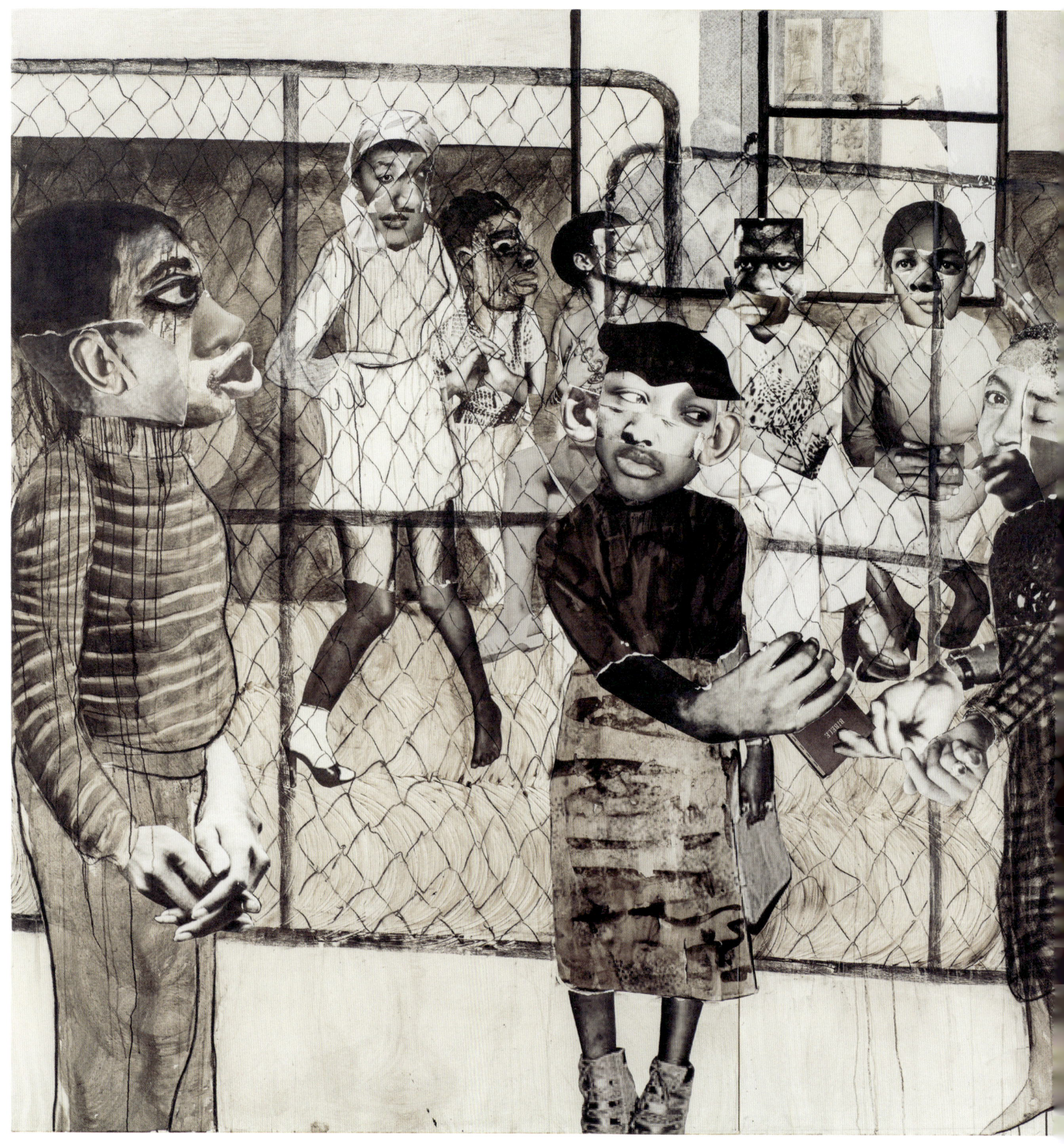

↑   **Sontaga (Sunday)**, 2021, collage, charcoal, ink and oil stick on canvas, 300 × 600 cm (118⅛ × 236¼ in)

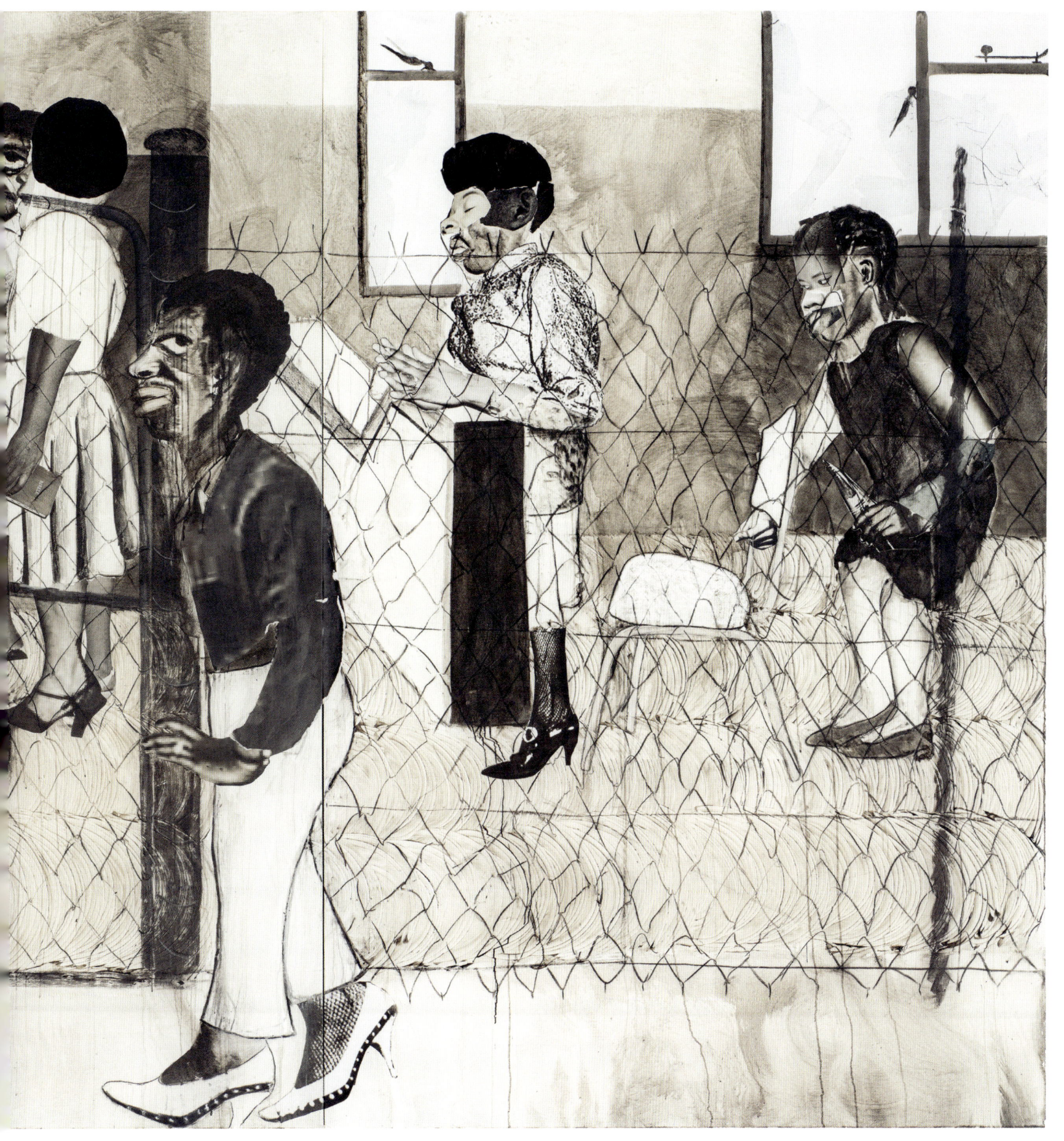

RAMI
MAYMON

While Rami Maymon only began creating handmade collages relatively recently, his practice – which spans photography, sculpture and installation – has long been dominated by a collagist approach. As well as sitting at the intersection of various media, his works employ collage as a formal and conceptual act. In referencing both international and Israeli art history, Maymon raises questions regarding originality, authenticity, canonization and the relationship between image and text. His ongoing series 'Further Reading' began in 2007 and comprises photographs in which art history books are used as ready-made sculptural and performative objects. Maymon then gradually shifted his focus to his local art history, using the pages of books themselves as a starting point for collage works. His 2019 exhibition 'Him-Self' at Mishkan Museum of Art in Ein Harod, Israel, included an installation recontextualizing objects from the museum's collection, as well as collages created using a deconstructed catalogue of the collection from 1970. In his hands, reproductions of the museum's artworks were almost entirely obscured by paint, ink and fragments of coloured papers, while their captions remained visible to indicate the original source, setting up a perplexing relationship to the newly formed abstract images. In *Untitled (A Jew)* (2018), for example, the caption reveals that the figure hidden under the solid shapes of white, black and pink paper is a 1934 drawing by the Ukraine-born Jewish painter Emmanuel Mané-Katz (1894–1962), titled *A Jew*. Maymon's manipulation obliterates Mané-Katz's fedora-wearing religious diasporic Jew, while hinting to the outline of its opposite – the secular Tzabar (born in Israel) Jew, with his forelock and wide-shouldered jacket. According to Liat Lavi in a text written to accompany the exhibition, this analytical yet aesthetic collagist act replaced the original artwork's visual value with its symbolic value, as revealed in the caption, while deconstructing the peripheral museum's focus on mainly Jewish-European artworks. The tension between the Orientalized local and Western modernist abstraction, characterizing Israeli art history, was also present in Maymon's 2018 exhibition 'Hunting West' at Inga gallery, Tel Aviv, which included works combining materials and references from the Middle East, the artist's immediate environment. *Untitled (Berlin, Andros)* (2018) features a postcard from the Neues Museum in Berlin, Germany, showing the eye of an Egyptian Nefertiti bust, attached to a piece of cardboard found in the Greek island of Andros. The composition and colours create a sculptural-surgical intersection between images, materials and values, as well as between locations and cultures that are historically submerged in relations of domination and desire. Using collage as a medium of appropriation, the work also raises questions regarding Western institutional appropriation and repatriation. Maymon's complex archaeological approach towards his original sources challenges how narratives and meanings are fixed through the photographic act and consecutive contextualization of reproductions. Drawing from collage's cardinal motivation to disassemble images into new contexts, his works awaken other works from their canonical dormancy. KEREN GOLDBERG

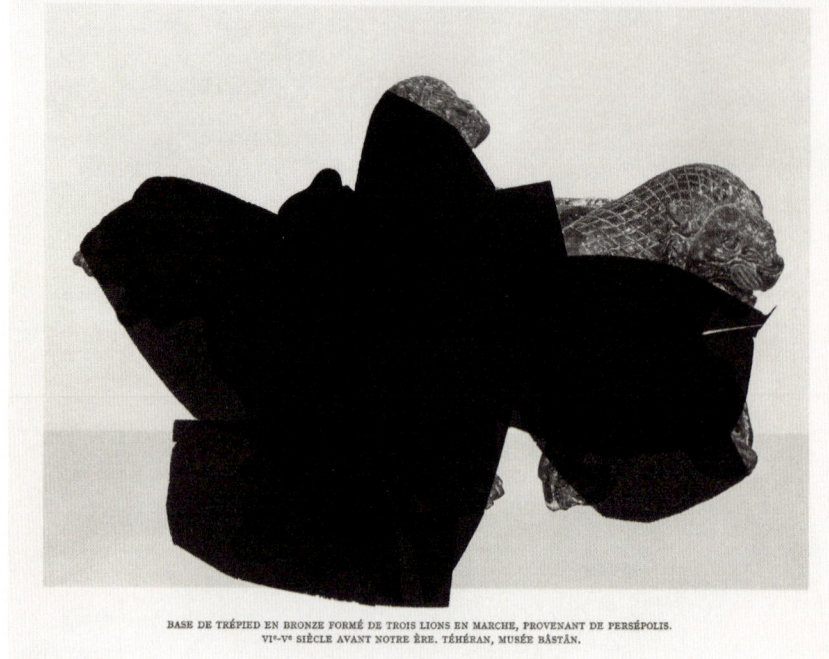

BASE DE TRÉPIED EN BRONZE FORMÉ DE TROIS LIONS EN MARCHE, PROVENANT DE PERSÉPOLIS.
VIᵉ–Vᵉ SIÈCLE AVANT NOTRE ÈRE. TÉHÉRAN, MUSÉE BÂSTÂN.

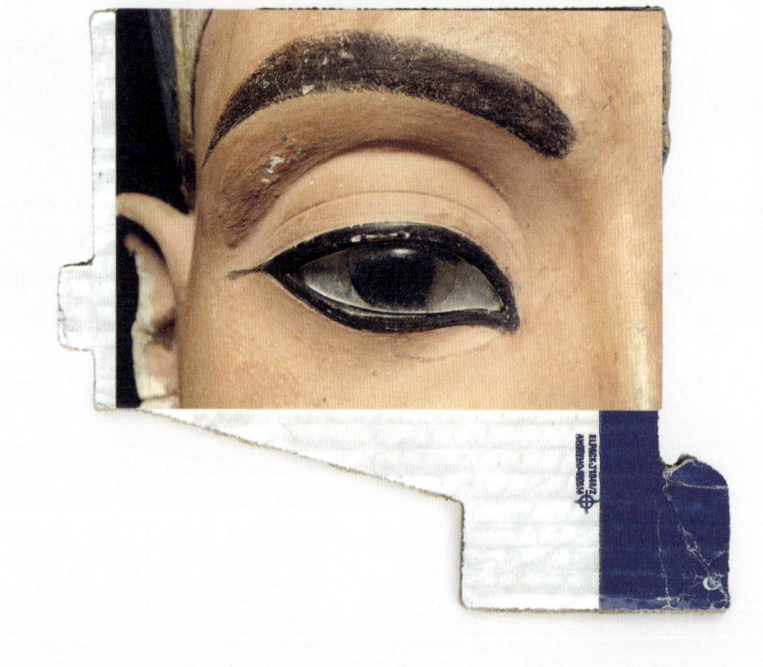

Born 1976, Tel Aviv, Israel. Lives in Tel Aviv.

↑↑ Untitled (Black lions), 2018, silkscreen print and carbon paper on inkjet print, 65 × 80 cm (25 ⅝ × 31½ in), private collection, Beijing, China

↑ Untitled (Berlin, Andros), 2018, postcard on found object, 14.4 × 16.5 cm (5 ⅝ × 6½ in)

↗ Untitled (Head of a girl), 2019, ink and paper cuts on book page, 40 × 29.6 cm (15 ¾ × 11 ⅝ in)

→ Untitled (A Jew), 2018, acrylic, ink and paper cuts on book page, 16.2 × 12 cm (6¼ × 4 ¾ in), private collection, Brussels, Belgium

→→ Untitled (Snake Charming), 2020, paper cuts and ink on postcard, 15 × 10.5 cm (5 ⅞ × 4 ⅛ in)

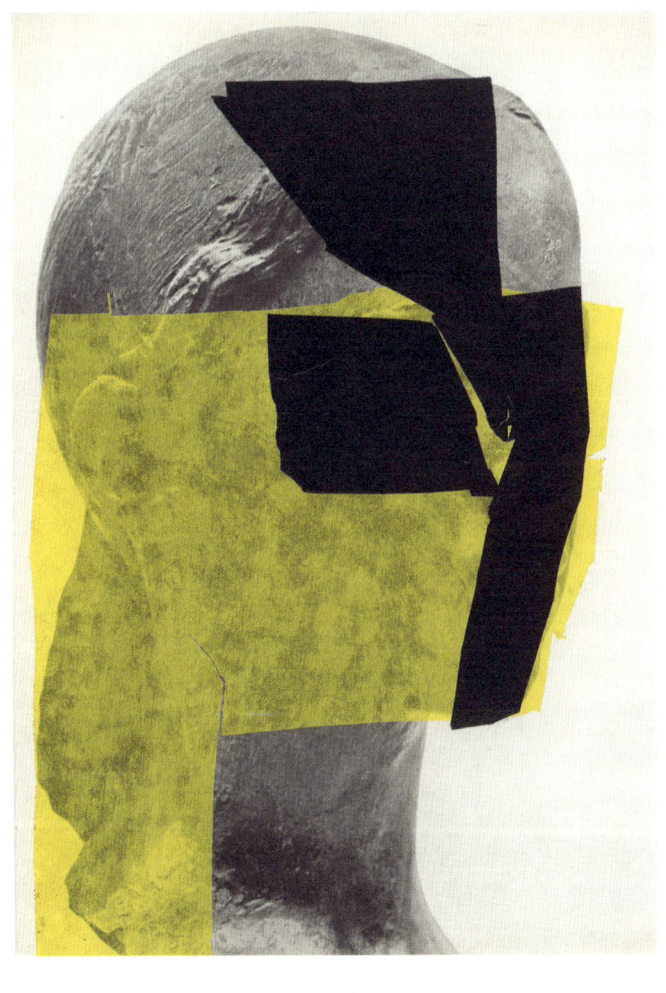

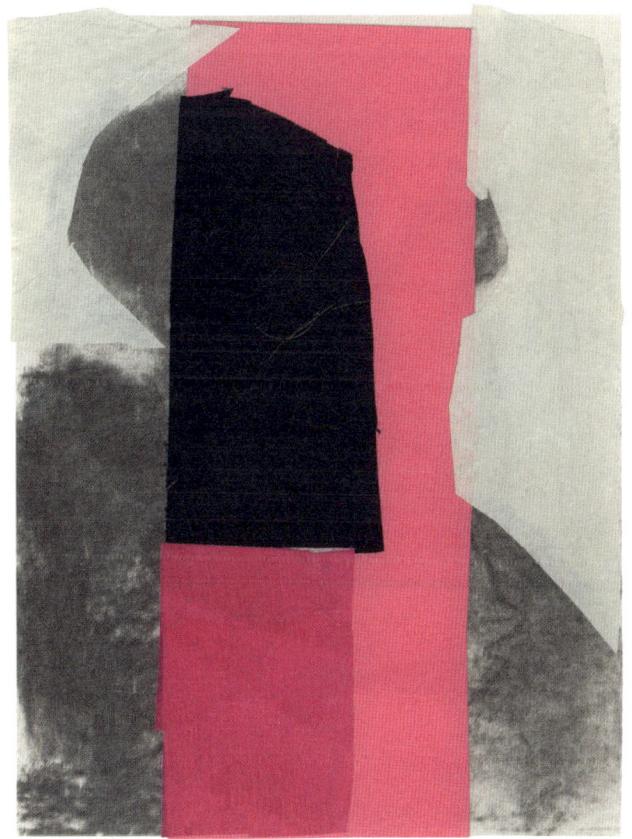

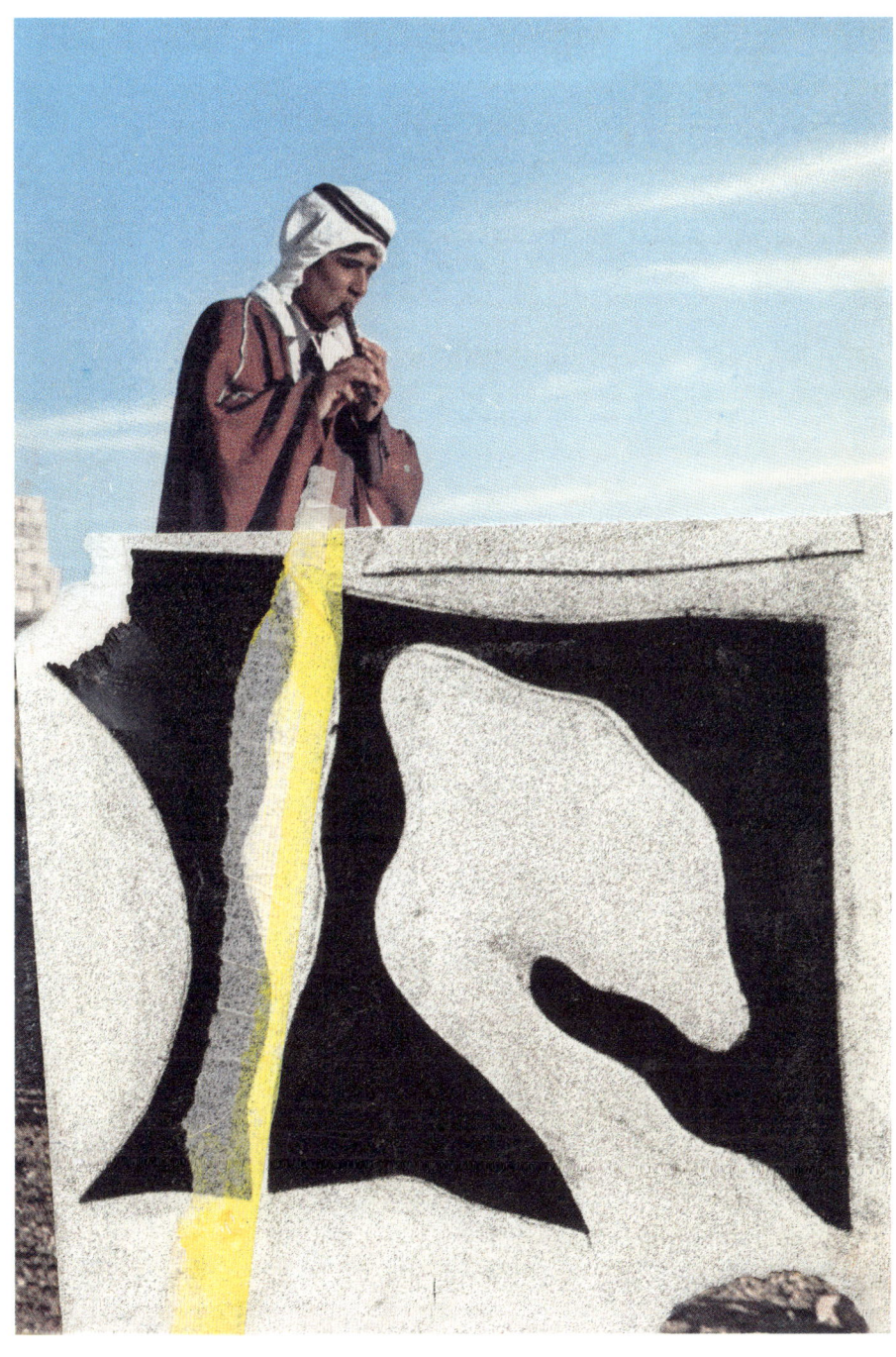

RAMI
MAYMON

LORNA MILLS

Quick, chaotic and moving with a cacophonous rhythm, Lorna Mills's art creates a viewing experience that parallels the movement of the internet. The net and new-media artist has been active since the early 1990s, and her practice has been punctuated by developments in technology and an increasing accessibility to online images that demonstrate what she describes as 'marginalized peculiarity'. ◄━━ Mills began experimenting with photo-based GIFs (digital files that contain a still or repetitively moving image) in 2005, and her practice has been predominantly dedicated to the format since, making Mills among the first generation of GIF artists who have defined the genre for many who have followed. Preferring an inchoate aesthetic, Mills roughly cuts and layers images ploughed from the subcultural corners of Reddit, Google+, Porn Fail and YouTube – 'I am drawn to gratuitous Internet filth,' she told *Artsy* in 2014. As such, there is invariably a psychosexual theme to these images, emphasized by the infinite jerking motion of the animated GIF. The bizarreness of sexuality online is also evoked by Mills's attraction to artificial products, such as rubber items and inflatables, that are rendered ridiculous, like the phallic tubemen mascots that feature in *Tiz war* (2015). ◄━━ Mills's practice also reveals an interest in the structure of things: the bleeding pixels and jagged edges of her works with their signature 'stairstep contours', and her use of what artist and writer Hito Steyerl (b. 1966) defined in 2009 as 'poor images,' throws the grids upon which these digital images rely into sharp relief. The vehicles stacked high, crushing and colliding in *Cerebral Concrete* (2019) demonstrate Mills's ongoing concern with the visceral effects of excess, explored in visual piles, dumps and repetitions. The limitations of the GIF also provide Mills with 'a lot of formal opportunities', as she said in a 2015 interview at the transmediale festival in Berlin, while also revealing their innate fabrication to the viewer, which could be taken as a metaphor for the way we perceive the world in a digitally networked culture. It has a levelling effect – Mills's source materials might be considered low culture and lo-fi, but they prompt questions about the order of the visual world and systems of value, since all art depends on a set of rules or structures. In this way, her collaged GIF frames align with the principles of more traditional media. ◄━━ Continuity and perpetuation are also concerns in her work, a quality of the looping GIF itself, but explored too through age-old themes, from sex to our primal nature. Animals and humans collide in *Petting Zoo: Noble Orphans #1* (2020), one of a series of works Mills has made under the 'Petting Zoo' banner, featuring a cast of creatures, cartoonish characters and human hands performing different 'petting' actions: a camel's lips are squished and squeezed, a dog chomps on a watermelon, a chicken peeks maniacally at a screen. As ever in the artist's work, what is funny at first soon becomes abject, a contemplation of the never-ending pathos of desire. ◄━━

CHARLOTTE JANSEN

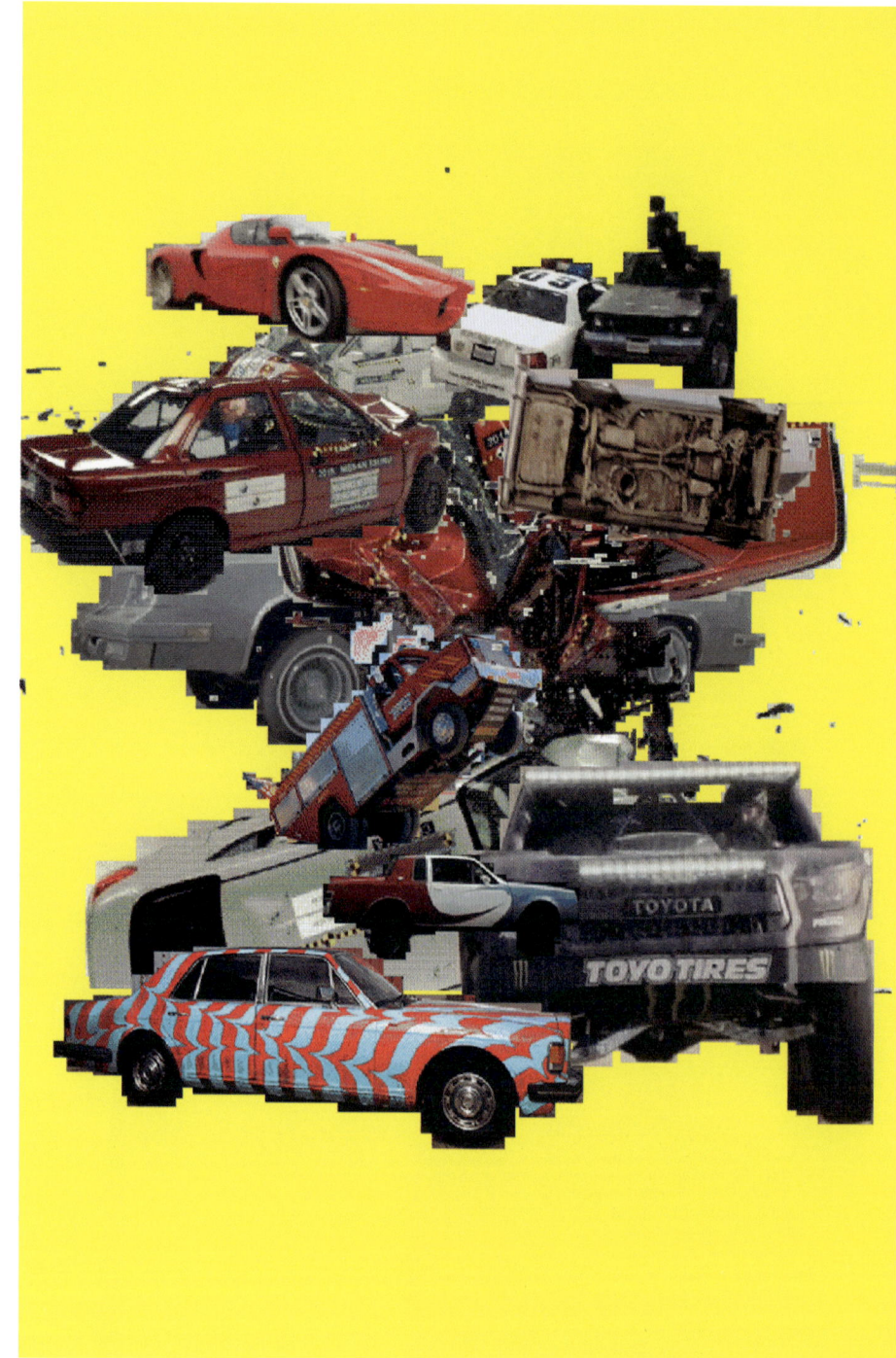

Born 1958, Yorkton, Saskatchewan, Canada. Lives in Toronto, Canada.

↑   Cerebral Concrete, 2019, still from animated gif, 1080 × 1620 px

↗   Tiz war, 2015, still from animated gif, 1920 × 1080 px

→   Petting Zoo: Noble Orphans #1, 2020, still from animated gif, 1920 × 1080 px, Thoma Foundation collection

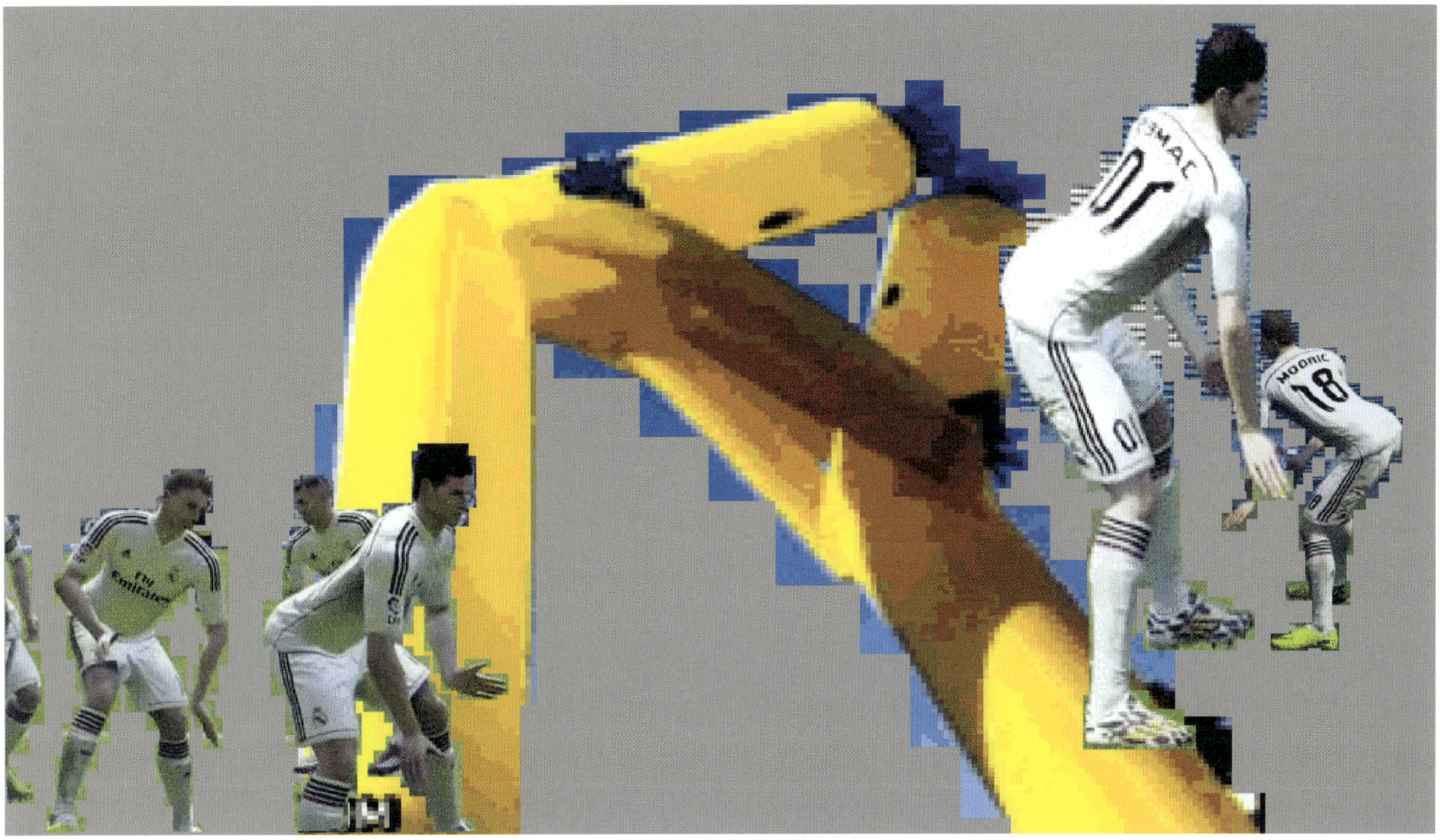

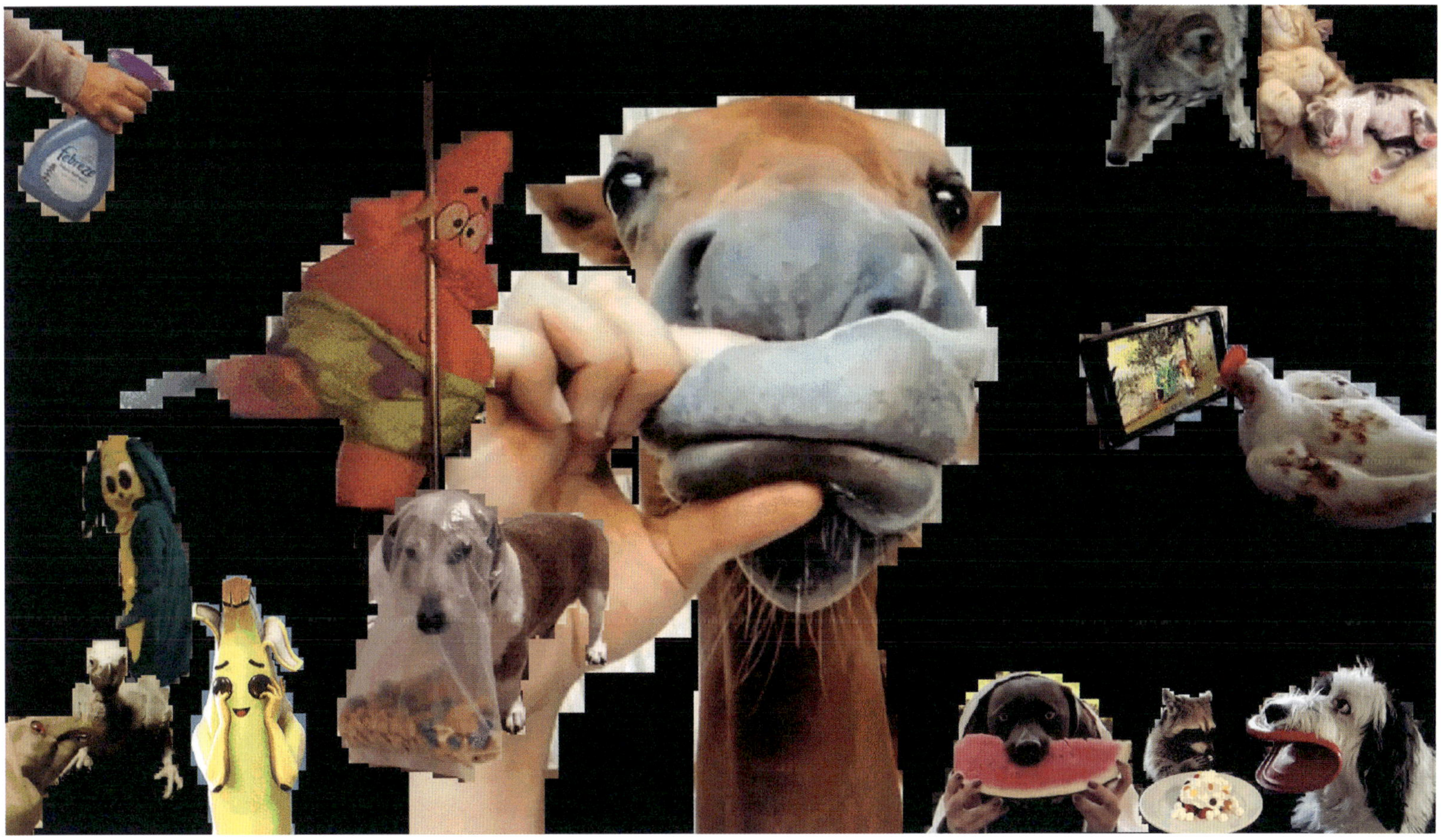

LORNA
MILLS

TROY MONTES MICHIE

Using images from old erotic magazines, as well as found and taken photographs, Troy Montes Michie creates interwoven collages and low-relief sculptures. Some of his works involve cutting, composing and layering paper elements – usually fragmented imagery of human bodies – which are then sewn together by machine with threads of contrasting colours. Unlike many forms of collage in which the means of adhering the image is hidden – glue pasted beneath an image to attach it to a ground – here it is on the very surface, making obvious the process of production and the fact of the image as a physical composite of once separate parts. In *Untitled (Brother to Brother)* (2020), the stitches appear like contours on a topographic map, turning the body parts beneath into a form of landscape. In other works the lines are vertical stripes, which act like bars behind which the subject is detained. In *Distorted in the Interest of Design* (2019) a standing figure is bent out of shape yet maintains their elegant, posture, one eye making contact with the viewer's gaze. The artist has overlaid the composition with fluttering, pearly lines in graphite, grease pencil and coloured pencil. Montes Michie seems to be playing with subjecthood: the figure is segmented by three suspended circles, forcing the viewer's eye to roam and reassemble its form. In an interview with *ARTnews* in 2022, the artist said, 'For me, the cut isn't about violence… it's more about thinking about our own contours.' He uses collage to reinvent our understanding of subject, and often the desirous nature of the source material he works with is made complex with each cut – the sensual protagonists exist on their own terms, in a visible flight of self-autonomy. In other types of collage work, Montes Michie dispenses with the zig-zag stitching and attaches elements together by more conventional means, while still giving importance to their edges. He grew up in the American border town of El Paso, Texas, explaining in the same interview how despite the international divide, 'I could see Mexico – the river and the bridges.' The border was visually dissolved by proximity, yet is still one of the most militarized and surveilled in the world, where identity becomes threatened and repossessed by state narratives. *Border as Frame* (2019) is a pictorial plane sliced into several sections, and combining a rich variety of textured material: papier-mâché, garment zippers, denim, acrylic, stretched linen. There are excerpts from newspapers and painted-over pages of publications. The figures included are coloured in, somewhat abject but still poised, as in the character sinking into a chair: we cannot see their face, but their posture is self-assured and coolly buoyant.

SKYE ARUNDHATI THOMAS

Born 1985, El Paso, Texas, USA. Lives in Brooklyn, New York, USA.

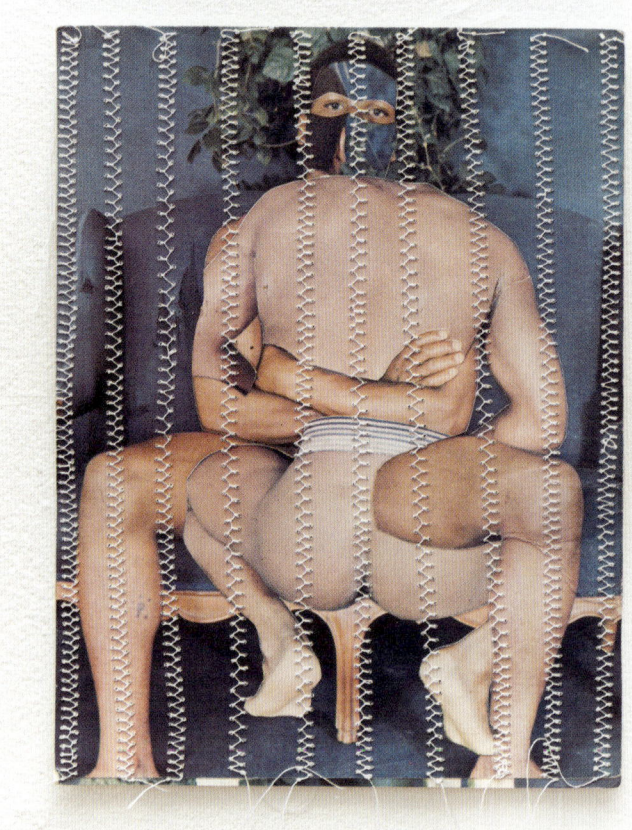

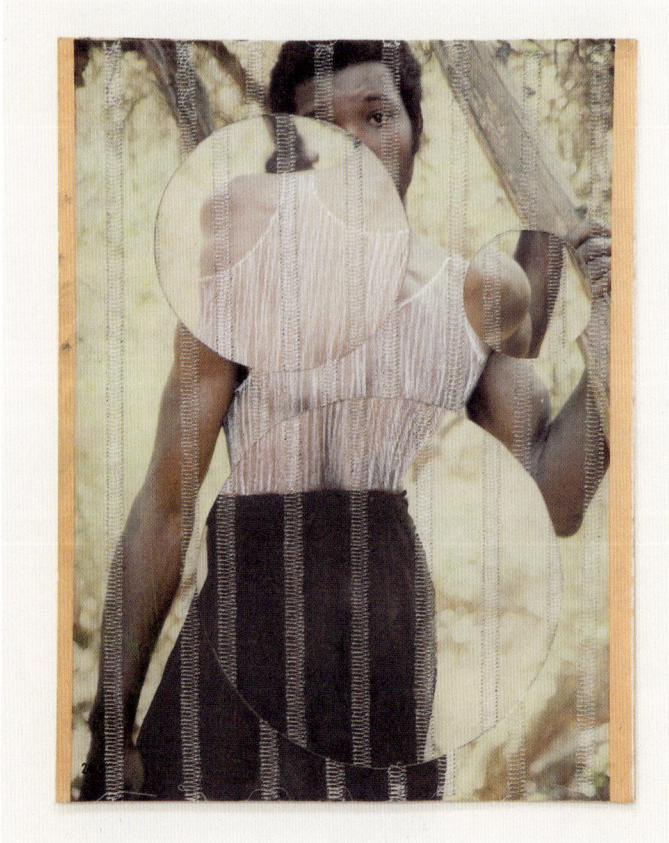

↑↑ **Untitled (Feeling Blue)**, 2020, cut paper and polyester thread on magazine paper, 27.9 × 21.6 cm (11 × 8½ in)

↑ **Distorted in the Interest of Design**, 2019, cut paper, graphite, coloured pencil, grease pencil and polyester thread on magazine paper, 27.9 × 21.6 cm (11 × 8½ in)

→ **Untitled (Brother to Brother)**, 2020, cut paper and polyester thread on magazine paper, 27.9 × 21.6 cm (11 × 8½ in)

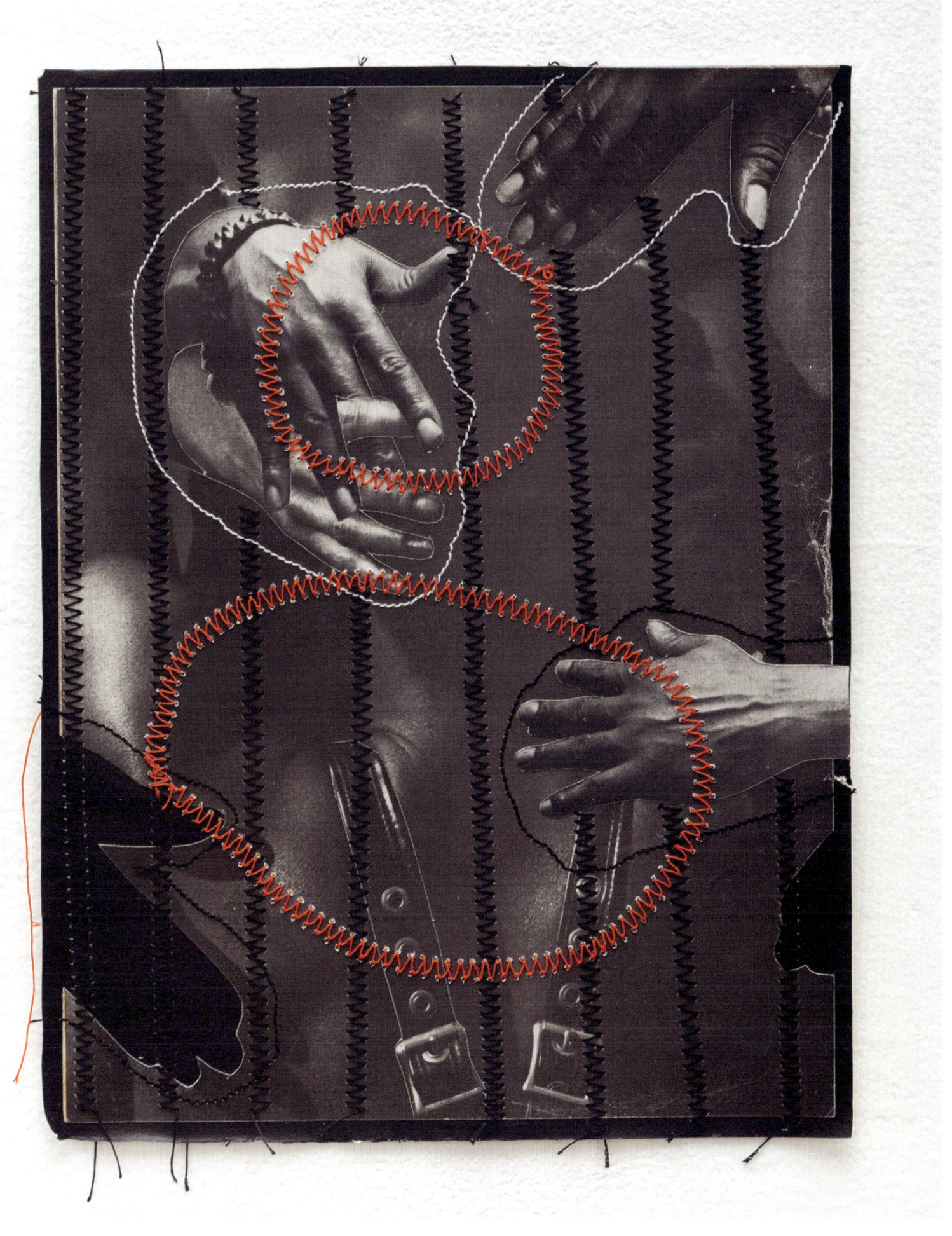

TROY
MONTES MICHIE

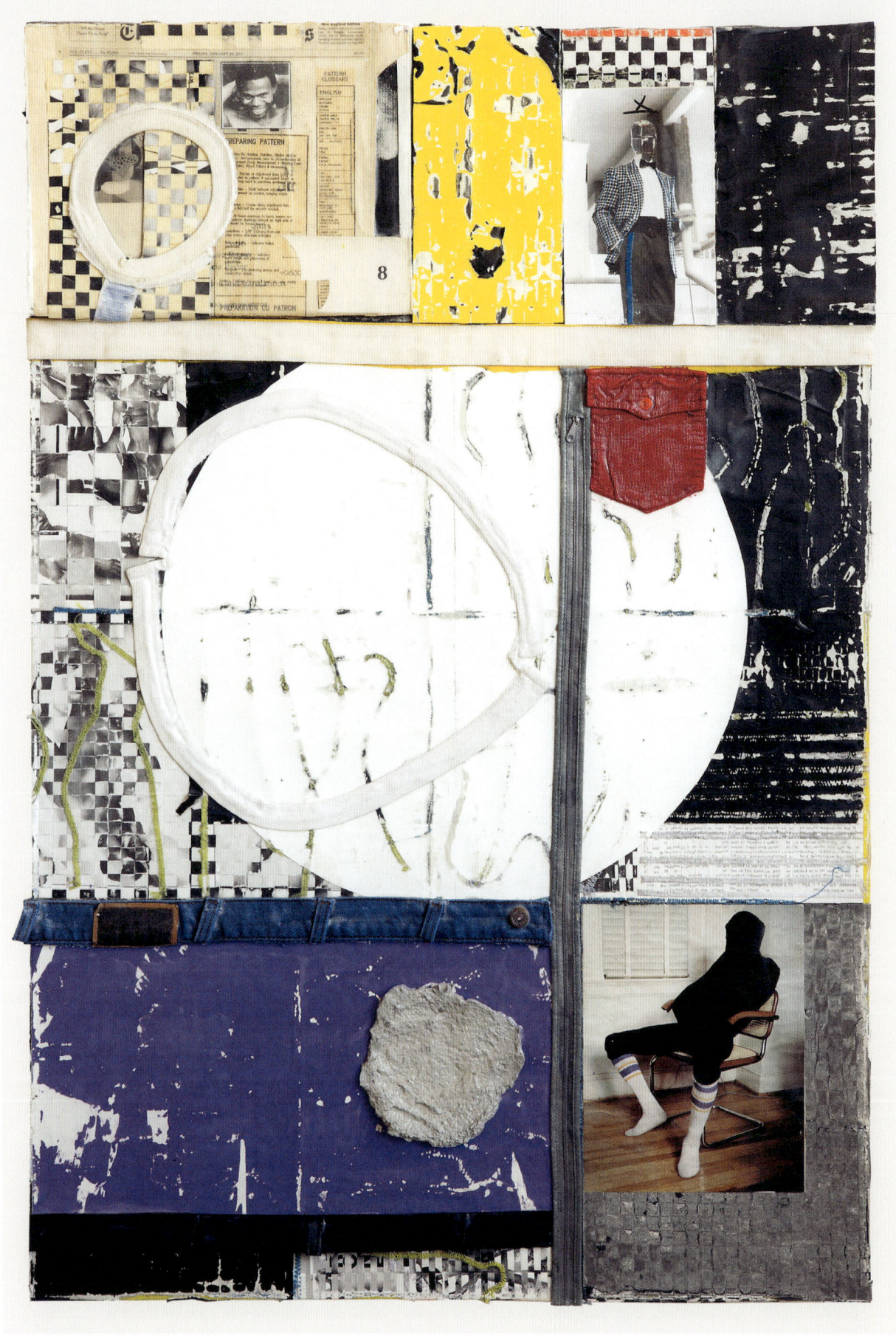

↑   **Border As Frame**, 2019, cut paper, photograph, polyester thread, papier-mâché, garment bag zipper, cut clothing, tape, cloth, graphite, ink, grease pencil, acrylic and woven paper on stretched linen, 121.9 × 83.8 × 2.5 cm (48 × 33 × 1 in)

→   **Constellations**, 2020, mixed media on canvas, 177.8 × 152.4 cm (70 × 60 in)

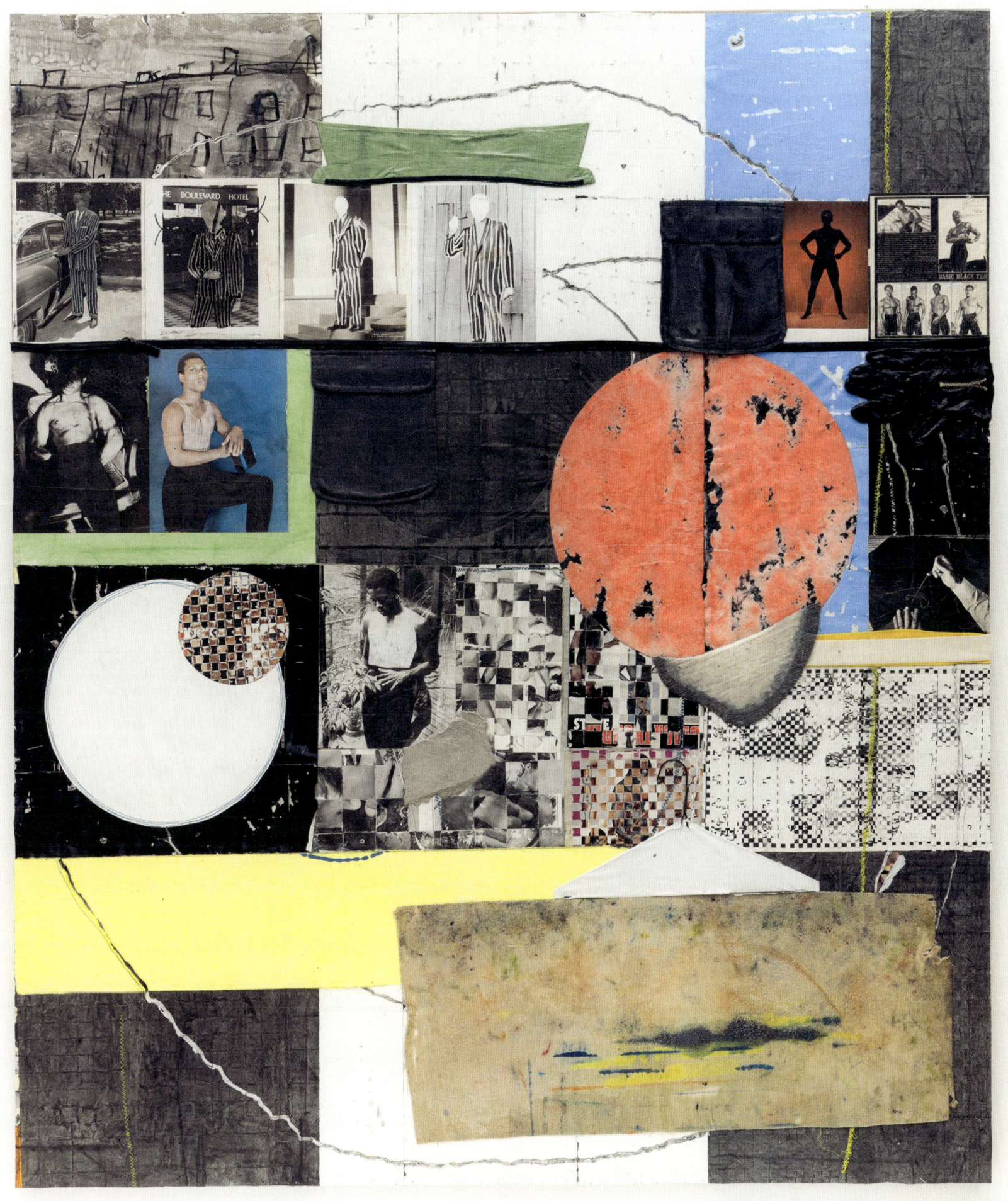

TROY MONTES MICHIE

SIMON MORETTI

According to Simon Moretti, all forms of communication are inevitably subjective. Even numbers, the most accurate symbols available to measure scientific information are never just fixed units, nor are they devoid of emotional baggage. They have shapes, a rhythm, and they tend to be linked with memorable dates loaded with personal meaning. Using collage as his primary strategy since the early 2000s, Moretti's work exposes links between knowledge, culture, memory and emotion. In *Untitled* of 2015, for example, a photocopy reproduction of an Egyptian sculpture from the late Eighteenth Dynasty (c.1340 BC) is cut out to remove the figure's wig – a symbol of her high social status – and replaced with a photograph depicting the mechanism of a large cathedral clock, an advertisement for watches from the *Financial Times* and a game of Sudoku. The resulting portrait is rich with associations, including formal resemblances between the absent depiction of hair in the chiselled stone and the giant clock mechanism that replaces it, and conceptual ones concerning the notion of commemoration and the effect of passing, or lost, time. Like many of Moretti's collages this work too behaves like a map, a grid or a board of associative thoughts, drawing on a particular tradition of artists such as Marcel Broodthaers (1924–76) and Alighiero Boetti (1940–94) and scholars including Aby Warburg (1866–1929) and André Malraux (1901–76), who sought to embrace language as well as photography in order to show formal resemblances between ideas, objects and even cultures that were previously latent or ignored. Seen within the context of this history, Moretti's work emphasizes the aesthetics of information and compares it with parallels from the realm of art and archaeology. This tendency is manifest in *Untitled* of 2016, where two photographic reproductions of sculptures made four hundred years apart from one another are placed side by side. The first is a sixteenth-century sculpture of Perseus captured at the moment after decapitating Medusa, and the second an abstract relief by Jean Arp titled *Siamois* (1960). The formal connection between the two artefacts relies both on their similar shapes and the manner in which Moretti has cut and positioned them. A background photograph of a sunset from a glossy magazine then serves as background to the two foreign bodies, now bound together as a pair of participants in an imagined theatrical play. And indeed, theatre is a useful image to have when trying to capture Moretti's approach to collage – a practice he considers free from the technical conventions of paper and glue and extends to his editorial and curatorial work, where multiple voices are combined and other artists are invited to display their work in conjunction with his own.

YUVAL ETGAR

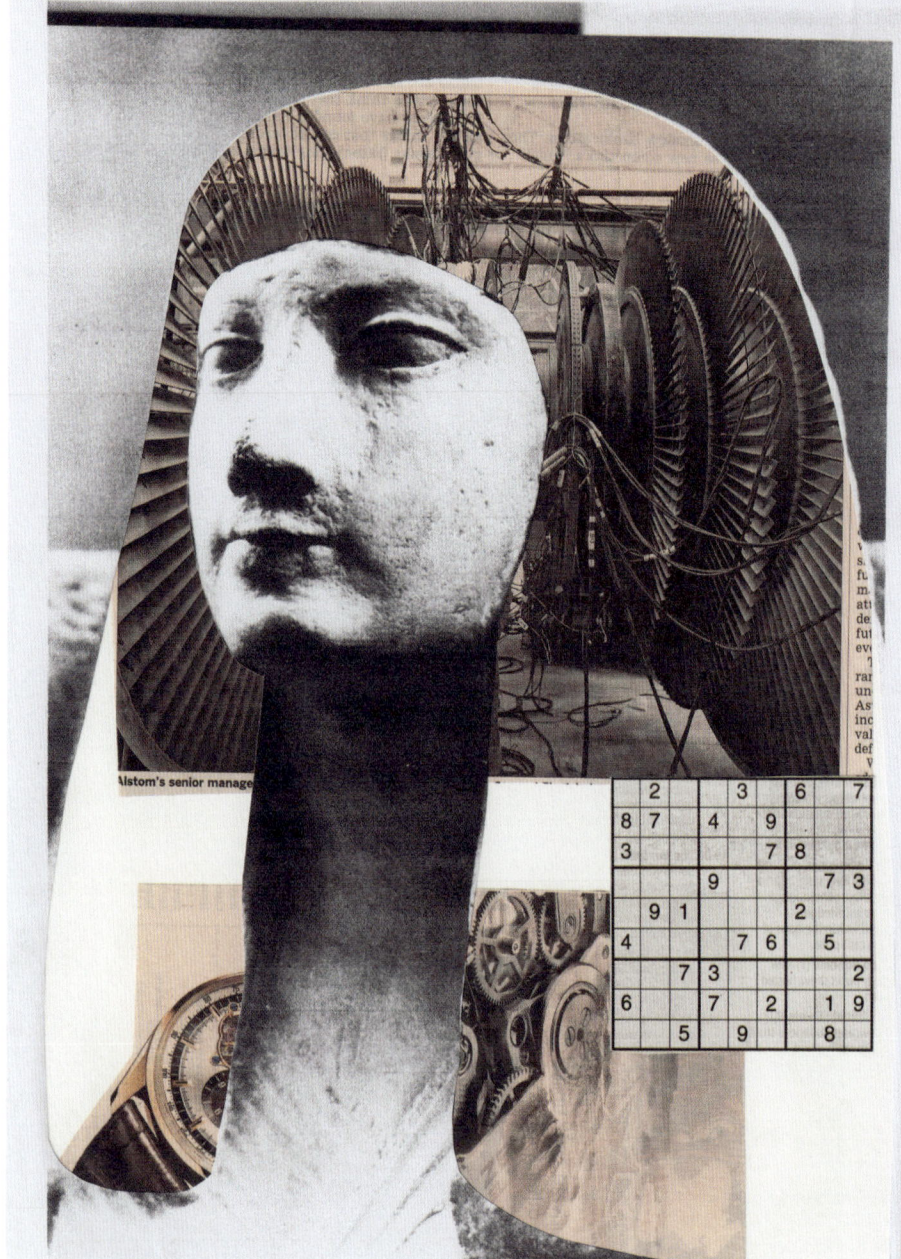

Born 1974, Bradford, UK. Lives in London, UK.

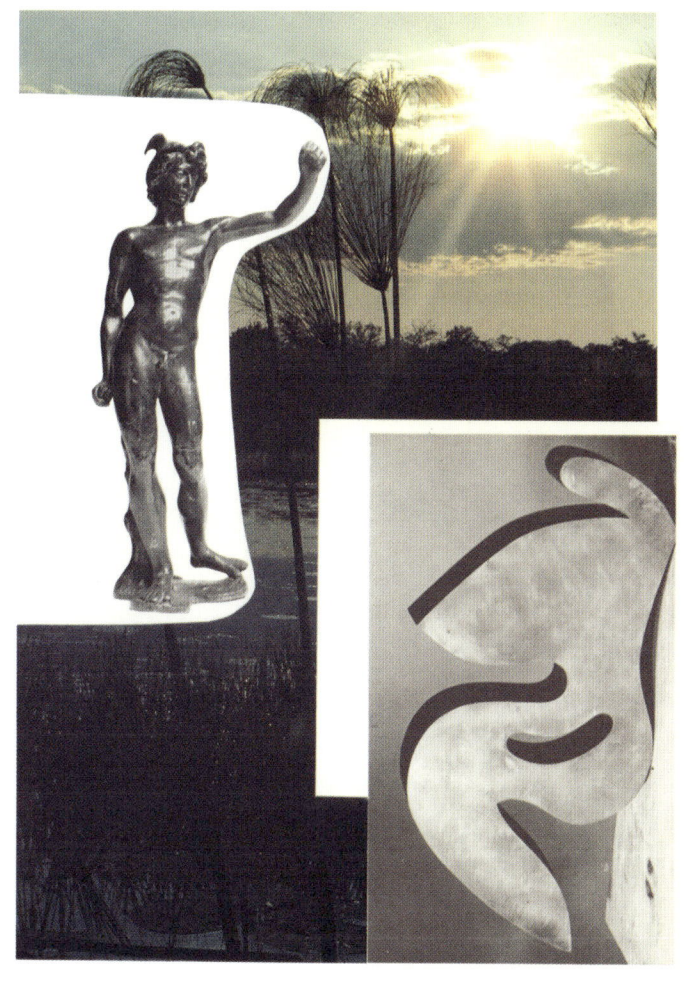

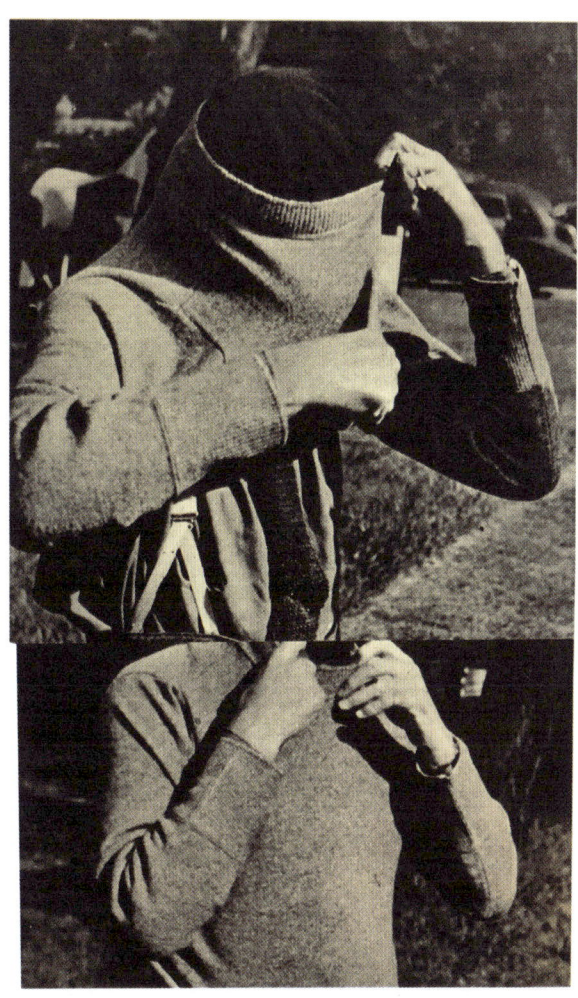

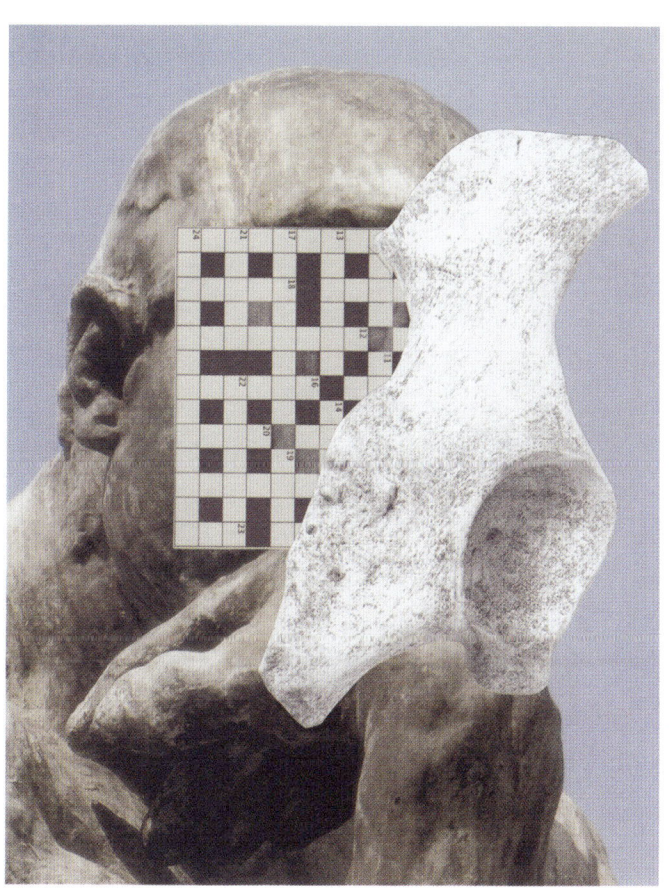

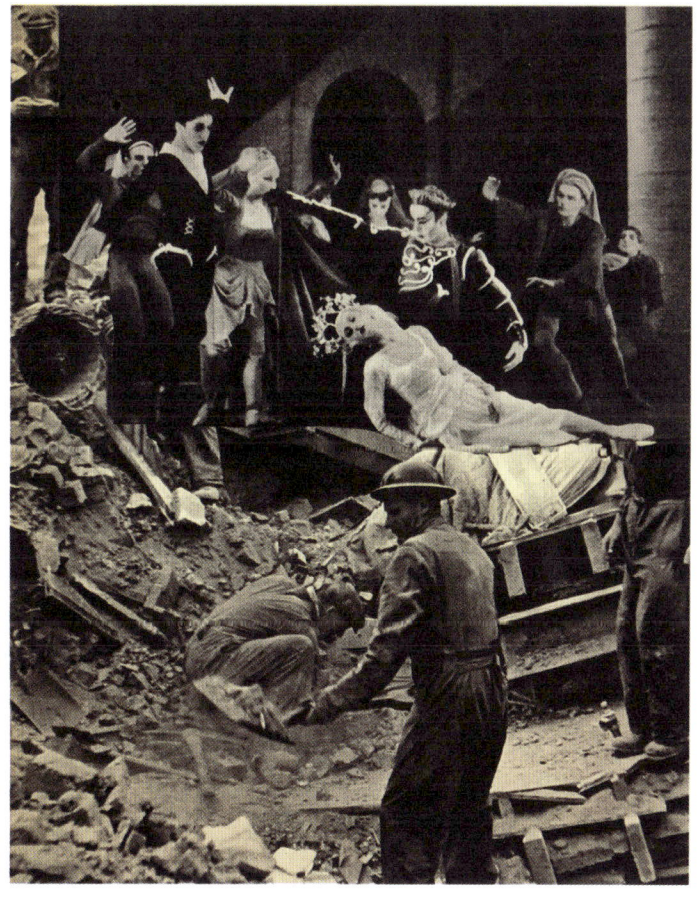

SIMON
MORETTI

WANGECHI MUTU

Internationally renowned for a practice that encompasses various techniques and mediums including sculpture, film, installation and collages, Wangechi Mutu's work features female hybrid creatures and vivid dreamscapes. The oxymoron that Swiss-Cameroonian curator Simon Njami described in a Creativity Pioneers podcast interview in April 2020 – 'reality is the best fiction ever' – can very much be applied to Mutu's sci-fi-influenced imagery. She consistently explores the interplay between fact and fiction while investigating the constitution of contemporary identities through historical references and archives. With a particular focus on preconceptions of the female body as a repository of alternative iconography, the artist proposes her vision of sexuality, social construction and colonialism in a highly individual form of mythmaking. ◢ Mutu's childhood on the outskirts of Nairobi with her father, a teacher obsessed with indigenous trees and storytelling, and a mother who was trained as a nurse-midwife but queasy about surgeries and dissection, profoundly informed the artist's practice. Her signature fabricated images are nimbly cut-out and collaged works populated by powerful hybridized figures sourced and carved from diverse visual registers. These include original photography, fashion magazines, erotic publications, medical books and *National Geographic* magazine.

◢ Mutu has created collages since 2001 when, having recently graduated from the MFA programme at Yale School of Art, she began a series of fragmented and constructed images called 'Pin-Ups'. Here Black female figures, some nude and others wearing seductive clothes, strike poses familiar from mass media as intended to be alluring, but which, on account of missing limbs, bloody stumps and peg-legs, are simultaneously gruesome. Since then, Mutu has continued to explore the potential of collage to enable a multiplicity of meanings and feelings to coexist at once. ◢ Allegory is central to her work as seen in *Forbidden Fruit picker* (2015), which was presented in 'All The World's Futures', the international exhibition at the 56th Venice Biennale (2015), curated by Okwui Enwezor. Centring a one-legged female protagonist dominated by a tree and seated in profile while still facing the viewer, the scene recalls the character of Myrrha from Greek mythology – who was transformed into a myrrh tree (also called African myrrh) after having had an incestuous relationship with her father – coupled with intimations of Eve's role in the biblical creation narrative. At once seductive when in human form or voracious in the shape of an arachnid as in *Eleven secrets* (2015), the female figure in Mutu's collages is blended with natural and unnatural elements impregnated with their own cultural interpretations that refute societal norms. ◢ *Green dream* (2015), in contrast, abandons the singular figure in favour of multiple elements, most notably African masks, kente cloth and flowering foliage. A swirling composition that leaves the viewer wondering which way is up, the work evokes the confusion between fiction and reality that typifies the dream state. ◢

JANINE GAËLLE DIEUDJI

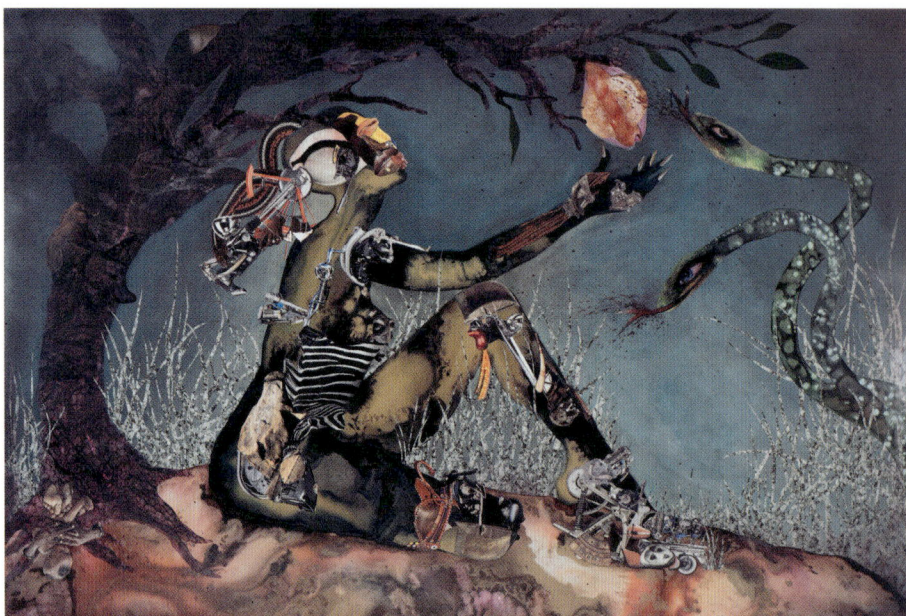

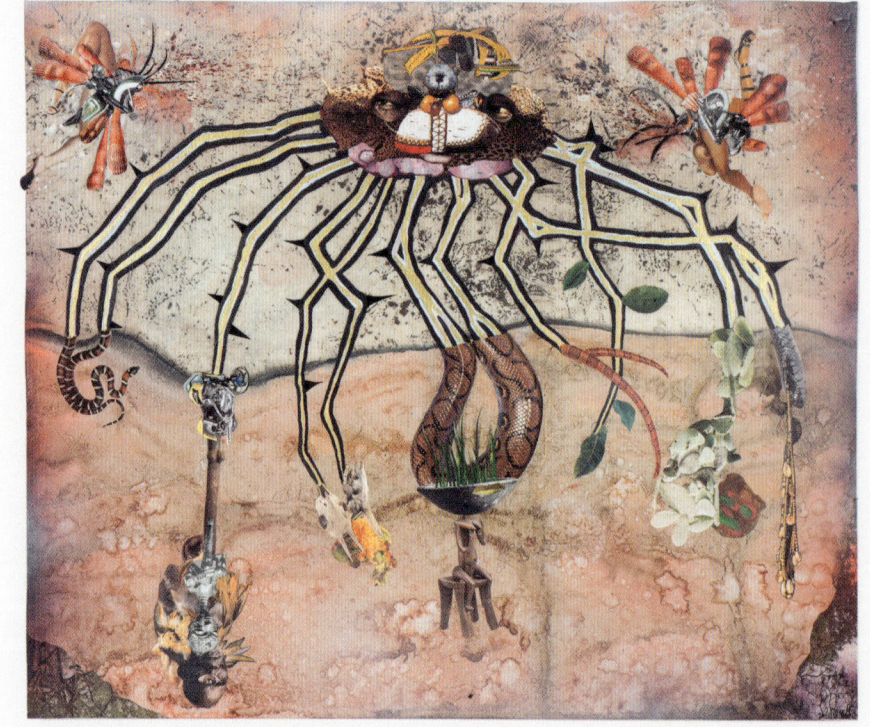

Born 1972, Nairobi, Kenya. Lives in New York, USA and Nairobi.

↑↑   **Forbidden Fruit picker**, 2015, collage painting on linoleum, 100.3 × 148.9 cm (39½ × 58⅝ in)

↑   **Eleven secrets**, 2015, collage on vinyl, 77.5 × 91.4 cm (30½ × 36 in)

→   **Green dream**, 2015, collage on linoleum, 61 × 45.8 cm (24 × 18 in)

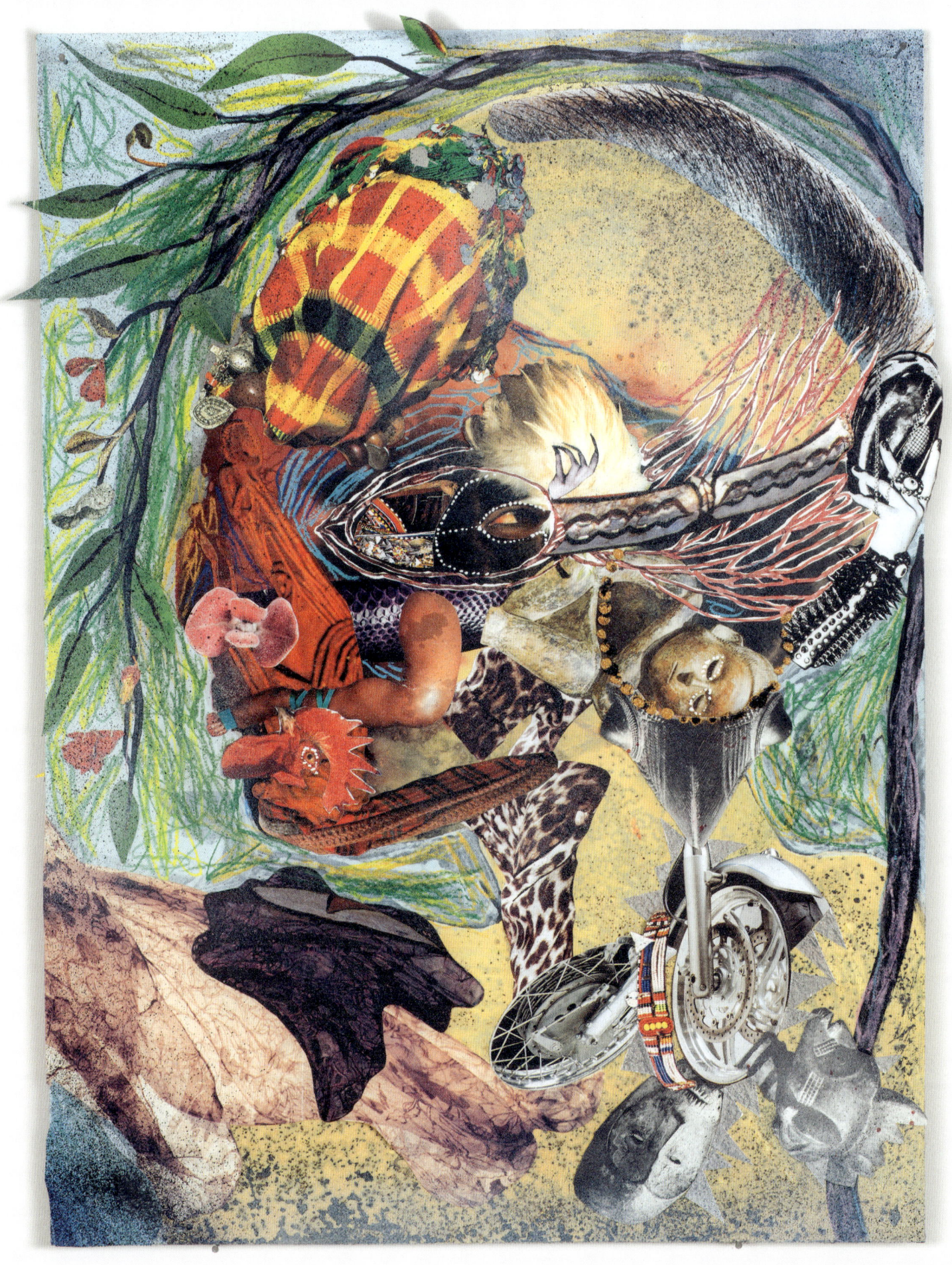

WANGECHI
MUTU

YAMINI NAYAR

Describing her work in a 2022 interview with the author as 'a hybrid photograph, a durational object, a composite, a collage', Yamini Nayar emphasizes how amalgamations define her approach. Her abstract photographic prints combine fragments of colour, texture and material, which together become imagined spaces in flux, seemingly morphing between states. In this sense, her work is inherently architectural, suggesting the built environment's capacity to hold and shape matter, as well as its relationship to the body – asking us to move in accordance with its parameters. Nayar's process starts with the building of assemblages using wood, plaster and paperboard, making wall-based or stand-alone sculptures that she then photographs. It is through the lens of the camera that the forms are transformed into sculptural scenes, winking at architecture. This does not necessarily happen in a linear trajectory; Nayar sometimes photographs the same construction at different phases of the building process, and even uses multiple exposures on one film. This results in photographs defined by fluidity: space in the process of becoming, shifting into something else. Take, for example, *Imprint* (2020), a print composed of numerous shots on one negative. Lines and geometric facets are layered and collaged in varying tones of black and white. There is the suggestion of architectural features such as a staircase, towers and domes. It is possible to visualize entering the space, taking step after step, venturing further and deeper into its layers: letting time dissolve. Nayar notes in the same interview how 'the final photograph sits at the in-between of dualities – flat vs. dimension, illusive vs. concrete, tactile and material vs. immaterial'. This is the crux of her approach to collage: using the constraints of photographic language (perspective, light, flatness) to create tensions between different states. As she poetically points out, 'I think of my photographs as being in the muddy middle.' Nayar's background in photography and sculpture – she took degrees in Fine Art at the School of Visual Arts in New York (2005) and the Rhode Island School of Design (1999) – underpins the way in which she challenges flatness, essentially using the camera to re-envisage the physicality of her method and the nature of construction. Works such as *Beginner's Mind* (2020), which hints at structural beams and protrusions, call to mind the twentieth-century artist Kurt Schwitters (1887–1948). His *Merzbau* (c.1923–37) – a walk-in collage comprised of columns, grottoes and found objects – blurred the line between art and life. Nayar cites this influence in relation to Plato's use of the *khôra*, a formless or transitory realm of non-being, alongside her childhood memories of self-built structures in southern India, to imagine built environments that both shape space and supportively hold us, as we feel out ways to move forwards into the unknown.

LOUISA ELDERTON

Born 1975, Rochester, New York, USA. Lives in New York and New Delhi, India.

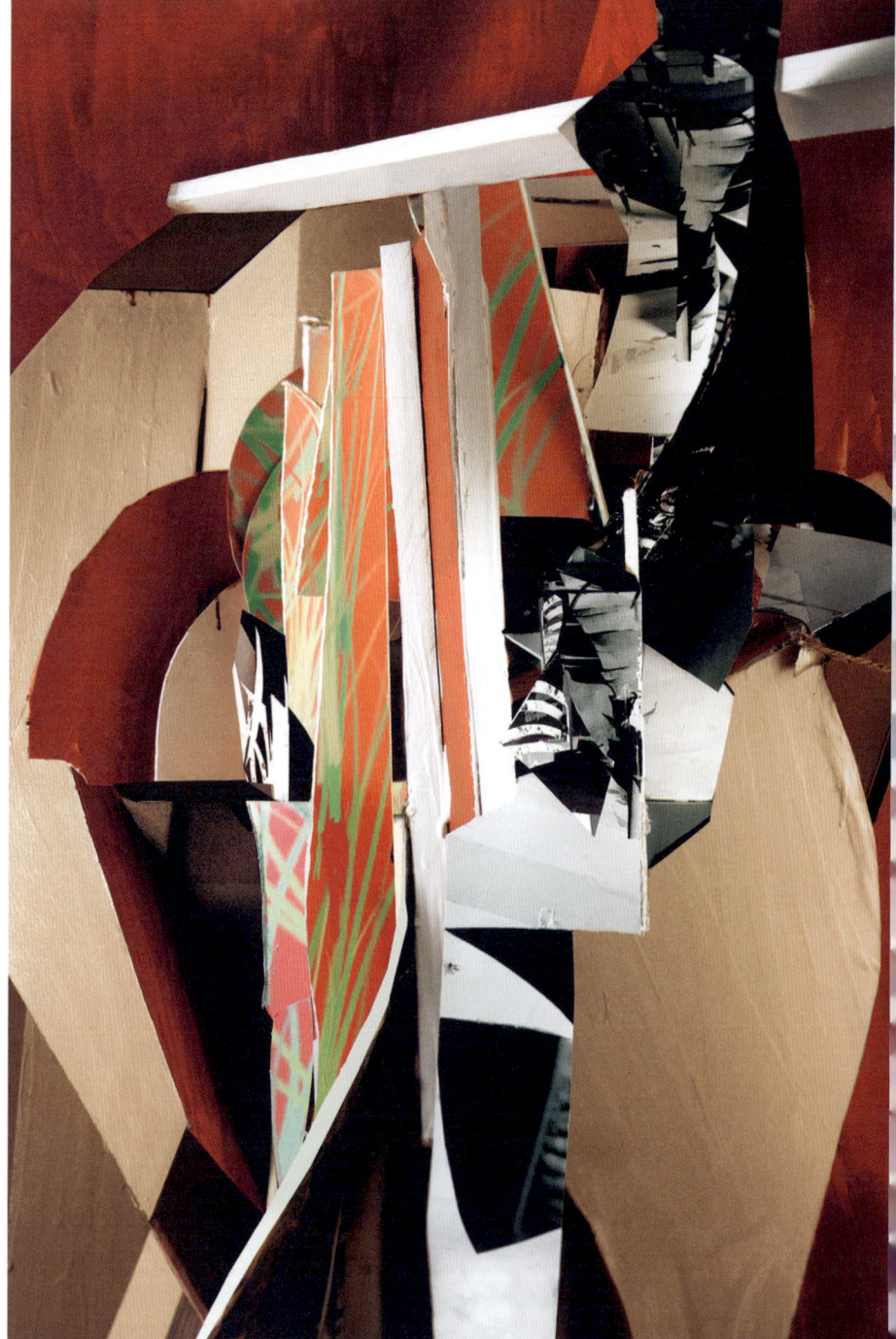

↑ Beginner's Mind, 2020, trichromatic C-print, 101.6 × 76.2 cm (40 × 30 in), edition of 5 + 1 AP

↗ Machine Living, 2018, archival pigment print, 83.2 × 101.6 cm (32¾ × 40 in), edition of 5 + 1 AP

→ Imprint, 2020, silver gelatin print, 45.8 × 35.6 cm (18 × 14 in), edition of 5 + 1 AP

→→ Garden for Laborers, 2015, C-print, 106.7 × 91.4 cm (42 × 36 in), edition of 5 + 2 AP

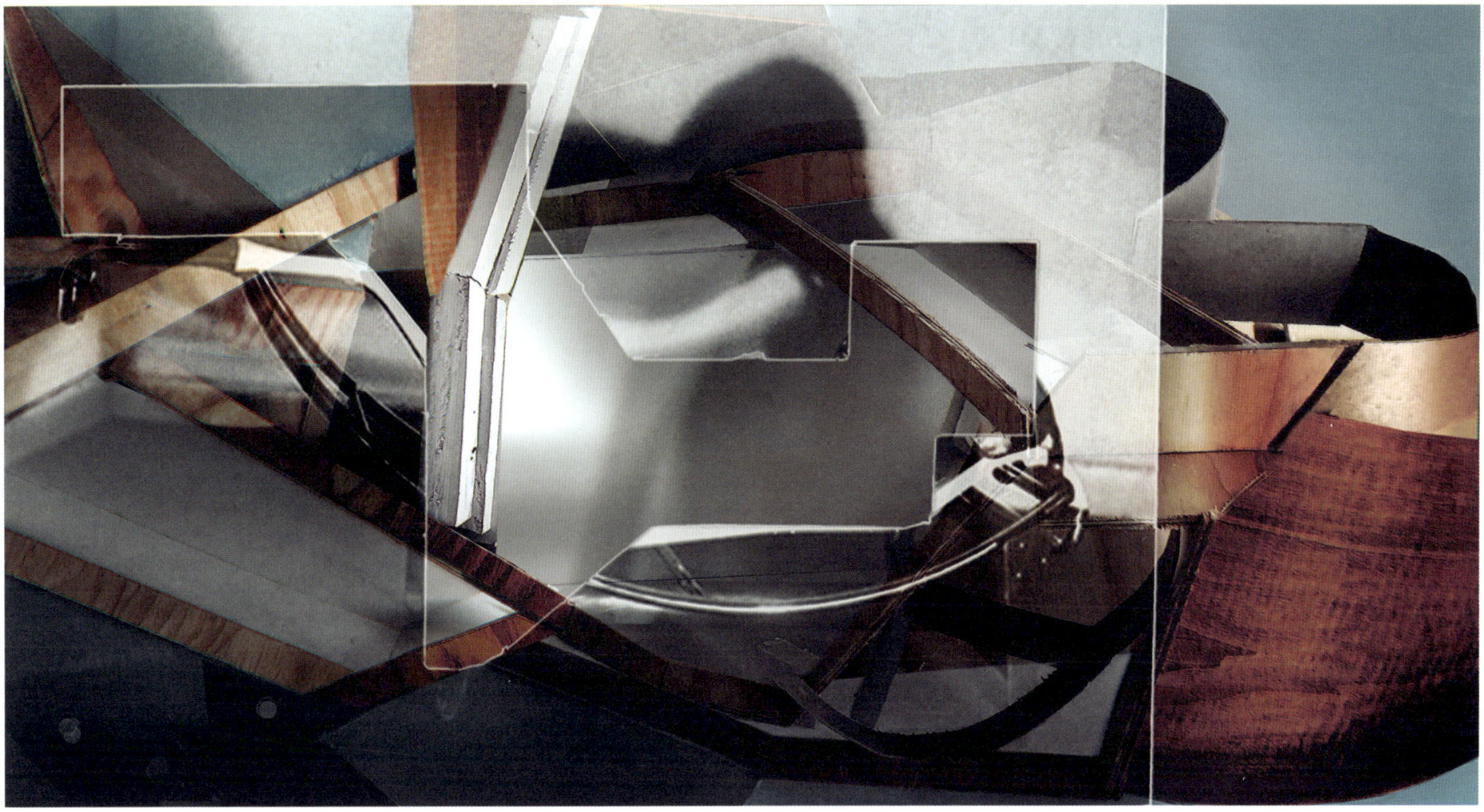

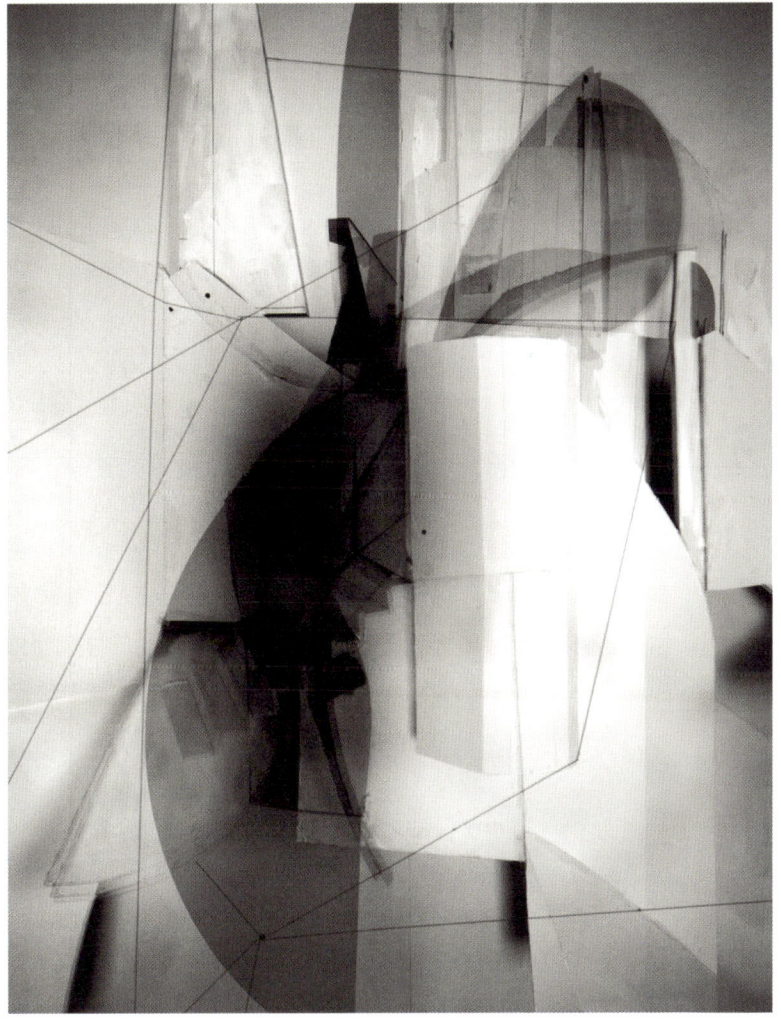

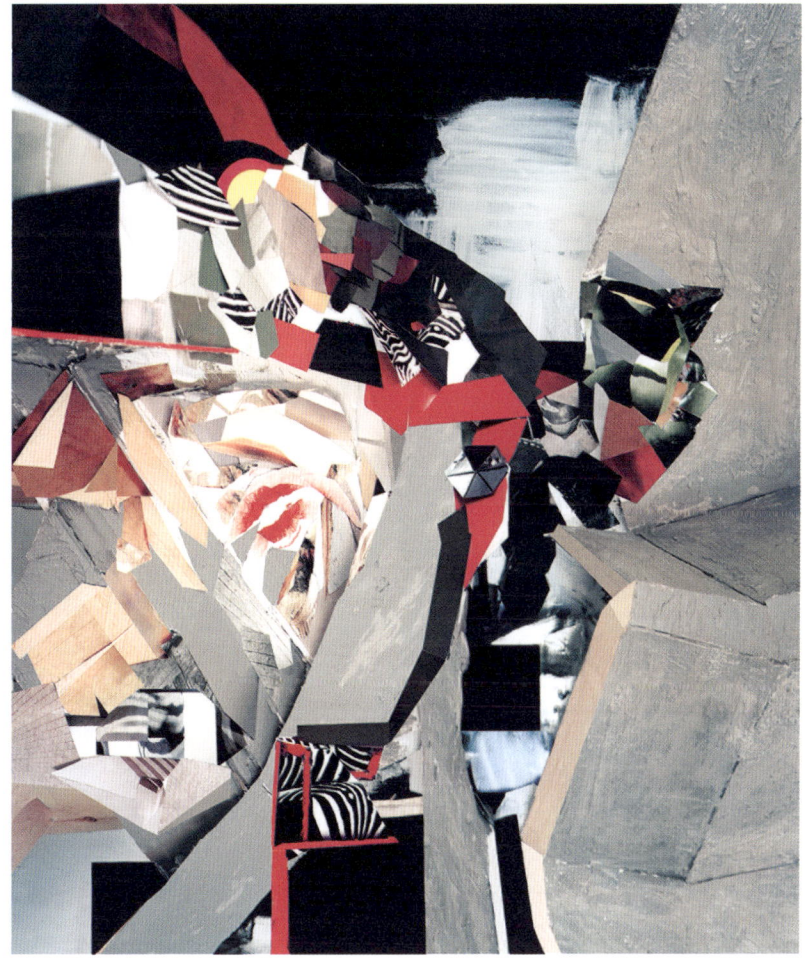

YAMINI
NAYAR

RASHAAD NEWSOME

For Rashaad Newsome, collage is not just a technique but also a conceptual strategy – in his artist's statement on his website he describes it as a method to 'construct a new cultural framework of power that does not find the oppression of others necessary'. Indeed, across his work, Newsome mixes and matches a range of practices including performance, sculpture, film, software engineering and community organizing, as well more conventional collage on paper, to mount a creative and often joyful resistance against dominant systems and categories of identity. This ambitious project is rooted in Newsome's own lived experiences within Black and queer communities, and draws deeply on the artistic canons of both – from traditional African rituals and ceremonial objects to the dance form of voguing. Newsome's celebration of Black and queer creativity is frequently placed in counterpoint to 'mainstream' white-centric culture and art history: take, for example, the opulent Baroque frames that Newsome uses to display his paper collages. These antique or custom frames are varnished using black 'candy paint' – a high-gloss type of paint usually applied to automobiles – in a reference to African American car culture in New Orleans. 'It functions as my version of gilt,' the artist explained in a 2016 interview with Antwaun Sargent for *Pelican Bomb*. The same strategy of appropriation and subversion is carried out within the frames, in unashamedly flashy collages that depict quasi-futuristic bodies – either standing individually or in groups – composed of layers of images from multiple sources. In *Look Back at It* (2016), the cut-out photographs of sculpted wooden African faces, scantily clad models in underwear and high heels, glistening costume jewellery and other found images are arranged to form four female figures, in a reference to Pablo Picasso's painting *Les Demoiselles d'Avignon* (1907). Picasso took inspiration from African and Oceanic art in the formation of his so-called 'primitivist' style. As the title of Newsome's collage indicates, *Look Back at It* reverses the artist's gaze, reimagining a landmark work of European modernism from an African diasporic perspective. In a 2022 online interview for the Southbank Centre, London, Newsome described the bodies that appear in his collages as 'cyborgian figures'. A cyborg is a hybrid being, made up of both organic and artificial elements, whose abilities are extended beyond normal human limits. In works such as *Thirst Trap* (2020), the artist builds his figures from a mix of gleaming luxury objects, cultural artefacts and perfectly groomed body parts – a nod to the consumerist logic that underpins contemporary capitalism. But for Newsome, collage is a way to push beyond this logic, and to create beings that transcend its limits. 'My hope is that they're somehow trying to break free of the frame, break free of what is projected onto us,' he said in the same interview. With his cyborgs, Newsome offers a blueprint for what liberation might look like – and it's totally fabulous.

GABRIELLE SCHWARZ

Born 1979, New Orleans, Louisiana, USA. Lives in Oakland, California and New York, USA.

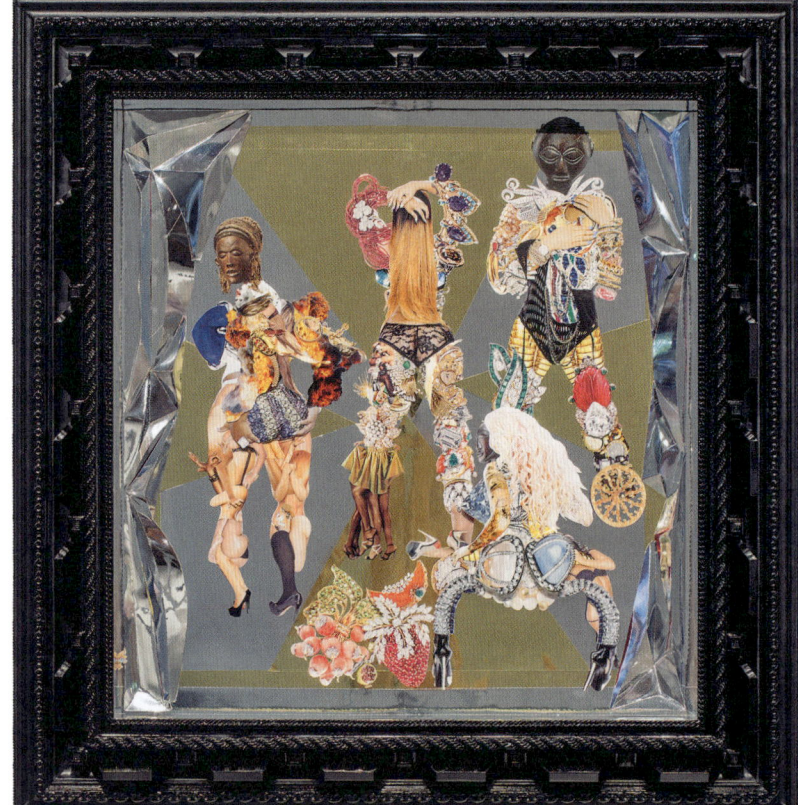

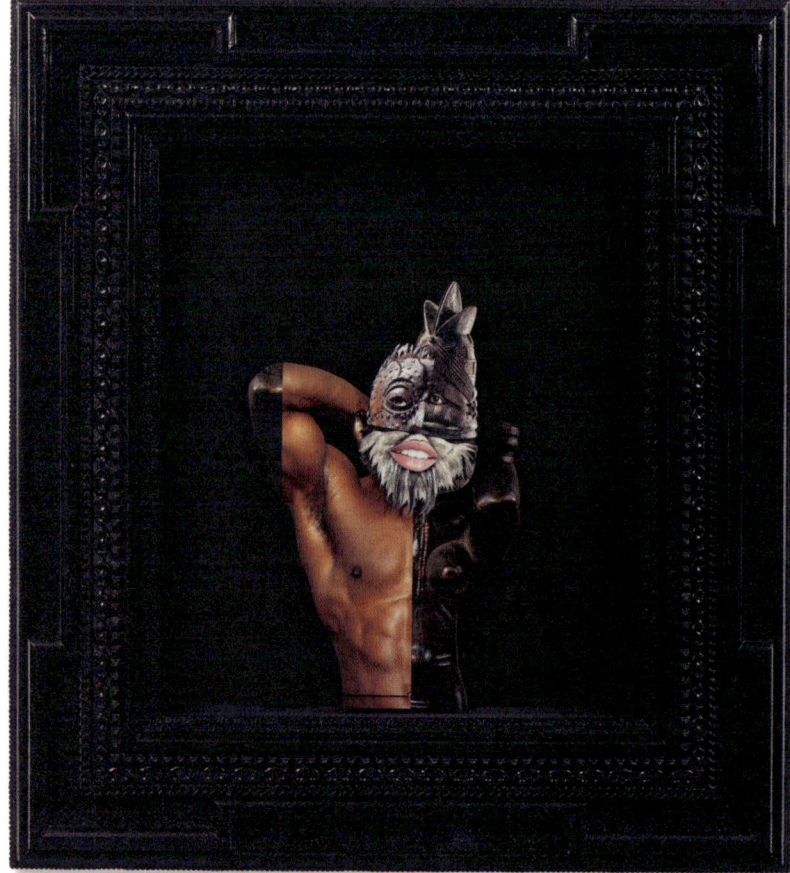

↑↑ **Look Back at It**, 2016, collage on paper in custom frame with leather, Swarovski crystal and automotive paint, 182.9 × 175.3 × 25.4 cm (72 × 69 × 10 in)

↑ **Thirst Trap**, 2020, collage on paper in custom mahogany and resin artist frame with automotive paint, 169.2 × 169.2 × 11.4 cm (66⅝ × 66⅝ × 4½ in)

→ **YAAAAAAS!**, 2016, collage in custom frame with leather and automotive paint, 183.5 × 183.5 × 12.7 cm (72¼ × 72¼ × 5 in)

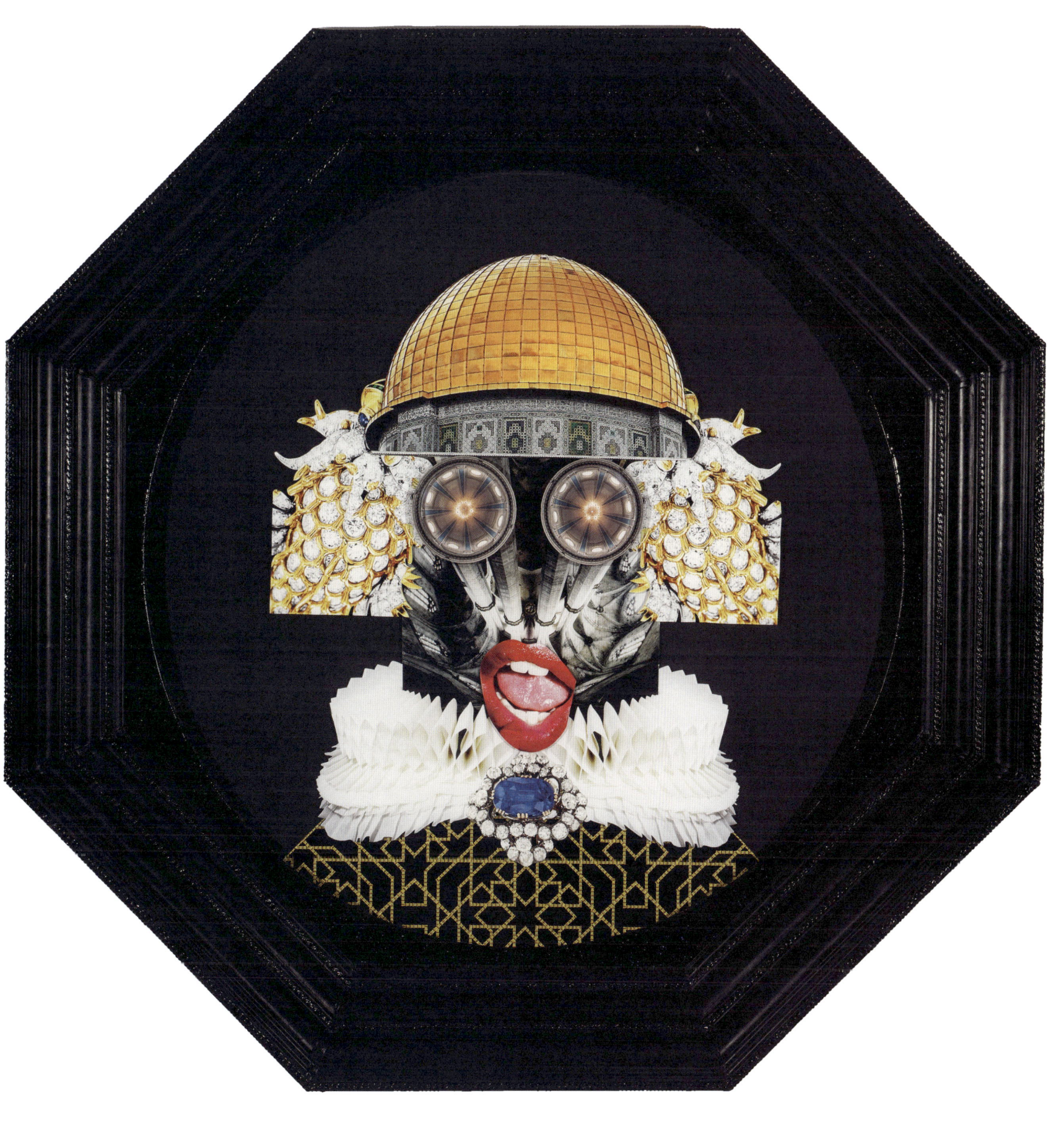

SAM
NHLENGETHWA

Works by Sam Nhlengethwa vividly recall history, revealing narratives of South Africa during the apartheid period and beyond, through a careful selection of images and a deft combination of materials. As well as painted sections, he employs elements from posters, newspapers, magazines and other publications to create scenes of people in interior and exterior settings – of life in the country's townships and cities. He explores diverse situations that prevail in his country, zoning in on individuals ranging from workers and politicians to artists and musicians, as well as identifiable landmarks. ◼ Many of his pieces depict workers, especially miners and commuters, in the shadow of high-rise buildings. Singularly and collectively, these reveal his skill for exposing the economic and financial situation of South Africans. *Headlines* (2016) shows a busy street in Johannesburg; Nhlengethwa captures pedestrians and porters on their beat, seemingly unperturbed by the dramatic headlines of the newspaper front pages that are pasted on walls or lampposts all around. The background is densely packed with buildings, with the Hillbrow Tower, a telecommunications tower that is one of the city's most recognizable buildings, in the distance. ◼ In view of the brutalities meted out to Black liberation movements by the apartheid regime, Nhlengethwa diverted his energies into politics and subsequently created pieces that commented on the cruelties of the period, including a famous re-enactment of the torture and subsequent killing of the anti-apartheid campaigner Steve Biko. He also addressed another of anti-apartheid's most well-known figures in *Winnie waiting for Madiba* (2018), which incorporates a photograph of a youthful Winnie Mandela in a spare interior, with a radio behind her. She is waiting calmly for her husband, Nelson Mandela, who was incarcerated for twenty-seven years for anti-apartheid activism in the early 1960s, before gaining freedom and going on to become President of South Africa. A sense of peace and tranquillity pervades Nhlengethwa's image, despite the fact that it highlights a moment in the long struggle for majority rule in the country. The theme of waiting is something Nhlengethwa has returned to repeatedly, creating portraits of people in various states of anticipation. ◼ Music is also a central theme of Nhlengethwa's work and life (he has a total of 4,000 records in his collection). He reveals the close link between music and art by incorporating images of album covers of the celebrated jazz and blues musicians who inspired him from an early age and became an intrinsic part of his work over the decades. *The Big Band* (2015) shows a twenty-piece jazz band with a woman vocalist. The artist adds veritas with the inclusion of curtains, a lighting rig and an audience. A sense of movement is created in the poses of the collaged figures and a sense of sound evoked by the placement of the saxophonists playing full blast in the foreground, revealing Nhlengethwa's long love for jazz in the process.

JOHN OWOO

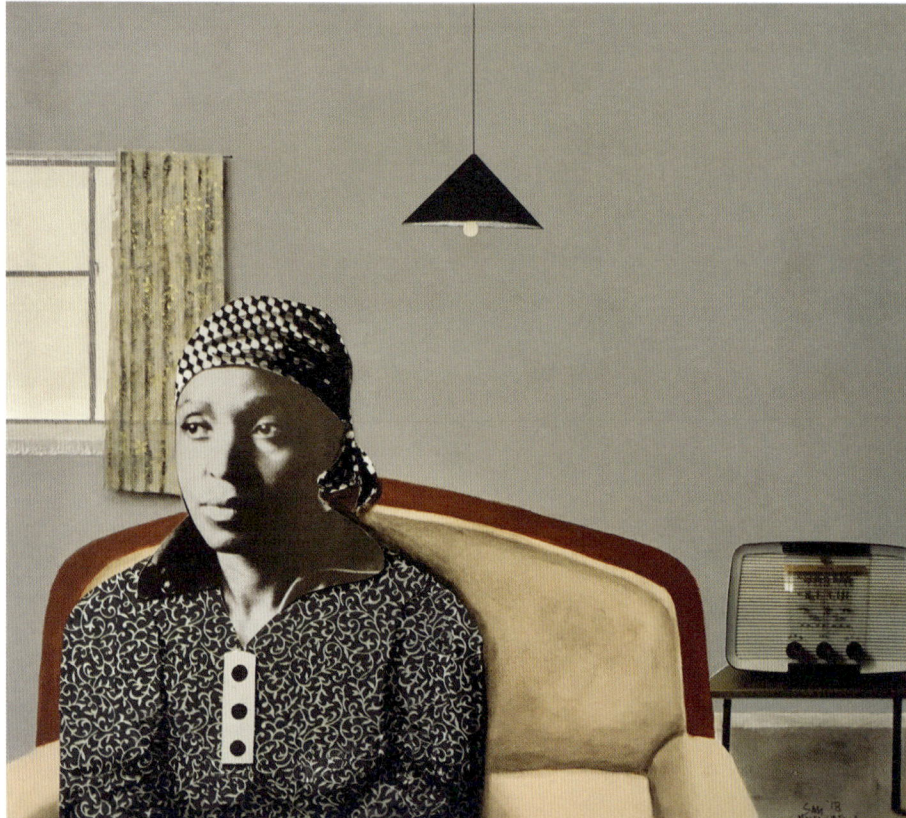

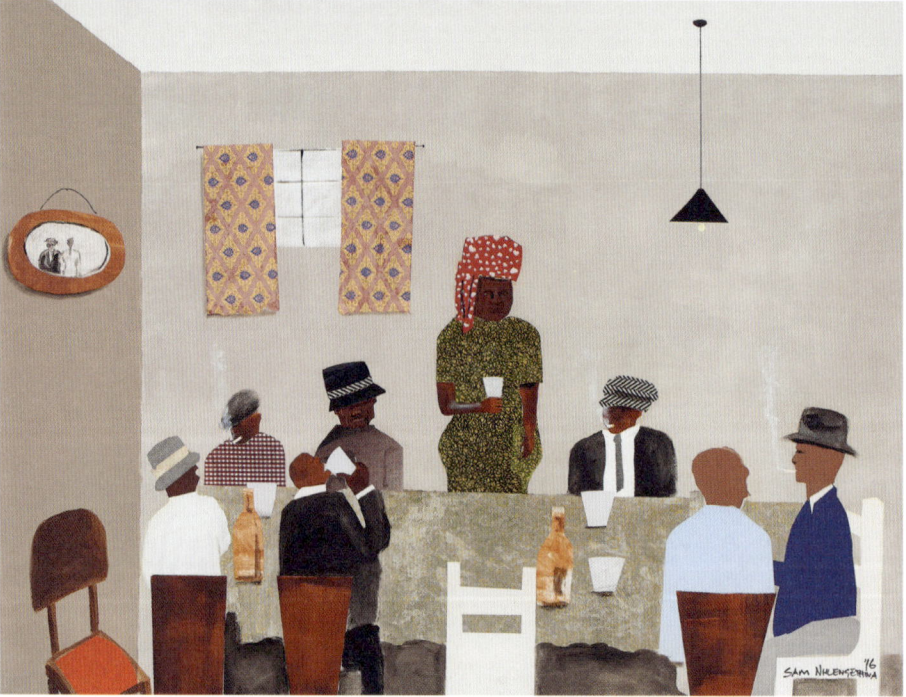

Born 1955, Payneville, Springs, South Africa. Lives in Johannesburg, South Africa.

↑↑ **Winnie waiting for Madiba**, 2018, oil and collage on canvas, 80 × 90 cm (31½ × 35⅜ in)

↑ **Shebeen Queen (Madi Curves)**, 2016, oil and collage on canvas, 120 × 160 cm (47¼ × 63 in)

→ **My daughter's grand piano**, 2020, oil and collage on canvas, 130 × 110 cm (51⅛ × 43¼ in)

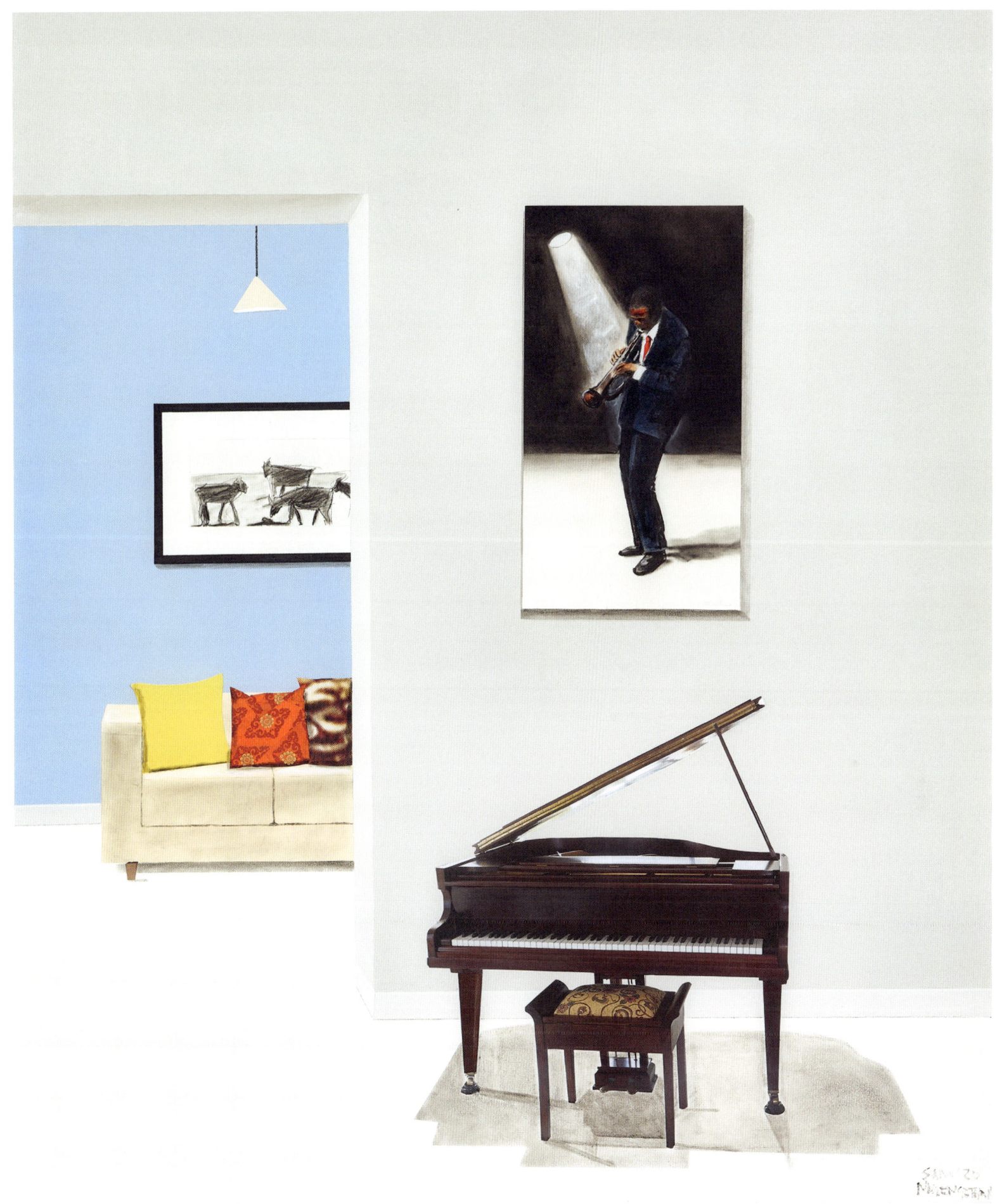

SAM NHLENGETHWA

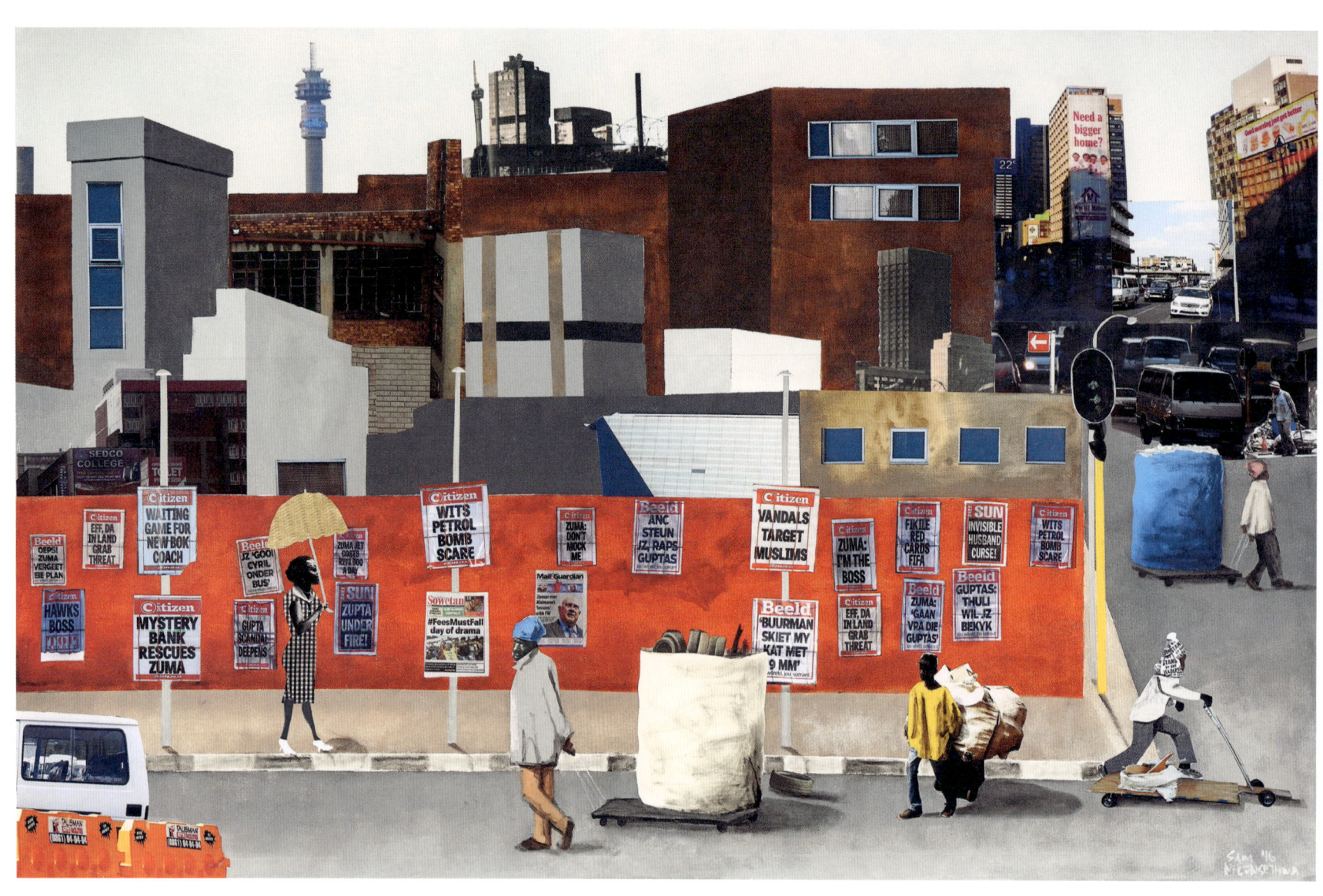

Headlines, 2016, collage, oil and acrylic on canvas, 140 × 220 cm (55⅛ × 86⅝ in)

The Big Band, 2015, oil and collage on canvas, triptych, each 199.8 × 100 × 4.8 cm (78⅝ × 39⅜ × 1⅞ in)

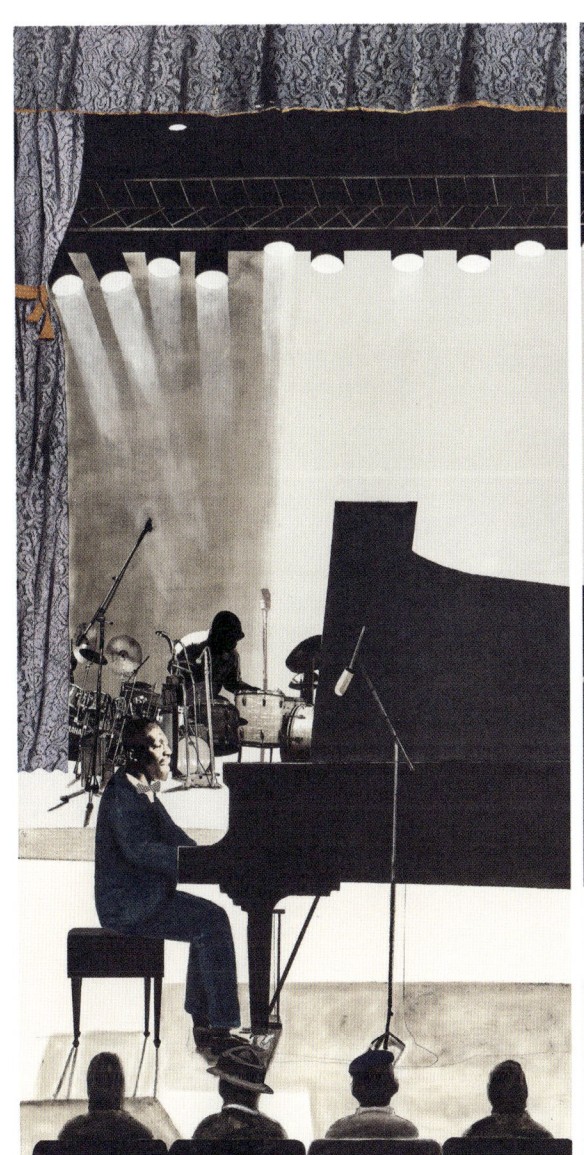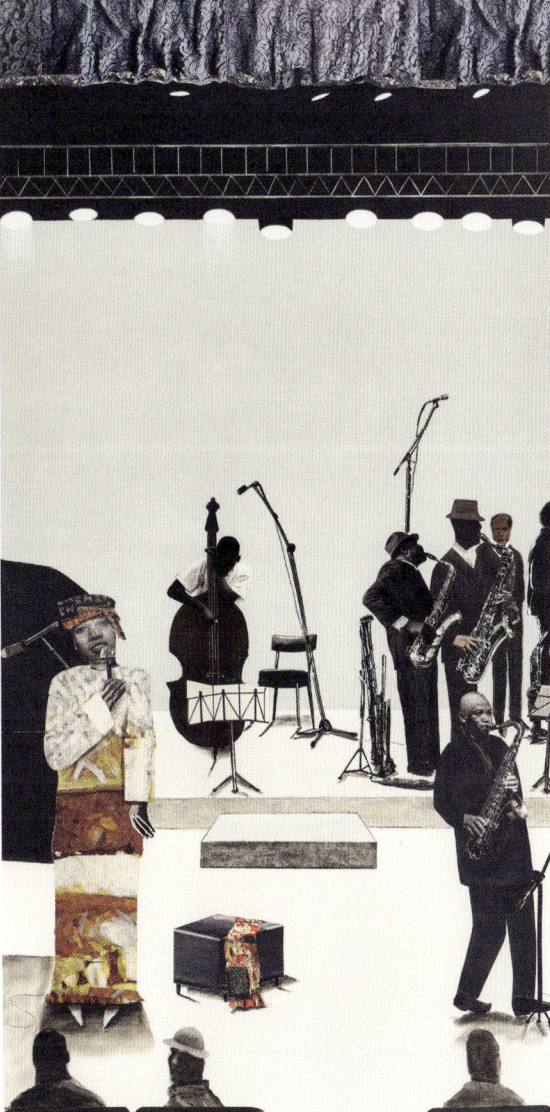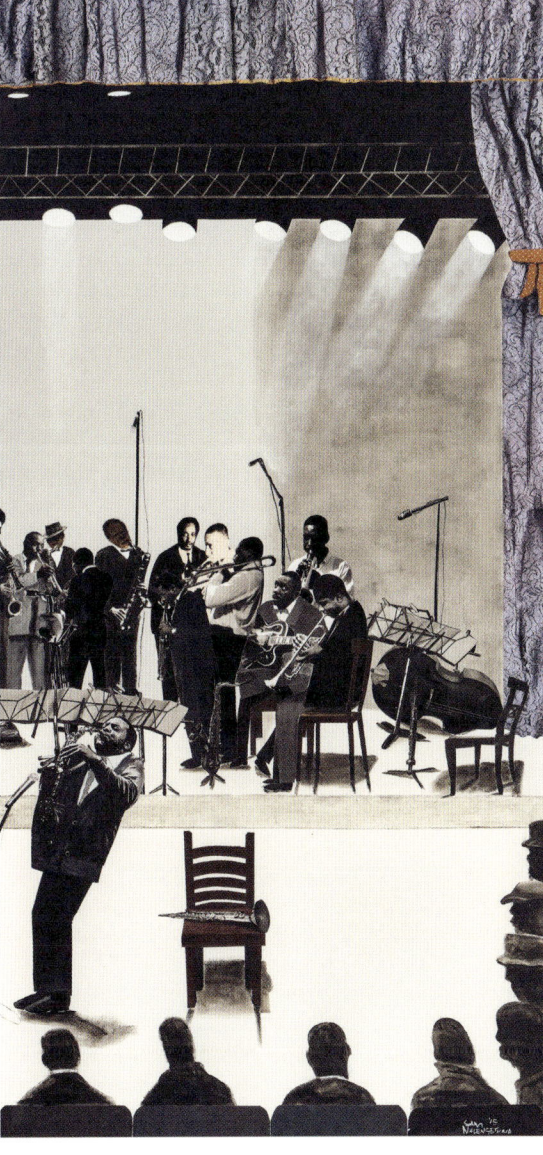

ZOHRA
OPOKU

The transformational merger of photography and textile practices into a unified statement has enabled Zohra Opoku to develop a graphically compelling and idiomatic approach to exploring her Afro-German identity. Opoku's heritage as a bi-racial child of a Ghanaian father and German mother figures prominently in her restless biography and underpins the monochrome works illustrated here. Opoku's parents met in 1975 in former East Germany while studying. Opoku's father returned to Ghana shortly after her birth. Her mother was prevented from following by the repressive German state and the artist grew up without knowing her father, who died in 2004. Opoku was made aware of her mixed-race heritage after German reunification, in 1990, when she was subjected to racist abuse. These factors informed her later decision to move to Accra and reconnect with her Ghanaian heritage, an experience that involved the discovery of Ghana's rich tradition of fabric design.

Fabric, noted art historian Silvia Forni in *The Textile Museum Journal* in 2021, is an essential element of Opoku's art, functioning both 'as material and as a conceptual framing of her practice'. Interested in textiles from a young age, Opoku studied fashion in Hamburg and briefly worked for Danish designer Henrik Vibskov. Fashion gave Opoku a practical grounding in collage as an improvisatory method involving the mixing and matching of diverse material elements. She learnt the basics of photography and of incorporating images into fabric. When she transitioned into art-making, photography became an important part of her repertoire. Her early portraits drew strongly from the poise of West African studio photography, with its strong emphasis on self-styling, status and cultural identity. Although an urban artist with a deep affection for hip hop, Opoku's portraits often integrate sacred trees and groves in acknowledgement of Ghana's polytheistic Akan religion. In 2014, during a residency in the Netherlands, Opoku printed one of her portraits onto cloth. It was a light-bulb moment. Two years later she presented an exhibition of photographs, projections and sculptural assemblies in Gallery 1957 in Accra. Titled 'Saasa', the exhibition included examples of Opoku's filigreed self-portraits shot in lush outdoor settings, some of them silkscreened onto cloth received from the artist's grandmother and displayed banner-style. The use of family heirlooms figured prominently again in Opoku's 2017 presentation by Sean Kelly Gallery at The Armory Show, New York – 'Unravelled Threads'. It was dominated by hanging textile collages screenprinted with images of the artist (including *One of Me II* and *Debie*, both 2017) and of her parents, notably her father in Asante royal dress. She also included letters and family photographs obtained from her father's Ghanaian family. The registration errors in the printed textiles are integral to their meaning as acts of translation and recovery. Opoku's more recent, colour-rich work exploring Egyptian symbols and beliefs extends the foundational strategies contained in her 'Unravelled Threads' series.

SEAN O'TOOLE

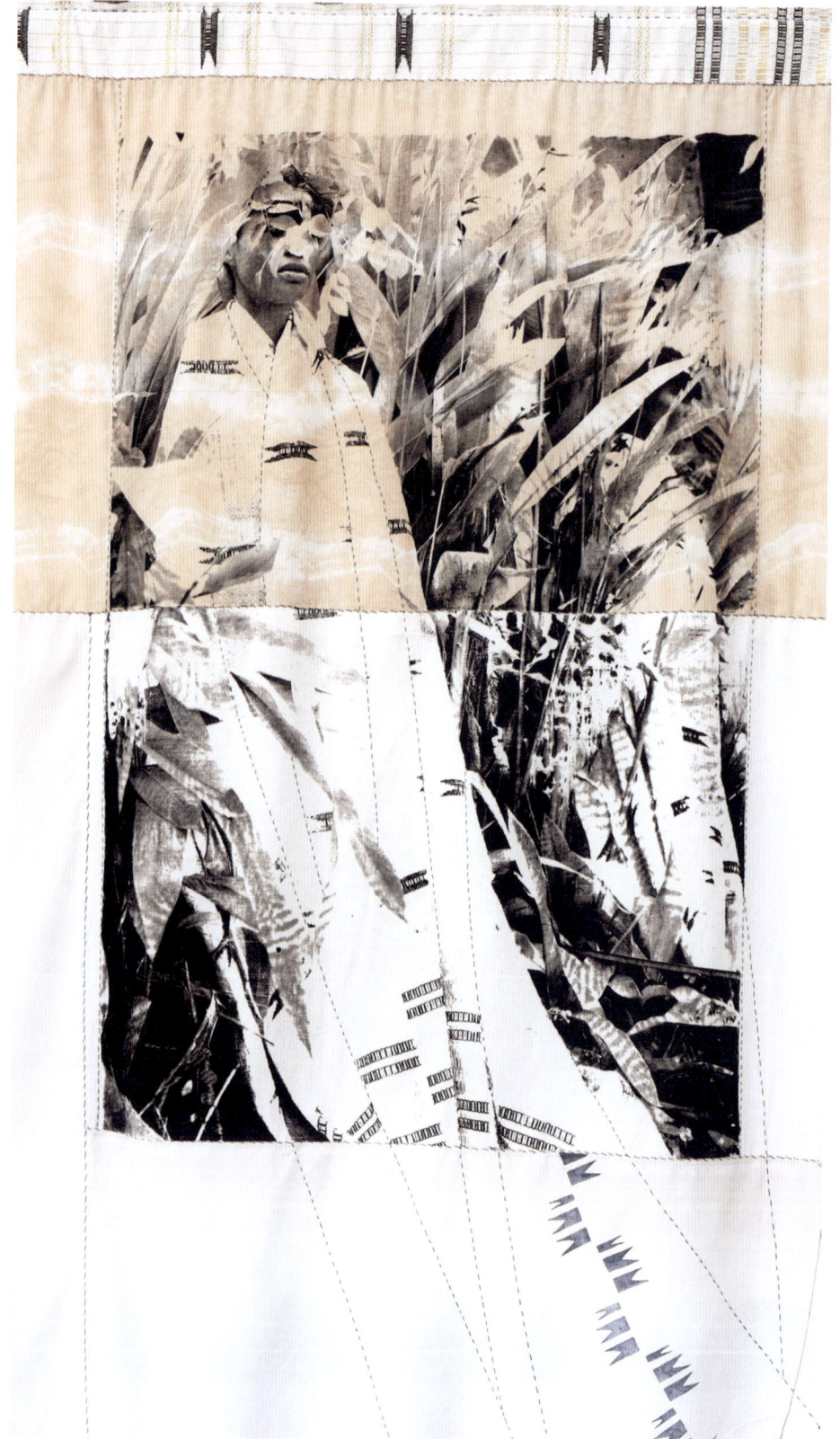

Born 1976, Altdöbern, Germany. Lives in Accra, Ghana.

↑   One of Me II, 2017, screenprint on textile, acrylic and thread, 219 × 145 cm (86¼ × 57⅛ in)

↗   Debie, 2017, screenprint on canvas and cotton, black tea dye, thread and acrylic, 230 × 140 cm (90½ × 55⅛ in)

↗↗ In Bob's Footsteps, 2017, screenprint on cotton, jeans and, thread, 282 × 200 cm (111⅛ × 78¾ in)

→   Kwame & Max, 2017–20, screenprint on denim, acrylic and thread, 160 × 165 cm (63 × 65 in)

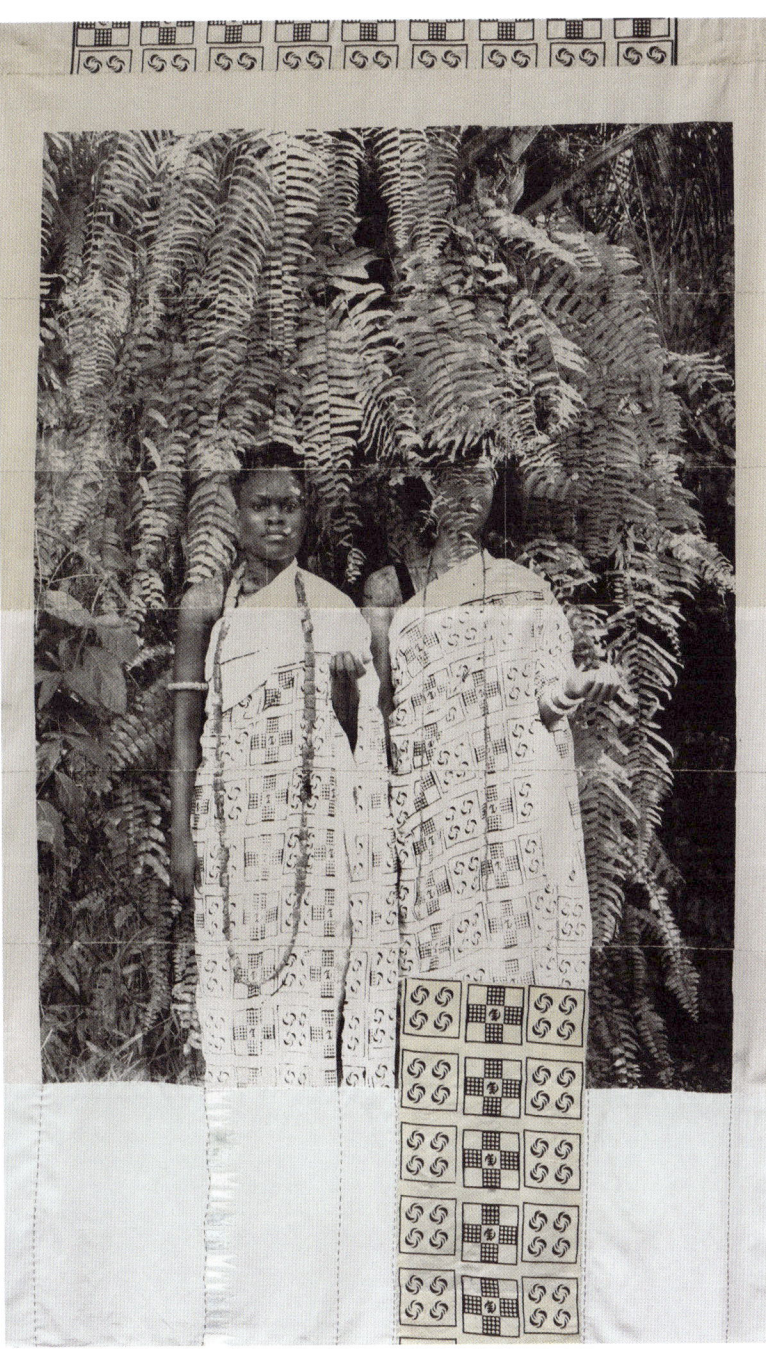

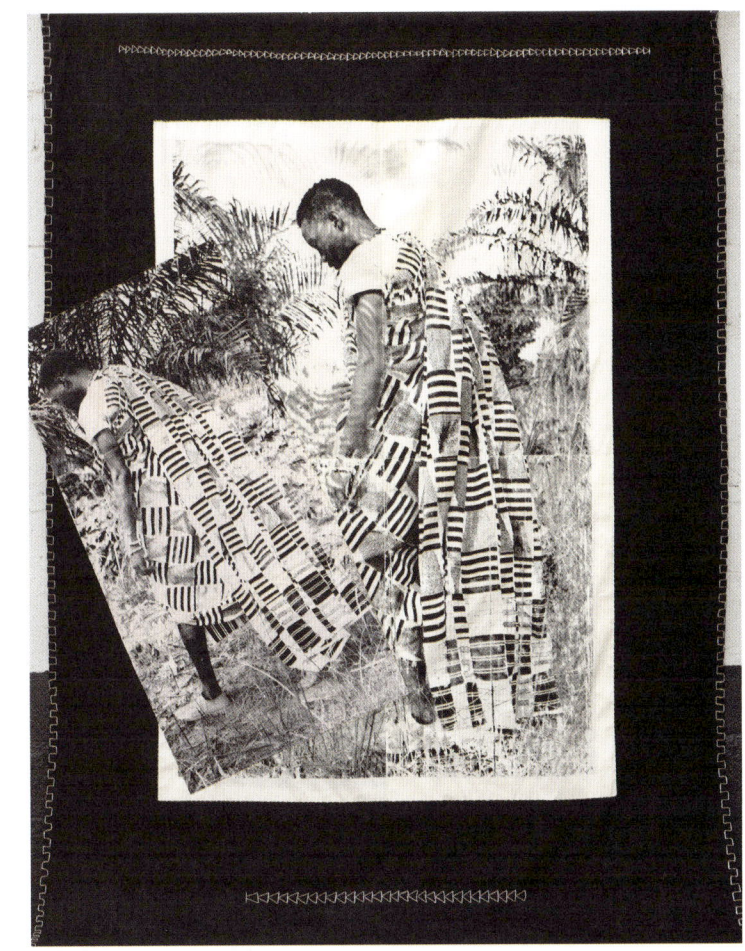

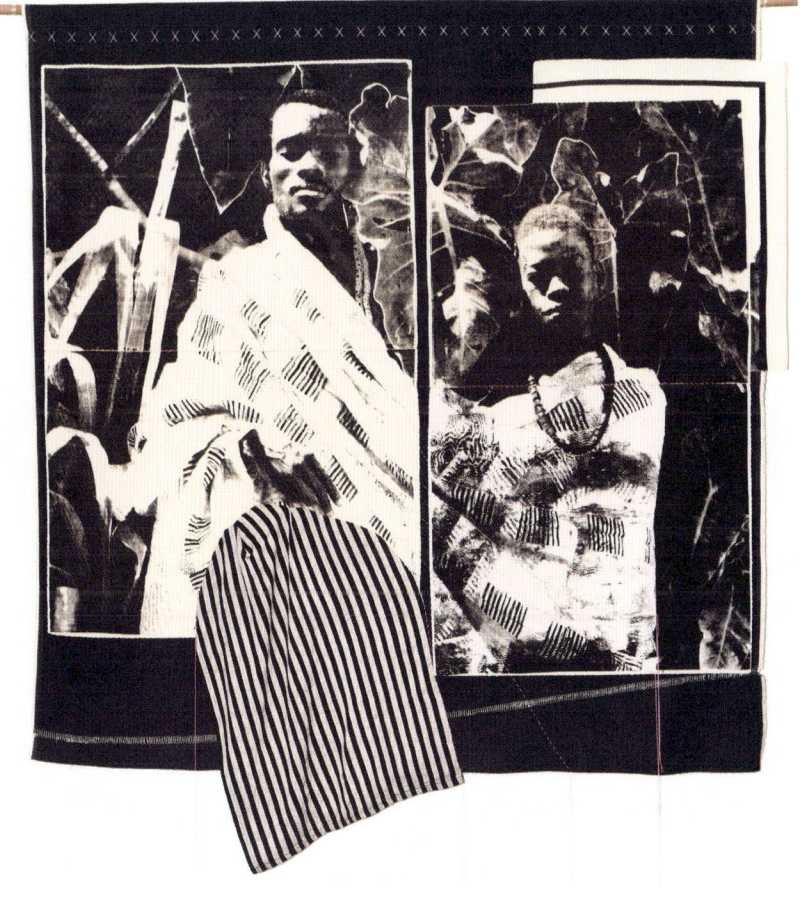

ZOHRA OPOKU

FRIDA ORUPABO

A sociologist and an artist, with a practice that spans photography, collage, sculpture and video, Frida Orupabo is largely focused on disrupting the prejudice historically directed towards Black women and their bodies. Postcolonial theory proposes a robust critique of the perpetuating account of modernity and its history, and yet, as contemporary politics reveal, the work of decolonization is far from resolved. The past, inevitably narrated by history, sets traps, and therefore the need for new forms of representation still holds. Orupabo's isolated, distorted or fragmented women consistently resist and subvert their historical objectification and give a voice to those who have too often been muffled, stifled and silenced. The figures in *Untitled* (2018), *Girl with blue dress*, *Mother and child in bed* and *Woman with gun* (all 2021) gaze defiantly and directly out of the frame to meet the viewer's eyes. In an online conversation with curator Elvira Dyangani Ose in October 2020, the artist described how 'When choosing images, I am looking for resistance or some type of tension, especially in the way a subject sees, or stares. It forces you to stop.' In her often lifesized collages, the artist weaves historical photographs of enslaved women mined from the cold stores of colonial archives with images plundered from online platforms including eBay, Tumblr, Pinterest and Instagram. Primarily presented as black-and-white images, occasional sections of bold colour reinforce their status as composite forms. Building on a legacy of African American, feminist scholars such as Moya Bailey – who coined the term 'Misogynoir' to describe the ways in which racist and misogynistic representations, particularly in visual culture and digital spaces, shape broader ideas about Black women – Orupabo salvages her subjects from the dominant histories of violence to reveal both their trauma and capacity for survival. A palpable and unnerving violence lingers at the surface of Orupabo's work, mirroring the physical force required to cut, tear and rip up images. The split-pins that secure Orupabo's sculptural accumulations in place once again renders explicit the violence wrought upon Black women's bodies as they have been prodded, probed and poked across centuries. Yet they also give the *figures* agency – their bodies are not fixed in one position as they would be with glue, but have the potential to move. Ultimately the process of cutting apart and reordering images parallels Orupabo's activist impulse to disrupt the status quo and develop new, alternative representations of empowerment. Rich with meaning and generative possibilities, Orupabo's subjects actively reimagine the world by engaging in powerful forms of resistance, disrupting mainstream narratives, subverting negative stereotypes and, in so doing, reclaim their agency. As she said in the same conversation, 'Resistance can also be seen in a position – how people sit or stand, how they dress, how they hold their hands... this is what I recognise in many of the images from the colonial archive – the anger and the quiet resistance.'

ALONA PARDO

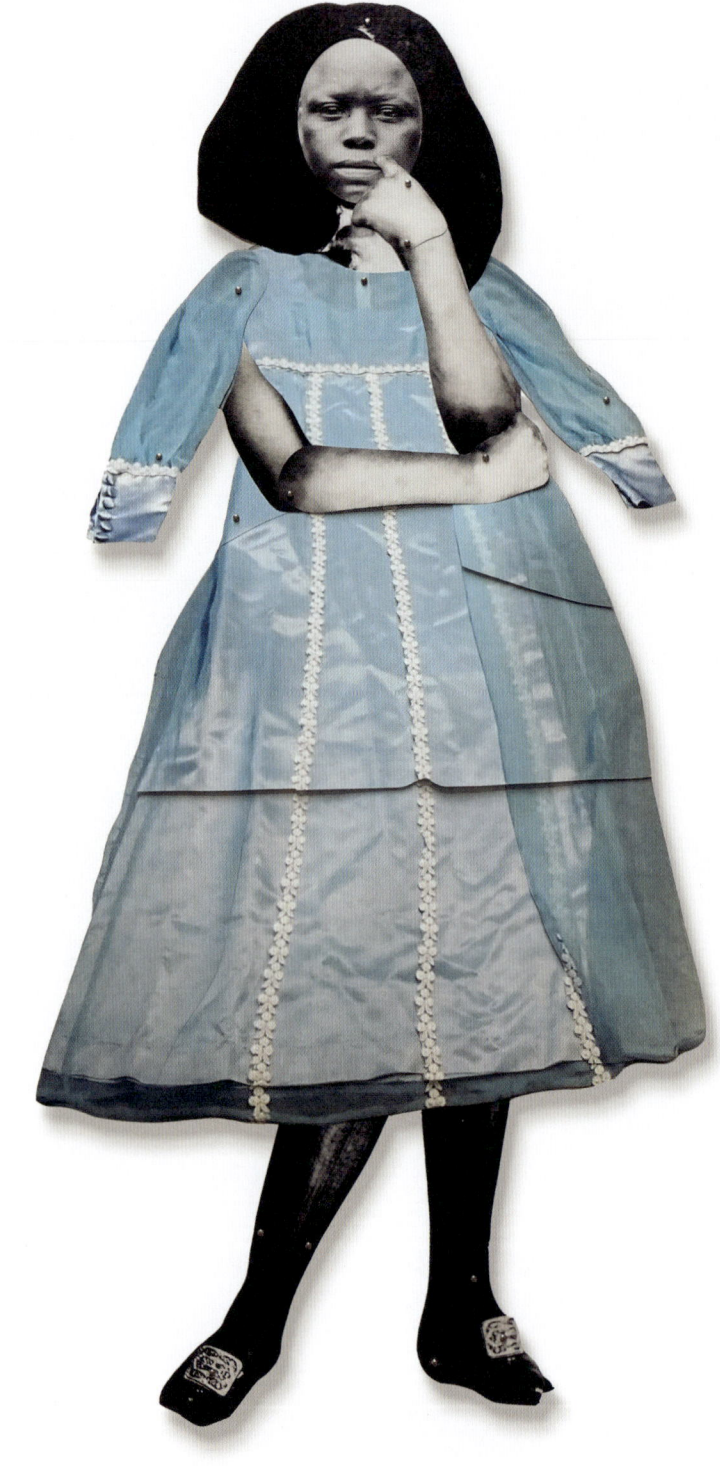

Born 1986, Sarpsborg, Norway. Lives in Oslo, Norway.

↑   **Girl with blue dress**, 2021, collage with paper pins, 164.5 × 88 cm (64¾ × 34⅝ in)

↗   **In bed**, 2020, collage with paper pins, 102 × 146 cm (40⅛ × 57½ in)

→   **Mother and child in bed**, 2021, collage with paper pins, 112 × 187 cm (44⅛ × 73⅝ in)

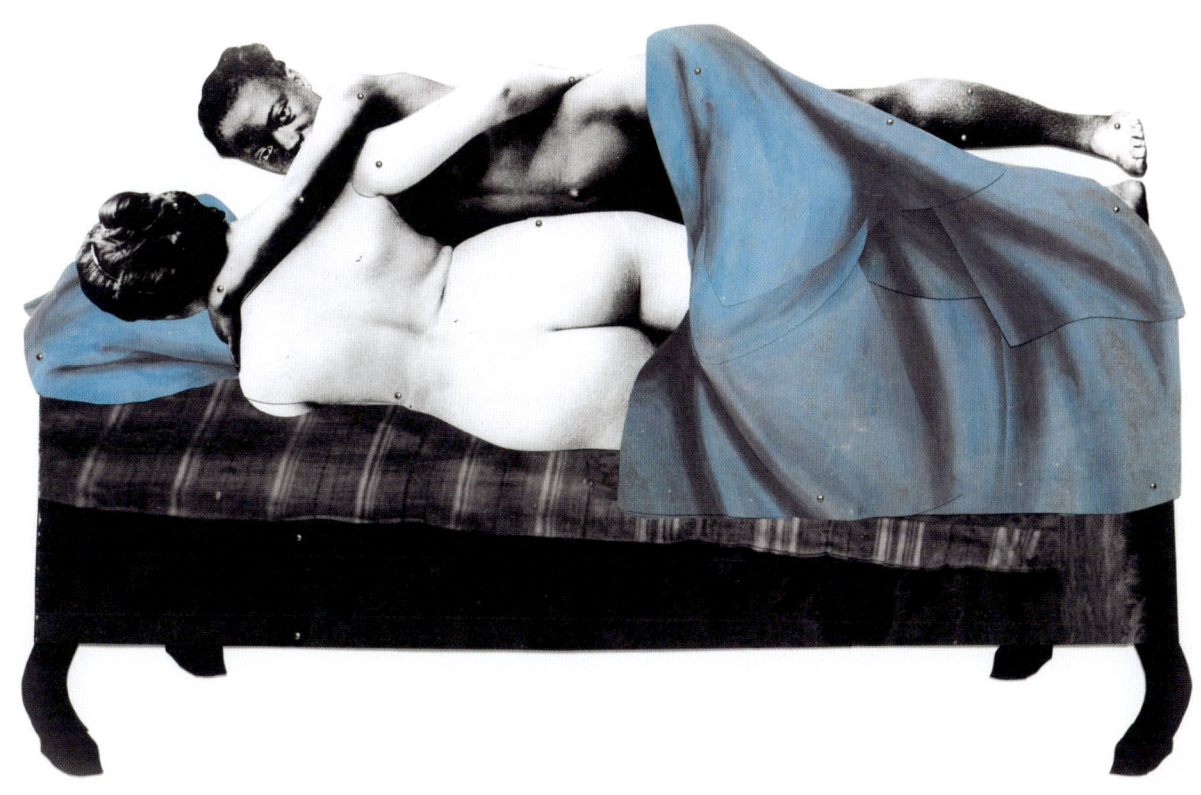

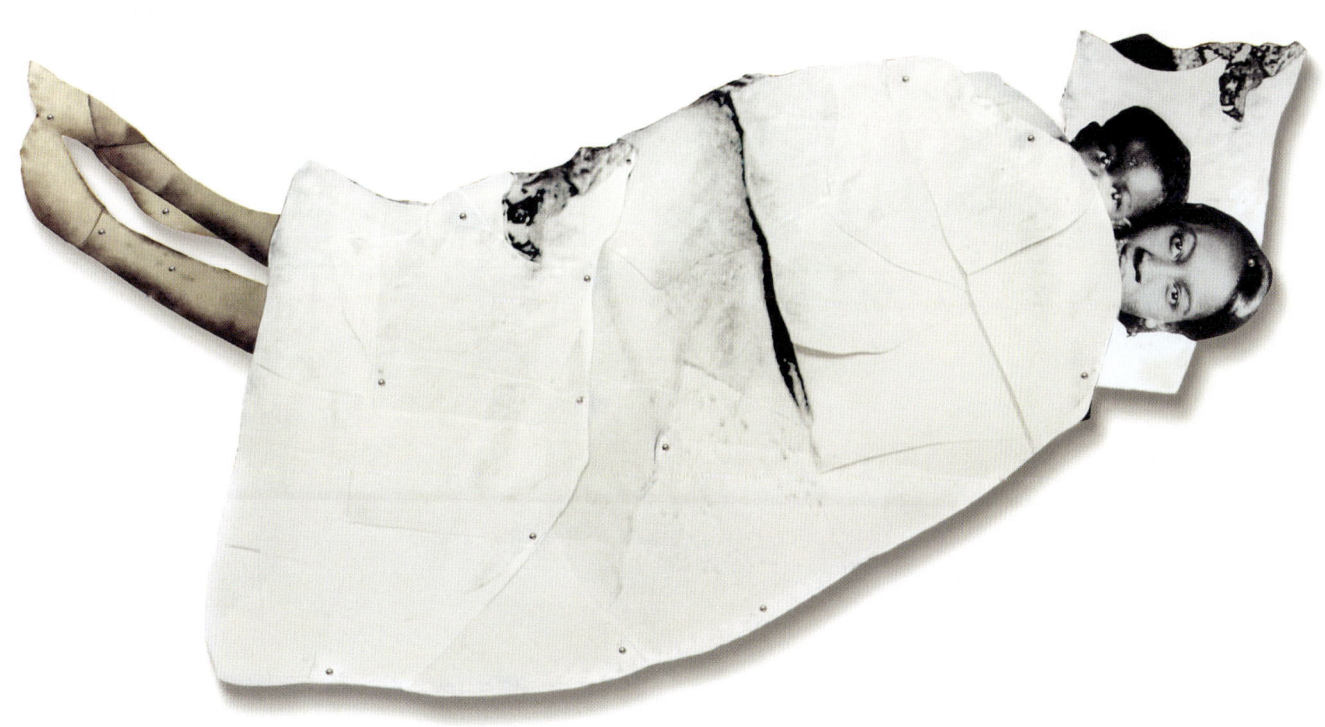

FRIDA
ORUPABO

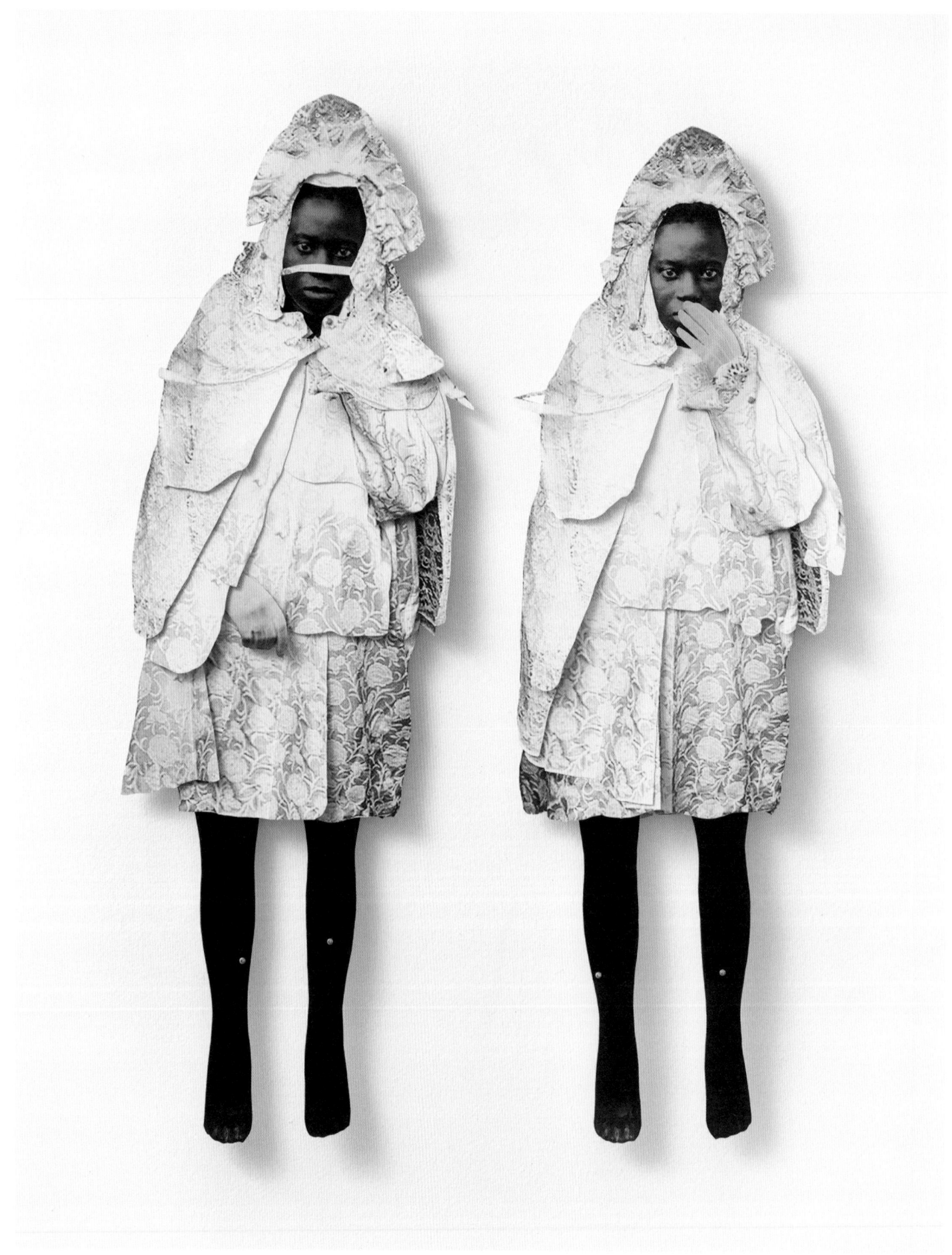

↑   **Untitled**, 2018, collage with paper pins mounted on aluminium, 2 parts each 123.5 × 80 cm
(48 ⅝ × 31 ½ in)

→   **Woman with gun**, 2021, collage with paper pins, 186 × 134.5 cm (73 ¼ × 53 in)

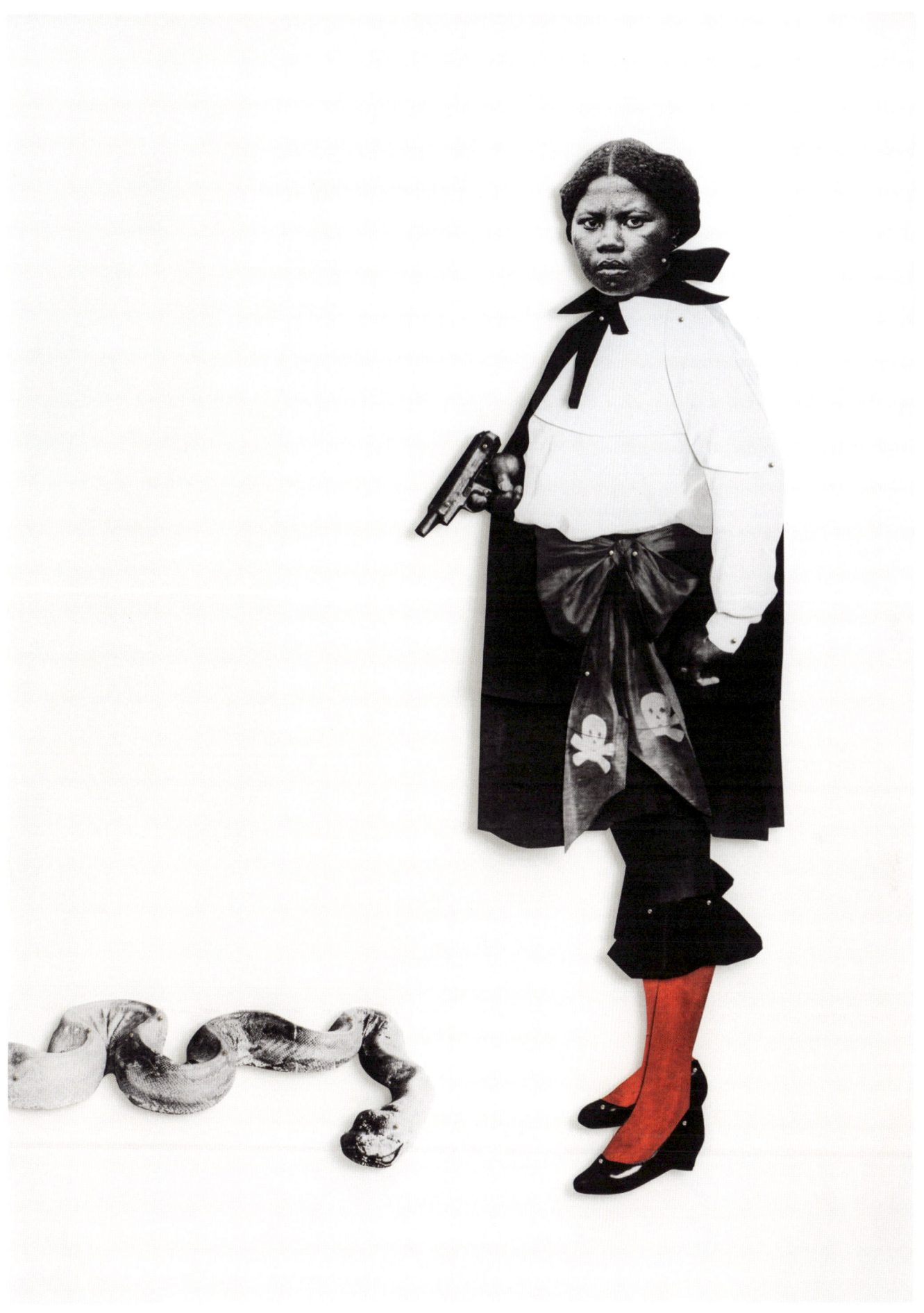

FRIDA
ORUPABO

JULIEN PACAUD

With a simplicity and boldness reminiscent of the work of early pioneers of modernism, such as László Moholy-Nagy (1895–1946), Julien Pacaud's compositions are harmoniously arranged to suggest a sense of iconic stillness, silence and balance. Sometimes this equilibrium is quite literal, as in the precarious bench on a diagonal rockface in *Authorized Perimeter* (2020) or the standing figure atop an overhead power line in *Catastrophe Lovers #9* (2019). While no obvious narrative is spelled out, the visual fragments invite the viewer to engage in a game of free association. Pacaud's collages possess an enigmatic quality: they are puzzles in search of a solution, allusions gesturing towards the elusive meaning of life itself. This existentialist dimension, which pervades the artist's output, might be the sum of his disparate past experiences as astrophysicist, international snooker player, hypnotist and Esperanto teacher. A passionate reader of sci-fi novels and obsessed with time travel, Pacaud claims that, regardless of the intention that brought them to life in the first place, his collages bear no prescriptive meaning. More broadly, the artist explores the tensions and overlays between past and present, time and space. His collages, which are created digitally rather than by cutting and gluing photographs from books and magazines, summon a sense of timelessness in which self-absorbed or meditative characters appear suspended, in defiance of the laws of gravity. Lunar, rocky or desert-like, Pacaud's landscapes suggest no specific geographical location, nor is the viewer offered many clues about the backstory of the figures that populate his worlds, aside from occasional clues granted by hairstyle or clothing. This disengagement from site-specific references casts the artist's collages as terse images of the mind – internal reflections or ethereal manifestations of fleeting moments of self-doubt. Ultimately, a sometimes unsettling and yet playful alteration of scale – at its most extreme with the oversized hand in *Cartography of Infinity #34* (2021) – grants Pacaud's collages the aura of a religious icon. As in medieval paintings, perspective may be flattened; what seems distant appears simultaneously close, and the most important elements loom large over understated details that are nonetheless critical to hold the image together. This sense of cohesiveness is important to Pacaud, who uses collage to master a sense of control over the chaos of everyday existence. Recurring linear elements and geometrical shapes – such as the rectangular prism in *Best Friends Forever* (2018) – enclose human bodies or connect them to other objects in space and allude to the rationalization of the uncontrollable flux of life itself. These elements may also point at the underlying cultural structures that hold our systems of core beliefs in place. More often, they seem to outline personal, cultural or social limitations. In this sense, Pacaud's collages also manifest the invisible, thus acquiring a transcendental value. At others they more readily allude to the potential trajectories of bodies in space – a way to further problematize the very nature of collage as a medium devoted to the reconfiguration of our experiences.

GIOVANNI ALOI

Born 1972, Chalon-sur-Saône, France. Lives in Paris, France.

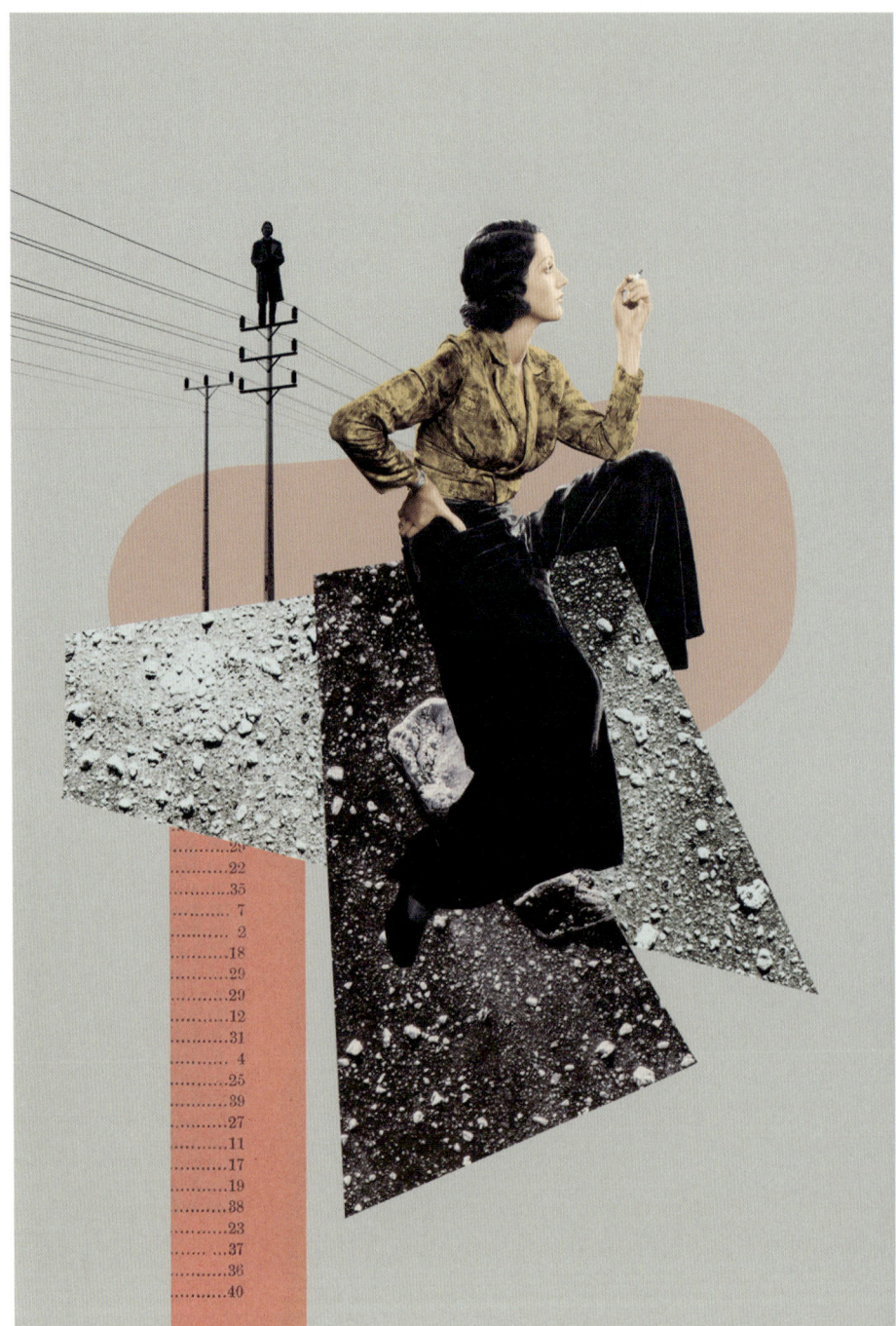

↑ Catastrophe Lovers #9, 2019, digital collage printed on 310 gsm fine art paper, 42 × 30 cm (16½ × 11¾ in)

↗ Authorized Perimeter, 2020, digital collage printed on 310 gsm fine art paper, 42 × 30 cm (16½ × 11¾ in)

↗↗ Cartography of Infinity #34, 2021, digital collage printed on 310 gsm fine art paper, 42 × 30 cm (16½ × 11¾ in)

→ Best Friends Forever, 2018, digital collage printed on 310 gsm fine art paper, 42 × 30 cm (16½ × 11¾ in)

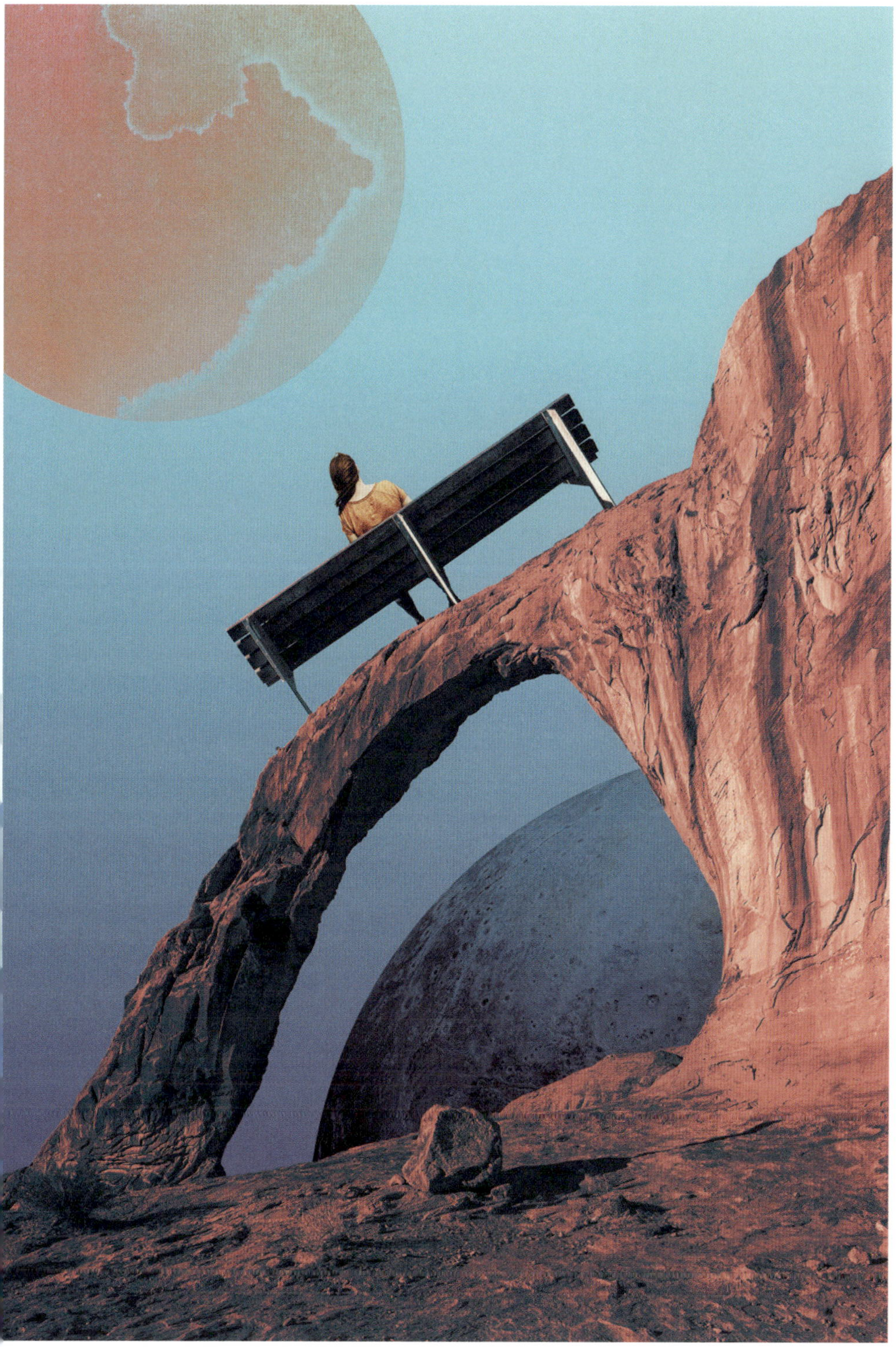

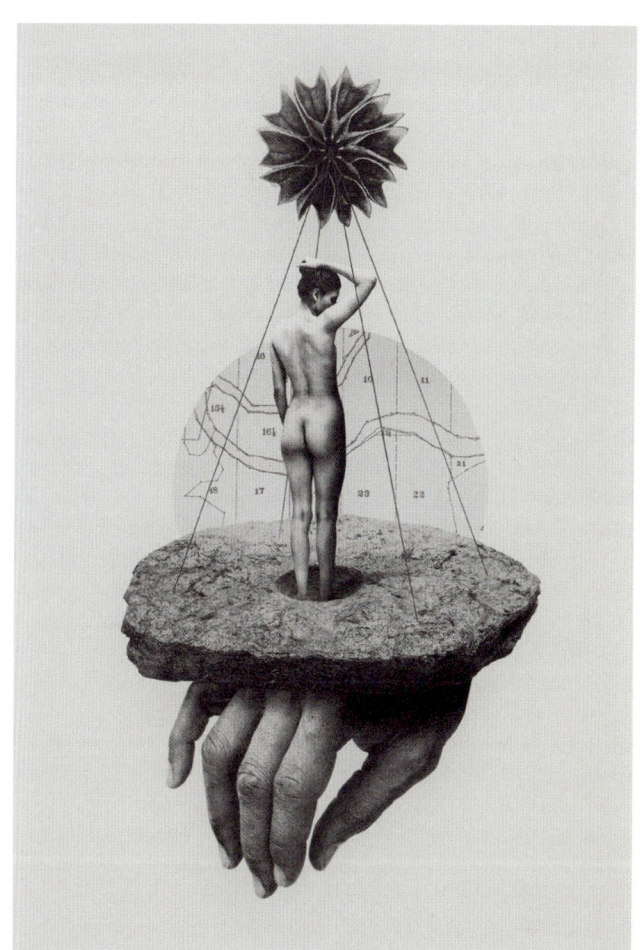

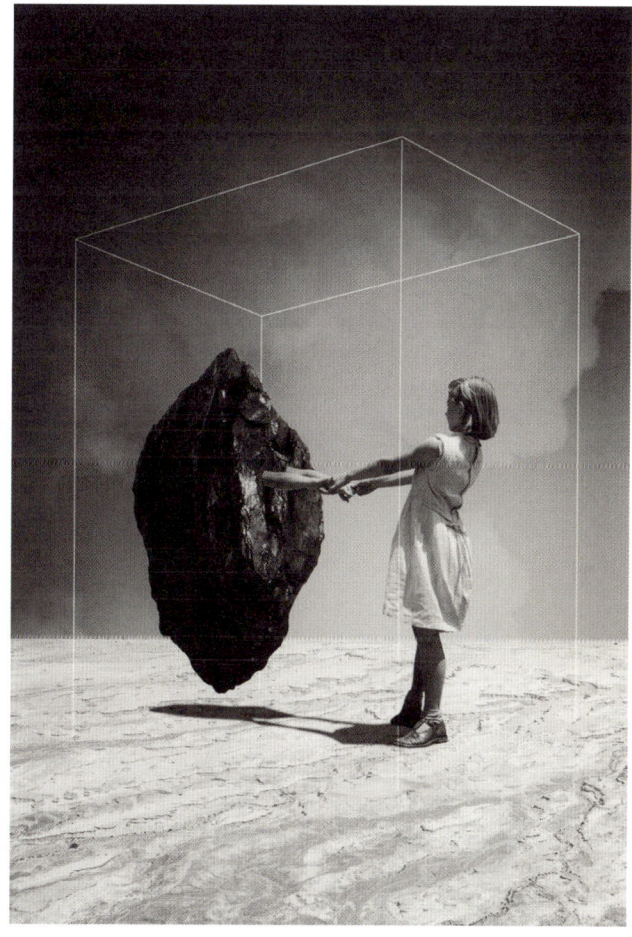

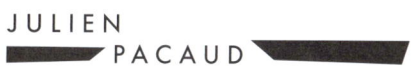

JULIEN
PACAUD

GIULIO PAOLINI

Giulio Paolini is frequently associated with the Italian art movement Arte Povera; he came to prominence through Germano Celant, the critic who pulled the movement together in a seminal exhibition in 1967, and indeed was born in the same year and city as him. However, Paolini's work is characterized less by the use of poor materials typical of Arte Povera than by the rigour with which he explores the concepts of art and the role of the artist, and how the viewer relates to them in turn. Quoted in an undated piece in *Wannenes* art magazine, he described himself as 'not so much oriented towards the taste of materials, but rather faithful to the roots of art history'. Far from Romanticism's ideal of the artist creating a personal vision from inner genius, Paolini sees himself more as a messenger pointing out what already exists.

His primary setting is very much the exhibition as the place of encounter: you might say that he is more a maker of exhibitions than of artworks, of 'theatres of evocation', to use art historian Maddalena Disch's term, in which he re-presents selections from a worldwide store of cultural mythologies and memories. Many of his sculptural installations succinctly trigger his concerns by using plaster casts of classical busts and figures to stand in for art history, artist and viewer – so it is no surprise that they reappear in collage form in *Le Nove Muse* (The Nine Muses, 2017). Is the artist the foregrounded muse pointing out the other eight, or is that the spectator? Typically, the two collapse. Either way, the muses are set in a landscape that seems more mathematical than topographic. The schematic lines of perspective delineated find an echo in the lines of sight applied in *Untitled* (2014–15): an artwork made up from people looking at artworks, which leaves them – or us – to take on the artist's role, as the paintings on the wall appear to have been left empty for filling in. Sometimes we see Paolini himself, but distanced: wearing sunglasses, allowing a stretcher to partially cover him, or – as in *Notti Bianche* (White Nights, 2015) – hiding his face. That collage revisits a work from 1990, in which the same evasive image of the artist is held in balance by a construction made from three blank canvases. This fits with his statement, published in 2022 by the Center for Italian Modern Art, New York, 'I cannot say why, but I have always manifested a degree of embarrassment in considering myself an artist… I feel more like a spectator than the creator I am.' Yet that pose is constructed in a very artful way. Don't look at these, one might imagine him saying playfully of his collages, look at the history of art instead – only for us to find it's too late, we've already been drawn in.

PAUL CAREY-KENT

Born 1940, Genoa, Italy. Lives in Turin, Italy.

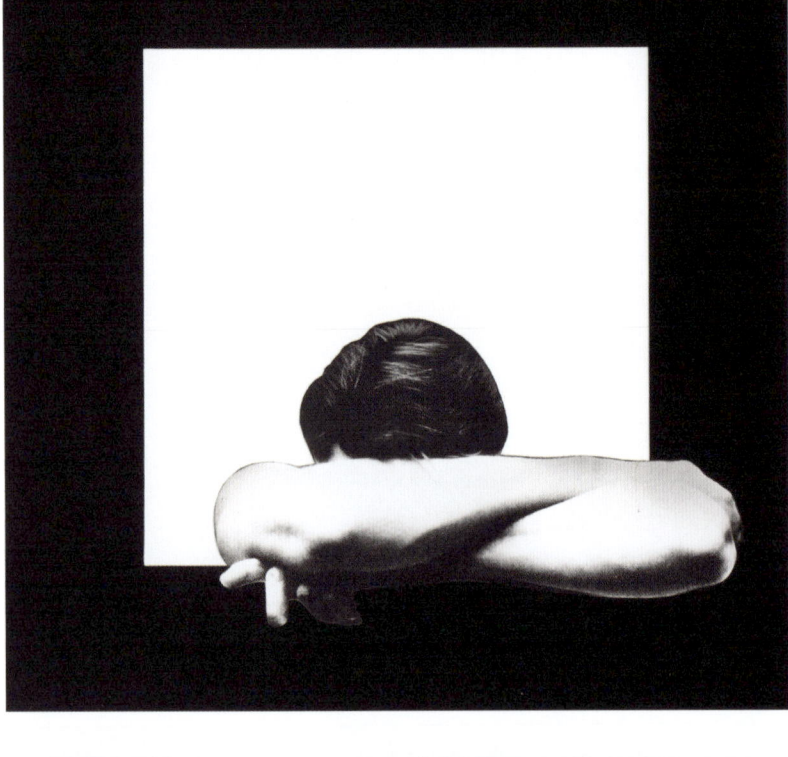

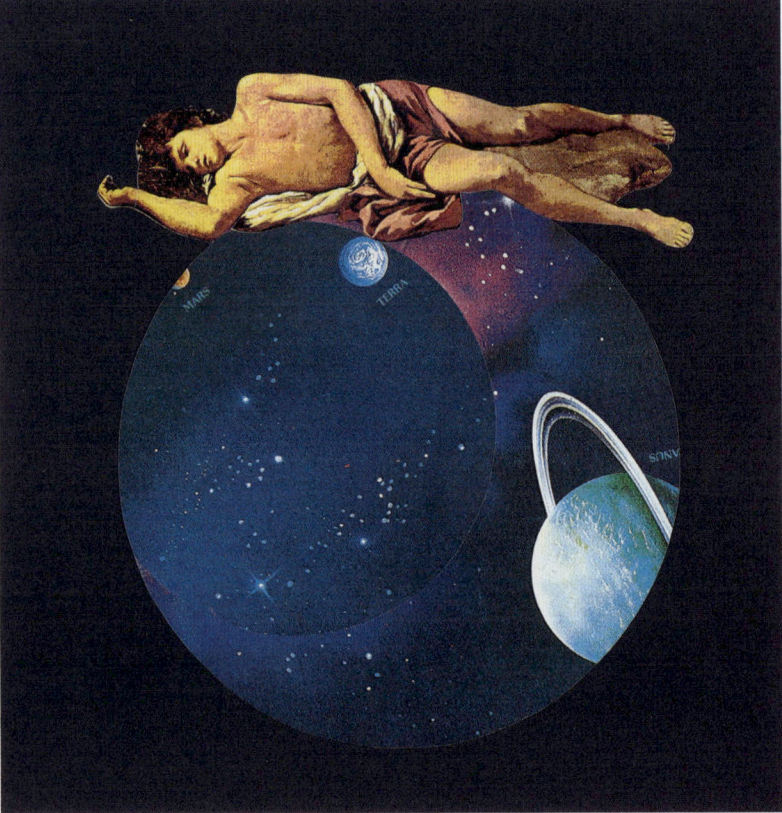

↑↑ Notti bianche (White Nights), 2015, collage on black passepartout, 60 × 60 cm (23 ⅝ × 23 ⅝ in), private collection

↑ Studio per 'Narciso' (Study for 'Narciso'), 2017, collage on black paper, 30 × 30 cm (11 ¾ × 11 ¾ in), private collection

↗ Zeusi e Parrasio (Zeuxis and Parrhasius), 2007–17, pencil and collage on paper, 62 × 91 cm (24 ⅜ × 3.5 ⅞ in), Françoise and Jean-Philippe Billarant Collection, Paris, France

→ Le nove Muse (The Nine Muses), 2017, pencil, black ink, red ink and collage on paper, 70 × 100 cm (27 ½ × 39 ⅜ in), private collection

→ → Untitled, 2014–15, pencil, red ink, black ink and collage on paper, 70 × 100 cm (27 ½ × 39 ⅜ in)

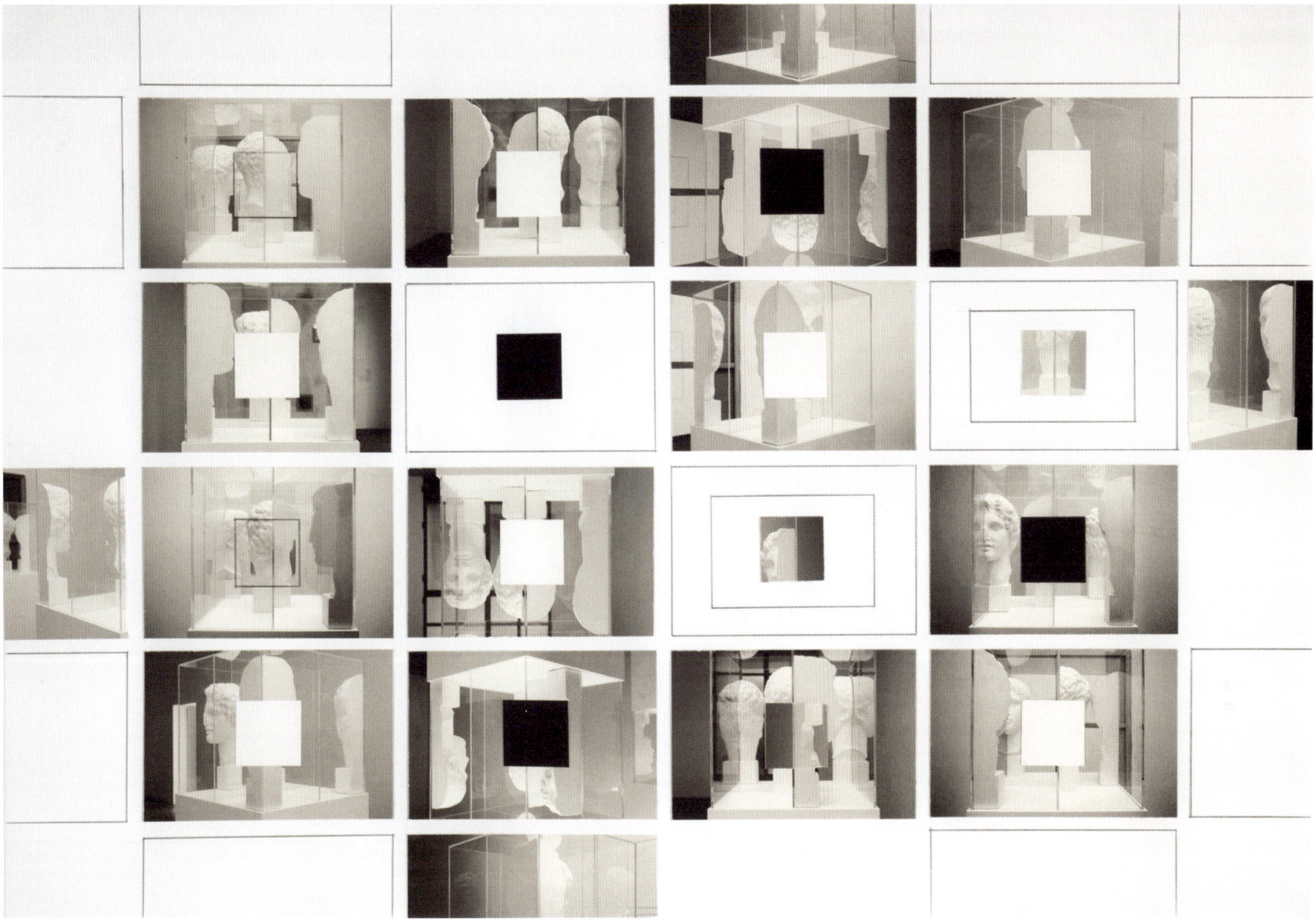

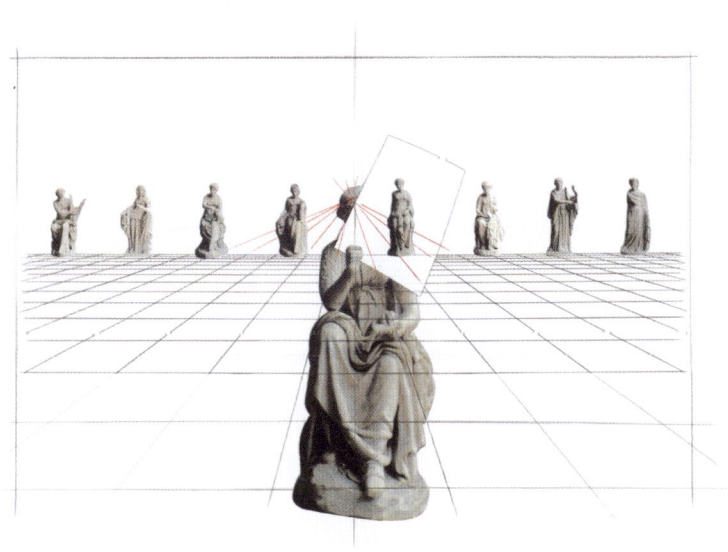

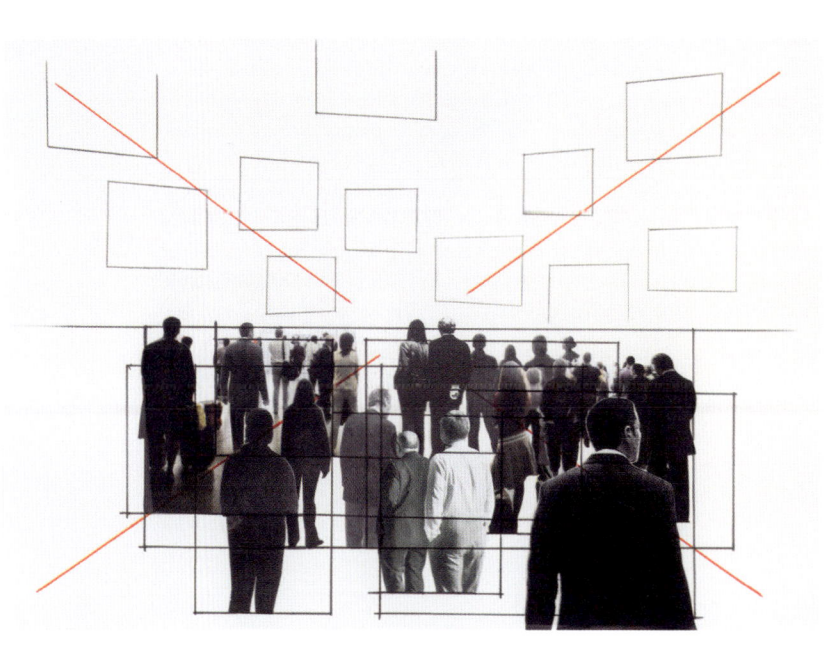

GIULIO PAOLINI

EBONY G. PATTERSON

Ebony G. Patterson's works are a trap. They lure the viewer in with their seductive lushness and intricacy, but open up difficult, important and timely conversations about race, class, gender and identity. Using embellished tapestry and mixed-media paper collages, Patterson creates visually dense works that one can get lost in. She titles them with lyrical and evocative phrases using ellipses and wordplay to reveal an interest in gaps and in dichotomies of meaning. ■ For her tapestry works, the production process is complex: she shoots and edits photographs, which are then cut up and arranged into compositions. These are reproduced as tapestries and she then uses collage, décollage (cutting away or removing elements) and layering of recognizable items of clothing and jewellery along with glitter, lace, flowers and feathers. The objects she incorporates represent Black and Brown bodies that are absent. Patterson creates an homage to those who have lost their lives to violence and injustice or to those who have been made invisible. Her use of everyday items allows her to represent the sitter as anonymous, rather than as a specific individual, thus representing the thousands who have perished, yet who deserve a moment of reverence. A work such as *found among the reeds-Dead Treez* (2015), can serve as an altar or shrine. It appears as though the person whose shoes are haphazardly lying on the floor has left in a hurry. The shoes – and the heavily embellished hats that stand out from the wall-based section above – can be interpreted as a symbol of a life lived then left behind. Yet the people who once wore them are not shown. These garments are redolent of the material possessions that loved ones leave behind, and there is a sense of community within Patterson's works, representing not only those who have gone, but those who remain. ■ In *...they stood in a time of unknowing... for those who bear/bare witness* (2018) Patterson reveals a more complete figure bending down, perhaps working or searching for something. Around the lower edges of the uneven shape are the haunting details of bare feet sticking out from the work. There is also a section of negative space that makes the composition disjointed, forcing the viewer's eye to keep moving throughout Patterson's signature textured details. It also draws attention to the wallpaper beneath, which is also designed by the artist to create a complete environment. ■ More recent works uses motifs of foliage and flora. As art historian Ksenia Soboleva wrote in *Brooklyn Rail* in 2022, 'Patterson continues to explore the garden as a multi-layered metaphor for the colonial histories embedded in the Caribbean landscape.' In paper-based compositions, such as *...a possum rises...* (2019), a digital print of flowers is adorned with butterflies and jewellery, but equally noticeable are the many holes and spaces where parts have been actively removed. The garden may exist as a site of beauty and life, but at the same time, it represents violence and loss. ■

MARITZA LACAYO

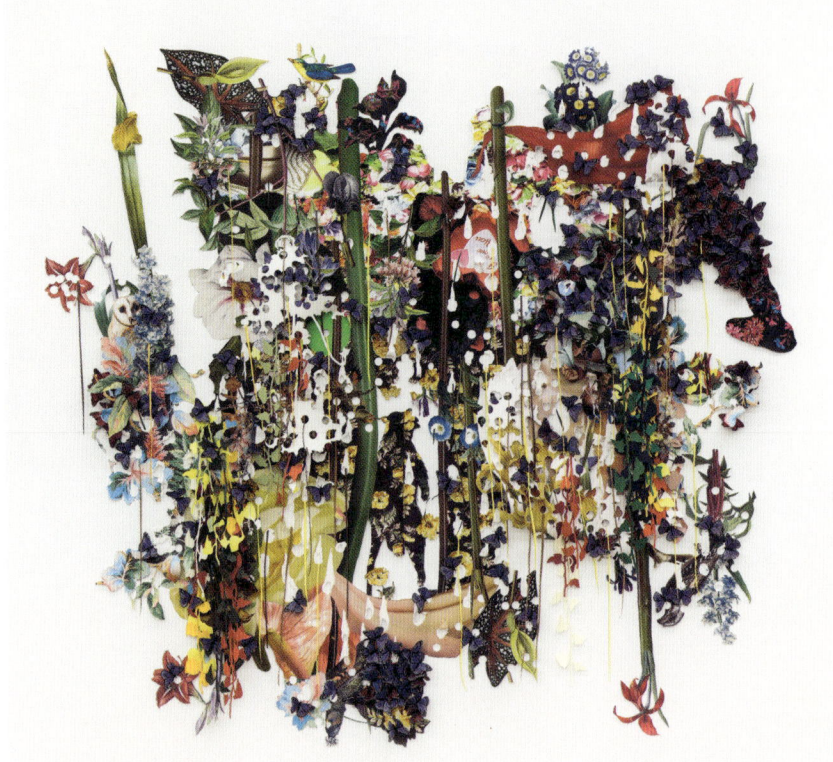

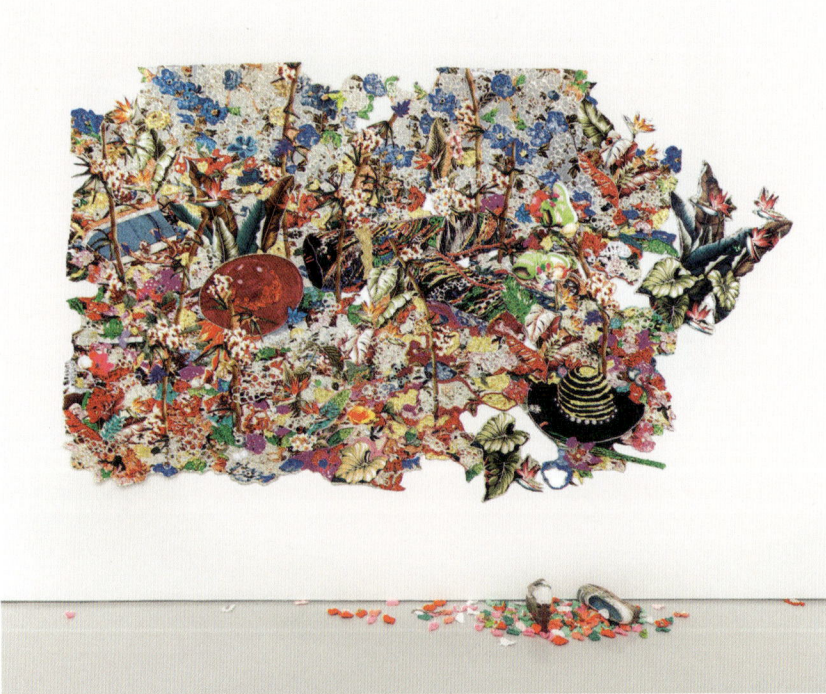

Born 1981, Kingston, Jamaica. Lives in Kingston and Chicago, Illinois, USA.

↑↑ ...a possum rises...a black bear falls...a pattoo takes watch...as children whisper through the leaves, 2019, digital print on archival watercolour paper with hand-cut and torn elements, fabric, poster board, acrylic gel medium, feathered butterflies and costume jewellery, 266.7 × 295.6 cm (105 × 116⅜ in)

↑ found among the reeds-Dead Treez, 2015, hand-cut jacquard woven photo tapestry with handmade shoes, knitted leaves, costume jewellery and mixed media, 259.1 × 365.8 cm (102 × 144 in)

↗ ...they stood in a time of unknowing... for those who bear/bare witness, 2018, hand-cut jacquard woven photo tapestry with glitter, appliqués, pins, embellishments, fabric, tassels, brooches, acrylic, glass pearls, beads and hand-cast heliconias on artist-designed fabric wallpaper, 386.1 × 508 cm (152 × 200 in)

→ ...love... (...when they grow up...), 2016, mixed media on hand-cut jacquard woven tapestry with appliqués, embellishments, brooches, plastic, glitter, fabric, stuffed toys and papier-mâché balloons on wallpaper fabric, 44.1 × 308.6 × 30.5 cm (112 × 121½ × 12 in), installation view, 'Live Uncertainty,' 32nd São Paulo Biennial, Brazil, 2016

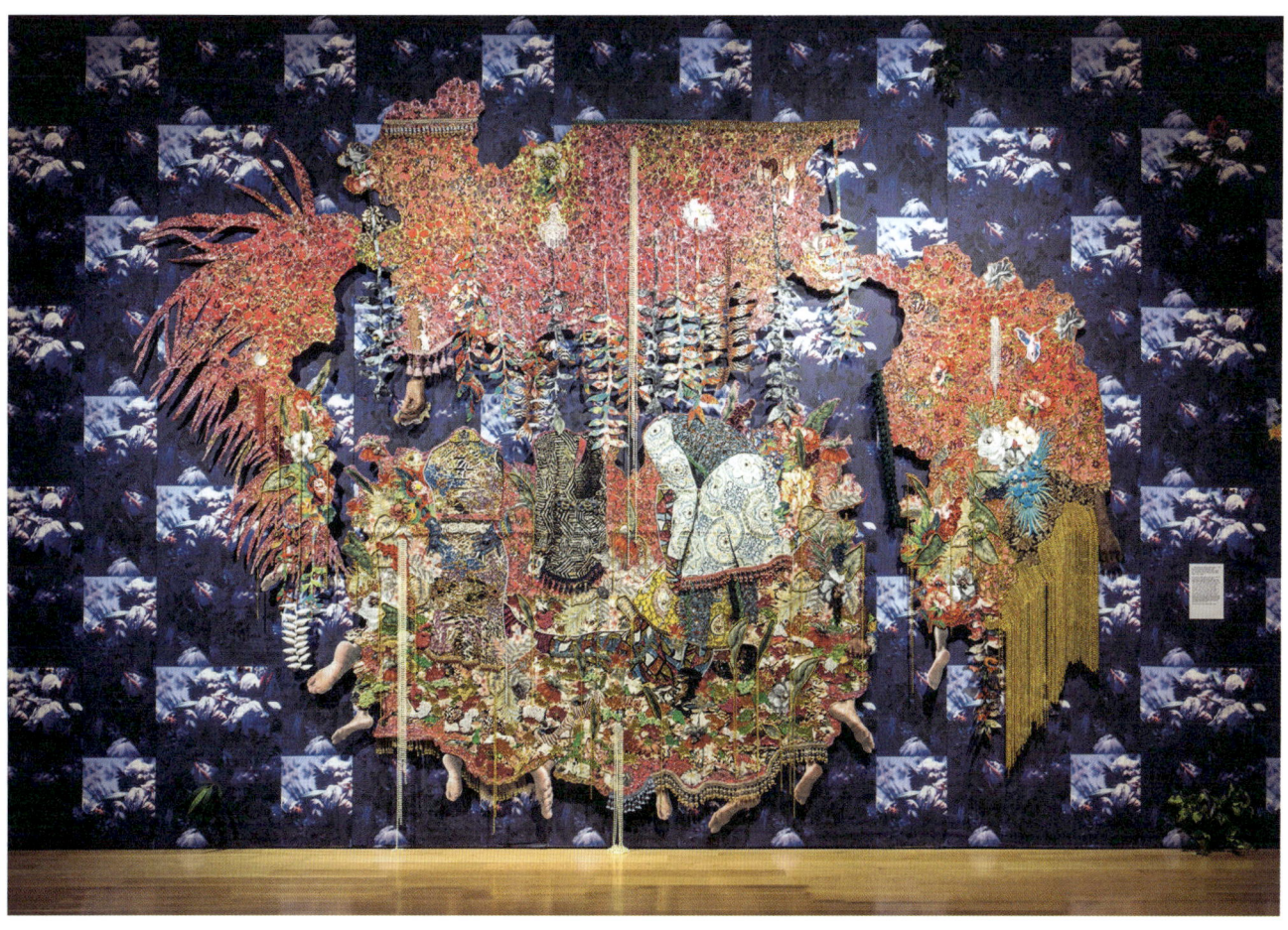

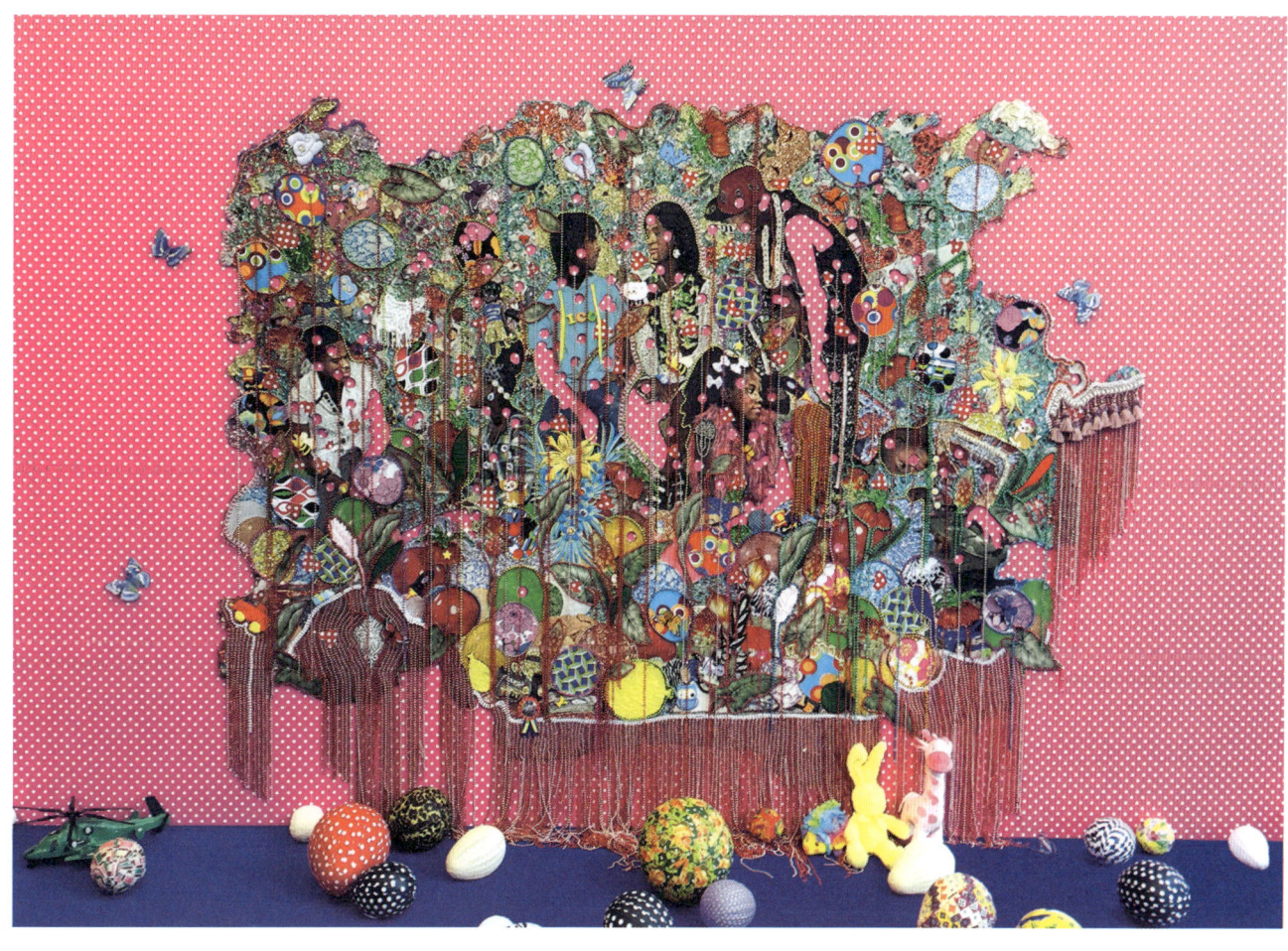

EBONY G.
PATTERSON

HEATHER PHILLIPSON

Classically trained as a pianist and violinist, and a published and award-winning poet, Heather Phillipson's career as a visual artist has united her interests in sound, language and representational imagery to great effect, winning her high-profile commissions including The Fourth Plinth in Trafalgar Square, London (2020–22), and museum exhibitions internationally. The thread that runs throughout her work is an interest in cutting up and reassembling – whether visually, in her videos and installations, or in audio form in the accompanying soundtracks and in her poetry. Describing her diverse practice in a 2014 interview with *Rhizome*, she stated, 'I think of it like a temporal collage or a physical musical composition – whether it's video editing or writing or walking between things in space, it's about the rhythm between the bits. And the bits are always colliding with or repelling or rubbing all over each other, synaesthetically.' Entering an installation by Phillipson is indeed a multisensory experience. She typically combines video, painted or printed imagery and sculptural elements that are often kinetic: either powered by motors or hanging loosely in space. One such example is *EAT HERE* (2015–16). Taking over the rotunda in Schirn Kunsthalle, Frankfurt – a 2017 *Artforum* review by Martin Herbert described how 'the minimalist atrium... never looked more maximalist' – the artist combined an existing video work with new elements to make a site-specific installation. The looped fifteen-minute, dual-screen video at its centre, *COMMISERATIONS!* (2015), is exemplary of digital collage. First shown within *un/fit 4 feeling* (2015) at the 14th Istanbul Biennial, the video – an exploration into the physiological heart as contrasted with its clichéd, symbolic representations – features images overlapping in quick succession and a soundtrack that is also layered, sampling from popular music and Phillipson's carefully performed narrations, in which word play and poetic non sequiturs drive the sequence forward. Surrounding the screens, she added a rotating Styrofoam foot, a spongy carpet, dangling black-edged cartoon drawings of spermatozoa, lightning bolts and wide-open eyes, and 'found' objects suspended on shock cords: tennis rackets and balls, hot water bottles, red stuffed waste-sacks and umbrellas. By reconfiguring older artworks to present them in different contexts, the entire installation becomes an exercise in collaging – new meanings borne of existing raw materials. In *RUPTURE NO 1: blowtorching the bitten peach* (2021), the artist's commission for the Duveen Galleries at Tate Britain, Phillipson turned her attention to wildlife and the extent to which the natural world is being critically threatened by the actions and inactions of humankind. Combining moving image, multi-channel audio, three- and two-dimensional artworks in a dense yet coherent installation, Phillipson succeeded in tackling pressing ecological issues in fresh ways. As the *Guardian* review by Adrian Searle concluded, 'this new work signals familiar concerns about the world's demise, and does so with as much inventiveness and wit as sorrow and dread. Phillipson makes catastrophe entertaining, but it is a bitter fruit.'

REBECCA MORRILL

Born 1978, London, UK. Lives in London.

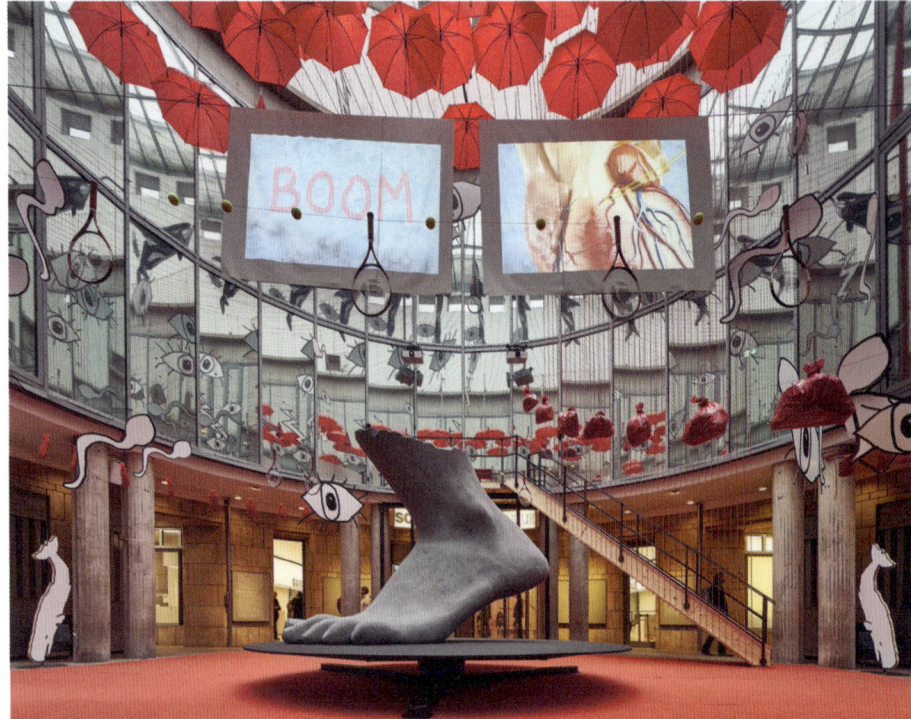

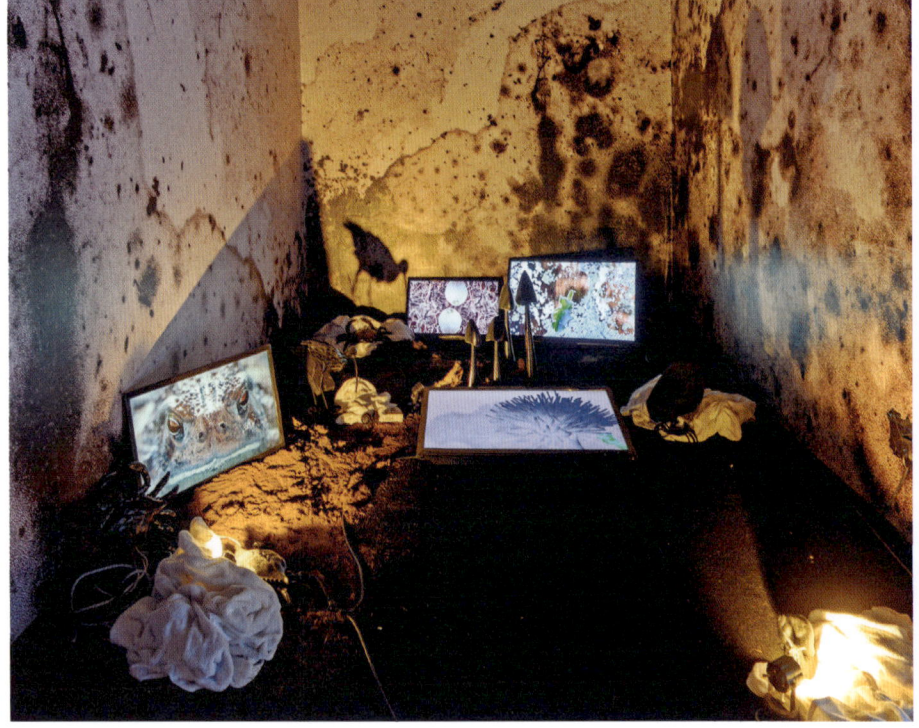

↑↑ EAT HERE, 2015–16, installation view, Schirn Kunsthalle, Frankfurt, Germany

↑ Cyclonic Palate Cleanser, 2019, installation view, 'Leaving the Echo Chamber', Sharjah Biennial 14, UAE

→ RUPTURE NO 1: blowtorching the bitten peach, 2021, installation view, Duveen Galleries commission, Tate Britain, London, UK

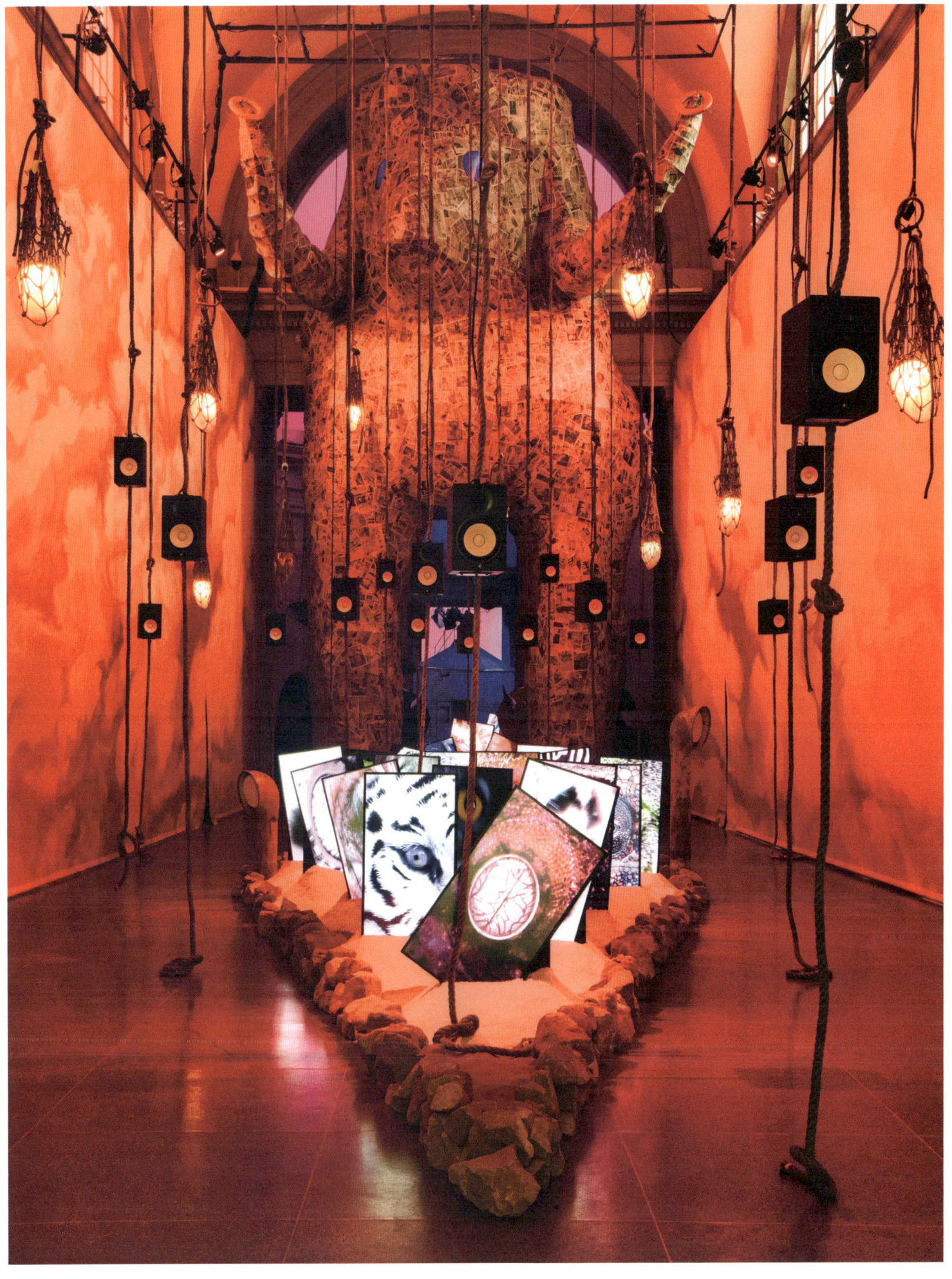

HEATHER
PHILLIPSON

PAULO NIMER PJOTA

Searching for points where the historic and contemporary come together, Paulo Nimer Pjota explains in 'Inside the Studio', a video interview of 2020, he looks 'for objects that are similar, both formally and conceptually'. This approach might be described as an investigatory collage across time, so it makes sense that he adopts collage principles in both his materials and in what he depicts. He paints on sheets of unprimed canvas and metal found on the streets of São Paulo, often pinning them together, and places objects cast in resin or bronze in front of them. Those objects play off the painted subjects and suggest a shrine of sorts. Embracing what might be considered 'high' and 'low' in the cultural mix, Pjota often combines classical artefacts with stickers, like those to be found on his local streets. In fact, he paints both – the apparent stickers with as much imitative realism as the vessels and statues. But the *trompe l'oeil* is countered in turn by a surface of scratches, dirt, footprints and splotches of paint – testament to the metal's discarded origins and the works' subsequent development on the studio floor. ◤ In *Nem Tudo Que Reluz é Ouro* (2018) – the Portuguese for 'All that glitters is not gold' – clownish sticker-faces bear witness to what appears to be a face-off between archetypal forms: Ancient Greek vases summon the history of Western civilization, African figurines evoke an alternative, chains the trauma of their combination. The gold backdrop is reserved for the African side, as if elevating its value. ◤ In the 2018 work *Jardim do Éden* (Garden of Eden), Adam and Eve appear as ancient figures who yet take on robotic qualities, while smiley stickers signal the prelapsarian condition. A row of bronze pomegranate-like pots, standing in for apples, presage the couple's fate. Pjota grew up in the Brazilian countryside and loves to travel, two factors feeding into the breadth of his references – as does music: he often takes his titles from songs, explaining on the occasion of his first solo exhibition in the UK, at Maureen Paley, London, in 2016 that 'If you think of the composition, you can imagine a rapper, sampling and repeating to produce the beat... I cut a part of the history and reproduce, cut another part and reproduce'. As curator and art historian Thierry Raspail has put it, 'in this floating, transitional space, between now and never, between what happens and what one thinks of it [Pjota] jumbles together his icons from here and elsewhere, African and Western, ancient and modern, in order to deterritorialize them.' ◤ Pjota's accumulations call to mind the surfeit of available images and information in the digital age, and the consequent impact on our identity formation, leaving the question: is he demonstrating the richness of our influences, or anatomizing the confusion their multiplicity can cause? ◣

PAUL CAREY-KENT

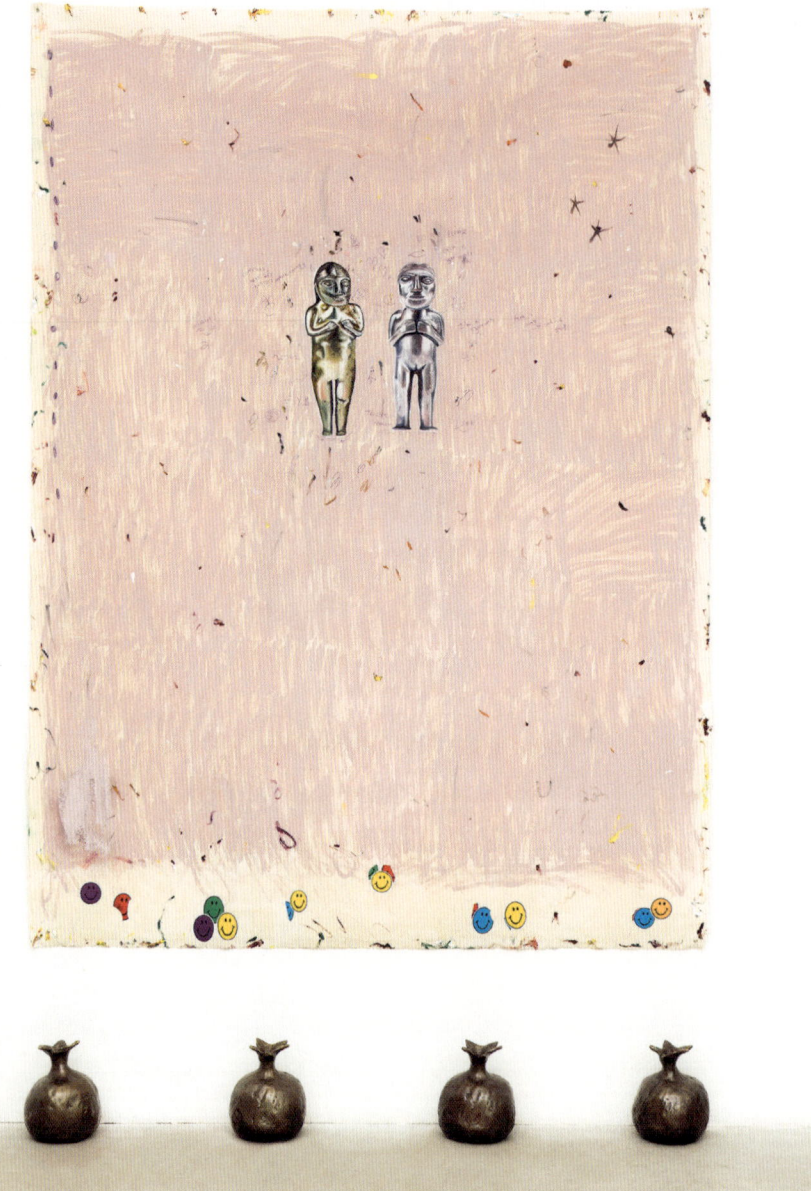

Born 1988, São José do Rio Preto, Brazil. Lives in São Paulo, Brazil.

↑   **Jardim do Éden (Garden of Eden)**, 2018, oil, acrylic and pen on canvas, 210 × 155 cm (82 ⅝ × 61 ⅛ in) + four bronze objects

→   **Ballet triadico 2 (Triadic Ballet 2)**, 2021, oil, tempera and acrylic on canvas, 260 × 210 cm (102 ⅜ × 82 ⅝ in) + iron support and bronze sculpture

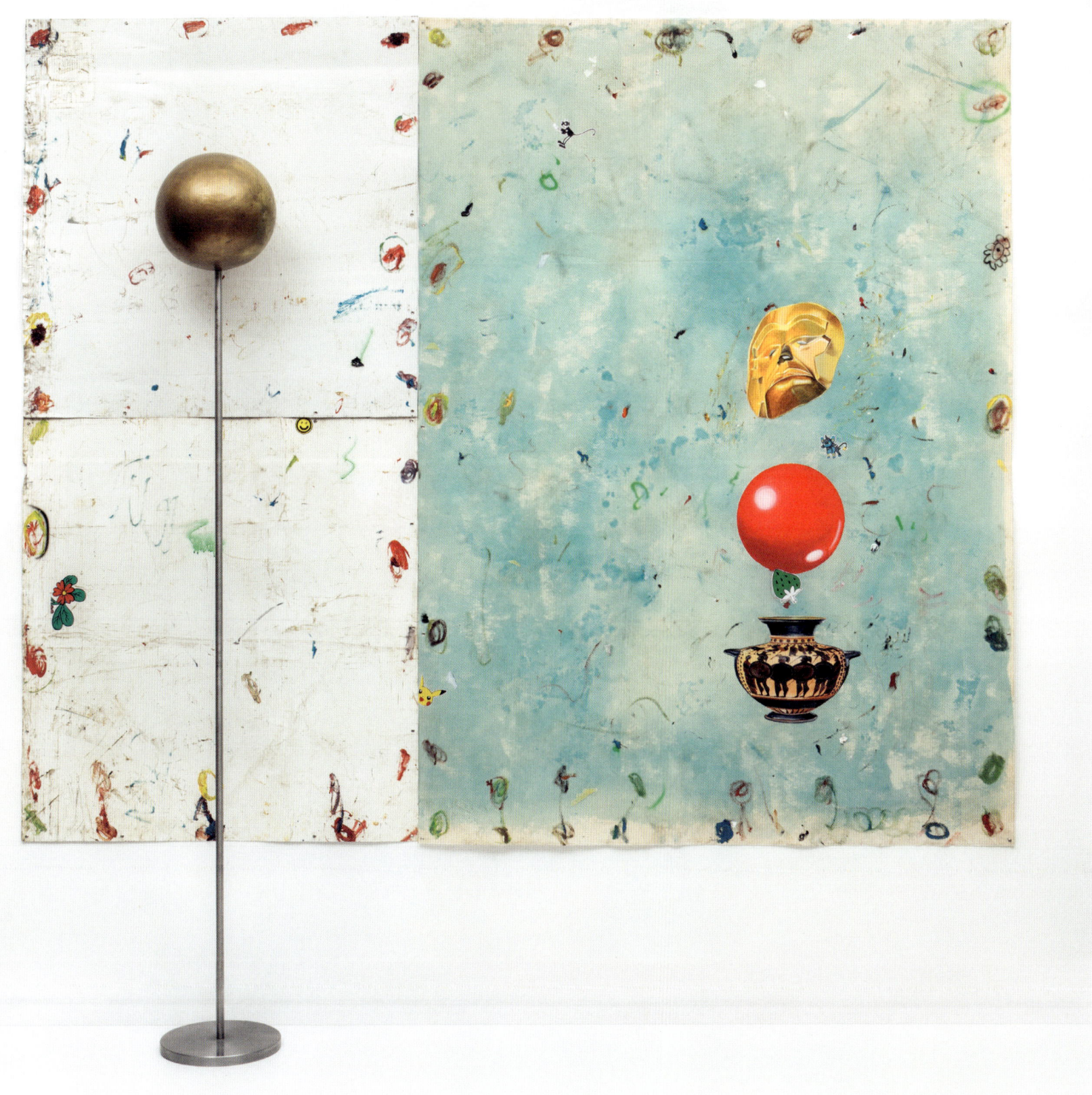

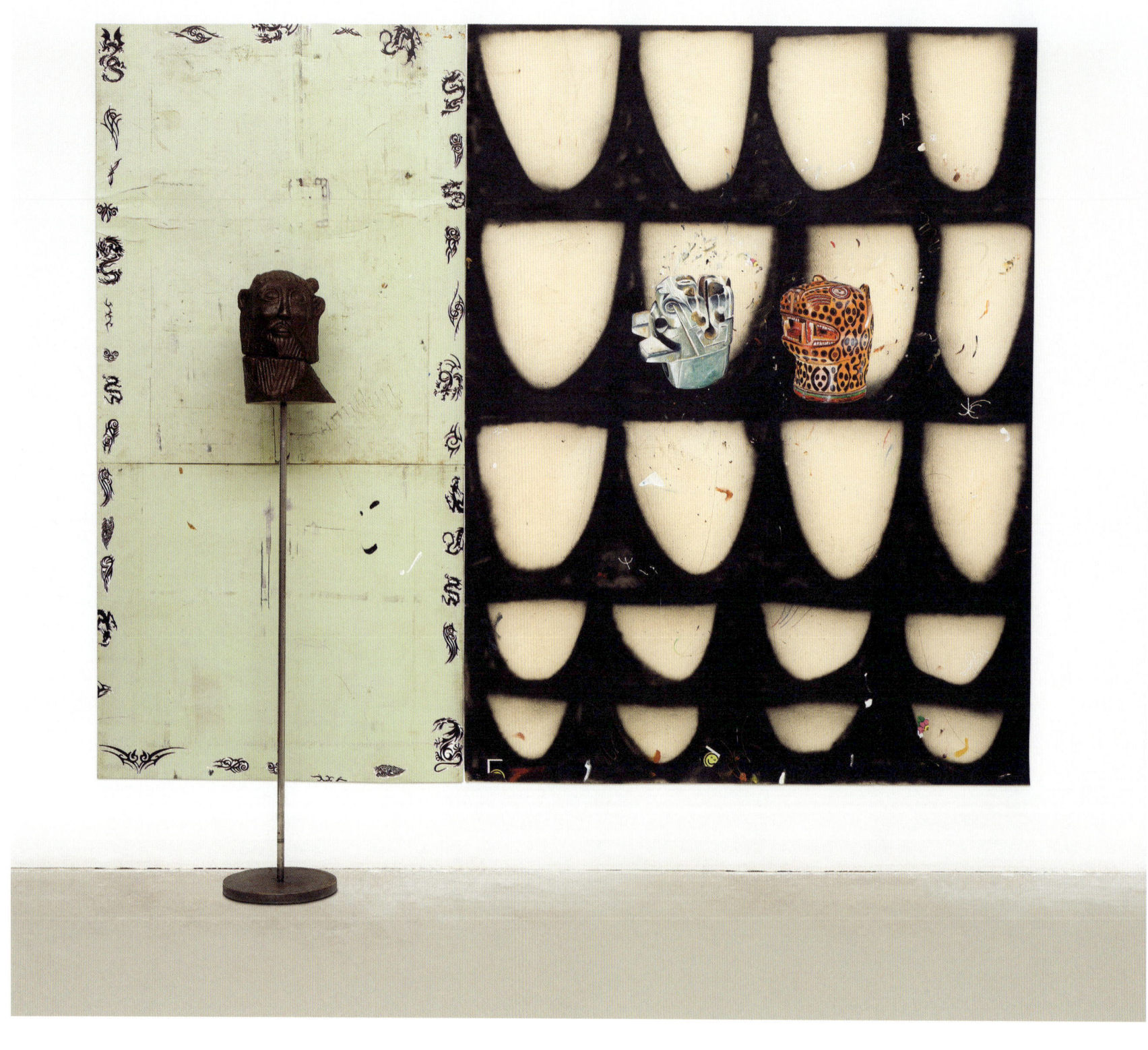

↑   **Yin Yang 2**, 2020, acrylic and oil on canvas, 201 × 256 cm (79 ⅛ × 100 ¾ in) + iron plate
    and bronze object

→   **Nem Tudo Que Reluz é Ouro (All That Glitters is Not Gold)**, 2018, oil, acrylic, pencil, pen on canvas
    and resin, 250 × 300 × 195 cm (98 ⅜ × 118 ⅛ × 72 ⅞ in)

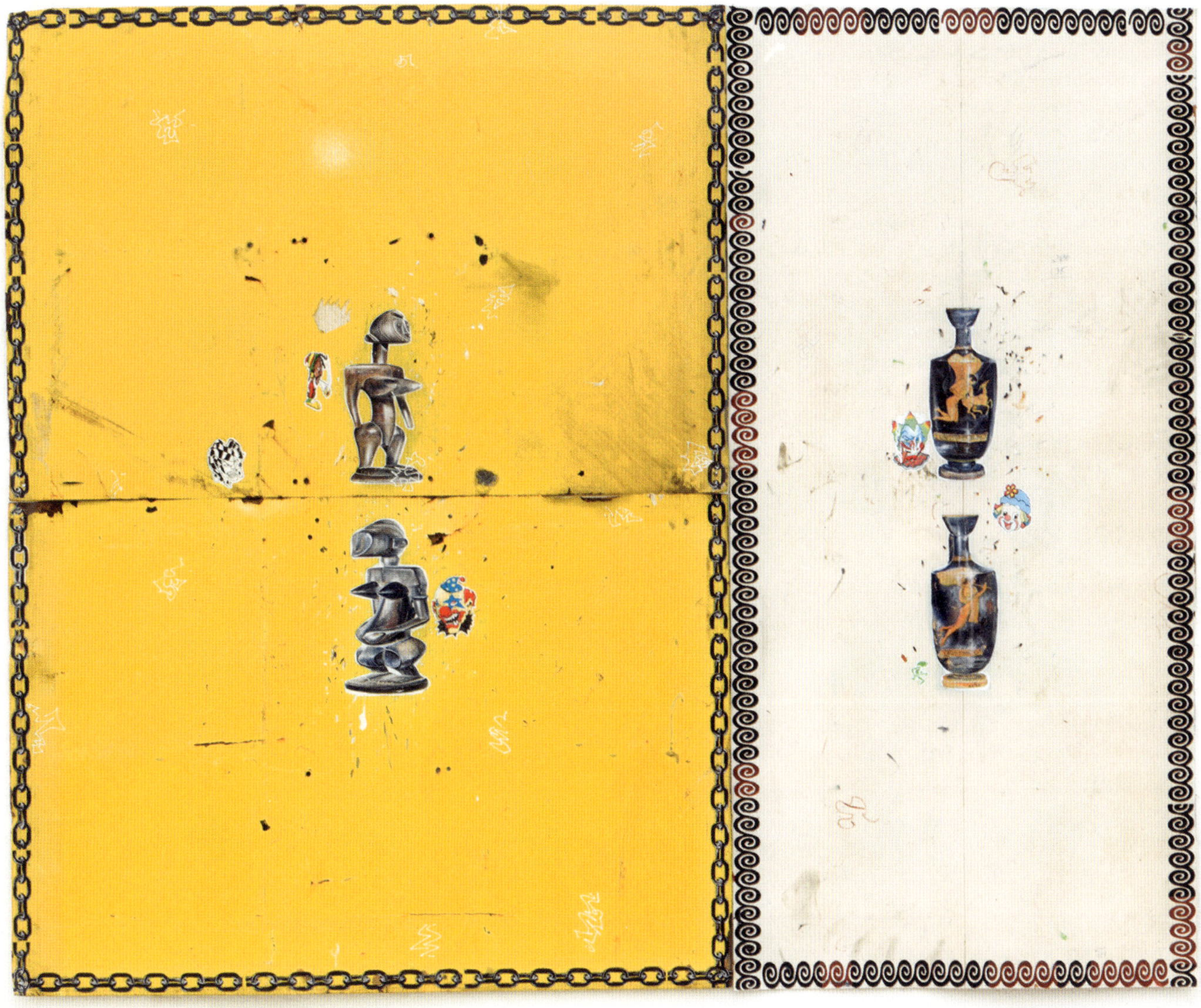

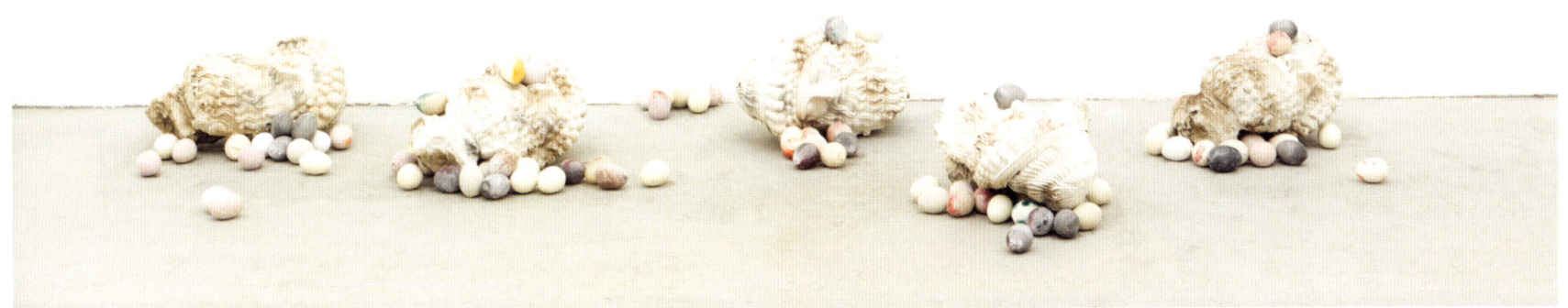

DAVID PLUNKERT

Rich, complex and filled with details, David Plunkert's collages echo the linear aesthetics and dynamic vertiginous axis typical of Constructivist art by Vladimir Tatlin (1885–1953) or Kazimir Malevich (1879–1935). This influence is evidenced in the muted colour palette that references the paper and image quality of early twentieth-century publications. Plunkert also openly acknowledges his debt to a range of groundbreaking creatives, from artists Pablo Picasso and Ben Shahn, through to graphic designers and illustrators Seymour Chwast and Paul Rand, to comic creator Jack Kirby. ■ Based on illustrations sourced from old printed publications, rather than online imagery or found photographs, Plunkert's collages are also directly informed by his passion for woodblock printing. His work frequently blends collage and drawing in seamless ways. The result is what the artist-illustrator called 'primitive pop surrealism with dust' in a 2014 interview with *designboom* – a recognizably retro aesthetic characterized by a distressed finish that evokes a veneer of historical heft. ■ For work that is going to reproduced in poster or print, Plunkert assembles and manipulates images digitally in Photoshop, while for gallery work, such as *Gentleman Monster* (2021), he tends to work directly with glue and paper, in the tradition of analogue collage. He usually mulls over ideas and begins to sketch with pen and paper until a graphic solution takes shape. As an artist working extensively in the publishing world, Plunkert regularly follows editorial briefs, so his priority is to produce memorable images that support text in creative and incisive ways rather than overpower it. As a result, his collages are bold and yet subtle, inviting keen observation while delivering swift and forceful punches. ■ A recurring theme in Plunkert's collages is the tension between the human and the machine that came to the fore in early modernist art movements such as Futurism and Vorticism but that still plays important roles in contemporary culture. As demonstrated in his 2015 'Architect' works for the American construction company Krekow Jennings, the human body appears fragmented – mechanical parts are inserted in ways that enhance human form, skills and potential. This account of modern life is deployed to great effect in the context of today's increasing mechanization and the resulting dehumanization of workers by corporations and institutions. It is therefore not a coincidence that Plunkert's men-machines should seem aloof and absent, hollowed out by the demands of a consumerist world – surrounded by a plethora of data and stimuli, a universe too complex to ever grasp fully and one that often alienates rather than enlightens. Geometric elements and diagrams intersect and connect Plunkert's cyborgs to the outside world while constellations and networks gesture towards the notion that everything, from visible matter to invisible capitalist powers, is ultimately interlinked. Often witty and sometimes sarcastic, Plunkert's collages serve as accessible social critique underpinned by political ideology. ━

GIOVANNI ALOI

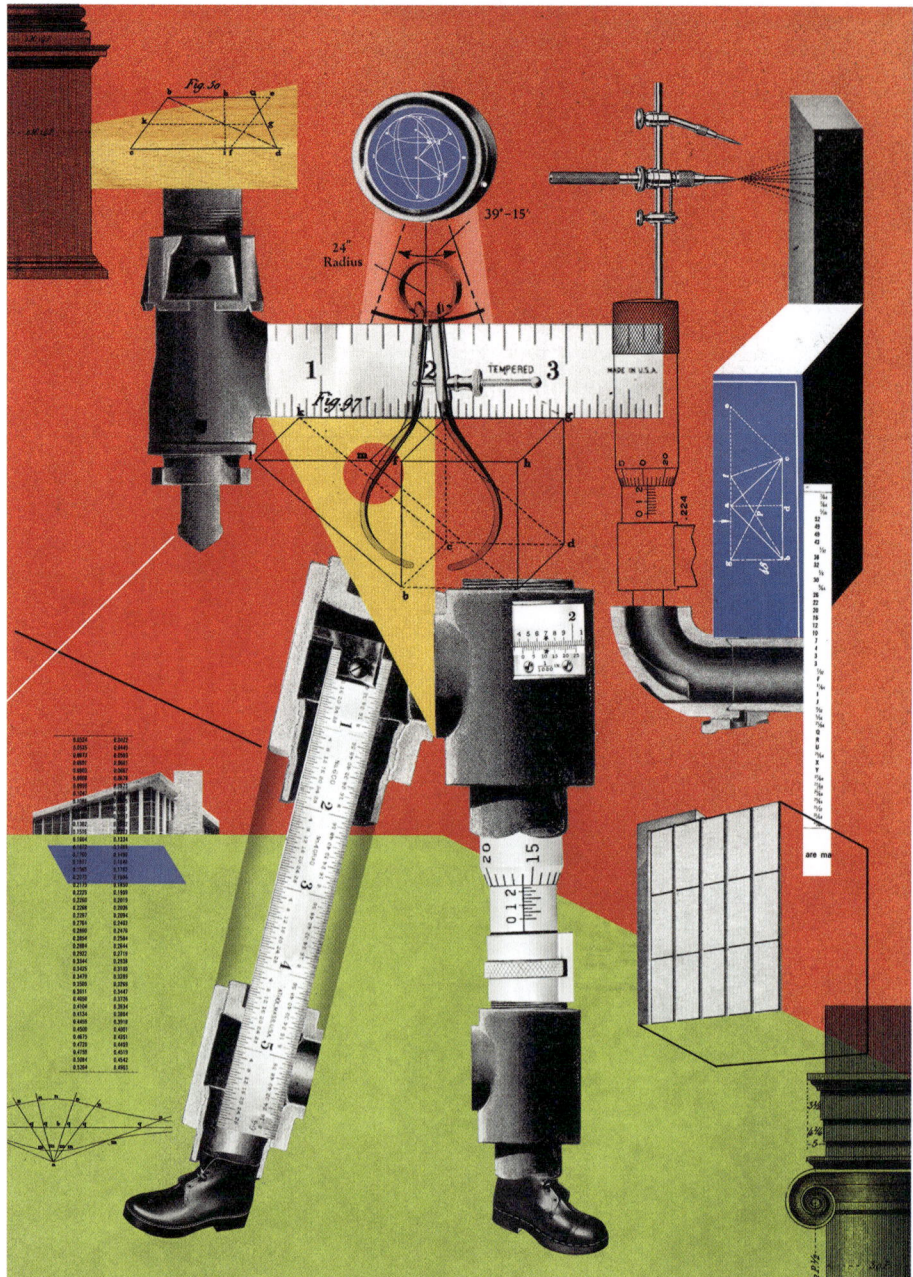

Born 1965, Frederick, Maryland, USA. Lives in Baltimore, Maryland, USA.

↑ **Architect 3**, 2015, digital mixed-media collage on paper, 38.1 × 27.9 cm (15 × 11 in), commissioned by Krekow Jennings

↗ **Architect 2**, 2015, digital mixed-media collage on paper, 38.1 × 27.9 cm (15 × 11 in), commissioned by Krekow Jennings

↗↗ **Gentleman Monster**, 2021, mixed-media paper collage with acrylic on wood panel, 61 × 45.7 cm (24 × 18 in)

→ **Looking Back**, 2020, digital mixed-media collage on paper, 101.6 × 76.2 cm (40 × 30 in)

→→ **Looking Forward**, 2020, digital mixed-media collage on paper, 101.6 × 76.2 cm (40 × 30 in)

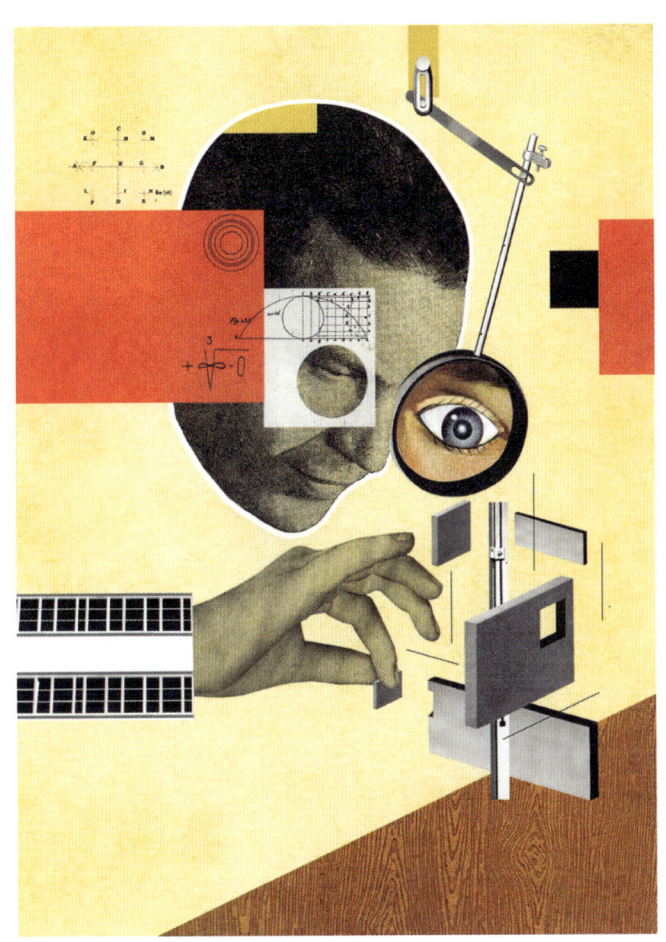
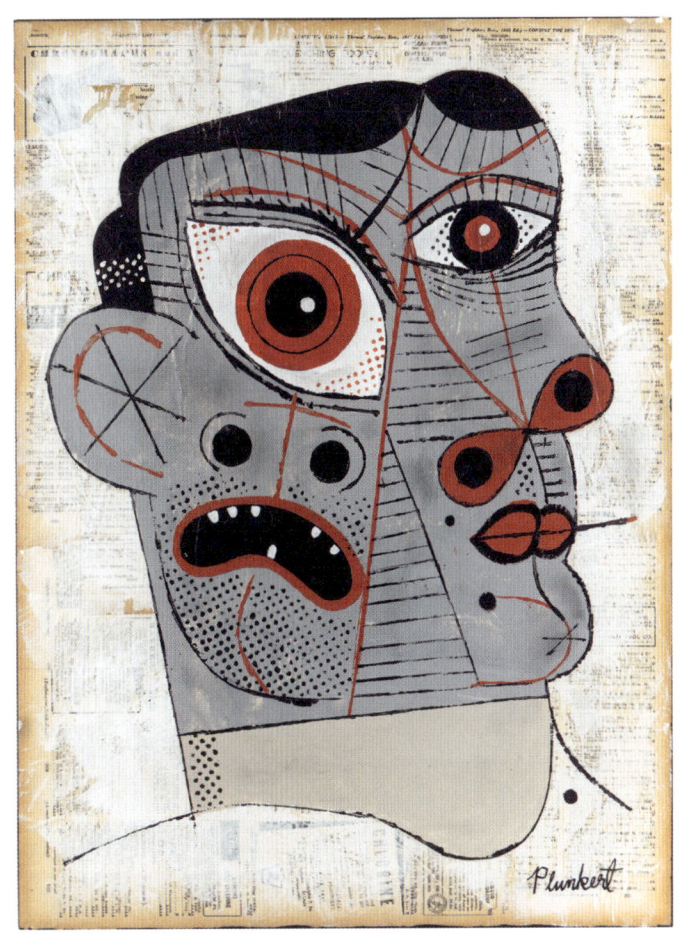
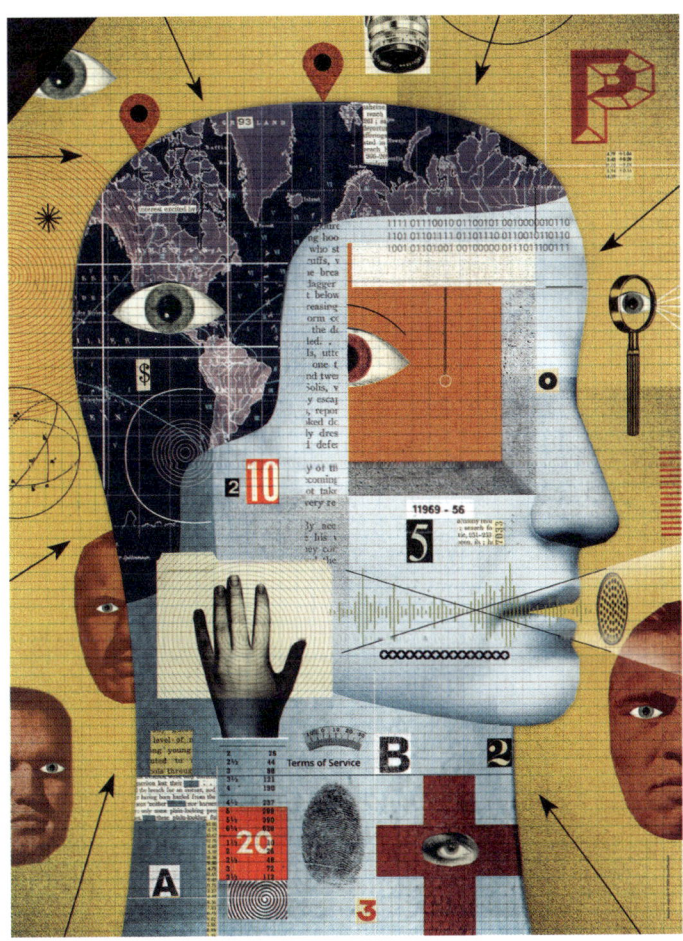
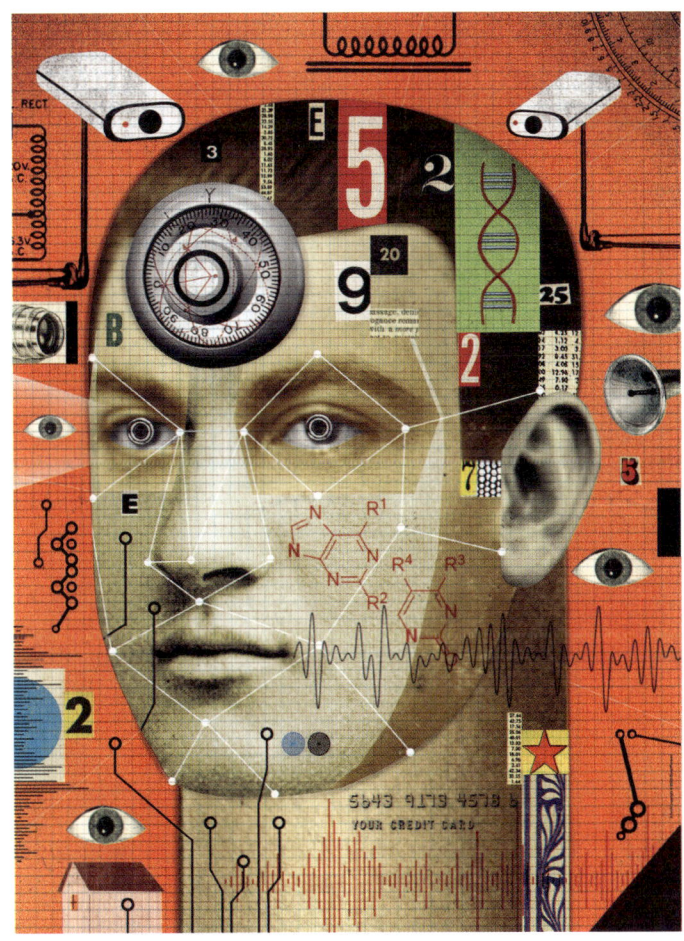

DAVID PLUNKERT

VENTURA PROFANA

The densely packed digital collages of Ventura Profana deal with the structures of patriarchal power, following a path of mass destruction that goes as far back as Babylon and continues into the present day. Fulminating against systemic dogma, doctrine and domination, collage is one of the modes Profana employs to dismantle what she depicts as closely interrelated forces, frequently using images connected to colonialism, imperialism, the military, architecture, environmental disaster and religious ceremonies. ◾ Rooted in her own experience of being raised in a Baptist family in Salvador in Bahia, Brazil during the 1990s and 2000s, Profana is preoccupied with religion – represented in her recurrent use of religious icons, symbols and figures, like the Pope who stands with his back emphatically turned to the viewer in the centre of O diabo é branco (Devil is White) (2020) observing a burning church. Other images suggest biblical-scale devastation, such as Hospital da Alma (Soul Hospital) (2020), in which scenes of floods, landfill and slums around the world swirl together in a heady, apocalyptic mix. Here, Profana plays with scale to create emotive tensions and emphasize ghoulish details: the twisted head of a broken doll floating in water looms larger than the two figures on a rescue boat. Often, by manipulating the source images taken from news reportage and documentary photography to heighten the drama and sense of widespread chaos, Profana also comments on the way collective violence against bodies becomes a form of entertainment. Among the various phallic symbols – from skyscrapers to the World Cup trophy – that appear in A Nova Era (The New Age) (2020) is a single plunging body, recognizable from The Falling Man (2001), a much reproduced image by photojournalist Richard Drew (b.1946) who captured a figure falling head first from the World Trade Center on 9/11. ◾ While critiquing the politics of the conservative Neo-Pentecostal Church and its particular influence within Brazil remains a fundamental part of Profana's ongoing research – which extends into performances, actions, music, installation, video and her spiritual practice as a missionary pastor – her collages also focus on other global faiths. In Concílio das Lamentações (Council of Lamentations) (2020) parallels between religious gatherings are explored through symmetries: the concentric circles of praying pilgrims at Mecca, mirroring a stadium below; clusters of bodies gathering at Jerusalem's Wailing Wall, juxtaposed with those visiting the holy site of Lalibela, Ethiopia. Despite the salient motifs of carnage and collapse, Profana refers to her collages in a 2021 video for the PIPA Prize as 'antidotes for a poison that is colonial'. As a Black trans woman, as an artist and as a pastor, Profana's concern is to prophesize, using the medium of collage and its implicit process of reconstitution to signal the end of the white, cisgender supremacy, projecting visions of a future in which non-conforming bodies are at the centre, or as the artist explains it 'to ensure fullness in dissident life, in trans life, in Black life'. ◾

CHARLOTTE JANSEN

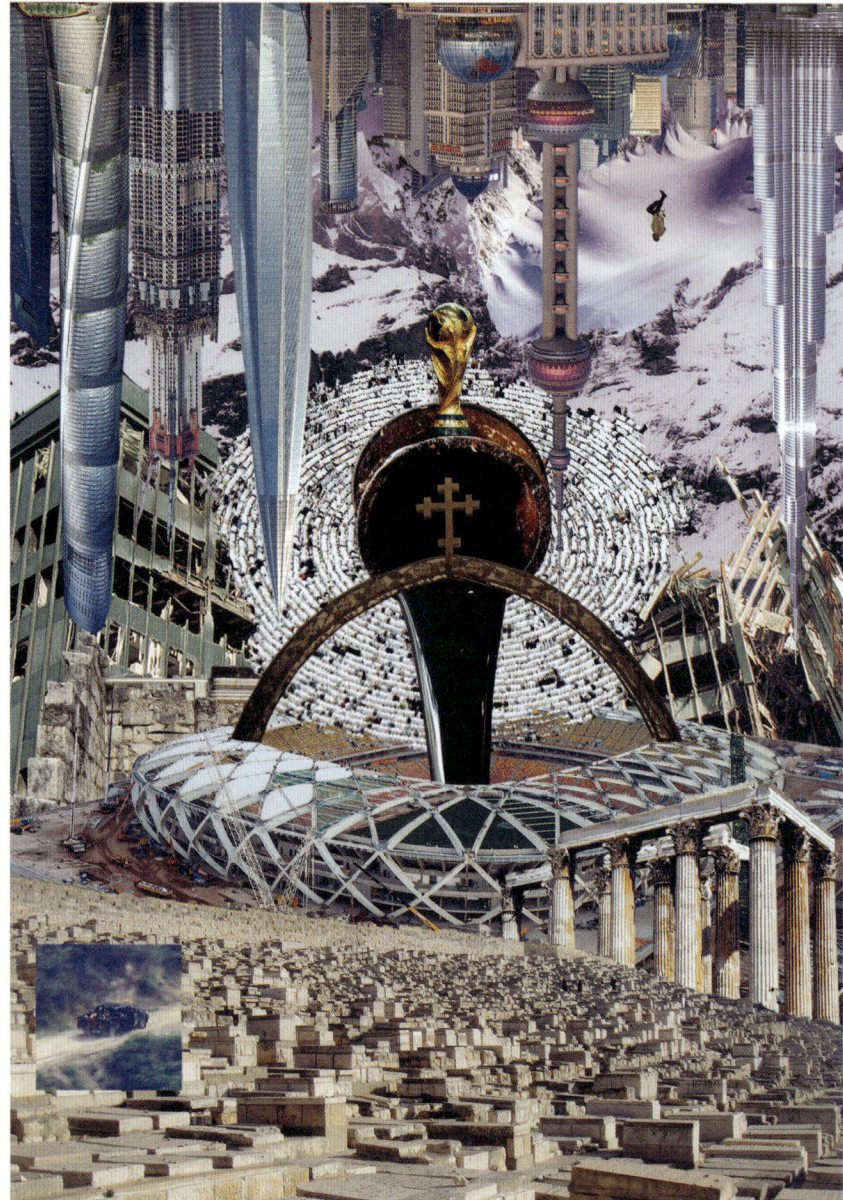

Born 1993, Salvador, Bahia, Brazil. Lives in Salvador.

↑ **A Nova Era (The New Age)**, from the series 'Sonda', 2020, digital collage, pigment printing (Canon Lucia Pró) on 200 gsm Hahnemühle Photo Matt Fibre paper, dark wood frame, with withdrawal, standard glass, chassis bottom and collage on PVC, 140 × 100 cm (55⅛ × 39⅜ in), commissioned by Instituto Moreira Salles, Bela Vista, São Paulo, Brazil

→ **Hospital da Alma (Soul Hospital)**, from the series 'Sonda', 2020, digital collage, pigment printing (Canon Lucia Pró) on 200 gsm Hahnemühle Photo Matt Fibre paper, dark wood frame, with withdrawal, standard glass, chassis bottom and collage on PVC, 110 × 70 cm (43¼ × 27½ in), commissioned by Instituto Moreira Salles, Bela Vista, São Paulo, Brazil

↗ **O diabo é branco (Devil is White)**, 2020, digital collage, pigment printing (Canon Lucia Pró) on 200 gsm Hahnemühle Photo Matt Fibre paper, dark wood frame, with withdrawal, standard glass, chassis bottom and collage on PVC, 110 × 70 cm (43¼ × 27½ in), commissioned by Instituto Moreira Salles, Bela Vista, São Paulo, Brazil

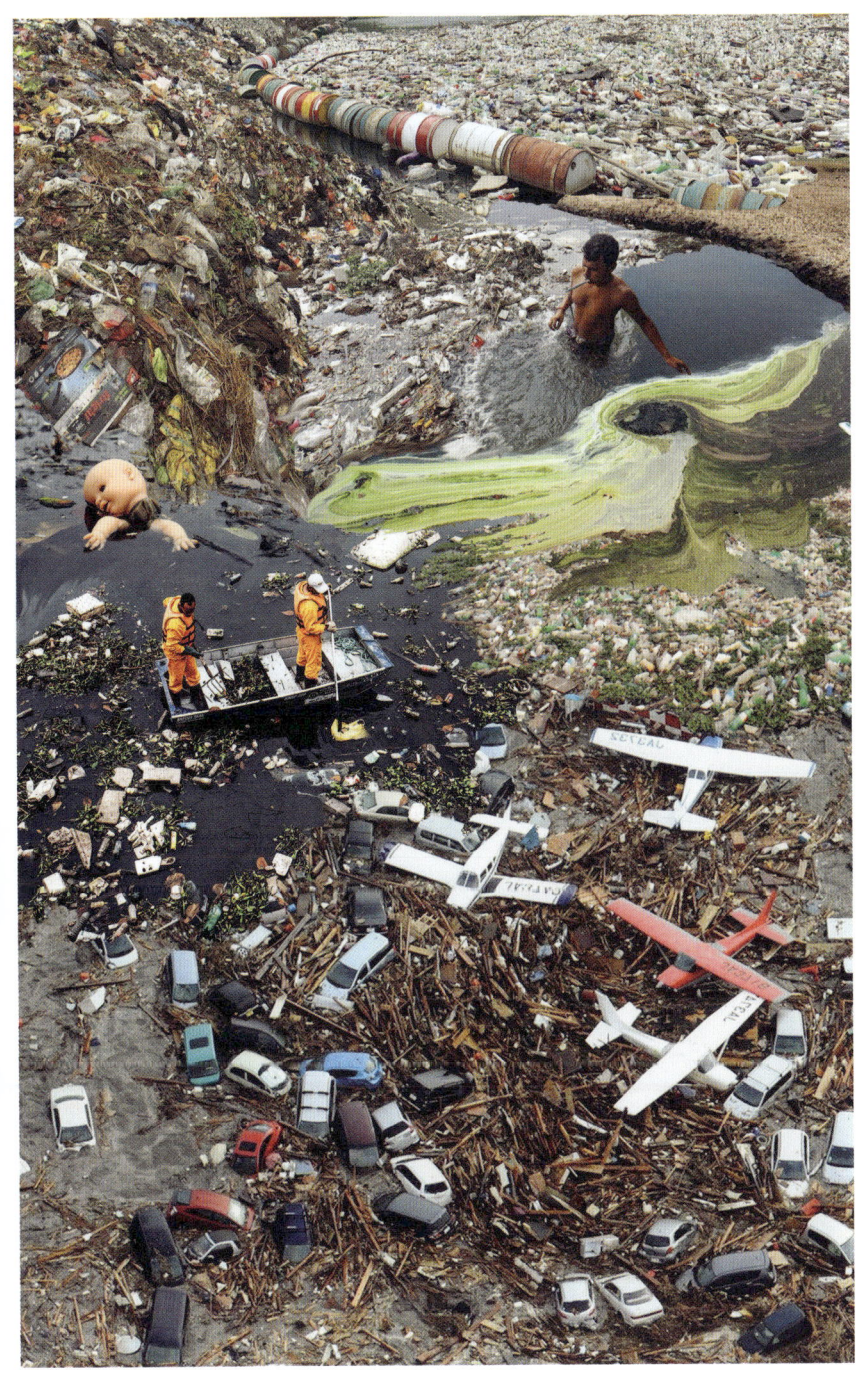

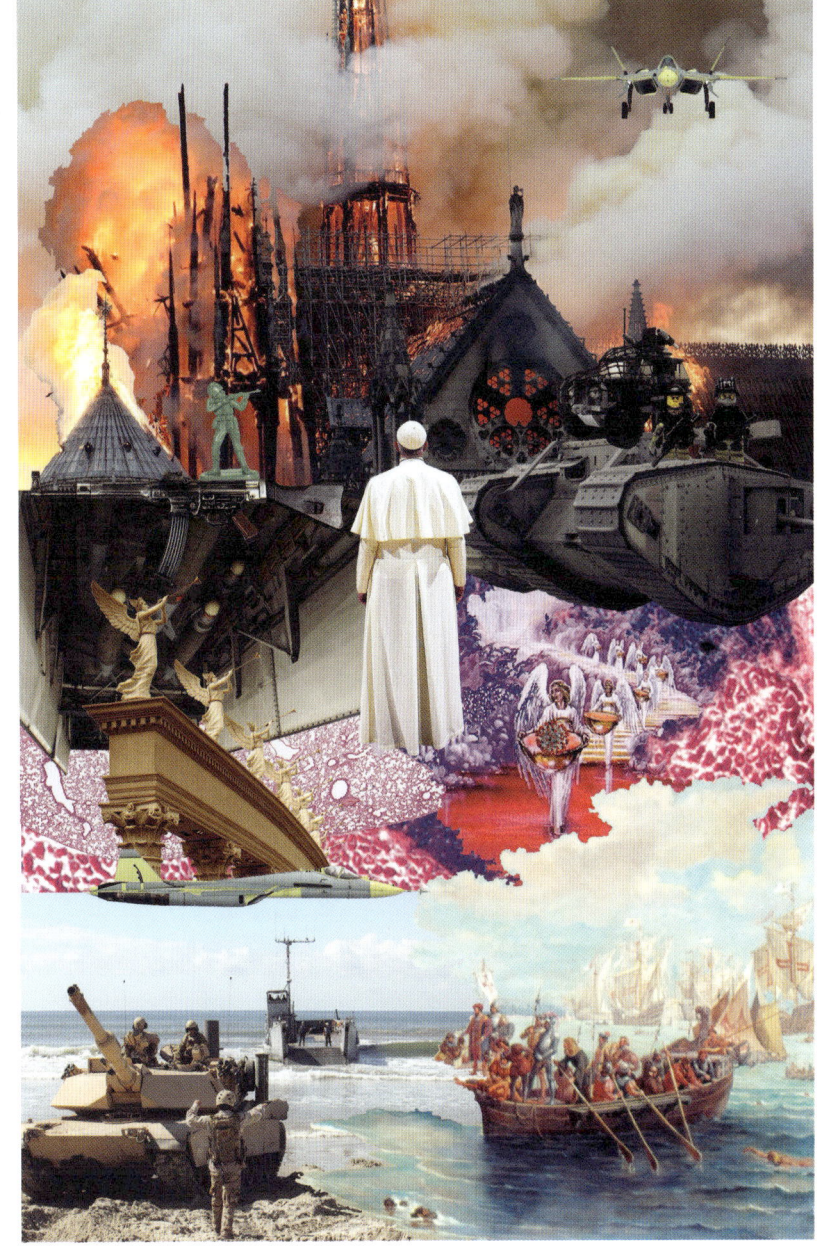

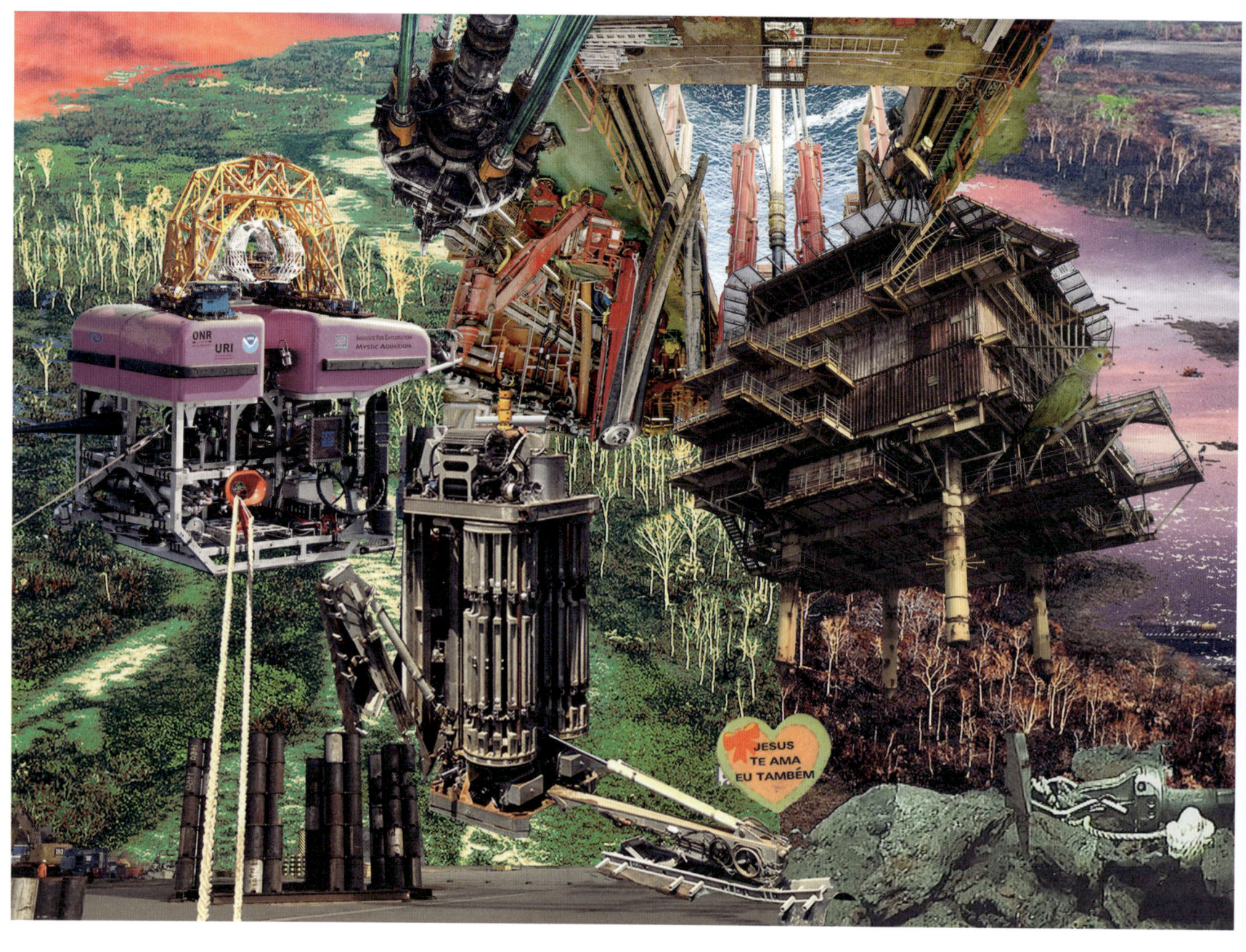

JESUS
TE AMA
EU TAMBÉM

↑   Ainda Que eu Ande pelo Mortífero Vale da Luz (Even though I walk through the deadly valley
    of light), 2021, digital collage, pigment printing on 350 gsm Hahnemühle Museum Etching paper, dark
    wood frame, with withdrawal, standard glass, chassis bottom and collage on aluminium, 60 × 110 cm
    (23 ⅝ × 43 ¼ in)

→   Concílio das Lamentações (Council of Lamentations), from the series 'Sonda', 2020, digital collage,
    pigment printing (Canon Lucia Pró) on 200 gsm Hahnemühle Photo Matt Fibre paper, dark wood frame,
    with withdrawal, standard glass, chassis bottom and collage on PVC, 140 × 100 cm (55 ⅛ × 39 ⅜ in),
    commissioned by Instituto Moreira Salles, Bela Vista, São Paulo, Brazil

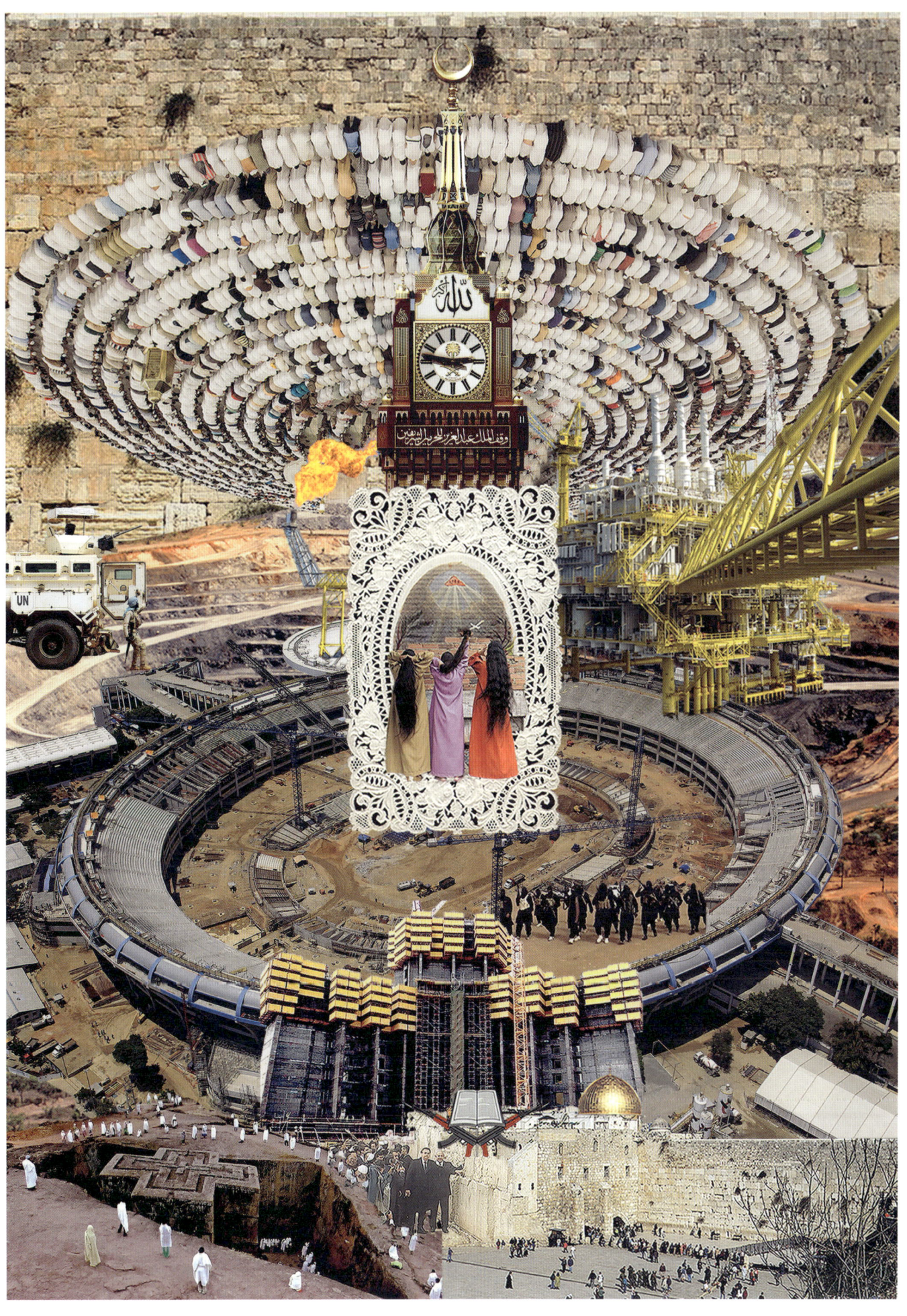

VENTURA
PROFANA

WALID RAAD

Often taking a conceptual approach to his work, Walid Raad demonstrates how collage makes the unthinkable possible and reveals cultural processes with a potency other media cannot match. Why is Margaret Thatcher's face glued to the daisy-like flower *Anacyclus* – an aphrodisiac plant said to enhance male virility? This image is part of *Plate 94* in the artist's collage series titled 'Better be watching the clouds', later remade as prints (2000/2017). It was produced for a fictional archive called 'The Atlas Group' – a project that ran between 1989 and 2004 – which comprised films, notebooks, diaries, photographs and artworks related to the Lebanese Civil War. ▪ This series uses re-envisioned pages from a photographic herbarium of native Middle Eastern flora. The headshots of local and international politicians involved in the Lebanese Civil War that took place between 1975 and 1990, resulting in an estimated 120,000 deaths, are glued at the centre of each flower – an incongruous juxta-position that produces an alternative kind of natural order. The images are accompanied by a (fictional) text, also written by Raad, which explains how the original plates were donated to the archive by a retired Lebanese Army officer, and trained botanist, called Fadwa Hassoun. According to the story, the country's intelligence department asked Hassoun to code-name military and political leaders according to the local flora. This system would allow residents to safely plot against them, undetected. ▪ The collages in this series of over 300 plates have a formulaic approach: the headshots are always black and white, so as to highlight their extraneity from the colourful vegetation, and each carefully retains the Latin name of the species and details the areas in which they grow. The artist's intervention is limited and restrained in order to retain a sense of dry wit and incisiveness. Given that his practice is concerned with physical and psychological violence perpetrated by military and political attacks that change the course of history, Raad's flowers ultimately raise important questions about national identity and question what is even native in the first place. The actions of military and political leaders impact the local land, peoples and ecosystems in irreversible ways, leaving indelible marks and forever changing the course of events. Their influence becomes part of the new nature that has replaced the local past, one that is imbedded in the indigenous wild vegetation. ▪ Another series of seven collages entitled 'We have never been so populated' (1997/2020) pictures ducks, chickens and pigeons as potential military weapons. The accompanying text explains how during the Lebanese wars, a right-wing Christian militia attempted (but ultimately failed) to breed species of invasive birds that would be sent to decimate the ecosystem of the enemies' territories. These simple and yet politically charged collages bring into question the very essence of history as a form of naturalized storytelling. What is objective and what is subjective? What happened and what didn't? ▪

GIOVANNI ALOI

Born 1967, Chbaniyeh, Lebanon. Lives in Beirut, Lebanon and New York, USA.

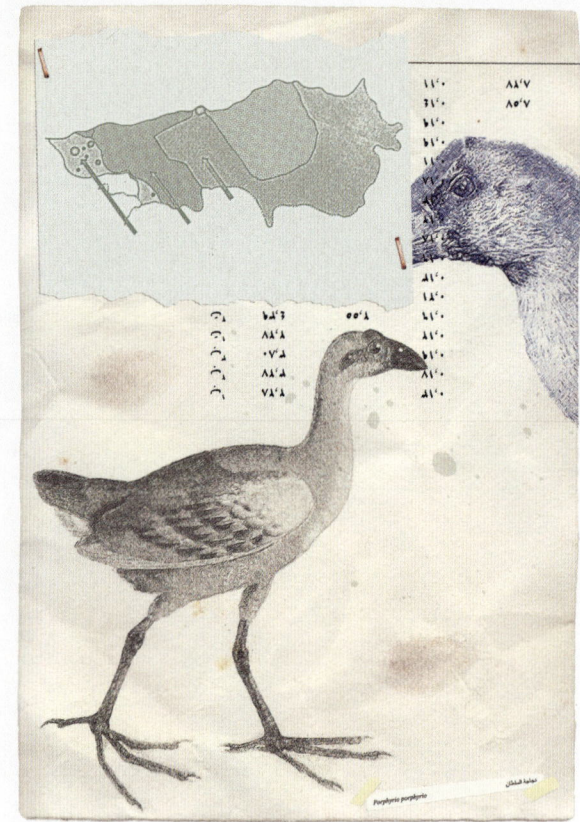

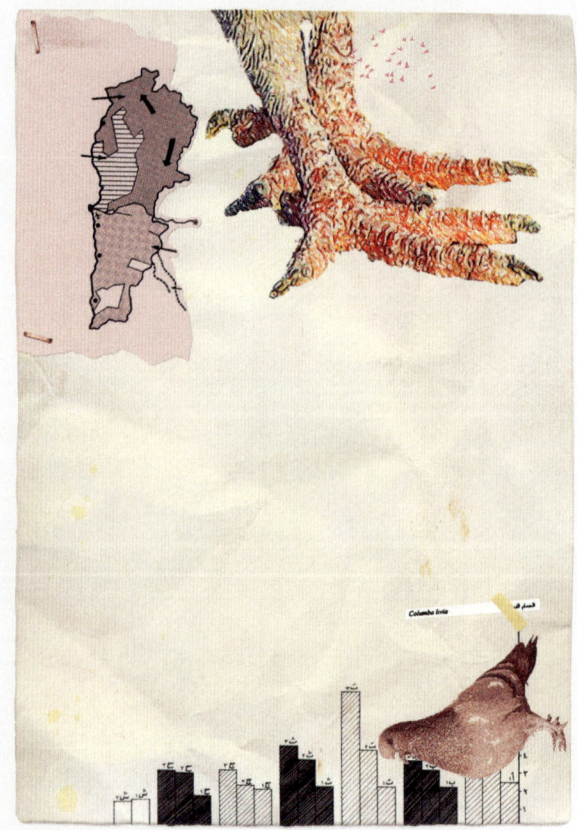

↑↑ We have never been so populated _Plate II, 1997/2020
↑ We have never been so populated _Plate III, 1997/2020
Both archival inkjet prints, each 82.2 × 58.7 cm (32⅜ × 23⅛ in)
↗ Better be watching the clouds_Plate 345, 2000/2017
↗↗ Better be watching the clouds_Plate 328, 2000/2017
→ Better be watching the clouds_Plate 339, 2000/2017
→→ Better be watching the clouds_Plate 94, 2000/2017
All pigmented inkjet prints, each 76.2 × 50.8 cm (30 × 20 in)

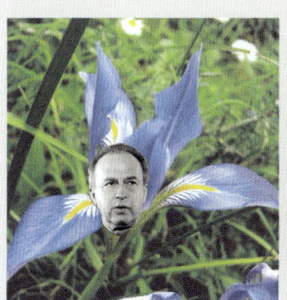

▲ *Iris unguicularis cretensis* (Janka) Mair. **Aandqet, Qoubaïyat, Akkar el-Aatiqa**. Woodland. EMR.
Cretan iris. IRIS DE CRÈTE. سوسن كريت

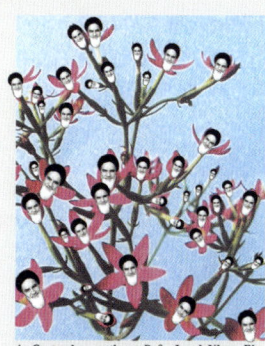

▲ *Romulea bulbocodium* (L.) Seb. & Mauri. **Sannine, Hamat, Qssaybeh, Aammiq, Kfar-houneh, Tawmat, Mlikh**. Various habitats.
Crocus-leaved romulea.
ROMULÉE BULBOCODE. حرملة

▼ *Romulea columnae* Seb. & Mauri. **Bintael, < Beit-Méri**. Woodland (altitude 550 m).
Sand crocus.
ROMULÉE DE COLUMNA. رومولية الرمل
A rigid tunic, spitted, with 2 bracts, downy bract.

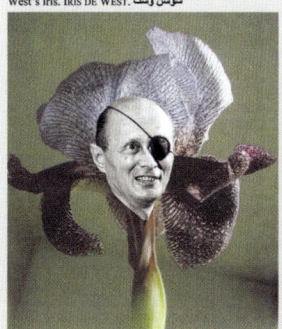

▼ *Iris westii* Dinsm. **Towmat Jezzine**. Rocky slopes.
End (Leb).
West's iris. IRIS DE WEST. سوسن وست

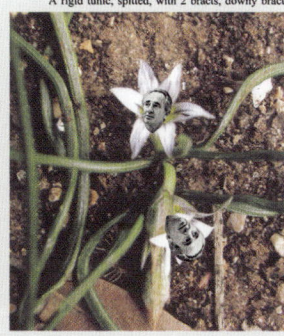

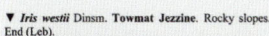

▲ *Centaurium erythraea* Rafn, **Jourd Njass, Eh-den, Harissa, Ras-el-Metn, Souq el-Gharb, Qoussaybeh, Aanout, Kfarfalous**. Woodland.
Common centaury.
PETITE-CENTAURÉE COMMUNE. قطريون شعر
Quadrangular stem branched at the top 20-60 cm;

▲ *Centaurium pulchellum* (Sw.) Druce, **Nakhl, Bqaakafra, Dbayeh, Bkhochtay, Boutmeh, Qlaiaa, Hasbaya**. Wet places.
Pretty centaury.
PETITE-CENTAURÉE ÉLÉGANTE. قطرانية
Branched stem ± quadrangular.

▼ *Centaurium spicatum* (L.) Fritsch, **Nakhl, Aamchit**.
Seashore.
Spiked centaury.
PETITE-CENTAURÉE EN ÉPI. حشيشة العطرب
Quadrangular in scarce spikes.

▼ *Centaurium maritimum* (L.) Fritsch, **Qoussay-beh**. Humid sandstones.
Sea centaury.
PETITE-CENTAURÉE MARITIME. قطريون بحري
Quadrangular stem sometimes simple.

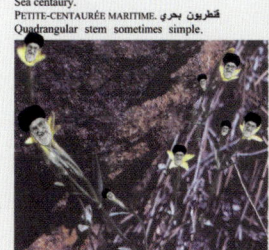
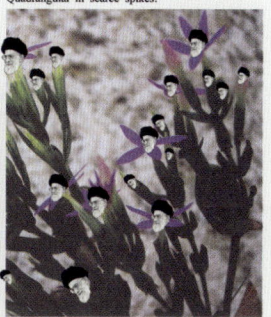

IRIDACEAE Hardy plant with underground stems, rhizomes, tubers or bulbs; 3 petals and 3 sepals with same colour, (tepal is an organ of perianth in which there is no difference between calyx and corolla) 3 stamens, 1 style, 3 stigmata, flowers often with enveloping bract.

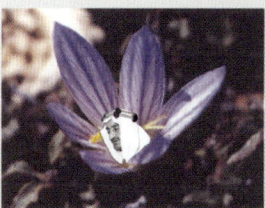

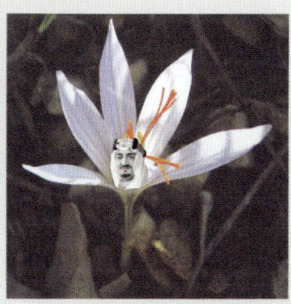

▲ *C. cancellatus damascenus* (Herb.) Mout. **Yanta, Qamouaa el-Hermel**. Dry places, mountains. EMR.
Damascus netted crocus.
CROCUS DE DAMAS EN TREILLIS. زعفران شبكي شامي
Dark tuber tunics are all lignified and thick.
▼ *Crocus graveolens* Boiss.& Reuter, **Beit Lahia, Yammouneh, Aabdine, Aalmane, Deir el Mouk-hallès, Ibl es-Saqi** Various grounds. EMR.
Heavy-scented crocus.
CROCUS À ODEUR FORTE. زعفران أبو ريحة
Membranous, brown tuber tunics, slightly dissected

▲ *C. cancellatus cilicicus* (Ky) Mouterde, **Qornet es-Saouda, Aabdine, Hasroun**. High mountains. EMR.
Cilician netted crocus.
CROCUS DE CILICIE EN TREILLIS. زعفران شبكي قيليقي

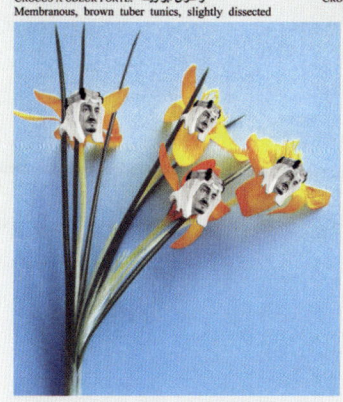

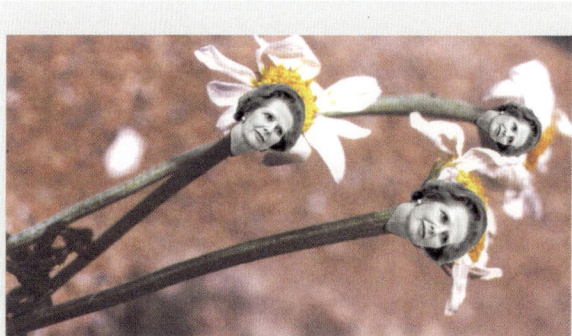

▲ *Anacyclus clavatus* (Desf.) Pers. **Aayha, Hasbaya, Nahr-Ibrahim**. Cultivated and naturalized.
Club-shaped anacyclus. ANACYCLE EN MASSUE. بيسوم
Pubescent plant, 20-40 cm; oblong, divided leaves; outer achenes with short auricles. Fl: 4-5.

▼ *Andryala integrifolia* L. **Aaramoun**. Fields.
Entire-leaved andryala.
ANDRYALE À FEUILLES ENTIÈRES. أندريالة كاملة الورق
Greyish, pubescent plant, 20-60 cm; rough pappus; disk holds bristles. Fl: 4-6.

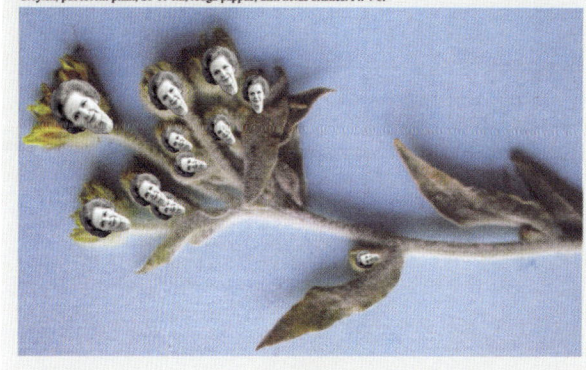

WALID
RAAD

TABITA
REZAIRE

Imaginative, celestial, environmental, spiritual, post-digital and humane, anarchic in assembly and in dissemination, Tabita Rezaire's collages appear as if a computer key has been pressed to automate an algorithm; however, they are deeply considered arrangements that speak to important issues. As in her wider practice that includes films, installations and performances, her collages cover themes relating to the ongoing legacies of patriarchy and colonialism. This includes what she frequently describes, speaking of the digital realm, as 'electronic colonialism'; the loss of ancestral knowledge; the deepening environmental crisis; the power imbalance between the Global North and South; and racism. Wellbeing is central to her vision, as she seeks out ways to heal the symptoms of our time by linking into knowledge and sources of experience that resist Western Enlightenment reductivism. She takes an intersectional position, is critical of the Anthropocene and embodies her own subject matter: she is a healer, yoga teacher and is currently training to be a farmer.

Rezaire centres the female experience, as reflected in *Sugar Walls Teardom* (2016) which includes an installation, film and digital collage prints that feature representations of the womb in the cut-and-paste style of internet aesthetics. The work examines the institutionalized and often violent use of women's bodies in medical and scientific research (historic and current). Rezaire explained in an online interview with Jack Radley for Berlin Art Link (2018): 'During slavery, Black womxn's bodies have been used and abused as commodities for laborious work in plantations, sexual slavery, reproductive exploitation and medical experiments.' Her intention is to give visibility, and in some instances names, to the women as an acknowledgement of their contribution, highlighting that still today Black women are excluded from discourses on the advancements of scientific, technological and medical knowledge. Shifting the gaze onto herself, the 'INNER FIRE' series comprises five collaged lifesize digital self-portraits that create archetypes of Black women, speaking to Rezaire's own experience of the aspirational and contradictory ideals around her identity. Each points to a different theme within her work, including anti-capitalism as seen in *INNER FIRE: BBHMM* (2016), with race, sex, spirituality and technology interwoven into the ideological systems of the compositions and the artist's body as a metaphor for resistance. The component parts of the collages are situated in an otherworldly digitized space, as with the majority of Rezaire's works, a mechanism that asks the viewer to look and interpret untethered from Western logic and framing. Rezaire's artistic practice allows for the possibilities of what Black identities and lives could be, while also revealing stereotypes and historical violations. The artworks we see are only one part of her creative life, which includes carrying out extensive research, self-training and creating networks with others. Hers is the kind of art-making – involving intellectual and emotional labour – that seeks to make real change in the world.

HABDA RASHID

Born 1989, Paris, France. Lives in Cayenne, French Guiana.

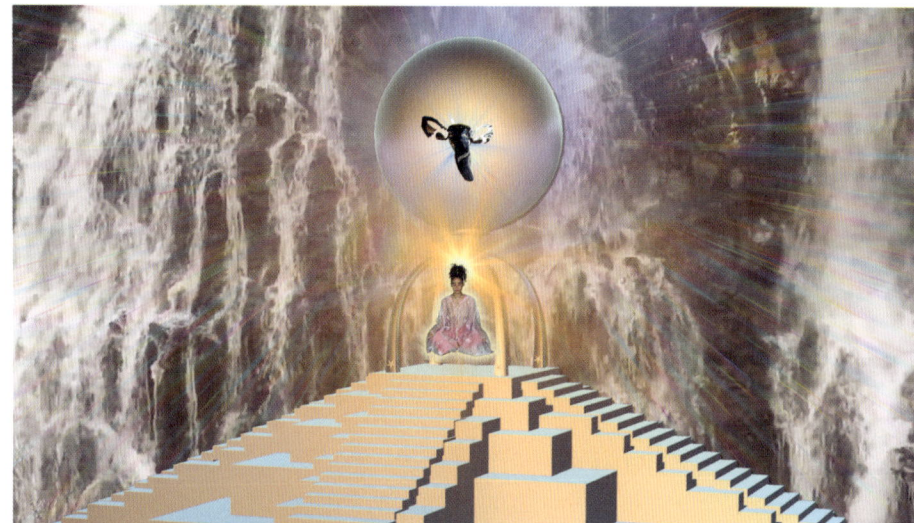

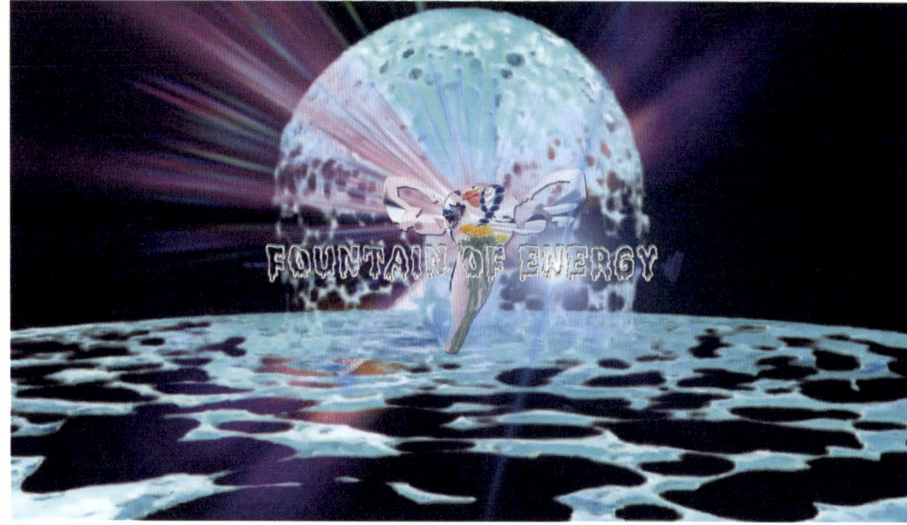

↑   Sugar Walls Teardom, 2016, stills from HD video – installation also includes gynaecological chair and mechanical arm, overall 218 × 162 × 85 cm (85¾ × 63¾ × 33½ in), edition of 3

↗   INNER FIRE: Pimp your Brain, 2017, Diasec print, 168.5 × 98.5 cm (66⅜ × 38¾ in), edition of 5

↗↗   INNER FIRE: BBHMM, 2016, Diasec print, 170 × 100 × 3.5 cm (66⅞ × 39⅜ × 1⅛ in), edition of 5

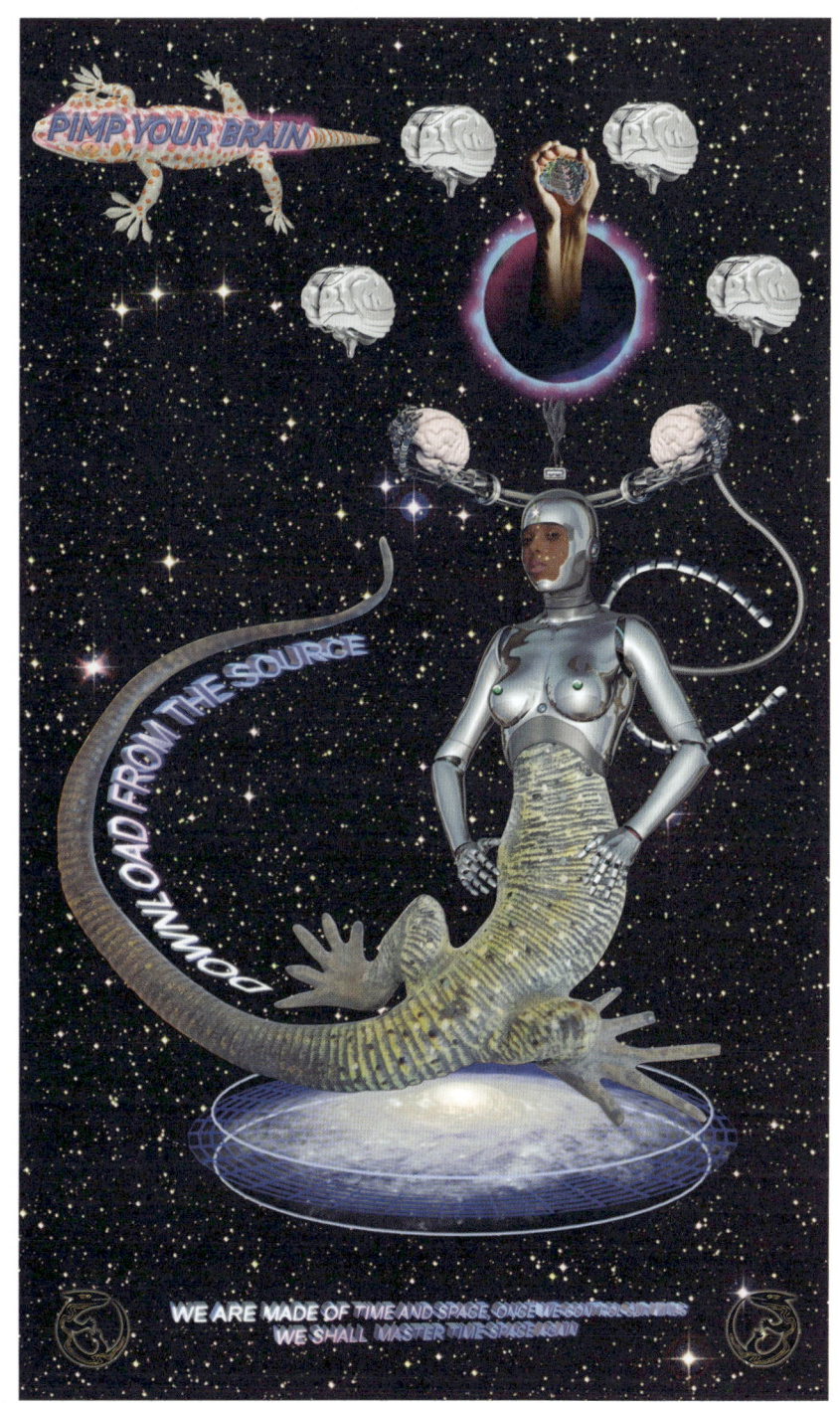

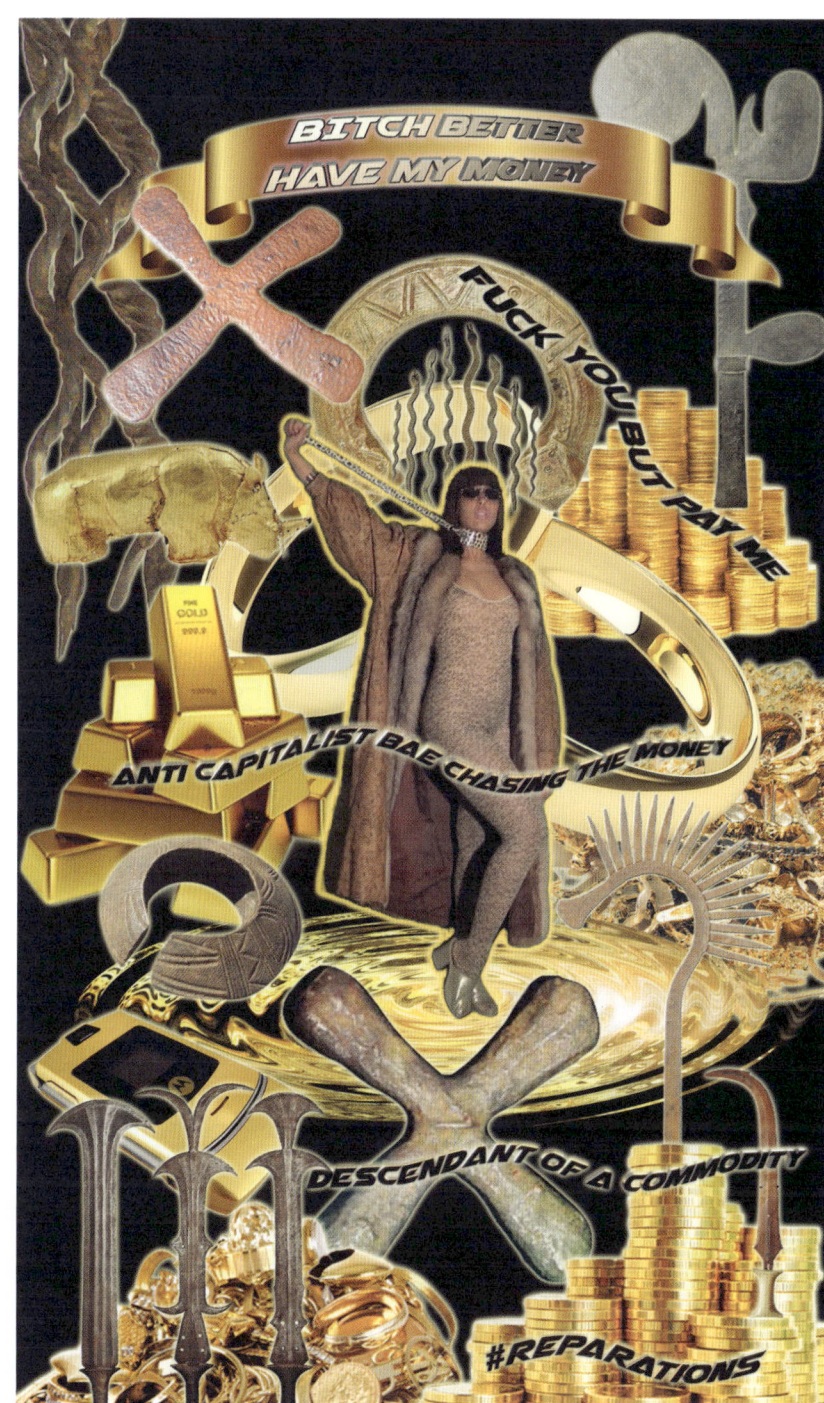

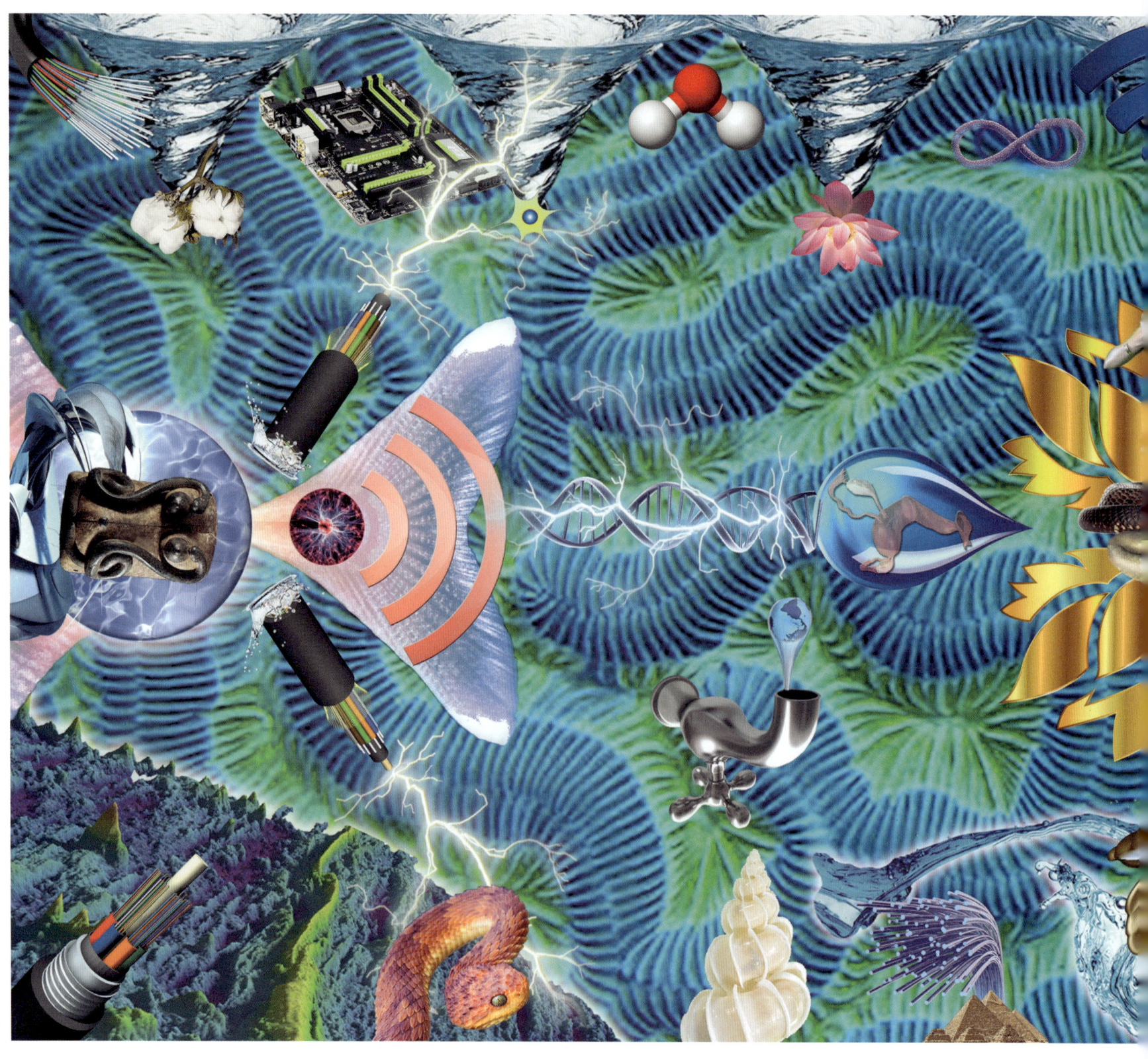

↑ **Dilo**, 2017, lightbox, 100 × 188 × 30.5 cm (39 ⅜ × 74 × 12 in), edition of 5

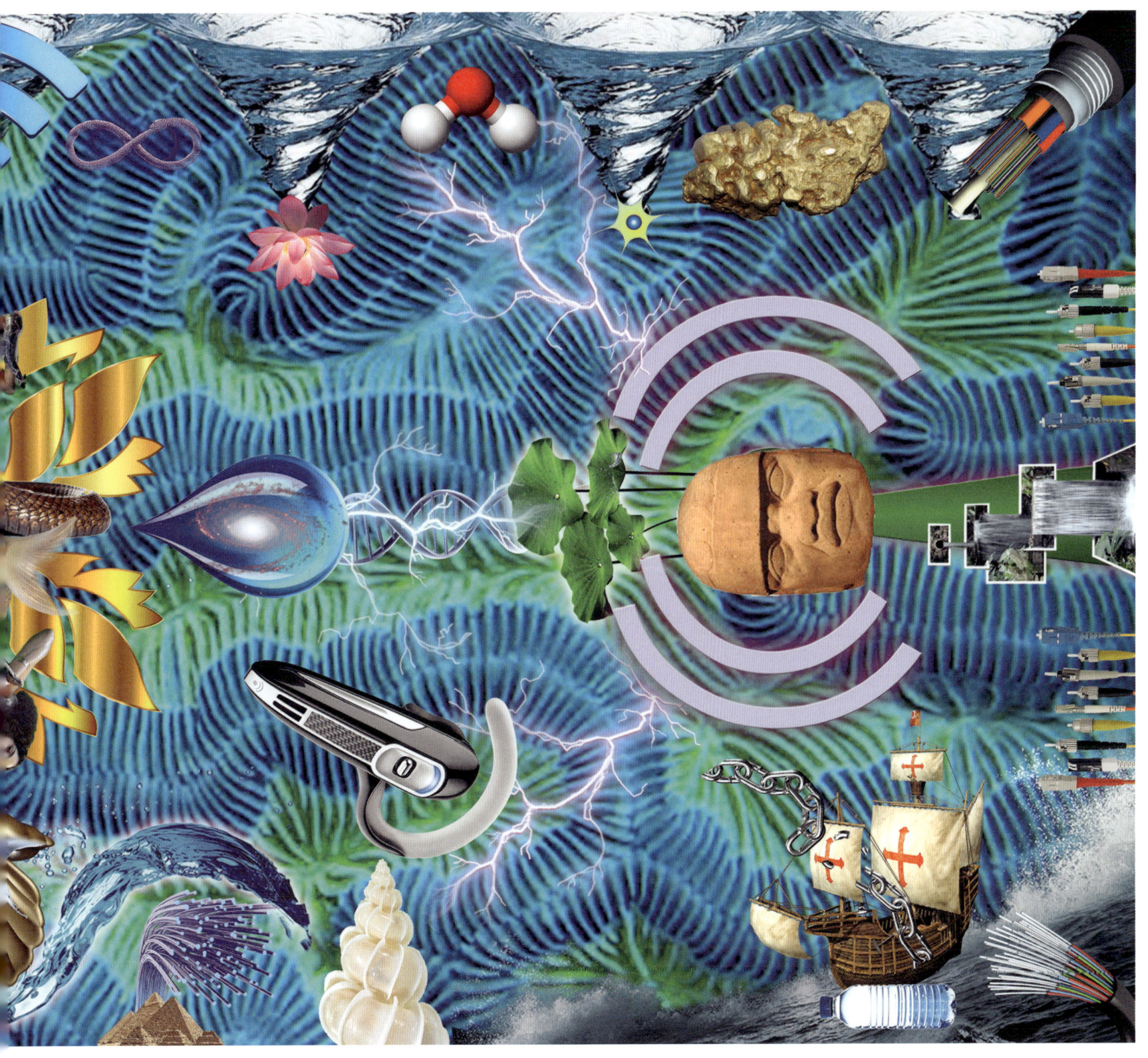

TABITA
REZAIRE

ANTONIO ROBERTS

Working primarily with audio, code and moving images, Antonio Roberts creates complex digital collages. On occasion, his work will also encompass the use of analogue materials such as MDF or stickers to create physical sculptures and installations. Concerned with network cultures, he explores the relationship between technology, authorship and copyright and the effect these have on the way we navigate and ultimately produce a sense of self in a digital age. *Visually Similar – Bust of a Young Woman* (2019) is a video that depicts a 3D scan of a Renaissance bust from the V&A museum collection in London. Cast in 1889 from an original made in the late fifteenth century, the bust has been scanned using open-source software that is free for anyone to use, adding to a sense of reproducibility for a digital age. In the video we see the bust rotating, her stoic face somewhat distorted by the abstract colours projected onto her. As she spins, images of contemporary and historic faces from multiple sources morph and blur into one another in the background. Contemporary images of the self, from TikTok, YouTube and advertising, are layered irreverently. The conflation of time, historicity and appearance are legible, pointing towards the changing nature of technology and its impact on how and why we offer ourselves out into the world visually. *Exposed* (2016) is a digital video presented as a website – complete with the graphic grey frame and 'tab' – that lattices together found imagery of online and offline signs prohibiting photography. It also includes images of military drone attacks and the mask of the hacker group Anonymous – at once a unifying symbol against any form of perceived oppression in today's society and also a mask that literally protects the wearer from contemporary surveillance technology. Yellow and orange clip art renderings of explosions and the ubiquitous bright red Google map pin punctuate this landscape, suggesting the interconnectedness of digital and 'real' landscapes. Flying silently above this cacophony of images is an ever-present white drone silhouette, 'monitoring' the action below. *Exposed* brings these discourses of the self, image and appearance into the political sphere. In it, the artist suggests that in an age of pervasive digital surveillance, it is impossible to extract the personal from immediate political contexts. When people offer their image to the world, they offer their data and therefore their very selves. In doing so, they willingly enter a sphere of corporate and political domination where their presence both inscribes them in global events and contributes to the effects of those events. In a sense, people no longer *are*, but instead constantly *become*. The making of oneself in one's own image happens in contested digital spaces and is always therefore at the mercy of the political forces that shape us all.

HANA NOORALI AND LYNTON TALBOT

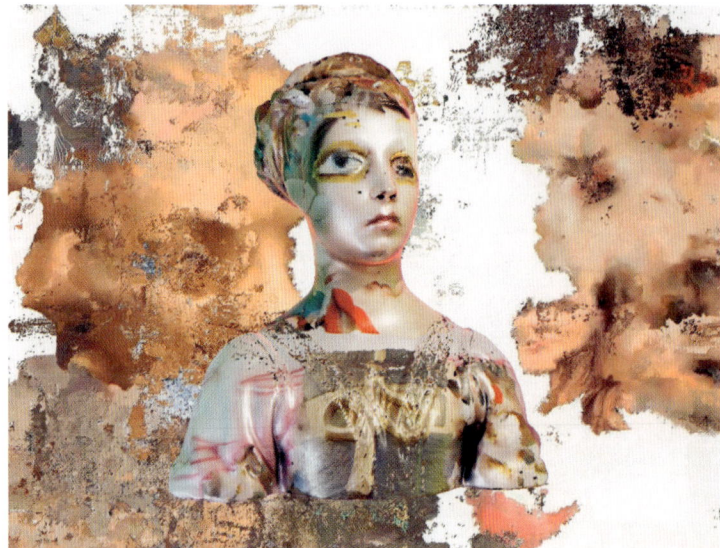

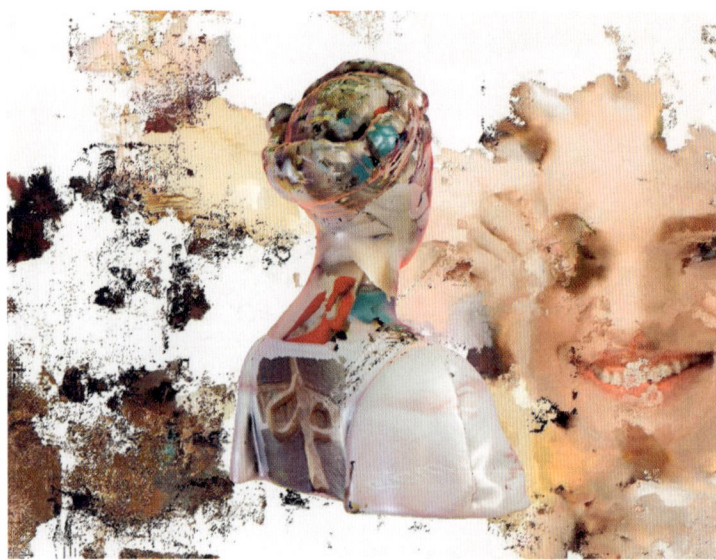

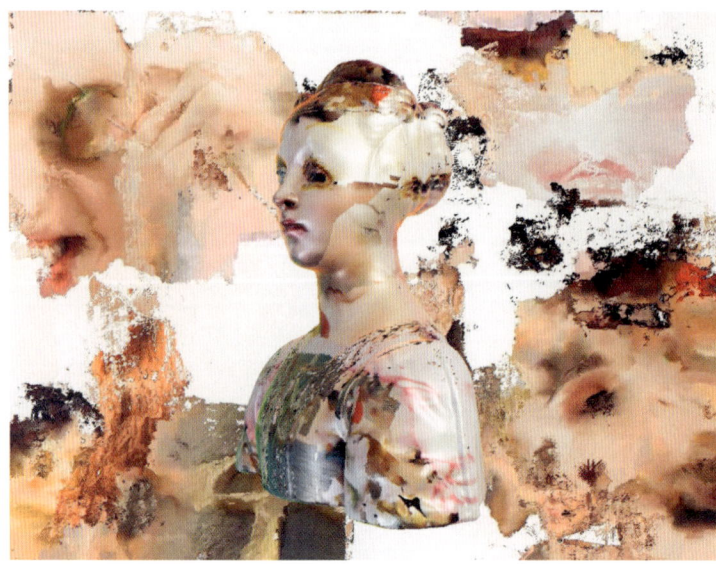

Born 1985, Leicester, UK. Lives in Birmingham, UK.

↑ **Visually Similar – Bust of a Young Woman**, 2019, stills from digital video, 1024 × 768 px

↗↗ **Exposed**, 2016, stills from website, dimensions variable

↗ **Sticker Book**, 2019, 3 of 18 vinyl stickers, left to right: 113.6 × 77.5 cm (44¾ × 30½ in); 79.5 × 99.5 cm (31¼ × 39¼ in); 113.7 × 79.6 cm (44¾ × 31⅜ in), installation view, 'WONDER – Where Reality And Imaginary Collide', Herbert Art Gallery and Museum, Coventry, UK

→ **Transformative Use**, 2016, stills from website, dimensions variable

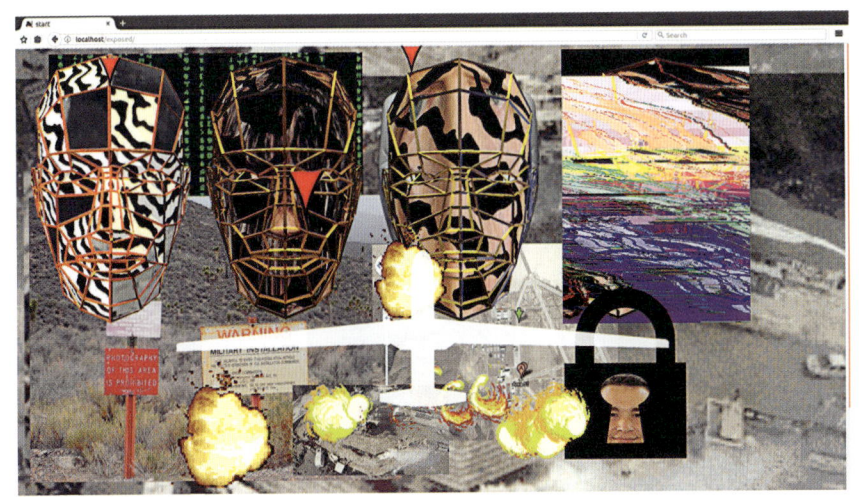
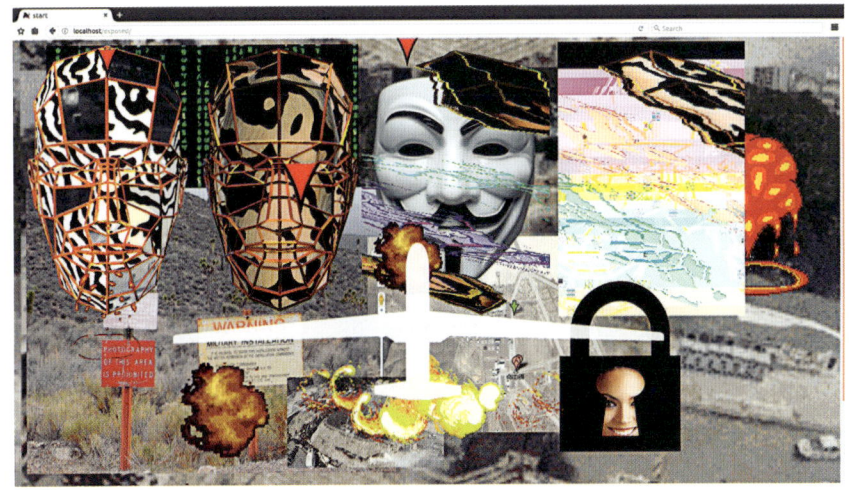
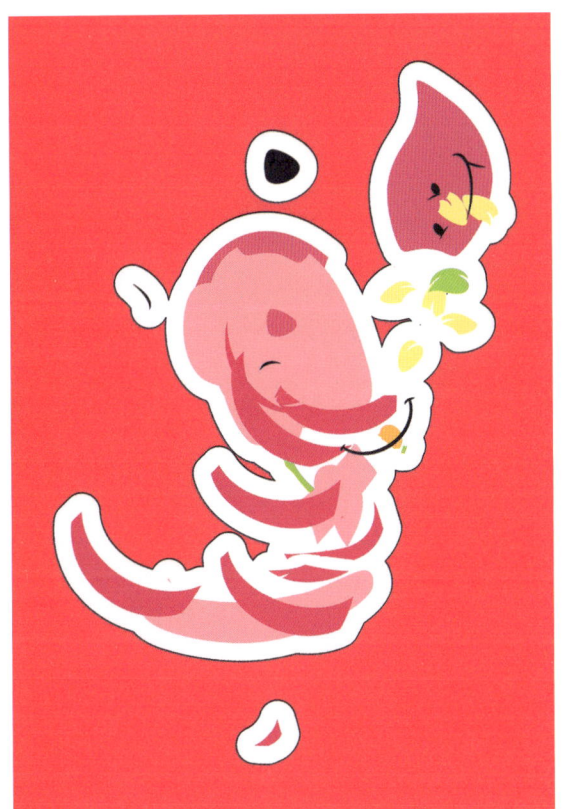
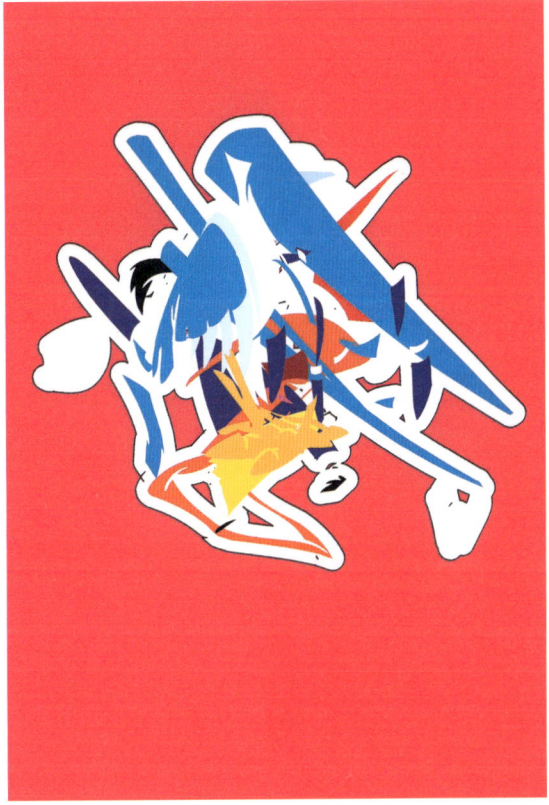
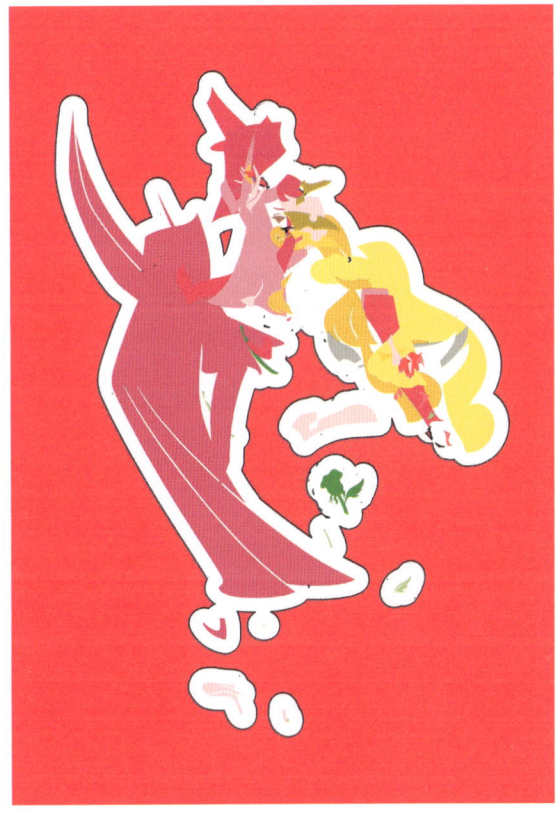
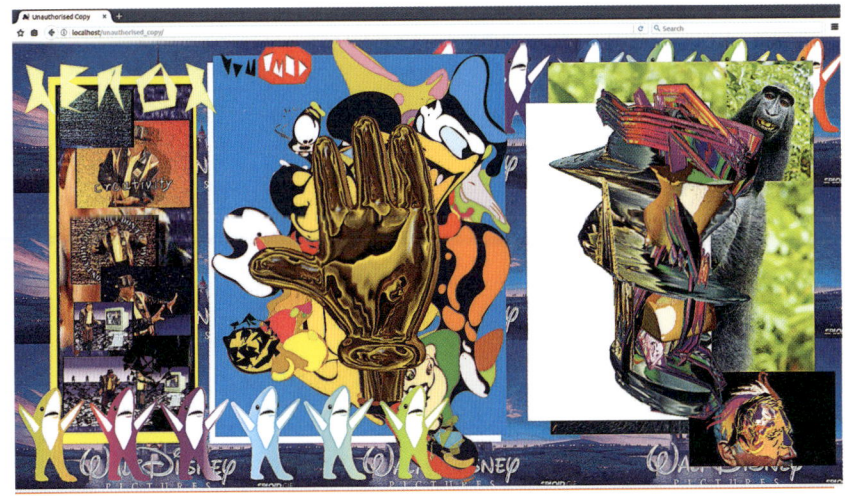
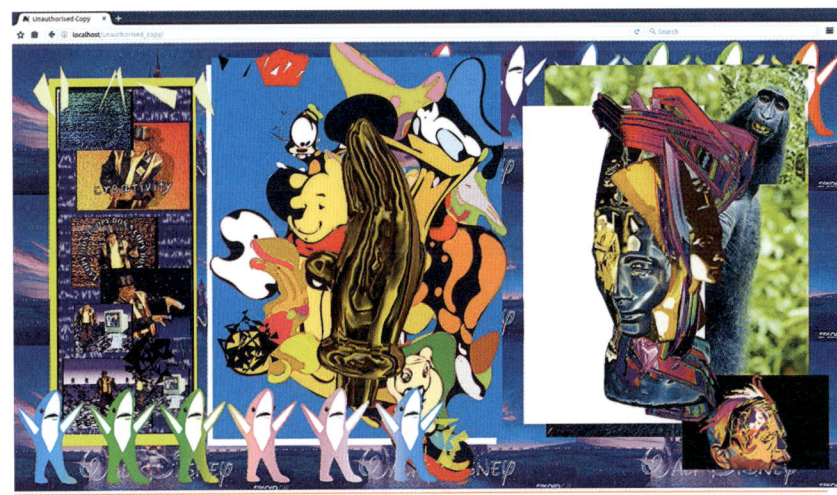

ANTONIO ROBERTS

DEBORAH ROBERTS

Blocks of vivid colour, outreached hands and animated patterns dance in stop-motion across Deborah Roberts's mix-media figurative collages of young Black Americans. With its history of disrupting, collage lends itself to temporal collisions, while its fissures expose complex and disordered relationships that evidence the malleability of life. Collage points to the potential for renewal and among its disordered parts lies hope. It is in this spirit that Roberts's works reveal and un-stick the complex identities that the vicissitudes of Western (white) history and society have imposed upon her Black subjects. Her figures, engaged in everyday activities, are isolated from the parapher-nalia of everyday life and positioned in a blank space synonymous with the white racialized gaze. Frozen while performing, these young people are strong – they want to be seen and to catch the viewer's gaze; at the same time, they demonstrate a vulnerability innate to all children, but of heightened relevance to Black youth pondering their futures. ▬▬▬ In *A long way to go* (2021) this is expressed by Roberts's empowering placement of the three young male figures across the full width of the canvas – they command our attention – however, the cartoon characters depicted on their caps and their composite faces reveal their true innocence and potential fragility. The black and white striped shirts worn by Roberts's youths, while having a formal optical presence, are reminiscent of both sports and prison apparel, drawing attention to society's criminalization and stereotyping of young Black boys and men. ▬▬ Cut-out images of adult bodily features are added into some collages, including those of notable Black figures such as civil rights activist Rosa Parks. Faces are constructed using multiple irregular sections, dispelling notions of singular or ideal identities – a style reminiscent of the facial composites of American artist Romare Bearden (1911–88), whose works also evoke the realities of African American life. ▬▬▶ Pointing to her own history in painting, interest in colour theory and in dialogue with Western art, Roberts creates imagined textile designs and blocks of deeply hued colours as clothing. In *Red, white and blue* (2018), two young girls, dressed in brightly coloured and heavily patterned outfits, stand back-to-back, each carrying a red boxing glove as a gesture of shared experience and defiance. The boxing glove is a motif that Roberts has used in several works to highlight the need for Black girls to confront racialized notions of beauty and the sexualization of Black bodies, particularly for girls. This is also expressed in *The burden* (2019), in which the cut-out image of a white girl's face is suggest-ive of a mask held in the young Black female's hand. Roberts's collages are empathetic records of the experience of Black American youth, whose bodies she constructs as containers of a turbulent history and, importantly, with the potential for a myriad of futures.

HABDA RASHID

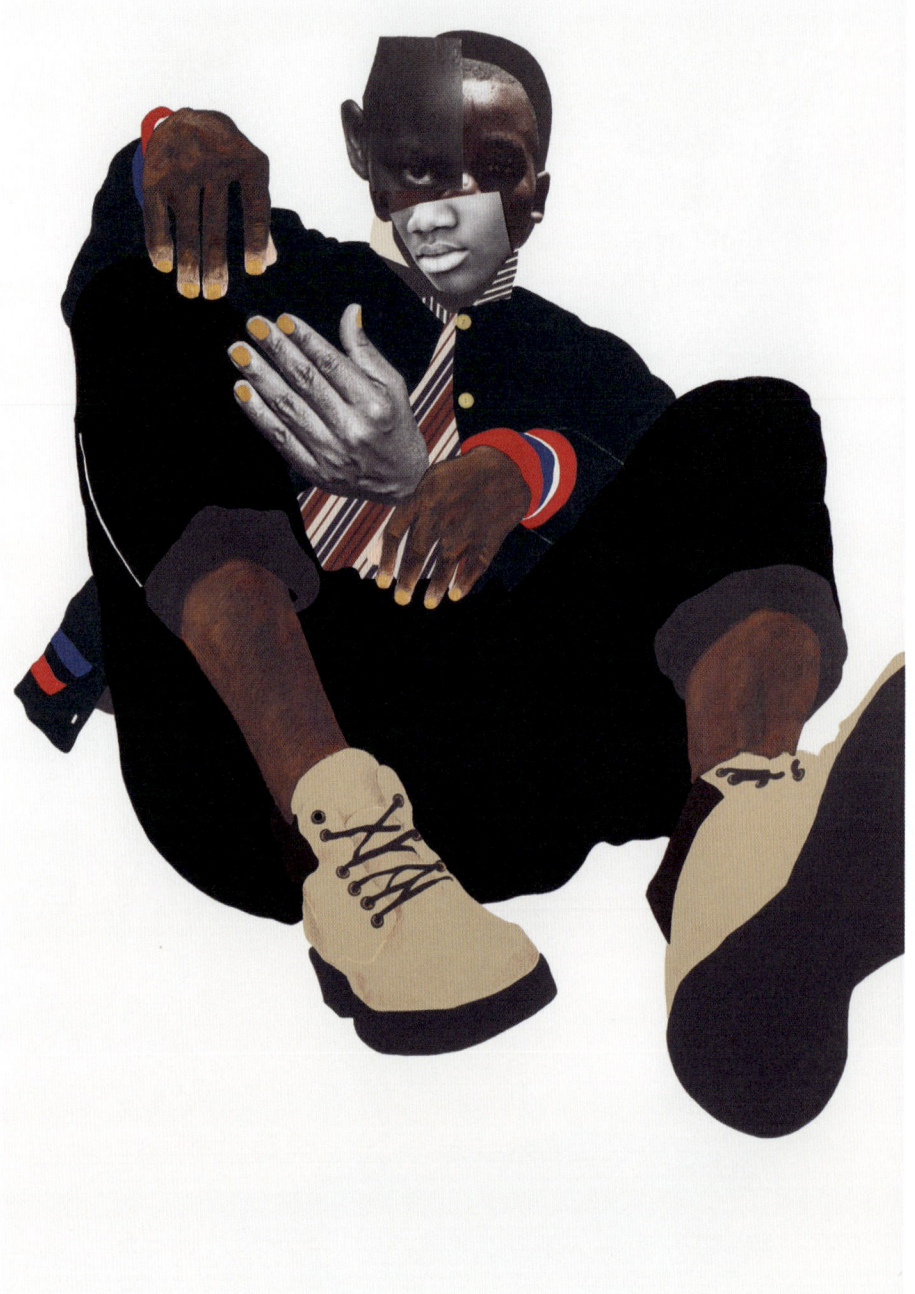

Born 1962, Austin, Texas, USA. Lives in Austin.

↑   **Jamal**, 2020, mixed media and collage on canvas, 165.1 × 114.3 cm (65 × 45 in), Solomon R. Guggenheim Museum, New York, USA

↗   **Red, white and blue**, 2018, mixed media and collage on canvas, 183 × 152.4 cm (72 × 60 in), SFMOMA, San Francisco, California, USA

↗↗ **The unseen**, 2020, mixed media and collage on canvas, 165 × 114.3 cm (65 × 45 in), private collection

→   **When you see me**, 2019, mixed media and collage on canvas, 165 × 304.8 cm (65 × 120 in), Dallas Museum of Art, Texas, USA

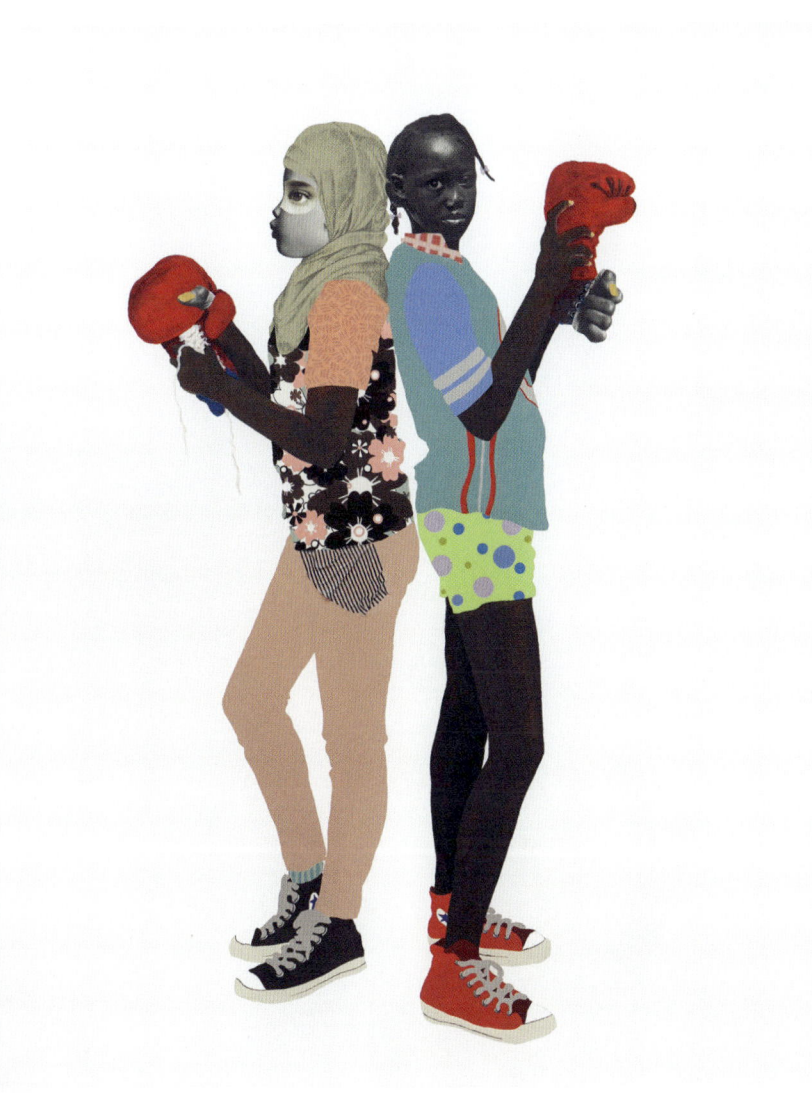
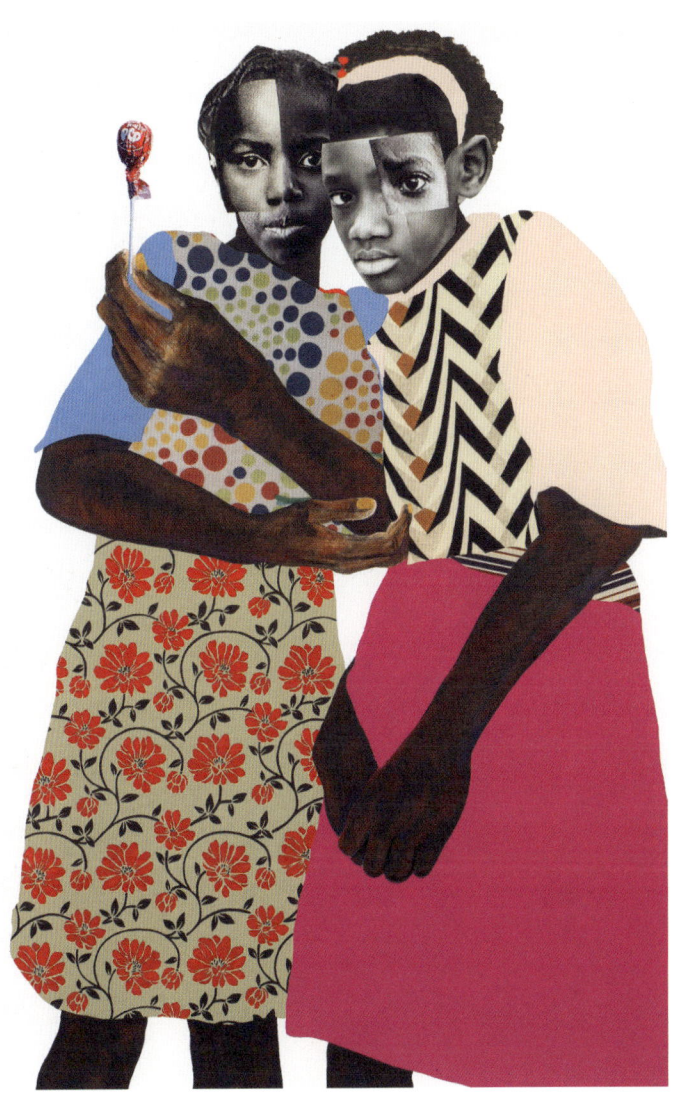
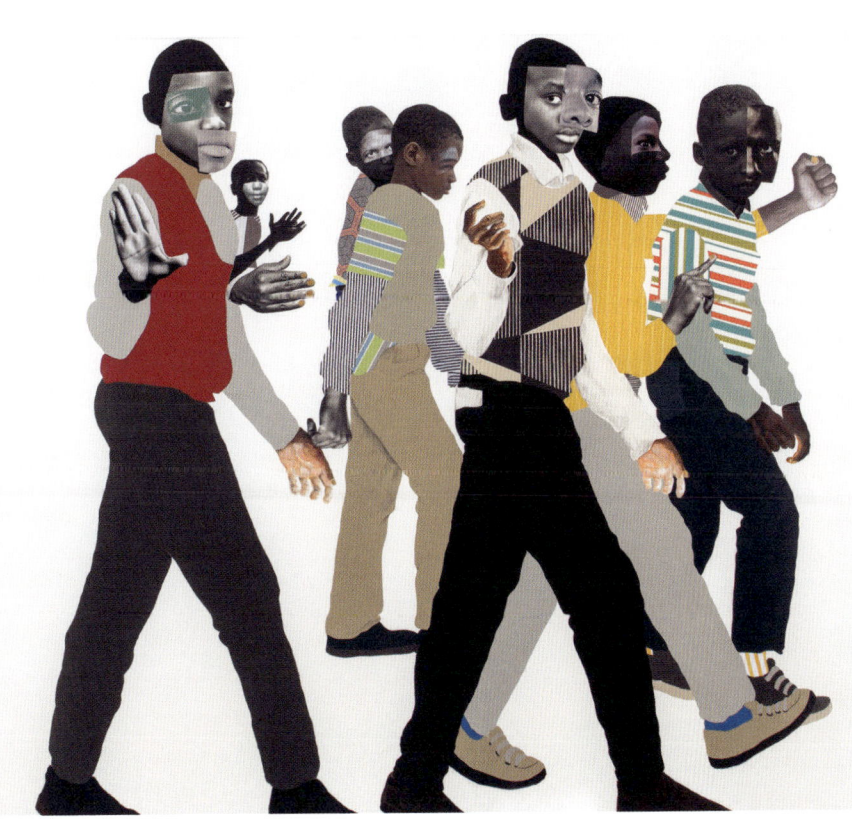

DEBORAH
ROBERTS

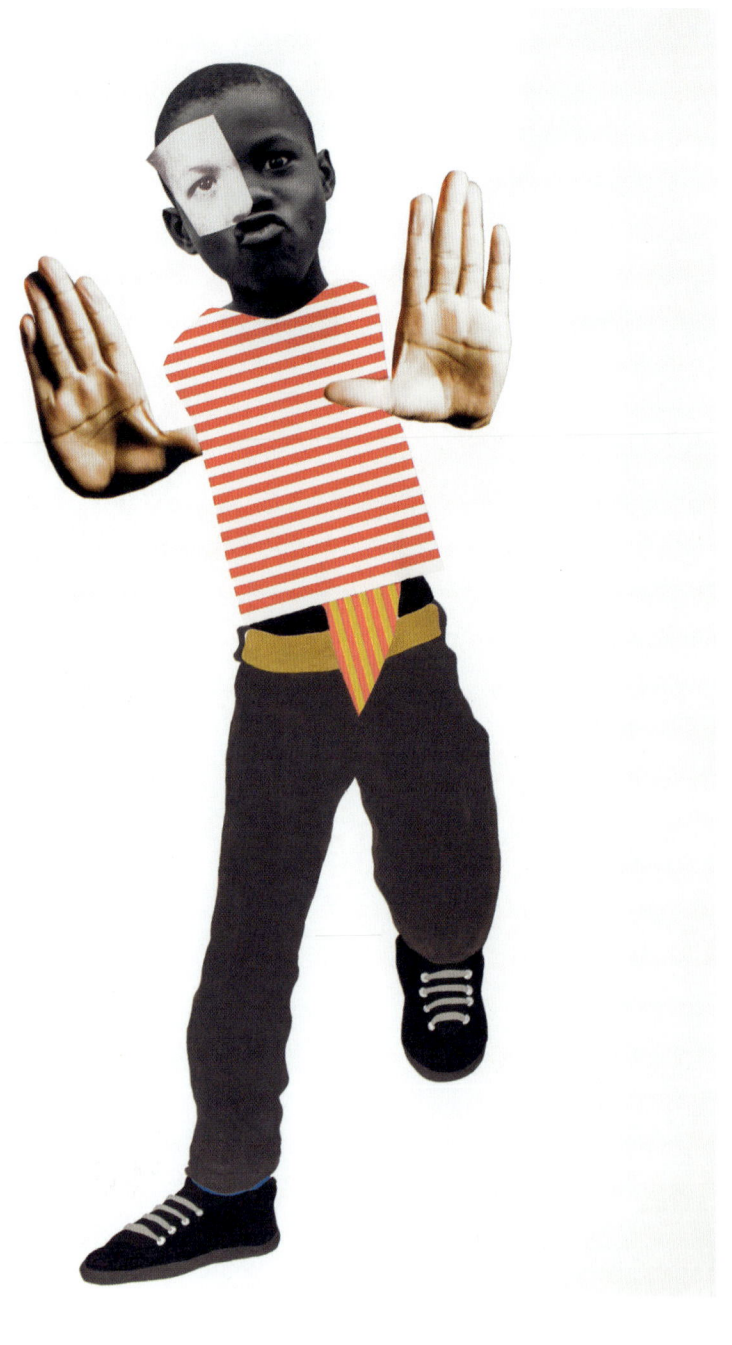

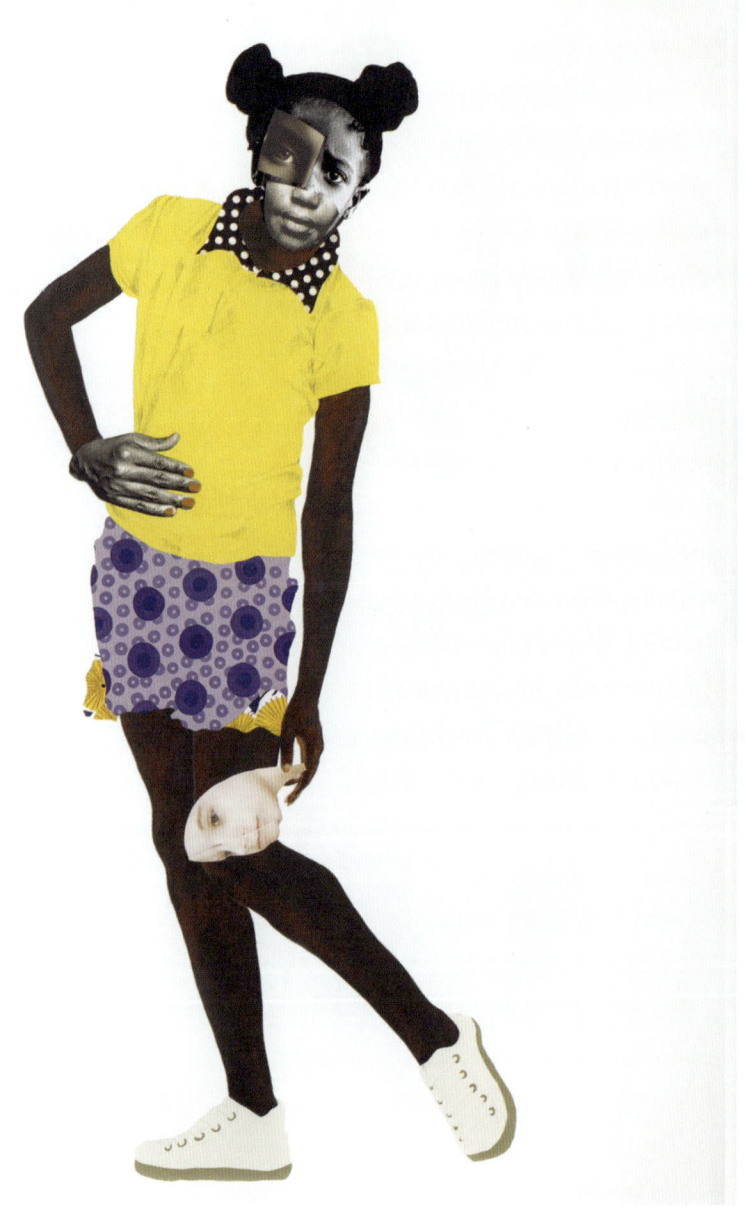

↖ **After the thunder (RR)**, 2019, mixed media and collage on paper, 111.8 × 81.3 cm (44 × 32 in)

↑ **The burden**, 2019, mixed media and collage on linen, 165 × 114.3 cm (65 × 45 in)

↗ **A long way to go**, 2021, mixed media and collage on canvas, 127 × 165.1 cm (50 × 65 in), private collection

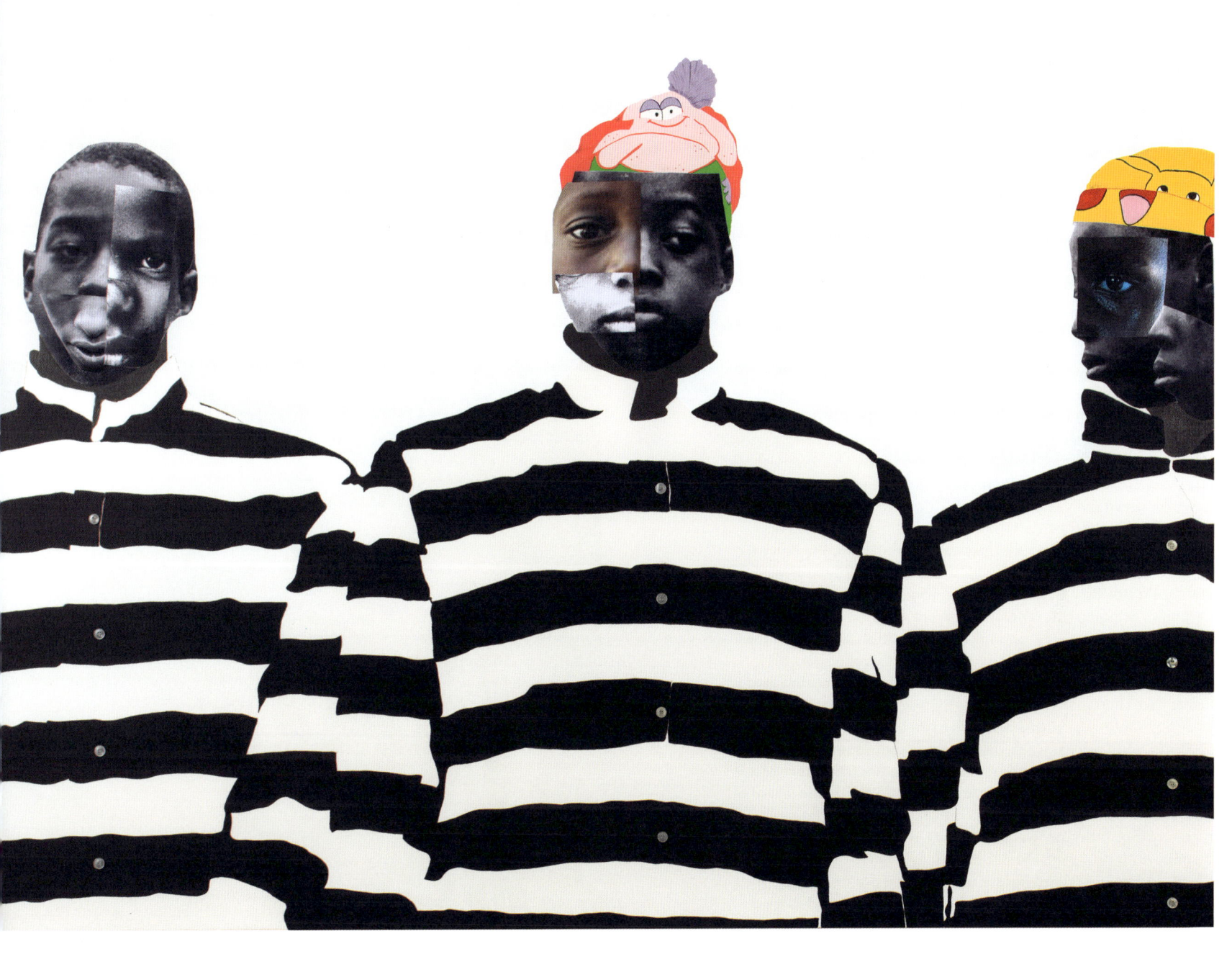

DEBORAH
ROBERTS

MARTHA ROSLER

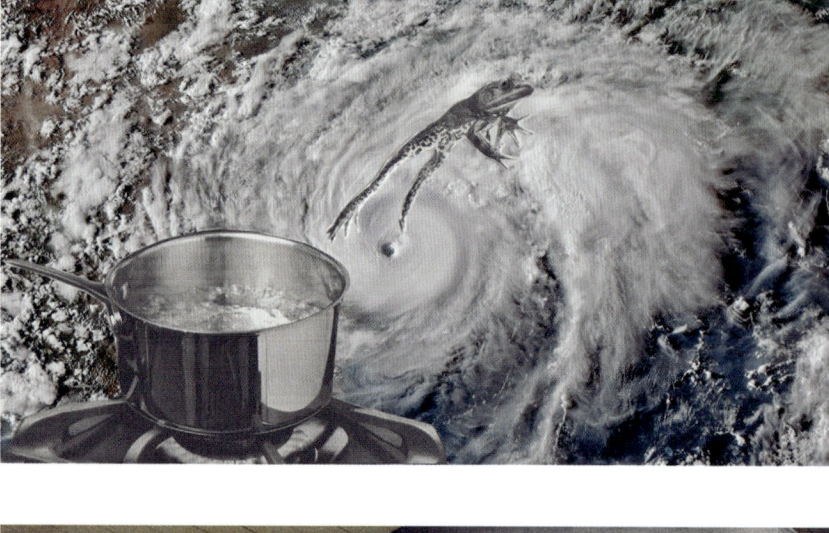

In politically punchy, excoriating and often hilarious photomontages – just one medium deployed by the multifaceted artist – Martha Rosler comments directly and critically on contemporary political and social issues, particularly in the United States context. Active since the 1960s, Rosler's work encompasses film, photography and performance, as well as activism, writing and lecturing; she has been a pioneer of photomontage, creating carefully choreographed images from pop culture sources such as advertising, mass media and fashion magazines to interrogate the role of visual culture and the machinations of the patriarchy. She often does so with an acerbic sense of humour, as in a work she produced after the ousting of the incumbent US president, *break for freedom (hurricane #1): on the electoral defeat of Donald Trump* (2020), which imagines the American people as an amphibian narrowly escaping being boiled alive. In the background, however, a hurricane swirls, leaving the viewer to ponder what fate lies ahead for this wretched frog. As Rosler, an outspoken critic of Trump throughout his presidency, told *Garage* magazine in 2018, 'the best way to deal with a tyrant is by laughter'. ◤ In the series 'House Beautiful: Bringing the War Home, New Series' (2004–8) Rosler returned to a theme that has preoccupied her work from the beginning – war. This group of works specifically addresses the US wars in Afghanistan and Iraq by incisively contrasting the jarring difference between scenes of destruction and displacement abroad with the domestic comfort of life in the US. The work reflects a strongly anti-war stance – a position also found in the earlier iteration of 'House Beautiful: Bringing the War Home', twenty photomontages Rosler produced between 1967 and 1972 in opposition to the Vietnam War that were initially published in underground papers and disseminated at anti-war protests. ◤ As in her earlier series, Rosler takes images of opulent private residences from the pages of popular interiors magazines such as *House Beautiful*, frequently focusing on female figures, and splices them seamlessly with scenes of destruction culled from the media depicting the wars in Afghanistan and Iraq. Rosler's cut-and-paste technique is crafted with precision so that the image appears to be a single seamless whole rather than a collage of different photographs. This is an important part of the effect, so that the familiar setting of the home and its perceived safety and privacy are upended by the violence and brutal reality of war – typically understood by the domestic Western consumer of images of war as something distant and separate but here felt in visceral, inescapable proximity. This is the prime motivation behind Rosler's use of collage: to communicate directly the notion, as she described in a 2017 conversation for *The Iris*, that 'we are not a here and a there. We are all one, and this is crucial.' ◤

CHARLOTTE JANSEN

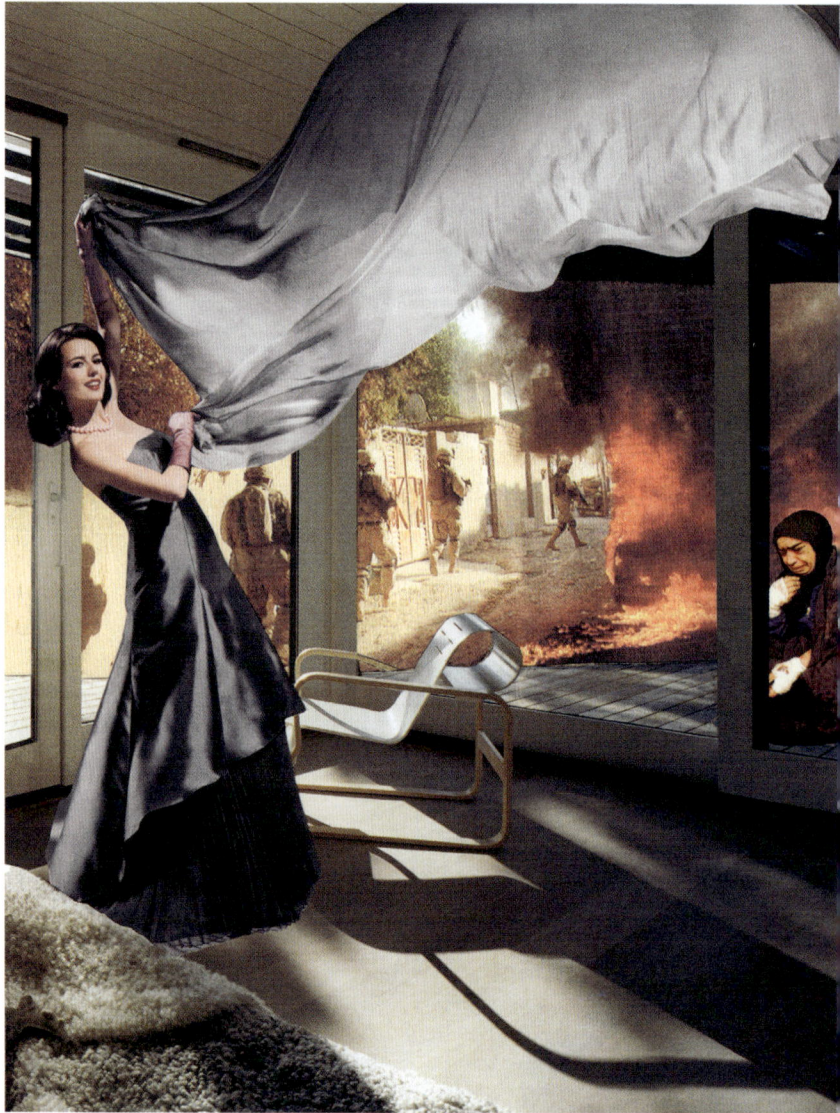

Born Brooklyn, New York, USA. Lives in Brooklyn.

↑↑ break for freedom (hurricane #1): on the electoral defeat of Donald Trump, 2020, photomontage

↑ **The Gray Drape**, 2008, from the series '**House Beautiful: Bringing the War Home, New Series**' (2004–8), photomontage, dimensions variable

↗ **Photo-Op**, 2004, from the series '**House Beautiful: Bringing the War Home, New Series**', (2004–8), photomontage, dimensions variable

↗↗ Vanitas, 2004, from the series '**House Beautiful: Bringing the War Home, New Series**', (2004–8), photomontage, dimensions variable

→ **Invasion**, 2008, from the series '**House Beautiful: Bringing the War Home, New Series**', (2004–8), photomontage, dimensions variable

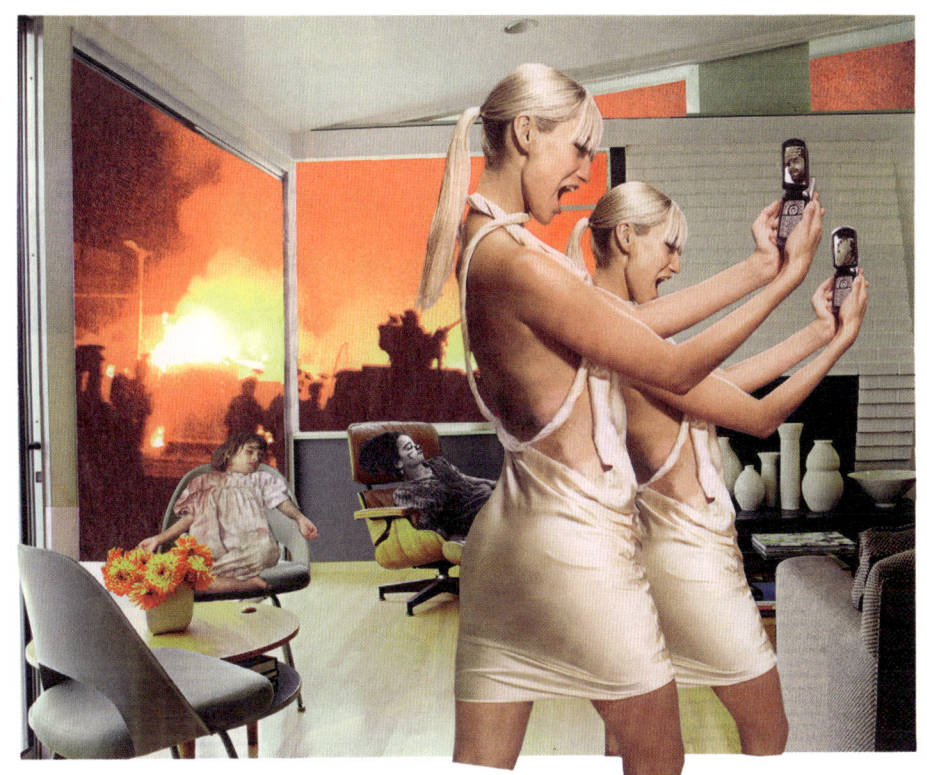

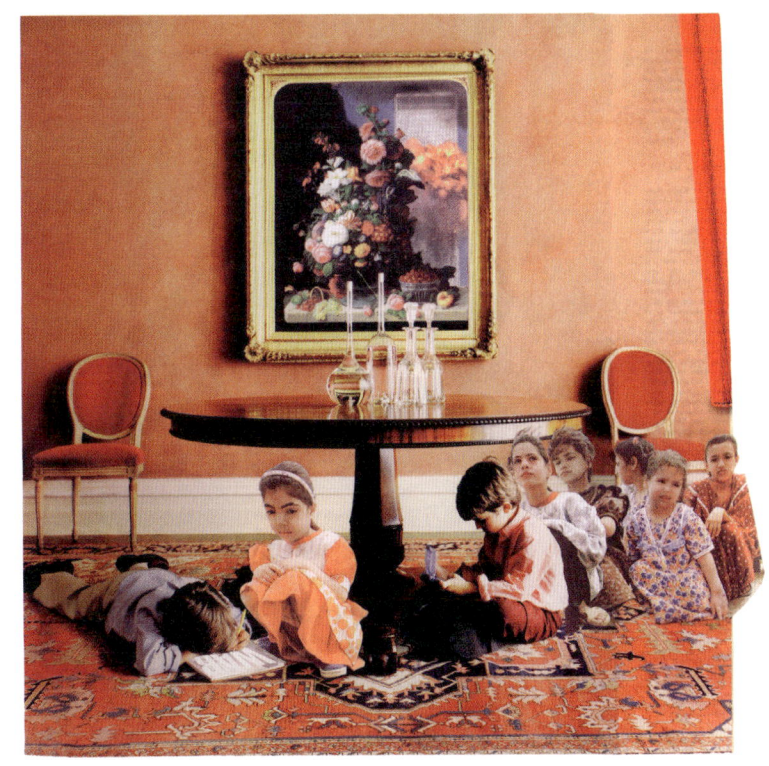

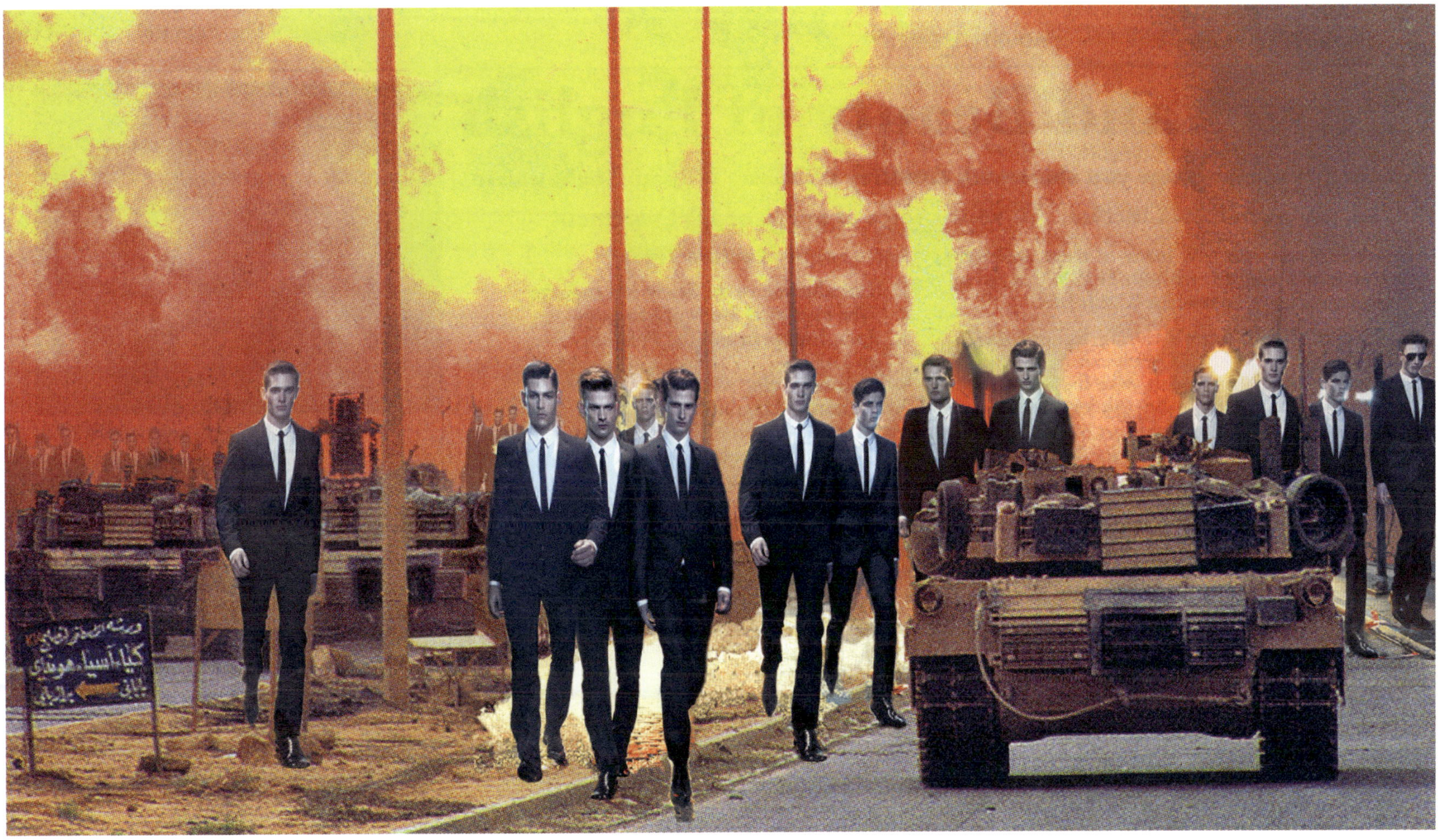

ANASTASIA
SAMOYLOVA

The collages – and overall practice – of Anastasia Samoylova carry us towards a sublime reckoning. Reality, according to the artist, may appear concrete but that is a mere fiction. Using images of the real world – its landforms, monuments and human interventions – Samoylova draws attention to the ways in which we make meaning. She studied interior design at the Russian State University for the Humanities in Moscow, a course that required building maquettes out of paper and then documenting the models through photographs. The act of flattening three dimensions into photographic imagery was foundational for her art practice: in her collages she fragments and rephotographs stock images taken by other photographers to create complex, kaleidoscopic compositions. In *Matterhorns* (2019) shots of the famed pyramidal peak are refracted across a glassy ground. The image is luminous, a hundred shades of bright glacier blue, and summons associations with travel postcards, looping screensavers, the endless, scrollable search results delivered by Google images. By layering and shrouding views of the Matterhorn, the work calls into question the very construction of a photographic image – what is included in the frame and what is left out – as well as the ways in which viewers rely upon images to understand reality. While many of us may never see the Matterhorn in person, we can nevertheless bring it to mind thanks to the thousands of versions of the mountain online, used in advertisements and made famous through the eponymous Disneyland ride. Photographs not only shape our understanding of the world, but they become the truth through which we experience it. Indeed, Samoylova first became interested in photography because of its inherent connections to reality, but over time she came to realize that this reality was but a construct. 'What attracted me to photography,' she said in a 2016 interview with *In the In-Between*, 'is that you can make up a world and produce a truthful record of it.' Similarly, the vertiginous *Grand Canyons* (2021), from the artist's 'Landscape Sublime' series, conjures the sensations of a deep descent, if not its actual likeness. Against an orangey-red ground, Samoylova has collaged ochre striations and rocky outcrops, each set within its own jagged frame. Alongside views of the titular canyons are silver cars tunnelling their way through the monumental and metaphorical landscape. Samoylova sees the environment as inextricably linked to consumerism, a relationship hinted at here in the ways in which the cars shatter the colossal expanse. *Grand Canyons*, like much of Samoylova's practice, seeks to negotiate the space between a sublime interaction and the truth of life on planet earth. Such terrain, according to the artist, is always in flux.
GRACE LINDEN

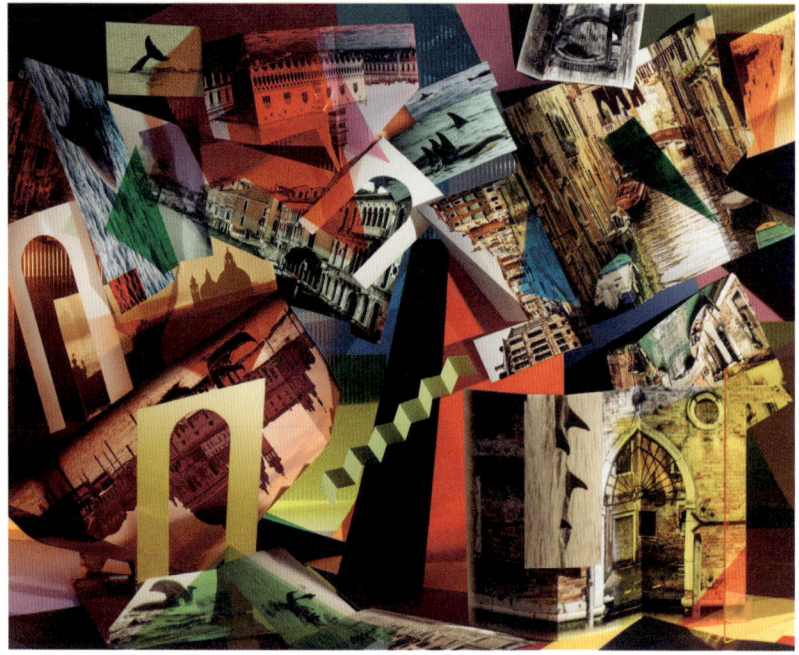

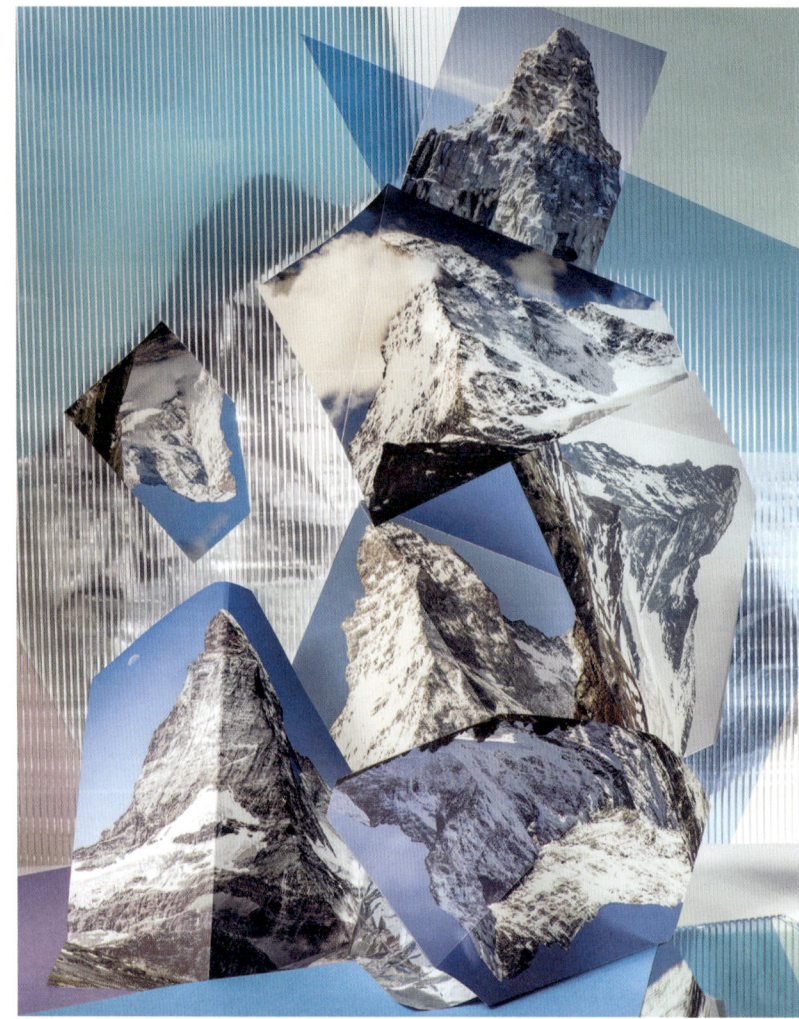

Born 1984, Moscow, Russia. Lives in Miami, Florida, USA.

↑↑ **Dolphins in Venice**, 2021, pigment print, 101.6 × 127 cm (40 × 50 in)

↑ **Matterhorns**, 2019, pigment print, 101.6 × 81 cm (40 × 32 in)

↗ **Yosemite**, from the 'Landscape Sublime' project, 2022, pigment print, 107 × 188 cm (42 × 74 in)

→ **Grand Canyons**, from the 'Landscape Sublime' project, 2021, pigment print, 101.6 × 322 cm (40 × 127 in)

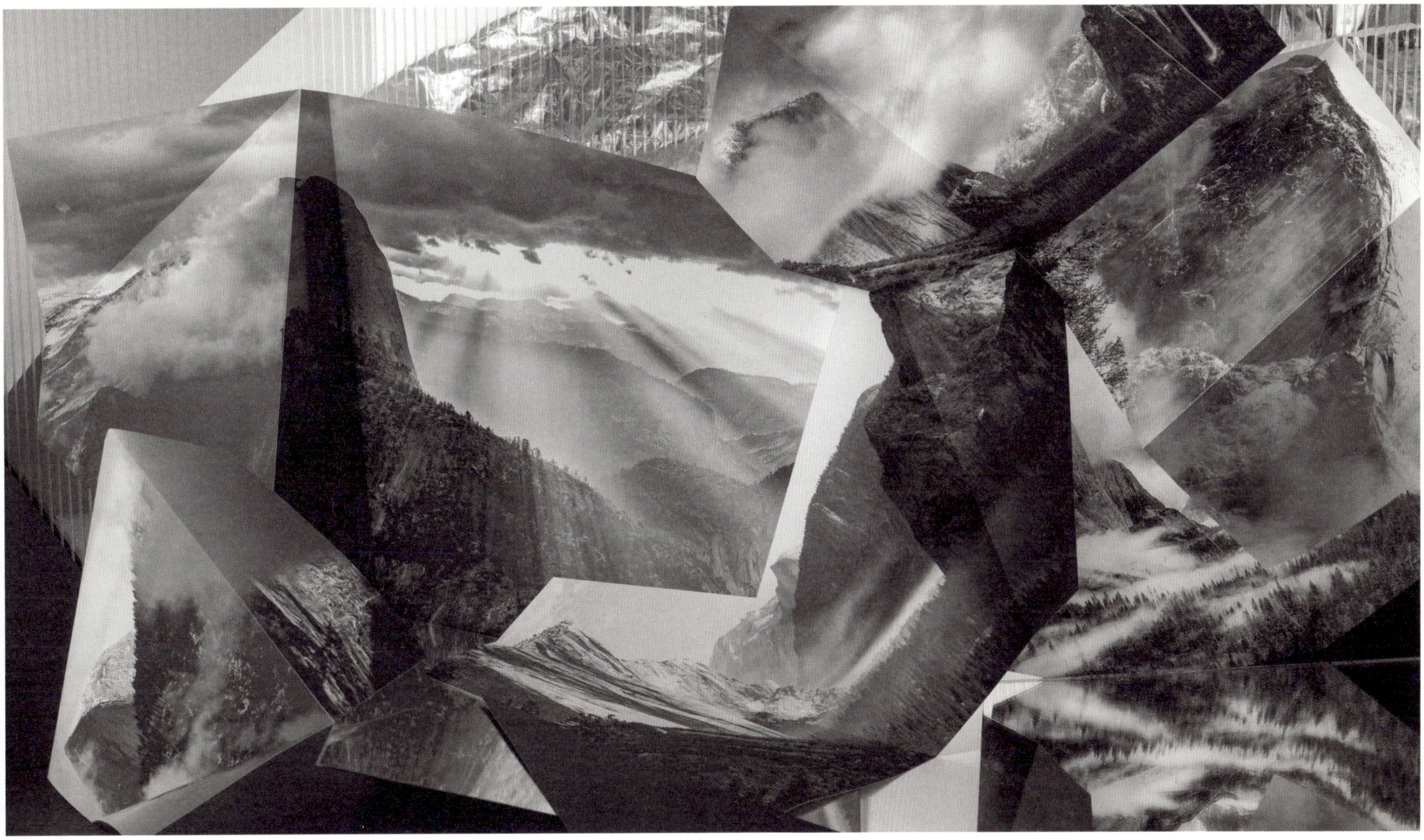

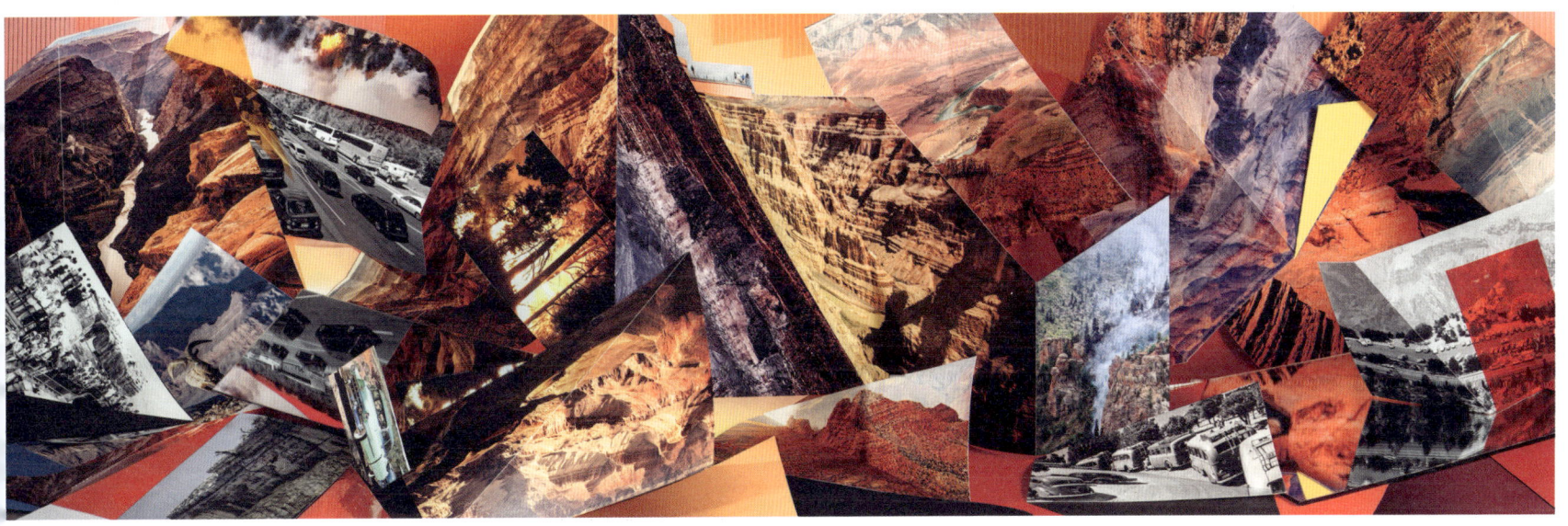

ANASTASIA
SAMOYLOVA

GABRIELLA SANCHEZ

While often described as paintings, Gabriella Sanchez's works involve overlapping and layered elements that make complex collaged compositions. Painting and drawing materials are combined with family photographs, fabric, glitter and even pieces of crochet and hand-embroidered lace made by Sanchez's grandmother, Lupe Ramirez, and members of her church sewing group, as seen in *Portrait Of Figures In Light II* (2021). Common across her practice is a desire to represent her experience of living in Los Angeles – a city with multicultural geneses and influences – and to add deeper complexities to the stories of those who sit at its margins by envisioning different outcomes for them. Fuchsia pinks, neon oranges and electric blues demand the viewer's attention, while the frenetic green strokes that recur in her works suggest growing grasses – a vision of renewal.

Sanchez studied graphic design and illustration, and worked on commercial projects before moving into art-making. Text – both dominant painted words and smaller handwritten phrases – appears in all her works. Whether rhyming (fine, line, define, refine) or in anagrams (from/form), it appears that Sanchez is interested in how words sound, and in their context-dependent meanings. Her use of contrasting typefaces is notable, and she is conscious of their pre-existing cultural associations: 'When, say, Ed Ruscha uses a gothic script, it has a different representational weight compared to when I use that same script,' she commented in a 2018 interview with *Galerie Magazine*. The words' placement is also carefully considered. In *Suitable* (2019), for example, gothic letters read 'suit', but the fact that they are aligned right, along with the work's title, suggests the viewer is not seeing the entire word. This work is a celebration of the artist's grandfather, a military veteran, who gained a sense of identity by placing importance on the presentation of his clothing. On the left of the work a small red circle draws attention to a baggy trouser cuff, a men's fashion style made notorious by the 1943 Zoot Suit Riots in Los Angeles. Young men, particularly Mexican Americans, were targeted for being 'unpatriotic' in their sartorial choices, ignoring the advised fabric rationing of the United States during the Second World War. Sanchez offers a new portrayal, highlighting their style and hinting by virtue of a red arrow at their being suitable 'for service' – arguably the most patriotic of roles.

The diptych *Define, Fine, Refine* (2020) reflects upon the multiple meanings associated with connecting hands – including greeting, praying and pulling away. The work uses screenshots from the cult 1993 girl gang movie *Mi Vida Loca (My Crazy Life)*, which are reinterpreted by being split with a gap left between. The words 'fine' in Helvetica, a bold typeface commonly used on street signs, and 'line' in gothic script emphasize the narrow space between different understandings of gestures, pushing the viewer to new ways of looking at togetherness.

AJ GIRARD

Born 1988, Pasadena, California, USA. Lives in Los Angeles, California, USA.

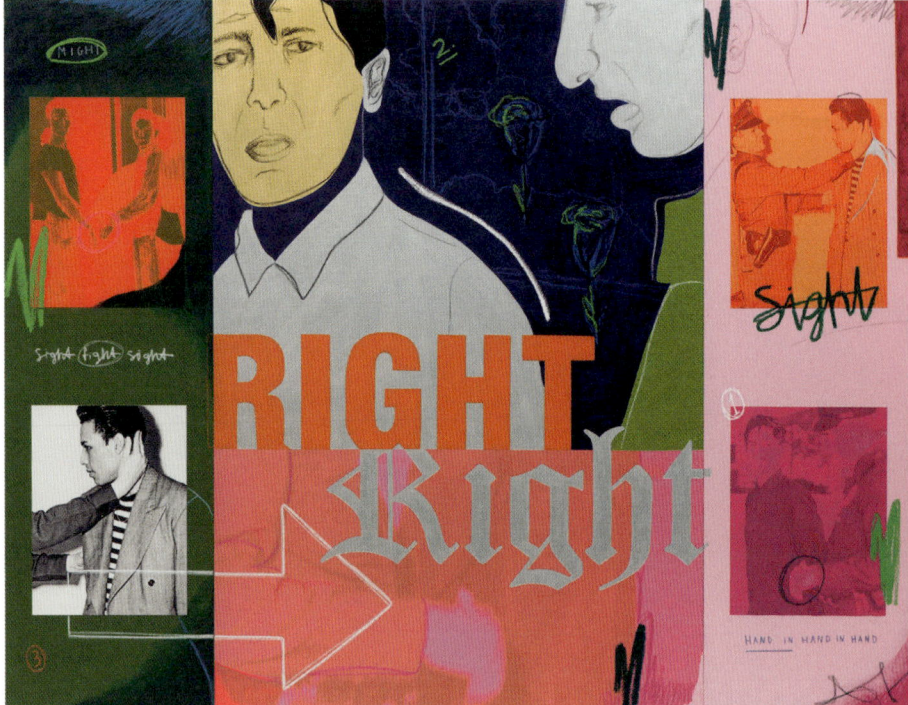

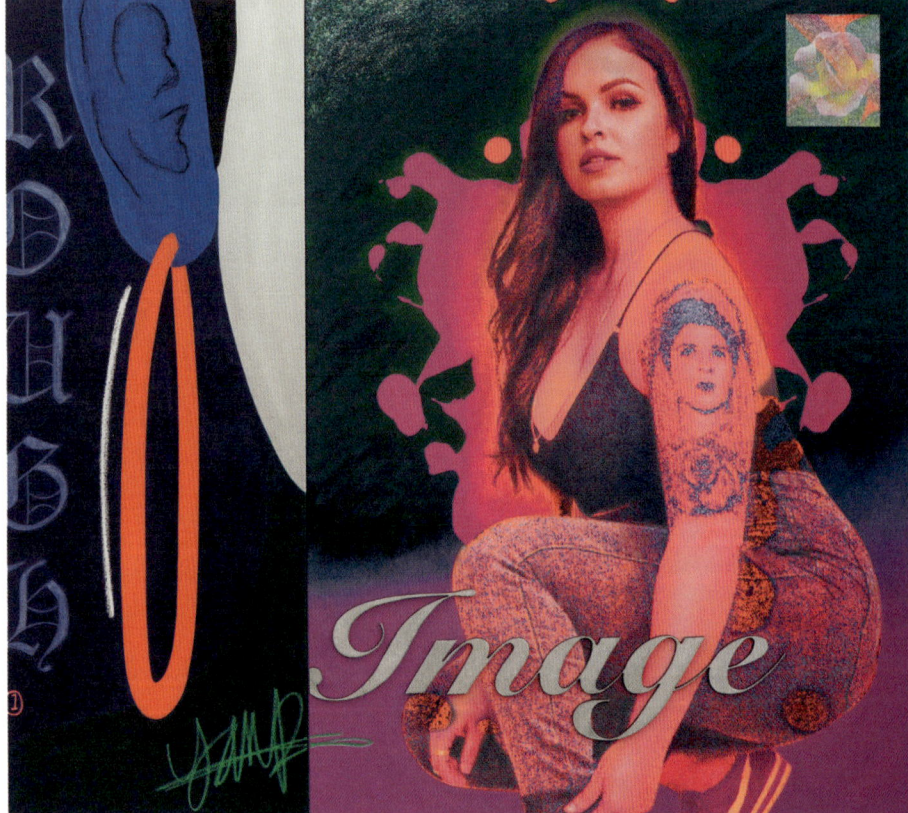

↑↑ **Down Is Up**, 2020, acrylic, oil stick, graphite, oil pastel and archival pigment prints on 3 canvases hung flush in a high-polished aluminium frame, overall 152.4 × 198.1 cm (60 × 78 in), Los Angeles County Museum of Art, USA

↑ **Rough / Image (A Cropped Image Of Yaz)**, 2020, house paint, acrylic, oil stick, glitter, oil pastel, archival pigment prints and galvanized steel on 2 canvases hung flush, diptych, 121.9 × 45.7 cm (48 × 18 in) and 121.9 × 91.4 cm (48 × 36 in)

↗ **Define, Fine, Refine**, 2020, acrylic, oil stick, graphite, oil pastel and archival pigment prints on 2 canvases in high-polished aluminium frames, diptych, each 152.4 × 121.9 cm (60 × 48 in)

→ **From / Veronica / Form**, 2020, house paint, acrylic, oil stick, spray paint, archival pigment prints and galvanized steel on 3 canvases hung flush, central canvas: 121.9 × 198.1 cm (48 × 78 in), outer canvases: 121.9 × 53.3 cm (48 × 21 in)

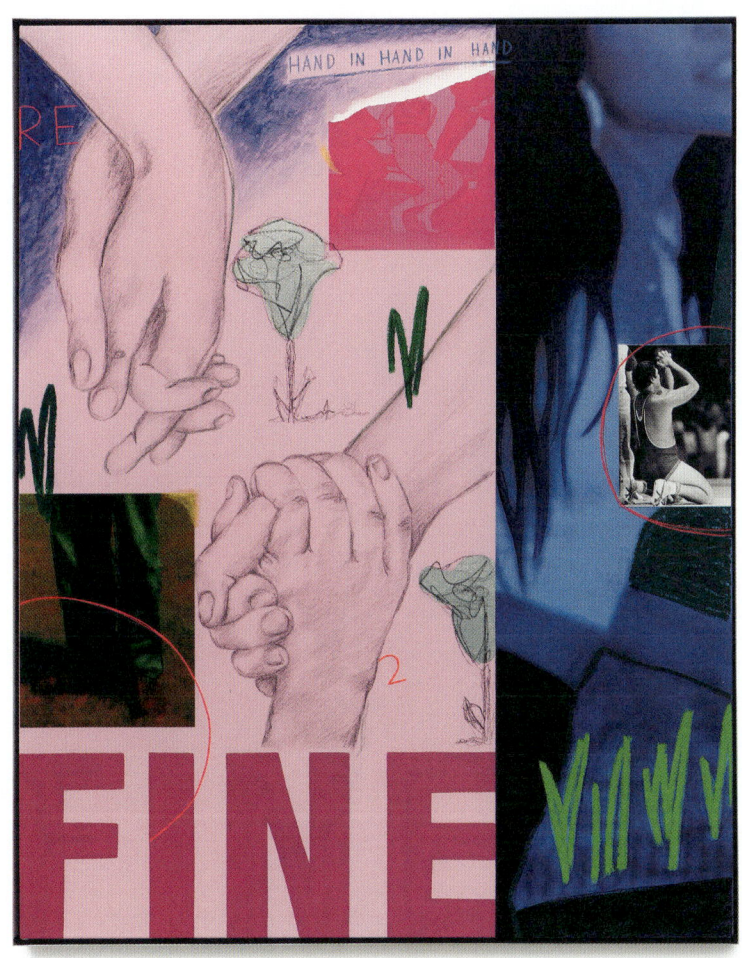

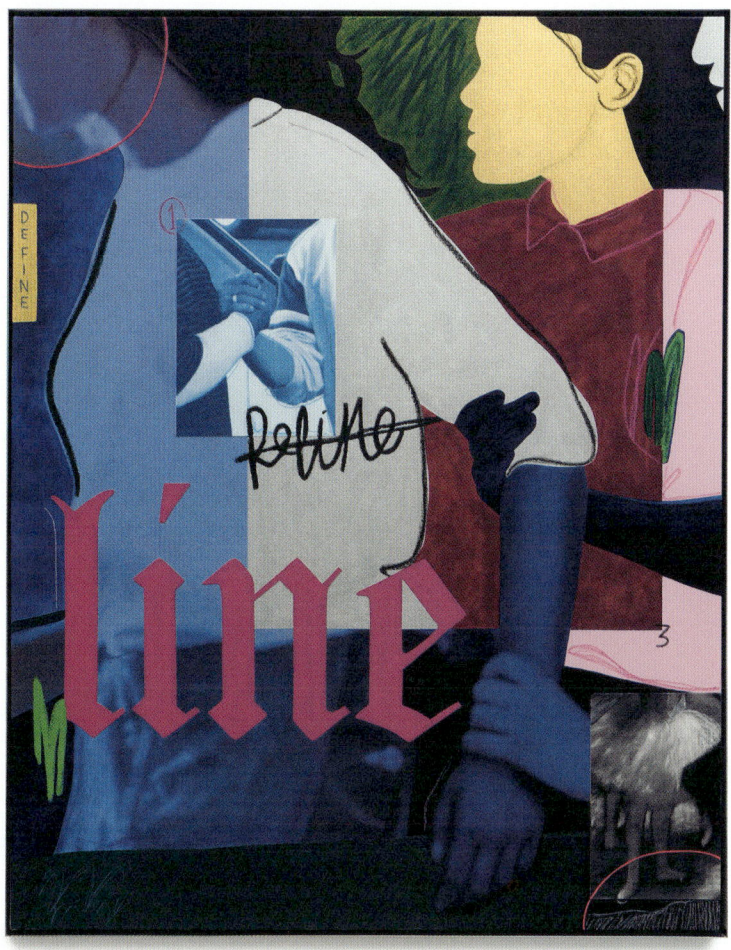

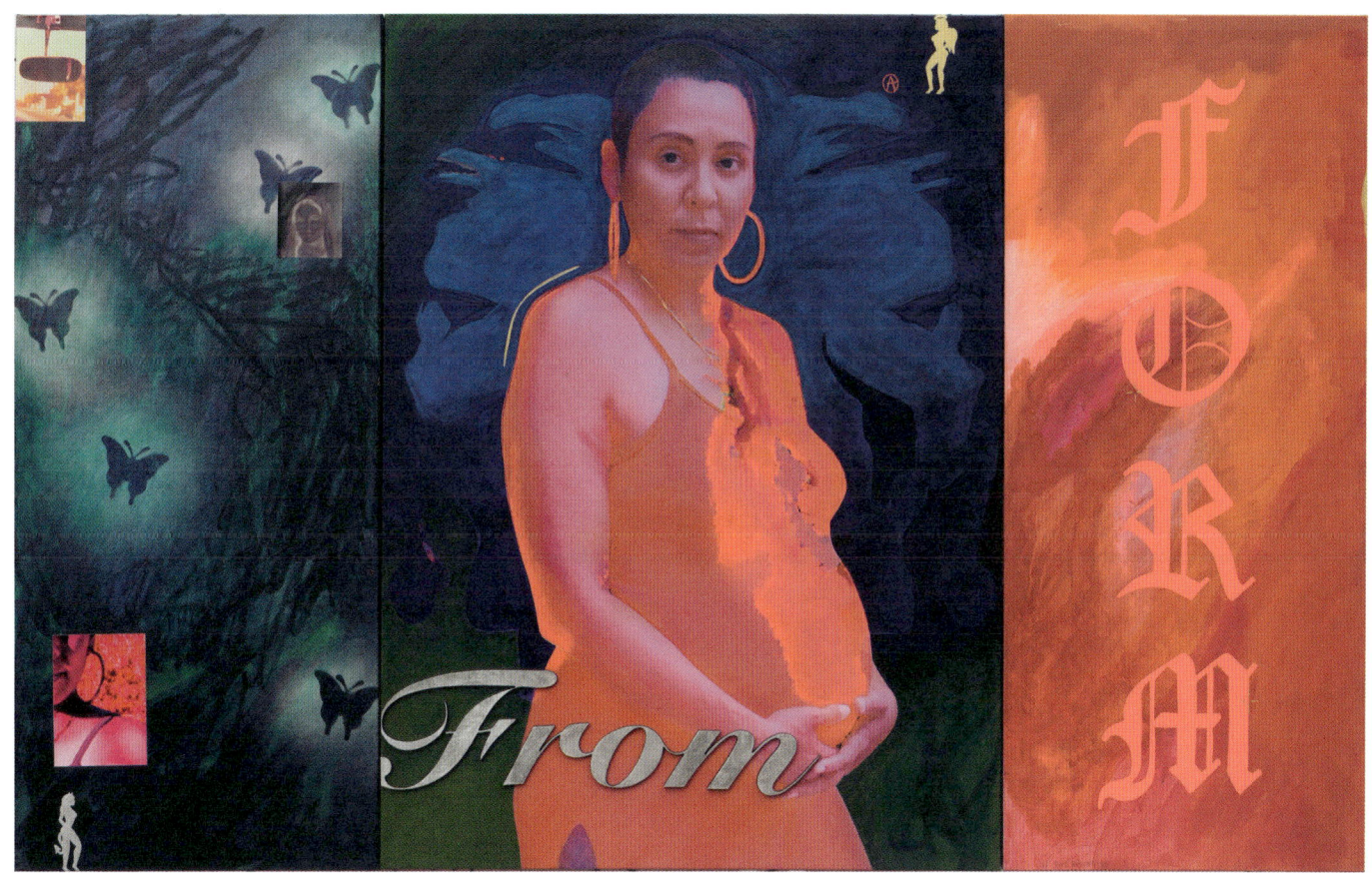

GABRIELLA
SANCHEZ

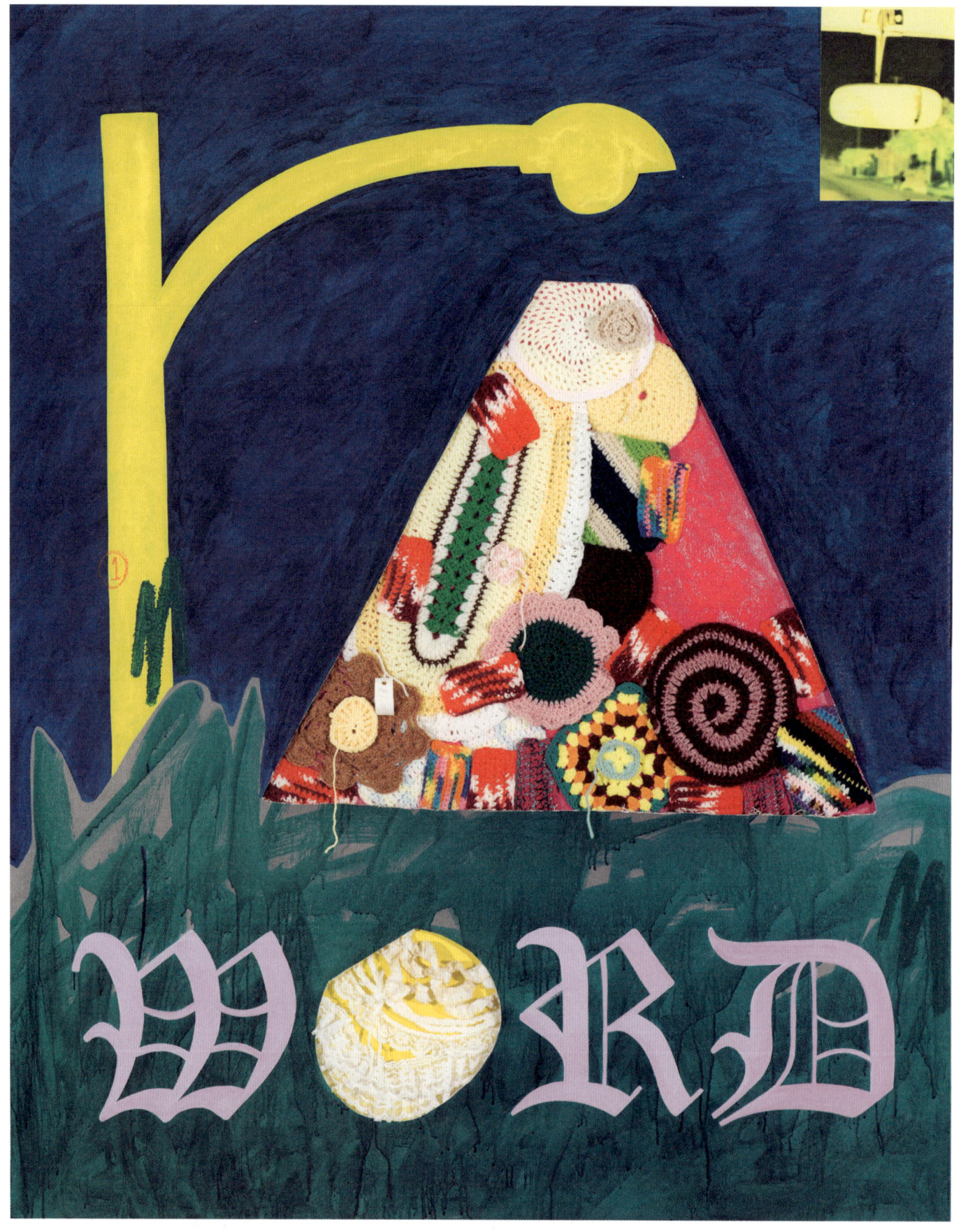

↑   **Portrait Of Figures In Light II**, 2021, acrylic, oil pastel, oil stick, house paint, archival photographic print on paper, lace, thread, yarn, fabric, crochet pieces and hand-embroidered lace from Sanchez's grandmother Lupe Ramirez and her church sewing group on nested canvases, 152.4 × 121.9 × 5 cm (60 × 48 × 2 in)

→   **Suitable**, 2019, acrylic, oil stick, graphite, oil pastel and archival pigment prints on canvas, 182.9 × 121.9 cm (72 × 48 in)

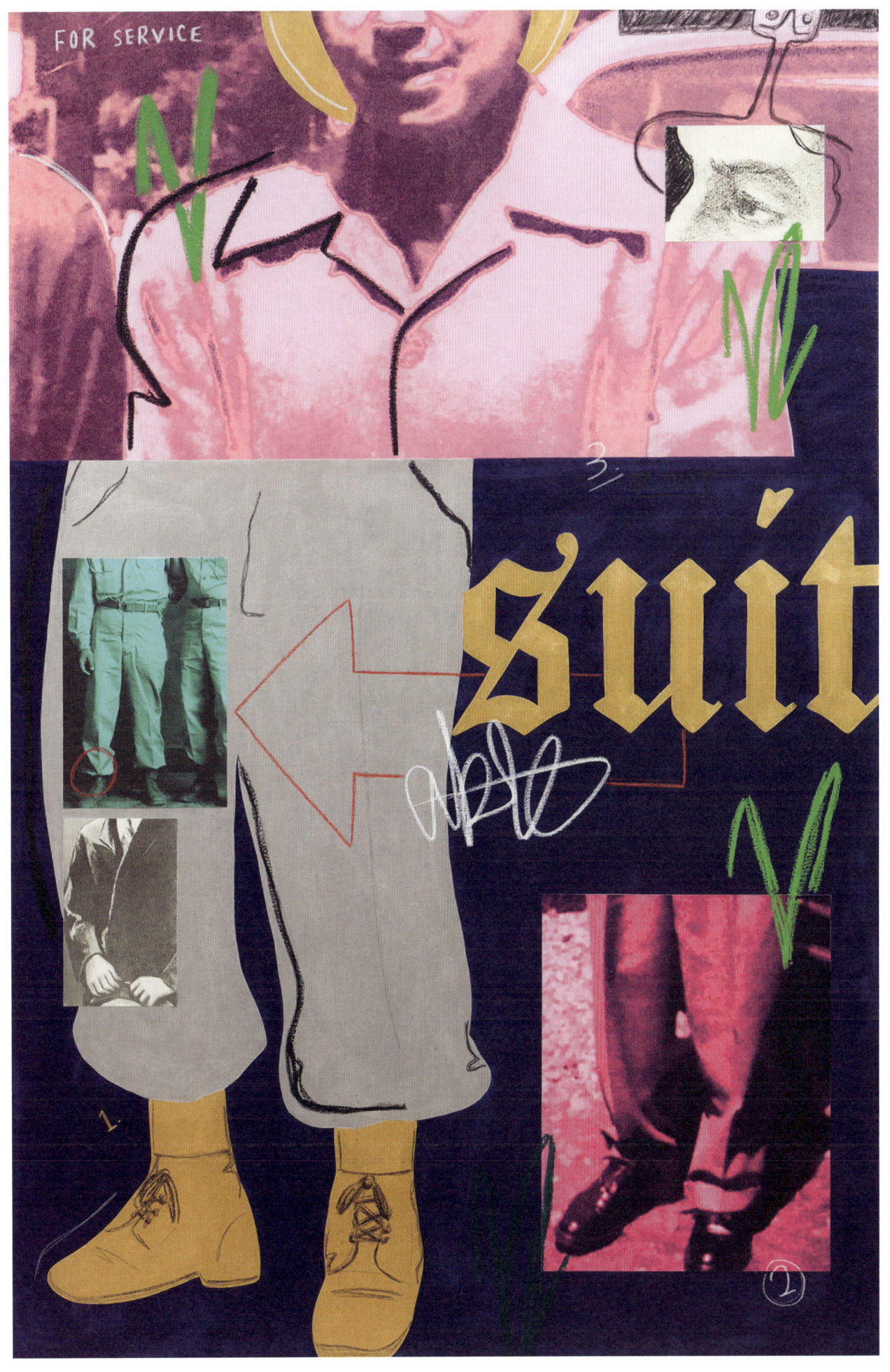

GABRIELLA
SANCHEZ

CHERELLE SAPPLETON

In a beguiling abstract language of hand-cut collages that play with scale, surface, colour and movement, Cherelle Sappleton investigates entrenched ideas about bodies – with a particular concern for Black female bodies. She began her artistic practice in performance, and elements of performativity, movement and action still percolate in her mixed-media collages. *YUM* (2018) is part of a body of work titled 'Hard Places', that borrows from approaches in abstract painting and explores themes of escape, fluidity and how to propose new ways of inhabiting, and looking at, bodies. Sappleton's process begins with cutting imagery from her collection of fashion and lifestyle magazines, creating collages on a small scale of between three to five centimetres (around one to two inches) that are then scanned and enlarged and composed in Photoshop, before being printed onto photographic paper at over a metre (more than three feet) in size; the artist then cuts these by hand, applies spray paint and fixes them only at certain points onto a base layer – some areas are left unattached allowing a sense of the possibility of shifting and movement. This effect is further emphasized when the works are displayed: shadows complicate their already layered surfaces, giving varying impressions of depth and dimension where some of the layers become visibly detached from the base – a vinyl layer printed with a fruit pattern that is commonplace and domestic yet seductive in its suggestion of succulence – visible through sunset shades of translucent spray paint that the artist has applied on top. This material aspect of Sappleton's work reflects her ongoing concern with how to represent bodies as free and in flux, creating a subjective experience rather than a fixed notion of a body as an immovable object. In doing so, Sappleton hopes to also restore pleasure, playfulness and sensuality, and elicit ways of feeling good in one's body. 'Hard Places' was made during a difficult period in the artist's personal life: *Fit* (2020) is an inward-looking work that addresses self-criticism. The title refers to both the idea of conformity and the ability to measure up to a standard, but also to the British slang for 'attractive'. Sappleton says that observing the diversity of bodies at a sex party she once attended prompted her to reflect on how standards surrounding physicality are essentially redundant – in the same way that such labels often don't match the lived experience of different genders, races, sexes. A leitmotif of striped leatherette that can be found in some of Sappleton's collages becomes a shorthand for 'restrictive binary thinking regarding difference generally – its smooth soft surface is a facsimile, appearing and feeling like leather and bringing with it a sensual and tactile quality,' the artist has explained on her website. 'Thinking about the problems of representing "blackness" and the (female) body, these works are attempts to find alternative ways to do so.'

CHARLOTTE JANSEN

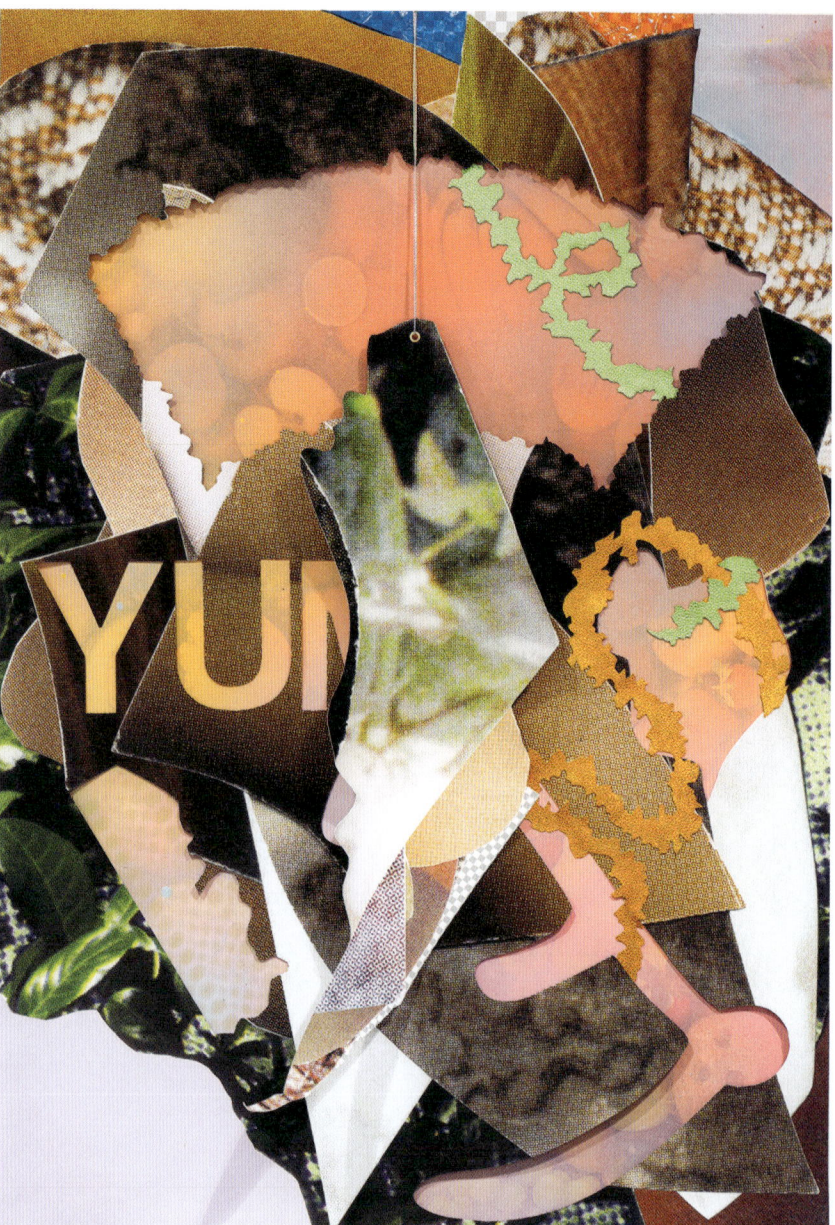

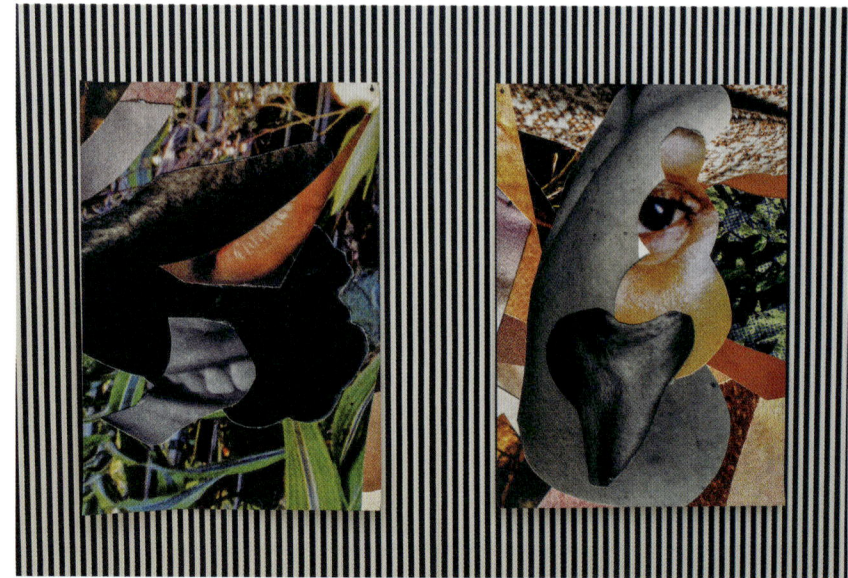

Born 1984, London, UK. Lives in Ramsgate, UK.

↑↑ **YUM**, 2018, mixed media, print, spray paint, vinyl and leatherette on wood, 118 × 84 cm (46½ × 33⅛ in)

↑ **Tea-leaf** and **Untitled**, 2020, giclée prints, each 118 × 84 cm (46½ × 33⅛ in), installation view, 'Among Other Things', Exeter Phoenix, UK, 2020

→ **Fit**, 2020, mixed media, giclée print, eyelets, leatherette and plasticized string on wood, 118 × 84 cm (46½ in × 33⅛)

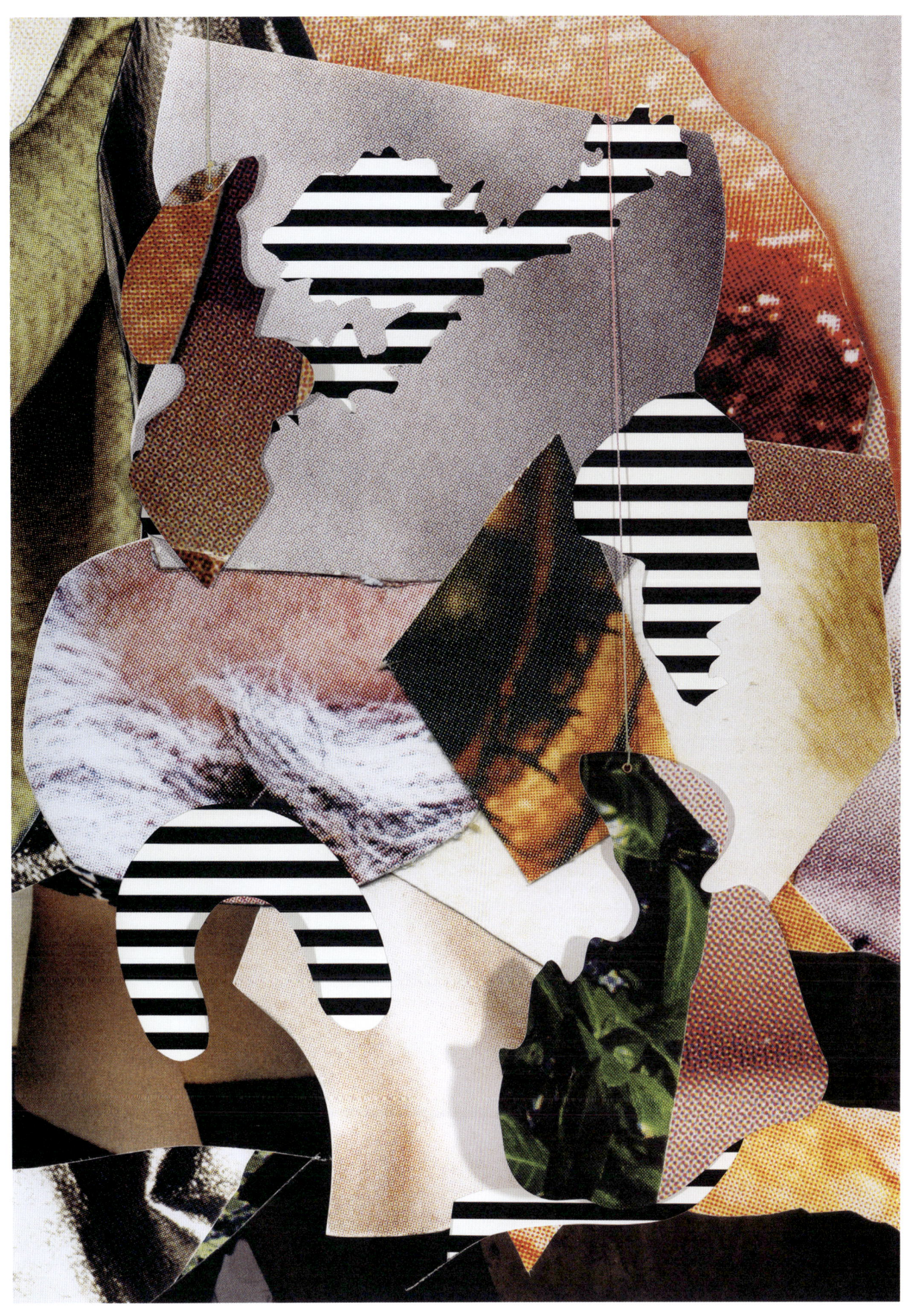

CHERELLE
SAPPLETON

Alongside peers including Sam Gilliam (1933–2022), Alma Thomas (1891–1978) and Jack Whitten (1939–2018), Raymond Saunders has been lauded since the 1960s, when he emerged as part of a generation of abstract painters who countered the ethos of the Black Arts Movement, in which representational work was considered the primary artistic vehicle in the struggle for libera- tion. The author of the self-published 1967 booklet *Black is a Color*, Saunders rejected what he saw as essentialist arguments that placed a burden on Black artists to express social politics in one specific way; at the time, the artist instead insisted on dramatizing social concerns through abstract painterly gestures. Often compared to Robert Rauschenberg (1925–2008) or Cy Twombly (1928–2011), Saunders's work is characterized by his penchant for amassing everyday detritus including found objects, magazine cut-outs and signage. He likewise has challenged the tropes of gestural abstract painting and the model of the self- expressive, heroic artist championed by Abstract Expressionism, but has done so by accumulating references that range from African American history and the classroom to improvisational jazz. ▬ Collage, painting and assemblage have remained three of Saunders's abiding interests; in more recent decades, these mediums have often included the use of dripped and textured pigments, chalk scratched on black backgrounds, flourishes in white pencil, scrawled-out simple equations, and fragments of childlike text. For rhythmic untitled works made between 2000 and 2015, he created detailed composite arrange- ments of found materials from everyday life, including scraps of patterned paper, doilies, age-worn puzzle pieces, magazine covers and a chess board. In an untitled piece from c.2000 (p.235), the tools for making art become components of the work: Saunders placed a paintbrush and set of coloured pencils directly on the surface of the panel alongside a Monopoly board, paper scraps and cast-off paintings of flowerpots. Here, the very tools of artmaking meld with ordinary things. ▬ The dramatic, mural-scale collaged work *Beauty in Darkness* (1993–9), made during the end of the apartheid era in South Africa in Saunders's Oakland studio, accumulates a patchwork of artists' tools, advertisements, children's literature and other ephemera relating to segregationist protocols, which are dynamically layered in fragments or otherwise cut up, reworked and shown emerging from a chalkboard background. The deconstructed nature of *Beauty in Darkness* draws attention to the gratuitous violence against Black people registered in the individual components of the piece in ways both spectacular and mundane. Seen as a whole, *Beauty in Darkness* is a hybrid object – it is indefinable as an example of one single artistic medium and evades one single interpretation. ▬

MADELINE WEISBURG

Born 1943, Pittsburgh, Pennsylvania, USA. Lives in Oakland, California, USA.

↑　Untitled, c.2000, mixed media on panel, 135 × 100 cm (53⅛ × 39⅜ in)

↗　Untitled, c.2000, mixed media on panel, 153 × 122 cm (60¼ × 48⅛ in)

→　Untitled, 2015, mixed media on panel, 121 × 89 cm (47⅝ × 35⅛ in)

→→　Untitled, 2000–10, mixed media on board, 121.9 × 90.2 cm (48 × 35½ in)

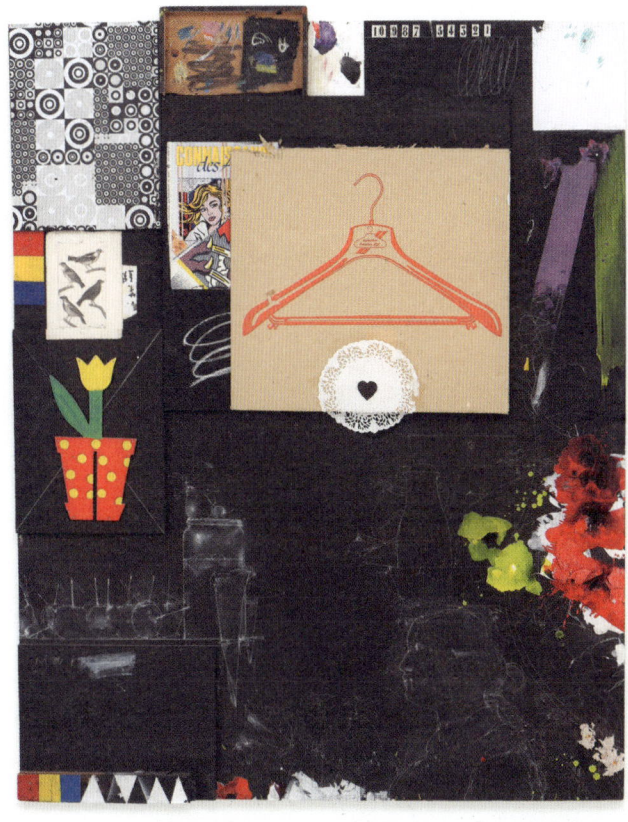

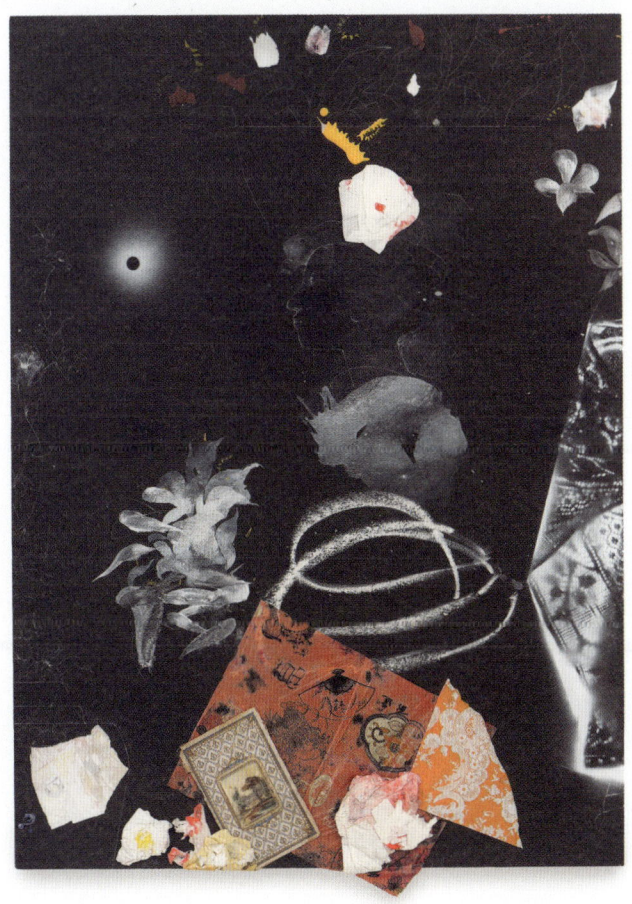

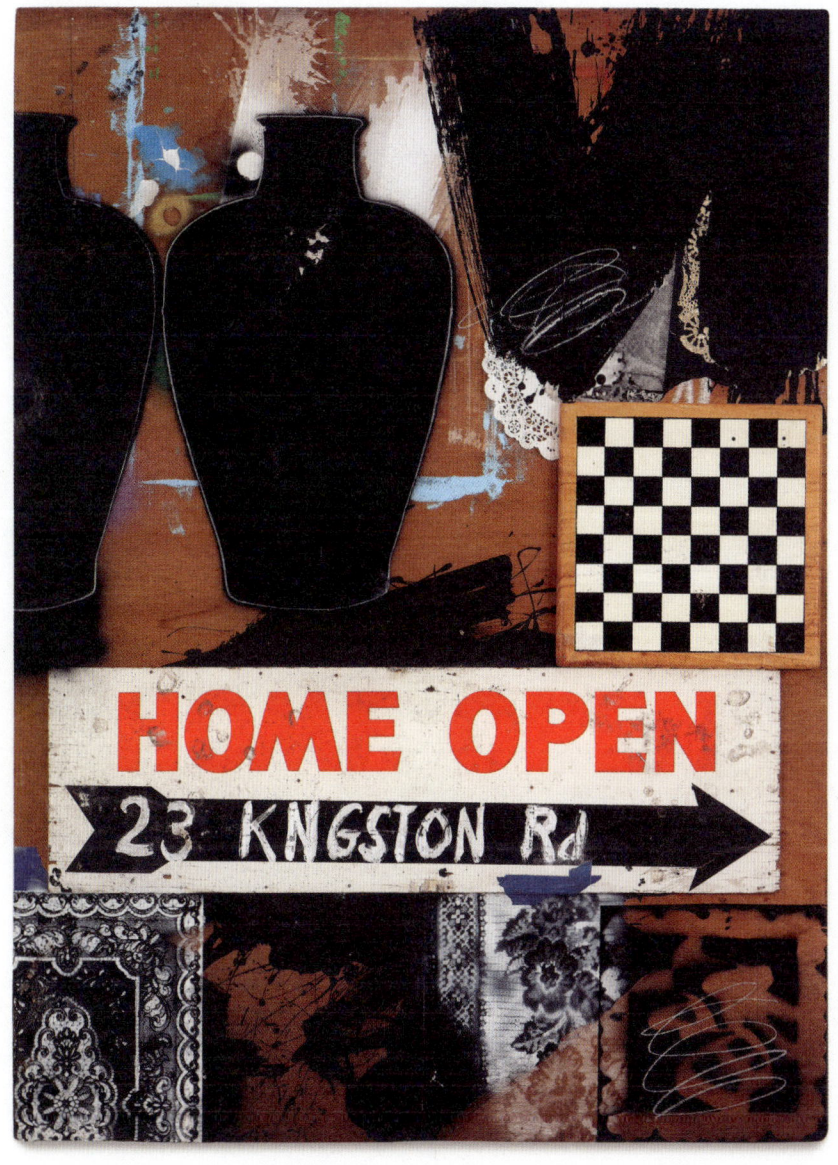

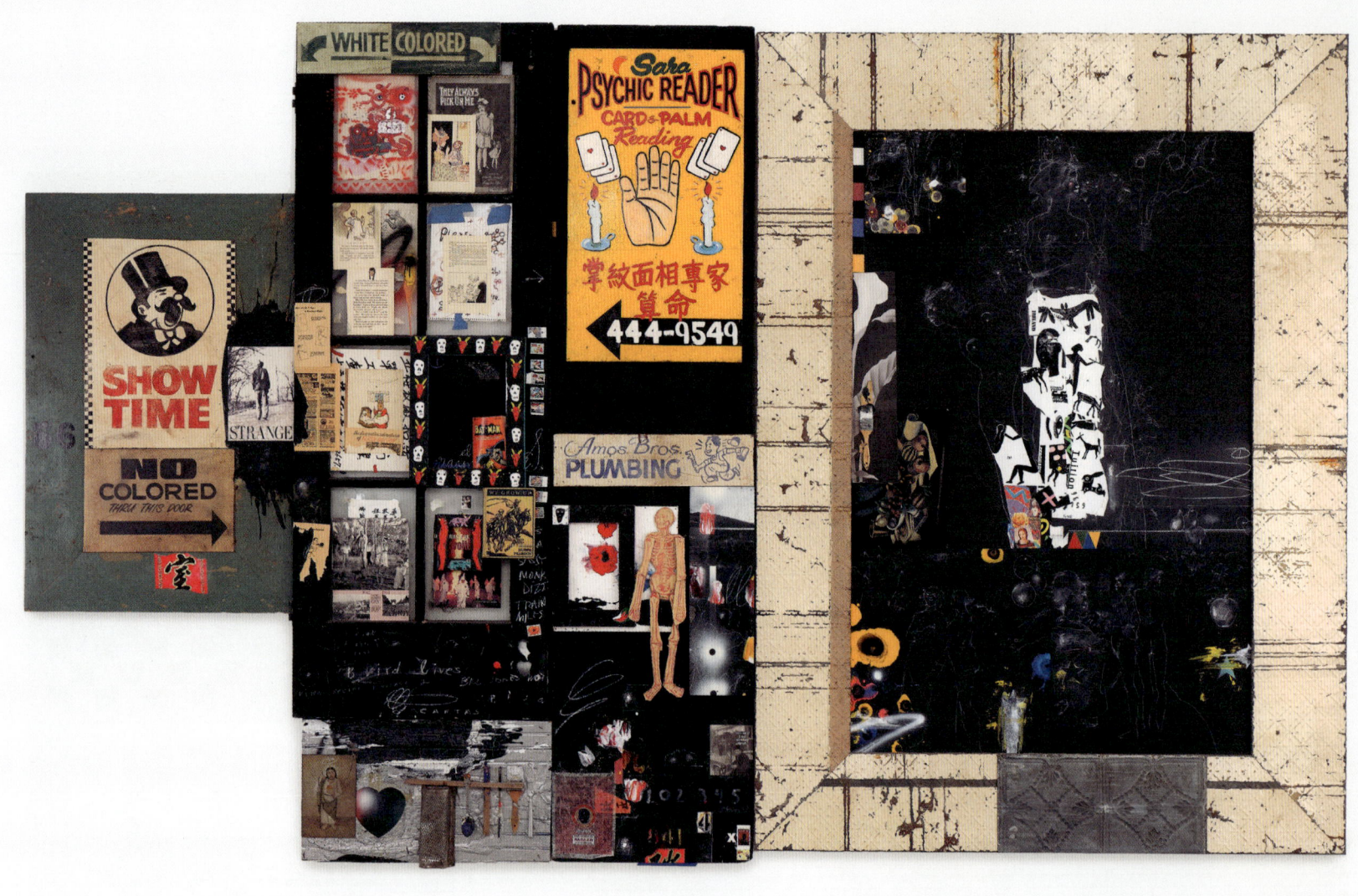

↑   **Beauty in Darkness**, 1993–9, mixed media and collage on board, 245.1 × 457.2 × 16.5 cm
(96½ × 180 × 6½ in)

→   **Untitled**, c.2000, mixed media on panel, 202 × 136 cm (79½ × 53½ in)

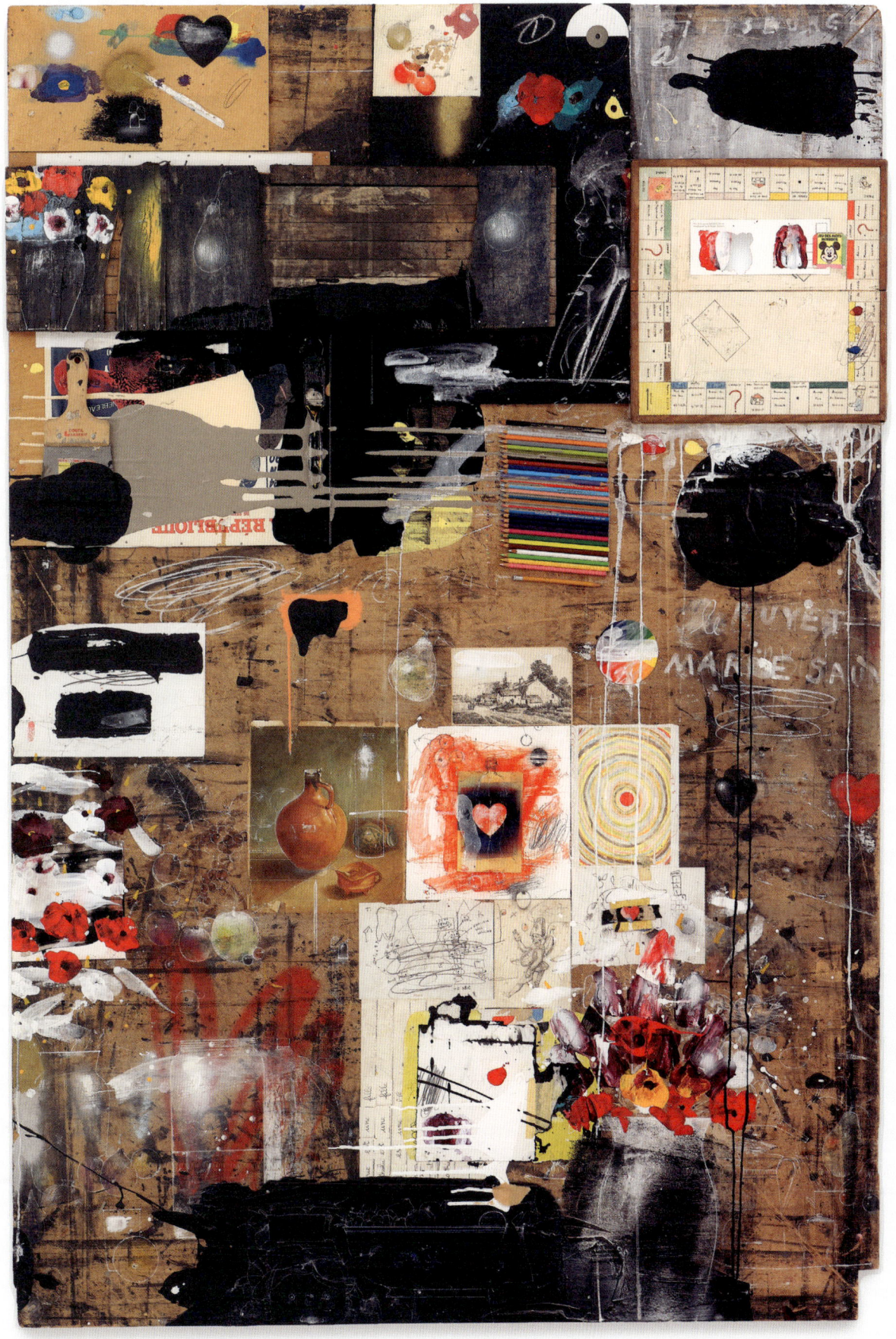

RAYMOND SAUNDERS

GERDA SCHEEPERS

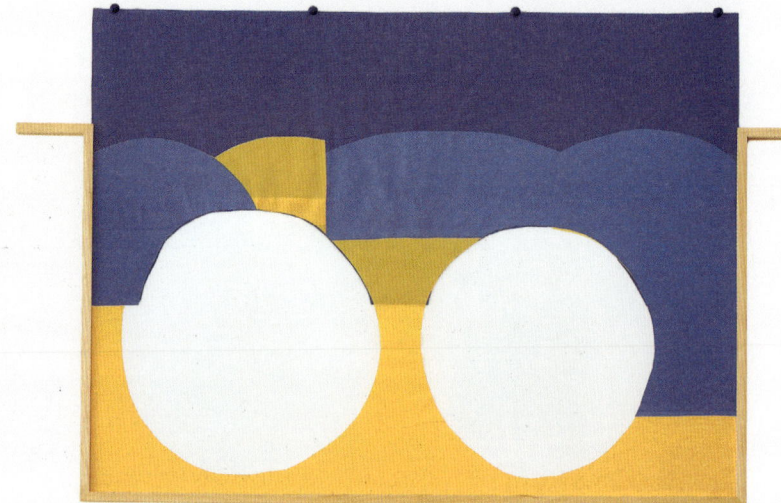

The collaged works of Gerda Scheepers are curiously ambiguous offerings: 'in between painting and sculpture, with slightly dishonest ambitions towards the performing arts, and actively jealous of the written or spoken,' as she wrote for her 2013 exhibition 'Talking About 12 Paintings' at blank projects in Cape Town. In her spare compositions, fabric becomes a pictorial and sculptural medium, giving shape and colour to Scheepers's preoccupations. Pulled, ruched and draped into familiar folds and forms, the artist's textile coverings are quietly humorous in their allusions to both upholstered furnishings and clothed bodies. That a neckline and soft shelving unit share the same pastel yellow tone in *Shirt Shelf Painting* (2021) suggests that bodies and household objects are perhaps not as dissimilar as one might assume – both similarly awkward forms to be dressed.

While Scheepers's broader thematic pursuits remain largely ambiguous, her compositions appear as much studies in fabric construction as in the arrangement of absences. Gaps and blank spaces recur as formal interludes across her collages, as in *The border's border* (2019) – with its oblong emptiness framed by patterned fabric – and *Holes for a flag or the sea* (2018), its two circular cut-outs staring blankly at the viewer. Both these collages, like many of the image-objects that populate the artist's practice, appear wholly ambivalent in their implications, as happenstance arrangements that find a precarious, imperfect balance. Reticent to explain her work, the artist reveals little of her intentions, offering only a material narration of her often opaque intrigues. In the artist's studio, 'possibilities and restrictions play themselves out,' as Scheepers said in the text for her 2016 exhibition 'Sitcom', also at blank projects. 'The works have to make do with what is available. They enter a struggle between possibilities and limitations and sometimes simply my inabilities.' Made within such constraints, material or otherwise, her collages frequently allude to the small, cumulative frustrations of daily life – slipcovers shrunk in the wash, a pair of shorts riding up, a fitted sheet that will not fit – the commonplace efforts of covering and otherwise concealing flesh and furniture. Something of this effort is mirrored in Scheepers's process: the artist unstitching and restitching her seams, tracing hesitations and revisions across her fabric forms. All her collages, Scheepers allows, are the product of a certain endurance. The resulting works appear as much as haphazard propositions for more robust iterations as they do the residue of past gestures and time spent. *History of a hand* (2019) recalls not only the absent image of an arm, cut from the canvas, but the hand of the artist gluing, sewing, pausing and persevering. There is a preparatory air to the composition, the sense of it having been fashioned from incident and off-cuts.

LUCIENNE BESTALL

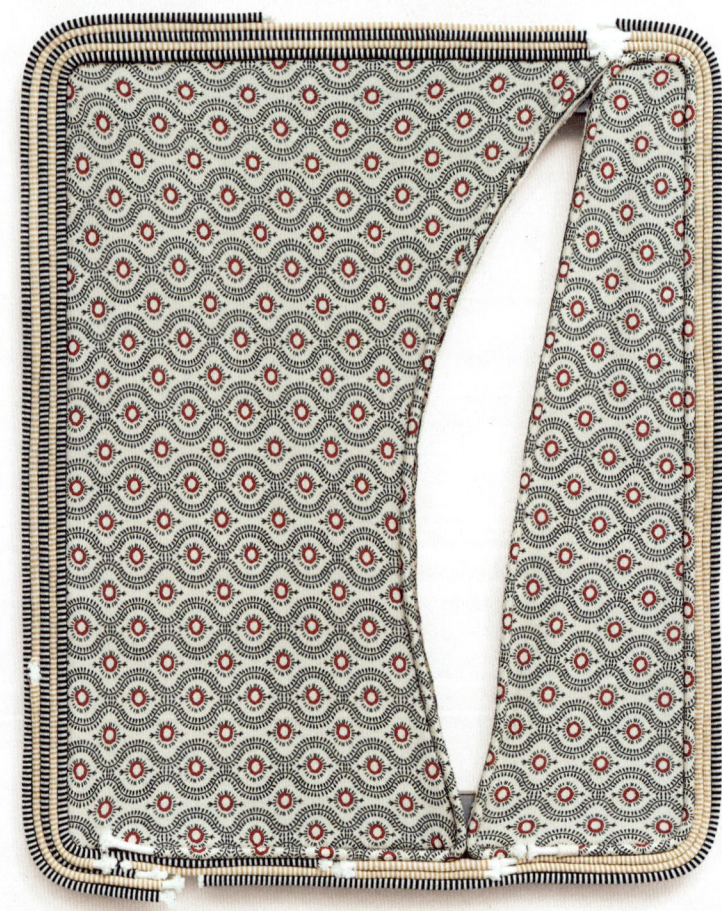

Born 1979, Tzaneen, South Africa. Lives in Cape Town, South Africa.

↑↑ **Holes for a flag or the sea**, 2018, wood, fabric, glass and papier-mâché, 155 × 254 cm (61 × 100 in)

↑ **The border's border**, 2019, fabric, rope and wood, 57 × 48 × 3 cm (22½ × 18⅞ × 1⅛ in)

↗ **History of a hand**, 2019, fabric, acrylic paint and wood, 110 × 62 cm (43¼ × 24⅜ in), private collection, Washington DC, USA

↗↗ **Inside Altar**, 2021, fabric collage on canvas, 90 × 70 cm (35⅜ × 27½ in)

→ **Shirt Shelf Painting**, 2021, fabric collage and acrylic on canvas, 70 × 90 cm (27½ × 35⅜ in)

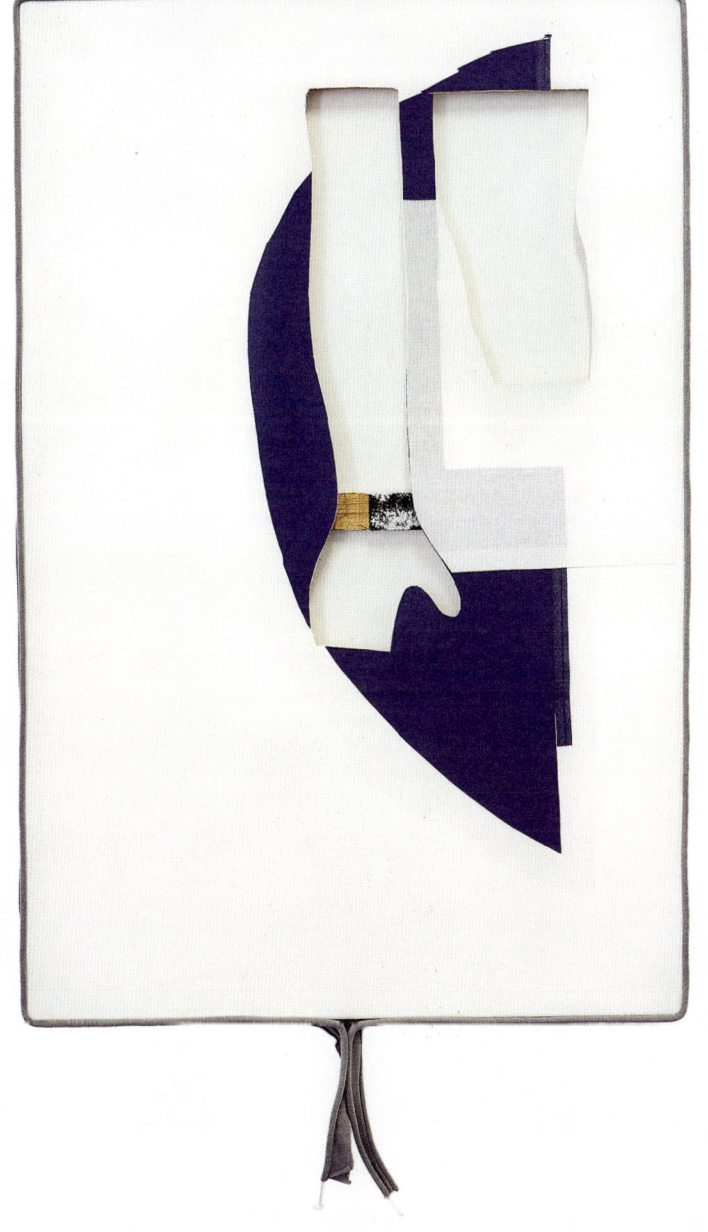

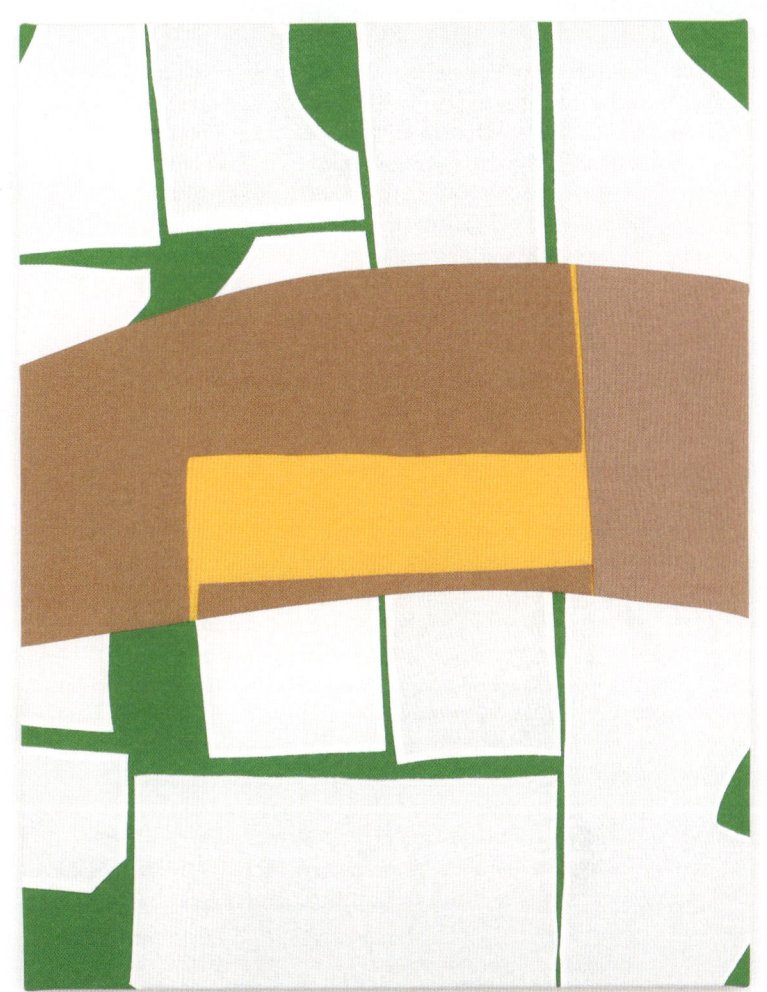

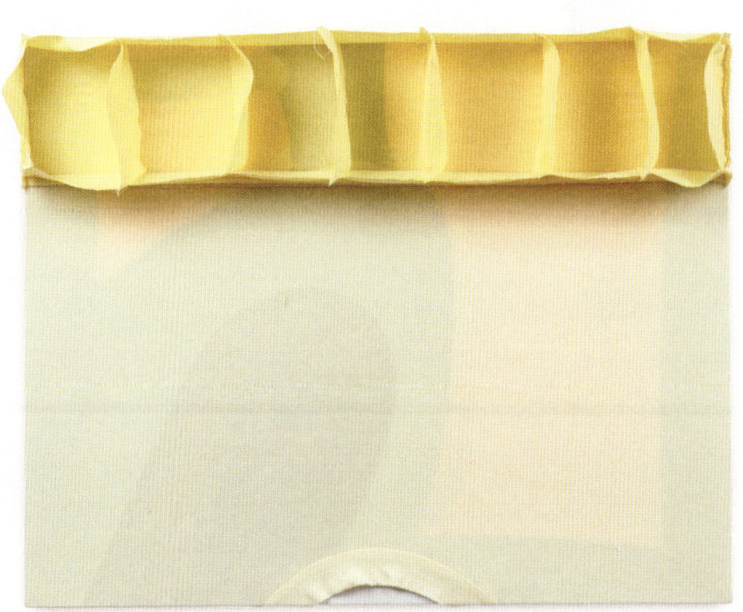

GERDA
SCHEEPERS

TSCHABALALA SELF

Utilizing various materials, techniques and approaches to collage including printmaking, painting, stencilling and stitching fabrics, Tschabalala Self examines issues around race and gender. She reflects on representations of the Black body in visual culture, while also introducing conversations about femininity and public space. Self regularly chooses anonymized women as her subjects, using collage as a way to reference the sitter's layered identity. Although the works initially appear as flat surfaces, the artist's use of varied materials creates a subtly textured surface that benefits from being viewed at close range. In *Half Full* (2022) Self depicts a woman looking over one shoulder, raised drink in hand, as though her attention has just been called by someone beyond the canvas at whom she now appears to be winking. The monochrome background offers no clues as to wider context and so the emphasis is concentrated on the figure and, in particular, her bold red clothing, which is brought to life by the use of sections of actual fabric. The work's title, while literally referencing the glass of wine depicted, also implies a metaphorical sense of positivity. Self is particularly interested in the ways in which some individuals (in essence, white men) are afforded agency and safety within public space, while others are not. With this in mind, she deliberately peoples her compositions with figures that are dynamic, unrestrained and able to express themselves freely – safely living, taking up space and enjoying boundless experiences. In *Tabled* (2021) Self reserves the use of fabrics for the figure as opposed to the checked tablecloth that dominates the composition, flattening any pictorial depth. Intricate lace is employed to emphasize sections of the figure and the facial features are modelled with different coloured fabrics. Typical in Self's work is the use of a theatrical shadow-like painted form behind her subjects, echoing their gestures and creating some dramatic depth within the composition. In *Tabled*, however, the black form appears in front of the figure's right foot, complicating the idea that it is a straightforward shadow – perhaps it represents a second self, or the subject's multifaceted existence. *Two Women 3* (2021) is one in a trio of works that were debuted at Baltimore Museum of Art, USA, in the artist's major solo exhibition 'Tschabalala Self: Be My Self' (2021). Made in response to a sculpture in the museum's permanent collection, *Two Women* (1907–8; originally titled *Two Negresses*) by Henri Matisse, in contrast to the still, silent bronze of embracing nudes who exist only to be gazed upon, Self's women are vibrant and self-possessed, described in a *Hyperallergic* review as 'torchless ladies of liberty that own the floor like Motown singers vying for center stage'.

MARITZA LACAYO

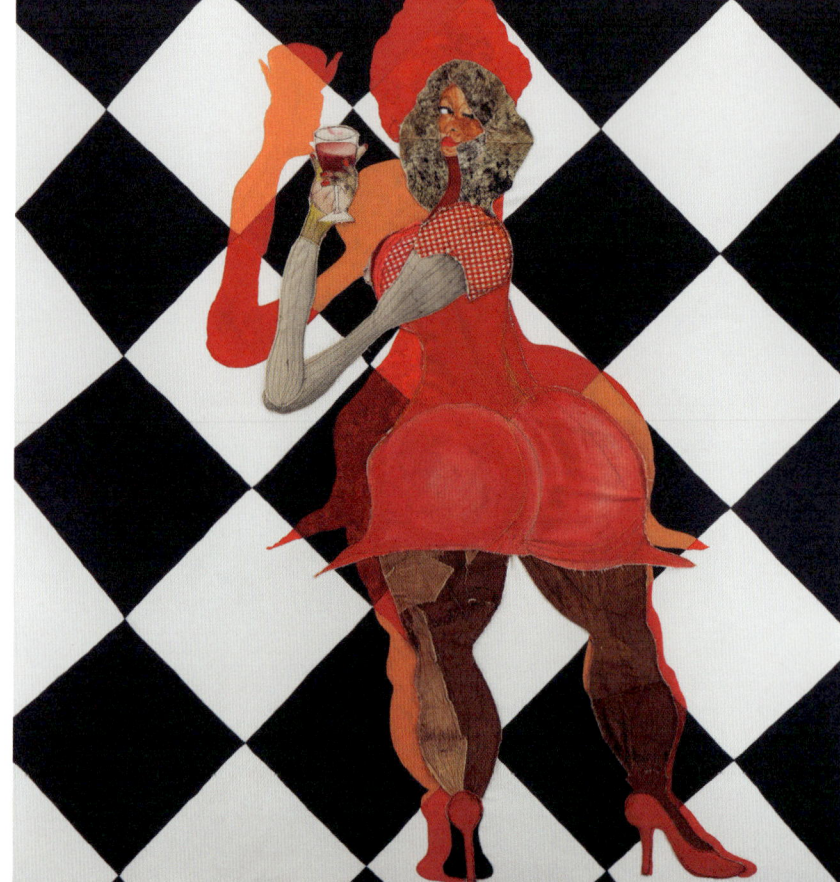

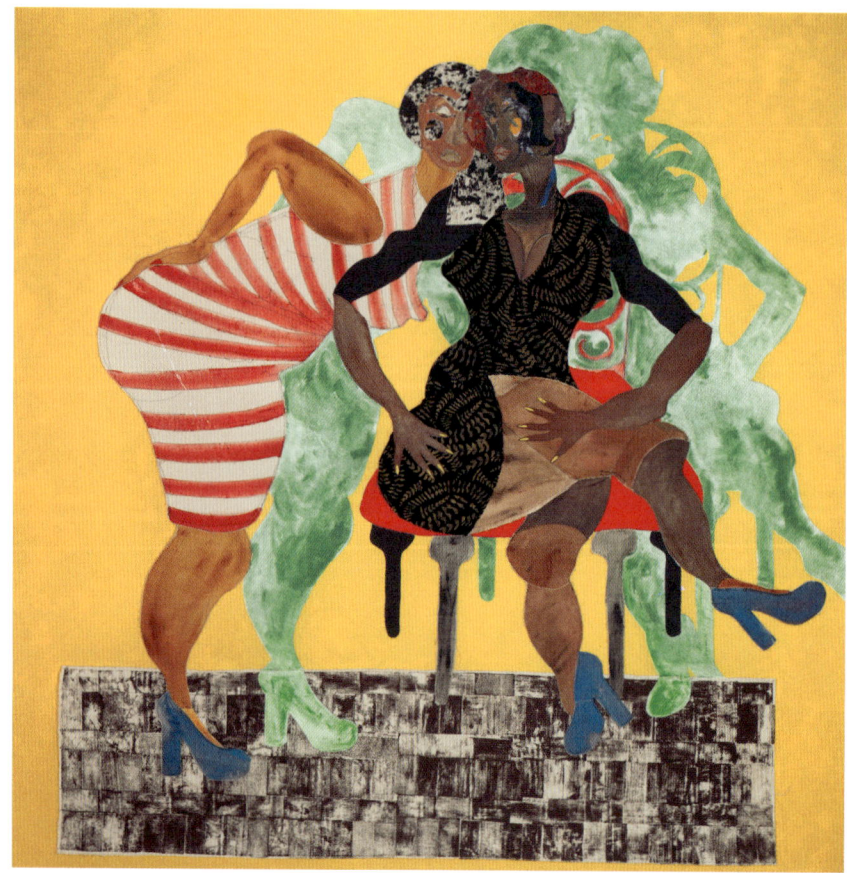

Born 1990, Harlem, New York, USA. Lives in New York and New Haven, Connecticut, USA.

↑↑ **Half Full**, 2022, acrylic, Flashe, assorted fabric, painted fabric, painted paper and thread on canvas, 213.4 × 203.2 × 2.5 cm (84 × 80 × 1 in)

↑ **Two Women 3**, 2021, tulle, lace, velvet, thread, acrylic paint, digital print on canvas and painted canvas on canvas, 243.8 × 243.8 cm (96 × 96 in)

→ **Tabled**, 2021, lace, fabric, oil, acrylic, dye and painted canvas on canvas, 213.4 × 182.9 cm (84 × 72 in)

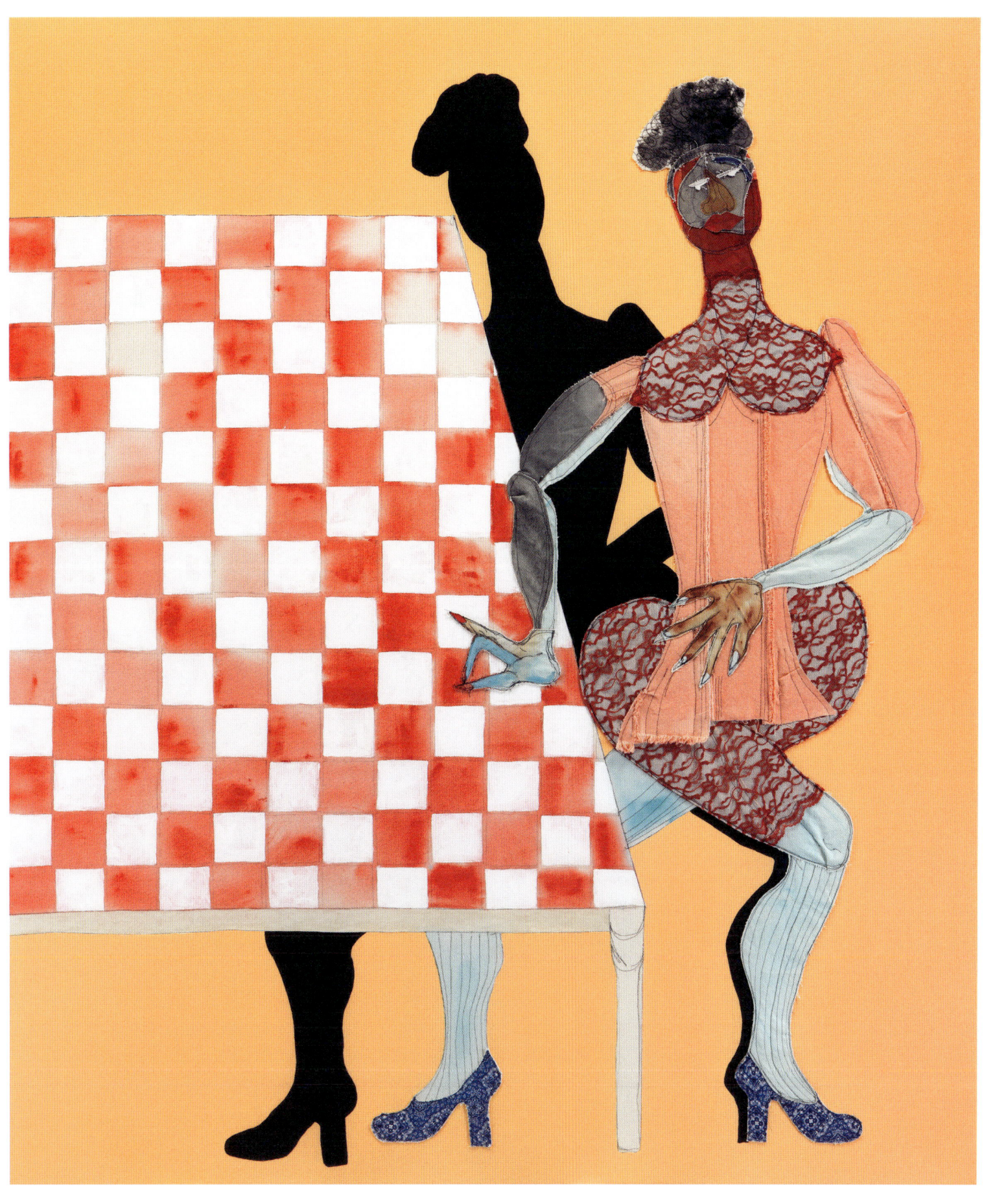

MARINELLA
SENATORE

In a practice that encompasses installation, video, performance, public art, photography, sculpture, neon and collage, Marinella Senatore's work is frequently performative and reflects on the political dimension of participation. She addresses various types of participation, both by audiences of art itself, but also by members of society more broadly, and considers oral histories, protest, ritual and the formation of social structures that govern us, among other topics. Influenced by artists such as Tim Rollins (1955–2017), Ana Mendieta (1948–85) and Felix Gonzalez-Torres (1957–96), her work can be situated within a lineage of such practices that utilize collective narratives as much as autobiographical experience. In this way, the aesthetics of resistance and the transformative power of social engagement are rendered more subjectively and vulnerably, inspiring an empathetic, collective outlook. ◢ 'Make it Shine' was the title of Senatore's solo exhibition at Mazzoleni gallery in Turin in late 2021. She also uses this title for the many artworks it included: for example, the brightly coloured nine-part collage comprising mixed media elements and paper cut-outs in a grid configuration. The panels range from boldly monochromatic to others suggesting more abstract motifs and formal arrangements of shape and colour. Some, however, depict silhouetted figures with a single arm raised, seemingly in a gesture of defiance or solidarity. In an echo to this, the text 'RISE UP' can be seen as a galvanizing call to the viewer. In the top left-hand panel, a hand is pointing in a less emphatic way towards something outside the frame. This iconography of hands is frequently deployed by Senatore and can be read as a portrait of the artist herself. In the bottom right panel, the text 'You + Me' is visible, and so the gentle extension of the hand can be read as an invitation, perhaps, to enter the work – the 'work' in this instance being the collage itself but also the act of collective solidarity. ◢ *Speak Easy Collage* (2017) is composed of twentieth-century brass band music scores, mosaic tiles, and other found imagery and materials. The title is derived from a larger 2013 video installation, which was produced by 1,200 citizens of Madrid, Spain (each of whom donated 1 Euro to finance the production of the work). Members of a neighbourhood association in Madrid as well as students from the city's Complutense University worked with trade and crafts people on all aspects of pre-production, from script writing to set design, to create a musical set in 1950s New York. *Speak Easy Collage* becomes a distillation of the video, working as documentation, evidence and, perhaps, contract: a metaphorical coming together of social and material elements to consider the place of community in art and art in community. ◢

HANA NOORALI AND LYNTON TALBOT

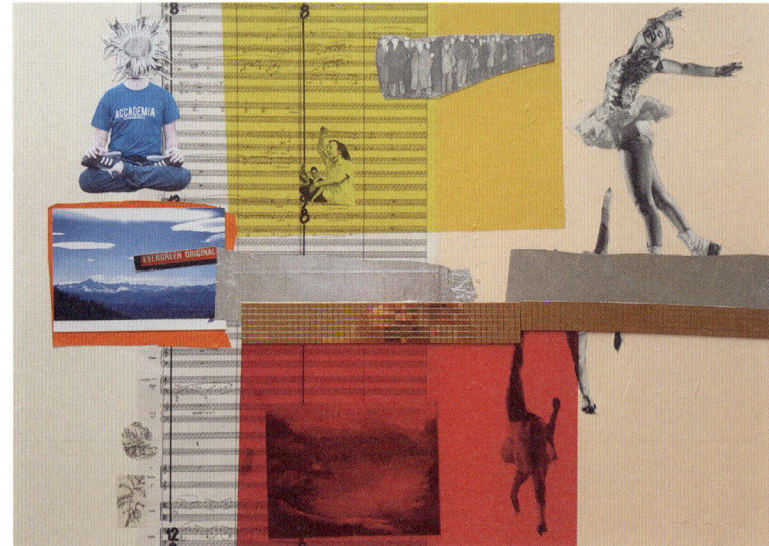

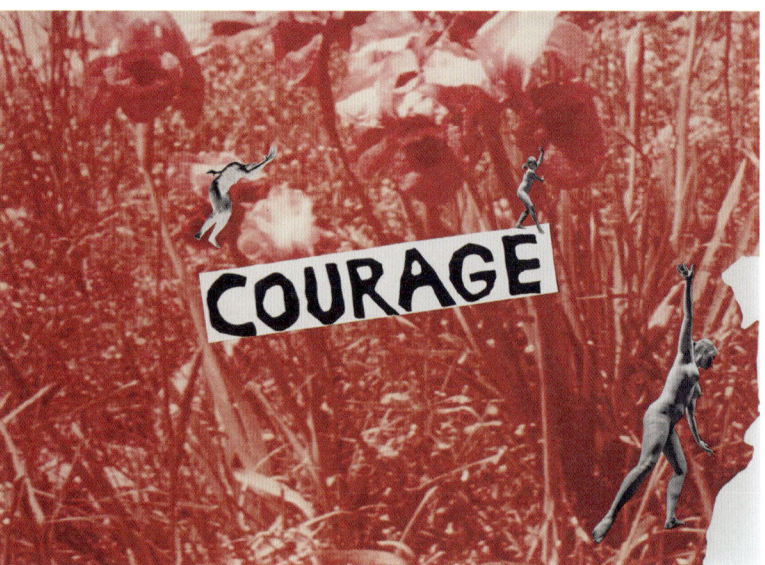

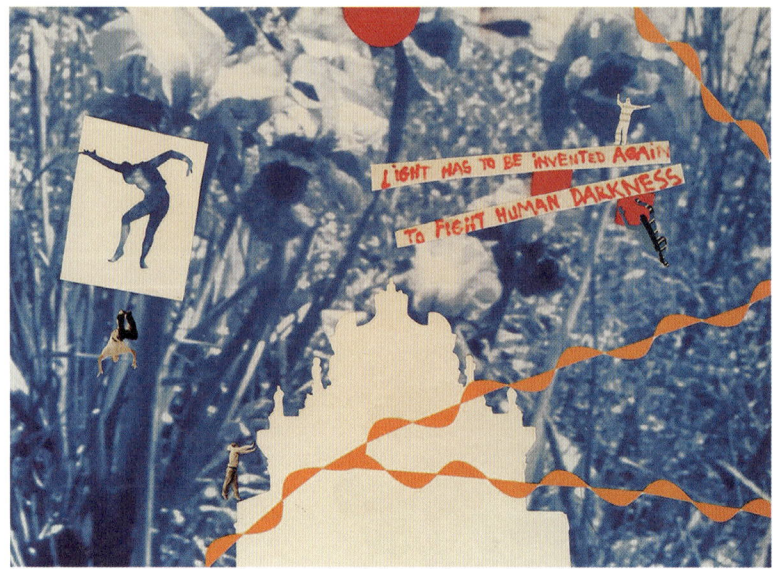

Born 1977, Cava de' Tirreni, Italy. Lives in Rome, Italy.

↑↑↑ **Speak Easy Collage**, 2017, collage and mixed media on acid-free vegetable cardboard, 50 × 70 cm (19¾ × 27½ in)

↑↑ **Make it Shine**, 2021, collage and mixed media on cotton paper, 50 × 70 cm (19¾ × 27½ in)

↑ **Make it Shine**, 2021, collage and mixed media on cotton paper, 50 × 70 cm (19¾ × 27½ in)

→ **Make it Shine**, 2021, collage and mixed media on cotton paper, 210 × 150 cm (82⅝ × 59⅛ in)

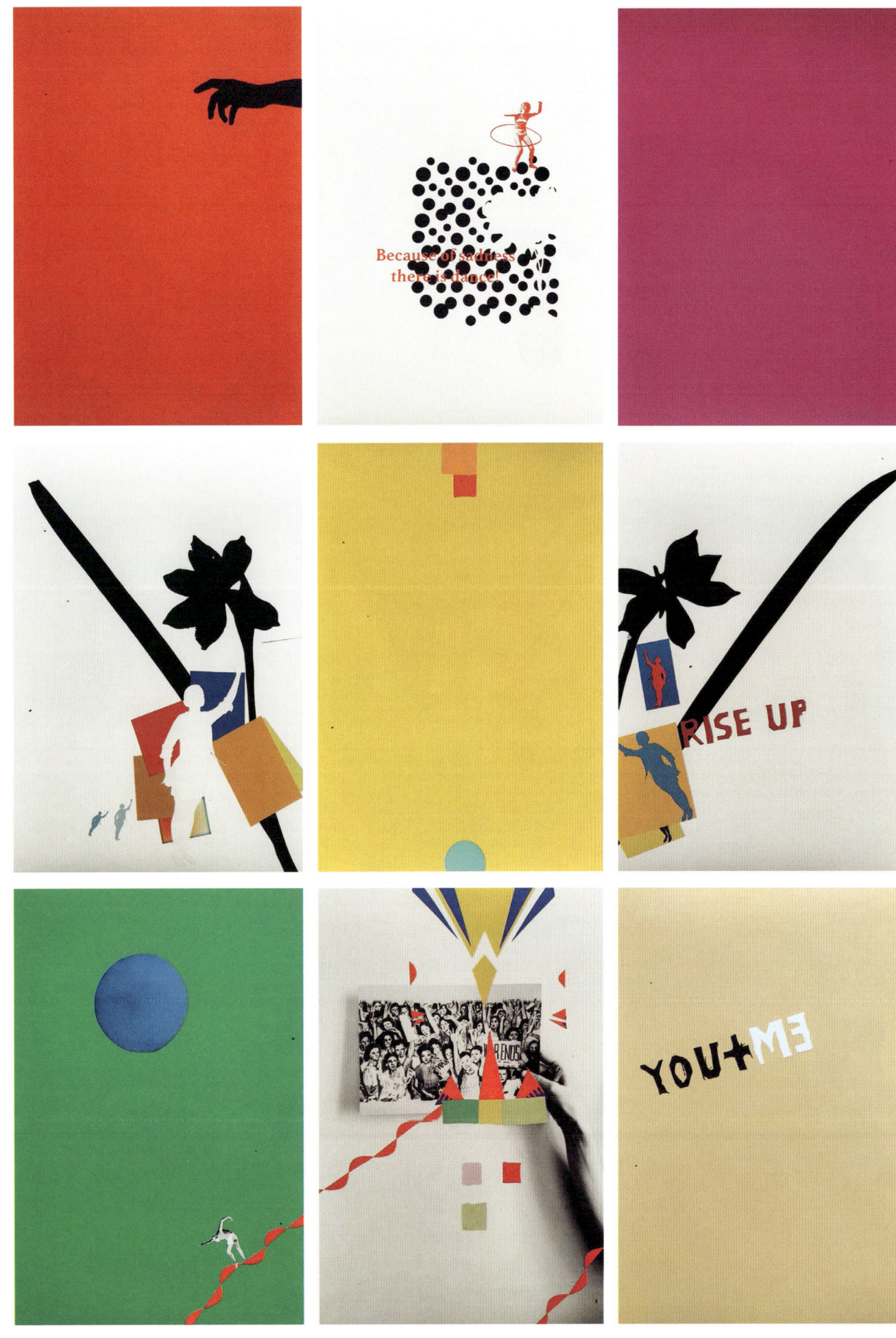

MARINELLA
SENATORE

AFRAH SHAFIQ

Afrah Shafiq's practice comprises installation, documentary, animation, sound and collage and explores folklore, mysticism, iconism and oral histories. Her research considers how these elements intersect and how they can be influenced by memory, national identity and ideology. Shafiq frequently mines archives containing ephemera of colonial histories and uses this material to bring to the fore more marginalized voices and overlooked histories. This is evident in *Sultana's Reality* (2017), an interactive, multimedia, web-based work, whose title is borrowed from a sci-fi and feminist short story published in 1905 by the Bengali activist and writer Rokeya Sakhawat Hossain. Resulting from the time Shafiq spent in the archives at the Centre for Studies in Social Sciences in Kolkata, India, *Sultana's Reality* deftly collages together contemporary and historical imagery including brightly coloured lithographs by Raja Ravi Varma (1848–1906), cinema posters, tarot, text, videos and interactive elements. The depiction of ordinary people and Hindu gods alongside the mythical, cinematic and prosaic materials poetically portrays different women's stories of protest that are housed in the archive, revealing their relationship to education in colonial India. The result is a hybrid, anachronistic digital lexicon that critiques the treatment of women during a particular time. An avatar visible on the left-hand side is a constant presence throughout the website. Perhaps this is representative of the artist herself, an attentive guide, marshalling us through this complex history using their access to other forms of knowledge so frequently belittled by colonial conquest. *Our Lady of I Can Be Anything You Want Me To* (2020) is an interactive browser-based work that incorporates sound, animation, text and custom-written code. It explores how the Marian (Virgin Mary) is portrayed globally across conflicting geographical locations and religions. The landing page holds a collaged-together image of an anthropomorphized pyramid shape, replete with a circuit-board eye and smile made from multi-coloured squares. Clip-art renderings of a slithering snake, a red rose and some bananas populate the base. Two kneeling people are holding candles. At the top is an ever-changing portrait made from found images of Marian. Clicking on the different squares reveals histories of the use of the name 'Mary': 'the marigold flower is named after Mary', 'before Mary existed it was the sacred flower of the indigenous people in Mexico'. With another click, we are invited to explore the relationship between Artificial Intelligence, divinity and being human by way of religious iconography, mandalas and text. Crucial to its understanding, however, is the fact that this work can be added to by the audience. Again, usurping the established Western notions of education – that favour a hierarchical model of disseminating knowledge from above – the work encourages the coming together of communal wisdoms as a type of production and dissemination in itself: shared knowledge as a form of collage.

HANA NOORALI AND LYNTON TALBOT

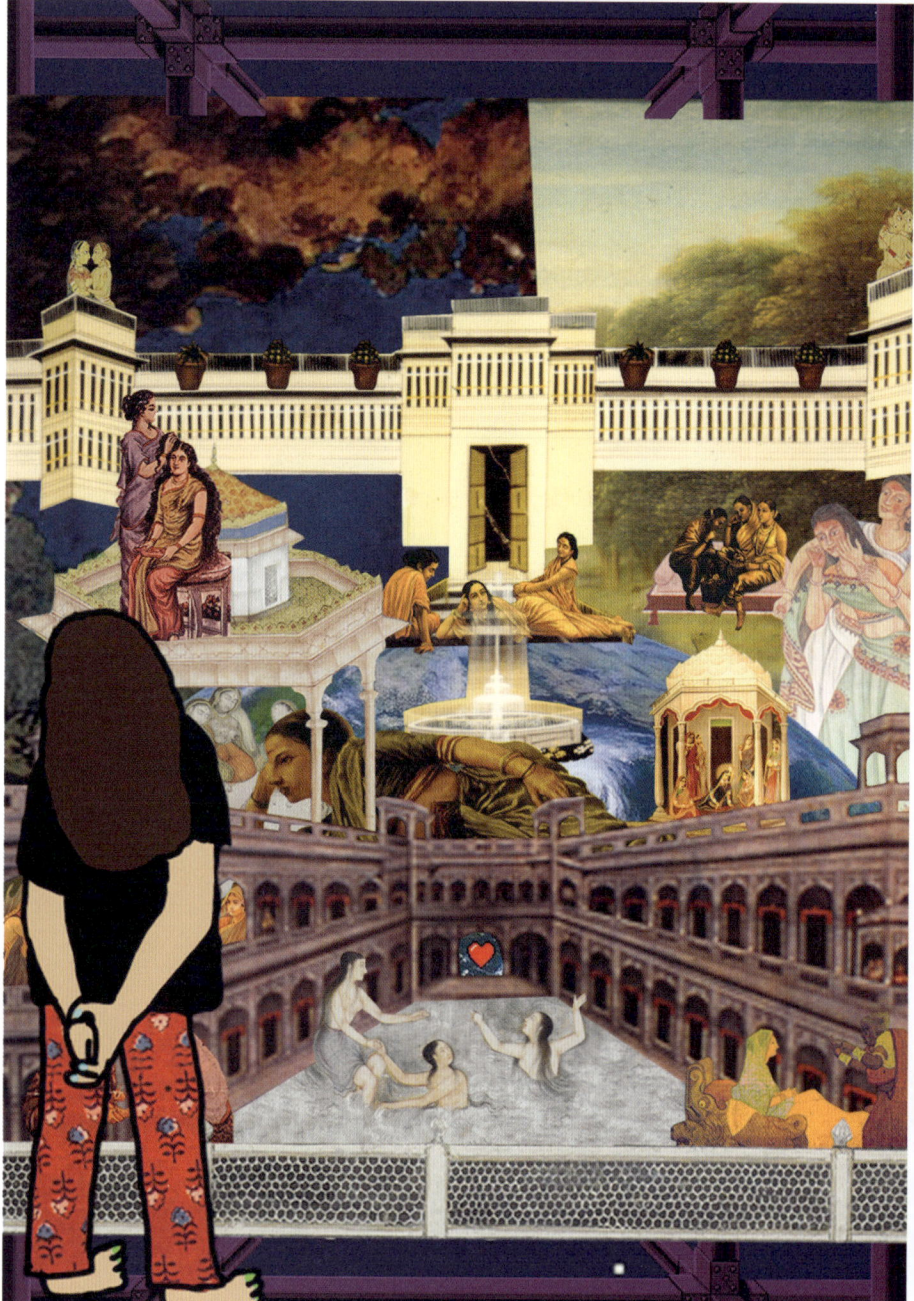

Born 1989, Mumbai, India. Lives in Goa, India.

↑ **An Inner World of Their Own (Except from Sultana's Reality)**, 2017, interactive multimedia installation (sound, animation, text, HTML) dimensions variable

↗ **Our Lady of I Can Be Anything You Want Me To**, 2020, video still, interactive browser-based work (sound, animation, text, custom code), dimensions variable

↗↗ **Same OR Different**, 2020, video still, interactive browser-based work (sound, animation, text, custom code), dimensions variable

→ **An Endless Afternoon Defragments (excerpt from st.itch)**, 2018, video still, multimedia patchwork, 26 scannable QR codes, 4-channel video, 13-minute loop, single channel sound, 139.7 × 139.7 × 17.8 cm (55 × 55 × 7 in)

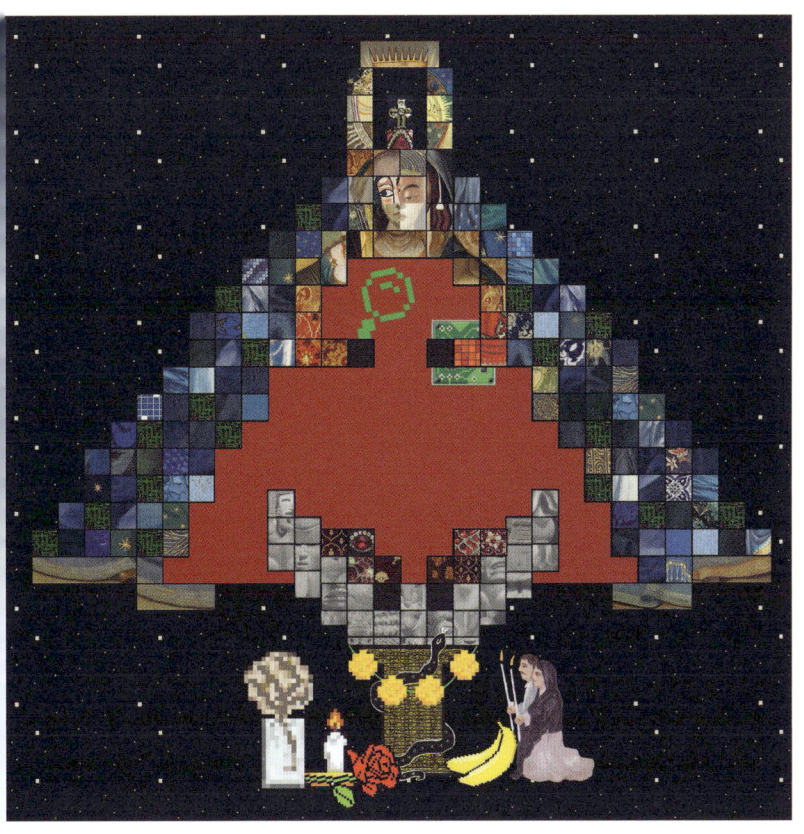

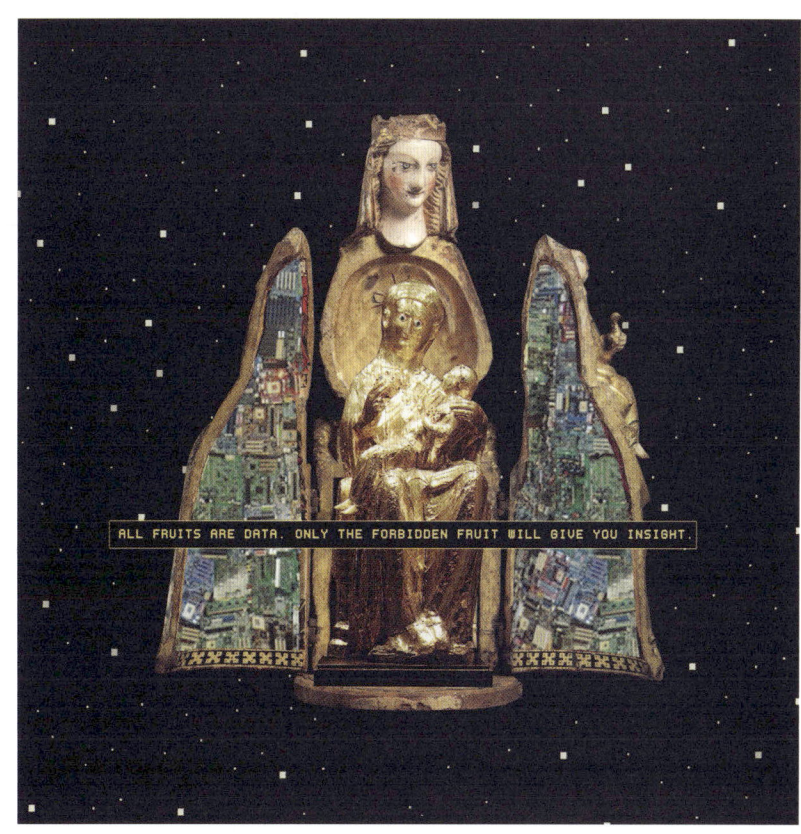

ALL FRUITS ARE DATA. ONLY THE FORBIDDEN FRUIT WILL GIVE YOU INSIGHT.

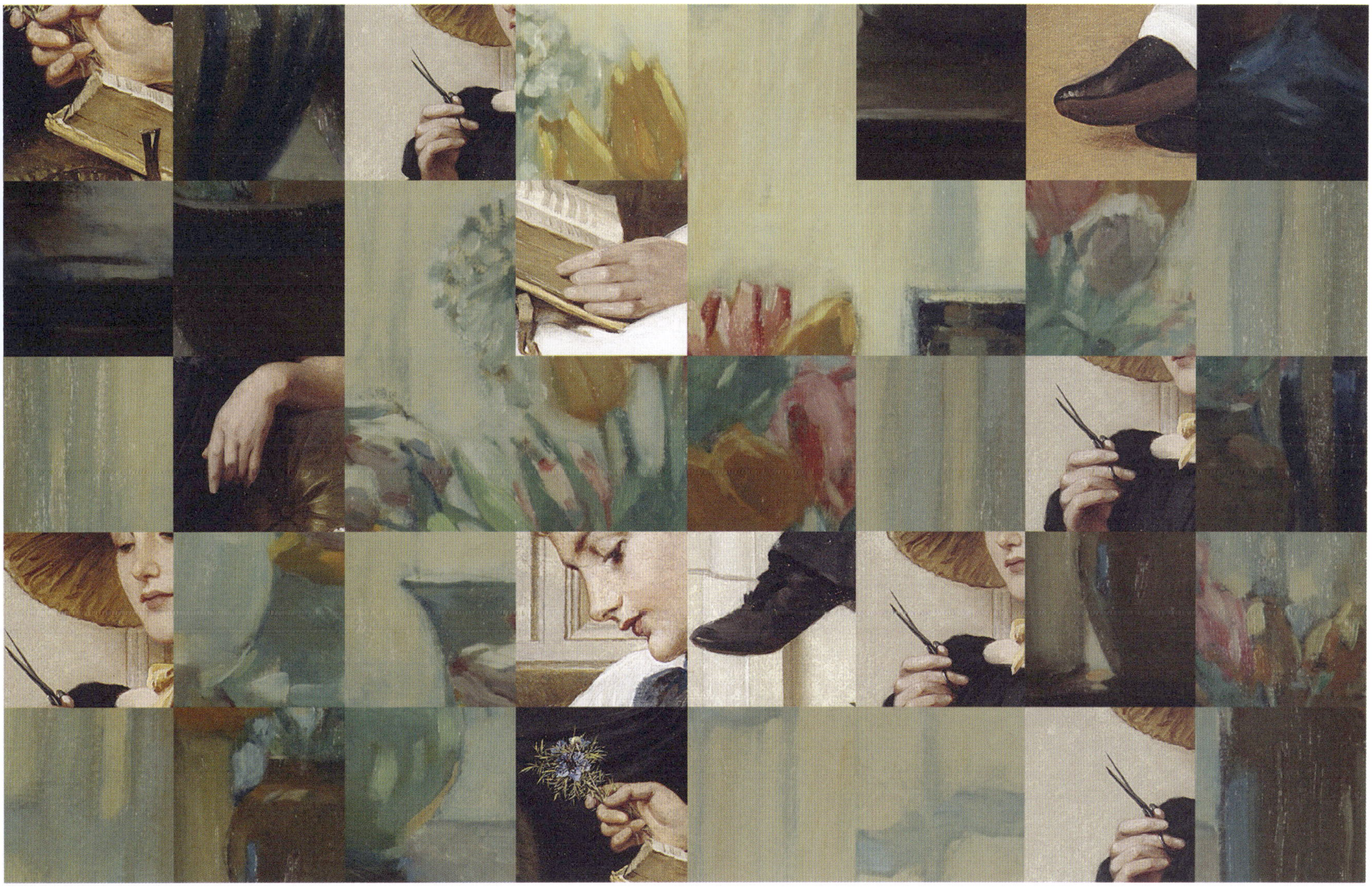

AFRAH
SHAFIQ

DEE SHAPIRO

Having entered the art world in her late thirties, Dee Shapiro soon became aligned with the Pattern and Decoration (P&D) movement of the mid-1970s. The movement arose in the United States due to awareness among its founding artists that the dominant art movements (particularly Minimalism and Conceptualism) were marginalizing abstract art that was deemed 'ornamental', which meant the exclusion of non-Western and feminine traditions. Often working with the same grid that Minimalist painters used to flatten perspective and remove any pictorial depth, P&D artists incorporated pattern from a broad range of global influences, echoing domestic designs of carpets, wallpapers, fabrics and quilts, yet positioning their output firmly in the realm of fine art. ■ Shapiro's early works reflected an interest in mathematical concerns and, in particular, the Fibonacci sequence, which she used as a means of developing abstract compositions. She initially produced paintings, which echoed the aesthetics of textiles in her evocation of knots made of pigment and chevron patterns that appeared like rows of knitting. She then moved towards a practice rooted in collage that uses fragments of textiles and other found patterns, and this became the major strand of her practice in the decades that followed. ■ One of the key proponents of P&D was Miriam Schapiro (1923–2015), who coined the term 'femmage' to describe artistic processes that combined elements of collage and assemblage but also drew on traditionally female crafts, including sewing, hooking, patching and appliquéing. It is an apt term to describe much of Shapiro's work, including the abstract compositions made in the last decade that combine geometric and biomorphic forms with patterned backgrounds and found objects. *Game Fun* (2020), for example, includes a chess piece, dominoes and Scrabble tiles, while *A Cycle of Rest* (2021) makes use of a small, repeating image of a reclining nude from art history, amid a constellation of colourful concentric circles. ◆ Since 2018, Shapiro has moved away from abstraction towards dramatically figurative works. These are inspired by some of the most iconic paintings of European art history, including Sandro Botticelli's *The Birth of Venus* (1485–6), Francisco de Goya's *The Naked Maja* (1795–1800) and Henri Rousseau's *The Dream* (1910). They take the form of irregular-shaped works on paper that incorporate sections of Shapiro's own paintings – cut up and reassembled – combined with elements of found patterns from sources including Japanese papers, book endpapers, tissue, fabrics and lace. Her figures' faces are replaced by images taken from magazines of celebrated and recognizable contemporary women: Amy Winehouse, Marilyn Monroe and, as seen in *My Standing Nude* (2022), Elizabeth Taylor, whose tilted head is placed on Paul Cézanne's *Standing Nude* (c.1898). By adding such famous faces, Shapiro draws a contrast with the anonymity of the women who originally modelled for these historic paintings. The effect is visually jarring and demonstrates the power of collage to create new meanings by the bringing together of disparate parts.

REBECCA MORRILL

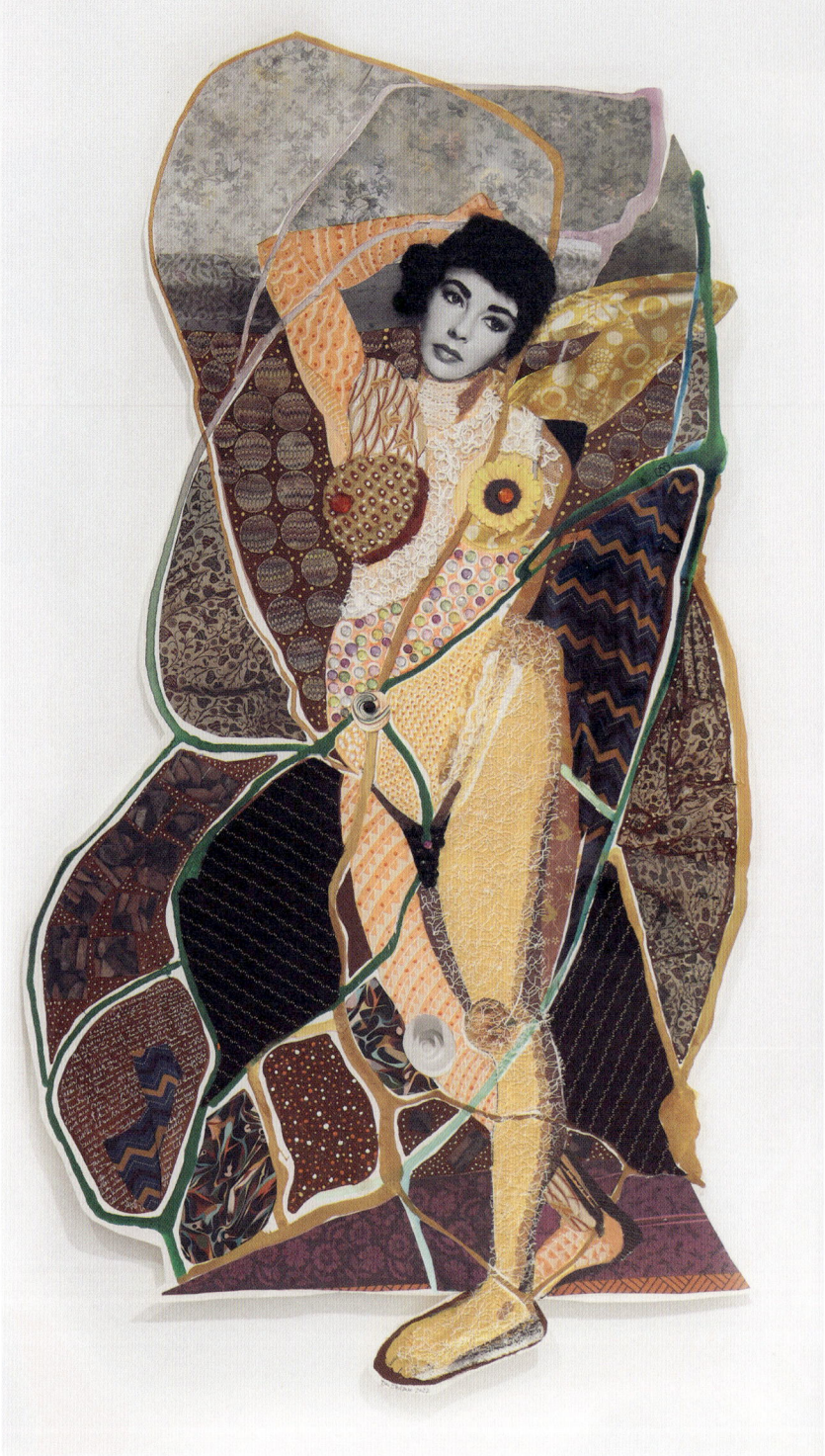

Born 1936, Brooklyn, New York, USA. Lives in New York, USA.

↑   **My Standing Nude**, 2022, mixed media on paper, 66 × 40.6 cm (26 × 16 in)

↗   **From Whence it Came**, 2020, mixed media on panel, 61 × 45.7 cm (24 × 18 in)

→   **Game Fun**, 2020, mixed media on panel, 61 × 45.7 cm (24 × 18 in)

→ →   **A Cycle of Rest**, 2021, mixed media on panel, 91.4 × 61 cm (36 × 24 in)

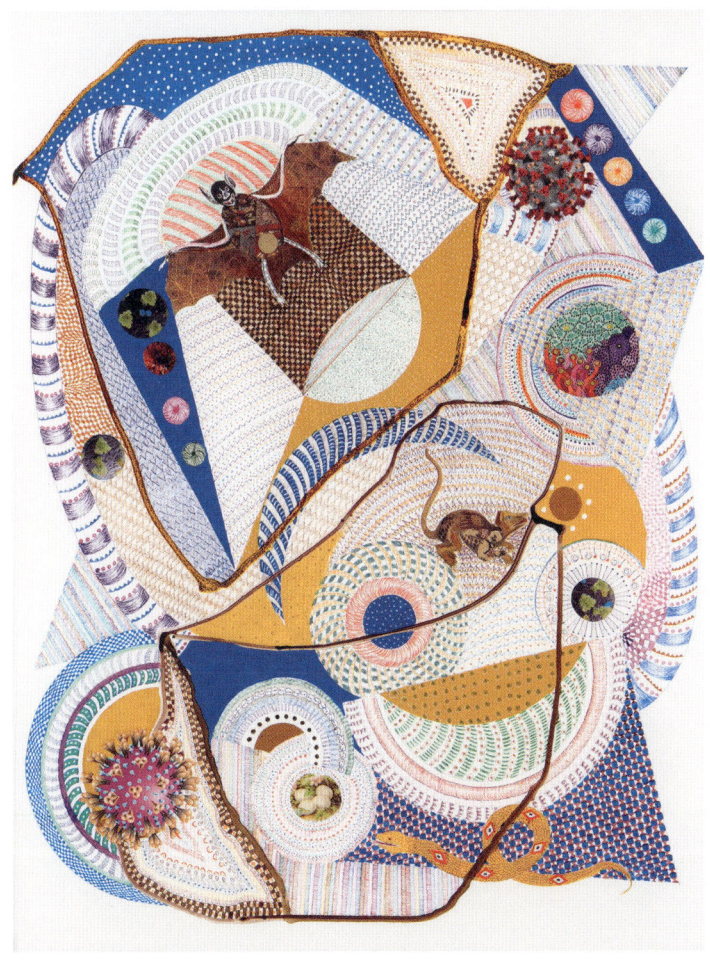

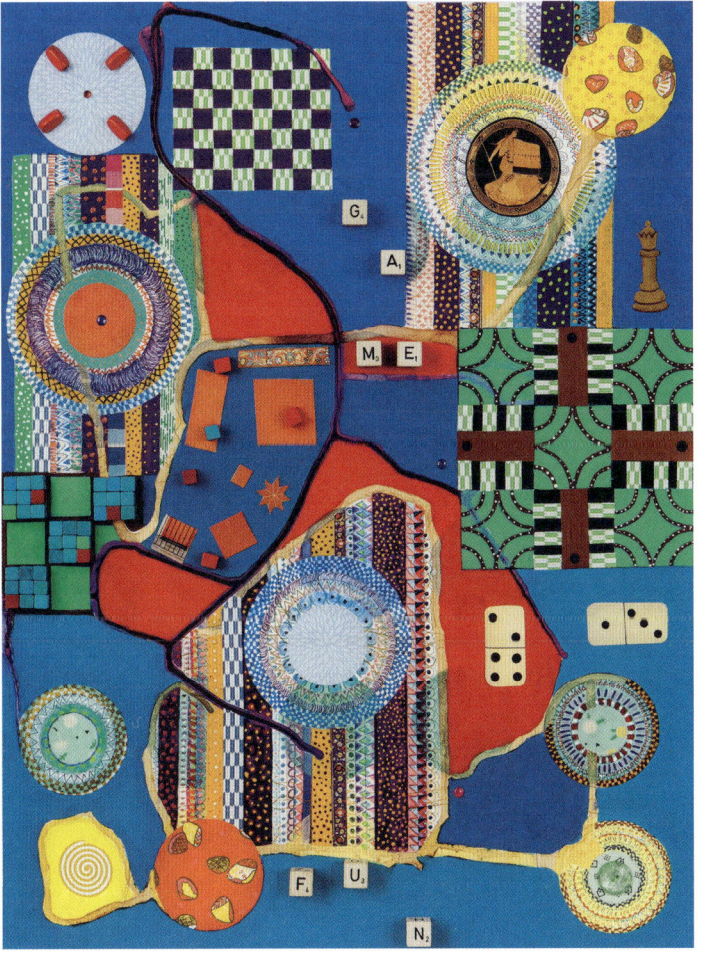

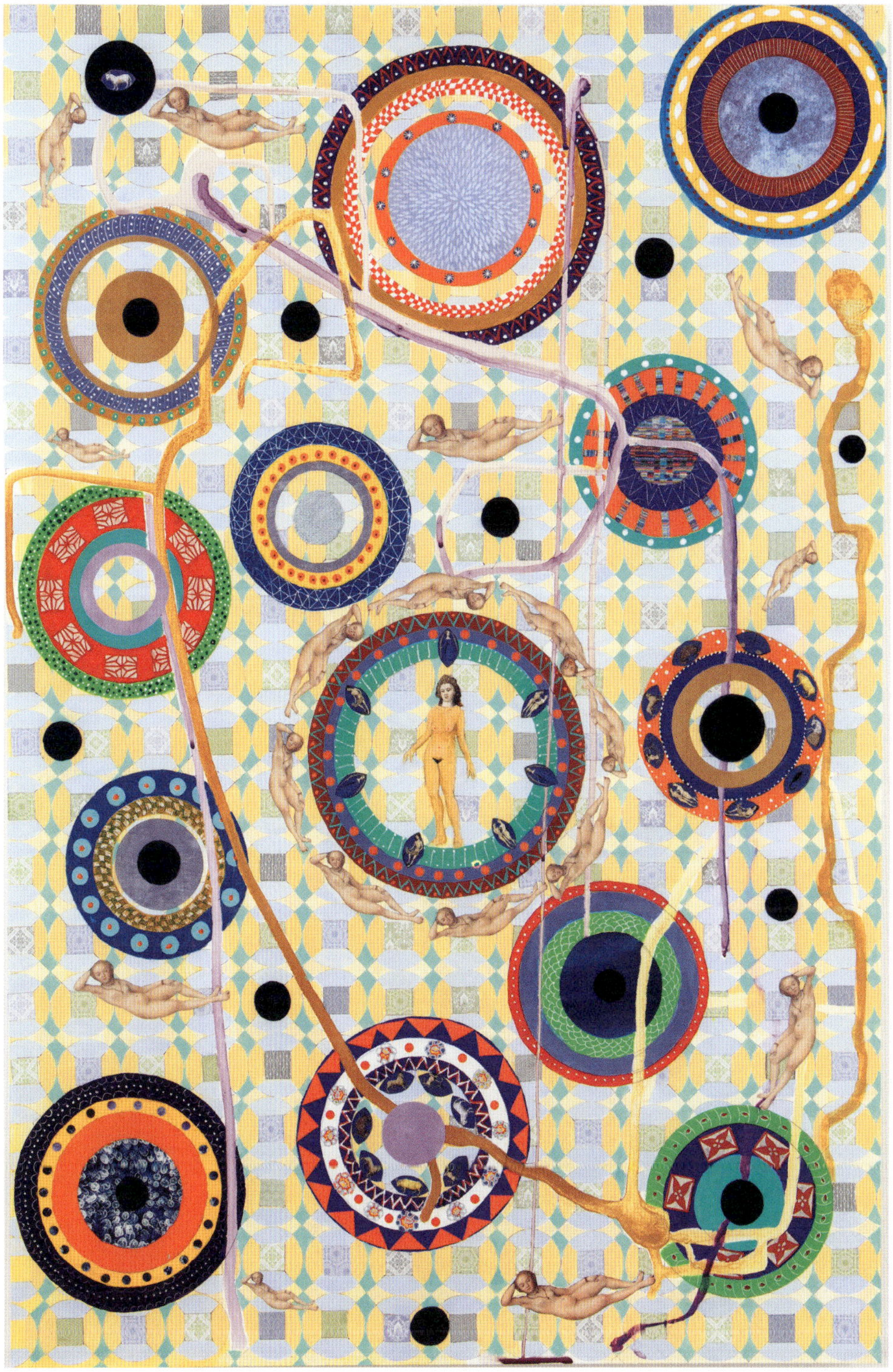

ERIN SHIRREFF

Erin Shirreff focuses on the inevitable gap between an object and its image. Consistent in her sculpture, photography and video is a process-oriented approach that invariably begins with a still image she finds online or, more often, in a book. Objects in reproduction appear flattened, still, one-sided and distanced from the viewer. Shirreff is interested in how we understand the unavailable side, how our perceptions work in relation to the limits of the photographic medium. It is a dynamic that runs parallel to the subject/object conundrum and, despite the uncertainty, she sees this gap as a generative, productive space. Shirreff has often used collage to juxtapose and cohere seemingly incompatible image fragments, in part to explore the veil of subjectivity that implicates photography, but also to play with the residue of physicality in two dimensions. For a group of works made in 2021 Shirreff pulled a range of reproductions from art history books designed and printed in the mid-twentieth century. She cropped selected images into suggestive fragments that carry remnants of materiality and colour, translating the pages to digital scans and enlarging them to the point of abstraction. The shift in scale highlights the physical presence of her source images, which are then printed onto a substrate of aluminium and cut into irregular shapes before being leant upright and layered within a deep frame, creating new pictorial-sculptural space from what began as conventional photographs of artworks. Shirreff's works are abstracted, yet specific; they are also seductively gorgeous. In *Alpha* (2021) bold zips of intense colour create a graphic rhythm: a band of cadmium red is central, yet integrated with cool sweeps of monochrome curves, echoing mid-century modern geometries. By dramatically increasing the scale of the reproduced half-tone and offset dot patterning, Shirreff creates multiple registers that visually cohere and simultaneously fall apart. Seemingly weightless, the scale of the images depicted on the cut-outs gives them a casual sense of spontaneity, but with the heft of substantial materiality – both pictured and extant. *New Moon Construction, Number 10* (2021) seems to reference the playful postmodern designs of the Italian design collective the Memphis Group (1980–7), the duck-egg blue in close proximity with mustard yellow enticing us to look closer at how her composition is constructed. Shirreff's collages often result in ad hoc, seemingly self-standing forms, as in *Standing fawn* (2021) or *Midday dilemma* (2022), that appear without context or definitive era, with just the suggestion of tubular structures. Shirreff is piecing together bits of history, activating a dated visual archive of objects, to assemble new forms that provoke us to ask how we read an image and how we claim to understand the recent past, especially as documented in print.

KATHLEEN MADDEN

Born 1975, Kelowna, Canada. Lives in Montreal, Canada.

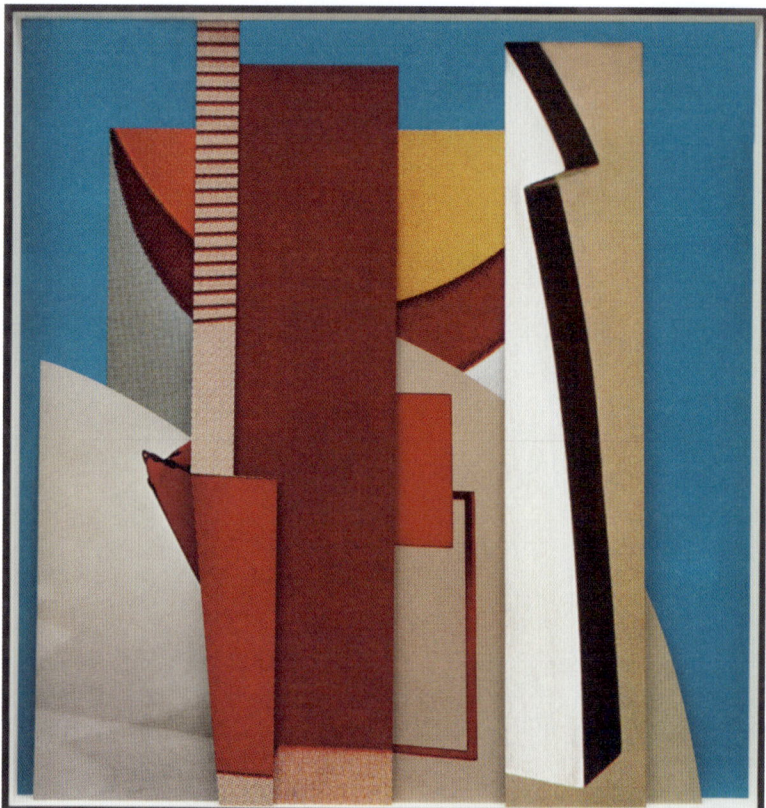

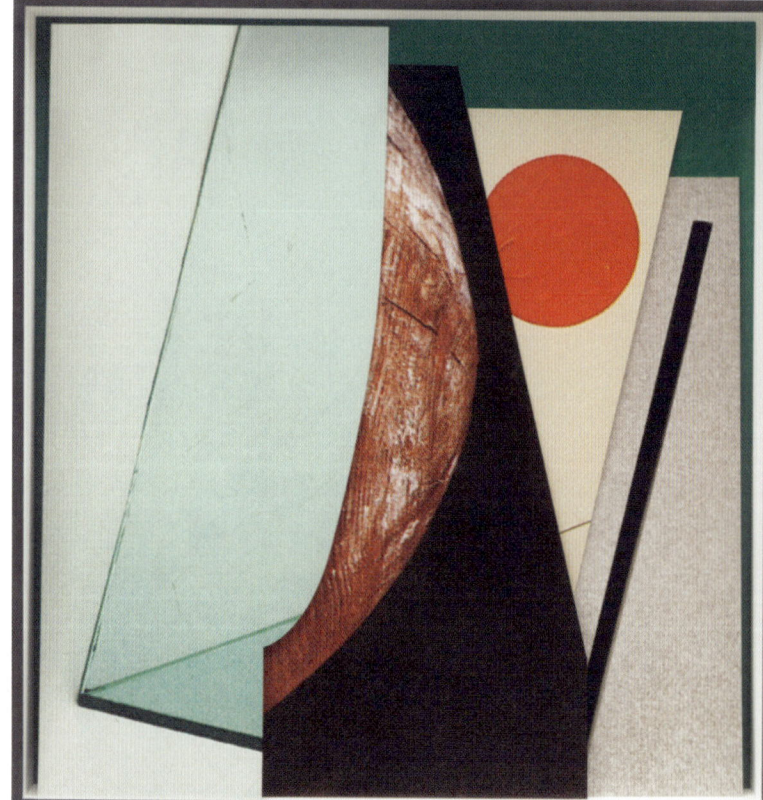

↑↑ New Moon Construction, Number 10, 2021, dye sublimation prints on aluminium and latex paint, 186.1 × 181 × 14.6 cm (73¼ × 71¼ × 5¾ in)

↑ Eyelit (glass), 2021, dye sublimation prints on aluminium and latex paint, 140.3 × 135.3 × 14.6 cm (55¼ × 53¼ × 5¾ in)

↗ Modern sculpture (green, red), 2021, dye sublimation prints on aluminium and latex paint, 182.2 × 154.3 × 14.6 cm (71¾ × 60¾ × 5¾ in)

↗↗ Alpha, 2021, dye sublimation prints on aluminium and latex paint, 181 × 153 × 14.6 cm (71¼ × 60¼ × 5¾ in)

→ Standing fawn, 2021, dye sublimation prints on aluminium and latex paint, 188.9 × 259.7 × 14.6 cm (74⅜ × 102¼ × 5¾ in)

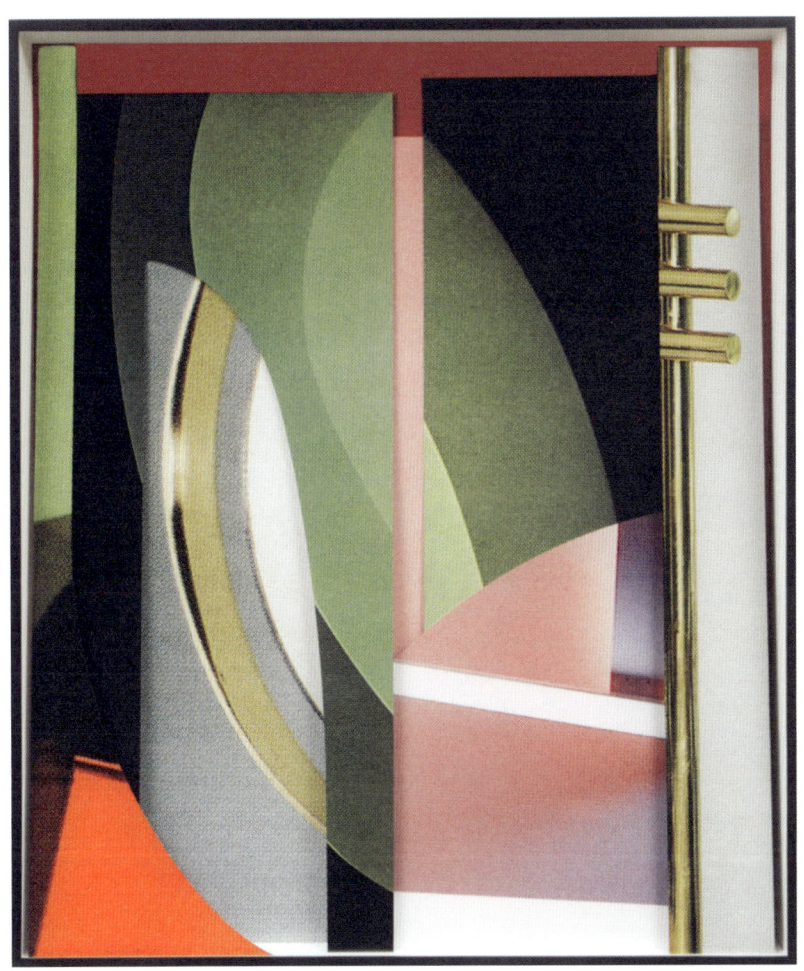
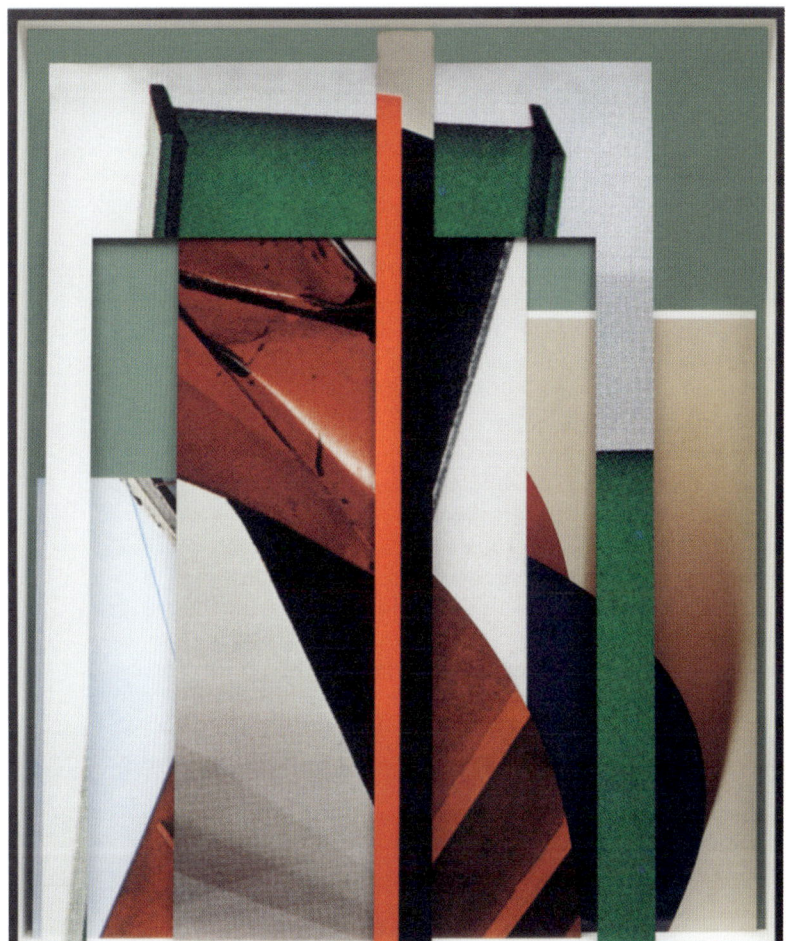
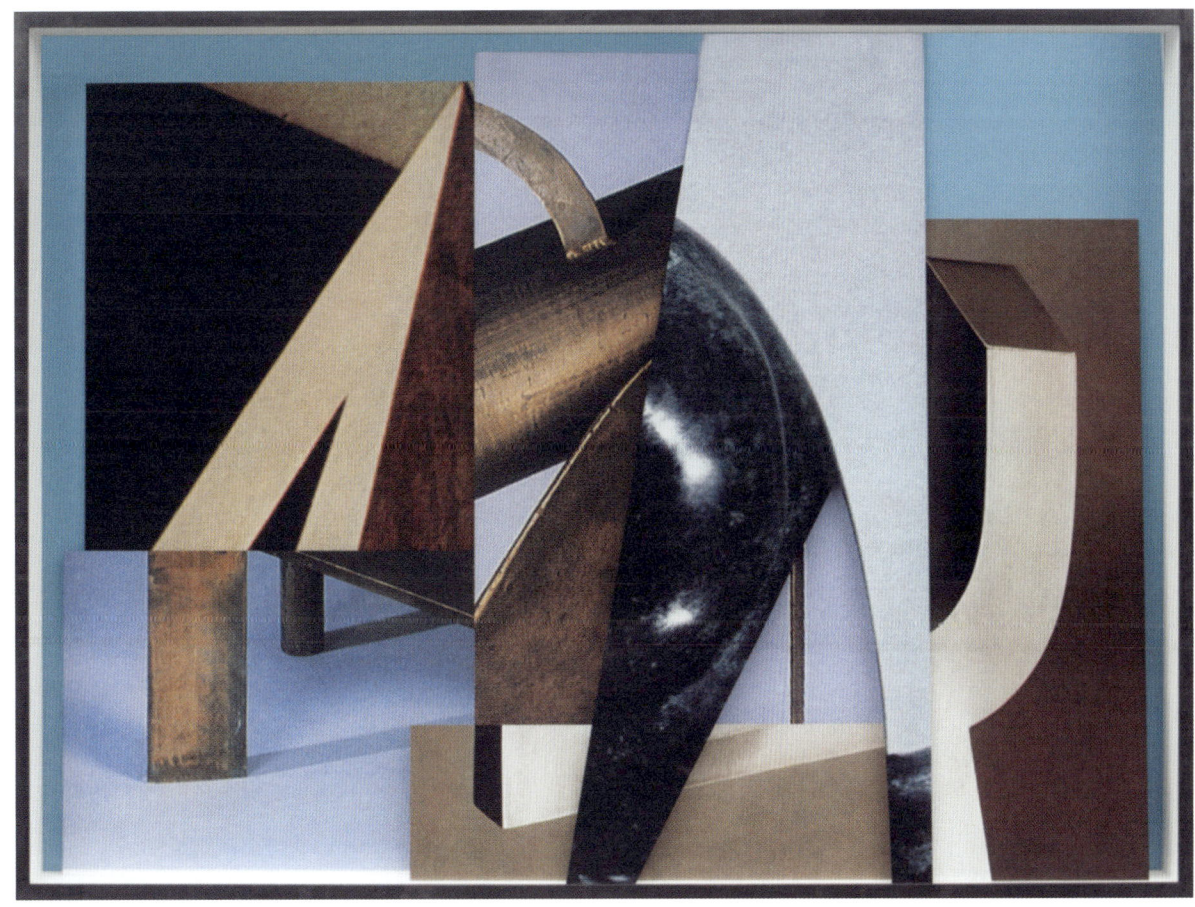

ERIN SHIRREFF

LORNA
SIMPSON

Photographs, whether taken by the artist or found images, have always been central to Lorna Simpson's practice. Rather than merely capturing the world through a lens, Simpson uses photography to question the nature of representation – in particular as it relates to categories of identity such as gender and race. Her earliest works, from the 1980s and 1990s, paired pictures of anonymous Black women and (less frequently) men with fragments of text, drawing attention to the ways in which meaning and narrative are formed. Although usually placed within the tradition of conceptual photography, these photo-and-text juxtapositions could also be thought of as budding experiments with collage. ■ Indeed, collage has since emerged as one of Simpson's primary mediums. 'The notion of fragmentation, especially of the body, is prevalent in our culture, and it's reflected in my works,' she told the *Paris Review* in an interview in 2015. Five years earlier the artist had come across her grandmother's collection of old *Ebony* and *Jet* magazines. Simpson began to cut out photographs from the pages of the magazines, embellishing them with watercolour and ink, layering them with images from other sources, or simply combining them to make new configurations, as in the fragmented women's faces of *Walk with me* (2020). Described in *Hyperallergic* in 2020 as 'a Cubist portrait in which multiple perspectives exist at once,' this analogue collage has a second iteration as a video work in which the faces are brought alive by blinking eyes, arching eyebrows and twitching mouths. ■ Simpson continues to collect vintage copies of *Ebony* and *Jet* alongside related printed matter from the 1930s to 1980s. 'For me, the images hearken back to my childhood, but are also a lens through which to see the past fifty years in American history,' Simpson told her interviewer in 2015. She uses this material to create distinctively otherworldly collages. In the 'Earth & Sky' series, for instance, the coiffures of glamorous models are overlaid with cut-out illustrations of precious stones. (The hair of African American women, how it is stigmatized or valorized, is a longstanding interest of Simpson's.) In more recent works such as *Stars from Dusk to Dawn* (2021), large swathes of the women's bodies are obscured by historic celestial maps, set against an inky blue sky rendered in pastel. ■ Echoing the Surrealists, in a 2018 video interview by Hauser & Wirth gallery Simpson described the activity of collage as 'a way for my subconscious to play' – discovering associations that have been formed on an unconscious level. In this sense, the collages are not intended to have a clear and fixed meaning. Rather, they reflect a process of breaking down appearances in order to create new images that are freed from the limits of conventional representation. There is something wondrously expansive about Simpson's collaged figures, with their elemental hairdos and intergalactic bodies. Put simply, they exist in a world where anything – anyone – is possible. ■

GABRIELLE SCHWARZ

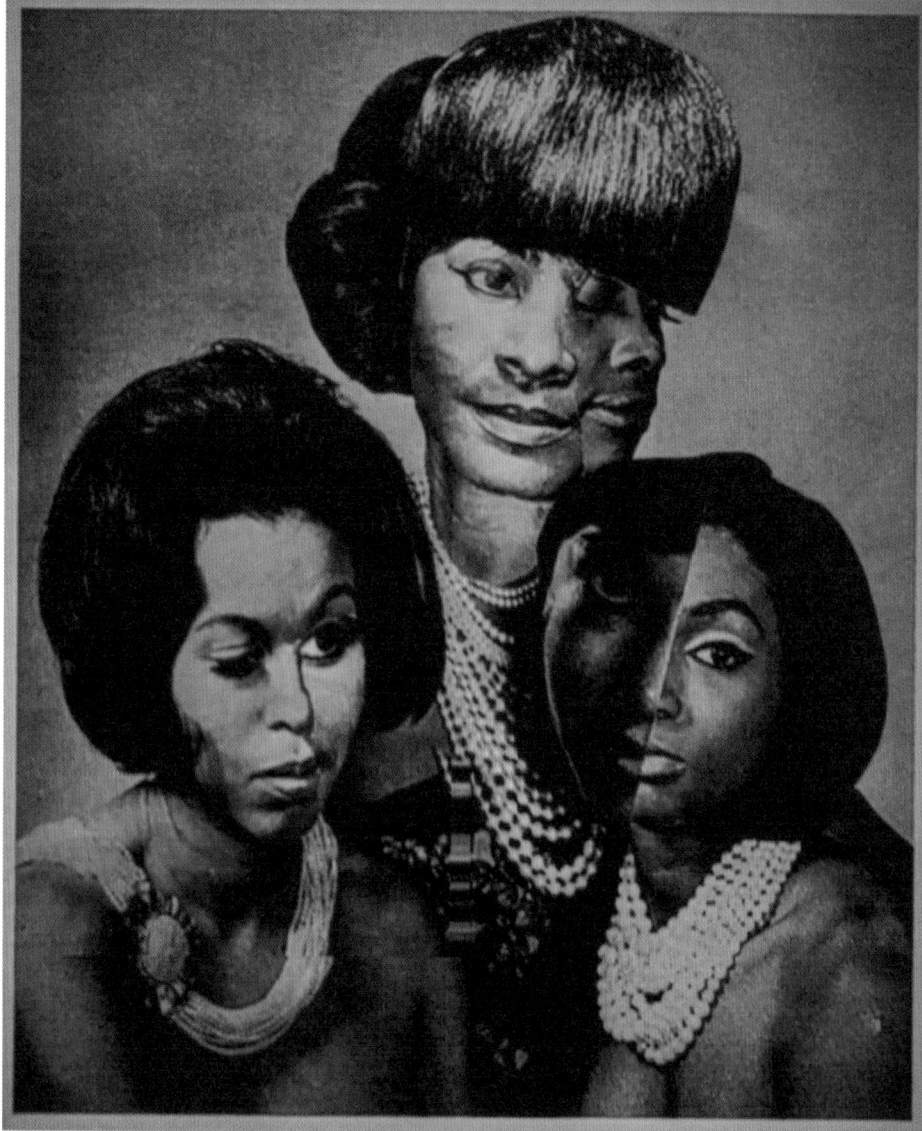

Born 1960, Brooklyn, New York, USA. Lives in Brooklyn.

↑   **Walk with me**, 2020, single-channel video installation, colour, silent, looped, 14 seconds

↗   **Stars from Dusk to Dawn** (detail), 2021, collage and pastel on handmade paper, 3 parts, each: 61 × 43.2 cm (24 × 17 in)

→   **Earth & Sky #24**, 2016, collage on paper, 27.9 × 21.6 cm (11 × 8½ in)

→ →   **Earth & Sky #10**, 2016, collage on paper, 27.9 × 21.6 cm (11 × 8½ in)

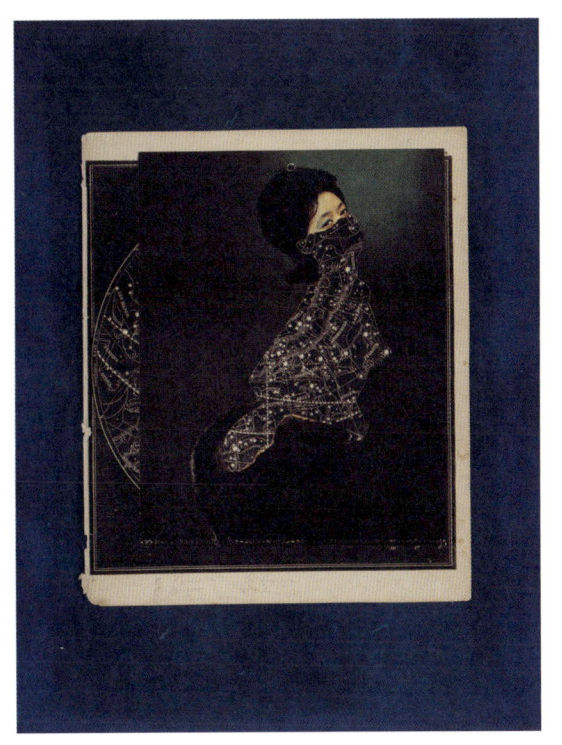
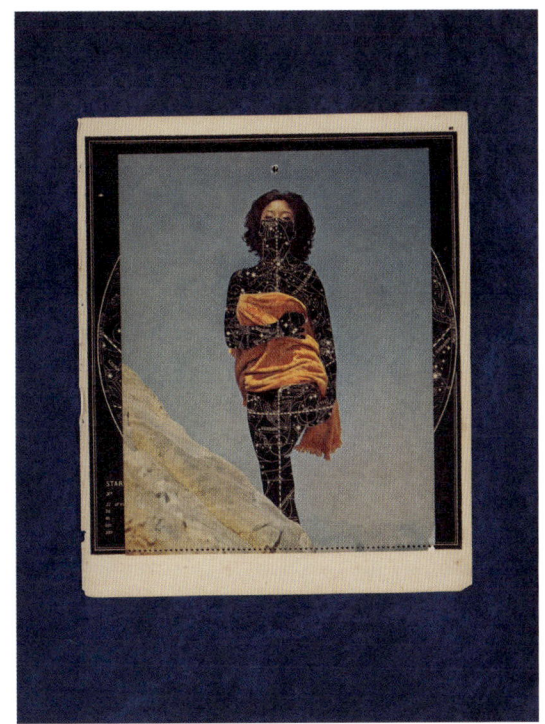
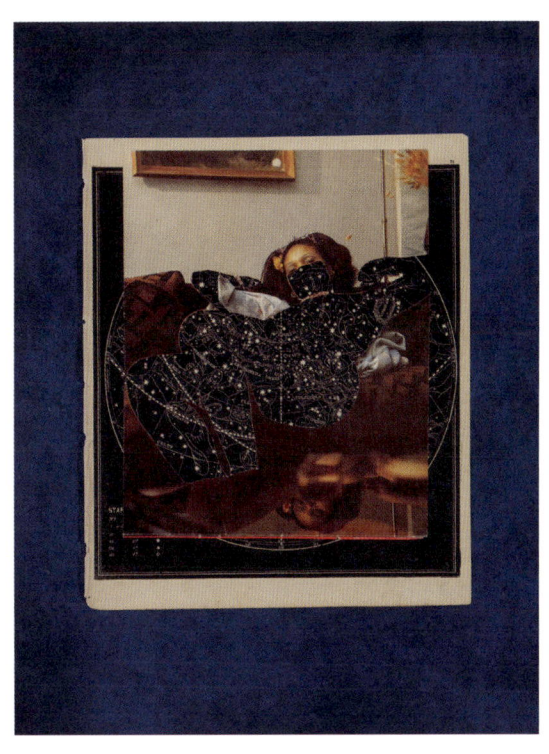
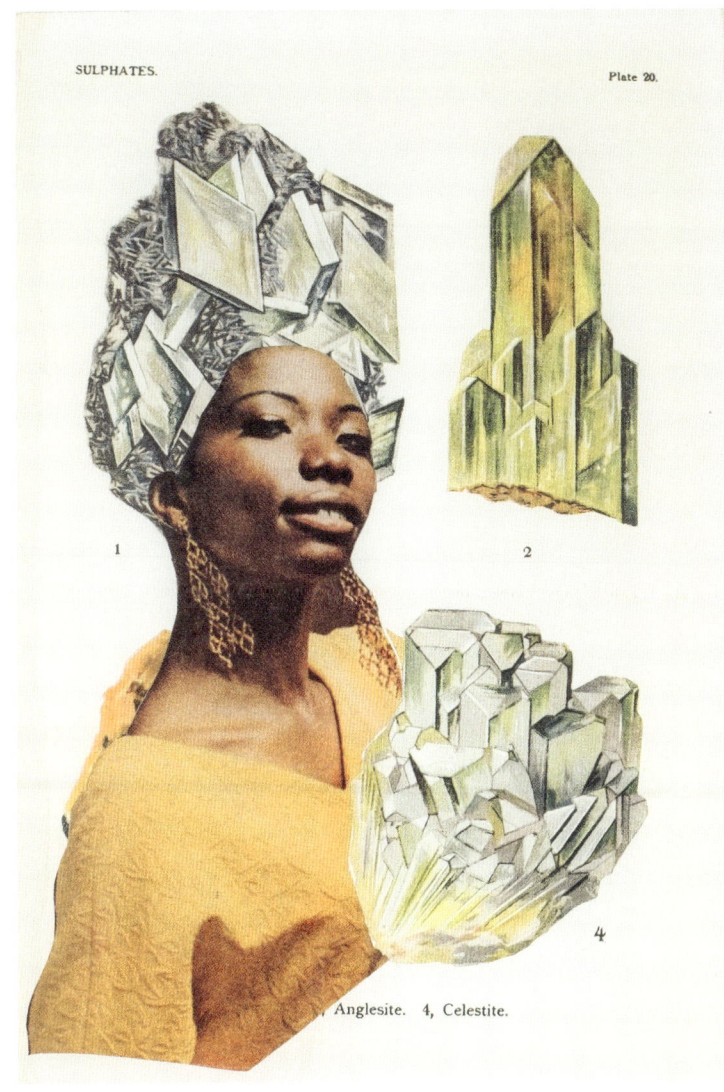

SULPHATES.   Plate 20.

1   2

Anglesite. 4, Celestite.

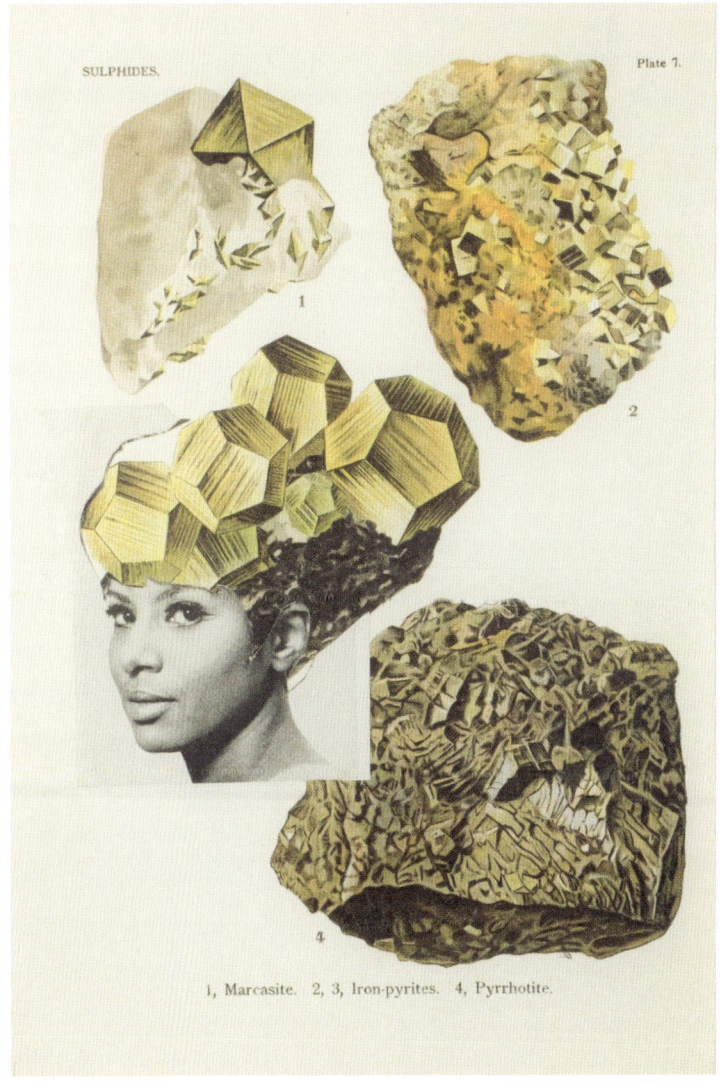

SULPHIDES.   Plate 7.

1

2

4

1, Marcasite. 2, 3, Iron-pyrites. 4, Pyrrhotite.

LORNA
SIMPSON

NYUGEN E. SMITH

Nyugen E. Smith is a first-generation Caribbean-American artist whose interdisciplinary work centres on how the legacy of colonialism affects today's world population through natural disasters, war, genocide and migration. He raises awareness of past and present struggles of Black and Brown communities by drawing on his experiences relating to his childhood home life and education, his studies in political science and his own mixed Haitian and Trinidadian heritage. ◤ In 2005 Smith started the 'Bundlehouse' series of paintings, drawings and sculptures, in which he bundles together various materials to create 'home'-like structures. These are conical shapes that resemble the make-shift constructions the artist had seen that same year in photographs of Ugandans displaced by ongoing war. The refugees' dwellings were made from a mixture of natural and synthetic materials, with the latter providing shelter from rain. In Smith's work, similar objects like plastic or fabric fragments, netting or artificial turf in vibrant colours – sometimes literally found in dumpsters – complement the sombre tones of earth pigments. In *Bundlehouse (Not a Fig-ment)* (2020) the four-legged shape at the centre sits on red and green concentric circles cut from paper, as in maps – where capital cities are marked in the same way – but which for Smith also denote spaces of energy. The structure is topped by magazine cut-outs of blue feathers and round eyes to suggest a flamboyant bird, which, like the nearby banana plant, points to both misguided notions of exoticism and issues around ongoing labour exploitation in the Global South. ◤ Throughout Smith's work, collaged fur, plastic beads and sequins invoke African and Caribbean spiritual practices that the artist has studied in situ and with a belief in their collective healing power. The references encompass Yoruba chief crowns and the carnival character Moko Jumbie, an ancestral spirit that protects Africans abducted into slavery as well as their diasporic descendants. ◤ The oversized yellow jerry can in *Bundlehouse (Like Oil + Water)* (2018) found its way into Smith's work after a trip to Tanzania, where he saw the containers being used for carrying water, repurposed from storing petrol. The sea occurs frequently as a metaphor for memory and history, especially the transatlantic slave trade, but also for climate change. While working on *Bundlehouse (Rising Into Something Else Again)* (2021) during the global lockdown, Smith said in an online post that 'we are at a moment in time as a society, where collectively, Black people are "'rising into something else". We also are living through a pivotal moment of a changing climate where water is bringing upon us an unprecedented level of devastation around the globe and within this, we are collectively "rising into something else".' ◼

PIA GOTTSCHALLER

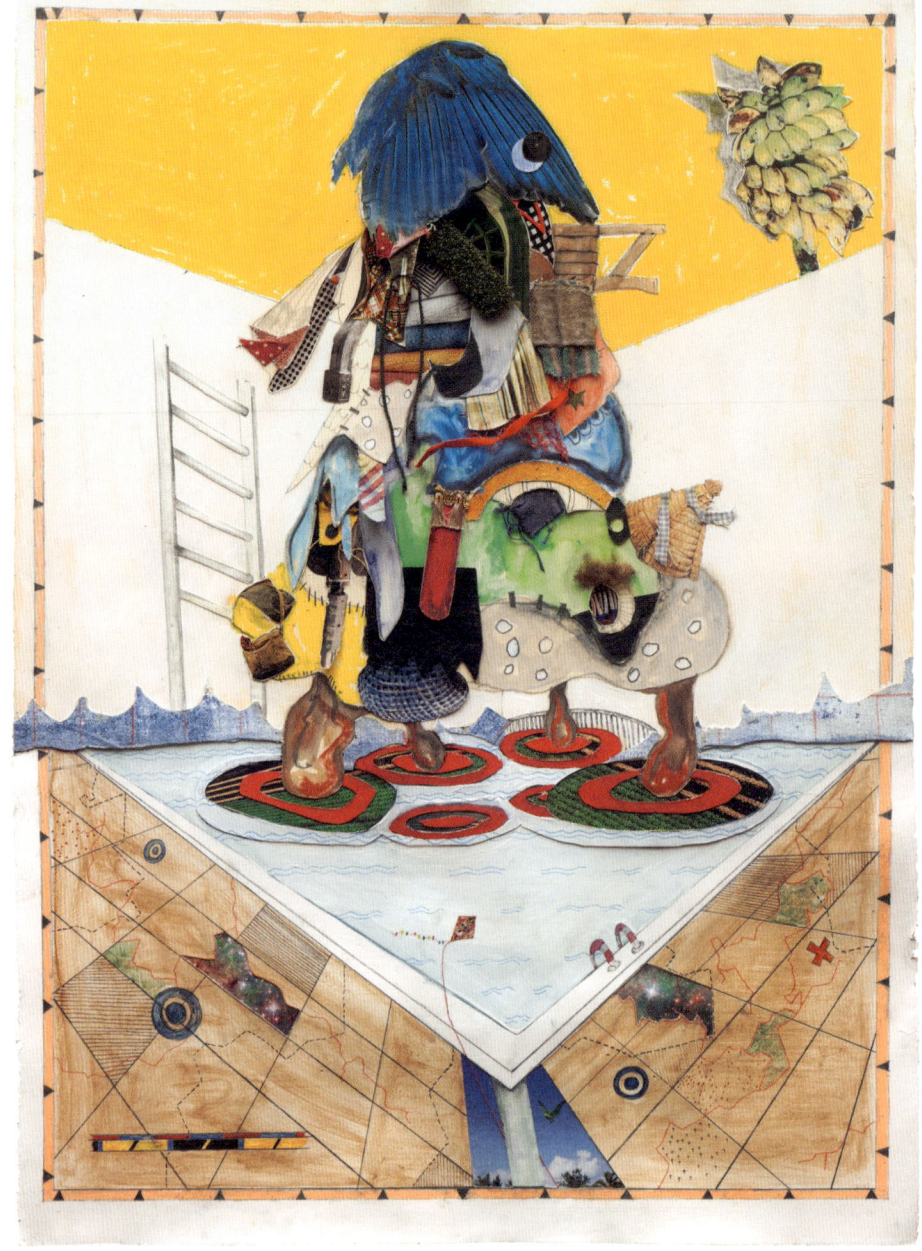

Born 1976, Jersey City, New Jersey, USA. Lives in Jersey City.

↑ **Bundlehouse (Not a Fig-ment)**, 2020, watercolour, acrylic, graphite, coloured pencil, lace, artificial turf, wool, thread, leather and collage on paper, 76.2 × 55.9 × 0.6 cm (30 × 22 × ¼ in), private collection

→ **Bundlehouse (Like Oil + Water)**, 2018, watercolour, acrylic, graphite, coloured pencil, lace, artificial turf, fur, plastic, leather and collage on paper, 109.2 × 91.4 × 5.1 cm (43 × 36 × 2 in), private collection

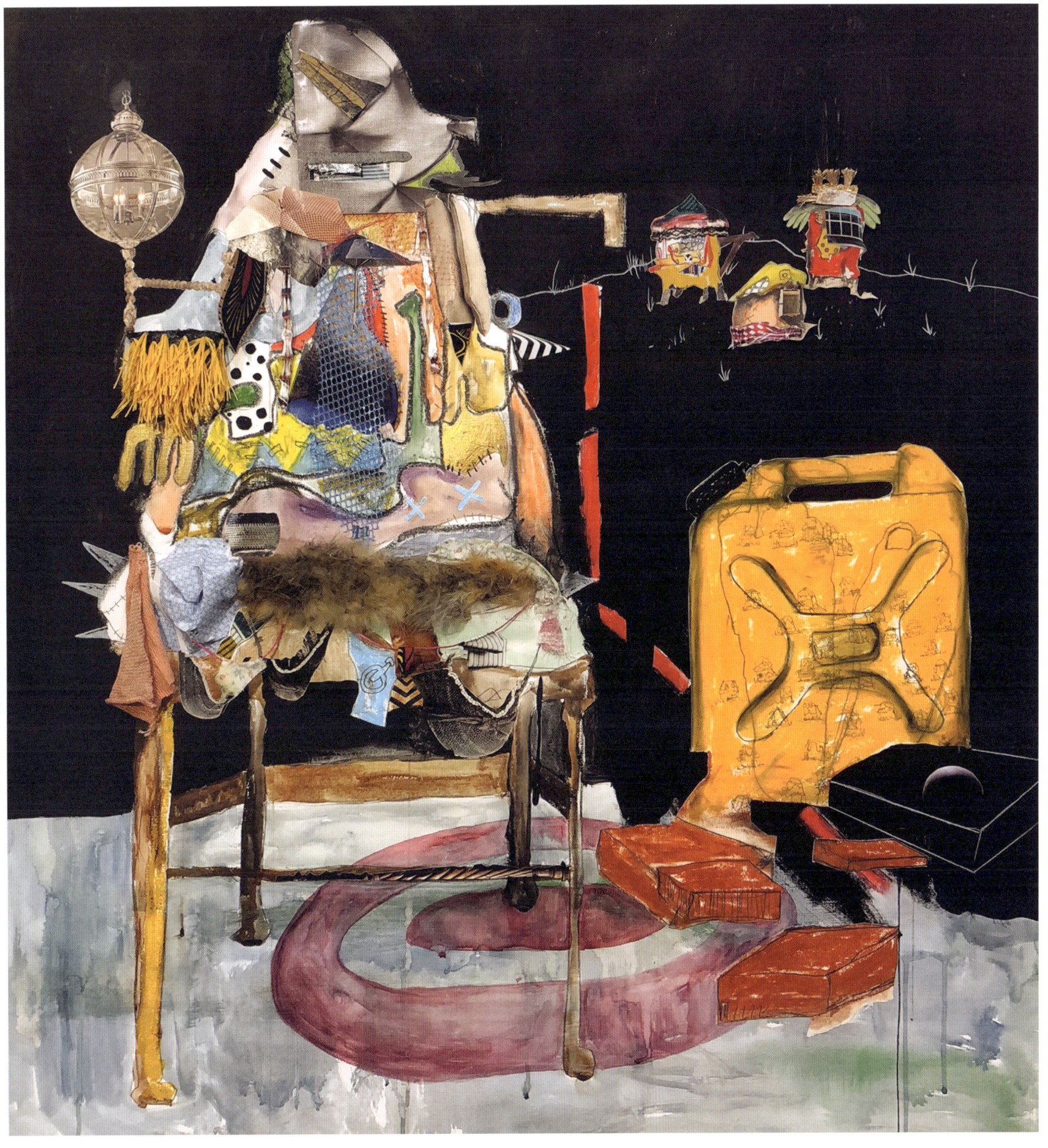

NYUGEN E. SMITH

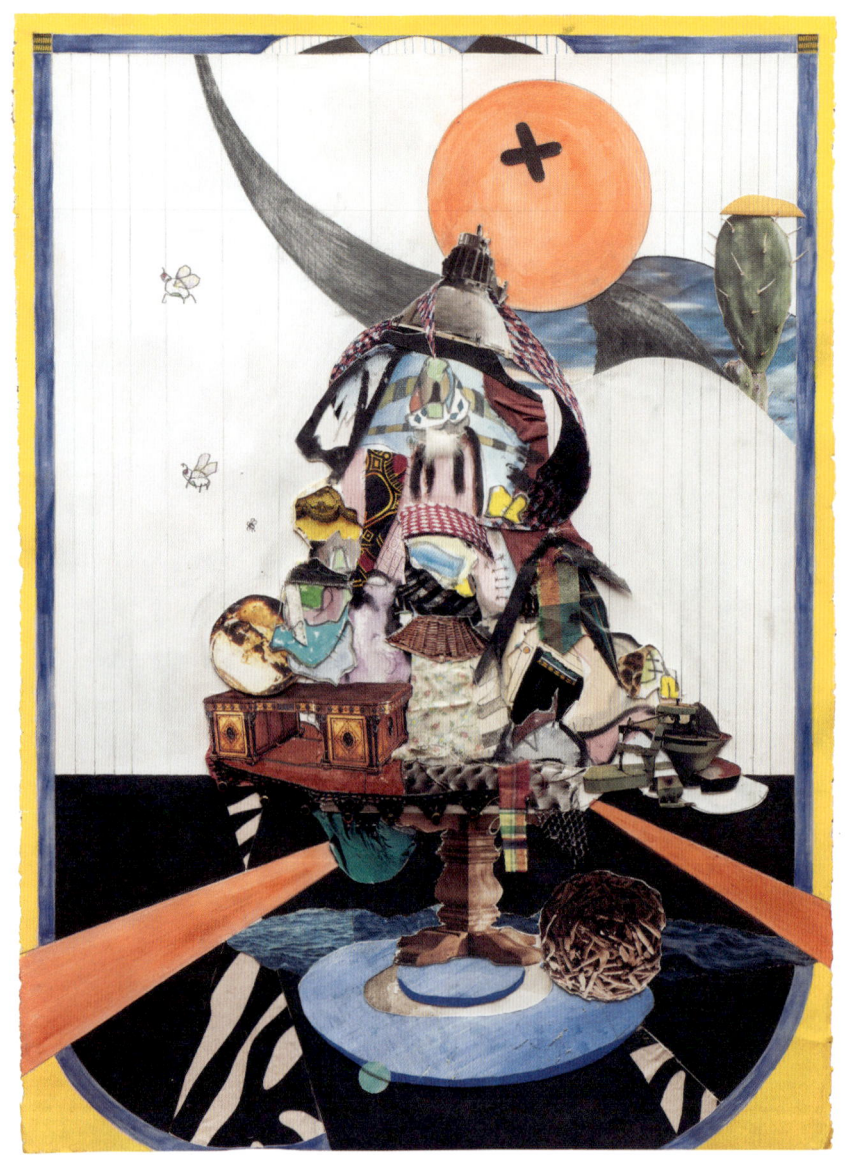

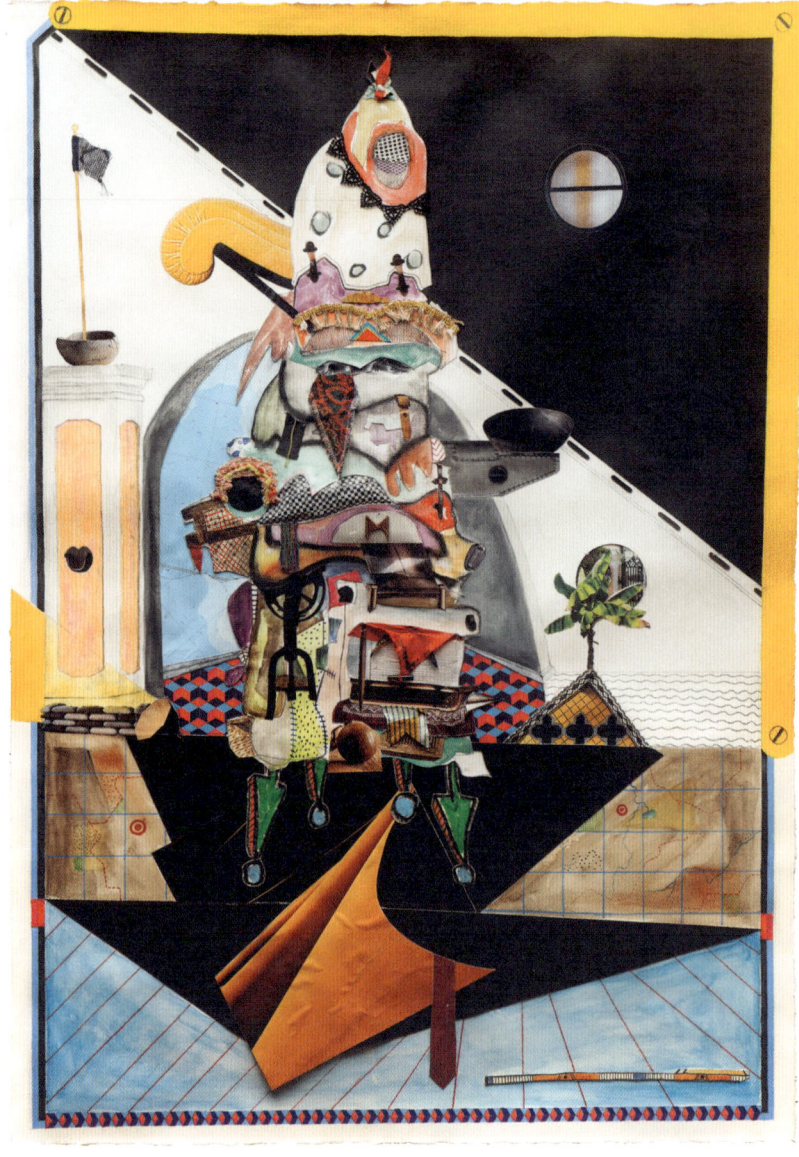

↖ **Bundlehouse (Table Talk)**, watercolour, acrylic, graphite, gesso, coloured pencil, lace, sequins, fabric, fur, plastic, leather and collage on paper, 76.2 × 55.9 × 0.6 cm (30 × 22 × ¼ in), private collection

↑ **Bundlehouse (At Thy Gates)**, 2021, watercolour, acrylic, graphite, coloured pencil, lace, plastic, leather and collage on paper, 105.4 × 74.9 × 0.6 cm (41½ × 29½ × ¼ in), private collection

↗ **Bundlehouse (Rising Into Something Else Again)**, 2021, watercolour, acrylic, graphite, coloured pencil, fur, bells, wire, canvas, plastic, leather, yarn, foam board, and collage on paper, 190.5 × 241.3 × 5.1 cm (75 × 95 × 2 in), Hudson Valley Museum of Contemporary Art, Peekskill, New York, USA

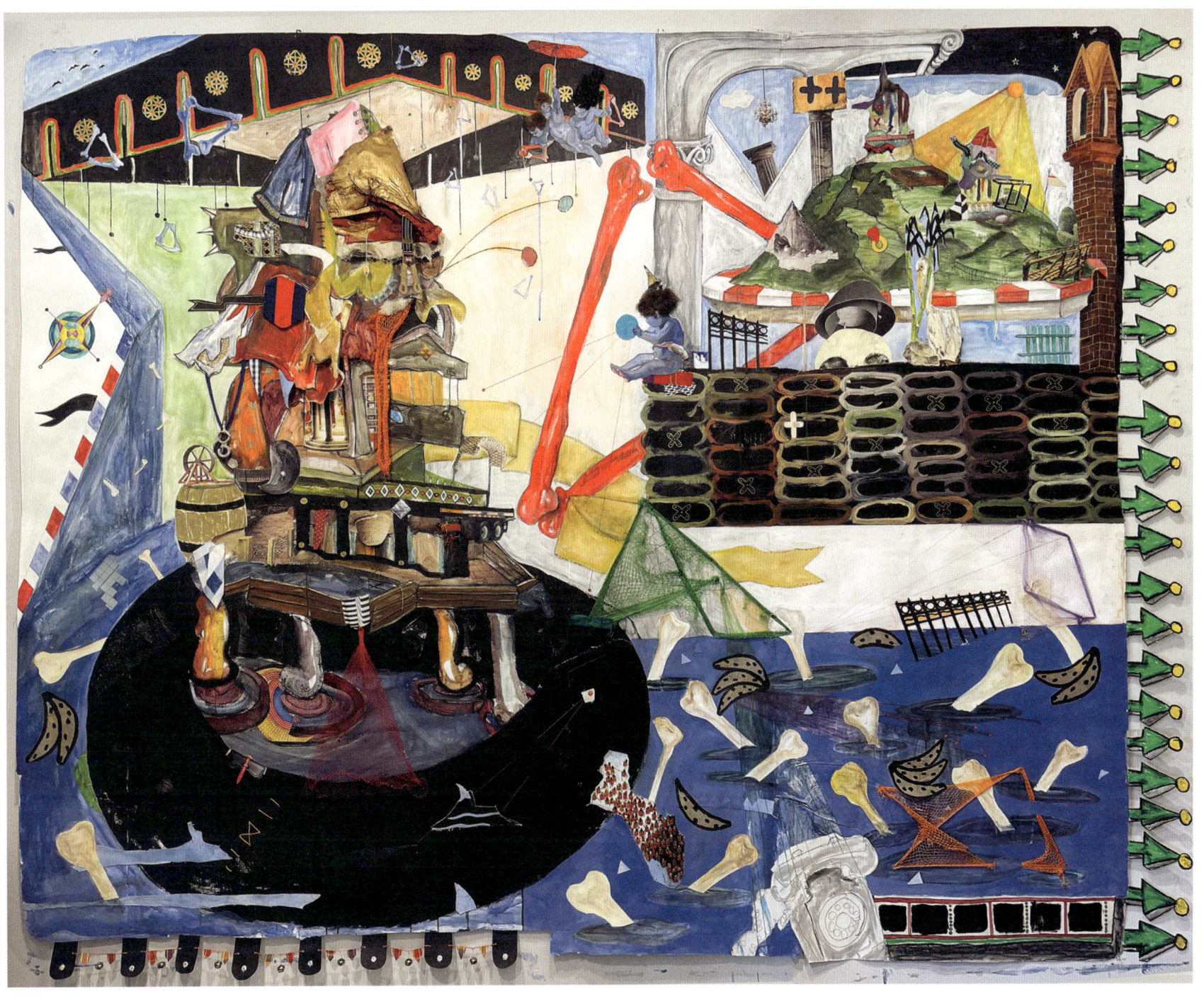

NYUGEN E. SMITH

EVA STENRAM

Photography has been both the subject and source material of Eva Stenram's work since the 1990s, when the artist began working with Photoshop software to digitally manipulate archival and analogue found photographs. Stenram has honed a signature style that evokes a nostalgic atmosphere, often incorporating vintage erotic and Pin-Up photography. Her sumptuous images contort the original photographs: backgrounds are brought into the fore, and figures are embedded or float, confounding the usual hierarchies of the photographic plane. In this deliberately disruptive process, Stenram questions the power dynamics of spectatorship, confronting questions of agency, control and ownership implied in the photographic act, while also acknowledging the complicity of both the artist and the viewer who indulges in the act of looking. *Drape XIV* (2015) is from Stenram's notable series 'Drape', which began in 2011, in which the artist set forth some of her preoccupying themes: in the digitally altered 1950s and 1960s negatives of Pin-Ups intended for publication in men's magazines, the desires of the intended original viewer – the male gazer – are exposed while the women subjects are concealed behind curtains. Though not entirely devoid of erotic frisson, with their tactile, sensual resonances, the pleasure of viewing these images is derived from the way they reveal how female sexuality is constructed and performed through pose, gesture and staging. Stenram is consistently interested in space, ominous interior settings and environments that conjure a certain sense of claustrophobia – from the domestic space of *Interior* (2021), with its doilies, teacups and shag-pile rug, to the dark grotto that engulfs the viewer in *Cave II*, part of a sequence of works created in 2021 using pictures from a 1970s book of landscapes in Germany. Spliced into this environment are human eyes – taken from vintage Pin-Up magazines – that slowly emerge from the glistening surface of the rock, their detached gaze both beckoning and blank. Stenram's exploration of these spaces may serve as metaphors for looking inwards, reaching for the recesses of the imagination – towards what cannot be seen – turning the photograph once more on its head. The artist takes delight and finds delectation in the aesthetics of image-making and the possibilities of creating strange and surreal new worlds by reinventing her source materials. Distinctive in its vibrant atmosphere is *Garden State (199)* (2019), a lush, dreamlike utopian vision of intimacy that combines a picture from a gardening book bought at a charity shop with bodies cut from vintage erotic magazines: the gesture conveyed in the interlocking, disembodied arms that extend out, representing, Stenram suggested in correspondence with the author, 'a desire to merge not just with each other, but with space itself'.

CHARLOTTE JANSEN

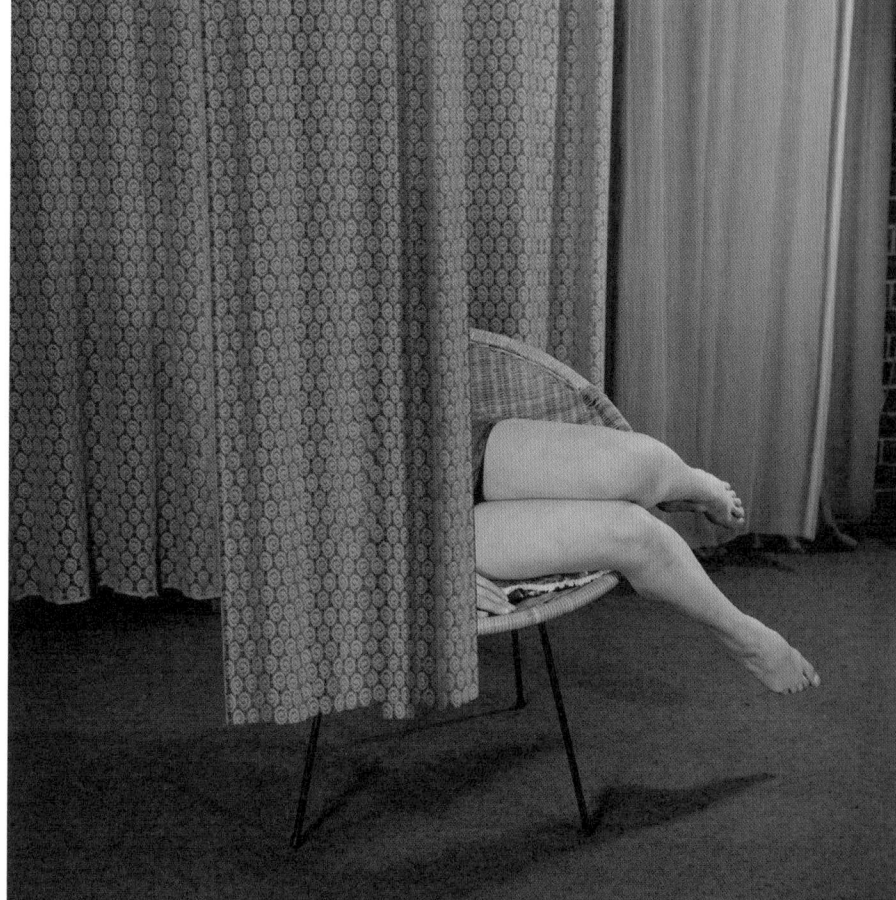

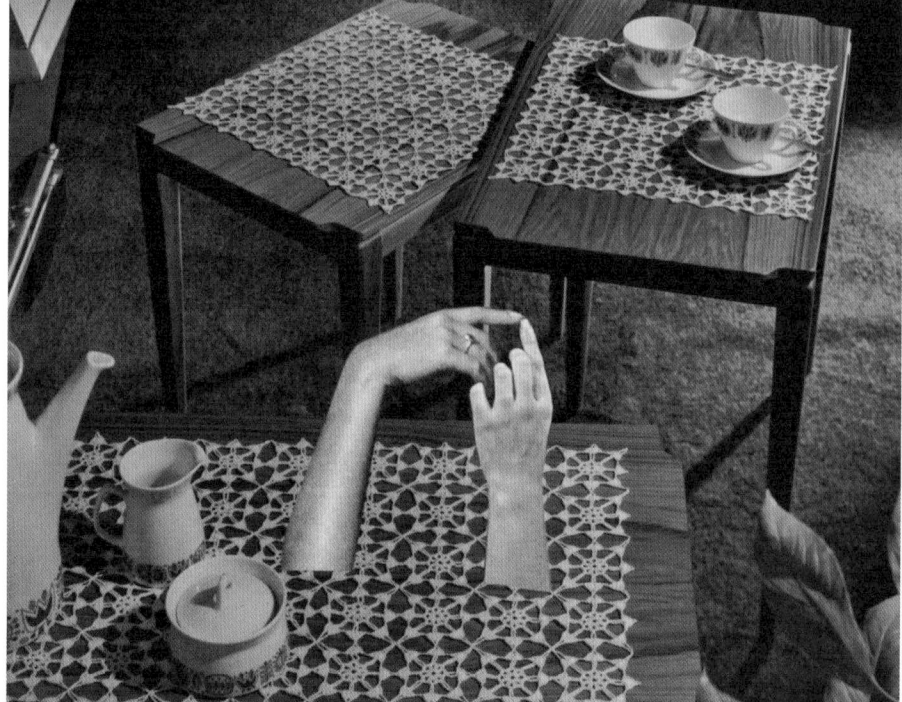

Born 1976, Stockholm, Sweden. Lives in Berlin, Germany.

↑↑ **Drape XIV**, 2015, silver gelatin print on fibre-based paper, 29.5 × 29.5 cm (11⅝ × 11⅝ in)

↑ **Interior**, 2021, Ditone pigment print on Hahnemühle Photo Rag Baryta, 11 × 14 cm (4¼ × 5½ in)

→ **Buds**, 2021, Ditone pigment print on Hahnemühle Photo Rag Baryta, 26.8 × 23 cm (10½ × 9 in)

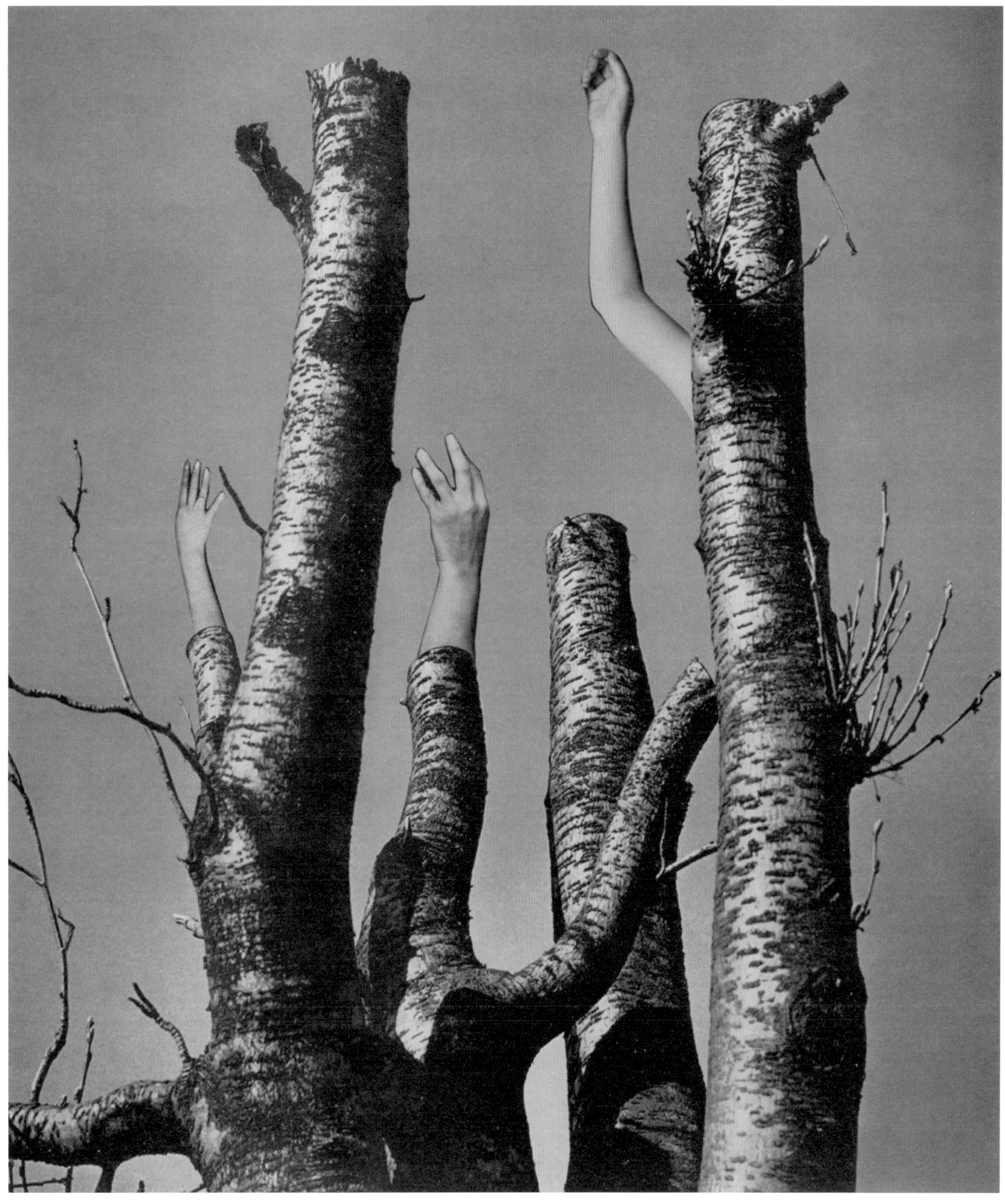

EVA
STENRAM

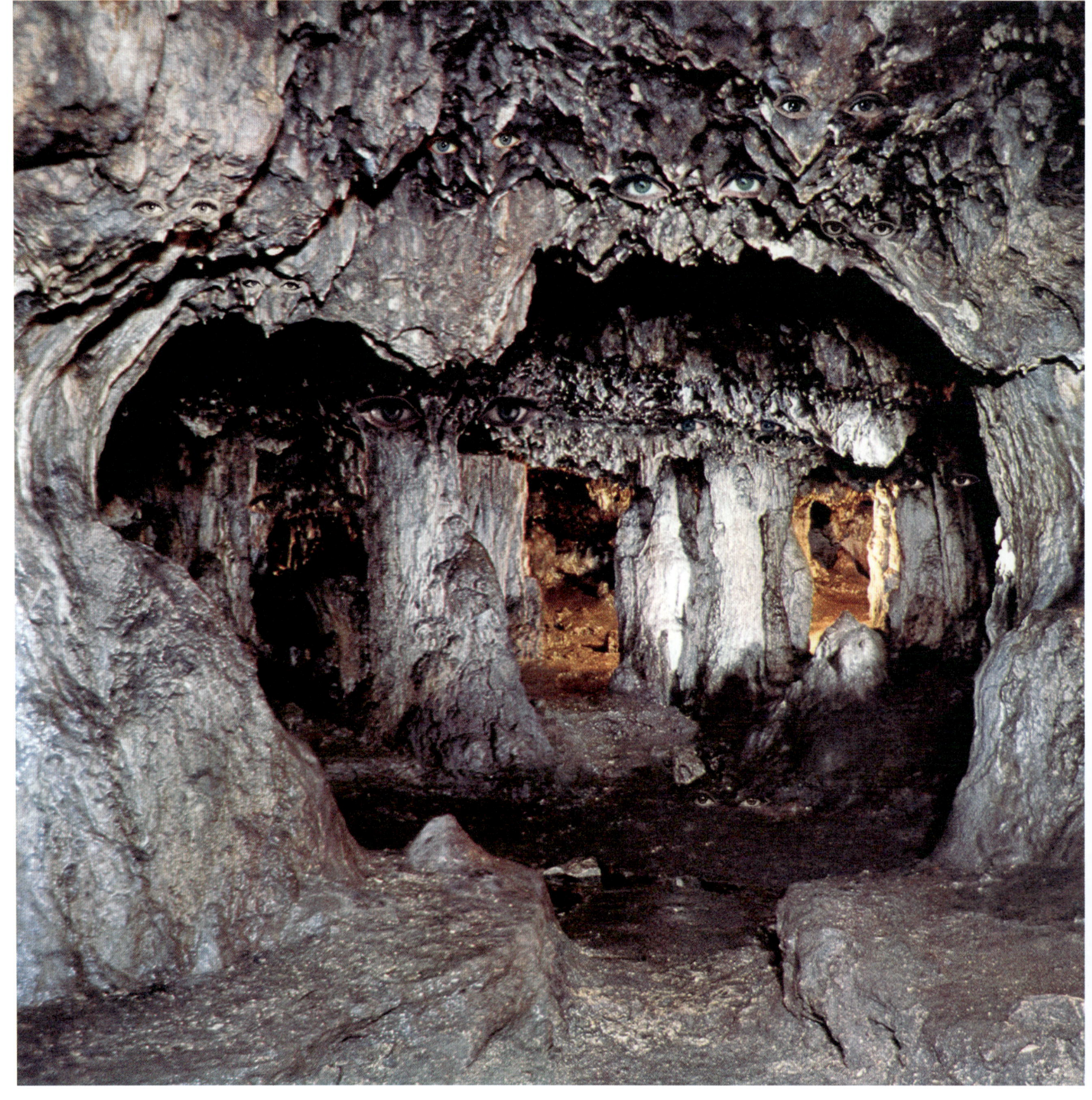

↑   **Cave II**, 2021, Ditone pigment print on Hahnemühle Photo Rag Baryta, 35 × 35.5 cm (13 ¾ × 14 in)

→   **Garden State (199)**, 2019, archival pigment print on Canson Infinity Paltine Fibre Rag,
40.6 × 30.5 cm (16 × 12 in)

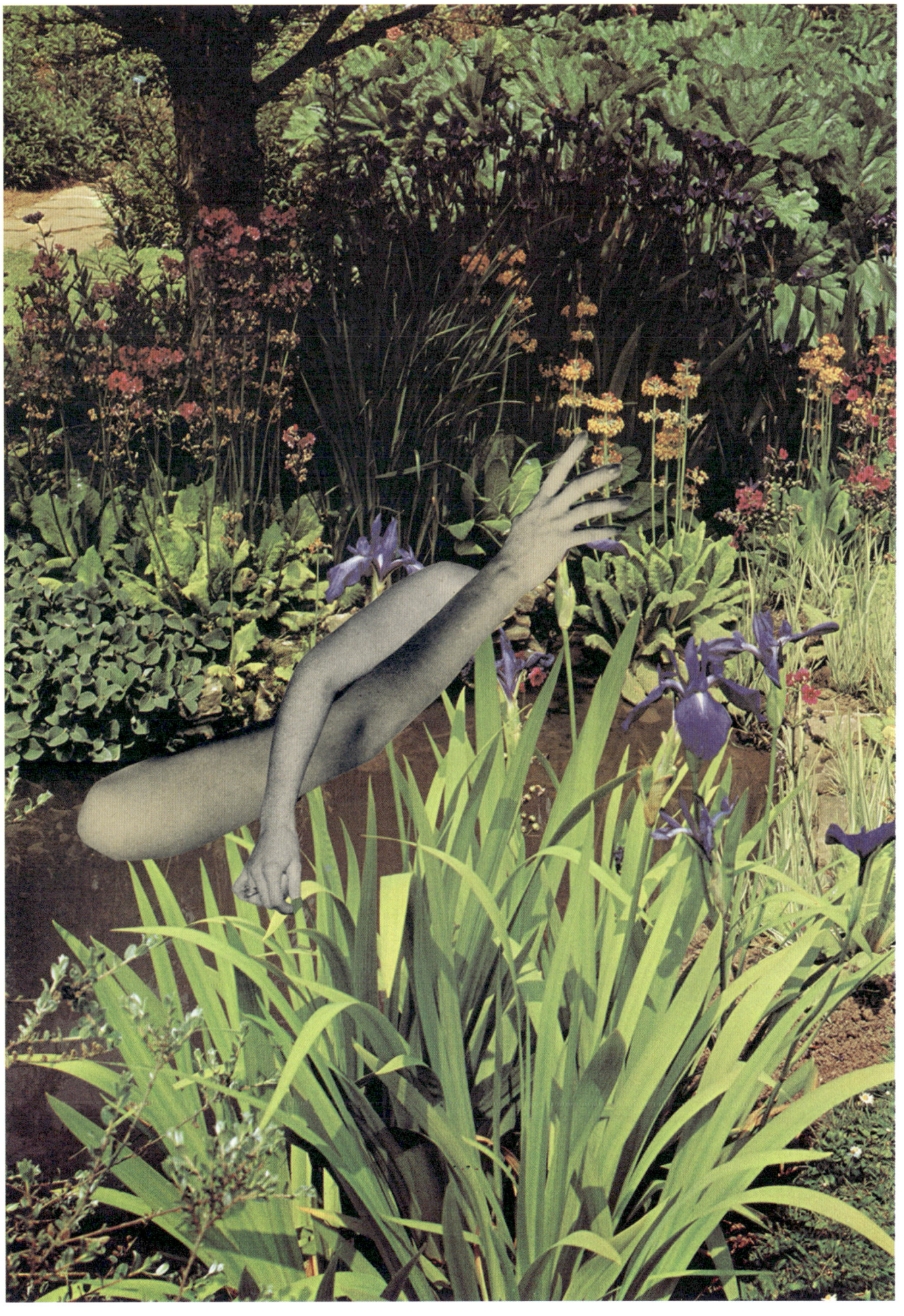

EVA
STENRAM

DIRK

STEWEN

Working on on paper, Dirk Stewen composes pieces that involve photography, sculpture, embroidery and drawing. He works from an archive of his own photographs, which continues to grow. These photographs are not necessarily taken with specific works in mind, but rather incorporated into them after some time has elapsed, each artwork being a culmination of a variety of methodsand archival references. *Untitled (Ich habe keine Lust auszugehen)*(2017) – which translates from German as 'I don't feel like going out' –is comprised of inkjet prints, dyed glassine and thread. Glassine is a pulpy substance with a glass-like appearance, but clouded and waxy, sometimes with a plastic sheen. Stewen has layered this onto the page in sky-blue spirals that float over marbled black ink, a characteristic typical of his work. ◣ The paper the artist chooses is often weathered, antiquated by time, or embellished, primarily by painting in watercolour on special pre-printed paper stocks. As part of his process, Stewen will expose photographic paper and soak it with black ink before stitching it onto the main support of a work. Sometimes loose threads will float out of the seam, left raw and uncut. Stewen's compositions have a surreal quality to them, and his use of textured and saturated papers feels akin to the darkroom experiments of the Surrealist photographers such as Man Ray (1890–1976) and Maurice Tabard (1897–1984). *Untitled (Ich habe keine Lust auszugehen)* is one of what the artist calls a 'confetti piece' – with attached painted circles that are also embroidered upon. *Untitled (Fuchskäfig)* (Fox Cage) (2018) combine inkjet prints with washes of gouache and markings in ink. It references museological display with an image of a sculpture in a vitrine – the fox of the title perhaps, its pointed ears parallel to its erect tail, its jaw open and panting. The image looks as though it has been solarized: the shadows turn light and the animal's eyes are whitened, appearing as two blazing voids. ◢ In *Untitled (Neptune Ave)* (2018) the artist's typically moody backdrop of blotting ink swirls is inset with an image of a streetscape. Cars pull into the setting, while pedestrians' hands clutch at the air. Over this float a number of cut spheres – perhaps versions of the planet to which the title refers. Stewen's work often carries the impetus of an optical illusion or of some kind of mystical puzzle, a geometry that invites being decoded, although they can also be appreciated for their high-spirited and yet serious approach to the formal anatomies of abstract picture-making. *NO HANDS* (2018) joins offset prints with inkjet, blurring the ink saturations of both techniques. In view – floating like smooth stone planets – are blue spirals that carry the mysterious energy of the innards of sea shells, and the mirror images of a recurring glass vase, casting a long shadow upon its plinth. There is a distinctive quality to Stewen's works, in their careful rally of practices that seem at once digital and handmade. ◣

SKYE ARUNDHATI THOMAS

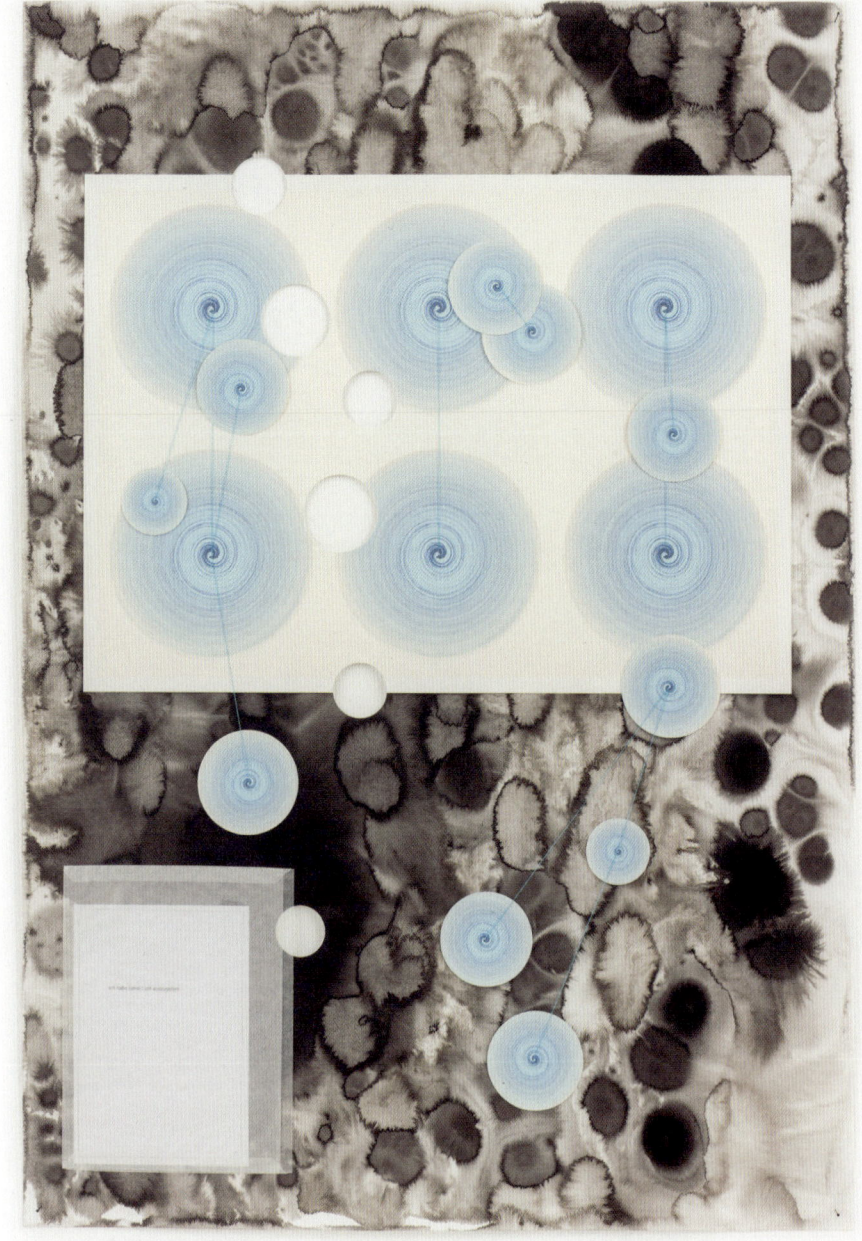

Born 1972, Dortmund, Germany. Lives in Hamburg, Germany.

↑ Untitled (Ich habe keine Lust auszugehen) (I don't feel like going out), 2017, ink, inkjet print, glassine and threads on paper, 100 × 70 cm (39 ⅜ × 27 ½ in)

↗↗ NO HANDS, 2018, ink, inkjet print and offset prints on paper, 100 × 70 cm (39 ⅜ × 27 ½ in)

→ Untitled (Fuchskäfig) (Fox Cage), 2018, inkjet prints, gouache and ink on paper, 100 × 70 cm (39 ⅜ × 27 ½ in)

→→ Untitled (Neptune Ave), 2018, ink and inkjet print on paper, 100 × 70 cm (39 ⅜ × 27 ½ in)

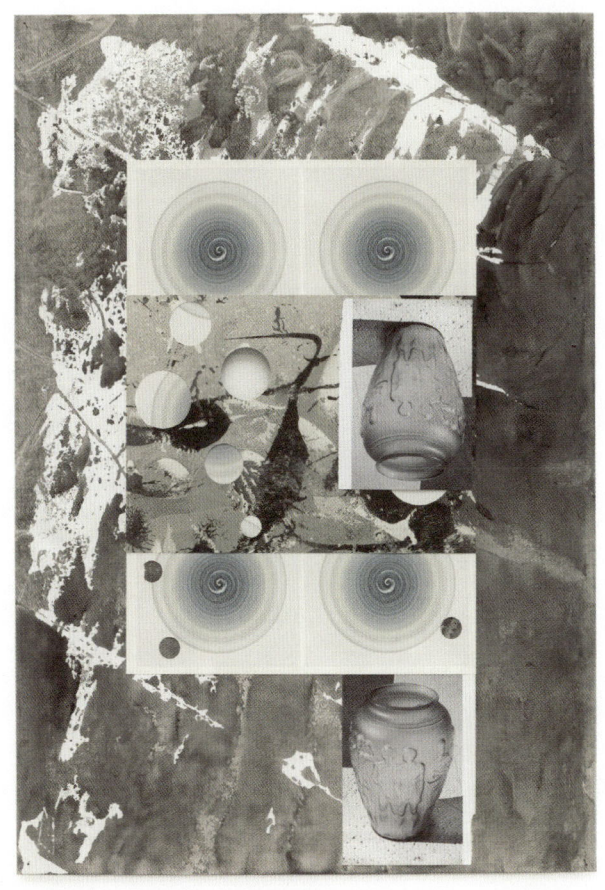

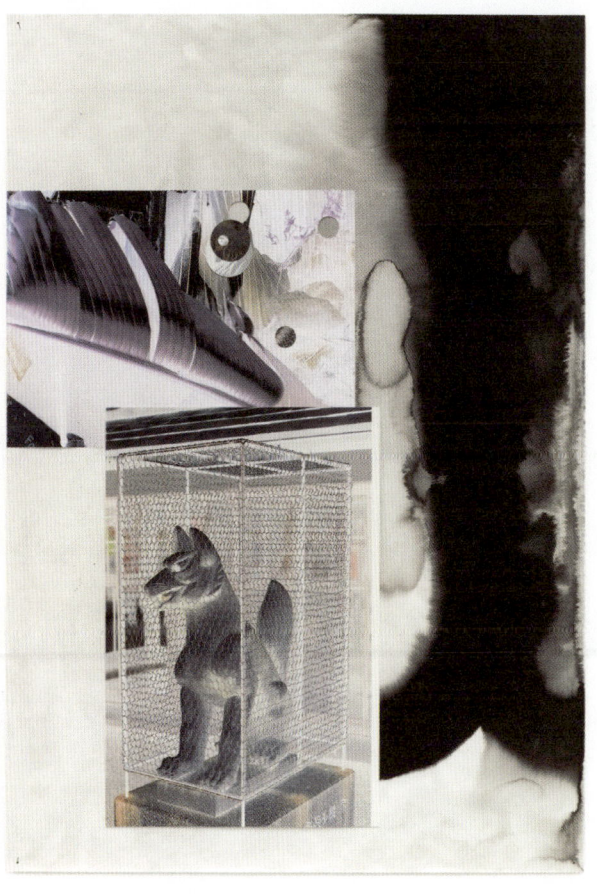

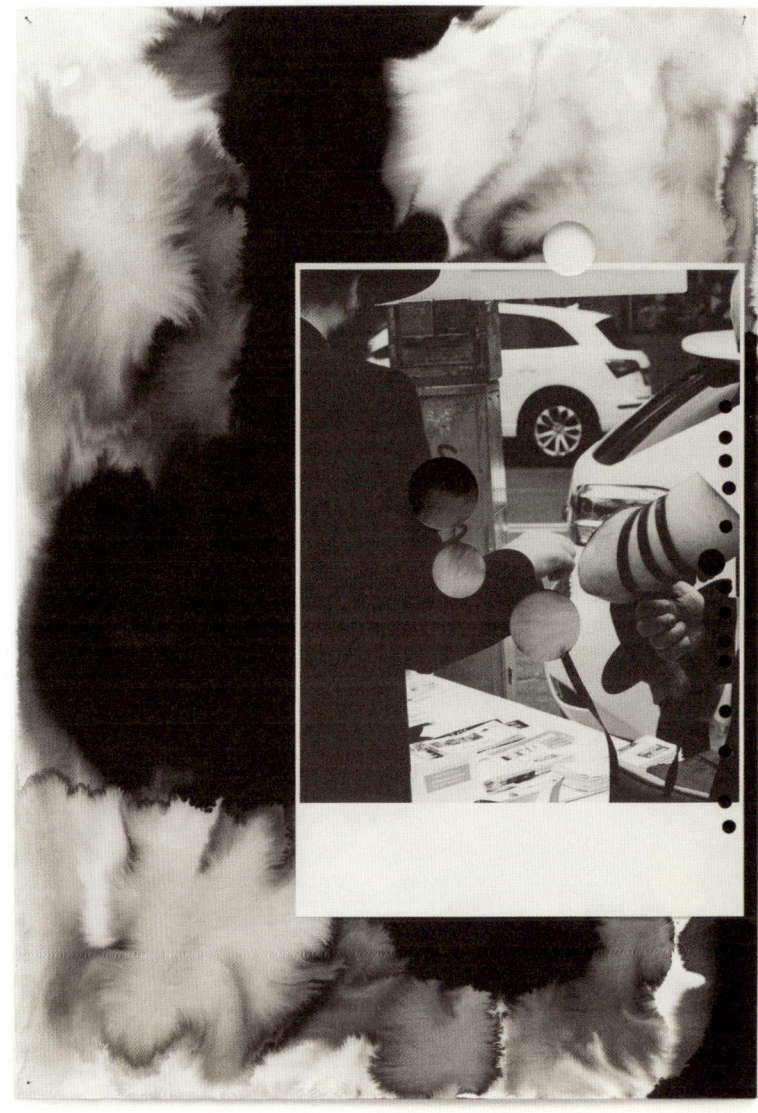

JOHN STEZAKER

Can a kiss be a good metaphor for collage? The coming together of two parts, according to John Stezaker, is all it takes. Since the mid-1970s Stezaker's work has aimed at unpacking the technical, formal and conceptual foundations of collage and creating an inventory of procedures and materials that are essential to it. His works in this form are recognizable for their reliance on two photographic elements juxtaposed to one another or enmeshed by a single straight or curved cut. His choice of source material, in turn, draws on found footage from the history of film, photography and tourism. ◢ Stezaker's 'Mask' and 'Insert' series, which are some of his best-known works, combine found postcards depicting natural landscapes (caves, cliffs, waterfalls) from the early decades of the twentieth century with film-still photographs from the 1940s and 1950s of the kind that are used to decorate the entrance lobbies of cinemas. Consider for example *Mask CLXXXIX* of 2016, where a portrait photograph depicting a mid-twentieth-century film star is partly covered by a postcard of a waterfall. Carefully matched, the relationship between the two images dictates the reading of the composition, where the actor's hair, and parts of her eye and nose perfectly merge with the natural cliff in several places and contrast in others. The result is at once grotesque, humorous and strangely familiar, as the gushing waters expose a hidden aspect that seemed to have been underlying the photographic portrait all along. ◢ But while 'Mask' relies on straight-line edges, reminiscent of the abrupt disjuncture of Cubist collages, other series rely on carefully executed curvilinear ones associated with the legacy of Surrealism, in which the joining of body parts and objects create fantastical creatures or hallucinatory situations. *Kiss I* of 2020 forms part of this group. In this work, Stezaker overlays two film-still photographs of kissing scenes, one in colour and the other in black and white. He has then carefully cut out the man's silhouette from the front image, hereby creating a confusing merger of lips, hands, colours and perspectival depth. A similar method characterizes his ongoing 'Double Shadow' series, where the dark background infiltrates the image, creating an anonymous placeholder for the viewer's imagination to fill. ◢ Having begun his engagement with collage in the mid-1970s, a time associated with the advent of postmodernist theory and digital technology, Stezaker remains determined that 'collage can only exist in… the age of mechanical reproduction', as he wrote in a 1977 essay accompanying his solo exhibition at The Photographers' Gallery, London. He further elaborates that the practice of cutting and pasting papers and photographs in the name of art is a direct outcome of modern technology, a way to respond, analyze and criticize the mass production and consumption of printed materials since the mid-nineteenth century – a gesture that now has great relevance to an even faster-paced flow of digital imagery. ◢
YUVAL ETGAR

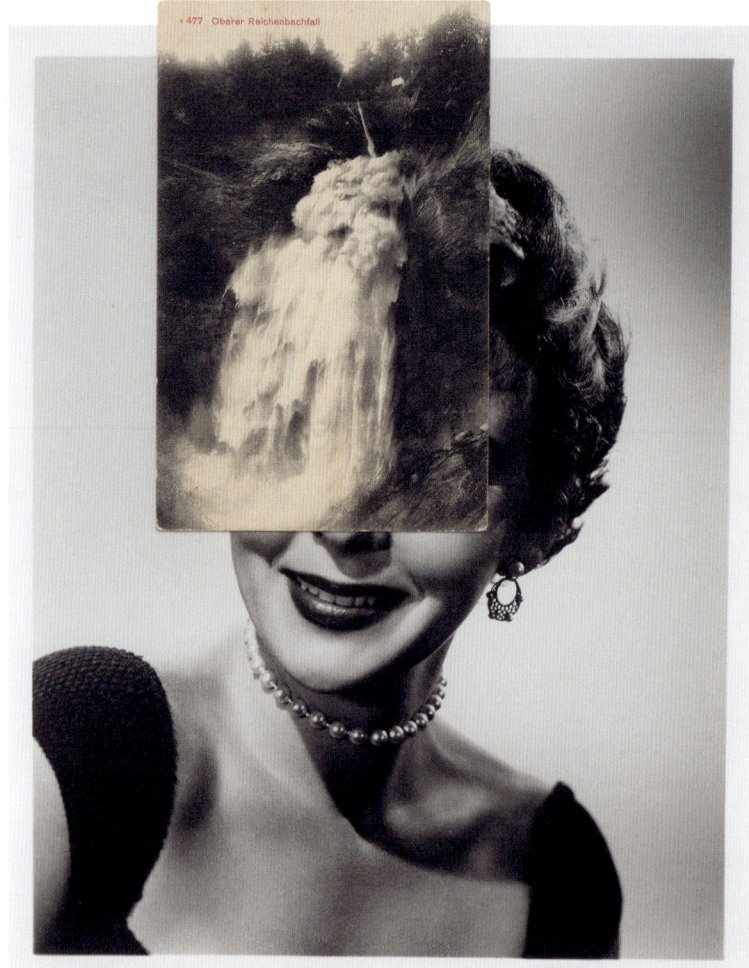

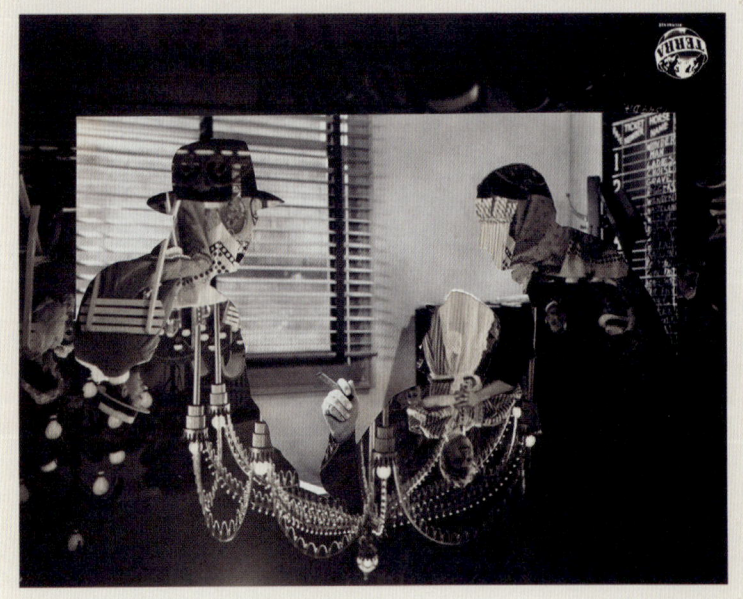

Born 1949, Worcester, UK. Lives in London, UK and St Leonards-on-Sea, UK.

↑↑ Mask CLXXXIX, 2016, collage, 25.4 × 20.5 cm (10 × 8 in)
↑   Double Shadow XLVI, 2015, collage, 23.5 × 29.7 cm (9¼ × 11¾ in)
→   Kiss I, 2020, collage, 32.2 × 29.5 cm (12⅝ × 11½ in)

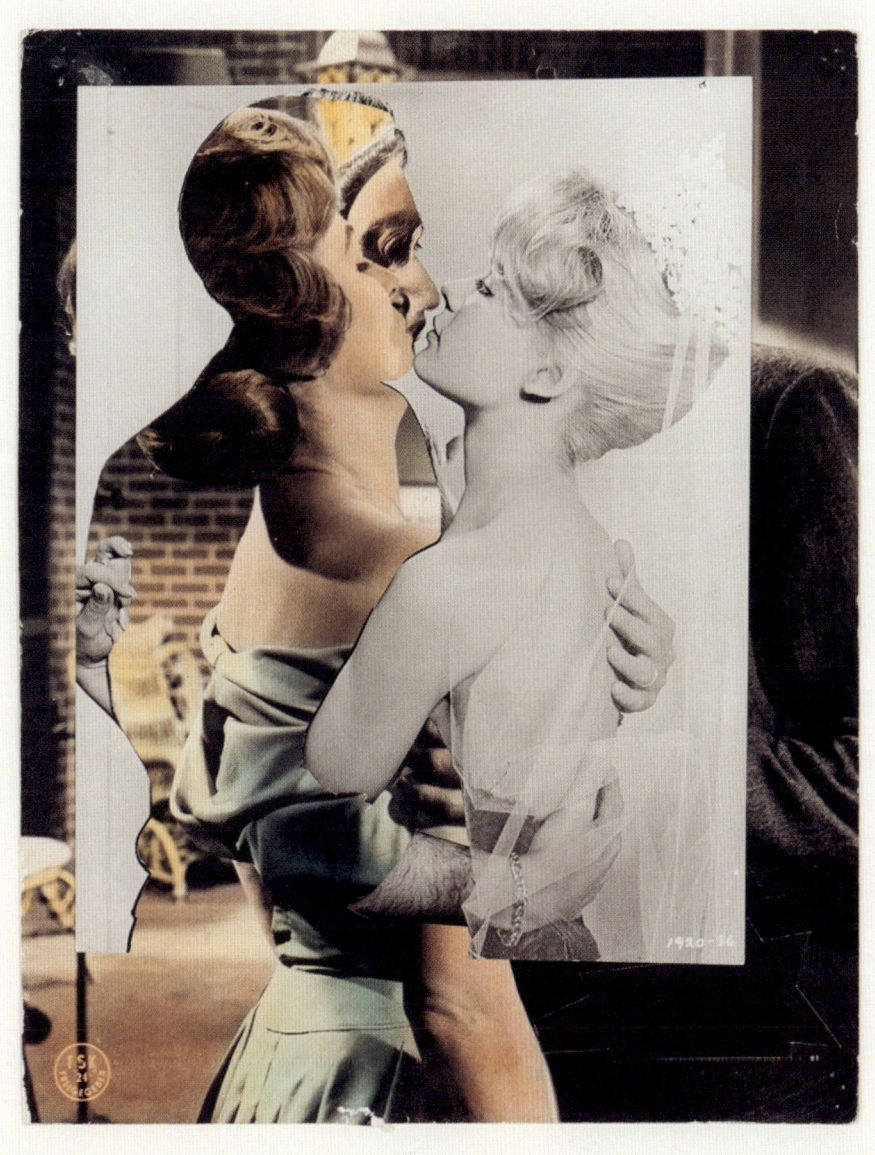

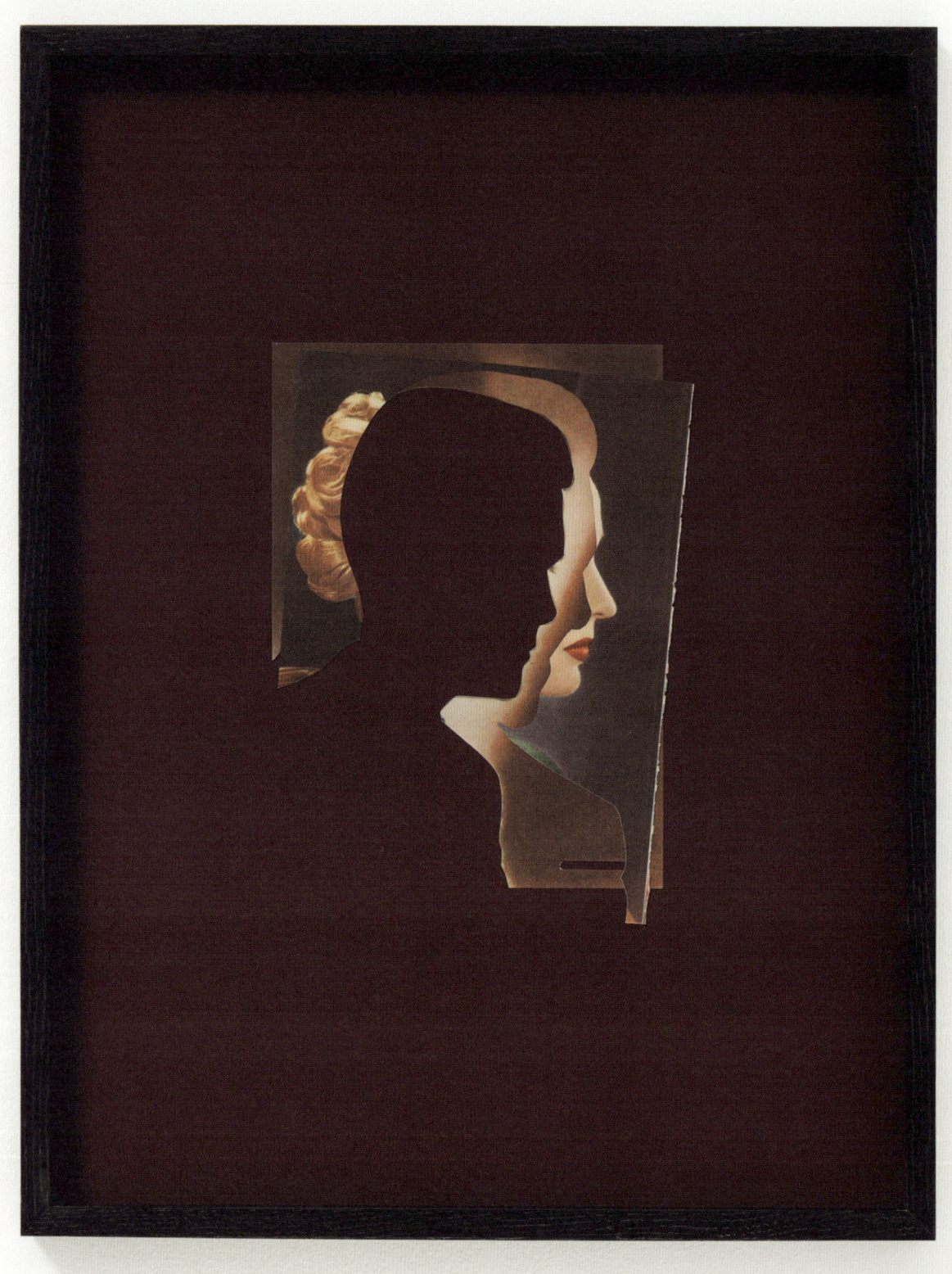

↑   **Double Shadow**, 2020, collage, 53.6 × 41.8 cm (21⅛ × 16⁷⁄₁₆ in)

↗   **Double Shadow**, 2021, collage, 53.6 × 41.8 cm (21⅛ × 16⁷⁄₁₆ in)

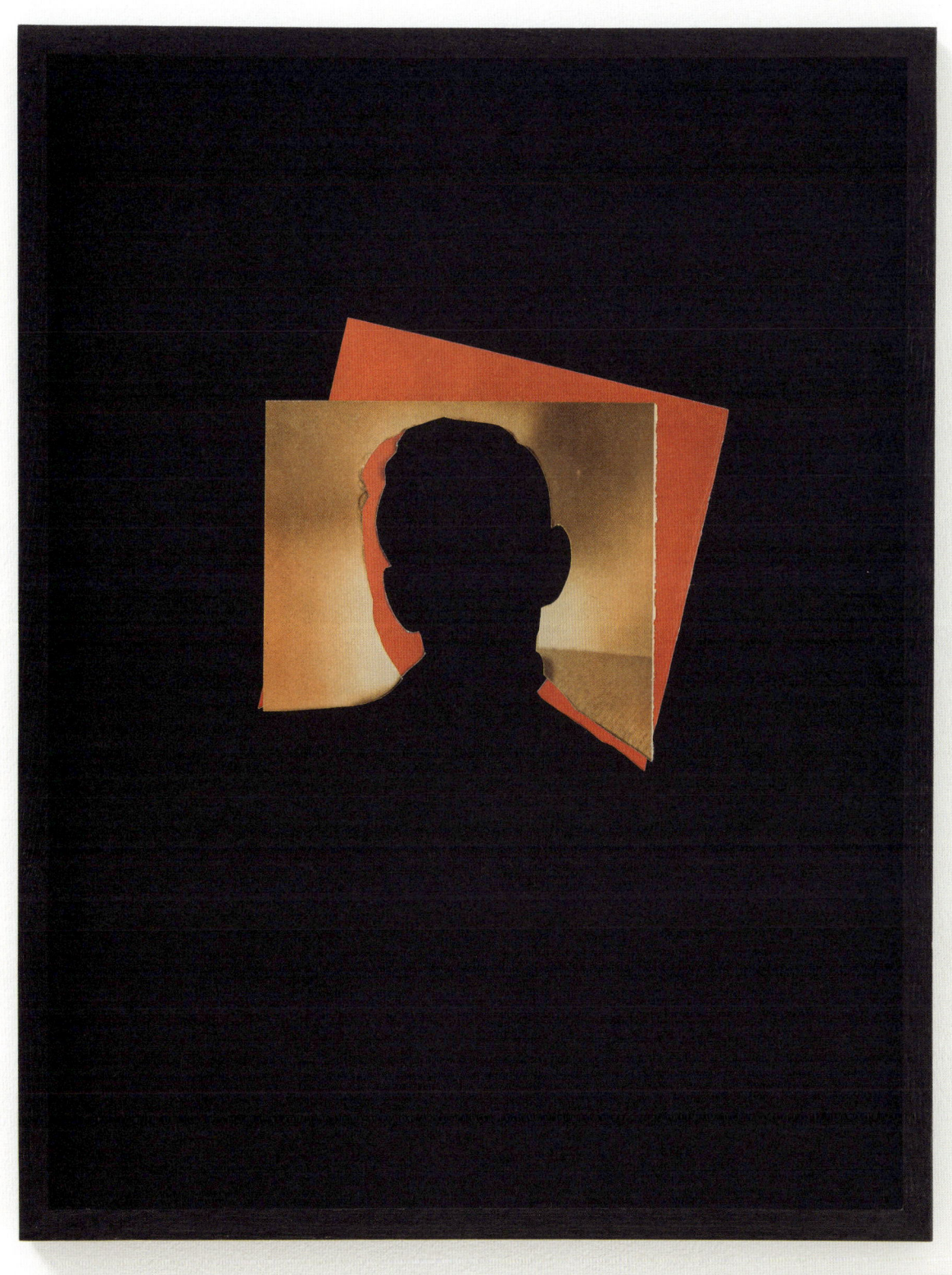

SITAARA STODEL

Found snapshots from the age of analogue photography are the principal material of Sitaara Stodel's synthetic studies of unpeopled domesticity. Sourced from markets and junk shops across Cape Town, in their raw form these discarded colour photographs mostly describe middle-class white experiences from mid- to late-twentieth-century South Africa – the apartheid years. Stodel's intervention in this fraught archive is twofold. Firstly, she cuts up the snapshots and deposits useful elements into separate folders labelled 'interior', 'exterior', 'walls', 'windows', 'doors', 'animals', 'cars', 'nature' and so on. The second step, making, is also procedural but ultimately transformative. Stodel's collages fall into two distinct groupings. Works like *Entrances* (2019) and *Be gentle* (2020) typify her use of over-lapping photos to evoke remembered environments from her youth. In contrast to these chaotic bricolages, the splayed compositional style of *Wake up and smell the flowers* (2021) is representative of a body of fantasy works depicting elements of an ideal home. Memory is integral in guiding her impressionistic arrangements. Even the pastel-coloured grounds are based on remembered hues from her youth. Whether densely layered or dispersed, Stodel's collages all reimagine aspects of her interrupted childhood and longer family history of displacement. The artist's father is a Muslim of Malaysian slave ancestry who was relocated from his childhood home by apartheid bureaucrats. Included among her Jewish mother's Dutch and English family are refugees from Nazi Europe. Stodel's parents divorced when she was two and the artist grew up with her mother, a clairvoyant who struggled economically. Rent was frequently a problem and the family often moved homes. By the time Stodel enrolled in art school, where she majored in photography, she had lived in over thirty different homes. During her art studies Stodel shunned digital processes in favour of exploring obsolete photo-graphy and darkroom techniques. These experiments also primed her interest in collage. She composed her first collages in 2014 from a stack of found photographs. Her teachers were impressed and advised her to continue. Stodel left art school with a clear sense of her medium and its narrative potential in relation to her biography. It nonetheless took her time to settle on her current aesthetic. Initially she blanked out the figures in her compositions as a way to acknowledge ethics around privacy and consent. Later she experimented with obscuring the figures with chocolate wrappers – a surrogate for gold leaf. She finally settled on excising them entirely from her compositions. Her interest is the scenography of suburban life. 'I don't see myself in the people I collect,' said Stodel in a 2022 interview with the author. 'I want to insert my own memories into these photographs.' To underscore their basis in suburban experience, Stodel sometimes presents her collages within domestic installations that amplify the scale and impact of her memory works.

SEAN O'TOOLE

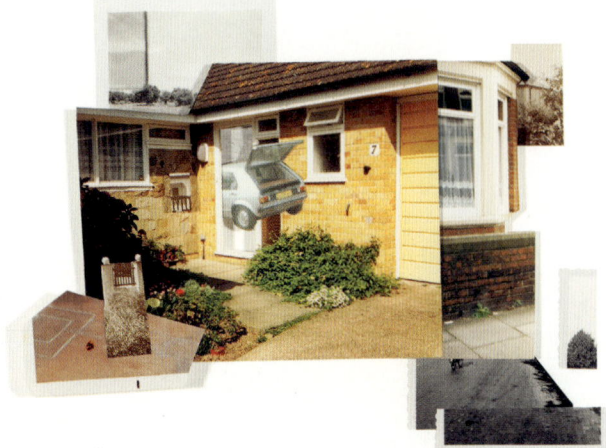

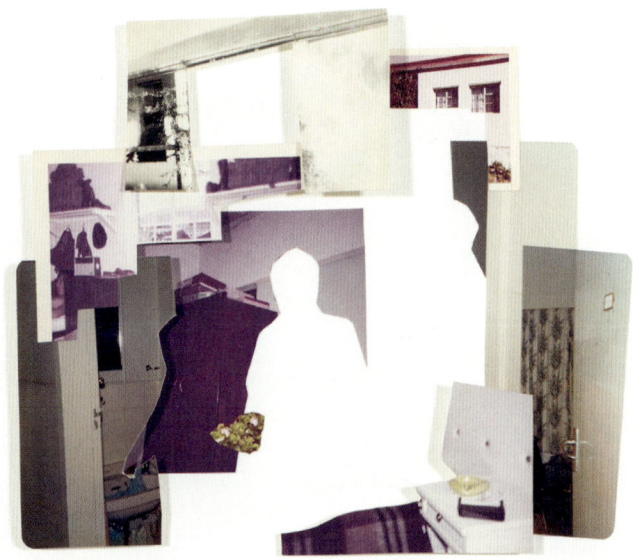

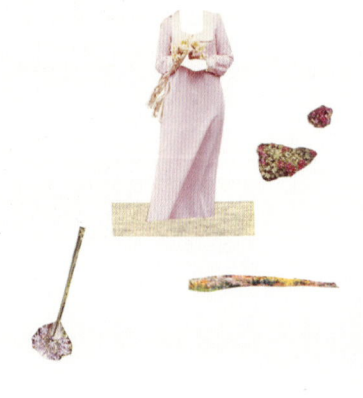

Born 1991, Cape Town, South Africa. Lives in Cape Town.

↑↑   **Entrances**, 2019, found photographs on Fabriano, 21 × 29.7 cm (8¼ × 11¾ in)

↑   **Be gentle**, 2020, found photographs on Fabriano, 28 × 21 cm (11 × 8¼ in)

→   **Wake up and smell the flowers**, 2021, found photographs on screenprinted archival mounting board, 49.5 × 42 cm (19⅜ × 16½ in)

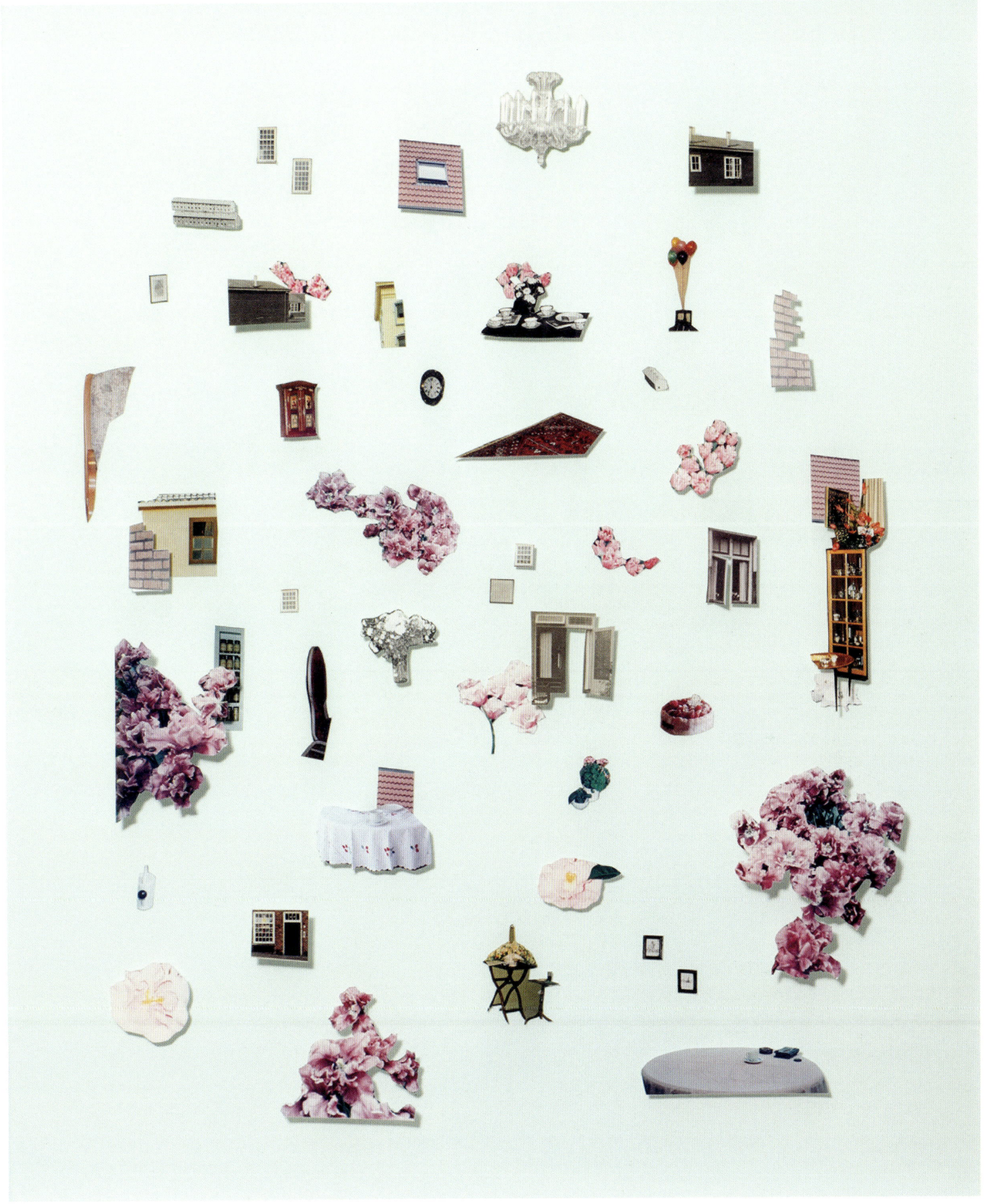

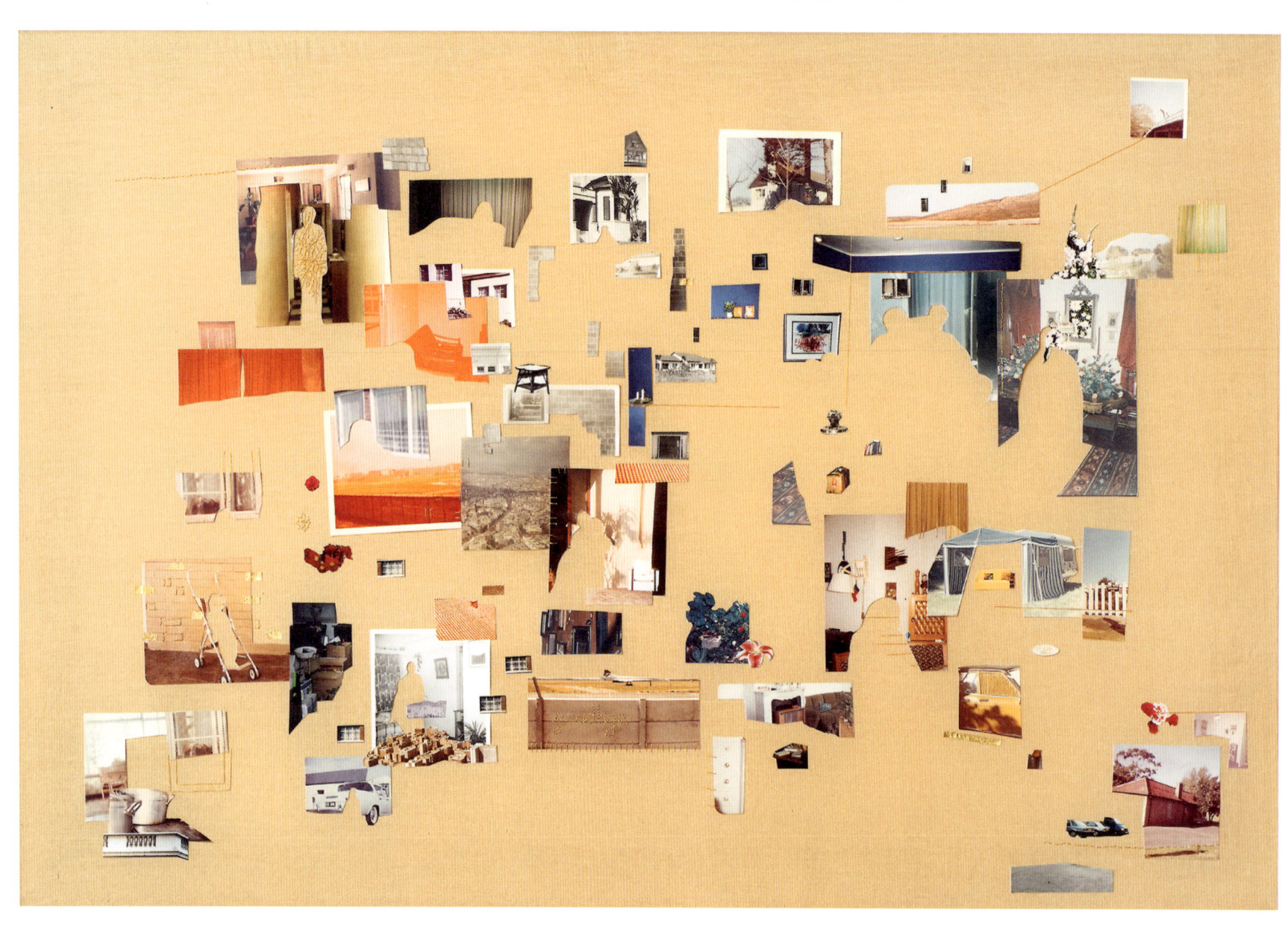

↑   **Goodbye, hello**, 2019, found photographs and gold thread on linen, 64 × 93 cm (25¼ × 36⅝ in)

↗   **Family reunion**, 2021, found photographs, gold thread and gold vinyl on linen, 91.5 × 121.5 cm
(36 × 47⅞ in)

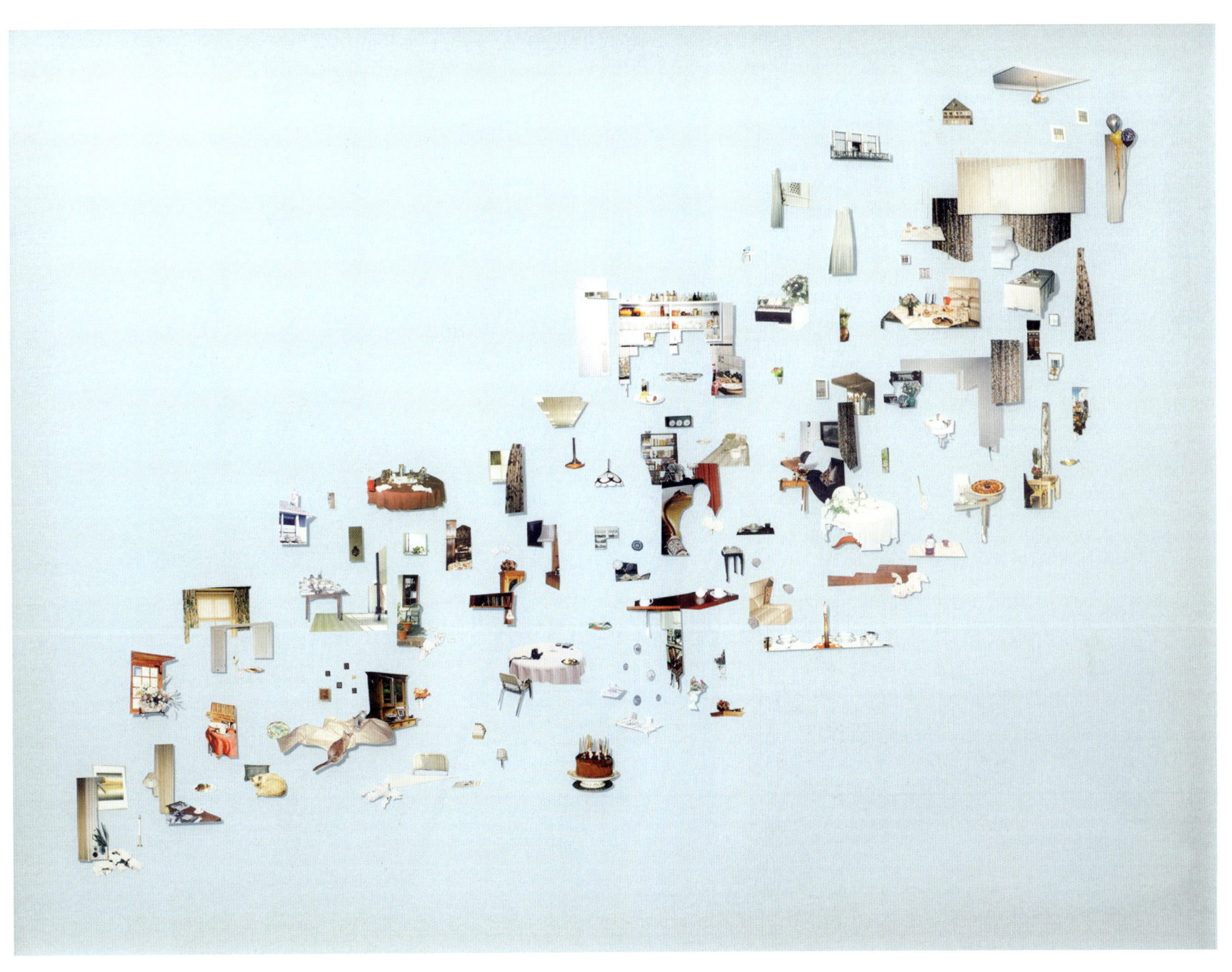

SITAARA
STODEL

MICKALENE THOMAS

Drawing on art history and popular culture, Mickalene Thomas creates collages that celebrate the beauty, sexuality and power of Black women. Her repertoire is broad, and viewers may encounter visual references as varied as the art historical movements of Neo-Classicism, Impressionism and the Harlem Renaissance, and popular culture, including the Blaxploitation film genre. Thomas inserts her figures into familiar compositions and poses found in historical works, but her women assume positions of power, staring confidently out of the picture plane. For *Clarivel Face Forward Gazing* (2020) Thomas depicts one of her repeated muses Clarivel in a casually reclined posture reminiscent of Édouard Manet's *Olympia* (1863) and, by extension, Titian's *Venus of Urbino* (c.1534). Subtle touches reinforce this connection, such as Clarivel similarly propping herself up on a cushion or Thomas cropping the ottoman in the foreground to mimic the draped bedding in Manet's painting. Olympia is already considered an audacious figure in the way she looks directly at the viewer, but Thomas ups the ante by showing Clarivel with her fingertips supporting her head in a look that could be interpreted as defiance, self-assuredness or even exasperation – either way, she exhibits undeniable confidence. ◼ Thomas is frequently inspired by people she knows as muses, but she also depicts well-known public figures such as Michelle Obama and Naomi Campbell. For her 'Jet Blue' series the artist featured women from *Jet*, an iconic Black weekly magazine in print between 1951 and 2014. The 'blue' portion of the title refers to the sexual content of the source photographs, which are taken from old *Jet* calendars. In her series, Thomas gives the models new context, sometimes choosing to obscure or pixelate the nude elements of the works. Instead, viewers focus on the women's beautiful smiles and the colourful world in which Thomas places them. On *Jet Blue #37* (2021), she adds rhinestones to accent the image, a material she has used repeatedly as an unabashed touch of glamour and sparkle. ◼ Equally captivating are the environments in which Thomas positions her figures. In *Interior: Green Couch with Red Flowers* (2017) the viewer is offered an unobstructed vision of the bold worlds she creates through layering cut-outs of photographs and patterns. The angle of the green floral sofa positions the observer as though peeking over the top to look upon a mid-century sitting room. The colours and prints – which are rather different from each other – are successfully tied together by their period appropriateness and Thomas's use of a complementary colour scheme. ◼ Thomas fortifies her work with history and popular culture in a way that creates multiple points of access and relatability for the viewer. Though her practice creates celebrations of Black women that are grounded in art history, she very much carves out space for her own point of view.

FERREN GIPSON

Born 1971, Camden, New Jersey, USA. Lives in New York, USA.

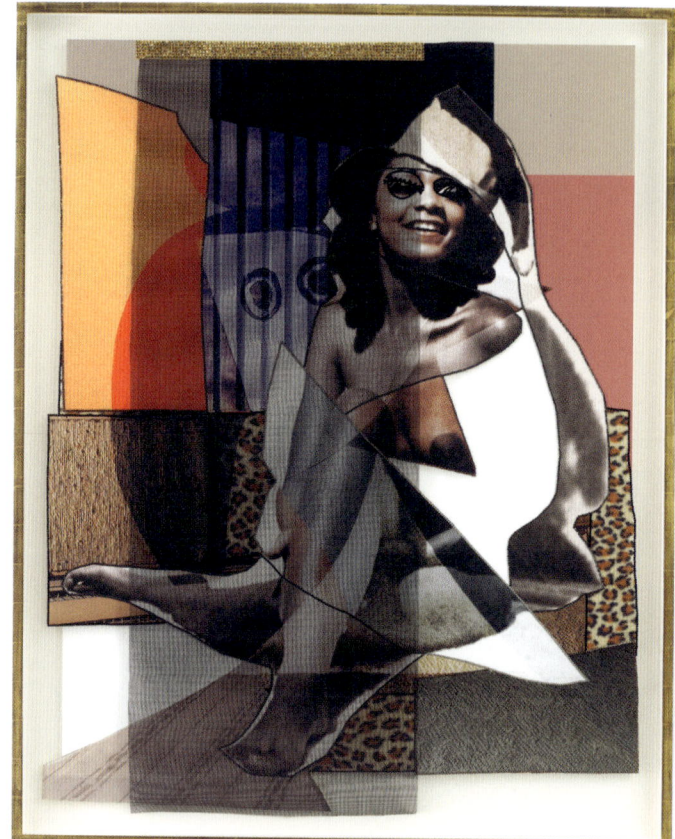

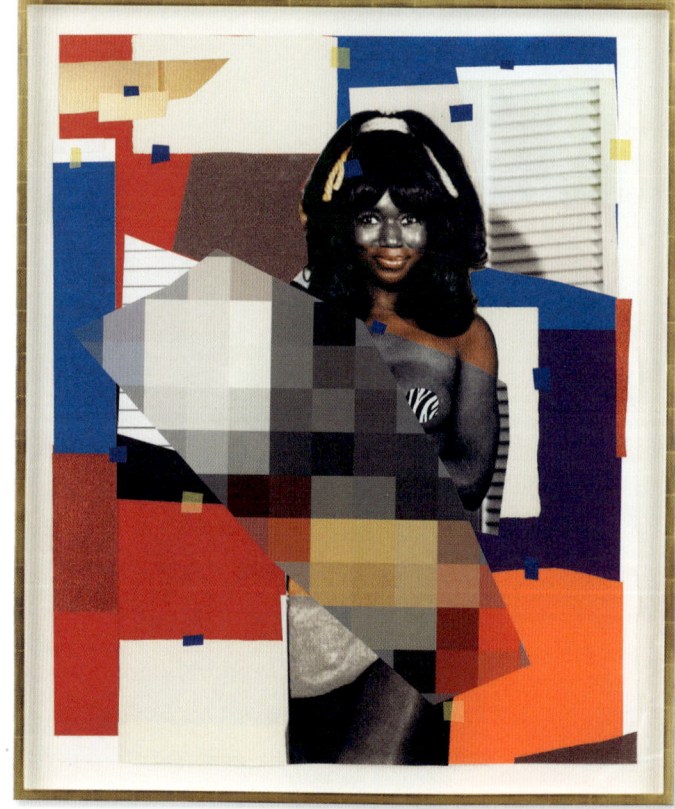

↑↑ **Jet Blue #37**, 2021, colour photograph, mixed-media paper, acrylic paint, rhinestones and fibreglass mesh on museum paper mounted on Dibond, framed 174.9 × 140.7 cm (68⅞ × 55⅜ in)

↑ **Jet Blue #7**, 2019, colour photograph, mixed-media paper, glitter and tape on hot press paper, framed 154.3 × 130.8 cm (60¾ × 51½ in)

↗ **Interior: Green Couch with Red Flowers**, 2017, colour photograph and paper collage on archival board, 17.1 × 28.6 cm (9 × 11¼ in)

→ **Clarivel Face Forward Gazing**, 2020, colour photograph and mixed-media paper, 22.9 × 28.6 cm (9 × 11¼ in)

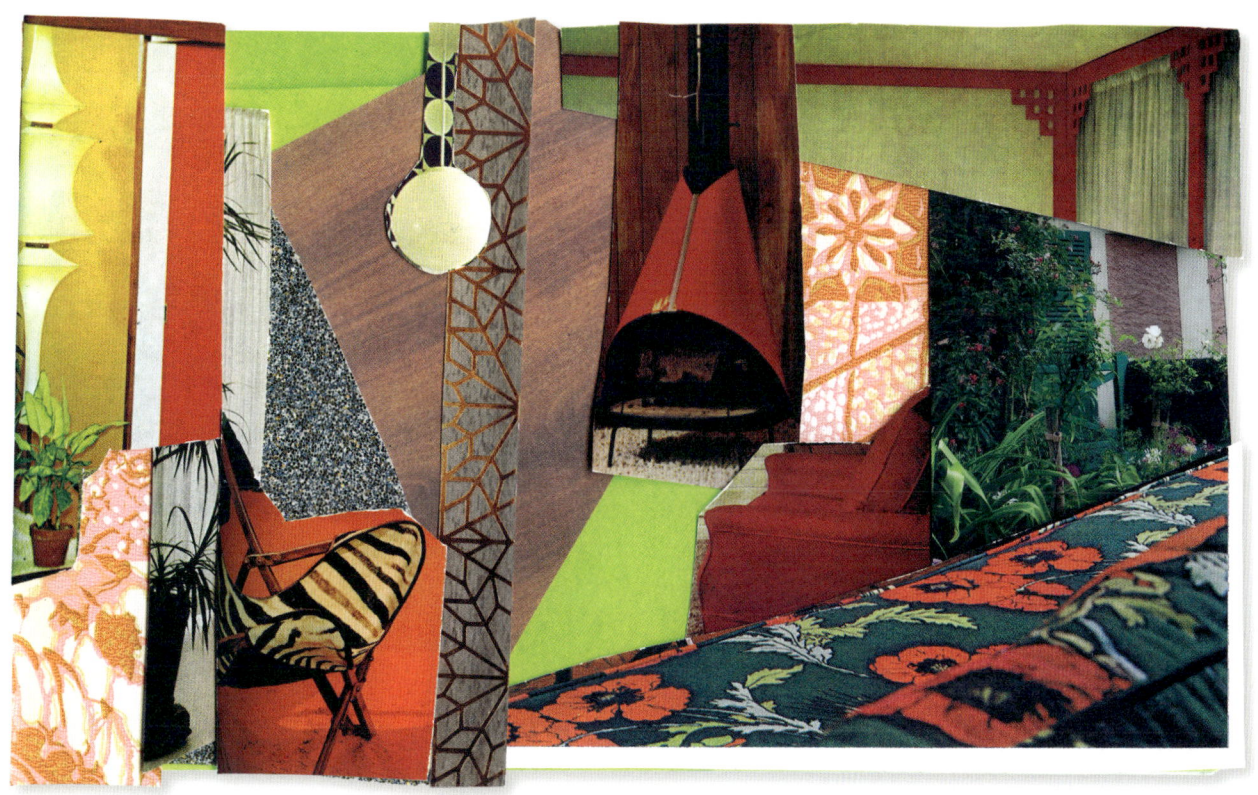

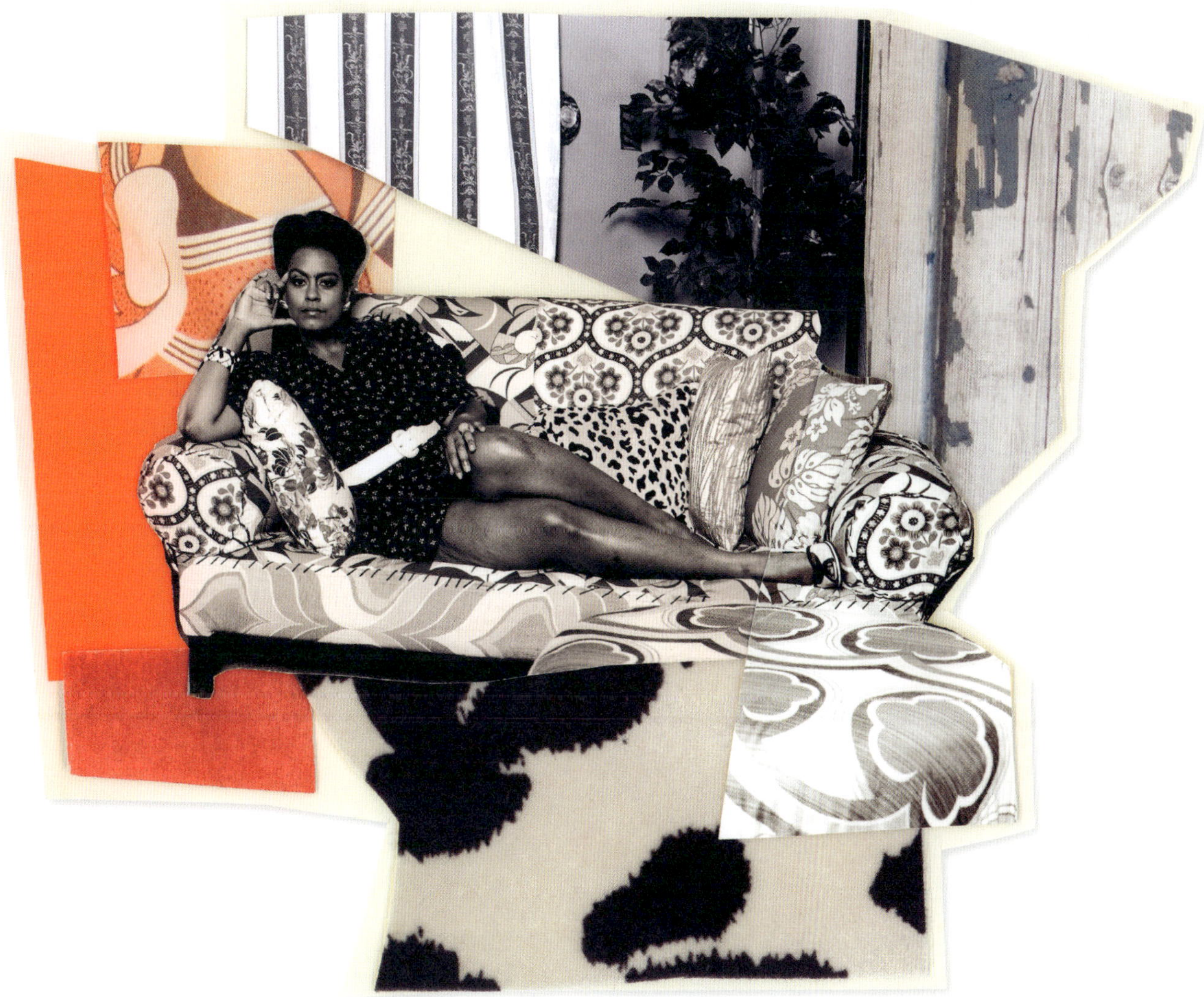

The political and economic crises of the present serve as raw material for subversion and critique in the work of Surajate Tongchua, whose multidisciplinary practice explores the impact of governmental policy on the lives of ordinary citizens. Probing the limits of how mass-media representation and political reportage mediate public life through live performances, sculptures and installations, as well as abstract collage, Tongchua interrogates the cultural heritage and contemporary politics of his native Thailand. ◢ Ruled for centuries as an absolute monarchy until a 1932 military revolt aided by Western imperialist influence established a constitutional democratic monarchy, Thailand has been subject to various coups d'état and changes to its constitution, abetted by military juntas. In May 2014, one such junta dissolved the caretaker government, imposing censorship laws, imprisoning dissidents and prominent political figures, and ultimately repealing the constitution; the junta's rule lasted until 2019, when general elections were held, with candidates from multiple parties running for positions. ◢ Initiated at the start of the military transition, Tongchua's series 'Priceless' draws from his experiences and observations of Thai society during this period, with a pointed focus on the financial implications of the junta's regime. When the transition was announced in May 2014, Tongchua began gathering receipts of financial transactions and expenses that he and his family had incurred, surmising that the tax payments he and other citizens made directly fuelled the junta's regime. ◢ In 2017, having amassed a plethora of financial documents, Tongchua put the materials through a paper shredder and began layering the now-illegible materials with acrylic paint to create abstract assemblages on canvas. The resulting collages, with their dense arrays of thin, multicoloured strips of paper, aesthetically recall the obfuscatory financial instruments of austerity – loosely resembling the dizzying vertical digits of stock market reports or horizontal ledgers and lines of code – with the shredded paper indexing the bureaucratic processes of the state. Combined with the repetitive, laborious and time-consuming process undertaken to create the works, the pieces establish the artist's pointed critique of the cyclical nature of Thailand's political regime and its exploitation of its citizens. ◢ Extending his critique further, in 2022 Tongchua created an untitled sculpture, consisting of a lone, dry branch in a large pot, both bedecked in papier-mâché made from a blend of Chinese newspapers in Thailand, social-science textbooks and receipts. As the artist remarked in a 2021 interview with the *Bangkok Post*, the work is a multi-layered critique – of the sympathetic relationship between Chinese-Thai investors and the government, and of the stagnation of both the Thai education system and the prosperity of its citizens. Deftly amalgamating these references in his work, Tongchua's abstractions prove that amid many forms of disaster, critique is both possible and urgently necessary.

TAUSIF NOOR

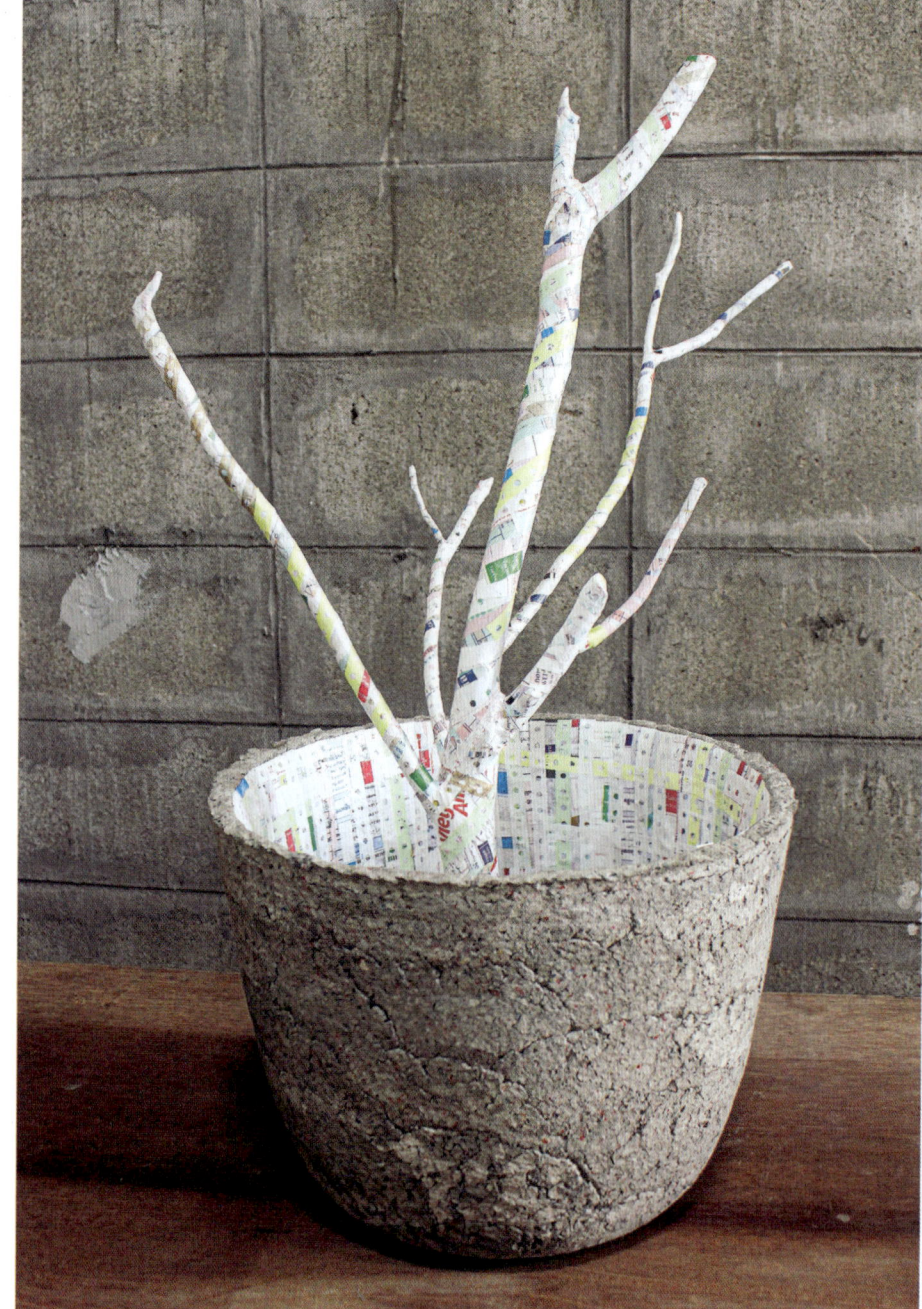

Born 1986, Bangkok, Thailand. Lives in Chiang Mai, Thailand.

↑ UNTITLED PRICELESS, 2022, papier-mâché, receipt paper and dry branch, 74.5 × 60 × 44 cm (29 ¼ × 23 ⅝ × 17 ¼ in)

↗ UNTITLED PRICELESS, 2019–21, acrylic and receipt paper on canvas, 180 × 200 cm (78 ¾ × 70 ¾ in)

↗↗ UNTITLED PRICELESS, 2019–21, acrylic and receipt paper on canvas, 120 × 100 cm (47 ¼ × 39 ⅜ in)

→ UNTITLED PRICELESS, 2019, acrylic and receipt paper on canvas, 70 × 140 cm (27 ½ × 55 ⅛ in)

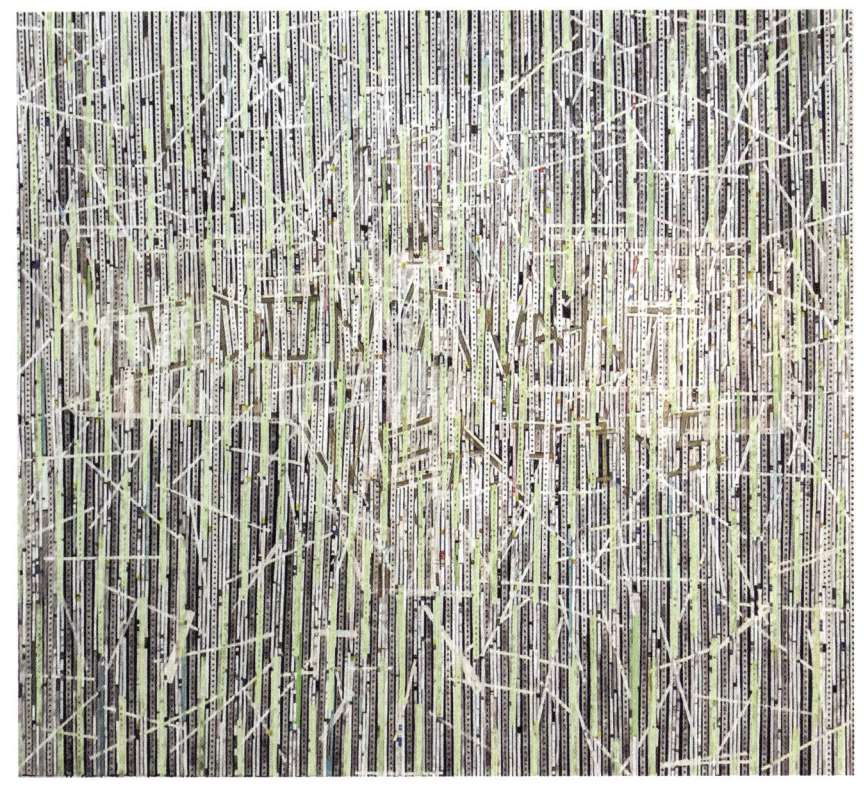

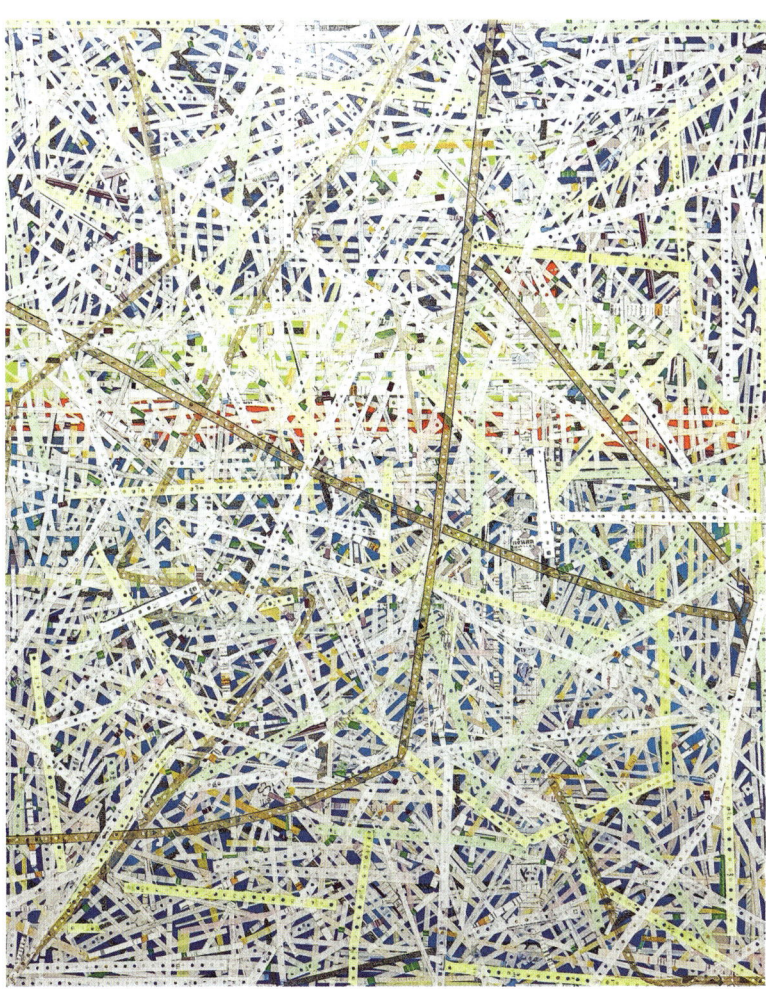

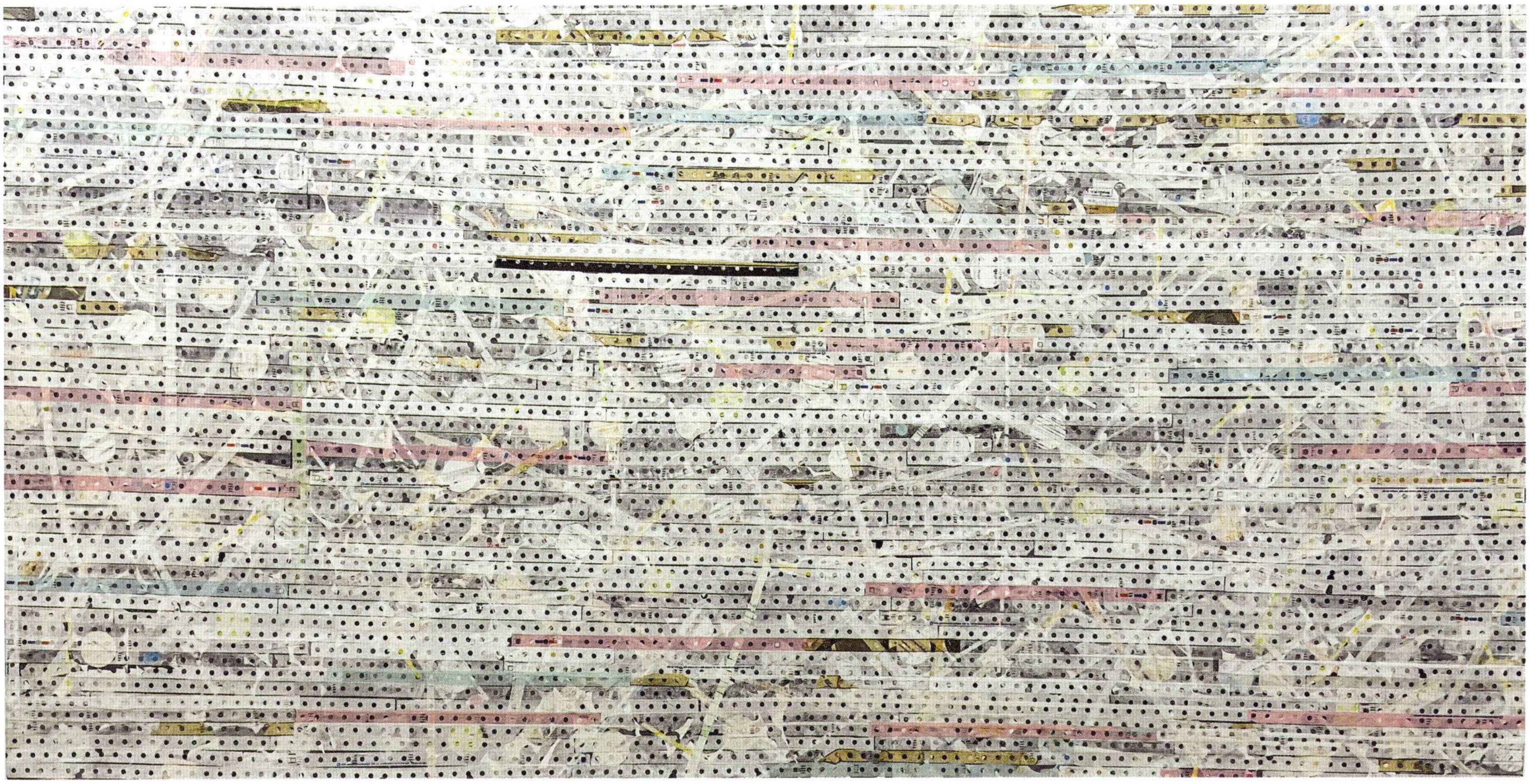

SURAJATE
TONGCHUA

SARA VANDERBEEK

The conceptual photographer Sara VanDerBeek is known for exploring the relationships between image and object. In earlier works she created sculptural forms that she photographed and then destroyed. She has since moved on to photographing objects in American and European museums, with a focus on artworks and artefacts relating to the female form. 'I wanted to explore figures that are already iconographic,' VanDerBeek told *Aperture* magazine in 2013. 'Although they are three-dimensional, I think of them almost as images.' Through composition, style and scale, her photographs place these historical works in the contemporary image space of the endless scroll. Her work is collage-like in its joining and overlapping of separate images and temporalities, and in its fusion of analogue and digital technologies.

To make her works, VanDerBeek first uses a camera with medium-format roll film and the existing light in a space. She circles each sculpture, carefully capturing all perspectives until she feels she has documented the whole. In the studio, she then digitally edits her images, combining different objects together and manipulating the colours – which are further enhanced through her use of a digital printing process called dye sublimation. She has a fondness for dusk-like hues, which give the figures an otherworldly quality, as seen in works such as the 'Women & Museums' series (2019). *Women & Museums IV* (2019) depicts the mask of a young woman used in Noh, a traditional form of Japanese theatre that dates back to the fourteenth century. Two-thirds of the work show the mask from slightly below, while the other third shows only a slice of the mask – its eye – from slightly above. Here VanDerBeek is adopting the techniques of Noh actors, who tilt the mask up or down to lighten or sadden its famously ambiguous expression. 'The series,' she explained to the *British Journal of Photography* in 2019, 'presents the roles and representations of women as a continuum that is fluid and evolving.' *Future Variations II* (2021) belongs to a development in the artist's practice, in which she presents her photographs as suspended kinetic sculptures. The work is composed of two independent panels that together depict a female torso. Each panel is printed on both sides and hangs from the ceiling by a thread. This presentation allows the viewer to walk around the work as they would the sculpture it depicts. The panels move according to air currents in the gallery – twisting and twirling, and sometimes aligning. The viewer's perception and understanding of the work moves with it, shifting between two dimensions and three dimensions – a single piece or a pair of photographs, a collage of overlapping images that are animated not on a screen, but in real space and time.

EDMÉE LEPERCQ

Born 1976, Baltimore, Maryland, USA. Lives in New York, USA.

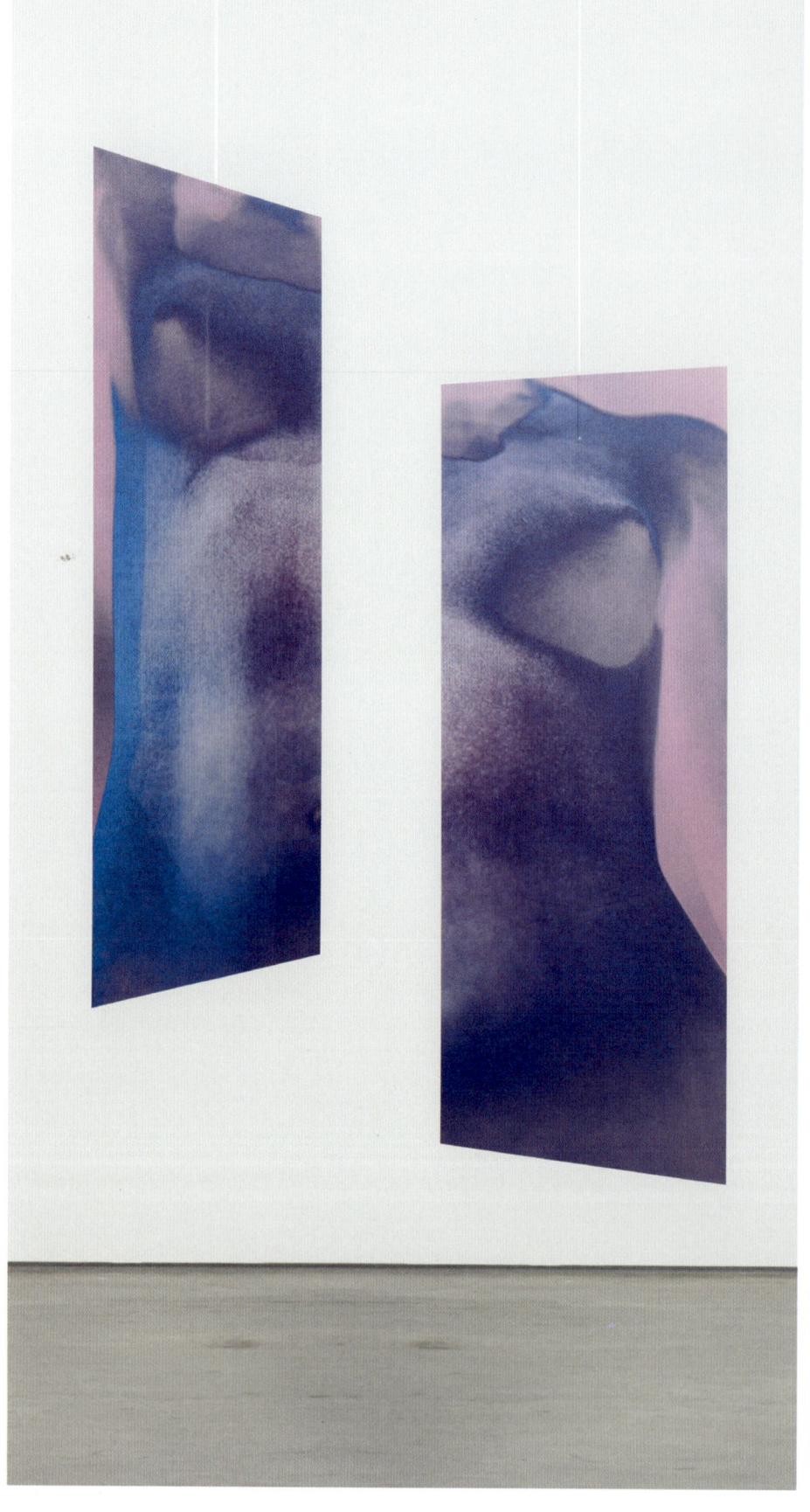

↑   Future Variations II, 2021, two-sided dye sublimation prints, each: 121.9 × 47 cm (48 × 18½ in)

→   Women & Museums IV, 2019, dye sublimation print, 243.8 × 121.9 cm (96 × 48 in), private collection

→→ Women & Museums I, 2019, dye sublimation print, 243.8 × 121.9 cm (96 × 48 in)

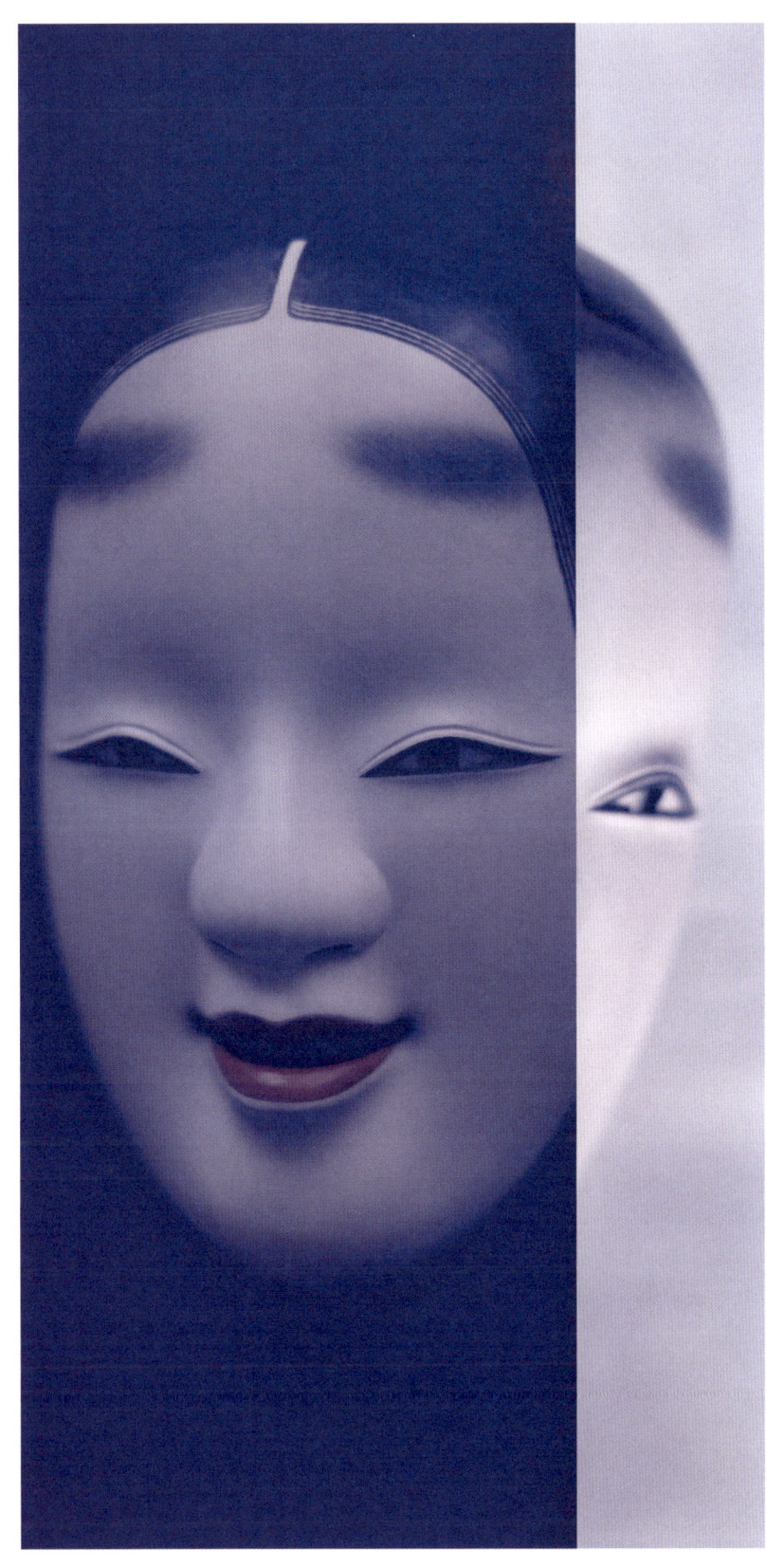
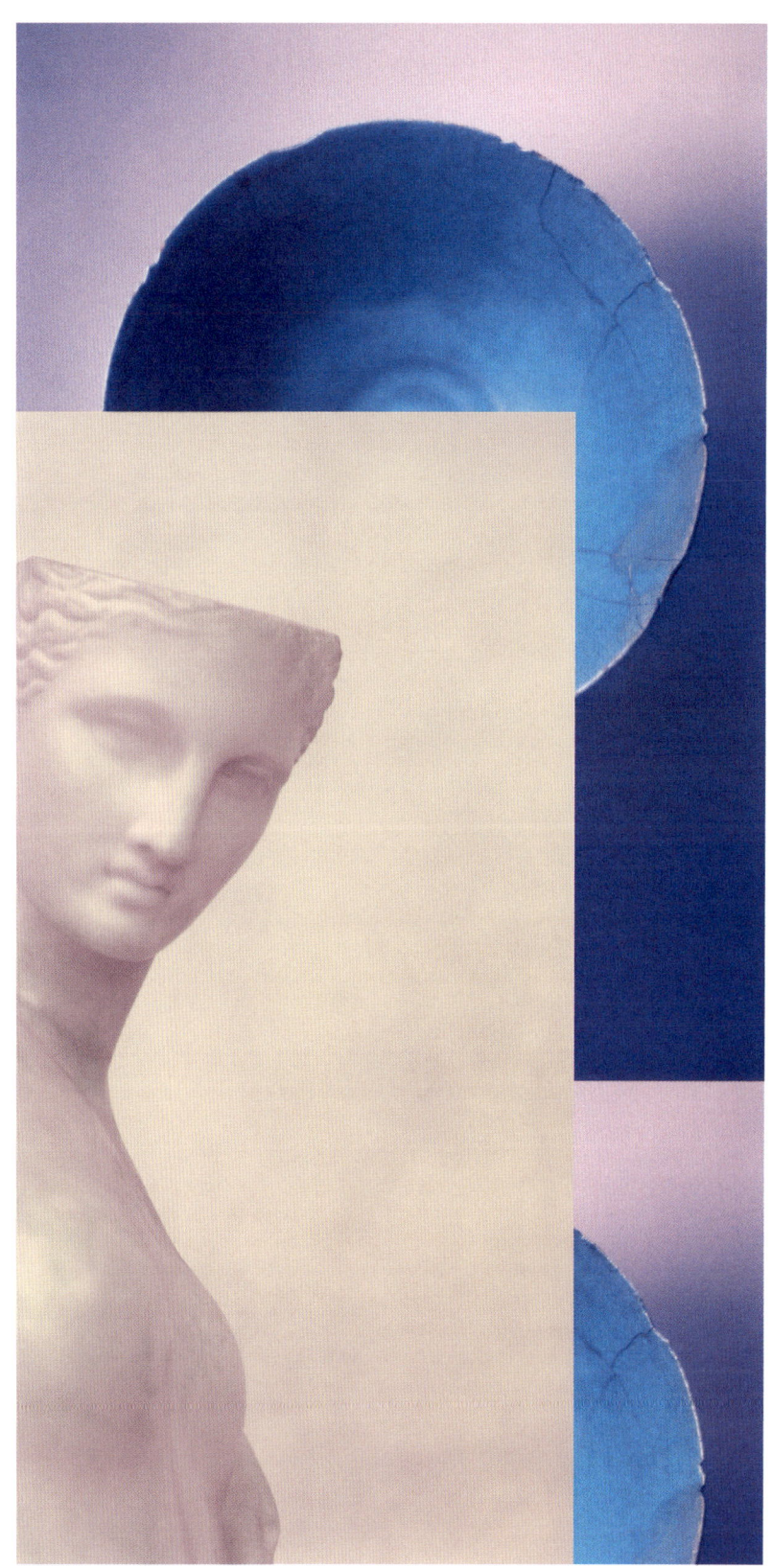

SARA VANDERBEEK

MAYA VARADARAJ

Looking to the diverse visual culture of South Asia, Maya Varadaraj examines the narratives defining female representation. Mining vintage advertisements, calendars and painted, embellished family photographs – common in Indian households – Varadaraj tackles questions of patriarchy, violence and the female experience as it relates to her south Indian upbringing. Although she was born in the United States and is based in New York, Varadaraj grew up in Coimbatore, in the south Indian state of Tamil Nadu. Her a dual inheritance profoundly impacted her understanding of power and gender dynamics. As she explained in a 2018 interview with *Juxtapoz*, 'While I was very aware of cultural obligations and expectations, I was rarely required to follow them. I think this allowed me to be sensitive to, but also critical of cultural processes.' Her distinctive visual vocabulary draws from both her own history and the specific reality of being female in India. In works such as *Imagine the Truth (2020)* we see two young girls whispering secrets to each other. Their bodies have been sliced into a series of concentric circles; they are imprisoned by their own existence. Yet elements of the composition endeavour to escape this circular trap – an arm, a ribbon, their long, lustrous hair – and likewise hands reach inwards as well, summoning images of the many-armed Hindu deities.

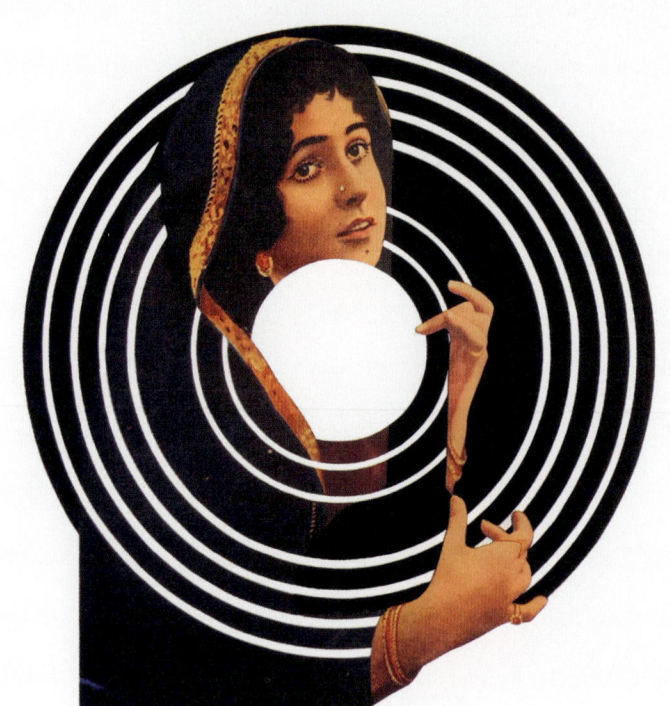

The corkscrew form returns again and again across Varadaraj's drawings and collages, a recognition of the psychological conditions of being a woman in this world. In *A Real Nervous Character* (2021) these infinite circles function more like radar, or a homing beacon, framing the work's protagonist: a single female who clasps her hands anxiously. As Athena rose from Zeus's brain in Classical Greek mythology, so too do two young women emerge from her head; but whether they represent unrealized dreams or simply her ancestors is not revealed. Under Varadaraj's deft hands, women are never absolutes but rather layered, complicated figures whose lives are shaped by the world's harsh realities. With a nod to the grotesque, she reflects such fluctuations and instability, the impossibility of arresting an entire life on paper, as seen in *It Was All Touch and Go For a While* (2020). Here, a woman, elegantly draped in vibrant textiles, sits at her dressing table powdering her face. But what face exactly? Hers has detached itself from her neck, meteor-like, streaking peachy-pink ahead of her. In spite of this disfiguration, the woman seems unperturbed, placidly applying her makeup. Acting as a shield again, circles of white obscure her body. While the work's title itself is tongue-in-cheek, it also suggests the unpredictability of the female experience – and the ways in which one is simultaneously both captain and passenger of one's own life.

GRACE LINDEN

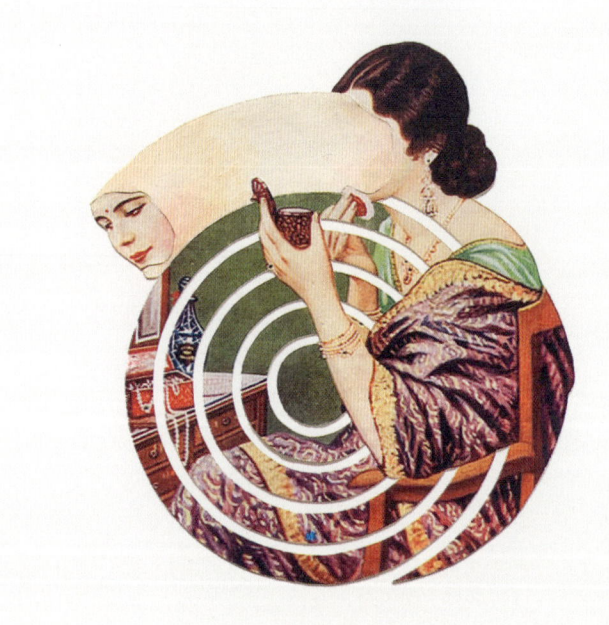

Born 1989, Orlando, Florida, USA. Lives in New York, USA.

↑↑ Pure Perfect Fifth, 2020
↑   It Was All Touch and Go For a While, 2020
↗   Imagine the Truth, 2020
↗↗ A Real Nervous Character, 2021
→   Oh, the Sights and Sounds, 2020
→→ A Pattern Began to Emerge, 2020
All archival printed paper adhered to archival paper, each: 45.7 × 45.7 cm (18 × 18 in)

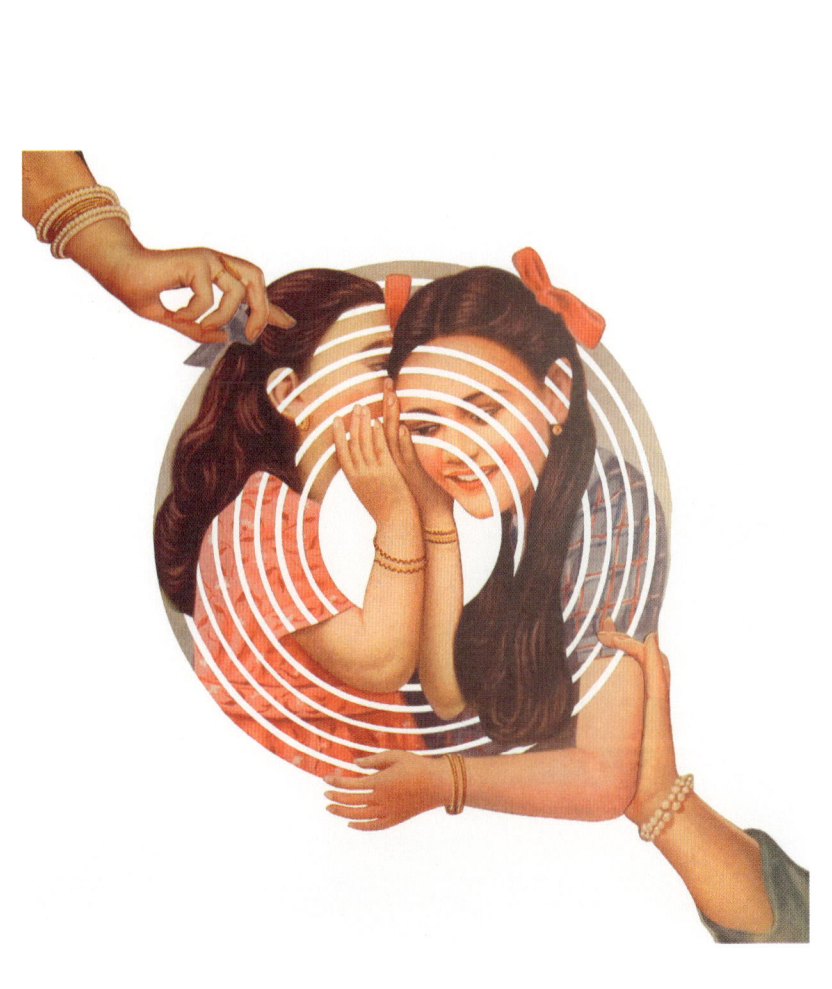

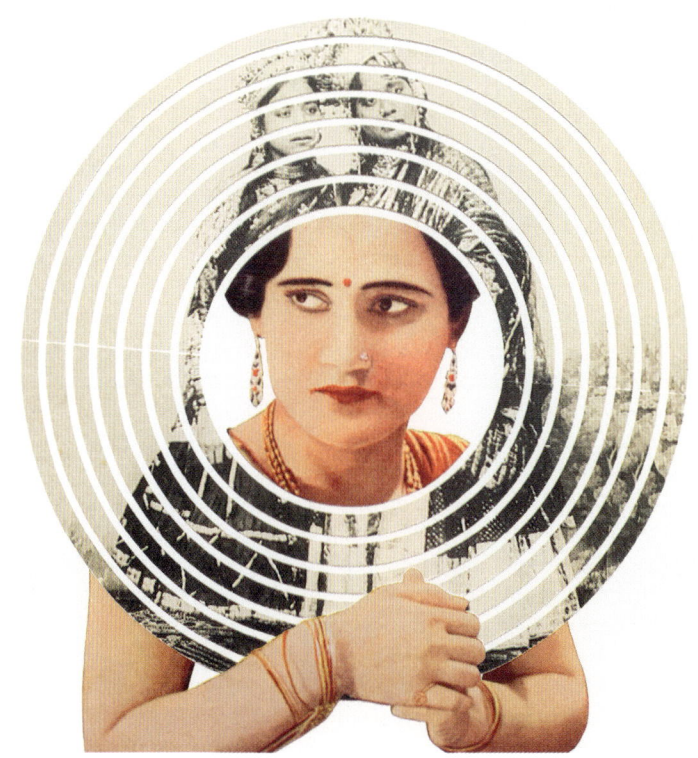

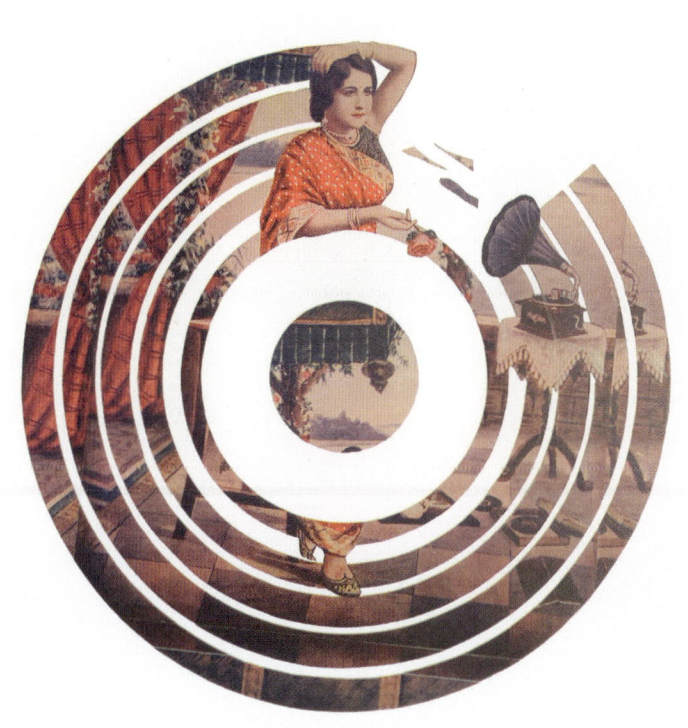

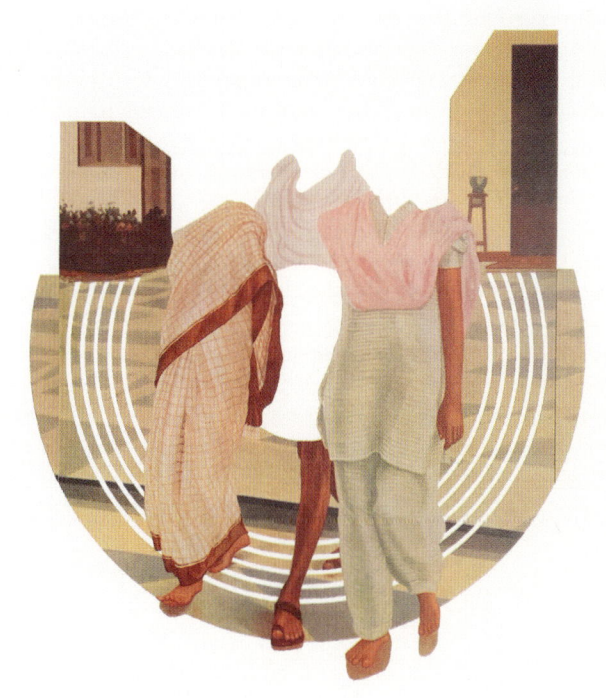

MAYA
VARADARAJ

SARA VATTANO

Characterized by surreal, imaginative fantasy, the collages of Sara Vattano drip with nostalgia for a bygone age. They invite us into a fanciful world of vintage wonder where the laws of physics hold little sway and every element is charged with cosmic meaning. Observing life through a lens of poetry, philosophy, art and literature, Vattano cites myriad reference points that range from Russian avant-garde cinema and jazz music to fairy tales, theatre, surrealism and, above all, architecture, a discipline she studied before coming to art. Accordingly, she insists on strong structures, both visually and conceptually. A geometric rigour underpins works such as Me (2022), a self-portrait produced for International Women's Day that shows the Sicilian artist perched on the edge of the moon, poised to dive into a starry abyss. Each intersecting element has personal significance: a watch representing her fascination with time, a ladder standing for agency, an empty mirror alluding to endless possibility and a large sprouting pencil that speaks to the importance of nurturing creativity. ◣▬ Searching for source material, the artist scours back-street antique shops that she hopes will yield a vintage photograph or inspiring object. Sometimes her searches are informed by a concept, at other times a chance find might spark a connection to a poem, a philosophical concept or memory. Back in the studio she builds up her fantastical digital collages and animations with software, piling on layer after layer of meaning. Likening the process to French author André Gide's 1893 concept of *mise en abyme* (stories within stories), the narratives she weaves have a veneer of accessibility yet remain enigmatic. Female protagonists, often with their faces obscured, are a staple of these works. In *Floating* (2017), we see a woman – lifted from a Neo-Classical painting by English painter John William Godward (1861–1922) – reclining on a blue whale hovering weightlessly above railway tracks. Inspired by Charles Baudelaire's enigmatic poem *Le Voyage* (1861), which addresses the futility of human efforts to escape time, the hallucinatory image reflects something of Vattano's yearnings to travel to yesteryear while tacitly acknowledging that such journeys are confined to fiction. ▬◣ A more abstract mode is adopted in the artist's introspective analogue collages, such as the intensely personal *Secrets* (2019). Made by hand with found objects during a period of great emotional tension, its disparate elements include a metal hinge, layers of overlapping papers and scraps, and the lid of a spice tin that, paired with a miniature antique frame, suggests a doorbell. A broken Sicilian tile painted with yellow sunflowers evokes the sufferings of Vincent van Gogh (1853–90), though there is also the suggestion of joy. Its ambivalence offers a glimpse into Vattano's psyche, though characteristically keeps its true meaning closely guarded. ▬◣

DAVID TRIGG

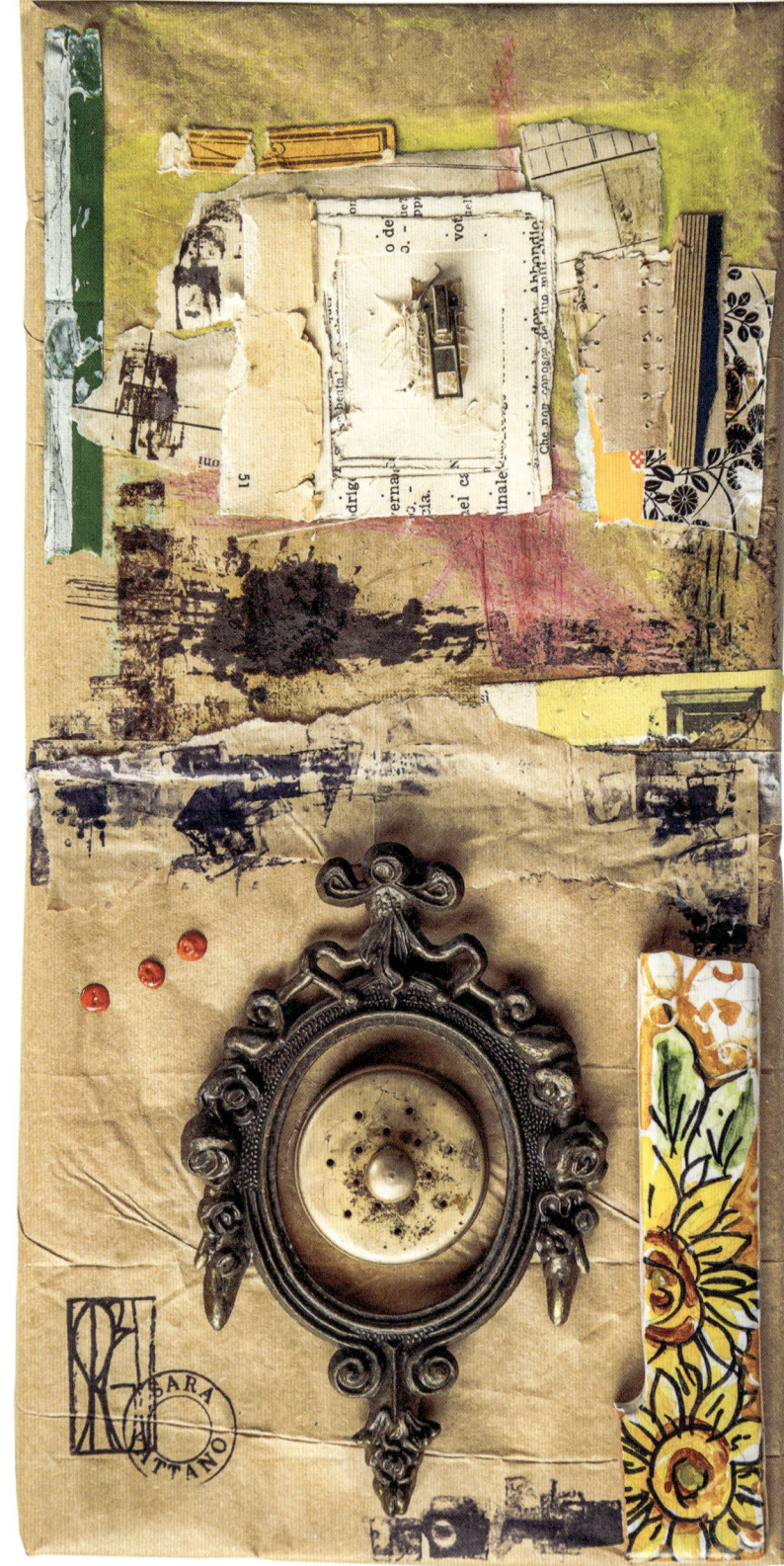

Born 1990, Agrigento, Sicily, Italy. Lives in Agrigento.

↑ **Secrets**, 2019, handmade analogue collage, 30 × 15 cm (11¾ × 5⅞ in)

↗ **Floating**, 2017, digital collage, 30 × 30 cm (11¾ × 11¾ in)

→ **Me**, 2022, digital collage, 70 × 50 cm (27½ × 19⅝ in)

↠ **Stretch union in pink**, 2022, digital collage, 70 × 50 cm (27½ × 19⅝ in)

↠→ **Green369**, 2022, digital collage, 100 × 70 cm (39⅜ × 27½ in)

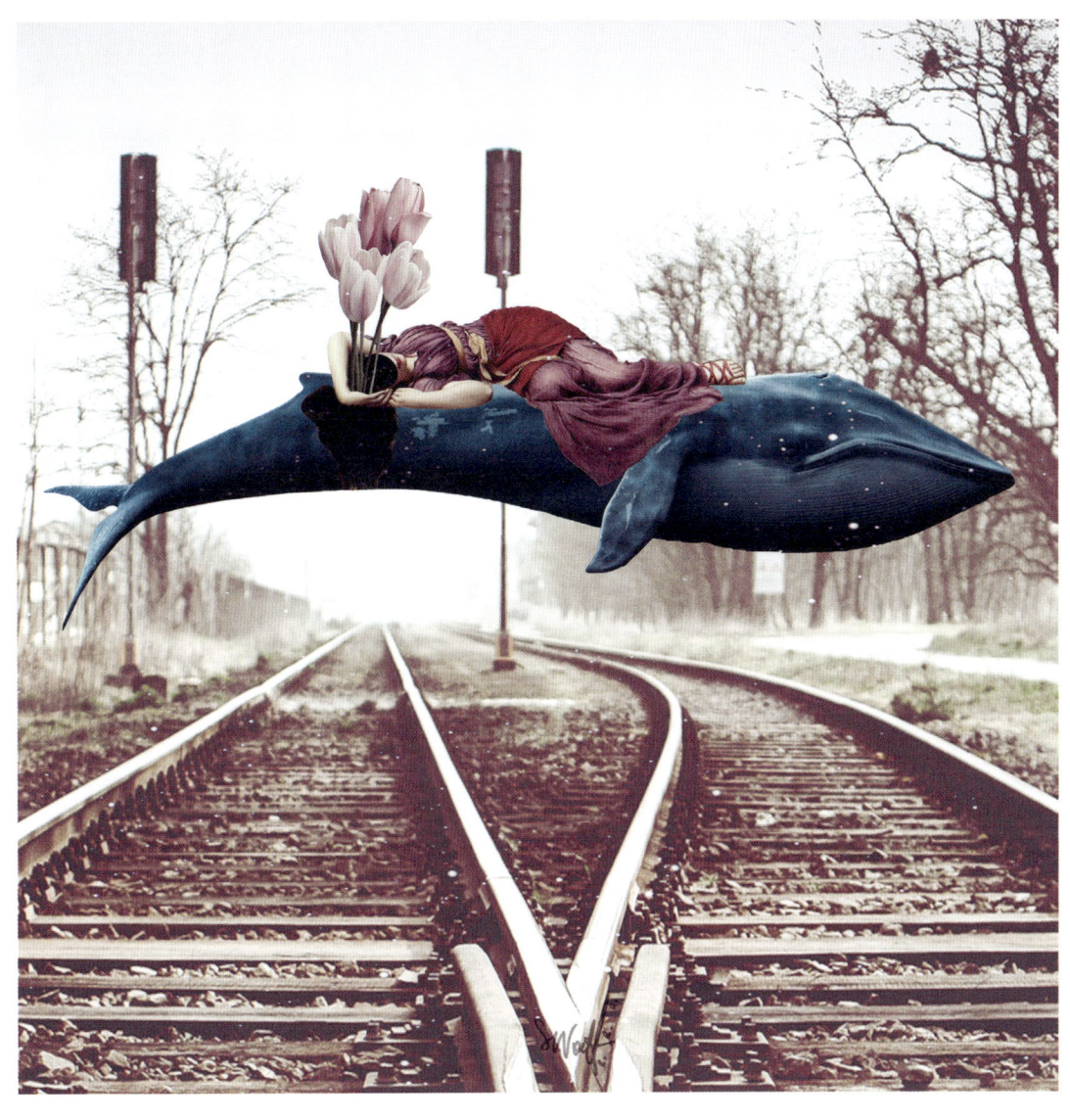

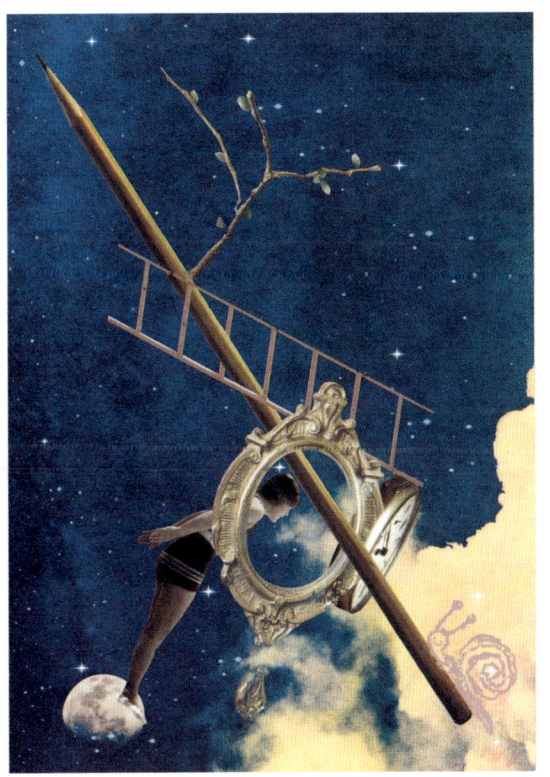

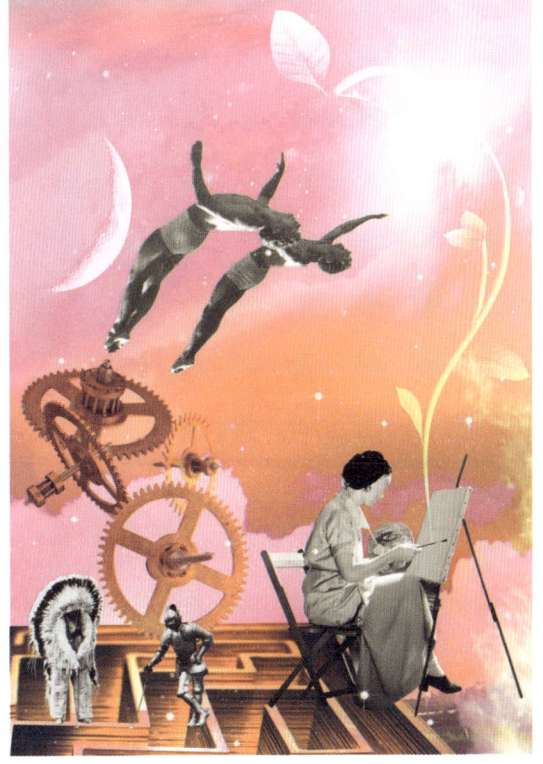

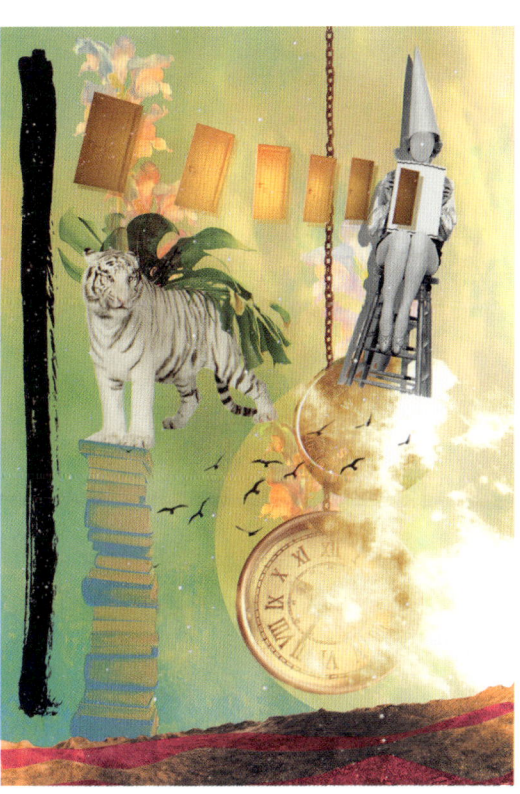

SARA

VATTANO

FRANCESCO VEZZOLI

Emotions run high in the art of Francesco Vezzoli. His is the language of melodrama: tears, blood, romance, glamour. The cast of characters is, fittingly, larger than life – from Hollywood A-listers to Roman emperors. Yet for Vezzoli these worlds of excess are deeply connected to reality. 'I am interested in the truth,' he has said, in a 2015 interview in the *Financial Times*. Skirting the line between satire and utmost seriousness, his works can be thought of as allegories: stories and images that hold up a mirror to contemporary society and culture. ◣ At the Venice Biennale of 2005, and again in 2007, Vezzoli drew attention for his spoof videos starring real celebrities – from a fake perfume ad with Natalie Portman and Michelle Williams to a presidential campaign facing off Sharon Stone and the philosopher Bernard-Henri Lévy. But the mediums of collage and embroidery have been equally central to his practice since the beginning. He first took up needle and thread in the mid-1990s while studying at Central Saint Martins in London, UK – partly motivated by the desire to distance himself from the heavily conceptual approach that dominated the 'Young British Artists' scene at the time. He began creating his now-signature canvases featuring laser-printed photographs – usually of famous women – embroidered with metallic thread to form streams of tears as early as 1999.

◣ In *Les Parapluies d'Avignon* (*The Umbrellas of Avignon*) (2015) Vezzoli layers the image even further. A black-and-white photograph of the actors Jean Vilar and Maria Casares, who played Lord and Lady Macbeth at the Festival of Avignon, France, in 1954, serves as the backdrop for cut-out images of Catherine Deneuve and Nino Castelnuovo, the stars of the 1964 French film *Les Parapluies de Cherbourg* (*The Umbrellas of Cherbourg*). Stitched onto the canvas, the faces of Deneuve and Castelnuovo become teardrops flowing from the eyes of Vilar and Casares. The same technique is deployed in *L'homme qui aimait les femmes (Isabelle)* (*The Man who Loved Women (Isabelle)*) (2021), a portrait of the French actor Isabelle Adjani originally created for a *Vanity Fair* cover, in a issue exploring themes of memory and twentieth-century European history. The collaged teardrops are made up of stills from Adjani's break-out film, *The Story of Adèle H* (1975).

◣ More recently Vezzoli has turned his attention from celebrity culture to the classical world and modern art history. This may seem like a startling shift but the same themes prevail: power, wealth, fame. In works such as *Homage to Cy Twombly: Self-Portrait as a Roman Statue Crying 'Paradise'* (2018) the recurring use of embroidery and collage also provides a sense of continuity. A lachrymal scrap of paper with a pattern reminiscent of the American artist's unruly abstractions rolls down the cheek of a classical bust that bears a strong resemblance to Vezzoli himself. It is a fitting self-portrait for an artist who has spent his career stitching together different worlds, both past and present. ◣

GABRIELLE SCHWARZ

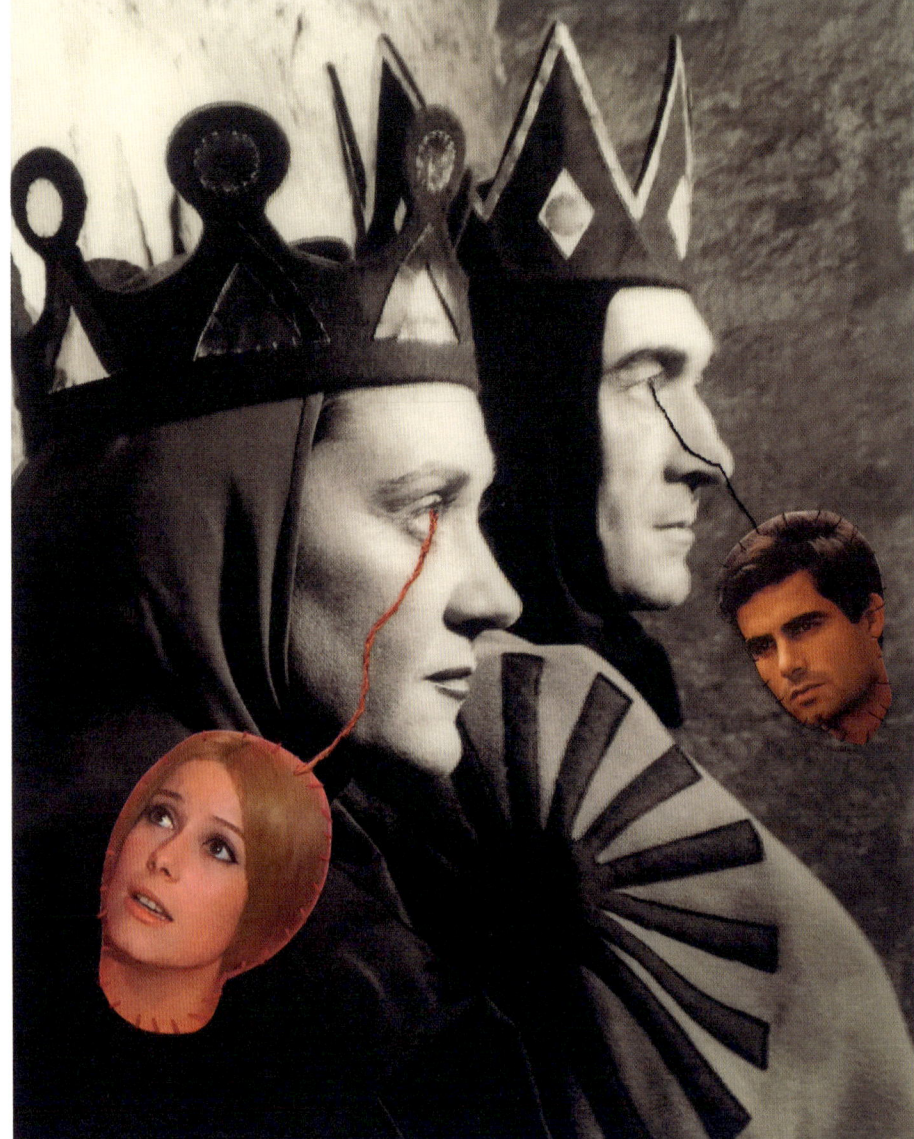

Born 1971, Brescia, Italy. Lives in Milan, Italy.

↑ Les Parapluies d'Avignon (The Umbrellas of Avignon), 2015, inkjet print on canvas, cotton, metallic embroidery and paper, 70 × 57 cm (27 ⅝ × 22½ in), Collection Lambert, Avignon, France

↗ Homage to Cy Twombly: Self-Portrait as a Roman Statue Crying 'Paradise', 2018, laser print on canvas, paper and crochet needlework, 60 × 51 cm (23 ⅝ × 20⅛ in)

→ Tears of Passion (My Life with Hadrian), 2022, oil on canvas and plaster collage, 42 × 30 cm (16½ × 11¾ in)

→→ L'homme qui aimait les femmes (Isabelle), (The Man who Loved Women (Isabelle)), 2021, inkjet print on canvas, metallic embroidery and paper, 64 × 52 cm (25¼ × 20½ in)

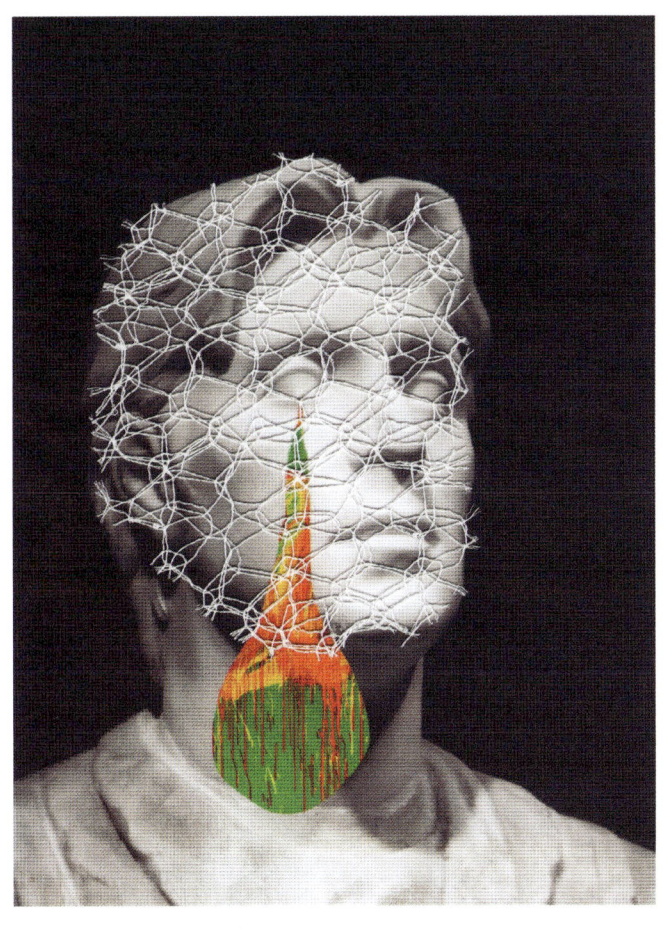

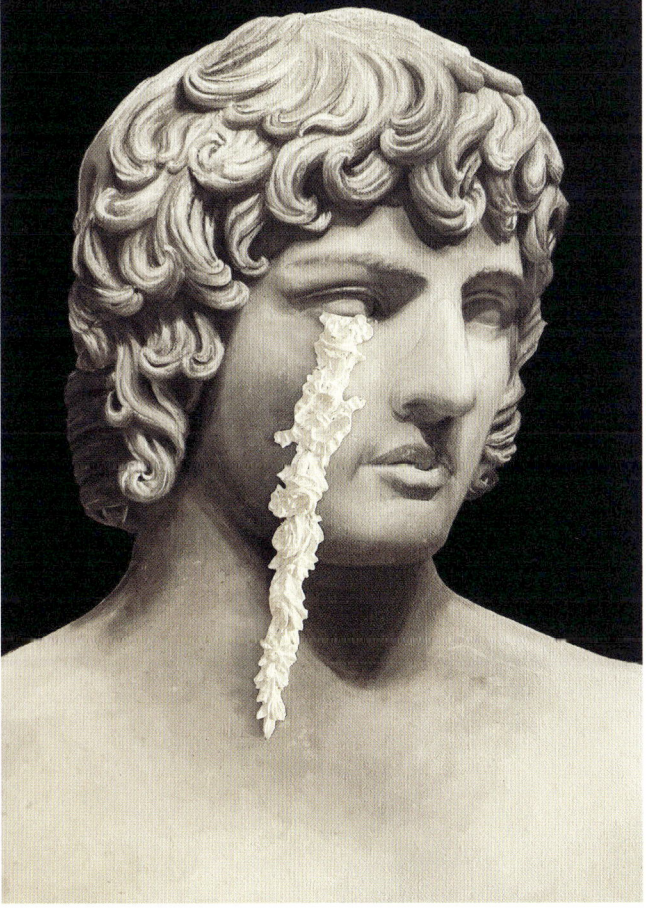

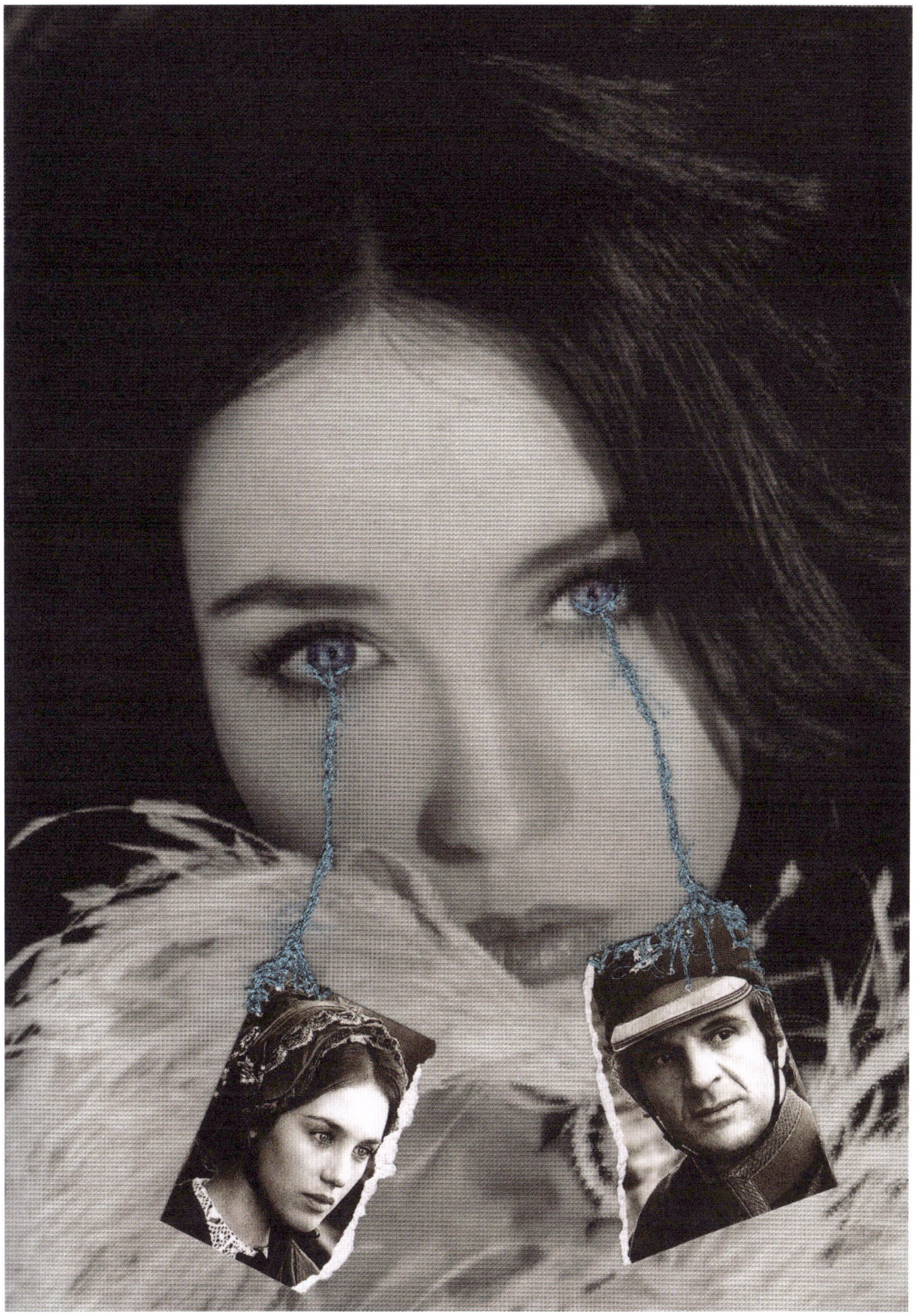

FRANCESCO VEZZOLI

To those who know her practice, Kara Walker's paper cuts are immediately recognizable: figures portrayed by way of silhouette, with their facial features, body characteristics and postures exaggerated to a point that hovers between caricature, the carnivalesque and the absurd. Envision a contemporary, politicized fusion of El Greco (1541–1614) and Pieter Bruegel the Elder (active 1550/1, died 1569) having a go at history but with ink, paper and scissors in lieu of tempera and oil. Silhouette is an ancient technique that became particularly popular in eighteenth-century Europe as a cheaper alternative to painted portraits. But in the hands of Walker, the centuries-old craft escapes the neat confines of the picture frame as well as the conventional delicacy of its subject matter. █ At times her sceneries sprawl over vast expanses, taking over an entire wall, as was the case with the work that first made her silhouettes known to the public, *Gone: An Historical Romance of a Civil War as It Occurred b'tween the Dusky Thighs of One Young Negress and Her Heart* (1994), a mural produced at the Drawing Center, New York. Other times they are more confined, such as the quietly disturbing *3am Vision* (2021), the size of which nevertheless almost mirrors that of its viewer. █ Drawing on her personal experience of relocating from California to Atlanta in her childhood, Walker's imagery frequently evokes the American Civil War years, drawing directly on historical documents or even past paintings. *The (Private) Memorial Garden of Grandison Harris* (2017) at once references the true story of the once enslaved then employed grave robber, Grandison Harris, who was tasked with illegally unearthing bodies for dissection at Georgia Medical College, while also nodding to Gustave Courbet's *Burial at Ornans* (1849–50). Sometimes her figures are more contemporary (one work features former US president Barack Obama in knickerbockers) or defy historicization altogether, as is the case in *Replacement Parts* (2021) where the medium of collage allows for a more sculptural and contorted version of Peter Paul Rubens's *Fall of the Damned* (1620). █ Walker's works dig into the shadows of particularly, but not exclusively, the American past, exposing the bodies and lives upon which modern wealth is built, fleshing out systemic racism, sexual transgressions and other taboos in the process. And yet the focus of her artistic probing is not history itself but more specifically the images which history has handed down to us. Walker rekindles the traditions of history and genre painting in the transitory mediums of paper, drawing, moving image and performance (even in her more recent ventures into monumental sculpture the material has been degradable) in order to expose the power of visual culture, highlighting how the images we make and inherit in turn affect the way we understand race, gender roles and identity more broadly. █

MARGRETHE TROENSEGAARD

Born 1969, Stockton, California, USA. Lives in New York, USA.

↑   **Replacement Parts**, 2021, oil stick on paper and Flashe on cut paper, 303.5 × 185.4 × 14 cm (119½ × 73 × 5½ in)

↗   **The (Private) Memorial Garden of Grandison Harris**, 2017, oil stick and Sumi ink on paper collaged on linen, diptych, overall 228.6 × 365.8 cm (90 × 144 in)

→   **3am Vision**, 2021, cut paper on paper, 49.5 × 158.1 cm (19½ × 62¼ in)

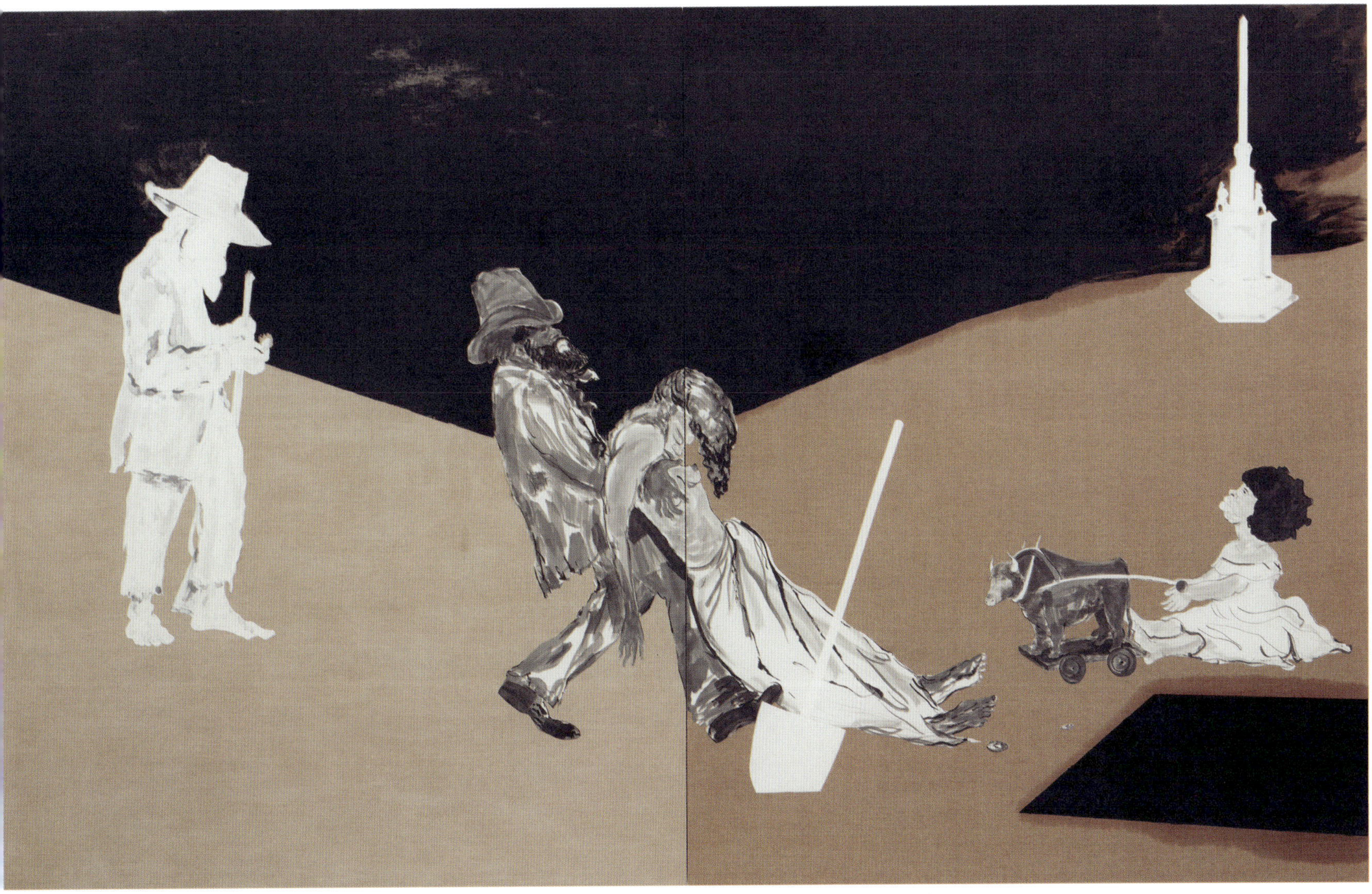

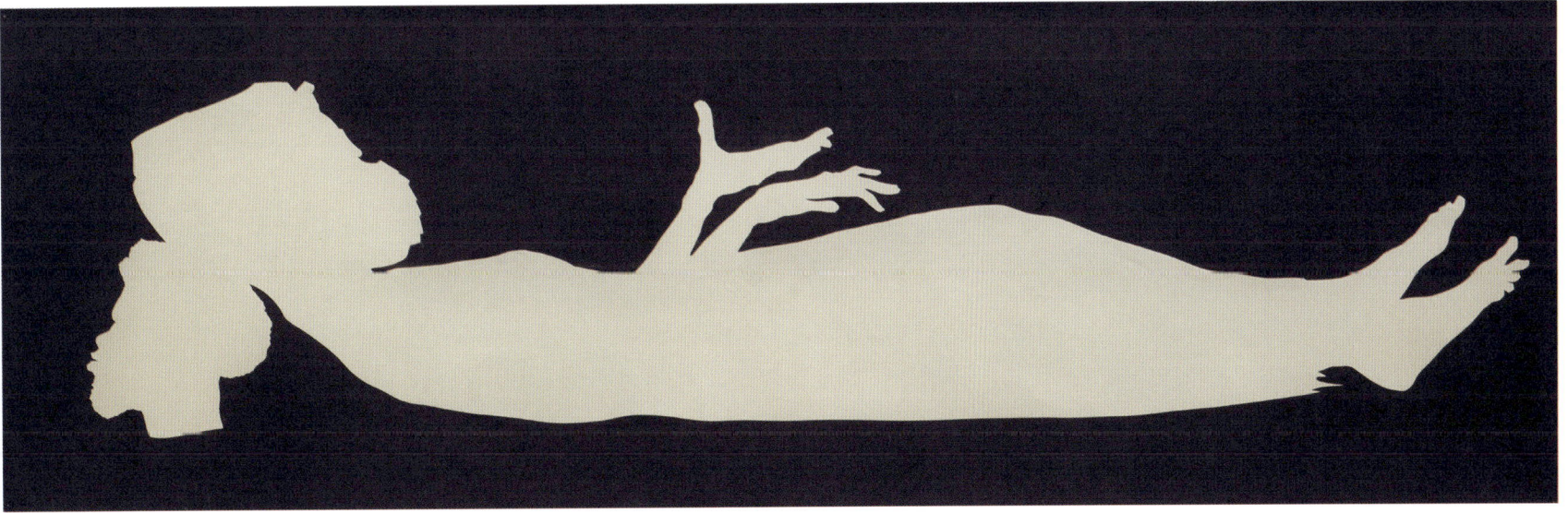

KARA WALKER

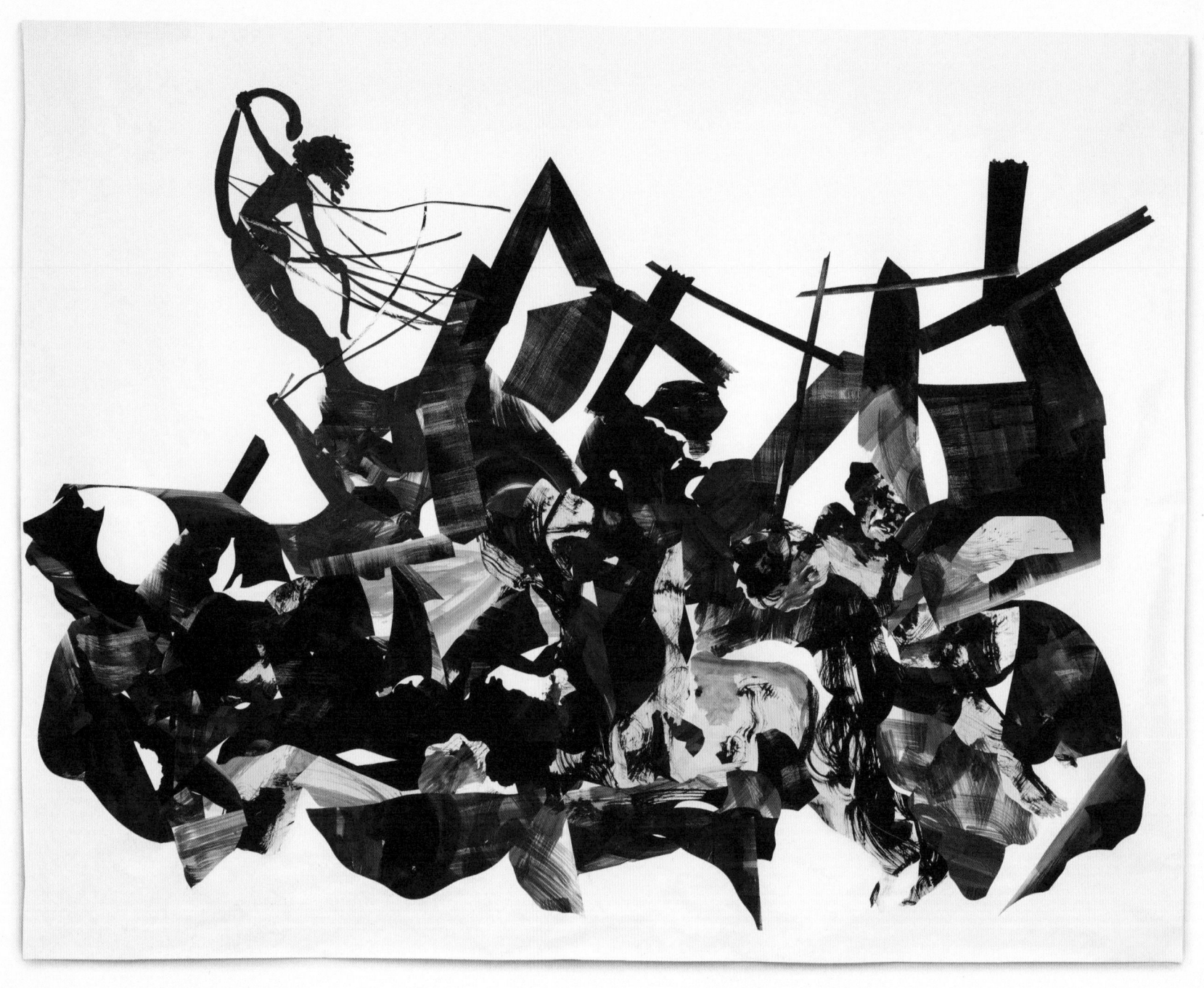

↑   **Rift of the Medusa**, 2017, gouache, Sumi ink and collage on paper with gessoed ground,
351.5 × 449.6 cm (138 ⅜ × 177 in)

→   **Uprising**, 2017, Sumi ink and collage on paper, 240 × 182.9 cm (94 ½ × 72 in)

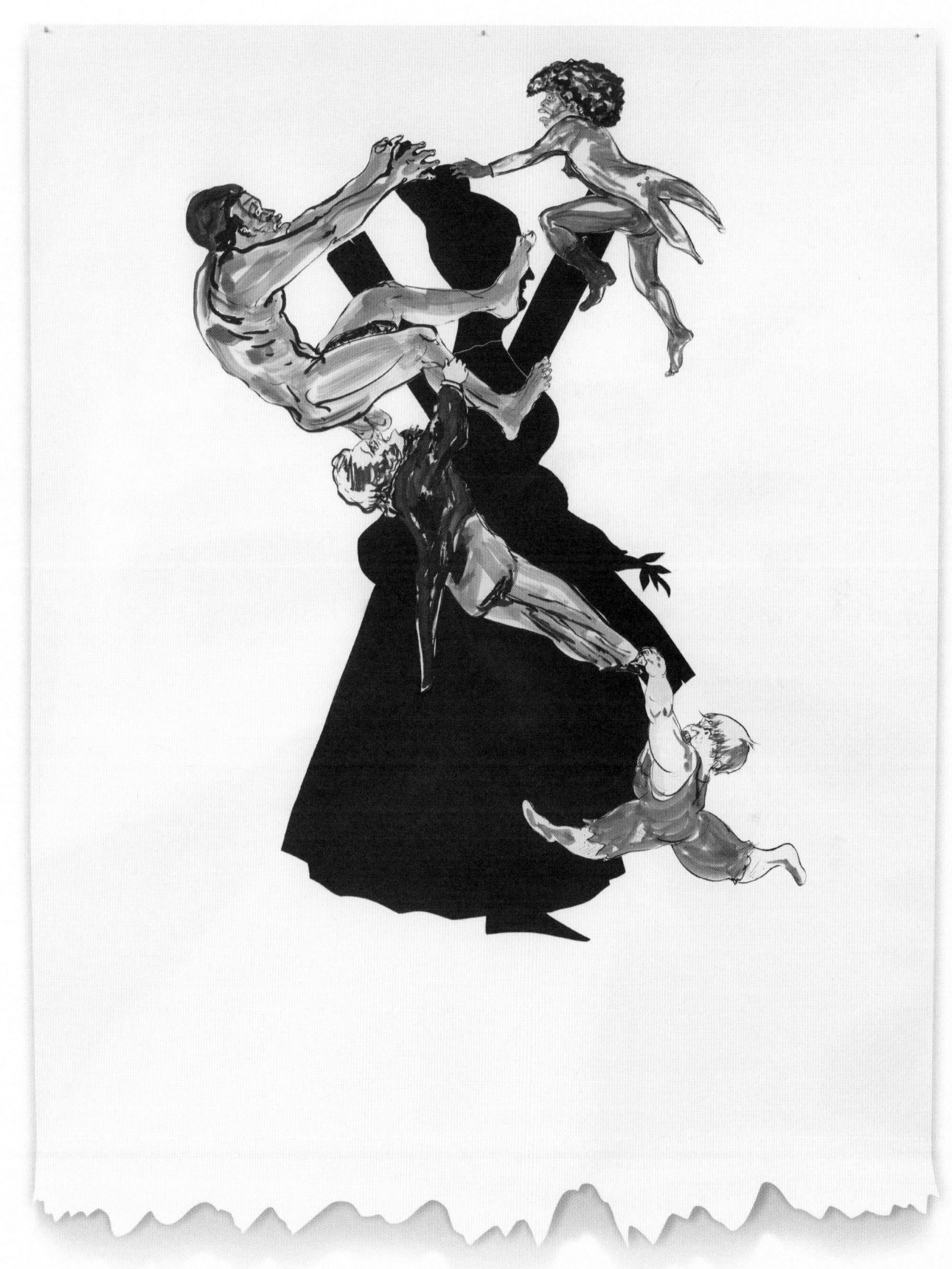

KARA
WALKER

KANDIS
WILLIAMS

In a 2020 interview with *Pin-Up Magazine*, Kandis Williams explained that she once considered her 'only practice to be liquidating photographic content, reducing a picture to the blur'. She was interested in German artist and educator Josef Albers's (1888–1976) thoughts on light and colour, and, as she described, 'how to demolish the architectonics of a photo'. Early in her career, she worked at scale, with wall-sized collages and intricate tableaux. Williams is a voracious reader and her research process is an extensive one, distilling all that she interacts with into her work through a process of continuous, and refined, deconstruction and rebuilding. Her works shift between video, collage, performance and literary readers. Williams is a publisher and co-founder of Cassandra Press, which she describes as a site for 'historical fantasies'. A central question runs through the many mediums and forms by which she makes work: 'What would the world look like if Black women were believed?' In a body of Xerox collages and ink on paper works from 2021, Williams presents outstretched limbs and the steady, delicate poses of contemporary Black dancers. The titles of the individual pieces sharply reveal their critical underpinnings; one goes: 'between cult and theatre lies the stage as moral institution', a quote from Bauhaus theorist and prop-master Oskar Schlemmer (1888–1943). Williams seems to pointedly ask: but whose stage is this? In *Black Box, 4 points: Horton, Ailey, McKayle contractions and expansions of drama from vernacular – arms outstretched and entangle* (2021) strong, grasping arms move towards each other in gentle lines across the page, at the centre of which two dancers are caught, mid-performance, with interlocked elbows. There is a flurry of movement around this calm, poised centre, showing Williams's distinct ability to create both dynamism and stillness in a single frame. In videos that accompany the work – entitled *Triadic Ballet* (2021) – Williams choreographs dancers to move across blank stages often marked by single lines. The dance – both in collage and in performance – is a mix of Native American Buffalo Dance, jazz, and even yoga. Williams described, in an interview with the *New York Times* in October 2021, how she is 'directing within [an] index of muscular and reflexive conditioning'. The movements skirt thresholds of technique, attitude and even pain, the artist showing how the body is capable of fundamental contradictions: pain can be deeply pleasurable, too. In *Hyper-interpretation – to be seated – figures sexualized and anonymized at rest, en largesse to stereotyping distribution* (2021) we see a single figure move through several resting positions, which Williams annotates by hand. This is a space animated by precision but also by an interiority, a concept that is important to Williams, who in the same interview stated that the notations are a manner by which to 'contemplate the dualism of the experience of being a performative Black body'.

SKYE ARUNDHATI THOMAS

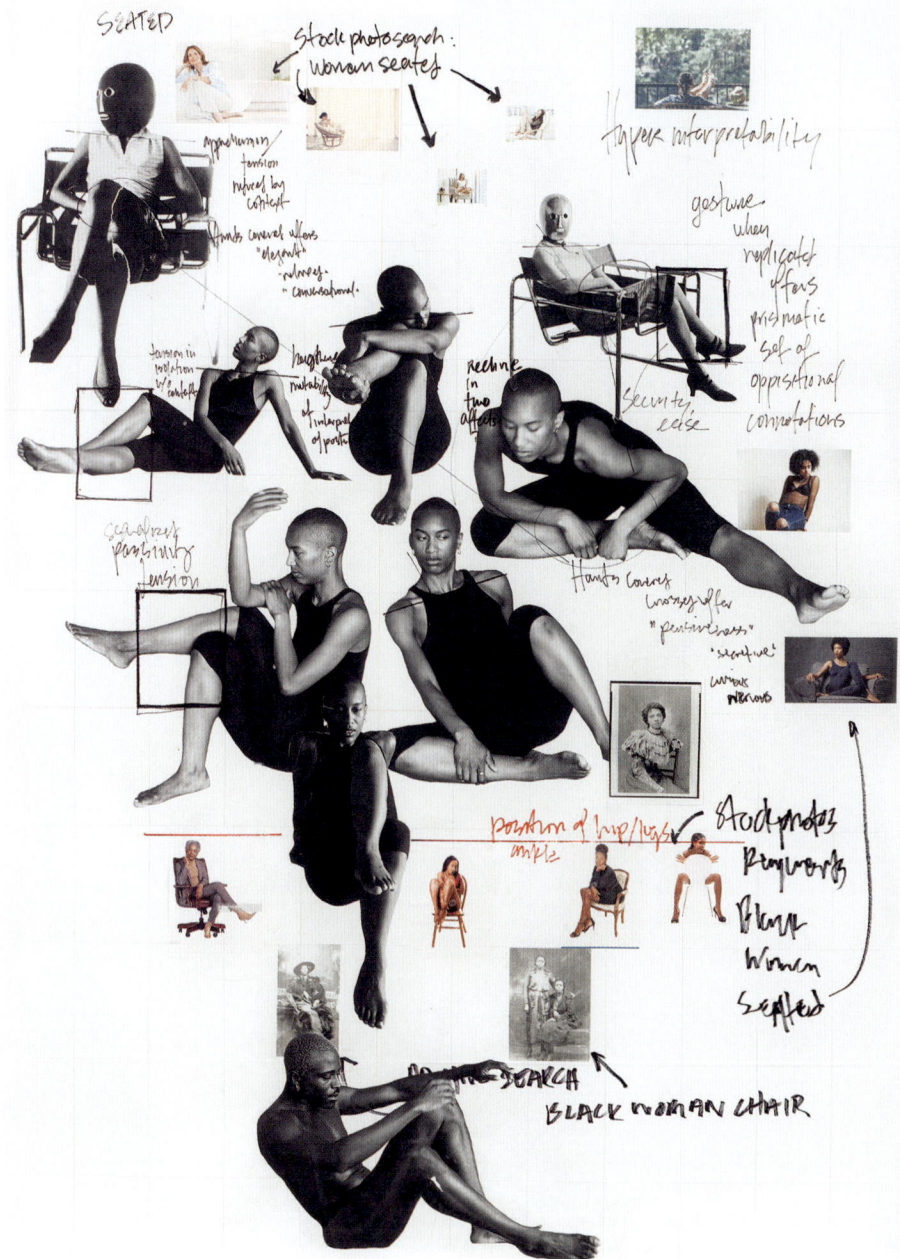

Born 1985, Baltimore, Maryland, USA. Lives in Brooklyn, New York, USA.

↑ Hyper-interpretation – to be seated – figures sexualized and anonymized at rest, en largesse to stereotyping distribution, 2021, Xerox collage and ink on paper, 162.6 × 121.1 cm (64 × 47 ⅝ in)

↗ Notes for Stage, Cult, and Popular Entertainment according to place, person, genre, speech, music, and dance, 2021, Xerox collage and ink on paper, 121.9 × 121.9 cm (48 × 48 in)

→ Lines of Contemplation: bitter, tense, angry, reserved, tormented (in thought) for Black and White, marble, bronze, and flesh, 2021, Xerox collage and ink on paper, 121.9 × 121.9 cm (48 × 48 in)

→→ Black Box, 4 points: Horton, Ailey, McKayle contractions and expansions of drama from vernacular – arms outstretched and entangle, 2021, Xerox collage and ink on paper, 105.4 × 74.9 cm (41½ × 29½ in)

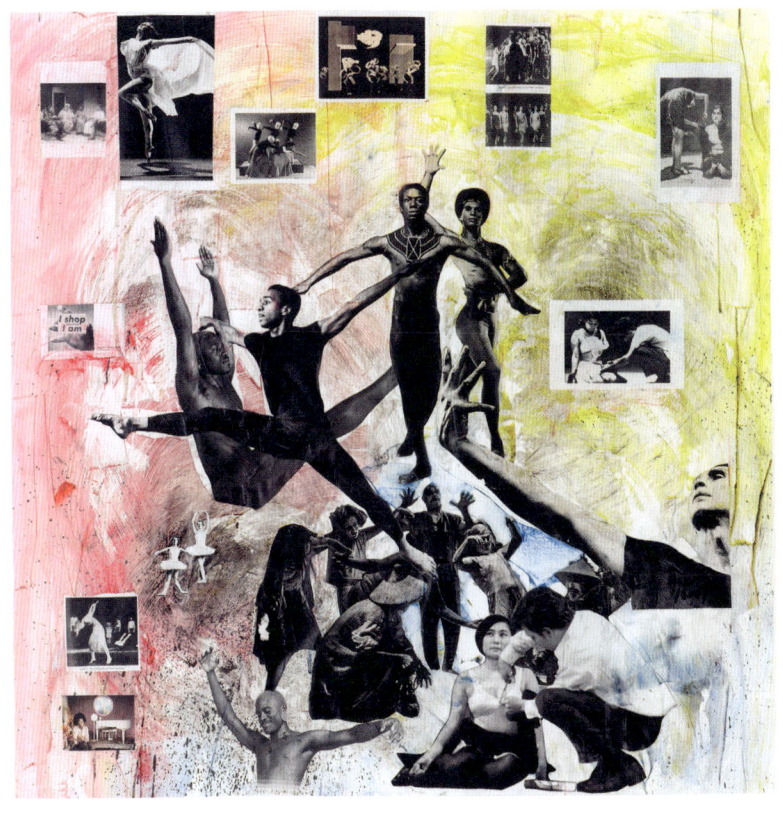

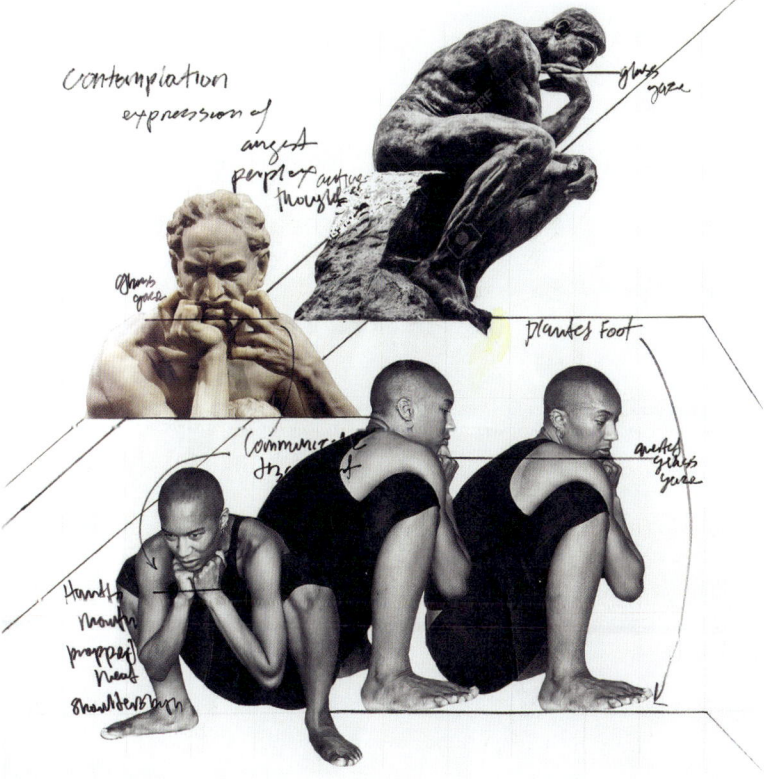

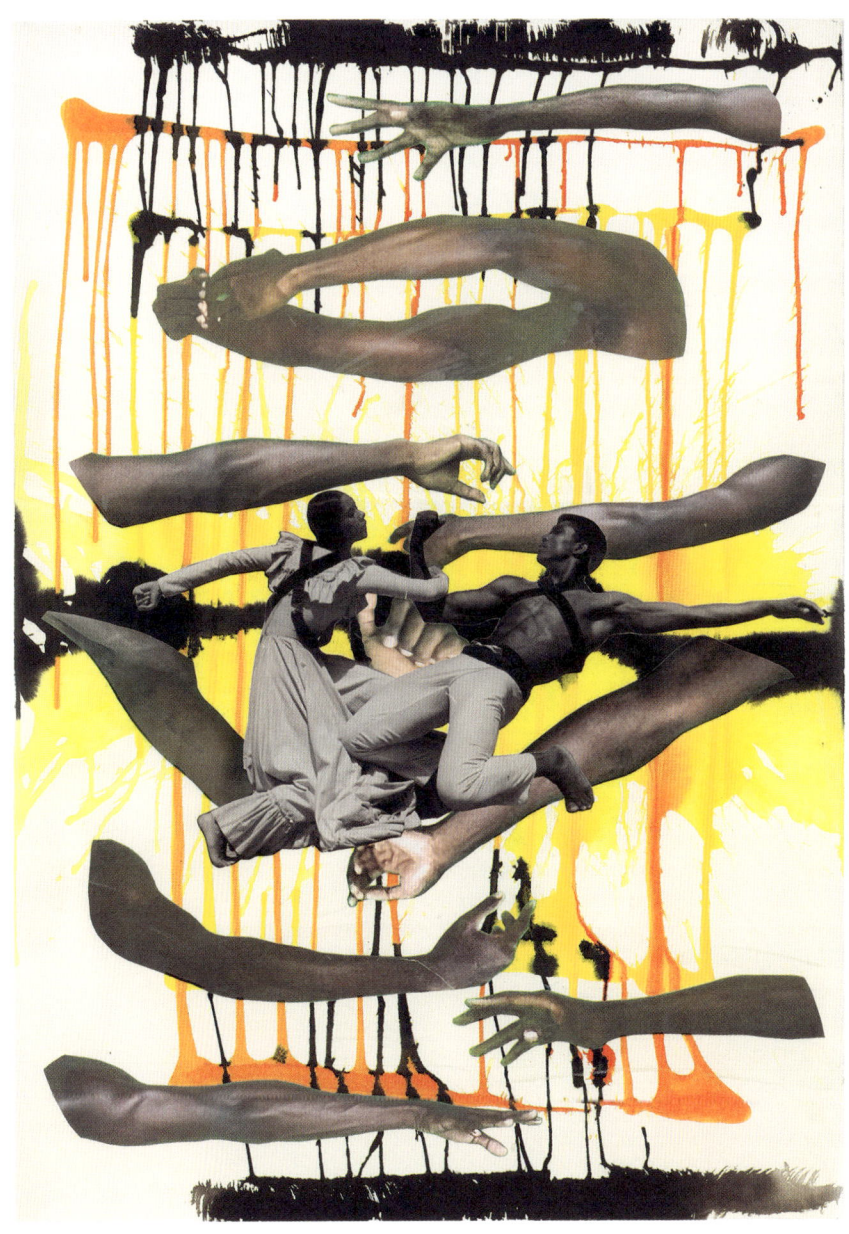

CARMEN WINANT

Though she is hardly alone among contemporary artists in giving way to what has been called an archival impulse, Carmen Winant sometimes follows the impulse much further than most others do. For instance, her 2018 project *My Birth*, as shown at New York's Museum of Modern Art that year, consisted of no less than 2,000 found photographic and photomechanical images (mostly, it would appear, from the 1970s and 1980s) taped to the walls, all having to do with women in the process or aftermath of giving birth – collage as a full-immersion experience. One might wonder if there is a sort of implicit (and implicitly feminist) pun at work in the piece – its printed photographs, exemplifying a medium of 'mechanical reproduction', standing in for processes of biological reproduction. But reproduction is not pure repetition: every birth is similar and every birth is unique. And yet, as Winant explained in a 2018 interview in *Vogue*, giving birth 'just feels so singular, like you're the only person who's ever gone through it' and yet 'images of strangers can act as a sort of a surrogate for me and for my body and my experience' – thus the singular possessive of the work's title. A more recent – and more compact – project is the 'Togethering' series of 2020. Again, the frame of reference is the heyday of the counterculture, the period just before Winant's own birth in 1983. The title, she explained to digital magazine *Topical Cream* in 2020, is a word coined by a group of 1970s lesbian separatists whose attempts at reinventing everyday life also included reconfiguring the language they used: 'They took new surnames (Hillwoman, Mountaingrove, Freedom, etc.), invented new words like herstory and moonstration, and created verbs like "visioning" and "togethering"'. At first glance, these framed conglomerations of found images adorned with colours applied with oil pastel offer a relatively conventionally composed and contained viewing experience, and yet enclosure by the frame is far from absolute. Many of the works in the series also include additional images hanging from delicate steel chains below the frame – a sort of reinvention of the predella of a medieval or Renaissance altarpiece with its sequence of images below the main scene. In *Togethering 4*, for instance, the images highlight sensations of touching – touching oneself and touching others. The dense arrangement comprises some forty pictures, few of which have the rectilinear edges of the pristine photographic print; their decorative patterning, with three slightly larger central images bordered by two layers of framing ones, recalls the practice of a hobbyist crafter more readily than it does the fine art tradition of modernist collage, deriving from Cubism and Dada, with its accent on shock and estrangement. Like Winant's choice of imagery, this formal choice asks us to reconsider how togethering – an implicit synonym for *collage*? – should be done.

BARRY SCHWABSKY

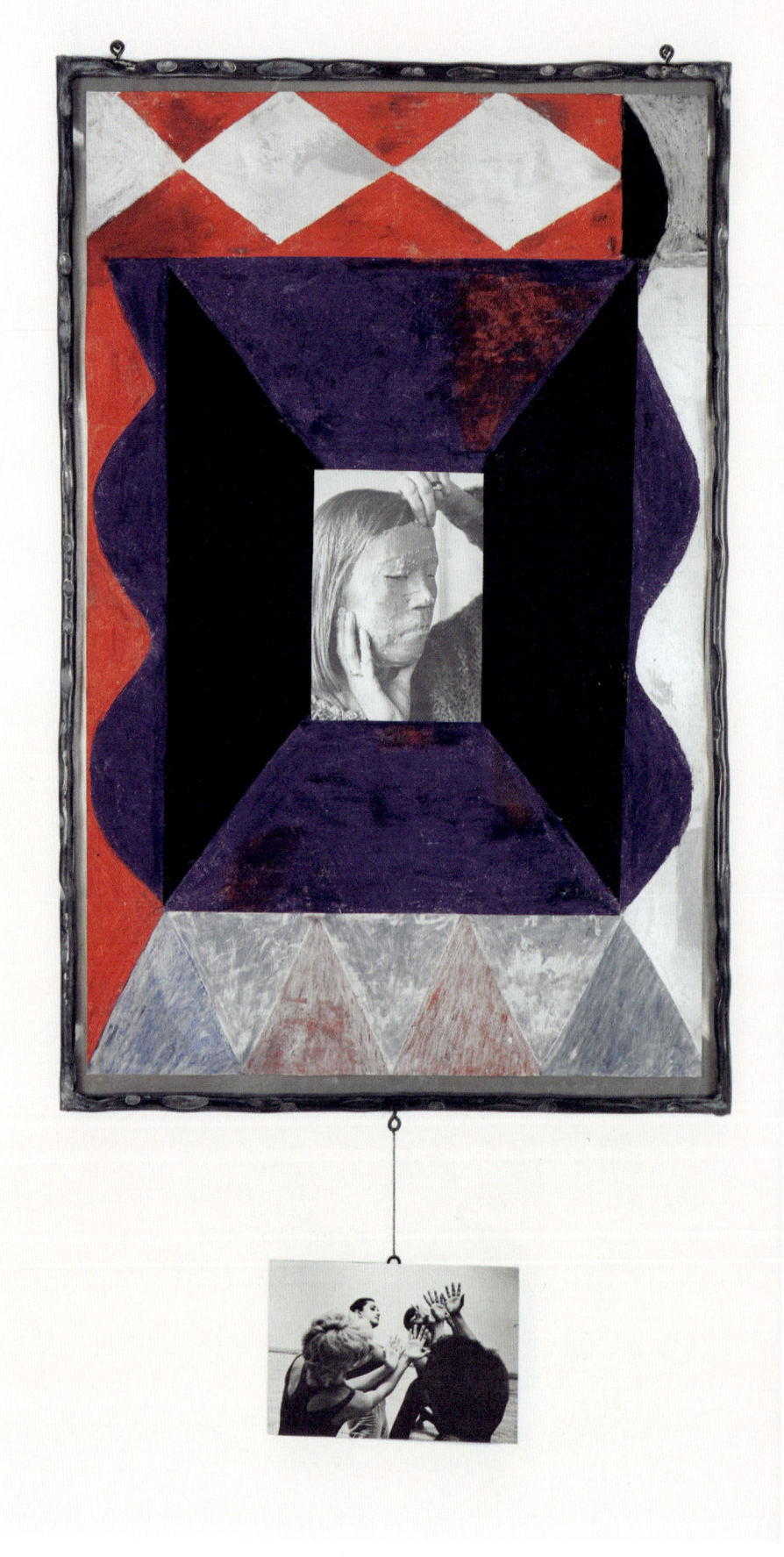

Born 1983, San Francisco, California, USA. Lives in Columbus, Ohio, USA.

↑ **Togethering 3**, 2020, oil pastel, found images on paper, steel chain, steel hanging plate and aluminium frame, 109.2 × 54.6 cm (43 × 21½ in)

→ **Togethering 1**, 2020, oil pastel, found images on paper, steel chain, steel hanging plate and aluminium frame, 139.7 × 78.7 cm (55 × 31 in)

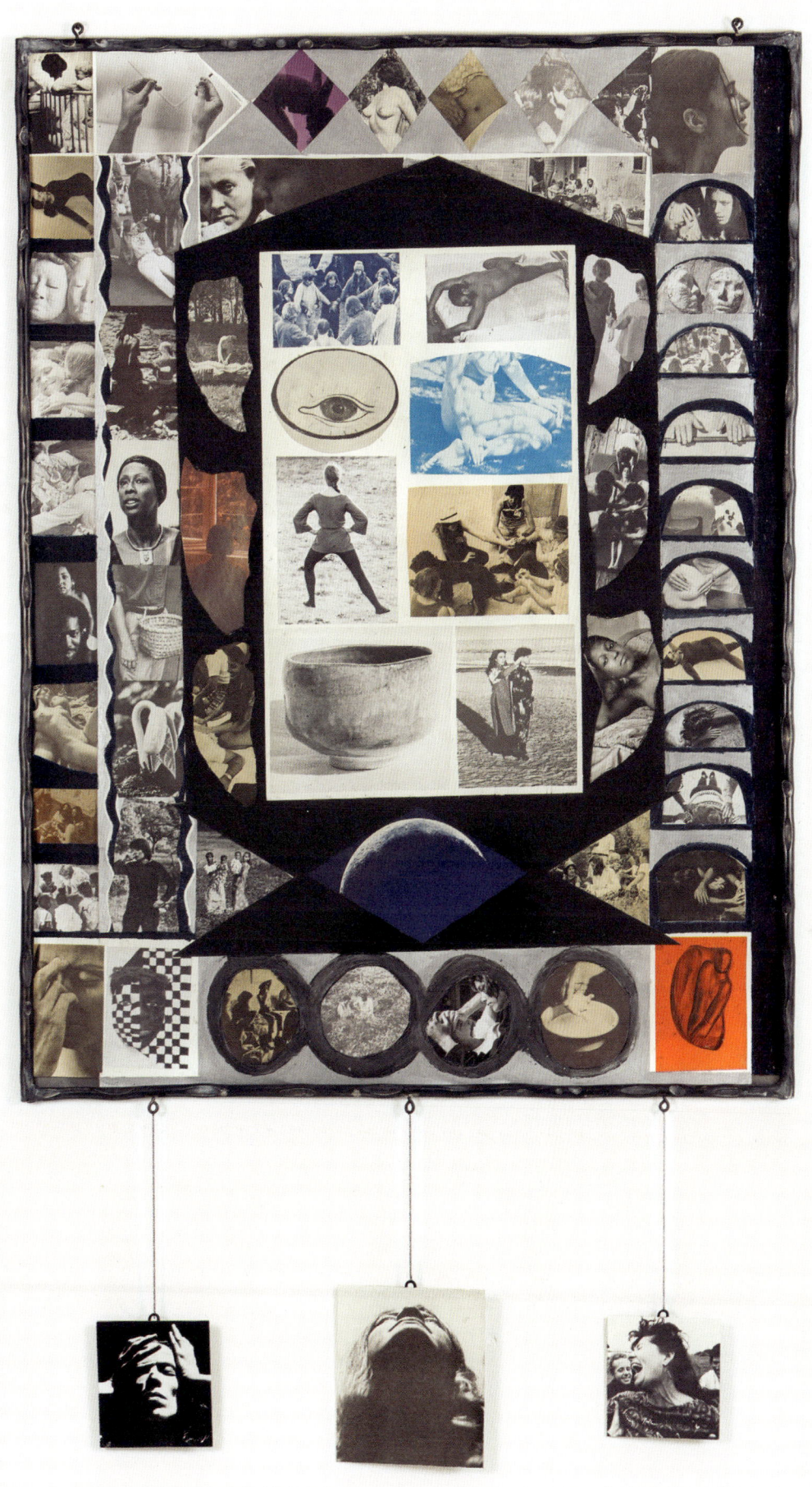

CARMEN WINANT

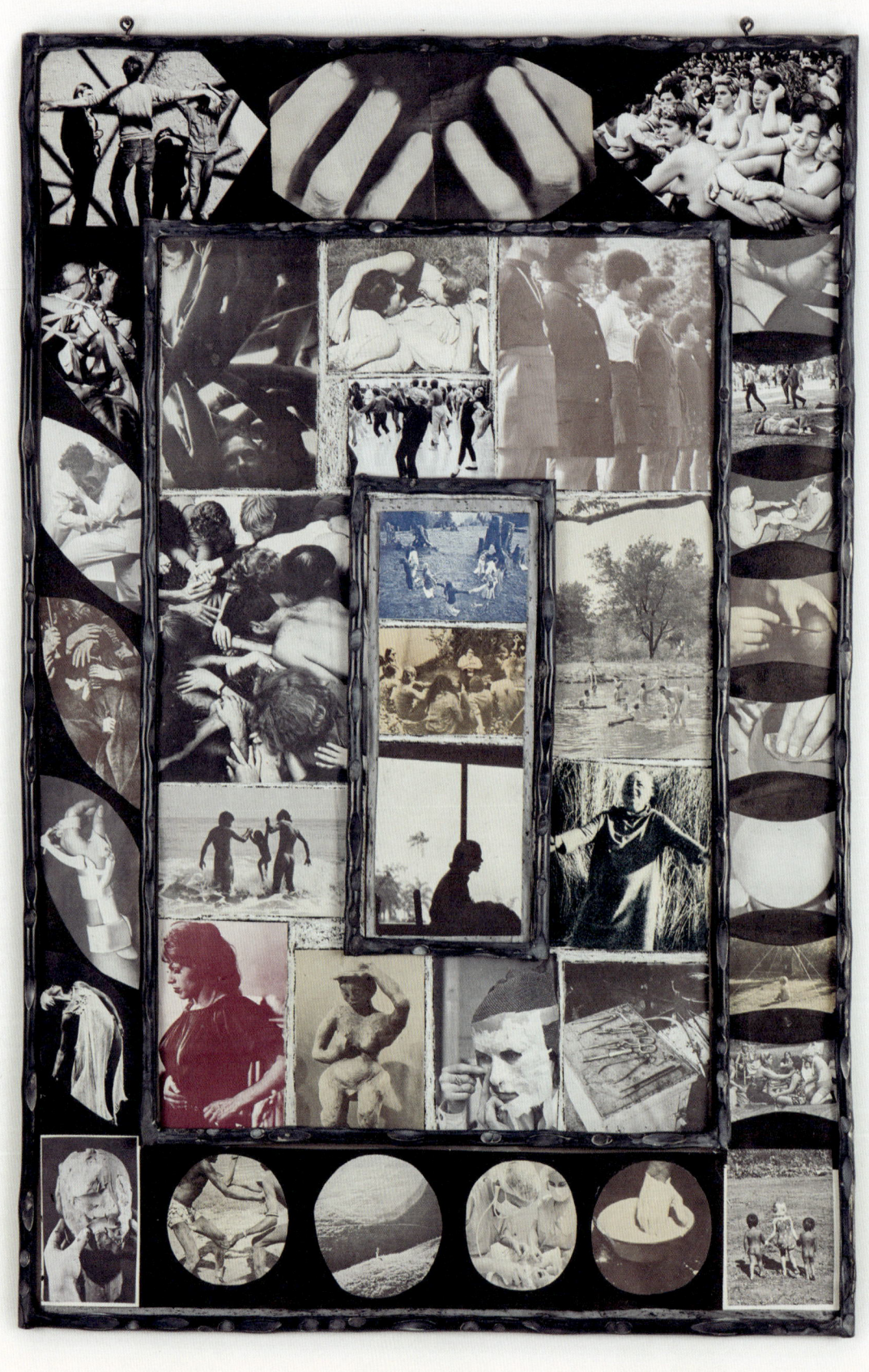

↑   **Togethering 9**, 2020, oil pastel, found images on paper, Sumi ink and aluminium frame, 104.1 × 68.6 cm (41 × 27 in)

→   **Togethering 4**, 2020, oil pastel, found images on paper and aluminium frame, 104.1 × 68.6 cm (41 × 27 in), Minneapolis Institute of Art, Minnesota, USA

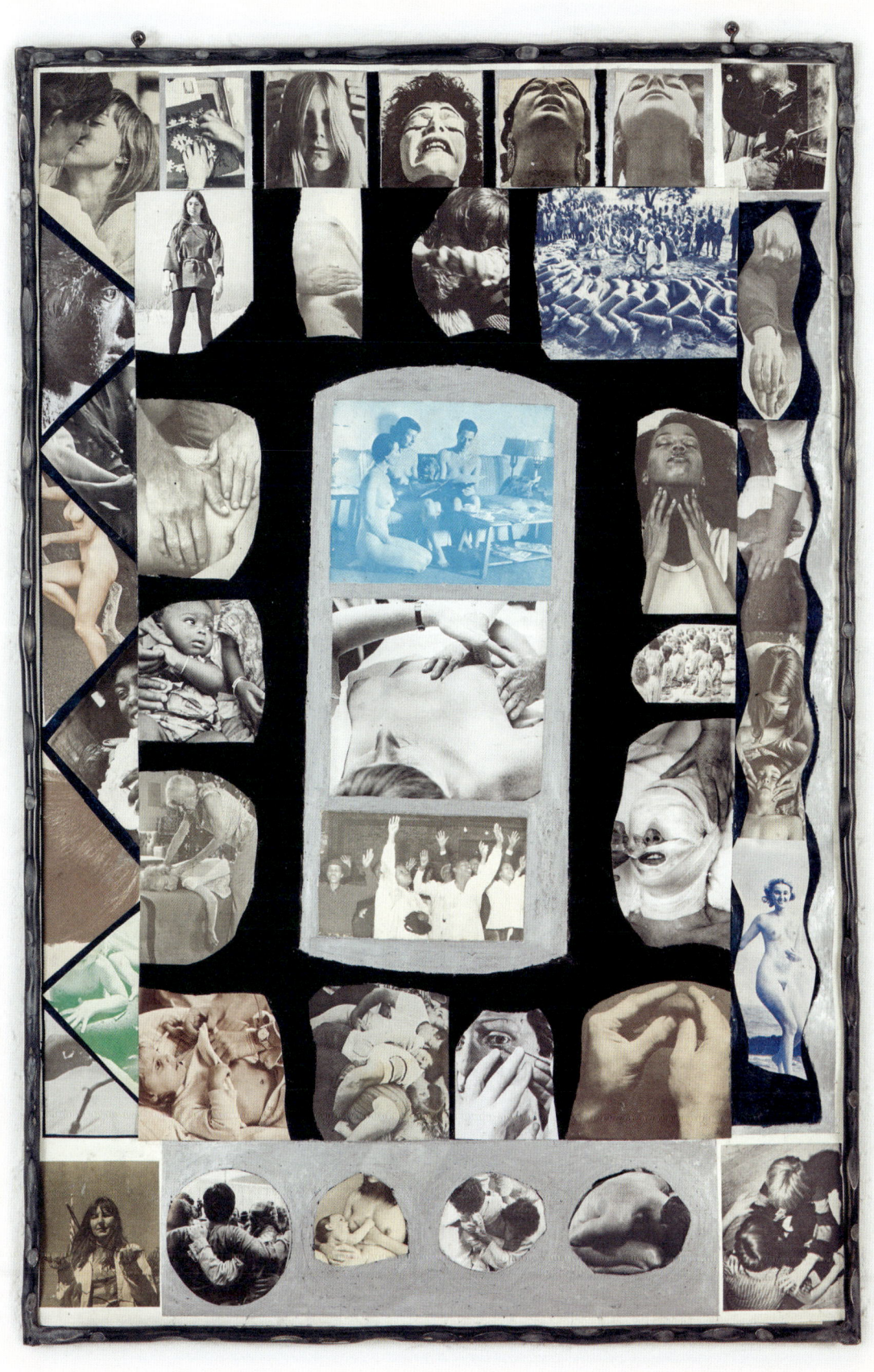

ANITA WITEK

Inhabiting the liminal space between architecture, photography and collage in their reliance on photographic depictions of built space, Anita Witek's three-dimensional constructions and environments partake in a fascinating history of artists who have explored this territory from different perspectives. Kurt Schwitters (1887–1948), Liubov Popova (1889–1924), Richard Hamilton (1922–2011) and Martha Rosler (pp.222–3) are but some of the names whose work informs Witek's practice. ▬ Since the late 1990s, shortly after her arrival in London, UK, as a student, Witek began exploring the phenomenology of built and lived environments. Her earliest project, *Polaroids of places that have never existed* (1998), came out of her search for accommodation in an expensive and poorly maintained city. The series is composed of clippings from real estate ads printed in newspaper supplements, exposing the incompatibility between typical agents' descriptions of properties on offer and the actual qualities of these places. By the early 2000s Witek made her first attempts at appropriating found photographic materials from architectural and lifestyle publications using slide and digital projections, trying to juxtapose found sources against the architectural background of the gallery space in series such as 'Before and After' (2003–6) and 'Retour en Forme' (2008). In the latter work, Witek presents 160 slides of 80 magazine pages that include photographs taken in professional studios. Having removed the central subjects from each picture, a series of neutral backdrops is all that remains. The slide projection then consists of photographs of these images as they pile up, serving as a testimony of an accumulated invisible space. ▬ The process of accumulation is fundamental to Witek's practice and generates a constant shift towards larger scale and more immersive experience of de- and reconstructed imaginative spaces. In her collages from 2009 onwards, such as *Make a Wish* (2016), *About Life* (2016) and *Clip* (2018), she enlarges photographic reproductions of surfaces, materials or built environments to create collages that sprawl across rooms, lobbies, offices, galleries or building facades to such a degree that they are described by the artist on her website as 'walk-in collages in space'. ▬ In the series 'Reset' (2016–19), for example, Witek included framed photographic collages alongside sculptural elements, furniture and partitions, all covered in photographs that depict cardboards and papers that she cut and manipulated to create shadows, layers and folds, and often planted into photographs of domestic interiors. Writing about her practice in *Originalausgabe / Original Issue* in 2012, curator Walter Moser suggests that in Witek's photographic collages 'the original semantics of the picture are "rewritten"... and are thereby open for new interpretation', albeit never a definitive one. And indeed, unlike many of Witek's predecessors in the field of architectural collage who explored the construction of space in symbolic, metaphoric or simulated ways, Witek's work is always both a picture and architecture. ▬

YUVAL ETGAR

Born 1970, Vienna, Austria. Lives in Vienna.

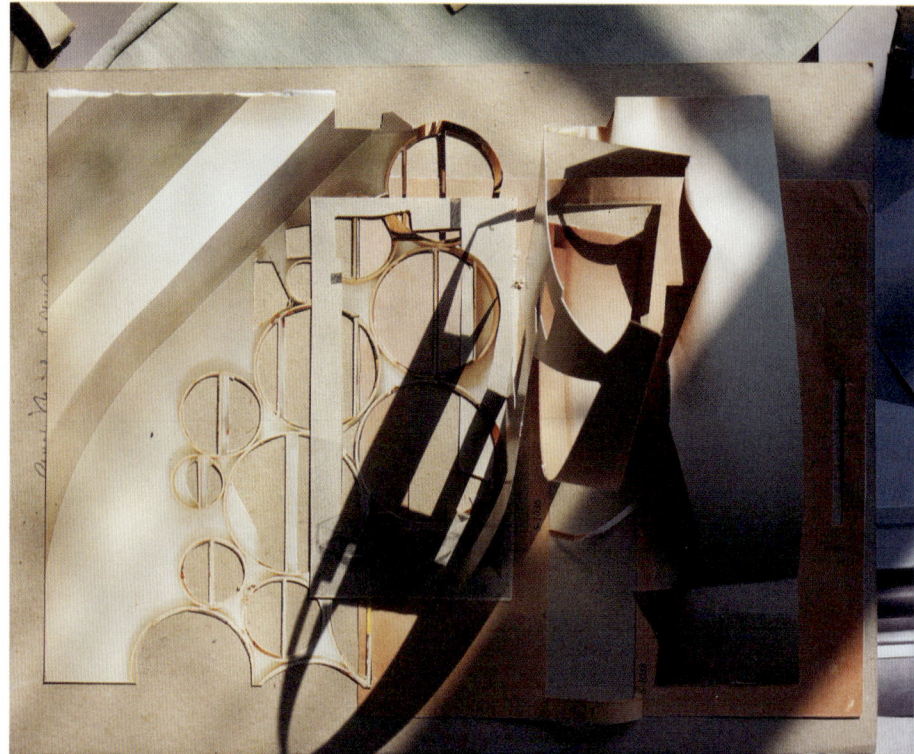

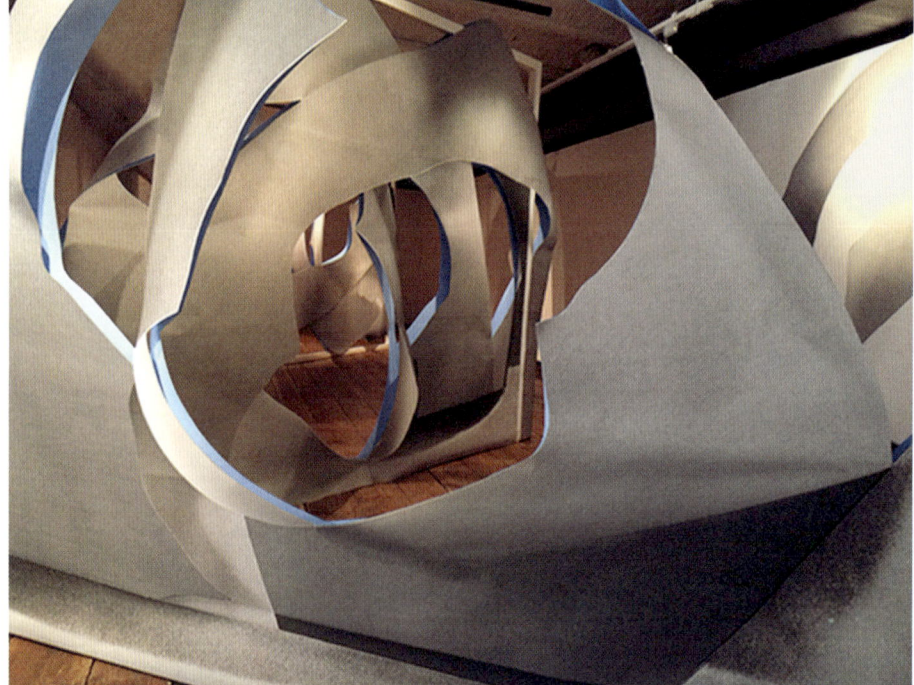

↑↑ **Reset (#3 / S.O.S.)**, 2016, hand-printed analogue C-type print, custom framed, 122 × 150 cm (48 × 59 in)

↑ **About Life**, 2016, latex print on photo paper in 9 parts, mounted on wooden frame and wall, 4 framed pieces: 400 × 350 cm (157 ½ × 137 ¾ in), wall piece: 700 × 350 cm (275 ⅝ × 137 ¾ in), installation view, Kunsthaus Wien, Vienna, Austria, 2016

↗ **Reset**, 2019, hand-printed analogue C-type prints, custom framed; paravent: wooden frame, fabric; lamp: marble, brass and print on technical foil, dimensions variable, installation view, 'Art Brussels with l'étrangère', Brussels, Belgium, 2019

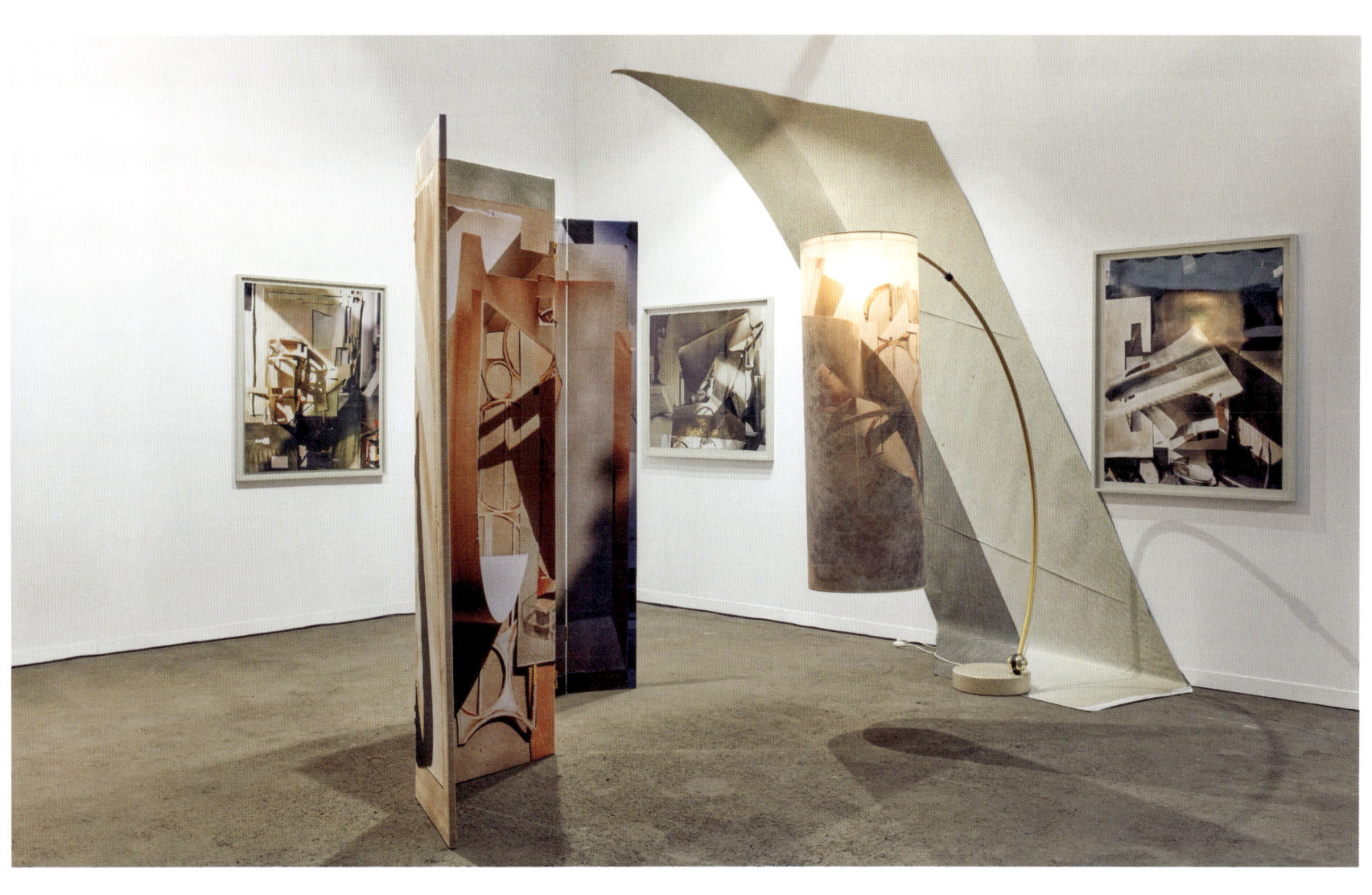

GUANYU XU

Guanyu Xu's temporary, site-specific installations can be considered as three-dimensional collages. Before dismantling them, he documents the installation on camera, subsequently creating photographic prints that are a seeming miscellany of excessive visual content. Xu's works are gentle inquisitions into the power relations between individuals and institutions, such as the family and the state. His works function as repositories of the fluid identities of the artist and his collaborators, which are disarticulated in space and time. The different viewpoints and perspectives within each print mobilize and tease the viewer's gaze and imagination, defying rigid interpretation. One such example is *Reanimated Bedroom* (2019) from the series 'Temporarily Censored Home' (2018–19). Having moved to the United States to attend the School of the Art Institute of Chicago, the artist created works when visiting his parents in China. Having never been allowed to hang posters on his bedroom walls as a child, he built an ephemeral installation – loaded with homosexual and queer visual tropes – in his childhood bedroom while his parents were out for the day. Coming from a typical patriarchal Beijing family, with a military officer father and civil servant mother, Xu makes a private protest against the suppression of his sexuality that is necessary within a conservative, heterosexual family.

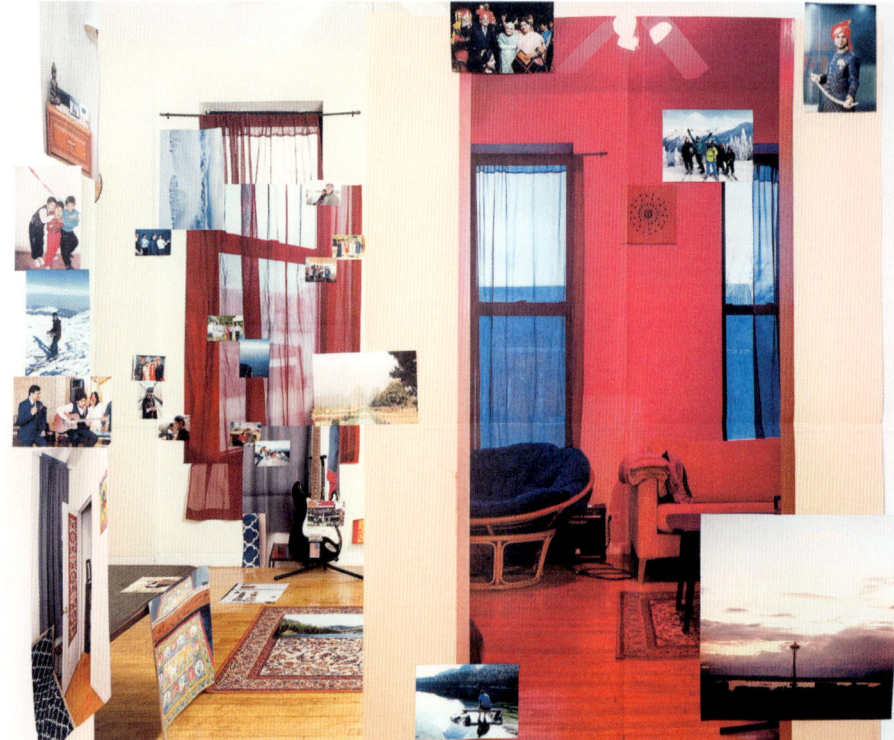

The work comprises an arrangement of diverse imagery: portraits of the artist and other gay men, photographs from family albums, and found images from the media, including political events from multiple locations in the world – a protest against alt-right in Munich, Germany, the back view of a soldier in Beijing, anti-Brexit posters in Brussels, Belgium, and a protest against Donald Trump in Chicago. Xu assembles a landscape of power dynamics where personal freedom and national ideology overlap. Conflicts are hidden under the peaceful facade, facilitating reflections on differences and contradictions. Four drawers are neatly aligned to balance the overall composition, while a large curtain-like print in the centre shows two digital representations of these drawers. This *mise en abyme* – the recurrence of an image within an image – allows a juxtaposition of two worlds in the same space, a sense of watching and being watched that is also strongly associated with self-censorship. *AK-08102008-05032021* (2021) is a work from Xu's series 'Resident Aliens', which he began in 2020. Temporary residents of the United States who have permission to remain via one of the country's various visa schemes become the subject matter for Xu's performative practice. The artist arranges the personal belongings of an individual in their room, along with imagery representing aspects of their lives, to create a collaged portrait within space. Due to ever-shifting immigration policies, each image emphasizes the temporary nature of the subject's situation: luggage may be unpacked, but any sense of security is constantly under threat.

POPPY DONGXUE WU

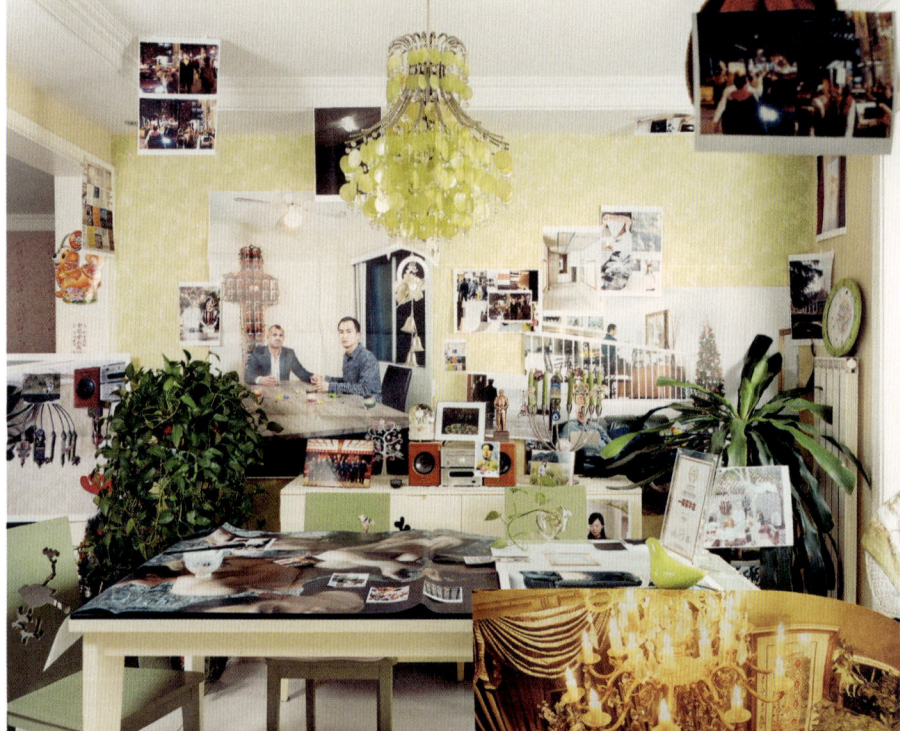

Born 1993, Beijing, China. Lives in Chicago, Illinois, USA.

↑↑ AK-08102008-05032021, 2021, archival pigment print, 101.6 × 127 cm (40 × 50 in)

↑ The Dining Room, 2018, archival pigment print, 101.6 × 127 cm (40 × 50 in)

↗ Reanimated Bedroom, 2019, archival pigment print, 101.6 × 127 cm (40 × 50 in)

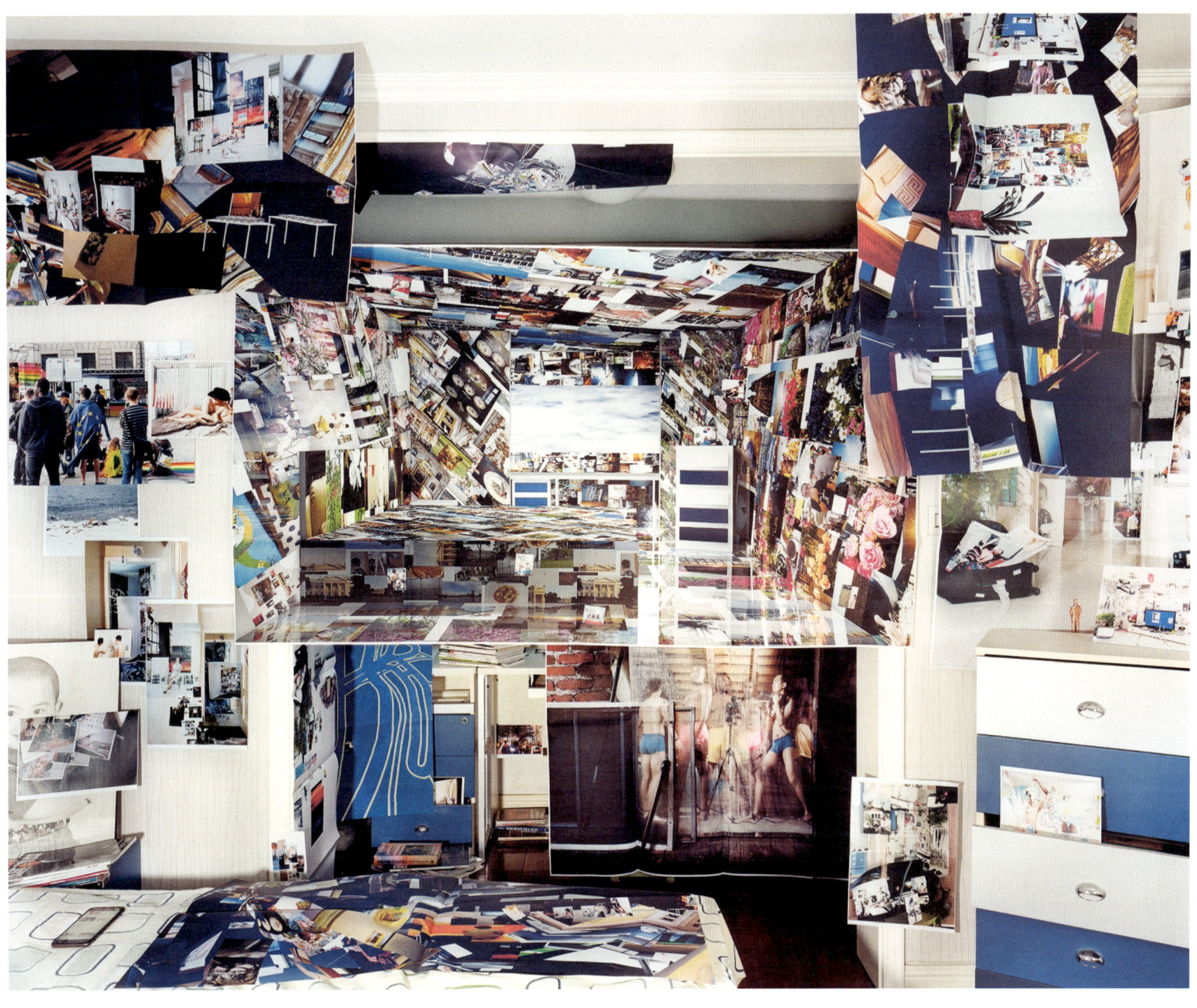

BILLIE

Z A N G E W A

The silk collages of Billie Zangewa examine human individuality from a feminist perspective, informed by her day-to-day experiences that revolve around dreams and realities, challenges and victories. Her works, which are hand-stitched using fragments of raw silk, are characterized by being unevenly shaped, creating the impression on various sides that a section of the picture has been either removed or deliberately excluded. ◢ Zangewa is particularly inspired by fashion photography, and places a great deal of attention on the clothes, costumes and textiles worn by her protagonists, as well as the wider environments they inhabit. Using different colours to model textures and the effects of lighting, her compositions are remarkably detailed, in ways more typically seen in photography or painting than textile art. ◢ While landscapes and cityscapes are prevalent in her work, she is particularly known for her figurative compositions that illuminate the gendered roles of women and men in the domestic sphere, the labour market, politics and the wider community. In her representations of female figures, she reflects on how they have been represented and consumed by the male gaze in visual culture and is concerned with the impact of that gaze on women's self-esteem. ◢ Many of her works are portraits and she often uses herself as subject. *In my solitude* (2018) portrays the artist absorbed in reading a book. The silhouetted plant in the foreground echoes the figures on the book's cover, perhaps making reference to Black subjectivity. While the reclining female figure is an art historical archetype, Zangewa's depiction can be seen as a quiet battle against such patriarchal tropes: her figure is clothed not nude, and in her comfortable pose and self-absorbed activity, she is not simply objectified for the viewer to consume. ◢ Indeed, Zangewa repeatedly calls for independence for all women, challenging society's expectations that they live by set standards or rules. *Every Woman* (2017) is geared at promoting female empowerment and demonstrates the artist's desire to tell stories through her own body and experiences. It shows her fashionably dressed, in high-heeled shoes, with artworks in the background and toys on the floor, revealing Zangewa's dual identity as artist and single mother. *Heart of the Home* (2020) portrays the artist and her son in their kitchen, in a pose that will be familiar to many parents. She stands behind him to assist or instruct him as he writes, or perhaps draws or paints. Zangewa represents the kitchen as a place of wide-ranging activities, beyond cooking and eating. In a *New York Times* article of 2021, she is quoted as saying, 'This is very much a post-Covid image of life, where domestic space has taken on so many different functions.' The work is a gentle commentary on women's domestic contributions, which are so often pushed to the background and undervalued.

J O H N   O W O O

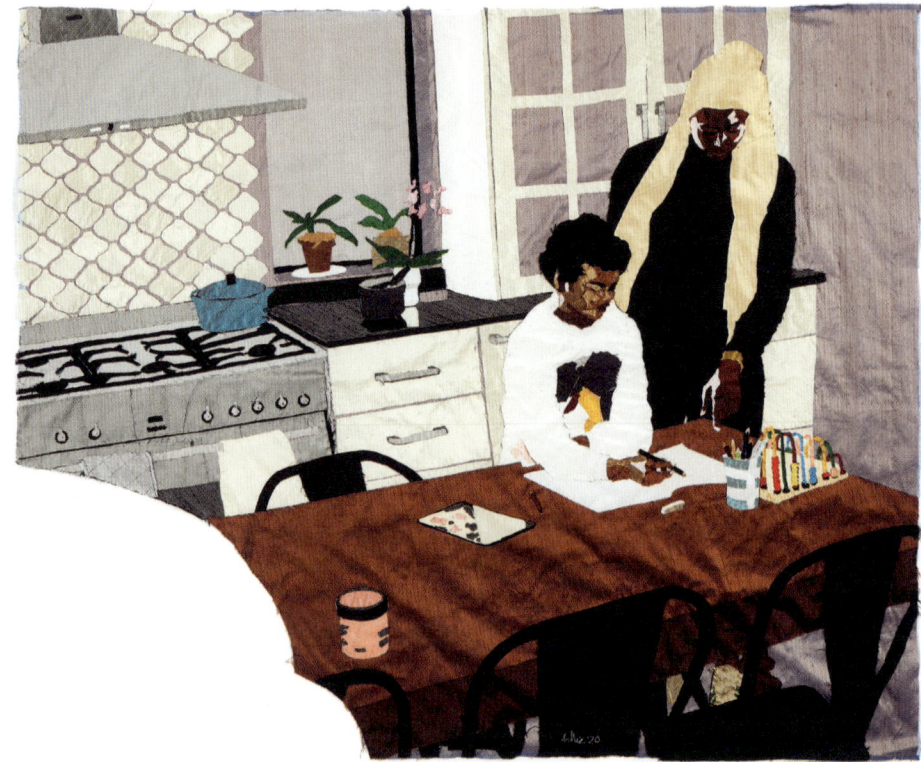

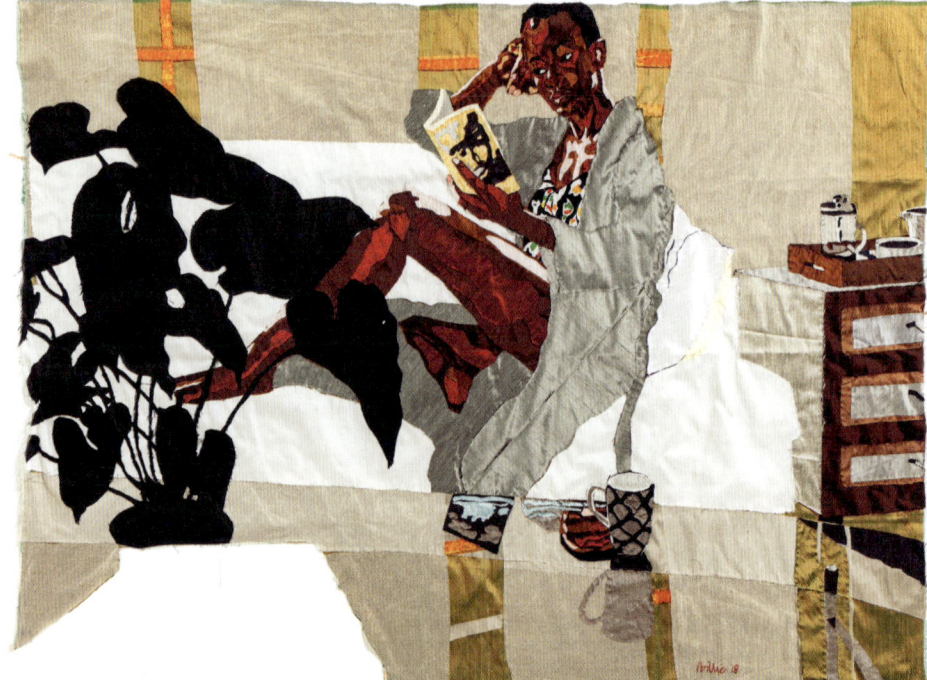

Born 1973, Blantyre, Malawi. Lives in Johannesburg, South Africa.

↑↑ **Heart of the Home**, 2020, hand-stitched silk collage, 114 × 140 cm (45 × 55 in)

↑ **In my solitude**, 2018, hand-stitched silk collage, 150 × 111 cm (59⅛ × 43¾ in), Centre Pompidou– Musée national d'art moderne, Paris, France

→ **Every Woman**, 2017, hand-stitched silk collage, 136 × 98.5 cm (53½ × 38¾ in)

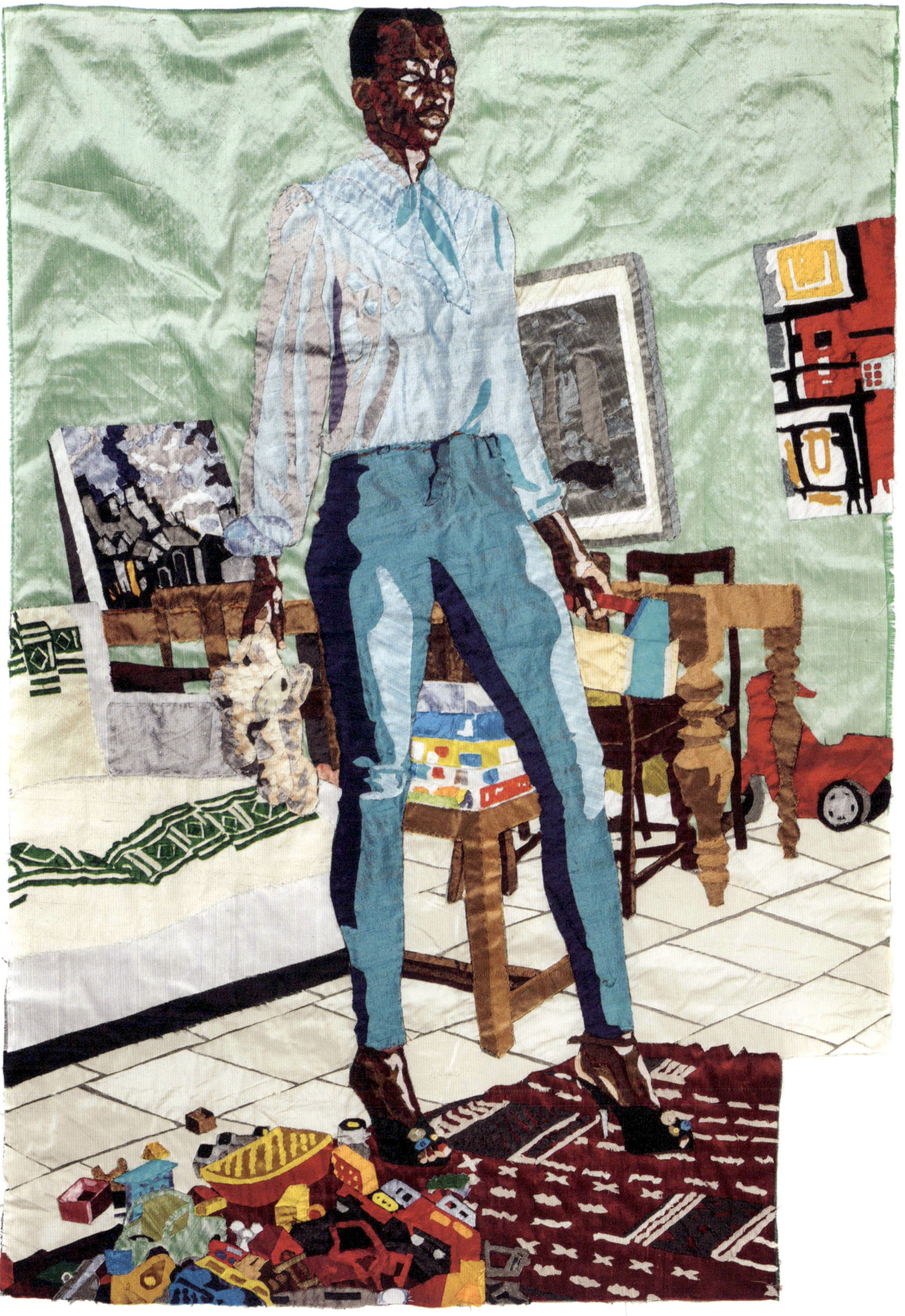

BILLIE ZANGEWA

ELIZABETH ZVONAR

Working with collage for more than twenty years, Elizabeth Zvonar scavenges the debris of twentieth-century visual culture to create witty images that prod at the patriarchal structures of Western culture while pondering the mysteries of existence. Her increasingly minimalistic works typically combine just two or three discrete elements, resulting in arresting images that bring her interests in art history and metaphysics into conjunction with feminist concerns. The artist likens her approach to puzzle solving, requiring restraint and contemplation in order to balance a work's aesthetic and conceptual aspects. Working initially on a small scale with hand-cut techniques, she scans, edits and digitally enlarges her collages before mounting them on aluminium, PVC or sheets of translucent silk that hang from gallery ceilings alongside her surreal sculptures. Zvonar's preference for succinct image-making developed from a desire to say more with less. Potential sources from vintage magazines, books and advertisements are often stumbled on by chance, followed by lengthy periods of deliberation over how images might be cropped, modified and melded with others from the files of clippings in her Vancouver studio. Sometimes pairings present themselves serendipitously, such as the combination of a Victor Vasarely (1906–97) Op art painting and an ancient Egyptian sculpture of a seated scribe in the large, floor-standing work, *Below Your Mind* (2016). Suggesting a psychedelic mushroom cloud exploding from the figure's head, the elements were sourced from H. W. Janson's *History of Art* (1962), a standard textbook in North America that has been critiqued by later art historians for not featuring a single woman artist. Taking aim at Janson's Eurocentric, white male perspective, Zvonar's work wryly critiques his skewed account. Frequently, Zvonar uses Photoshop to edit her imagery, a programme with seemingly boundless possibilities that she considers analogous to the unfathomable nature of the universe. In *Photography Is Hard* (2019), the background is digitally airbrushed white, emphasizing the disembodied arms and camera lens that jostle with a 1945 portrait of English socialite Pauline Tennant by British painter Lucian Freud (1922–2011). A casual reading suggests a questioning of the male gaze's control over female bodies, but its title playfully alludes to the stifling legacy that Vancouver's post-conceptual photographers of the 1980s and 1990s (including Vikky Alexander, Stan Douglas, Rodney Graham and Jeff Wall) have had on Zvonar's generation. Photoshop was also used to modify *Dali's Dalliance* (2022), in which a blazing trashcan fire exploding from an egg in the Surrealist artist's hand is precariously balanced by Athena, Greek goddess of wisdom, war and handicraft. Emblematic of a bygone generation of towering male artists, Salvador Dalí (1904–89) is an ambivalent figure for Zvonar – problematic yet strangely compelling. Although the collaged elements derive from 1970s magazines, the work is an apt metaphor for the bewildering contradictions of early twenty-first-century life, where chaos and wonder materialize at every turn.

DAVID TRIGG

Born 1972, Thunder Bay, Canada. Lives in Vancouver, Canada.

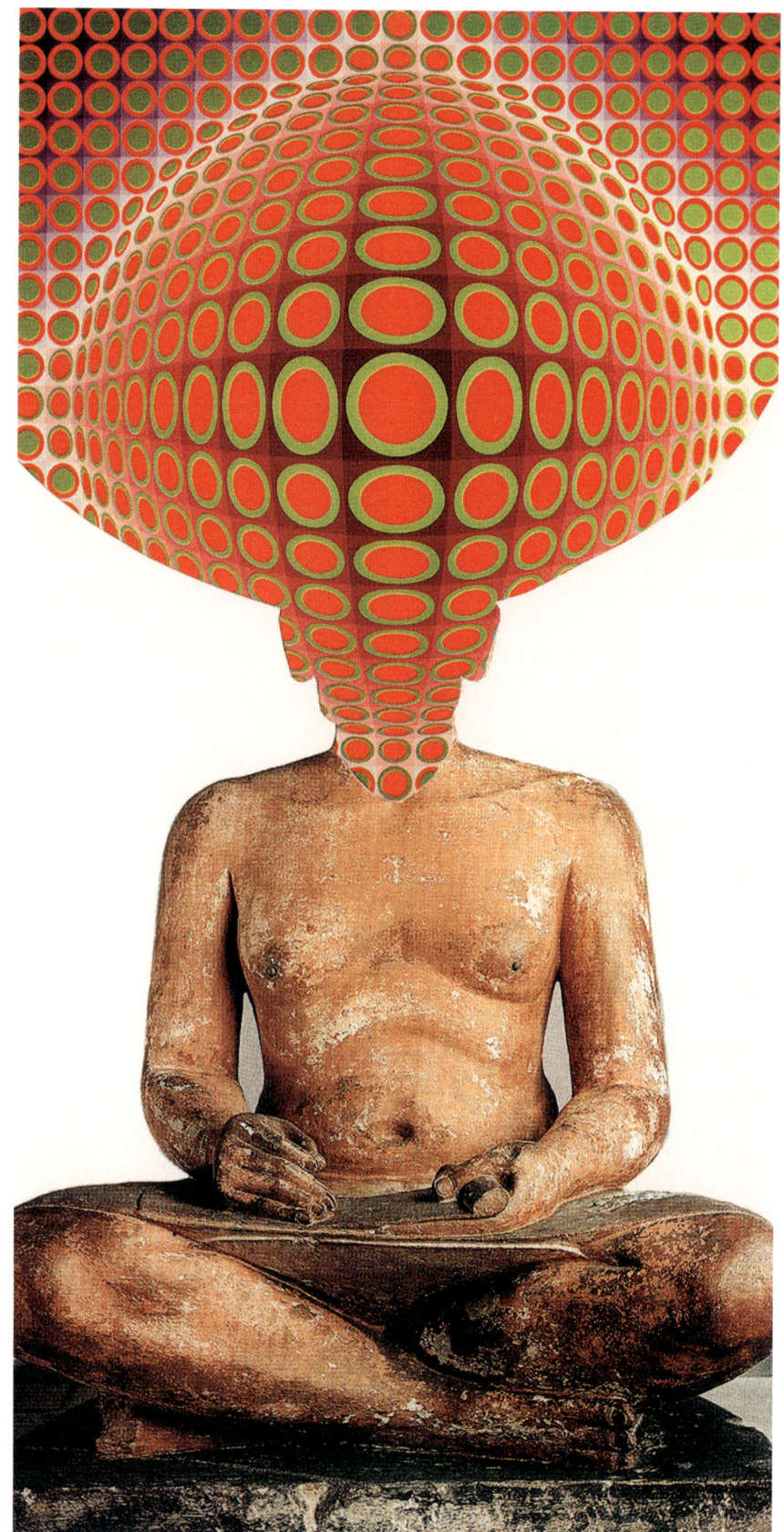

↑   **Below Your Mind**, 2016, inkjet print of hand-cut collage, scanned and enlarged, 213 × 109 cm (84 × 43 in)

↗   **Clear Eyes Full Hearts**, 2019, inkjet print of hand-cut collage, scanned and enlarged, 66 × 48 cm (26 × 19 in)

↗↗ **Watermelon Sugar**, 2021, inkjet print of hand-cut collage with digital alterations, 64 × 51 cm (25 × 20 in)

→   **Photography Is Hard**, 2019, inkjet print of hand-cut collage with digital alterations, 150 × 117 cm (59 × 46in)

→ → **Magic Hands**, 2022, inkjet print of hand-cut collage, 38 × 36 cm (15 × 14 in)

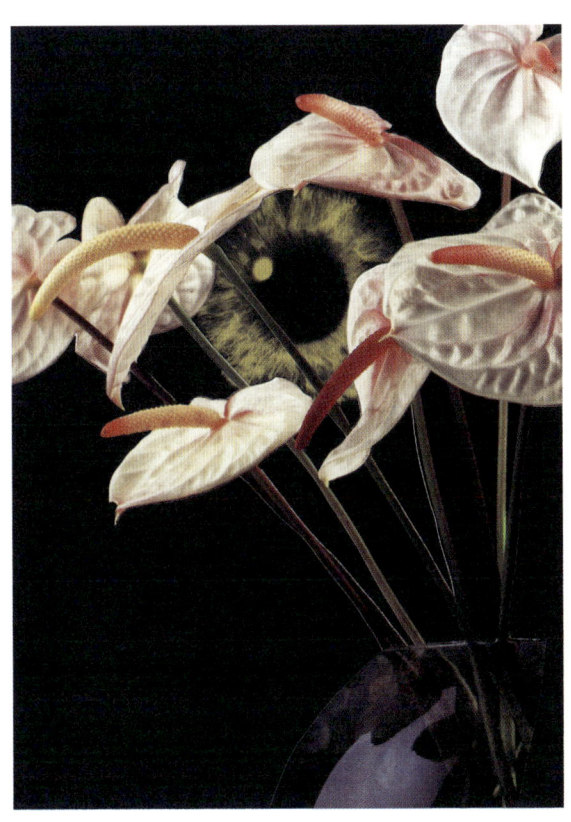
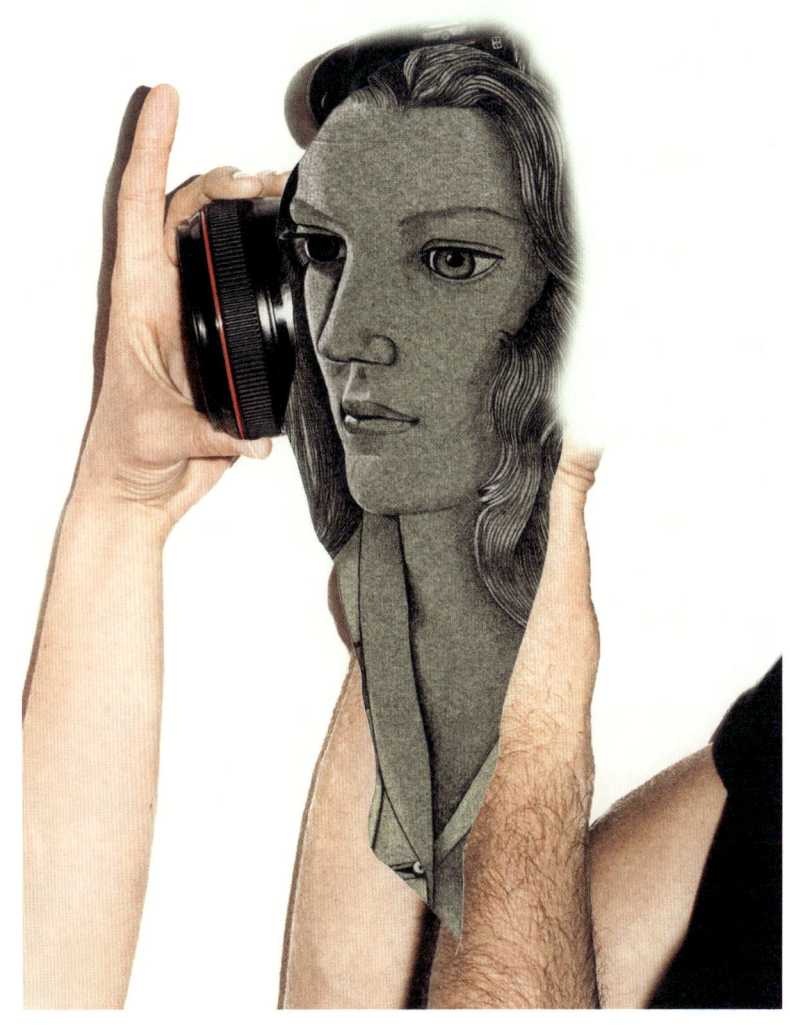
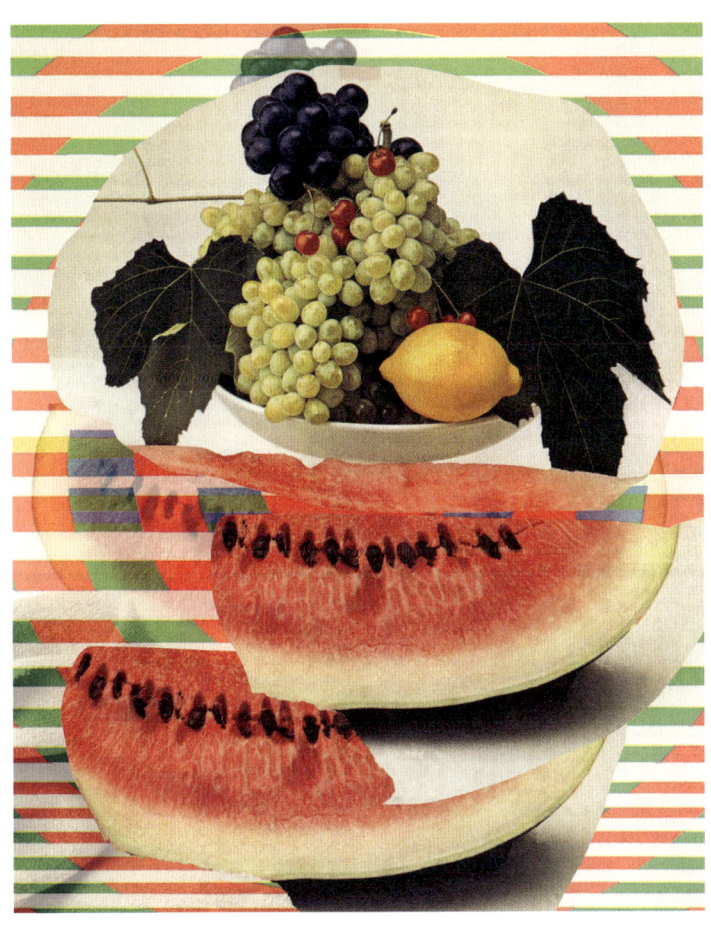
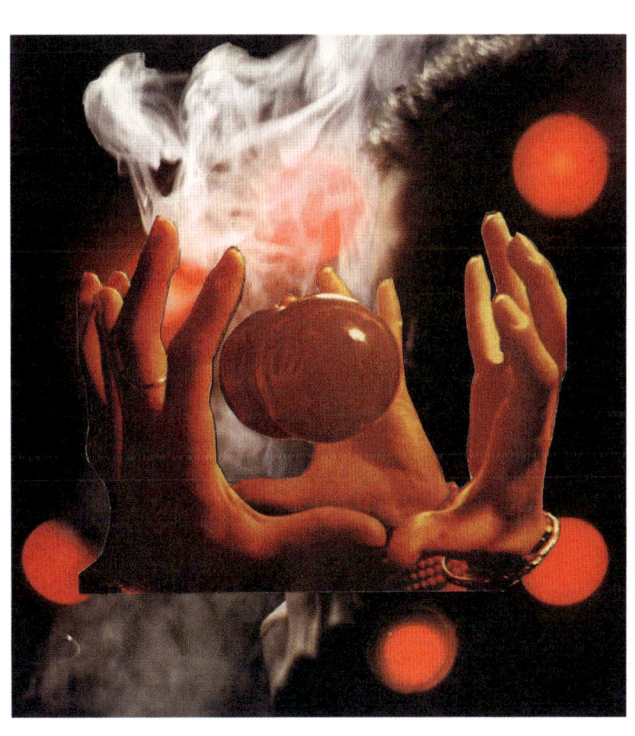

ELIZABETH ZVONAR

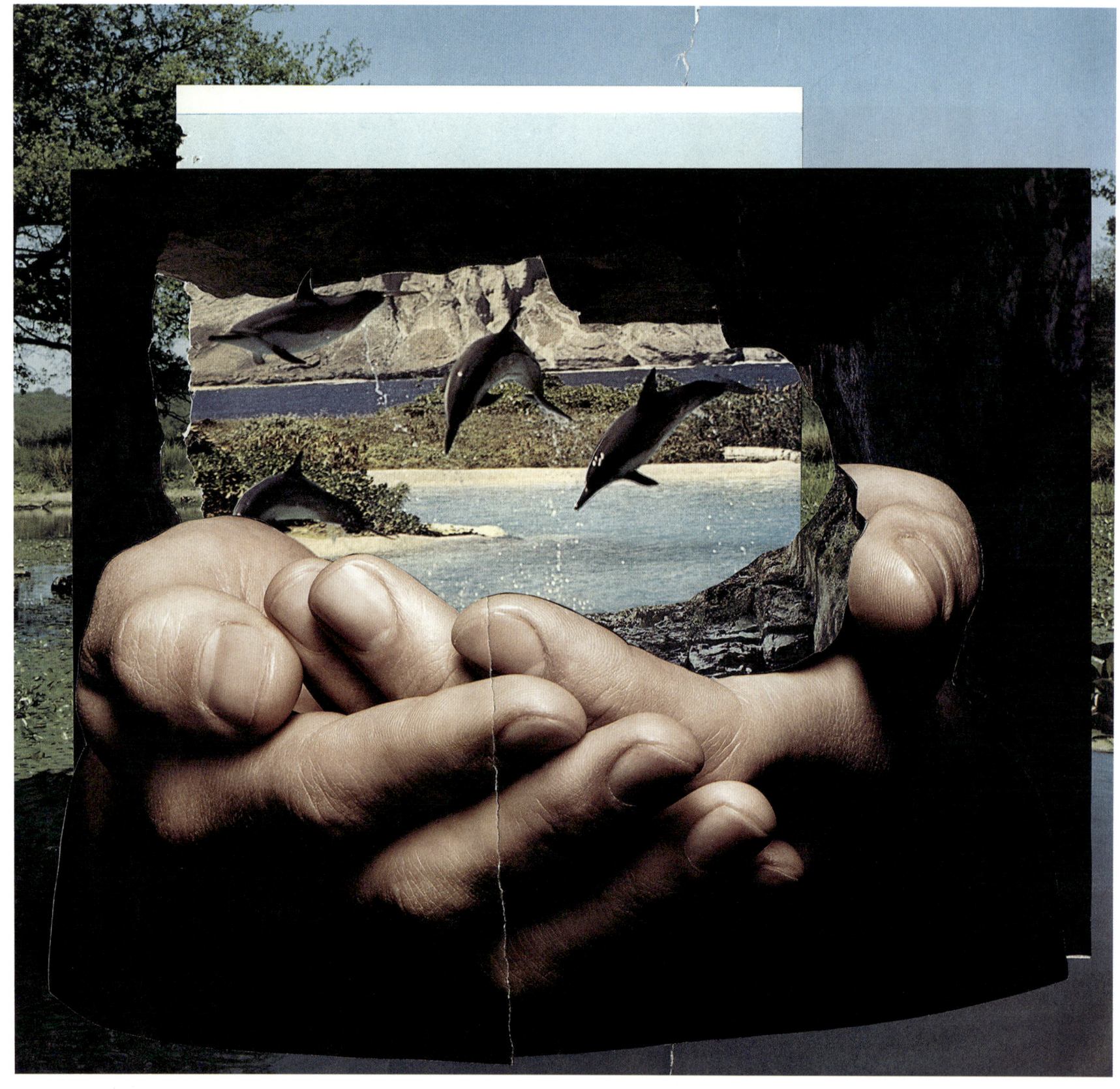

↑   **Divine Intervention**, 2016, inkjet print of hand-cut collage, 61 × 64 cm (24 × 25 in)

→   **Dali's Dalliance**, 2022, inkjet print of hand-cut collage with digital alteration, 51 × 46 cm (20 × 18 in)

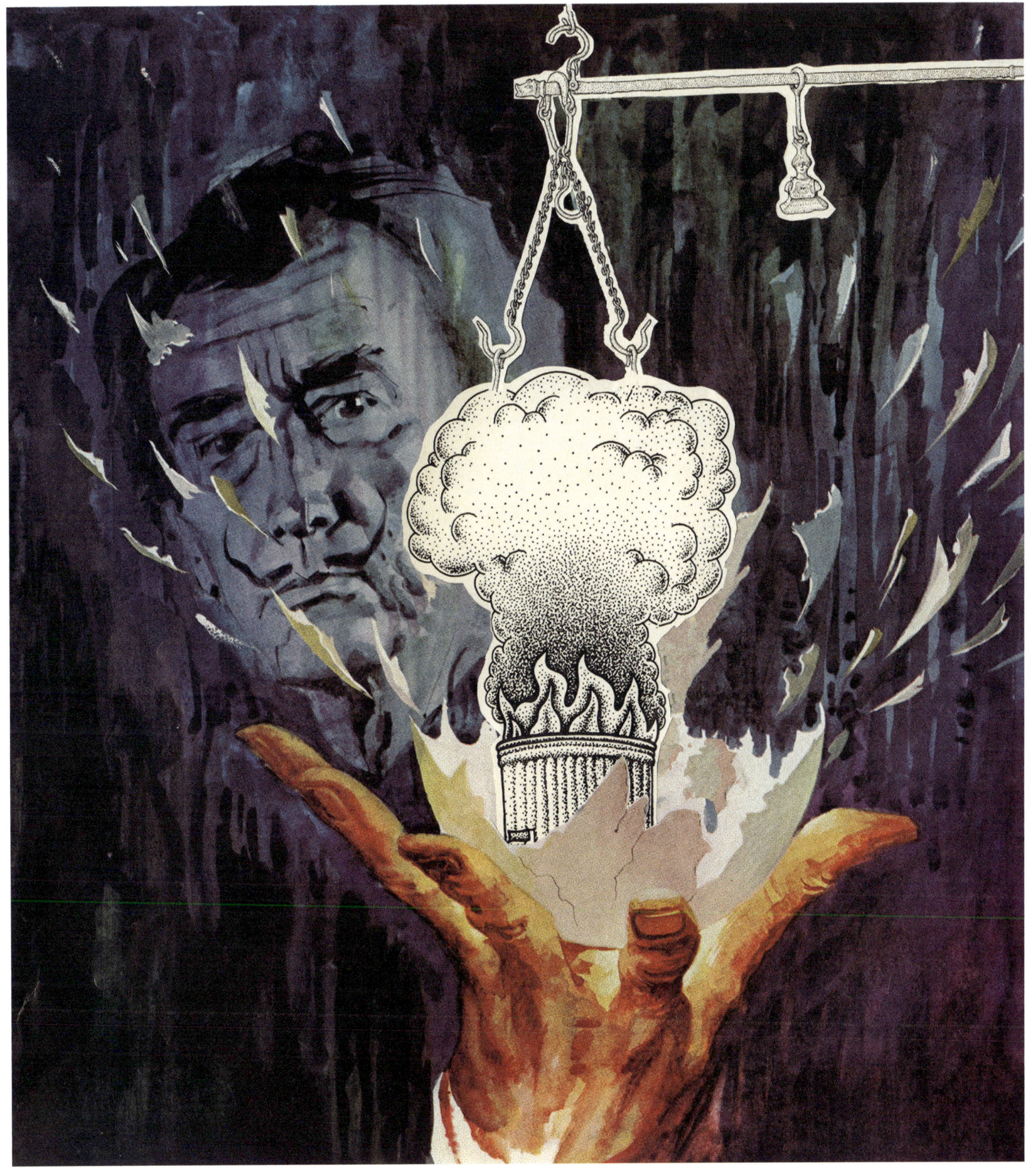

ELIZABETH ZVONAR